Date Due

Unless Recalled Earlier

FEB 18 2002

CODING
PROCESSES IN
HUMAN MEMORY

THE EXPERIMENTAL PSYCHOLOGY SERIES

Arthur W. Melton · Consulting Editor

MELTON AND MARTIN · *Coding Processes in Human Memory, 1972*

CODING PROCESSES IN HUMAN MEMORY

Edited by ARTHUR W. MELTON and EDWIN MARTIN

UNIVERSITY OF MICHIGAN, ANN ARBOR, MICHIGAN

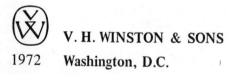

V. H. WINSTON & SONS

1972   Washington, D.C.

DISTRIBUTED BY THE HALSTED PRESS DIVISION OF

JOHN WILEY & SONS
New York   Toronto   London   Sydney

BF
371
C56

V. H. Winston & Sons, Inc., Publishers
1511 K St. N.W., Washington, D.C. 20005

Distributed solely by Halsted Press Division, John Wiley & Sons, Inc.,
New York.

ISBN 0-470-59335-0

Library of Congress Catalog Card Number: 72-5431

Printed in the United States of America

CONTENTS

LIST OF CONTRIBUTORS

Numbers in parentheses indicate the pages on which the authors' contributions begin.

Fred Attneave, University of Oregon, Eugene, Oregon. (283)

Robert A. Bjork, University of Michigan, Ann Arbor, Michigan. (217)

Gordon H. Bower, Stanford University, Stanford, California. (85)

W. K. Estes, The Rockefeller University, New York, New York. (161)

Wendell R. Garner, Yale University, New Haven, Connecticut. (261)

Earl Hunt, University of Washington, Seattle, Washington. (237)

Neal F. Johnson, The Ohio State University, Columbus, Ohio. (125)

Alvin M. Liberman, Haskins Laboratories and Yale University, New Haven, Connecticut, and University of Connecticut, Storrs, Connecticut. (307)

Tom Love, University of Washington, Seattle, Washington. (237)

Edwin Martin, University of Michigan, Ann Arbor, Michigan. (59)

Ignatius G. Mattingly, Haskins Laboratories, New Haven, Connecticut, and University of Connecticut, Storrs, Connecticut. (307)

George A. Miller, The Rockefeller University, New York, New York, and Institute for Advanced Study, Princeton, New Jersey. (335)

Allen Newell, Carnegie-Mellon University, Pittsburgh, Pennsylvania. (373)

Michael I. Posner, University of Oregon, Eugene, Oregon. (25)

Jack Richardson, State University of New York at Binghamton, Binghamton, New York. (45)

Michael T. Turvey, Haskins Laboratories, New Haven, Connecticut, and University of Connecticut, Storrs, Connecticut. (307)

Benton J. Underwood, Northwestern University, Evanston, Illinois. (1)

Robert E. Warren, University of Oregon, Eugene, Oregon. (25)

Delos D. Wickens, The Ohio State University, Columbus, Ohio. (191)

ACKNOWLEDGMENT

The papers published in the present volume represent the proceedings of a research workshop on coding processes in human memory held at Woods Hole, Massachusetts, in August, 1971. The workshop was arranged under the auspices of the Committee on Basic Research in Education, which was funded by a contract between the United States Office of Education and the National Academy of Sciences-National Research Council. The Committee was jointly sponsored by the National Academy of Education and the National Academy of Sciences.

PREFACE

During the past ten years, the topic of human memory has captured an inordinate amount of experimental and theoretical attention. This has been a period of excitement, of discovery, and of competing theoretical interpretations. These we believe to be symptoms of a Kuhnian "paradigm shift" within the science of human learning and memory, with the structure and function of coding processes as the focus of the new paradigm. If this conception of the importance of coding notions is valid, it seems obvious that there must be important consequences for the application of the science of human learning and memory to the control of learning processes in educational settings. Equally obvious, in our view, is the need to promote intensive, directional examination of the concept of coding in a variety of experimental-theoretical contexts, this by a representative group of scientists who, by prior use of coding concepts, are committed to the elaboration or refinement of coding theory. With the sponsorship of the Committee on Basic Research in Education and the advisory assistance of G. H. Bower, M. I. Posner, and D. D. Wickens, the papers in this volume were presented and discussed at Woods Hole, Massachusetts, during the week of August 2, 1971.

Conceptual paradigm shifts have a way of sneaking up on scientists. Such seems to be the case with coding theory in the analysis of human learning and memory. During the decade prior to 1962 there was the vigorous controversy between all-or-none and cumulative strength conceptions of the association of events. Movement toward the resolution of this issue came through recognition that the association between two nominal events—the stimulus and response terms of paired associates—could be manipulated in ways that would involve one, two, or three gross component learning processes: stimulus discrimination learning, response learning, and associative learning between the products of stimulus discrimination and response learning. At the very least, it became clear that the issue of strength versus all-or-none had to be faced for these component learning processes, and this forced attention to questions about what it was that was being learned—stored in memory—when a single event or a pair of to-be-associated events occurred. Meanwhile, during the latter part of this same decade there was a sharp revival of interest in short-term memory and the beginnings of a methodological revolution that allowed the observation of very-short-term memory and long-term memory under comparable conditions. Again, the theoretical questions about memory for experienced events or associations between events quickly focussed on questions about what was stored in memory.

By 1963 the roots were firmly established for a decade of research and theory about questions of what is stored at the time of learning and the relations between such storage events and the holding processes of memory, as reflected in recognition, recall, and transfer tests. There are three developments within the past decade that make the paradigm shift self-evident. One is methodological, and a continuation at an ever more rapid pace of what was started in the preceding decade: The traditional multitrial learning of serial and paired-associate lists was supplemented with a wide variety of precise methods for observing the learning and retention of individual verbal items or pairs. These methods allow much more exact control of the duration of single learning periods, the spacing of learning periods, the kind and difficulty of information processing activities that precede or follow a learning period, and the information-processing context of the learning, the test for retention, or both. As a consequence of this flexibility of method it has become possible to ask, and answer, probing questions about what is stored in memory and about the way what is stored affects retrieval.

A second major development within the last decade is in the pretheoretic conceptions used as the base for development of specific theories. The traditional association theory, which dealt with associative dispositions between input and output events according to a conditioned-response analogy, has given way to theories in which the learner is conceived to be an active processor of input events (stimuli) and selector of output events (responses), with the products of learning being conceived as stored perceptual or cognitive events (event traces) and relations between them (associations). With this emphasis on the structure of what is learned, the major theoretical controversy shifted from that of all-or-none versus cumulative strength (although by no means resolved) to a revival of the controversy about association as the basis of organization versus organization as the basis of association. Although reminiscent of the earlier conflict between association theory and Gestalt theory, the important difference is that these contemporary theoretic preconceptions are being tested in experiments that reflect the enriched methodology of the field and with recognition that the issue must be formulated in terms of central—as contrasted with peripheral—events.

The first two developments that have been mentioned are two reliable symptoms of the intellectual release that has occurred with the breaking of the traditional constraints on systematic thought about human learning and memory. The coding concept and the many terminological variants of the idea of coding—encoding, recoding, decoding, functional stimuli, "chunks," subjective units—is the third. The core intent of this idea is that between the external world and a human's memorial representation of that external world there operate certain processes that translate external information into internal information. These processes may in part be selective, or elaborative, or transformational; some may be optional while others are obligatory; the speech code that translates an acoustic signal into a phonemic representation has a different "grammar" than does the process that finds in memory a semantic marker; and so on through the basic considerations covered in the 15 chapters of this book. A major purpose of this book is to exhibit and explicate the uses of the new concept of coding, without imposing formal constraints on those who find the term fitting to their needs and intent.

The implication of these chapters is that the critical determinants of learning and remembering are to be found in the coding response to an experienced event, pair of events, or sequence of events. Further, it is implied that coding responses have their components and structure determined by the preexisting structure of the brain, whether built-in or acquired, as well as by transient factors such as information-processing sets, whether generated by context, instructions, or self-instruction in combination with habit. In our view, this turn to questions about coding and coding processes exemplifies the new paradigm of the science of human learning and memory because it may well provide the theory that incorporates the truths of both the association theory and organizational traditions as well as the truths of all-or-none theory and cumulative strength theory. At this point in time, it is a fact that proponents of all of these theoretic positions are employing the language of coding processes and code structures.

If our assessment of the situation is correct, learning and memory theory will experience an integrative advance that was never before possible. However, there is another effect of coding concepts that will benefit psychology immediately and in the long term. This is the multiplication of the substantive and conceptual contacts between the learning-memory area and other areas of research concerned with human performance. For example, if memory entails coding processes, then such processes must have domains from which they receive information; to better understand how the processes work, we need to know something of the nature of those domains; once the interface between a process and its input domain becomes an everyday topic, the two hitherto disparate areas will become one area. In other words, boundaries between certain topical areas tend to disappear. A casual glance at the table of contents of this book reveals the spectrum of consideration involved in the notion of coding. There is clearly a definite commitment toward coordinating the theoretical concepts of perception, memory, and learning; it is clear that these topical areas cannot long persist as separate, noninteracting enterprises. Although not given emphasis here, the same may be predicted for attention, problem solving, and thinking.

Even though some of the chapters in this volume are important contributions to a theory of coding and others examine some fundamental questions about coding processes, there is as yet no formal statement of a general coding theory of learning and memory here or elsewhere. There is also no agreed-to taxonomy of coding processes of importance in learning and memory. Therefore it is, in our opinion, premature to insist that psychological coding theory abide by some constraints on the term *coding,* particularly as such constraints might derive from well-formed and tested models of information transmission and transformation in physical systems.

For example, Shannon distinguishes between an input process and an encoding process, where an encoding process is one in which the form of the information is changed, as from acoustical to electrical, or from continuous to digital. Other processes, such as noise exclusion, are not considered encoding processes in such physical models. In contrast, psychological encoding encompasses "representational responses" as components of a coding response, and stimulus selection, an exclusion process, is considered an important functional characteristic of encoding.

While it would be nice to coordinate the principles of psychological coding theory with those of information theory whenever possible, such should not be a constraint on the development of psychological coding theory. As the term is now being used by psychologists, it has strong mentalistic overtones. Those who speak of coding, coding responses, or coding processes are referring to happenings within the individual. These happenings may be iconic representational responses, associated naming responses, or a variety of elaborative responses in the form of word-word associations, memory images, constructed images or sentences, or feelings. There is, however, no necessity that these components of a coding response to a nominal event be conscious or reportable; nor need there be any serious dependence on introspection as a method for identifying the structural properties of a coding response. Instead, coding is a construct, with components and temporal dependencies between components to be defined by objective indices or converging experimental operations; in short, by the armamentarium of methods the objective psychologist previously applied to draw inferences about associations or organization at the level of nominal stimuli and responses.

We think the chapters in this book make important contributions to the development of a theory of coding processes in human learning and memory. We wish to thank the participants for the successful completion of the venture, and also the Committee on Basic Research in Education, National Research Council, and the Office of Education, Department of Health, Education, and Welfare, for support of the venture.

Arthur W. Melton
Edwin Martin

May 11, 1972

CODING
PROCESSES IN
HUMAN MEMORY

1
ARE WE OVERLOADING MEMORY?[1]

Benton J. Underwood
Northwestern University

Ten years ago it might have been said that most conceptualizations of memory were impoverished or simplistic in that they did not at all reflect the variety of memory phenomena evident even to the casual observer. If an increase in the size of the technical or semitechnical behavioral vocabulary signals escape from conceptual poverty, we have become liberated. Memories now have attributes, organization, and structure; there are storage systems, retrieval systems, and control systems. We have iconic, echoic, primary, secondary, and short-, medium-, and long-term memories. There are addresses, readout rules, and holding mechanisms; memories may be available but not accessible (or is it the other way?). Our memories are filled with T-stacks, implicit associational responses, natural-language mediators, images, multiple traces, tags, kernel sentences, markers, relational rules, verbal loops, and one-buns. Surely, it is only fitting that the workers in the field of memory should have available such an enormously rich and flexible vocabulary to provide the topic the awe it so rightfully deserves.

To focus on coding theory is to focus on the meaning and implications of many of the terms listed somewhat haphazardly above. These terms have, in at least a descriptive or metaphorical sense, been used to reflect points or processes of interest as an environmental event becomes a candidate for a memory (encoded), how its code is stored, and how the fact that a memory has been established can be made public (decoded).

Encoding, as the term is used in this paper, refers to three different processes, two of which are types of transformations. First, the event to be remembered may be transformed in some way so that at least superficially the transformed representation differs appreciably from the event. Among the transformations that

[1] The author's research is supported by the Office of Naval Research through Contract N00014-67-A-0356-0010.

are possible are those involving addition, subtraction, and, if the event allows it, a reordering of the elements. Usually such a transformation will occur if as a consequence the event corresponds more closely to the contents of memories that already exist. To illustrate: The consonant syllable RCH may be added to, becoming RICH; the passive sentence may be subtracted from (words removed), becoming an active sentence; the nonsense syllable TEP may be stored as PET, representing a reordering of the elements.

The second type of transformation involves a complete change in the type of representation of the event. A concrete noun may be stored as a visual image of the object symbolized by the noun. In reverse, the picture of an object may be stored as a word .

The third process involved in encoding includes all of the additional information that becomes a part of the memory. Transformations always require such additional information if correct decoding is to occur. But, a wide variety of other types of information may also become a part of the memory even if the stored representation of the event is, so to speak, isomorphic to the event. A minimum amount of such additional information must be a part of the memory; without it, no memory could be said to exist, for it could not be made public (retrieved). A fairly complete catalogue of the types of additional information which *may* be a part of the memory was included in an earlier publication, the various types of information being called the various attributes (Underwood, 1969).

The intent of this paper may now be sketched. An examination will be made of five different topics or areas that are integral parts of the recent work on coding, although there is no close relationship among the topics. One of the questions that will be faced occasionally is whether or not we are overloading memory with our theoretical notions. But, more generally, the essay is intended as (*a*) an evaluation of the rapport between fact and theory, and (*b*) a status report on our dealings with some old but fundamental issues of memory.

THE MULTIPLICITY AND AUTOMATICITY OF ENCODING

By far the most comprehensive and integrated work on the encoding of attributes has been produced by Wickens and his students. A large amount of empirical data, as well as a theoretical framework, has been presented in a paper that must be considered a landmark in the work on memory (Wickens, 1970). It is to Wickens' great credit that he does not hesitate to reach for general conclusions to characterize fully the implications of his data as he sees them. Two of these conclusions, the multiplicity of codes and the automaticity of encoding, are the central topics for the discussion in this section.

The method used by Wickens and his students will be spoken of as the release-from-PI (proactive inhibition) technique. It is a clever adaptation of a method devised originally by Peterson and Peterson (1959) for quite different purposes, and although the technique is fully described by Wickens (this volume), a short summary seems necessary in order to facilitate the subsequent discussion. For most of the work involving word attributes, the method consists of presenting successive triads of words with the recall of each triad taken after 20 seconds. The retention interval, of course, is filled with a rehearsal-preventing task. The words in each successive triad are related in some fashion, for example, all are animal names or all are "good" words as determined by Semantic-Differential ratings. Recall performance decreases systematically with each successive triad, a feature that is often described as a PI buildup. Then, for a final triad, the common characteristics of the words are changed, for example, three vegetable names or three "bad" words are presented. If the retention of this final triad shows an increase (over a control), it is described as release from PI. The release is interpreted to mean that with the change in the dominant attribute the composition of the memory changes, and the interference that had been produced by the common attribute of the earlier triads is eliminated or reduced in amount.

Whenever a PI release is obtained it is concluded that the subjects were encoding heavily or predominantly on the same attribute on successive triads during the PI buildup. Thus, the identification of an encoding attribute depends upon the conjunction of a PI buildup and a PI release. An impressive array of evidence is presented on various attributes. There are wide differences in the amount of release associated with the attributes and for one (parts of speech) essentially no release was obtained.

We may first examine two alternative interpretations of the basic findings. It might be concluded that the so-called PI buildup is due to poorer and poorer learning of each successive triad. Similarly, the so-called PI release might be due to the fact that the final triad was simply learned better than the earlier ones. However, this alternative interpretation would not require a change in the basic implication of the findings. Thus, the poorer and poorer learning may be due to interference produced by the common encoding attribute, and the better learning on the test item due to a change away from the interfering, common attribute.

A question may also be raised concerning the independence of the various attributes studied. Words differ on so many different dimensions that it is probably not possible to equate them on all but the one of interest. But, even if there is some contamination across attributes the implication would be only that there are fewer encoding attributes than represented. At the same time there may be other attributes of the words which have never been put to experimental test. In fact, there must be at least one, for in the study on parts of speech (verbs and adjectives) the PI buildup was very heavy but there was no release. If the logic is to be consistent, some common attribute among the triads must have been responsible for the PI. If this could be discovered it would be another to add to the already long list of attributes on which encoding is seen to occur.

In terms of the distinctions made earlier, the Wickens-type encoding is of the third type, the adding of information. His studies include tests not of only the semantic attributes but also orthographic attributes (e.g., length of word) and relatively incidental attributes such as the size of the slide background on which the word triad is presented. Considering only the semantic attributes, it would appear that release from PI could be demonstrated for any attribute that could be reliably scaled by the subjects. Using items from one end of the scale for the buildup series and those from the other end for the PI release test should always produce positive results. In short, any attribute of a word that is a part of the memory for that word (before the word is presented in the experimental situation) is likely to be shown to be an encoding attribute when subjected to the Wickens procedure.

We may now consider the general conclusions reached as a consequence of these experiments (Wickens, 1970, p. 12):

> In the split second while the symbol is processed by the individual, it is granted a locus on many of these dimensions or aspects—encoded, in short, in a multiplicity of ways. . . . The process of encoding symbols into these multiple dimensions is done—I believe—with tremendous alacrity and proficiency, the entries into many different attributes being achieved almost simultaneously, and with the deftness and automaticity associated only with a highly practiced skill.

It is clear that Wickens assumes that the multiplicity and the automaticity holds for the single word, for example, for each word in an unrelated list of words; and it would be of no consequence how rapidly the words were presented provided the subject had sufficient time to perceive each of them. As a means of focusing the subsequent discussion, it may be said now that an argument will be advanced against the multiplicity-automaticity hypothesis.

There is reason to believe that the Wickens technique will overestimate the number of attributes *normally* encoded when a single word occurs in a learning task. There is considerable evidence, for example, that categorization by sense impressions will be minimal or absent unless the subject is instructed about the categories (Hudson, 1968; Underwood & Richardson, 1956; Wood & Underwood, 1967). This suggests that a form of instruction is occurring during the PI buildup, an instruction that is usually called priming. If just one word in a triad of words elicits the categorical response appropriate to all words in the triad and to other triads, there is an increase in the likelihood that subsequent words will also be perceived as belonging to the category. Wickens considered the possibility that priming occurred but rejected the idea on the basis of certain transfer data. He noted, for example, that in an experiment in which the stimulus terms in two lists were identical, with the response terms for corresponding pairs belonging to the same taxonomic category (e.g., *head, arm*), positive transfer occurred. This suggests that *head* might have been encoded as "body part" during first-list learning thereby facilitating the acquisition of the response word from the same category during second-list learning. There are at least two alternative interpretations. First, there may be a direct association between the two words that produced the transfer. Second, the categorization of the first-list response into a body part may not have occurred until the second list was presented, that is, a form of priming occurred in this experiment.

Whatever interpretation is eventually shown to be appropriate, it seems necessary to hold open the possibility that the PI-buildup technique produces priming and thereby we may overestimate the number of encoding attributes that are elicited when the single word is presented, as in a free-recall task with unrelated words. Certainly in the case of sense impressions the encoding is not automatic in many situations. This may or may not be true for other attributes, although subjectively speaking it is most difficult to understand how certain of the words given common scaling on the Semantic Differential dimensions would produce a common attribute, and produce it quickly. But, as Wickens ... individual's consciousness may be circumvented in some of ... process.

There is no evidence from the Wickens-type studies that words a ... encoded on semantic attributes during the short period of presentation of ... the learning task (but see Wickens, this volume). Each experiment examin ... the influence of a single attribute and, if priming was heavy, it may have been the only attribute involved. We do not know that a given subject encoded any word on more than one attribute. In fact, one of the most pressing needs we have is for data that will help reach a decision on this issue. There are studies that indicate that a subject can encode in a multiple fashion (e.g., Bregman, 1968) but again the nature of the procedures has been such that the subject is essentially instructed to encode in particular ways. If an instructional procedure has any influence on the nature of the encoding on semantic attributes it may be used to argue against the automaticity of encoding and to demonstrate that the subject can use particular attributes in encoding, but again, we are not thereby informed about the encoding multiplicity that occurs for the single word in a list of unrelated words.

It may be that the PI-release technique leads to a misconception concerning the number of different attributes involved in establishing a laboratory memory and in that sense we are overloading memory. It should be evident that long-term memory carries a great deal of information about a word, or about the object it symbolizes, information that can in total be said to be its meaning. Under appropriate conditions, much of this information can be generated by the subject. The question that has been raised concerns the amount of this information that is automatically involved in the memories we observe being formed in the laboratory.

Finally, it should be noted that if we accept the ideas of multiplicity and automaticity of encoding literally, we have not only eliminated the intentional-incidental learning distinction, but have also enormously reduced the flexibility we can exercise in developing theoretical formulations relating the role of memory attributes to learning, that is, to the establishing of new memories. But, of course, it is an open question as to whether or not the memory attributes identified by the Wickens procedure are in a fundamental way involved in new learning that we study in the laboratory. As will be seen later, there may be situations in which they are not so involved. At the very minimum, however, there is the problem of explaining how the responses to the verbal units (from which the presence of semantic attributes are inferred) have been learned in the first place.

RECALL VERSUS RECOGNITION

Sooner, or later, any theory of coding must come to grips with the meaning of recognition measures as contrasted with recall measures. On the one hand, we may assert that the usual quantitative differences observed between recall and recognition scores are just that and no more. They are not, this assertion would include, indicative of any fundamental difference in the operation of memory mechanisms. This position has current adherents: "The findings ... make it increasingly difficult, in our opinion, to cling to the view that there is something inherently different about processes of recall and recognition...." (Tulving & Thomson, 1971, p. 123).

On the other hand, we might assert that differences in recognition and recall *do* represent fundamental information about memory and, indeed, that an examination of these differences is one of the more productive techniques we have for understanding the workings of memories. It is the intent of this section to develop this position. As will be seen, the position one takes on the recognition-versus-recall issue has implications for the handling of other problems.

Operationally, of course, recall and recognition procedures are quite distinct. In one case we ask, "What was that word?"; in the other, "Is this that word?" However, we are quite aware that operational distinctions need not reflect process distinctions. Nevertheless, in this case such a process distinction may be critical. In recall a part of the memory *must* include mechanisms for retrieval; this is simply not the case for recognition. We can construct what may seem at first to be an intermediate case. For example, if the words in a free-recall list were all two syllables in length, we might supply the first syllable of each word as a cue for recall, and such a procedure would probably give higher "recall" than without such aid. But, what would this mean? It certainly would not mean that the subject normally uses the first syllable of the word as the retrieval cue, or, even if he did, it does not tell us the retrieval cue for producing the first syllable. As will be seen in the next section, our knowledge of retrieval mechanisms may have been somewhat distorted by the use of such contrived experiments. In any event, it will be assumed here that the operational distinction between recall and recognition must reflect also a process difference in the memory mechanisms.

The distinction to be drawn must be clear at the outset. If a subject is given a list of words under instructions that he will be given a memory test, the composition of the memory established for a word is, obviously, quite independent of the nature of the memory test actually given. We assume, however, that the attributes of the memory utilized on a recognition test may not include some that are absolutely essential for the recall task. To this end, we have earlier distinguished between discriminative attributes and retrieval attributes (Underwood, 1969). The discriminative attributes are primarily responsible for recognition decisions, while recall involves both retrieval and discriminative attributes. To say this and no more is merely to make a convenient dichotomy to handle differences between recall and recognition. It is necessary to characterize the two classes further. This cannot be done with complete satisfaction. It is believed, however, that associative attributes, attributes that link one word with another, or that link the words with a particular situational context, are responsible for retrieval. However, as will be discussed in the next section, our ignorance concerning subject-produced retrieval cues is profound. The discriminative attributes, including the temporal, spatial, and frequency attributes, are assumed to be primarily responsible for discriminations among memories and as such are primarily responsible for recognition performance. We do not believe that these attributes can, except in the most contrived situations, serve as retrieval mechanisms. Preeminent among these discriminative attributes is the frequency attribute, which, we have assumed, is the dominant information used for recognition decisions (Underwood & Freund, 1970). A clear distinction between discrimination and retrieval has been recently demonstrated by Zechmeister (1972) for spatial information. The subject was given a long prose passage on pages that were clearly divided into quadrants. After the subject studied this passage it was discovered that the particular quadrant in which a certain fact was given could be identified with far greater than chance expectations even though the subject had not anticipated such a test. However, when other subjects were given the quadrant location of a particular fact and were asked to recall it, knowledge of the spatial position did not enhance recall.

In spite of the fact, therefore, that no clean and nonoverlapping distinction can be made between discriminative attributes and retrieval attributes, there seems to be usefulness in maintaining the distinction, and by identifying some attributes that are relatively pure cases it is possible to give some operational meaning to the distinction.

It was stated earlier that if a subject is given a list of words to learn under instructions that he will be given a memory test, the composition of his memory cannot be dependent upon the type of test given. This would not be true if the subject made an assumption about the nature of the test to be given and if he could, by directing his learning attempts, mold the memory to fit the type of test anticipated. Students may tell us that they study differently for a multiple-choice test than for an essay or short-answer test, but there does not seem to be substantial evidence that relates the subject's prelearning expectation concerning the nature of the test and his recall and recognition performance. It may or it may not be possible for the subject to influence appreciably the composition of the memory with regard to the balance between retrieval and discriminative attributes. In any event, as noted earlier, a description of recall as given by a number of writers to the effect that it requires both production and discrimination seems appropriate. The discriminative attributes monitor the units produced by the retrieval attributes. The discriminative attributes are involved in the decisions that "this word is appropriate" and "this one is not appropriate." The infrequency of intrusions requires this monitoring process and the appearance of an intrusion represents a discriminative failure in the same sense as does a false positive on a recognition test. In the same manner, it is highly probable that correct recall can occur without correct recognition. This is to say, for example, that in free recall the subject may retrieve a word that was in fact in the list but the word is rejected as not having been in the list. Evidence for this type of discriminative failure would never appear in the free-recall protocol but it does appear on a recognition test.

If we knew with any certainty the nature of the retrieval process—the attributes involved—it might be possible to conclude that there is simply no overlap in the processes involved in response production (retrieval) and the attributes involved in making decisions as to the appropriateness of inappropriateness of the words produced (recognition). Without such information, it would be foolish to insist that there is no overlap in the processes. In fact, some evidence indicates that associations, normally identified with recall, may play at least a "supporting" role in recognition (e.g., Wolford, 1971). But the logical analysis of the situation (as given above), as well as certain types of data, give a strong recommendation against ignoring the possibility that the recall-recognition process distinction may provide an excellent basis for understanding coding processes. Certain data will be advanced which, it is believed, further support the recommendation for separation.

Several investigators (e.g., Kintsch, 1970) have noted that certain variables that have a profound effect on recall have relatively little effect on recognition. Three further types of evidence bearing on the distinction between recognition and recall will be emphasized. First, Bower and Bostrom (1968) have shown that very little retroactive and proactive inhibition occur in recognition memory when the interference is of a within-list type. The recognition of a pair, A–B, is uninfluenced by following it in the list or preceding it in the list with an A–C pair. Although there is no corresponding recall evidence for this paradigm in a within-list design, it is known that a paradigm that normally produces less interference between lists (A–B, C–B) has a severe interfering effect within a word list (Underwood, Freund, & Jurca, 1969).

One might anticipate that the composition of memory would be influenced by intentional versus incidental learning instructions. However, as long as the subject perceives the units presented for learning under the two types of instructions, there does not seem to be any way to prevent certain discriminative attributes, particularly the frequency attribute, from becoming a part of the memory. Recognition memory does not appear to change as a function of the intentional-incidental instructional variable, even for a paired-associate task (e.g., Estes & DaPolito, 1967). It is possible, under special circumstances, to get equivalent free recall under intentional and incidental instructions (e.g., Mechanic & Mechanic, 1967), but as the Estes-DaPolito study shows, this does not occur for the paired-associate task under the conditions in which recognition is equivalent following intentional and incidental instructions.

Finally, if the attributes involved in recall and recognition are in complete overlap in terms of their function, the correlation between recognition and recall scores for subjects given both types of tasks should be substantial. Evidence from our laboratory (unpublished) shows that these correlations, while positive, are quite low between word recognition and free-recall of words. These findings suggest (a) that subjects differ to some extent in the composition of the encoded attributes, and (b) that the effectiveness of the composition for performance depends on the nature of the memory test. It is unfortunate that subjects do not produce more intrusions in free recall. In terms of the general conception of free recall outlined earlier, it must be predicted that the number of intrusions and recognition errors would be highly correlated since both represent a failure in the discriminative attributes of memory.

In summary, it may be reemphasized that it seems quite inappropriate at the present time to conclude that the operational distinction between recall and recognition is not representative of information of value for understanding the coding processes.

RETRIEVAL IN FREE RECALL

In a relatively short period of time (as research time within a discipline is measured), the free-recall task has become a major source of data and theory. On the one hand, theorists who wish to stress the organizational characteristics of memory (e.g., Mandler, 1967) have found the task a sympathetic one. On the other hand, the task has also been frequently used in an effort to mediate an understanding of how the individual item is stored in memory, and how it may be retrieved. An evaluation of the methods and outcomes of the latter studies is the primary purpose of this section. Essentially, these studies involve the use of external cues provided by the experimenter, the intent being to produce words from the free-recall list. It will be concluded that these studies have been based on a conception of multiple encoding to a degree that probably far exceeds reality. The emphasis will be on studies of single-trial free recall.

Two classes of cues have been used in attempts to understand the nature of the retrieval processes in free recall. One class may be thought of as vertical cues in that they consist of features or elements of the task as such. Examples would be serial position and other items in the list. The second class is made up of horizontal cues in that these cues are not a part of the list but are rather the assumed implicit associative responses elicited by individual words or by two or more words. As can be seen, this type of study implies that the free-recall task is in fact very similar to a paired-associate task but in which the stimulus for each response is assumed.

Vertical Cuing

Vertical cuing studies have been unable to add significantly to recall, hence have been unproductive in a positive sense, that is, we have not learned much about the nature of the retrieval processes the subject normally uses in free recall. Consider the Slamecka (1968) studies.

The subject was initially given two learning trials on a free-recall task. Then, the investigator presented a certain number of words from the list and the subjects were instructed to recall as many of the remaining words as possible. A control group simply recalled as many of the words from the total list as possible. The comparison in performance was made on the items not given as cues to the experimental group. In no case was the recall of the experimental group superior to that of the control. In the most extreme study, Slamecka presented his experimental subjects 29 of the 30 words from the list to observe the effect on the recall of the one missing word. Again, the frequency with which this thirtieth word was recalled was no greater for the experimental than for the control group. In a further study the subjects were first allowed to free recall, and then words from the list were supplied to see if further recall would result. None did.

The latter procedure was used by Freund and Underwood (1969), with various kinds of learning instructions (to emphasize various potential cues) and these were orthogonal to the types of cues provided at recall. Although some influence on learning was produced by the differences in instructions, apparently resulting from the subject's attempts to emphasize the cues he was instructed to emphasize, the cuing following unaided recall produced no significant change in overall recall. It was as if the subject had produced all of the words he could produce and none of the cues afforded him changed this. It did not seem unreasonable to assume, in accordance with an earlier conclusion by Cofer (1967), that normal recall had exhausted the storage and that insofar as the cues used were realistic ones, there was no storage-retrieval discrepancy.

The use of one word from a list to cue one or more other words from the same list seems to be conceptually sound. Words *do* get associated, or at least become consistently ordered during learning; otherwise, subjective organization would not develop. There is the possibility that consistent serial ordering does not mean item-to-item associations and that free recall may be reflecting the same enigma that appears in standard serial learning. However this may be, the fact is that the studies have shown that cuing by other words from the list has not appreciably influenced retrieval. Either one word from a list is not an effective cue for another word from the list, or all such words having a functional associative relationship with another word in the list were recalled by the subject and cuing beyond this was of no consequence.

Horizontal Cuing

As mentioned earlier, horizontal cuing uses a paired-associate model of free recall. When a word is presented in a free-recall task certain implicit associative responses (IARs) may occur to the word. We do not know that a word normally elicits multiple associative responses, and it may well be that some words will not elicit any. But the fact that some words may elicit an associative response implicitly now seems beyond reasonable doubt. Insofar as such simple and direct associations are bidirectional, recall might be aided. If the subject, at recall, "thinks of" the IAR he may be able to produce the word actually presented him. This would require a discrimination between the IAR and the word presented or an intrusion may result. Indeed, the few intrusions that do occur probably result from such a discrimination breakdown. In one sense the IAR route to recall—the paired-associate route—is reasonable and in another sense, unreasonable. If the subject can "get to" a correct word either via the IAR or via some other attribute, the probabilities of recalling the word should be increased. The notion is unreasonable in the sense that if each word elicits at least one verbal IAR, the total memory load is doubled and, as suggested above, the problem of discriminating between the words presented and those not presented (but implicitly produced) could also be severe.

Let us assume, in spite of the above reservations, that the IAR mechanism is one way by which a word may be recalled. How do we test this assumption? One possible way is to present a strong associate of each word to be recalled at the time of recall. Thus, if *white* is a word in the list, we could present the word *black* at the time of recall basing this procedure upon the reasonable assumption that for many subjects *black* is a likely IAR to *white*. Recall is enhanced (as compared with no cue or a weak IAR cue) by such procedures (Thomson & Tulving, 1970).

What are we to make of such findings as we attempt to understand how retrieval processes work in normal free recall? The present answer to this question is that we are not learning about retrieval processes in free recall by the horizontal cuing approach. The procedure circumvents entirely the natural production or retrieval

phase. A strong natural associate is used to produce a response the subject may t ....
evaluate for correctness by the attributes used in making such recognition decisions.
For those subjects who produce the expected associate to the cue, it is essentially
comparable to providing the word and requesting a decision as to whether or not it
had been in the list. If indeed the appropriate IAR had occurred during learning,
the probability of producing the list word by presenting the cue may be increased
(over the probabilities expected from word-association norms). It is of interest,
furthermore, to know that it appears possible to decrease the likelihood that a
primary associate will be elicited by the cue when certain contextual restraints are
introduced during the learning phase. But, it is not evident that we are learning
about the retrieval mechanisms the subject applies to the free-recall task.

It is always appropriate, of course, and often necessary, to contrive particular
situations for experimental purposes. But, we must be reasonably certain that the
contrived situation does not differ fundamentally from the situation that has
produced the phenomena we are trying to explain. Consider the study by Freund
and Underwood (1970). During learning the subject was presented two words
together, one of which he was instructed to learn. He was told that the other was
provided as a possible memory aid or as a possible retrieval cue (the two words were
strong restricted-type associates, e.g., *moon-round*). The evidence suggested that we
were able to influence the composition of the memory for a small number of items.
This was indicated by the fact that cuing did produce some additional recall
following completely free recall. But, here again, the evidence told us nothing about
how free recall took place for the words the subject had produced without aid.
Furthermore, the effectiveness of the cue was only demonstrated by what is
essentially a recognition test, and, as concluded earlier, this does not tell us how the
subject goes through recall and recognition when left to his own devices.

There is one further horizontal cuing situation that, perhaps, might seem to
adhere more closely to the true free-recall task, hence, the results of which may be
more informative concerning retrieval mechanisms. This is the situation in which
categorized lists are used (e.g., Tulving & Pearlstone, 1966). The evidence on
clustering makes it reasonably sure that the category name occurs as an IAR during
the learning, and is also involved in the retrieval of the individual words. Now, if the
subject fails to recall any words from a given category, presentation of the category
name will result in recall of at least some of the words from that category. Yet, if it
is sound to assume that recall of the category instances is normally produced via the
category name, the most critical question concerns the failure to recall the category
name. Why is he able to retrieve the category name in some cases and not in others?
The category name occupies the same logical status as does the individual word in
an unrelated list.

A Change in Direction

The above comments have been critical of the cuing studies if these studies are
viewed as vehicles by which we have tried to understand retrieval processes in free
recall. Vertical cuing, which seems to be the most realistic approach conceptually,
has not been productive of information from which we might infer the manner in
which the subject produces words from a free-recall list. Once again, perhaps, the

use of cuing has resulted from a conception of memory that is overloaded with attributes or in which certain of the attributes (including some of the associative attributes) are irrelevant or epiphenomenal to the usual free-recall processes. It may be appropriate and timely to suggest a change in the direction of our thinking, albeit a change that will undoubtedly appear regressive to some since it emphasizes the older, more traditional approach to problems in verbal learning. Yet, as Postman (1971) has demonstrated, some of the traditional notions still have vigorous theoretical potential. In molding this approach, three types of observations are considered important. Each will be considered in turn.

However we go beyond it in our explanatory attempts, it is patent that we must start with the fact that rehearsal frequency is fundamental. The Rundus and Atkinson data (1970) are impressive on this score. If we assume that the subjects in single-trial free recall normally do implicitly what they did explicitly in the Rundus-Atkinson study, there can be no doubt that recall and frequency of rehearsal of a word are directly related. The primacy effect seems to be due entirely to the fact that the initial serial positions provide a convenient and near universally used basis for serial rehearsal. In a study in our laboratory (as yet unpublished), the subjects were allowed to pace themselves through a long list of unrelated words. The subjects were told they would receive only one trial before recall, and that they should govern how long each slide for each word remained on the screen. The data show that the time for each item increased sharply for the first six serial positions, followed by a drop. This suggests that with each additional word it took longer and longer for the subject to accomplish his rehearsal of the items in the initial positions.

Not only is it believed that rehearsal frequency should be used as a keystone in developing a theory of single-trial free recall for unrelated lists, but also that it represents a fundamental consideration when we ask about the incorporation of the effects of certain task variables. This is to say that the first approach is to ask how a particular variable might increase the rehearsal frequency. For categorized lists, the IAR (category name) is given several implicit frequency inputs (rehearsals), the number depending upon the number of category instances and the frequency with which the IAR occurs to each. If frequency and recall are directly related, the category name should indeed have a high probability of recall. Furthermore, in at least some cases, it appears that the category name serves as a convenient mediator for rehearsal of words representing the category instances (Wood & Underwood, 1967). If words within a list have direct associative connections, for example, *table* and *chair,* the appearance of one may result in the implicit rehearsal of the other. In short, whenever we discover a variable that influences single-trial free recall learning, it would always seem appropriate to ask first whether or not the variable might influence rehearsal attempts. The more fundamental question of explanation is, of course, how rehearsal frequency is so directly tied to the probability of recall. More on this matter later.

As a second type of observation, an observation believed relevant to any interpretation of single-trial free recall learning, consider the behavior of the subject at recall. Reference is made specifically to the speed with which the subject produces (orally or in writing) the words he is capable of recalling. It is as if there is a bus load of people all trying to get out the door at the same time, and the number involved for long lists (or a big bus?) is far greater than could occupy the theoretical short-term memory. Murdock and Okada (1970) have quantified this behavior for oral recall and their data show clearly the "burst" of words the subject initially emits. Furthermore, they show that if 10 seconds pass without the subject recalling a word, the chances that he will subsequently recall one are essentially nil.

These observations on recall behavior are described for one purpose, namely, to indicate that such behavior does not suggest complex retrieval functions. They do not suggest that for each word produced the subject is somehow supplying himself with a cue that is different for each word as implied by the paired-associate model of cuing. Rather, it is as if the subject has a pool of words he "spews" out without, so to speak, any particular stimulus being involved.

The third observation actually represents several points from which a single factor will emerge. Tulving (1968) has pointed out that in one sense when a subject is asked to learn a list of words for free recall, learning of the words is not required. If the words are common ones, the subject has already learned them. The learning that is required involves separating his repertoire of words into two pools, one being appropriate to the experimental situation, the other not. This can be done on the basis of the discriminative attributes involved in recognition. The critical theoretical problem with which we are dealing is how the subject learns to *produce* the words appropriate to the situation.

It is known that certain types of memory information can be quickly and near perfectly acquired in the experimental situation even though this information does not coincide, or indeed may conflict, with information acquired from previous experiences outside of the laboratory. For example, if subjects are asked to judge the frequency with which words have been presented in a long free-recall type list, these judgments are completely uninfluenced by the frequency information the subject carries with him as derived from other sources (Underwood, Zimmerman, & Freund, 1971). This can only mean that there is an association between the words and the experimental situation, at least with regard to frequency information.

The cuing studies reviewed earlier have examined two possible environments as possible sources of retrieval cues for free recall. Results were essentially negative with regard to the environment of the list per se, although these findings do not eliminate this source for the words which the subject recalled. The second environment has been the implicit linguistic environment. The only fact that seems clear from the consideration of such studies is that the implicit linguistic environment can increase the rehearsal frequency of words within the list. Somewhat by default, perhaps, the remaining environment must be involved in a fundamental way in single-trial free recall, and the only remaining environment is the experimental context. And this is the third point, namely, that the words are associated with the experimental context and that the context is a primary eliciting stimulus.

If frequency information concerning a word can be associated with a particular context, why cannot the word per se also enter into such an association, with the probabilities of this occurring being directly related to the situational frequency? To speak of experimental context is subject to many age-old criticisms. We cannot use context in an entirely literal fashion, perhaps, since the change in the experimental room to quite a different room has little influence on recall. But, physical change more closely associated with the process of presenting the words may be involved (just as such physical changes influence the performance in the release-from-PI procedures). Further, however, and probably most important, context must include all psychological reactions of the subject. It must include his reactions to the instructions; it must include any strategy of learning he imposes on himself, or has imposed on him; it must include any affective reactions, including those elicited by the words. All such reactions become a part of the context, and probably the critical part.

Given that words can be associated to the context as indicated, the rapidity with which the words are emitted at recall becomes reasonable. The subject does not have different retrieval cues for each word; most are associated with the stimulus complex. This does not deny the role of other supplementary cues, such as serial position, nor does it deny that some words get associated with each other so that if one is recalled the other will be also. Such associations must be expected on the same grounds that words become associated with contextual factors, that is, frequency of occurrence together in the rehearsal pattern.

Two further problems must be considered briefly in concluding this section. The major criticism in the past against the notion of contextual involvement in learning has been that it does not lead to analytical research. However, it appears now that techniques are available to make the enterprise somewhat more productive. The fact that heavy unlearning occurs when two successive unrelated lists are learned not only may be used in support of the contextual interpretation (the context is the A term in the A–B, A–C paradigm), but also suggests that the influence of the variation in contextual factors between two lists can be gauged by the changes in the amount of unlearning.

The second problem deals with the role of rehearsal frequency. How does rehearsal result in better recall? One may take the position that events get associated by contiguity and the more frequent this contiguity, the greater the likelihood that a functional association will be manifest in performance. Wallace (1970) has made a strong case for this interpretation in handling a number of the phenomena observed in free-recall learning.

It has seemed at one time to the writer (Underwood, 1969) that increased performance over trials might be accounted for by either of two possibilities, both being based on the notion of horizontal cuing as a model for free recall. One possibility was that across trials more and more associative retrieval cues were implicitly occurring so that avenues of access to the word to be recalled were increased. The other possibility was that a single associative attribute became stronger and stronger with trials. It does not seem now that either of these possibilities can be considered seriously. In addition to the arguments raised earlier against the horizontal cuing notion, we (Mrs. Linda Esrov and myself) have collected enough data to convince us that these notions were not worth pursuing. In one case subjects were given a different parenthetical associative word cue for each word on each trial, and in another, the same parenthetical cue over all trials. All cues were reasonable in the sense that they might well have been produced implicitly by the subject if this was in fact what he did when left to his own devices. The idea of the experiment was simply to make sure he produced them on each occurrence of the word. However, as compared with a control condition (no cues), free recall did not differ over trials. The reports of the subjects led us to believe that they really did not want to be bothered with such extra material. Again, perhaps, it indicates that our theoretical conceptions overloaded the memory.

To pursue the matter of the influence of repetition over trials is beyond the scope of this paper. It has become obvious, however, that were it to be pursued, the emphasis would be on the role of some of the older concepts, as direct associations by frequency and contiguity, and not on elaborate search, cuing, and coding processes.

NATURAL LANGUAGE MEDIATORS (NLMs)

Although natural language mediation has been studied with formal mediation paradigms, the use of the abbreviation (NLM) and the major thrust of the topic in contemporary literature has come from studies in which the reports of the subject form the basic data. The paired-associate model has been most frequently used, and the reported NLMs are usually of the first and third types of encoding as identified in the early section of this paper. Thus, transformations may occur in either or both of the two terms, or the two items may remain intact but with some inserted (by the subject) intermediary term linking the two. The transformations usually occur when low-meaningful units are used. The fact of interest is the correlation between reported use of mediators and the ease of learning (e.g., Montague & Wearing, 1967).

Extent of NLMs

When an investigator asks his subjects to report NLMs at some point in the learning, it is customary to find that NLMs cannot be reported for all pairs; such pairs are said to be learned by rote. Most investigators have taken the reports of rote-learned items at face value, that is, they have assumed that reports of NLMs and failures to report NLMs are equally valid. However, some (e.g., Prytulak, 1971) have argued that only the reports of NLMs are valid, and that failures to report an NLM cannot be taken as evidence that an NLM was not or had not been present. Certain evidence would argue against this position. Montague and Kiess (1968) asked their subjects to report NLMs for syllable pairs in a scaling, not a learning, study. For each pair the subject was allowed 15 seconds to write down the associative device suggested by the two units; they were to search for a means to link the two. Almost any linking device was accepted by the experimenters as representing an NLM. Yet, even with the long interval to search, NLMs were reported for only 60 percent of the pairs. Furthermore, frequency of reported NLMs is directly related to the meaningfulness of the material. It is, perhaps, remotely possible that when an NLM is not reported there really was one present but the subject was not aware of it, or that the content of the NLM was such that the subject feared to report it. On the other hand, it may well be possible that reports of NLMs are not always valid; the subject may view the situation somewhat as an intelligence test where reporting an NLM is believed to be a good thing. Or, as Montague and Kiess (1968) point out, the subject may simply construct an NLM to please the experimenter.

If our intent is to seek general principles of learning, it does not seem appropriate to start with the assumption that all verbal learning is mediated by NLMs. By so doing we are forced to ask how the mediator was learned and in this regress there must be some point or time in the history of the subject where verbal habits were learned without mediation. Let us leave open the possibility that we can study pure associative learning with the college student.

The Meaning of NLMs

Mediators have been reported by subjects as long as verbal-learning experiments have been conducted. But always, as is true at the present, the experimenters have recognized the delicacy of the situation for drawing cause-effect conclusions. The basic issue may be illustrated. Suppose a stimulus term is RYT and the response term CEZ. The subject might report that the stimulus term made him think of *rat* and the response term, *cheese*. Now, the problem is that these two transformations may occur without entering into the learning; RYT and CEZ could be directly associated. Consider a parallel case with a pair of words, *mouse* and *cracker*. The stimulus term may produce the implicit response *rat*, the response term the implicit response *cheese*. But that these events occurred does not mean that they were responsible for the learning. Yet, undoubtedly a report of such transformations would be tabulated as an NLM. This is not to imply that NLMs are not involved in a causal way in learning; some reported NLMs are extremely compelling. But it must be realized (most investigators do) that transformations and so-called mediators may be reported that are entirely epiphenomenal to the learning. A more complete comprehension of the issue may be obtained by a further examination of the work of Montague and Kiess (1968). These investigators developed an associability scale (AS) following the procedure noted above in which subjects were given 15 seconds to find a means of linking two syllables. This scale was shown to be highly reliable. However, when pairs varying in AS values were used in experiments on learning, some unexpected findings emerged.

In the first experiment, with four lists differing in mean AS value, the differences in learning the four lists failed to achieve statistical reliability. This was true in spite of the fact that reported NLMs following learning increased sharply from 27 percent to 59 percent as AS increased across the four lists. In this case, therefore, reported NLMs and learning were not correlated. In a second experiment, using only two lists with relatively extreme values on the AS scale, a comparable set of data emerged. In a third experiment the exposure time of the pairs was increased from 2 to 5 seconds and the difference in trials to learn the two lists was statistically reliable (7.31 versus 5.68 trials to criterion). Thus, under some conditions the relationship between learning and the AS scale will be found, but it is certainly not a striking one. At the same time, the AS scale predicts reported mediators in the learning situation with great precision. Such data can only underline the caution that must underlie possible interpretations of the NLMs. However, neither of two possible interpretations of such data can allow a fundamental role of NLMs in determining the rate of learning. If NLMs as reported are assumed to be the true mechanisms by which the learning occurred, then it must be concluded that NLMs have only a small effect on the rate at which the learning occurs. A second possible conclusion is that NLMs are irrelevant to the learning and the low correlation between reported NLMs and learning is to be attributed to some other characteristic of the pairs.

There is a more general issue that should be mentioned at this time. The differences among verbal units, particularly nonsense and consonant syllables, which we often speak of as meaningfulness, can be described quantitatively in a number of different ways. Thus, we can speak of number of associates produced, pronunciability, approximation of letter sequences to those in words, number of transformations required to produce a stable NLM, and so on. All of these scales are quite highly correlated with learning and with each other. But, as we found a number of years ago (Underwood & Schulz, 1960), to move from the operations involved in quantifying these scales to a sound theoretical base is a very hazardous and discouraging undertaking. A subject, under appropriate instructions, can perceive many differences among verbal units and can express these reliably on the various scales we use. We are compelled, it seems, to search for a theoretical solution for learning by examining the implications of the scaled characteristic for learning. This approach has simply not provided the solution. The mistake we make, it may be ventured, is to assume that the behavior of the subject in accomplishing the scaling has a direct and fundamental representation in his learning behavior. This approach will not work and we would be wise to abandon it and search for the solution at a different level of theoretical thought.

The "Dropout" of NLMs

It has been observed that reported NLMs may decrease in frequency late in the learning of a list (Adams & McIntyre, 1967). If NLMs are fundamentally involved in learning, this finding is astounding and certainly requires the use of explanatory notions which are not readily apparent. Consider the simple case where X is a mediator between A and B, A-X-B. Once X starts to occur in the sequence, continued trials should, it would seem, increase the probabilities that it would continue to occur, not decrease them. It is inadequate merely to say that it drops out because it is adaptive for the organism; principles of learning should make its occurrence more and more probable. Some resolution is required. Two different cases will be considered. The first is based on the assumption that the mediator is truly mediating the learning, the second upon the assumption that the mediator is epiphenomenal.

An explanation for the dropout of a true mediator would seem to require getting the nominal response term to occur prior to the mediator so that it occurs in temporal contiguity with the stimulus term, or its encoded version. The X-B association can be thought of as a two-unit serial chain. In Mackay's (1971) recent work on spoonerisms he has several demonstrations of the fact that the second term may be made to occur before the first if it is the stressed element in the chain. It would seem that B is clearly the stressed element in the X-B chain. It is the only one of the two that has to be produced overtly for the experimenter's benefit This mechanism, therefore, may allow the B term to move ahead of X, thereby becoming contiguous with A and, consequently, develop its own direct association with A.

Even if this suggested explanation for the dropping of our true NLMs has merit, it is not clear why the subject would forget the mediator unless some extinction takes place. An account of how mediators may drop out is of interest for the understanding of mediation in situations in addition to those involving NLMs. It seems likely that in certain transfer paradigms, for example, identical stimuli and highly associated response terms, the second list is learned by mediation from the first-list response to the second. Subjects have, as in the case of NLMs, reported that the mediator dropped out in later trials (Barnes & Underwood, 1959). It also may be noted that in this paradigm we usually observe a curious little depression in performance after several trials of initial high positive transfer on the second list. There are several possible ways to account for this, but if it is true that the mediator is dropping out, the subject is actually changing to a newer and perhaps weaker association.

For the present discussion we have assumed the truth of the statement that mediators do drop out. It should be noted that there are situations where this does not occur even with extended responding (Richardson, 1967). However, the habits involved (linking of sequential letters in the alphabet) were of long standing and this may have prevented the collapse of the chain.

As the second case we will assume that the NLMs are epiphenomenal and ask how the reports of dropouts could be explained. Assume the stimulus term RCH produces the implicit mediator *rich*. To say that this is epiphenomenal is to say that a direct association could be established between RCH and the response term even though the *rich* is occurring as an implicit response. However, as the direct association between RCH and the response term develops, unlearning of the implicit response should occur because an A-B, A-C paradigm is formed. The unlearning results in forgetting and the subject, later in learning, will be unable to report that the so-called NLM had been present.

Conclusion

We cannot conclude, of course, that NLMs may not at times be fundamentally involved in learning. Experimenters can provide the subject with mediators that will facilitate performance. Yet there are situations in which, from the experimenter's point of view, mediation with strongly established laboratory associations would have markedly reduced the difficulty of the learning task of the moment and still there was no evidence that the subject utilized such mediation (Underwood & Ekstrand, 1968). Such observations again caution against putting too much theoretically into the subject's memory mechanisms.

FORGETTING

Given that a memory is established, the study of forgetting deals with its persistence over time. Theories of forgetting (at the behavioral level) have used the concept of interference as a pivotal one, with other concepts being subsidiary in that they were employed to account for variations in the amount of interference. A brief review of the status of the theory will form the background against which several comments emphasizing the implications for coding theory may be made.

As is well known, the emphasis on interference as a focal concept in forgetting theory arose from the work on proactive and retroactive inhibition. It may not be fully realized that transfer effects in learning, and retroactive and proactive inhibition, are exclusively concerned with associative attributes of memory for memories that have been established in the laboratory. The use of various transfer paradigms and a variety of similarity manipulations have generated a considerable body of knowledge concerning the roles played by implicit associative responses; that is, when they may interfere with or facilitate learning, when they may serve as mediators, and when they are of no consequence.

The results of a closely related area of endeavor seem equally well known. When the mechanisms and outcomes of implicit associative interference derived from laboratory studies were extended to incorporate associative attributes learned outside the laboratory, the data have given at best only scant support to the validity of the extension. More than a decade has passed since the generalized formulation was advanced (Underwood & Postman, 1960). The theory explicitly anticipates differences in forgetting of appreciable magnitude when certain task variables are manipulated. It anticipates these because the occurrence of implicit associative attributes learned outside the laboratory should result in particular interference paradigms that in turn have quite predictable consequences when manipulated in the laboratory. The rate of forgetting of single lists of different types do not have the variance expected by the theory. In fact, insofar as there are constants for behavior, rate of forgetting of the single list seems to be one.

One might evaluate this outcome by offering commiserations, or one might conclude that the theory and its failure have only a parochial interest. However, the implications of this ten-year history go far beyond the particular theory involved and certainly relate in a basic way to the theme of this volume.

The theory as formulated, and many of the tests made of it, were based upon a conception of memory in which simple and direct associations were the critical ingredients in the analysis. Perhaps this pretheoretical assumption is the basis for the inadequacies of the theory. It might be maintained that interference within the laboratory may be productively analyzed by emphasizing simple associations because the nature of the tasks used emphasize learning of this kind. But (to continue), learning outside the laboratory results in memories that are far more elaborate in terms of images, mediators, organizations, and so on. These memories represent a level of encoding so different from the laboratory associations that any interaction between the two would not be expected.

Available data give no significant support to this line of reasoning. When differential encoding procedures are induced in learning the same task, the constancy in the rate of forgetting continues to be observed. Three diverse examples may be noted. Delin (1969), using serial lists, gave varying instructions for learning, the instructions differing in the way in which mnemonics should be used. There were seven types of instructions; at one extreme, those commonly given for rote learning, and at the other extreme instructions for the use of bizarre imagery.

These instructions did produce differences in learning but there was no interaction between the instructional conditions and the observed forgetting over time even up to 15 weeks.

Olton (1969) used fifth-grade school children and induced the use of short sentences to learn the two terms in a paired-associate list, a technique sometimes referred to as sentential facilitation. Learning was more rapid for the subjects given these sentence frames than for those not given them, but there was no difference in the rate of forgetting over a week. Epstein (1972) used three-word sentences or a random string of three words as response terms in paired-associate lists. Rate of learning differed in the expected way but there was no interaction between the type of response term and the length of the retention interval.

Such studies give no support to the idea that the composition of the memory, in terms of the attributes that make it up, is fundamentally involved in differences in rate of forgetting. In certain cases where a mnemonic is used, one might predict more rapid forgetting than without the mnemonic. If, for example, an NLM is used to link a pair of words, there is one more element in the memory than is true for a direct association. If forgetting may occur as a consequence of the loss of any one element, the more rapid forgetting of the mediated pair might be expected. This probabilistic expectation appears to have no support in the available data, although one could always posit counteracting factors.

There is a further way to view the differences between laboratory learning and the learning that has occurred outside the laboratory. The laboratory may isolate the subject so that his natural habits and memory attributes do not enter into the interference with the laboratory task in the way assumed by the theory. There is no way to gauge the extent of the interaction between the verbal habits the subject brings with him to the laboratory and the habits he acquires in the laboratory. However, in study after study the learning has been influenced in the expected way, as if the natural habits were "in" the laboratory and behaving as expected. A few of these studies, but not most, allow an alternative interpretation in terms of the lack of preestablished associations rather than interference from such associations. But, beyond reasonable doubt, we must conclude that the laboratory does not produce isolation to the extent that there is no interaction between established habits and the habits required to learn the laboratory task. Learning is influenced by these established habits, rate of forgetting is not.

Some of us have long believed that in making comparisons of retention for lists in which task variables are manipulated it is necessary to carry the learning to the same level. The reason, of course, is that level of learning is itself a potent variable determining retention and so must be neutralized. This usually means that the different tasks are given different numbers of trials or different amounts of learning time. Are we, in our insistence upon equal levels of learning, in some way adding or subtracting memory attributes in such a way as to neutralize the effects on retention of the variable being manipulated? If so, it is not apparent. That the method of inducing the learning may have some relevance is suggested in a study by Amster, Keppel, and Myer (1970). In this study an adjusted learning technique was used in taking subjects learning lists of different difficulty to the same criterion. The data on retention gave strong support to the theory, which assumes that the natural language habits will interfere with the habits learned in the laboratory. However, it has not been possible thus far to comprehend how this change in the procedure is related to the theoretical mechanisms assumed by the theory. Nevertheless, this is one lead that must be pursued.

Some summary evaluative comments will be made. It would not seem that interference theory has overloaded the memory with mechanisms. Even when these are expanded in number and kind, the basic problem remains. The data that have proven so intractable to interference theory must be viewed with concern by anyone interested in memory, whether his sympathies lie with the interference approach or with some other. Tasks in which a variety of encoding processes are used in establishing the memory are not forgotten at different rates. Lists of high meaningfulness, low meaningfulness, high similarity, low similarity, and so on, are all forgotten at the same rate. Further, individual differences in rate of forgetting are minimal (Underwood, 1964). Do these facts mean what they appear to mean, namely, that a wide variety of mechanisms used in establishing memories, memories that must be encoded differently, have no consequence for long-term retention? Or does it mean that underlying all of these memories there is one, powerful, common constituent that is responsible for the observed constant rate of forgetting and that remains uninfluenced by particular manipulations suggested by extant theory? One cannot but conclude that the problem is of critical centrality and that its solution is no longer the sole responsibility of the interference theorist.

SUMMARY COMMENT

Some problems in the handling of coding mechanisms in five different research areas have been evaluated. One possible conclusion kept emerging, a conclusion that might characterize many of our theoretical approaches: Our models and theories are overloading the subject's memory. This should not be taken to mean that many different mechanisms and attributes have not been involved in establishing the many, many memories which form the basis of the intellect of the young adult. But there are no grounds for the assumption that all of these attributes and mechanisms come instantaneously into play when we present a simple verbal learning task to the subject in the laboratory. Our theories must to some extent provide for selective encoding. Furthermore, even if certain attributes, particularly the associative attributes, are present at the time a new memory is formed, it is by no means a certainty that they are involved in a fundamental way in the learning that is observed.

REFERENCES

Adams, J. A., & McIntyre, J. S. Natural language mediation and all-or-none learning. *Canadian Journal of Psychology*, 1967, **21**, 436-449.

Amster, H., Keppel, G., & Meyer, A. Learning and retention of letter pairs as a function of association strength. *American Journal of Psychology*, 1970, **83**, 22-39.

Barnes, J. M., & Underwood, B. J. "Fate" of first-list associations in transfer theory. *Journal of Experimental Psychology*, 1959, **58**, 97-105.

Bower, G. H., & Bostrom, A. Absence of within-list PI and RI in short-term recognition memory. *Psychonomic Science*, 1968, 10, 211-212.

Bregman, A. S. Forgetting curves with semantic, phonetic, graphic, and contiguity cues. *Journal of Experimental Psychology*, 1968, 78, 539-546.

Cofer, C. N. Does conceptual organization influence the amount retained in immediate recall? In B. Kleinmuntz (Ed.), *Concepts and the structure of memory*. New York: Wiley, 1967. Pp. 181-214.

Delin, P. S. Learning and retention of English words with successive approximations to a complex mnemonic instruction. *Psychonomic Science*, 1969, 17, 87-89.

Epstein, W. Retention of sentences, anomalous sequences and random sequences. *American Journal of Psychology*, 1972, 85, 21-30.

Estes, W. K., & DaPolito, F. Independent variation of information storage and retrieval processes in paired-associate learning. *Journal of Experimental Psychology*, 1967, 75, 18-26.

Freund, J. S., & Underwood, B. J. Storage and retrieval cues in free recall learning. *Journal of Experimental Psychology*, 1969, 81, 49-53.

Freund, J. S., & Underwood, B. J. Restricted associates as cues in free recall. *Journal of Verbal Learning and Verbal Behavior*, 1970, 9, 136-141.

Hudson, R. L. Category clustering as a function of level of information and number of stimulus presentations. *Journal of Verbal Learning and Verbal Behavior*, 1968, 7, 1106-1108.

Kintsch, W. *Learning, memory, and conceptual processes*. New York: Wiley, 1970.

MacKay, D. G. Stress pre-entry in motor systems. *American Journal of Psychology*, 1971, 84, 35-51.

Mandler, G. Organization and memory. In K. W. Spence & J. T. Spence (Eds.), *The psychology of learning and motivation*, Vol. 1. New York: Academic Press, 1967. Pp. 327-372.

Mechanic, A., & Mechanic, J. D. Response activities and the mechanism of selectivity in incidental learning. *Journal of Verbal Learning and Verbal Behavior*, 1967, 6, 389-397.

Montague, W. E., & Kiess, H. O. The associability of CVC pairs. *Journal of Experimental Psychology Monograph*, 1968, 78, (October, Pt. 2), 1-21.

Montague, W. E., & Wearing, A. J. The complexity of natural language mediators and its relation to paired-associate learning. *Psychonomic Science*, 1967, 7, 135-136.

Murdock, B. B., Jr., & Okada, R. Interresponse times in single-trial free recall. *Journal of Experimental Psychology*, 1970, 86, 263-267.

Olton, R. M. The effect of a mnemonic upon the retention of paired-associate verbal material. *Journal of Verbal Learning and Verbal Behavior*, 1969, 8, 43-48.

Peterson, L. R., & Peterson, M. J. Short-term retention of individual verbal items. *Journal of Experimental Psychology*, 1959, 54, 157-173.

Postman, L. Organization and interference. *Psychological Review*, 1971, 78, 290-302.

Prytulak, L. S. Natural language mediation. *Cognitive Psychology*, 1971, 2, 1-56.

Richardson, J. Latencies of implicit associative responses and the effect of the anticipation interval on mediated transfer. *Journal of Verbal Learning and Verbal Behavior*, 1967, 6, 819-826.

Rundus, D., & Atkinson, R. C. Rehearsal processes in free recall: A procedure for direct observation. *Journal of Verbal Learning and Verbal Behavior*, 1970, 9, 99-105.

Slamecka, N. J. An examination of trace storage in free recall. *Journal of Experimental Psychology*, 1968, 76, 504-513.

Thomson, D. M., & Tulving, E. Associative encoding and retrieval: Weak and strong cues. *Journal of Experimental Psychology*, 1970, 86, 255-262.

Tulving, E. Theoretical issues in free recall. In T. R. Dixon & D. L. Horton (Eds.), *Verbal behavior and general behavior theory*. Englewood Cliffs: Prentice-Hall, 1968. Pp. 2-36.

Tulving, E., & Pearlstone, Z. Availability versus accessibility of information in memory for words. *Journal of Experimental Psychology*, 1966, 5, 381-391.

Tulving, E., & Thomson, D. M. Retrieval processes in recognition memory: Effects of associative context. *Journal of Experimental Psychology*, 1971, 87, 116-124.

Underwood, B. J. Degree of learning and the measurement of forgetting. *Journal of Verbal Learning and Verbal Behavior*, 1964, 3, 112-129.

Underwood, B. J. Attributes of memory. *Psychological Review*, 1969, 76, 559-573.

Underwood, B. J., & Ekstrand, B. R. Differentiation among stimuli as a factor in transfer performance. *Journal of Verbal Learning and Verbal Behavior*, 1968, 7, 172-175.

Underwood, B. J., & Freund, J. S. Testing effects in the recognition of words. *Journal of Verbal Learning and Verbal Behavior*, 1970, 9, 117-125.

Underwood, B. J., Freund, J. S., & Jurca, N. H. The influence of number of response terms on paired-associate learning, transfer, and proactive inhibition. *Journal of Verbal Learning and Verbal Behavior*, 1969, 8, 369-377.

Underwood, B. J., & Postman, L. Extraexperimental sources of interference in forgetting. *Psychological Review*, 1960, 67, 73-95.

Underwood, B. J., & Richardson, J. Verbal concept learning as a function of instructions and dominance level. *Journal of Experimental Psychology*, 1956, 51, 229-238.

Underwood, B. J., & Schulz, R. W. *Meaningfulness and verbal learning.* Philadelphia: Lippincott, 1960.

Underwood, B. J., Zimmerman, J., & Freund, J. S. Retention of frequency information with observations on recognition and recall. *Journal of Experimental Psychology*, 1971, 87, 149-162.

Wallace, W. P. Consistency of emission order in free recall. *Journal of Verbal Learning and Verbal Behavior*, 1970, 9, 58-68.

Wickens, D. D. Encoding categories of words: An empirical approach to meaning. *Psychological Review*, 1970, 77, 1-15.

Wolford, G. Function of distinct associations for paired-associate performance. *Psychological Review*, 1971, 78, 303-313.

Wood, G., & Underwood, B. J. Implicit responses and conceptual similarity. *Journal of Verbal Learning and Verbal Behavior*, 1967, 6, 1-10.

Zechmeister, E. B. Memory for place on the page. *Journal of Educational Psychology*, 1972, in press.

2
TRACES, CONCEPTS, AND CONSCIOUS CONSTRUCTIONS[1]

Michael I. Posner and Robert E. Warren
University of Oregon

Studies of the perception of letters (Posner, 1969), words (Schaeffer & Wallace, 1969), and sentences (Collins & Quillian, 1969; Clark & Chase, 1972; Foss, 1969) have begun to reveal the complex sequence of mental operations involved in coding such material. A word (e.g., *plant*) is first of all a physical code which uniquely represents details of the structure of the print or accent in which it is presented. A hundred milliseconds or so later it is also represented as part of a "name" which is in itself indifferent to mode of presentation. Still later it may be related to semantic structures having to do with flowers and vegetables or with labor unions and factories. By appropriate techniques it is possible to study, not only the time relations of these codings, but also the attention demands of the production and preservation of each code. One of us has reviewed elsewhere the evidence that leads to this conception (Posner, 1969; Posner & Keele, 1970; Posner, Lewis & Conrad, in press). Our studies indicate that successive codings are laid down and maintained in parallel. That is, the name code of a word is extracted from its physical code, but it does not replace the physical code. Rather, both remain present and compete for the limited rehearsal capacity of the subject (Posner, 1969).

In this paper we wish to explore the idea that each stage of coding gives rise to a code which, under favorable conditions, may be stored in long-term memory. Corresponding to the physical code of a particular item is a trace that preserves the

[1] The preparation of this paper was supported in part by National Science Foundation Grant GB 21021 and by the Advanced Research Projects Agency of the Department of Defense as monitored by the Air Force Office of Scientific Research under Contract No. F44620-67C-0099.

The authors are very much indebted to the many people whose ideas about encoding and memory are represented here. In particular, the valuable theoretical insights and experimental demonstrations by our colleagues N. Frost, D. Hintzman, R. Hyman, S. W. Keele, J. Lewis, and G. Reicher who have often allowed us to quote from as yet unpublished papers.

individual character of that experience. The temporal sequence of such items serves as a memory system of our individual experiences. Although perhaps incomplete and difficult to retrieve, this memory system underlies our limited ability to recognize and recreate the detailed structure of our own past experience. Recently, Hintzman and Block (1970) have revived the term "trace column," used earlier by Koffka (1935) as a name for a memory system of this type.

Studies of encoding show that input information quickly contacts memory units that serve to identify and provide a name or meaning for it. The presentation of a visual word is followed by the activation of a visual trace system, the word name and related words. Morton (1969) has called the memory units related to word recognition "logogens." More generally these units may be called concepts since they can be activated by numerous inputs which differ in physical character. These concepts serve as a means of storing the general character of past experience. The associations built up between these concepts constitute much of our knowledge about words and familiar objects. Experience organizes these concepts into structures. For example, the logogens or concepts corresponding to the digit names are themselves organized by association into a list ordered by magnitude. Different views of the same face are also organized into a complex structure that allows us to become increasingly able to recognize the face despite distortion. The retention of an experience will be affected by the kind of structures it activates. Experimental psychologists and others have proposed a number of different types of structure and have begun to explore the consequences of differences in structure for memory and thought. Some types of structure are reviewed in a later section.

The usual view of the relation of long-term memory and perception is outlined in the upper panel of Figure 1. According to this view we must first perceive an item consciously before it contacts long-term memory. However, studies of coding show that actual performance resembles the diagram in the lower panel. What we perceive is crucially dependent upon the structure imposed upon input by information in long-term memory. For example, a word is perceived as a whole (Reicher, 1969; Krueger, 1970) because it is a unit within long-term memory. The view outlined in the lower panel of Figure 1 suggests that there is an important distinction between those habitual structures that are contacted automatically by input and that, therefore, affect our conscious experience, and those structures that may be activated only as a result of conscious effort. It seems to us that multiattribute theories of memory badly need to consider this distinction (Bower, 1967; Wickens, 1970) or they might seem to imply an organism with virtually unlimited capacity for classification. Such a view runs counter to the limits usually found in studies of even highly automated performance. Indeed, in this volume Underwood has proposed somewhat the same idea by suggesting that the priming that takes place in the PI release paradigm may lead to an overestimation of the amount of automatic encoding. Wickens' new experiments on subliminal perception (this volume) are clearly designed to develop a stronger method for testing which categorizations are made at input. We explore this issue in the final section of this chapter.

In summary, we wish to consider four propositions about the role of coding in memory. First, each stage of encoding gives rise to a memory appropriate to the

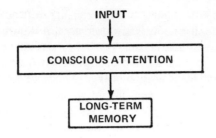

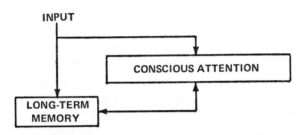

FIG. 1. Upper panel portrays the idea of long-term memory following after conscious attention. This model stresses long-term memory in the sense of storage of new information. The lower panel portrays the idea of consciousness as the result of the interaction of input and long-term memory. This model stresses the role of long-term memory in perception and recognition.

code created at that stage. Second, new codes do not obliterate previous codes. Third, retention of each code depends upon the degree of concentration that a subject invests in a given code. Finally, the memories that represent the various codes may be differentially available to different types of retrieval operations. In order to review data relevant to each proposition we have divided the remainder of the paper into three sections, each dealing with one level of the encoding process. The next section (Traces) deals with what is stored concerning the physical code of a particular input item. The following section (Concepts) considers the coding imposed by structures that are activated automatically by the input. In the final section (Conscious Constructions) the relationship between automatic coding and conscious processing is examined.

TRACES

The study of memory involves two different traditions. One group of investigators has studied highly accurate iconic representations of input information (Crowder & Morton, 1969; Sperling, 1960). This group works quite closely with the input. They tend to probe memory at very brief time intervals and use large amounts of information so as to avoid elaborate recoding. Another group presents information more slowly thus allowing elaborate conscious recoding and rehearsal (see, for example, papers in Slamecka, 1967). They tend to ignore input modality and focus on semantic information. As a consequence of these methods, it has been widely held that short-term memory is based on physical features of the stimulus and long-term memory on abstracted codes. This appears to us to represent a confusion between two quite different questions (Posner, 1967).

Fortunately this strict identification of type of code with temporal parameters is breaking down. Since studies of encoding of visual words and letters suggest that name codes are available at least by .5 second after visual presentation and superordinate semantic information at least by 1 second, there is ample opportunity in most short-term memory studies for the effects of semantic codes to appear. Indeed, Shulman (1970) has shown that semantic effects in short-term memory increase as the list presentation rate is lowered from 350 to 1400 milliseconds per item provided the subject is given a reason for dealing with semantic information. His data fit very well with the idea that semantic information accrues over intervals of a second and that the subject can attend on physical, name, or semantic codes.

In a number of studies (Posner, 1969) it was shown that a visually presented letter is recoded into its name, but that both the physical and name codes remain available in memory. If the subject's attention is drawn to the categorized information (name code), the physical code is lost more rapidly than if attention is placed upon the physical information. More recent studies have shown that the physical code may remain present for many seconds (Cohen, 1969; Kroll, Parks, Parkinson, Bieber, & Johnson, 1970). Even when physical and name matches are made equally efficient in terms of reaction time, operations that affect name match times may leave the physical match times unaffected, thus suggesting that the physical code is still present (Cohen, 1969; Kroll, et al., 1970). Recently, the same method has revealed evidence for a physical code of an aurally presented letter lasting for several seconds (Coltheart & Allard, 1971). All these studies seem to show the same basic thing. Both physical codes and recategorizations are available within a second or so after input. Task structure determines what the subject will choose to emphasize.

Most of these studies involve intervals of time that would fall within the domain of short-term memory. However, retention of the physical characteristics of a particular input is not only short term. If information about the physical character of the acoustic code were only preserved for a short period of time, how would we ever learn to recognize accent? Evidence that subjects can generate a physical code of a letter or face from its name (Posner, 1969; Tversky, 1969) also suggests the presence of material in long-term memory that must be based upon storage of the trace of the input and not only upon categorizations.

Frost (1971b) has directly extended the analysis of visual and name codes into long-term memory. In her experiments subjects are shown a series of line drawings. One group expects to have to recognize the specific drawings from pictures of the same class while another thinks it is to recall the names of the drawings. Fifteen minutes later both groups receive a reaction time (RT) test in which they are to classify each drawing as to whether it is of the same object as they saw before. Some of the drawings are physically identical to those seen during training, some are rotated so they are physically different but have the same name, and others are from a different class altogether. The recognition group gives significantly shorter

RTs and fewer errors to physical identity matches than to those that have been rotated. The recall group has equal RTs to rotated and identical pictures, but fewer errors to the physically identical test items. These data fit rather well with a theory (Posner, 1969) in which both physical and name information is stored and retrieval goes on in parallel but with times related to the degree of concentration given to a code.

Other data suggest that detailed information about the temporal context in which items are presented must be preserved for a considerable period of time. These studies involve the method of "memory judgment." In these studies (Hintzman, 1970; Hintzman & Block, 1970) the subject is presented a long list of words which he is informed will be tested later. After being presented with the list he is required to make judgments about the words he received. For example, he may be required to recall the modality of entry of the information, the position in the list, the number of times the given word is presented, or the spacing (i.e., the number of items that intervene between a given word and its repetition). What is impressive is the ability of the subject to report the exact details of information concerning the list. According to most strength doctrines of memory (e.g., Wickelgren, 1970) different repetitions of the same item are pooled so that they either do not represent temporal information at all or temporal information must be inferred from the set of associations to which words are related. However, the results of the Hintzman studies argue quite strongly that words are encoded both by time and by the modality of entry.

It is possible that retention is maintained by an elaborate tagging system at the time of entry. However, given that the subjects never knew what they were to recall this seems unlikely. Moreover, recently Hintzman (cited in Underwood, 1971) has been able to show that subjects can say which of two repetitions of an item was visual and which auditory by placing each repetition at its position in the list. In order for this to be done the "tags" of modality and position would both have to be associated not only to the abstracted word, but also to each other. As the extent of tagging required to deal with such judgments gets more complex, it seems simpler to propose that the actual time record of events is recorded in much the same way as is done in a tape recorder. In this way temporal information could be obtained directly by reference to the list positions entered on the tape. Doubtless Hintzman's experimental method, which involves a long series of words with only the vaguest instructions as to what to remember, encourages subjects to remember the material in a way that is as veridical to presentation as possible. For example, one would expect relatively little effort to rehearse or organize the list in this kind of experiment. These are the conditions under which much of our daily experiences are stored.

Of course, tape recorder memories have been proposed before in psychology and they fail because they provide little organization of information for retrieval. For example, it is well known that as list length increases the probability of recall drops. A tape recorder memory would maximize that kind of difficulty. Moreover, the advantage of repetition of an item could only be on the probability of retrieval since no individual trace would be strengthened. Thus, one hardly feels that such a memory system could be the whole answer to the problem of human memory. However, it might well serve as one component of our long-term memory.

A trace column system might be useful mainly as a means of recording a rough history of the past for the purposes of recognition. In order to contact such memories in the absence of appropriate external stimuli, it might be necessary to build elaborate reconstructions that could serve to stimulate their retrieval. Indeed, subjects often report that they can remember experiences in vivid detail after an extended effort to recreate the stimulus conditions present when they occurred (Tomkins, 1970).

Much of the information stored in memory is context free. The motor programs that allow me to type these words need not be closely associated to the temporal context in which they were learned. Our knowledge about the world is organized in a way that is quite free of the detailed temporal and spatial context in which it was learned. We turn now to an analysis of the concepts that tend to summarize the content of our past experience in the form of such knowledge.

CONCEPTS

Logogens

In viewing the form "A" three stimulus codes are available in memory within a brief period. One is the trace of the particular form, the second is the trace system (logogen) activated by the visual form, and the third is the logogen of the letter name [a]. Experiments have shown that the two types of logogens are isolable systems that can be separately manipulated by appropriate operations (Posner, Lewis, & Conrad, in press; Frost, 1971b). Our memory of the experience may be viewed as a complex combination of these three codes. Several experiments have given us clues concerning how these various codes enter into our later recall or recognition.

It is well known that memory is often distorted in the direction of convention. Our retention of a picture of a teacup, for example, is influenced not only by the trace of the particular teacup we have seen, but by other teacups that have defined our experience of the category. These effects have played a role in recent studies of visual memory. For example, Frost (1971a) found recognition errors to be in the direction of orientations most frequent or conventional. Bahrick and Boucher (1968) found that recall probability for picture names was quite independent of the ability to recognize the particular item seen, although subjects appeared to use a visual memory of some sort. The usual way to handle these data is to suppose that the trace of the picture shown to the subject is distorted in the direction of past experience. What we are suggesting is that the concept that is activated by a given picture is as much a component of the memory as the trace of the input presented on that trial. How much of later recollection is influenced by the trace of the item presented and how much by the association to the concept will depend upon factors related to the subject's attention at the time and to the retrieval operation.

Many theories of memory have stressed the importance of past experience in our retention of any new information (Bartlett, 1932; Underwood, 1957). Sometimes the influence is decremental (e.g., proactive interference) and sometimes incremental (e.g., meaningfulness). One difficulty in understanding the influence of past experience upon memory is that we know little about the structure of internal trace systems. In recent years psychologists and others have been proposing a variety of internal structures that might serve to summarize past experience. We review some of these ideas in the next section. We do not feel that the issue is so much a matter of choosing which is *the* right structure as it is in understanding what the consequences of different types of structure are for memory and thought.[2]

Structures

Lists. A subject may be given any arbitrary list of items to hold in memory. In such a list each item serves as an individual element. If the subject is then given a single probe and asked to indicate as quickly as possible whether it is a member of the set, his response time is an increasing function of list size (Sternberg, 1970). The functions so obtained are reasonably linear and can be characterized by a slope that is often about 35 milliseconds per item. This rate seems to hold for practiced subjects using many different kinds of material that approximate letters in complexity (Sternberg, 1970).

However, a rather different picture emerges when the list is not arbitrary but is one that corresponds to a structure in long-term memory. For example, Morin, DeRosa, and Stultz (1967) cite studies in which subjects indicated whether a probe digit was a member of the set 3, 4, 5, 6. Here the positive set is connected as a list within long-term memory. The data are not very well characterized by a search rate; rather, the subject seems able to estimate the distance from the list boundary to the probe. Probes that are near the boundaries are responded to slowly and those far away, rapidly. It is as though the probe can be tested against the list as a whole.

A similar result is obtained in studies of visual search. If asked to search through a field of digits for letters or a field of letters for digits, the search time seems to be relatively independent of the size of the target set (Brand, 1971). Moreover, when Neisser (1967, p. 70) had subjects search for one of 10 targets he found that search time became relatively independent of the number of target items after many days of practice. Neisser explained his result by suggesting that the subject develops a series of special tests that allow him to filter out all but the target-set letters at a low level of processing. An explanation that appears to us to better fit the search data is to suppose that lists that are well integrated in memory can be tested as a whole. The subject interrogates the entire list as though it were a single item in memory. This might be followed by a scan of the list if the task requires the subject to name the particular target item or to achieve a high level of accuracy.

---

[2]Simon (1969) has suggested that all internal structures, even those which give rise to visual images, can be handled by the same overall list language. We do not dispute the point, but believe that for experimental psychology the important issue is whether different psychological consequences can be found corresponding to different structures. For example, images are different than verbal lists if, as Brooks (1968) has shown, the former are disrupted by new visual input while the latter are not. The structures we discuss here are thought to differ in this sense.

ma. A number of investigators have suggested a type of structure that might best be called a schema (Attneave, 1957). This structure differs from what we have been calling a list because it is typified by a central tendency that may be said to stand for the structure. Most work on schema formation has involved visual patterns (Bregman & Charness, 1970; Evans, 1967; Posner & Keele, 1968; Reed, 1970). In some of these studies the subject is taught to classify a set of exemplars that are distortions of a single prototype pattern. At the end of learning the subject behaves as though he had extracted a representation of the prototype, which in fact has never before been seen (Posner & Keele, 1968; Reed, 1970). This is shown by his ability to classify the prototype with as great accuracy and speed as the memorized distortions and by his tendency to recognize the prototype as having been seen before. The prototype is thought to stand for or represent the list. Thus it would be expected that the prototype would resemble the subject's drawing or image of the list, although this has never been clearly shown.

An extension of the schema idea to very poorly learned patterns and linguistic ideas has been illustrated in the work of Bransford and Franks (1971). In these studies subjects are shown a set of geometric forms or a series of sentences. Each instance is a distortion of some prototypical pattern or sentence. In the case of sentences the prototype contains the general or common ideas of the sentence set. Their studies show that subjects "recognize" the prototype as having occurred before more often than the items that have actually been presented.

These experiments seem to illustrate the tendency of the memory system to abstract the commonalities among different instances and to erect a structure that emphasizes those commonalities. At low levels of learning, the instances from which the common schema has been abstracted may not even be recognized; at higher levels of learning these seem to help form the boundary of the structure.

Hierarchies. Another type of memory structure that has been discussed a good deal recently is a hierarchical memory (Collins & Quillian, 1969; Schaeffer & Wallace, 1969). This system is based on the assignment of a given word to a hierarchy of superordinates. There is a good deal of evidence that supports the idea that the time taken to classify two words is longer the farther apart they are in such a hierarchy. That is, it is faster to say that a canary is a bird than that it is an animal. Unfortunately, there are also findings that do not fit so well. For example, it takes longer to say that *a daisy is not a bird* than it does to say that *gold is not a bird* (Schaeffer & Wallace, 1969). The common category "living" seems to interfere with a judgment that is supposed to be made at a lower level.

One particularly attractive notion of the hierarchy is the view that properties may be assigned only to a particular level. That is, the property "flies" is assigned only to *bird* and need not be repeated for *canary* (cognitive storage economy). This property is not only economical but fits with some common human characteristics such as stereotyping and overgeneralization. We know that the cognitive economy notion does not fit all the data obtained with these kinds of materials (Conrad, 1972). However, it may still tell us something important about a possible consequence of this kind of structure.

Spaces. The term "concept" has most often been studied where the instances have been defined by values along discrete dimensions (Bourne, 1966). Miller

(1967) discusses the relationship between structures in which every instance has a value on each dimension or feature (paradigmatic) and those, like the hierarchies discussed above, that have no consistent set of features for each entry (taxonomic). Spatial structures (Osgood, Suci, & Tannenbaum, 1957; Pollio, 1964; Romney & D'andrade, 1964) are usually paradigmatic in this sense.

Spatial structures have been used to account for the connotative aspect of words as obtained from ratings of the Semantic Differential. Pollio (1964) has shown that the latency of word associations can be predicted from the distance of the words in a semantic space. Spatial models have also been applied to kinship terms (Romney & D'andrade, 1964). The valuable aspect of a spatial structure is that it allows for a natural definition of distance (Hyman & Well, 1967) and if the subject is aware of the dimensions he is able to recognize and produce an infinite number of new instances defined within the structure.

The main distinction we would like to stress between spatial and hierarchical structures is the relative importance of the features or dimensions. In the Collins and Quillian (1969) system the features or properties at each node become active only as a result of the activation of the noun. On the other hand, in a spatial structure the item is a point along a set of dimensions and activation spreads in the space defined by the dimensions. The dimensions are primary. Wickens (this volume) suggests a spatial structure for word recognition when he supposes that the word will be activated following a number of semantic dimensions. Of course, it is also possible to develop structures that are compromises between hierarchies and spaces (Deese, 1970).

There seem to be obvious cognitive differences between a hierarchical and a spatial structure. For example, in a hierarchical structure the difference between subordination and superordination is important, but not in a spatial structure. This difference may have psychological consequences; for example, obtaining the name of a visual letter (superordination) may be an automatic process that is essentially unavoidable, but generating a visual form of a letter from the letter name may be an optional process that requires central processing capacity. It is possible that this distinction between abstraction and generation extends more widely. In the next section we turn to an effort to understand the experimental distinctions between structures.

Automatic Processing and Structure

The obvious objection to a comparative analysis of mental structure is that memory can be sorted on any basis whatsoever, so why single out certain kinds of organization and call them structures? This seems to be what Deese (1970) means to imply when he says

> we might suppose that at least theoretically, a complete and well organized tree or table could be invented for the lexicon of any language. Unfortunately that is not true. The reason is that semantic markers or attributes are easy to invent.... There are literally endless numbers of other ways in which we could characterize everything in the universe [p. 92.]

It is not our goal to deal with the lexicon of a language. We intend instead to ask what kinds of structure subjects have in their minds *before* they are asked to make a classification. Clearly a subject can tell you all the yellow things he knows and all those beginning with the letter R and perhaps eventually all those whose third letter is K, so why should we not assume that his memory system reflects these structures?

The more traditional methods for the analysis of cognitive structure involve some variety of word association (Deese, 1970) or sorting behavior (Miller, 1967, this volume). We have no objection to these methods but wish to propose a rather different basis for the definition of memory structure. In the free association experiment the subject is asked to emit the first response that comes to mind after a stimulus. In some cases his response comes effortlessly, in other cases only after a conscious search. Is it not possible that these represent rather different processes? The free association and sorting methods combine them together in a complex way. When we say that a structure exists in memory we are really saying that one item will activate another in a quite direct and simple way even perhaps when the subject does not intend for it to occur. If we had methods to tap structure uninfluenced by conscious search, we might reflect the structure of memory more simply.

To illustrate the problem of levels of analysis let me take an example from another domain of psychological research. Beck (1966) has shown that slope or angle is a most crucial variable in determining what items will be grouped together perceptually. For example, a field of tilted Ts will be seen as grouped together and quite distinct from a field of upright Ts. On the other hand, when overall slant is held constant, as in comparing an L with a T, grouping is poor. At the level of neural processing at which grouping takes place, similarity depends more upon slant than upon the item having the same name or even the same visual pattern. Nonetheless, if asked to rate overall similarity, subjects will say that a T and a tilted T are more similar than a T and an L. In such judgments subjects are influenced more by the form correspondence than by slope. By analogy we need methods for studying memory structures which reflect the activation pattern as uninfluenced as possible by higher level processes.

How can we study automatic processes as distinguished from those that involve conscious search? Even the definition of "automatic" is a difficult matter, and yet without such a distinction it appears impossible to develop a meaningful analysis of structure. Our effort to analyze this problem has involved the notion of a single limited-capacity central processing system that integrates signals from all modalities. When this system is occupied by any signal, its capacity is reduced for dealing with any other signal or mental operation that requires its use. This idea is similar to that proposed by Broadbent's single channel theory (1958) and modified by Moray's (1967) allocatable processor. However, we believe that many complex mental operations that are learned and that require time can be performed outside this system (Posner & Keele, 1970; Posner & Klein, 1971). For our purposes the use of this system becomes the central definition of a "conscious process" and its non-use defines what is meant by "automatic." We believe that such an operational definition may prove too narrow unless it can be shown that operations that are automatic in this sense also meet other intuitive notions of automatic, such as being performed without intention, awareness, or storage. However, it should be noted that automatic in our sense does not imply that the operations are innate or unlearned, nor that they are performed without requiring time, nor that they *could not* also be performed using the limited capacity system. Moreover, a process that is automatic in a particular context may not be so in a different context.

In the remainder of this section we try to illustrate some experiments that have attempted to study automatic operations. In the following section (Conscious Constructions) we try to deal with the relation of such automatic operations with the operations of the central processor.

Suppose you are asked to name the color of ink in which the word *red* is written. It is easy to show that without intending to do so you look up the name of the word and this interferes with your naming of the ink color (Stroop effect). Moreover, Keele (1972) has shown that this lookup of the name goes on in parallel with the processing of the ink color and interferes only at the stage of vocal output. Thus we argue that the relationship between a word and its name is automatic in the sense that no conscious processing is needed to connect the visual input with the ultimate stimulation of the logogen.

An extension of the Stroop method can be applied to show the reality of the hierarchical structure. Warren (1970) has shown that the aural presentation of three related words (*elm, oak, maple*) activates both their own names and the category name *tree*. The ability to name the color of the ink in which the word *tree* is printed is impaired over appropriate control RTs after hearing the three priming words. The impairment appears to be even greater for the words themselves than for the category. Our assumption is that the task does not require the activation of the category name and thus the subject does not intend to do so. Thus the category must be activated by virtue of a preexisting structure. We would argue that the contact of the visually presented word with memory goes on without any involvement of the central processor. Thus the effect ought to occur even when the subject's attention is elsewhere. This has not been demonstrated in the experiments described above. However, Lewis (1970 a, b) has shown that a visual or aural word presented on an unattended channel will influence the processing of a word on the attended channel. MacKay (1972) has shown that a word on the unattended channel will serve to disambiguate an attended sentence. MacKay's work suggests that there are definite limits to this process. The deep structure of an unattended message does not appear to disambiguate an attended sentence.

Similar evidence may be used to argue for the reality of the schematic structure in memory. If the schema were derived at the time of retrieval from the individual exemplars, one would expect the response to it to take longer, and one would expect the subject to judge that the pattern, though a reasonable one, had not in fact occurred before. The absence of these results in recognition memory studies (Bransford & Franks, 1971; Posner, 1969) lends credence to the idea of a schematic structure present within the memory system.

Recently, Atkinson and Juola (1971) have proposed a two stage model of recognition experiments. The first stage involves contact between input and long-term memory necessary to assign a recognition strength to the input. This stage is rapid, error prone, and independent of the number of items in the recognition list. The second stage is a search of the area of memory located in the first stage. This model is very much what would be supposed if the first stage were an interrogation of an integrated area or structure in memory that took place without involvement of the central processor. The processor is then able to search among the items in that location. Since the processor has limited capacity, the time to search will be a function of the number of items to be searched.

CONSCIOUS CONSTRUCTIONS

The analysis made in the last section depends upon our ability to distinguish automatic encodings from those based upon conscious processes. One of us (Posner & Boies, 1971) has been trying to develop such an analysis. In this view one component of attention involves the limited capacity mechanism capable of integrating and transforming information from different modalities. It is the characteristics of this system that produce the serial character and widespread interference effects in tasks for which highly developed learned structures are not present.

Doubtless, such conscious processes have an important role in memory storage, particularly for later recall. For example, it has been widely assumed that rehearsal (Reitman, 1971) is a mental operation that places a load upon the limited capacity system. When the subject rehearses he is relatively refractory to the processing of other signals provided such processing also requires access to the central processor. Other complex strategies for memorizing such as grouping stimuli, developing images, or using natural language mediators (except perhaps for mnemonic systems practiced to a very high level of skill) also require conscious attention in our sense.

We are only at the beginning of efforts to understand the relationship between the automatic encodings described in the previous section and the conscious processing involved in rehearsing and developing mediators. This is a central problem for the relationship of coding to memory. Once an item reaches the mechanisms responsible for consciousness the constraints upon encoding are probably drastically altered. According to this view, encoding that takes place prior to conscious processing is markedly constrained by habit and by sets established prior to presentation. Only a limited range of codings that have been well learned can occur. Once an item is conscious the range of possible codings must become much larger. This is not to argue that conscious processing is unlawful or free of the influence of past experience, but only that it is flexible and no more constrained by past experience than any other form of thinking. On the other hand, constraints of a different type are present. Since the central processor is of limited capacity such processing tends to be serial. Each operation effectively uses a part of the processor's capacity for a given length of time. For this reason such processing ought to be subject to rather strict time constraints, much more so than the basically parallel encodings discussed in the last section.

What determines what occupies the limited capacity mechanism, and when? In other words, what kind of encoding is likely to require consciousness? The answer to this question depends upon a number of factors many of which we are very far from understanding. For example, it depends heavily upon the level of alertness of the subject. A very alert subject will tend to bring the conscious mechanism into his processing at an early stage. He thus becomes aware of the signal before some of the automatic structures are activated. If he is in an RT task he is able to respond more quickly than when he is not alert, but only at the risk of making more errors (Posner, Buggie, & Summers, 1971). Moreover, if the subject knows that a stimulus is significant, in the sense that it is to be followed shortly by a cue to respond or will remain present only very briefly, the conscious mechanism begins to operate on the signal very quickly. On the other hand, if time allows, the subject may withold consciousness and allow encoding to proceed very far in an automatic way (Posner & Klein, 1971).

How can we observe the interactions between encoding and conscious processing? Most of our analysis comes from studies that use a probe technique (Posner & Boies, 1971; Posner & Keele, 1970; Posner & Klein, 1971). The primary task is a visual letter-matching task that can be divided into an encoding phase and a matching phase. During the encoding phase only one letter is presented and no overt response is required until the second letter appears. Delays in RT to respond to an auditory probe task are taken as evidence that processing the primary task requires the limited-capacity mechanism. The results suggest that, given sufficient time, the subject encodes the first letter in terms of obtaining the letter name without causing interference with the probe. This result fits well with other evidence that encoding processes can be performed in parallel (Hawkins, 1969; Keele, 1972; Posner & Boies, 1971).

Encoding is followed by a marked interference with processing the probe. This occurs at a time when the subject is thought to be consciously processing the retrieved products of encoding (Posner & Klein, 1971). The time for this interference and its extent is heavily under control of such things as first-letter duration, the interval between letters, complexity of transformation required on the first letter, and other factors. Thus the relationship between encoding and conscious processing is quite complex and very flexible. The probe RT appears to mirror these complexities.

Although the probe method has provided much of the evidence for the conclusions we have suggested, there have been other techniques that seem to support them. Perhaps the most interesting example of the relation between encoding and conscious processing comes from the use of subjects who are highly skilled as encoders of information. An example is DeGroot's (1965) work on master chess players. This has recently been extended to people with high levels of skill in sight reading music (Reicher & Haller, 1971). DeGroot studied the ability of the master chess player to reproduce a complex chess position after a 5-second exposure. One interesting finding was that the chess masters invariably paused several seconds after being exposed to the stimulus before starting to recall. Less skilled players began to reproduce the board immediately, before losing the little they could retain. This same observation was made more formally by Reicher and Haller (1971) who found that differences between levels of ability in sight reading music only emerged if there was a delay between input and recall.

What goes on during this delay? The answer is not provided by data and thus is speculative. However, it is possible to extend the analysis that was appropriate to simpler levels of encoding. Such an extension would suggest that during this time the spatial input information is recoded into complex meaningful chunks by activating structures the master has stored in memory. Because of the complexity of the material these encodings require considerable time, but because they do not involve conscious attention they can proceed in parallel. When the reorganization is finished the master can rehearse the information in a few meaningful chunks which can be reproduced.

This account is similar to that used by Miller (1956) to explain how a reorganization of binary into octal digits could aid recall. In a similar way skilled readers of prose report themselves to be unaware of all encoding short of the meaning of the passage being read (Bower, 1970; Kolers, 1970). Conscious attention seems to be reserved in this case for the highest level code. Despite the inability to report such encodings, they may still occur, but at a high skill level insufficient attention is given to store them. More direct evidence supporting the view of automatic encoding, extended in time, comes from the retention of random and meaningful letter strings. Crawford, Hunt, and Peake (1966) showed that the ability to report the letters contained in a briefly exposed sentence is an increasing function of time delay. This "inverse forgetting" suggests that if the subject is forced to tap into the automatic encoding process too soon he will either interfere with it or fill his active memory with codes that are less useful for his final report.

Repetition

It would appear particularly important for the development of coding theory to have methods to trace in detail the coding of an individual item from the moment of input through long-term memory. A possible way would be to find a phenomenon that can be studied in detail over time. Such a phenomenon is the effect of repeating an item twice in succession (repetition effect). The study of repetition has taken place in widely different literatures, but if one attempts to put these together it is possible to trace its effect from initial encoding through long-term memory.[3]

One of the more persistent findings in the literature of long-term memory is that a word that is presented twice in succession will be retained more poorly in long-term memory than if the repetitions were distributed (Melton, 1970). It has also been shown that short-term memory for an immediately repeated word is somewhat better than would be the case if its repetition had been distributed (Peterson, Wampler, Kirkpatrick, & Saltzman, 1963).

There is also reasonably good evidence that reaction time to a repetition is faster than it would be if the item had not just been presented (Hyman, 1953; Keele, 1969). Moreover, there is reason to suppose that this advantage is due to stimulus and not response repetition (Hawkins & Hosking, 1969). A special case of this finding is that in a successive letter-matching task, response to a repetition (same response) becomes progressively faster than to a nonrepetition (different response) as the interval between letters increases from 0 to 500 milliseconds (Posner & Boies, 1971). This last finding is striking since no overt response is made to the first

---

[3] We are grateful to D. Hintzman for pointing out this relationship.

stimulus, thus the differences do not appear to be due to response accessibility but rather to encoding of the second letter. Finally, we have found recently (Posner, Buggie, & Summers, 1971) that the vertex evoked potential components occurring from 200 to 250 milliseconds after the second letter are reduced when it is a repetition. See Table 1 for a summary of these results.

TABLE 1

Effects of Repetition and Nonrepetition of an Item upon
Psychological Measurements that Occur at Varying
Intervals Following the Item

Time After Input	Repetition	Nonrepetition
.2 - .3 sec.	Small vertex evoked potential	Large vertex evoked potential
.3 - .5 sec.	Fast reaction time	Slow reaction time
2 - 5 sec.	Strong short-term memory	Weak short-term memory
2 - 5 min.	Weak long-term memory	Strong long-term memory

Note. The data are selected from a variety of studies cited in the text.

Thus it is clear that a repeated stimulus is already being handled differently by 200 milliseconds after input and that this difference is still found when the item is probed several minutes later. I think this constellation of results is an exciting one for coding theory, because it provides an example of an effect that can be followed over the whole range of processing.

Besides the methodological implications, the results suggest to us the following. Reaction time to a stimulus and retention of that stimulus in short-term memory depend upon the degree of activation of a logogen or internal structure. When a stimulus repeats itself, activation is high, and thus RT is short and short-term memory is good. However, a stimulus handled at this level does not receive the more complex conscious processing that goes to a nonrepetition. The vertex evoked potential and the long-term memory component might be tied in with this higher level of processing. There is reasonable evidence from other sources to suggest that vertex evoked potential enhancement is related to attentional states. Thus it seems reasonable that the enhanced processing of a nonrepetition would show up both in vertex evoked potential size and in long-term memory.

In short, RT and short-term memory seem related to logogen activation, while vertex evoked potential and long-term memory seem to depend upon an additional response that relates to what we have been calling conscious attention. Hopefully, new data will provide some support for this speculative analysis.

SUMMARY

This paper has been an effort to review evidence on the automatic and conscious components of the coding process as they affect later retention. We have suggested that long-term memory may involve storage of the trace of an item in relatively pure form, retention of structures activated automatically by the input, or memory for conscious constructions developed in response to input. Which code is retained will depend upon how the subject uses his limited capacity in the period following the input. He may use it to maintain the physical code, to process the automatic encodings, or to develop new codes. We reviewed briefly some of the ways automatic coding is constrained by memorial structures. Our efforts to analyze the relationships between automatic encoding and conscious processing were quite fragmentary and speculative, but the convergence of evidence from a variety of sources and of techniques suggests that a deeper understanding is possible.

REFERENCES

Atkinson, R. C., & Juola, J. F. Factors influencing speed and accuracy of word recognition. Technical Report No. 177, Institute for Mathematical Studies in the Social Sciences, Stanford University, Stanford, California, 1971.

Attneave, F. Transfer of experience with a class-schema to identification learning of patterns and shapes. *Journal of Experimental Psychology,* 1957, 54, 81-88.

Bahrick, H. P., & Boucher, B. Retention of visual and verbal codes of the same stimuli. *Journal of Experimental Psychology,* 1968, 78, 417-422.

Bartlett, F. C. *Remembering.* Cambridge: Cambridge University Press, 1932.

Beck, J. Effect of orientation and of shape similarity on perceptual grouping. *Perception & Psychophysics,* 1966, 1, 300-302.

Bourne, L. E. *Human conceptual behavior.* Boston: Allyn & Bacon, 1966.

Bower, G. H. Multicomponent theory of the memory trace. In K. W. Spence & J. T. Spence (Eds.), *The psychology of learning and motivation.* New York: Academic Press, 1967. Pp. 229-325.

Bower, T. G. R. Reading by eye. In H. Levin & J. Williams (Eds.), *Basic studies in reading.* New York: Basic Books, 1970.

Brand, J. Classification without identification in visual search. *Quarterly Journal of Experimental Psychology,* 1971, 23, 178-186.

Bransford, J. D., & Franks, J. J. The abstraction of linguistic ideas. *Cognitive Psychology,* 1971, 2, 331-350.

Bregman, A. S., & Charness, N. Schema plus transformations in visual pattern recognition. Paper presented at the meeting of the Eastern Psychological Association, Atlantic City, April, 1970.

Broadbent, D. E. *Perception and communication.* London: Pergamon Press, 1958.

Brooks, L. R. Spatial and verbal components of the act of recall. *Canadian Journal of Psychology,* 1968, 22, 349-368.

Clark, H. H., & Chase, W. G. On mental comparisons of sentences and pictures. *Cognitive Psychology,* 1972, in press.

Cohen, G. Some evidence for parallel comparisons in a letter recognition task. *Quarterly Journal of Experimental Psychology,* 1969, 21, 277-279.

Collins, A. M., & Quillian, M. R. Retrieval time from semantic memory. *Journal of Verbal Learning and Verbal Behavior,* 1969, 8, 240-247.

Coltheart, M., & Allard, F. Physical and name codes of heard letters. Paper presented at the meeting of the Psychonomic Society, St. Louis, November, 1971.

Conrad, C. Cognitive economy in semantic memory. *Journal of Experimental Psychology,* 1972, **92**, 149-154.

Crawford, J., Hunt, E., & Peake, G. Inverse forgetting in short-term memory. *Journal of Experimental Psychology,* 1966, **72**, 415-422.

Crowder, R. G., & Morton, J. Precategorical acoustic storage. *Perception & Psychophysics,* 1969, **5**, 365-373.

Deese, J. *Psycholinguistics.* Boston: Allyn & Bacon, 1970.

DeGroot, A. D. *Thought and choice in chess.* The Hague: Mouton, 1965.

Evans, S. H. A brief statement of schema theory. *Psychonomic Science,* 1967, **8**, 87-88.

Foss, D. J. Decision processes during sentence comprehension: Effects of lexical item difficulty and position upon decision times. *Journal of Verbal Learning and Verbal Behavior,* 1969, **8**, 457-462.

Frost, N. A. H. Clustering by visual shape in the free recall of pictorial stimuli. *Journal of Experimental Psychology,* 1971, 88, 409-413. (a)

Frost, N. A. H. Interaction of visual and semantic codes in long-term memory. Unpublished doctoral dissertation, University of Oregon, 1971. (b)

Hawkins, H. L. Parallel processing in complex visual discrimination. *Perception & Psychophysics,* 1969, **5**, 56-64.

Hawkins, H. L., & Hosking, K. Stimulus probability as a determinant of discrete choice reaction time. *Journal of Experimental Psychology,* 1969, **83**, 434-440.

Hintzman, D. L., Effects of repetition and exposure duration on memory. *Journal of Experimental Psychology,* 1970, **83**, 435-444.

Hintzman, D. L., & Block, R. A. Memory judgments and the effects of spacing. *Journal of Verbal Learning and Verbal Behavior,* 1970, **9**, 561-565.

Hyman, R. Stimulus information as a determinant of reaction time. *Journal of Experimental Psychology,* 1953, **45**, 188-196.

Hyman, R., & Well, A. Judgments of similarity and spatial models. *Perception & Psychophysics,* 1967, **2**, 233-248.

Keele, S. W. The repetition effect: A memory dependent process. *Journal of Experimental Psychology,* 1969, **80**, 243-248.

Keele, S. W. Attention demands of memory retrieval. *Journal of Experimental Psychology,* 1972, in press.

Kolers, P. A. Three stages of reading. In H. Levin & J. Williams (Eds.), *Basic studies in reading.* New York: Basic Books, 1970.

Koffka, K. *Principles of Gestalt psychology.* New York: Harcourt Brace, 1935.

Kroll, N. E. A., Parks, T., Parkinson, S. Z., Bieber, S. L., & Johnson, A. L. Short-term memory while shadowing: Recall of visually and of aurally presented letters. *Journal of Experimental Psychology,* 1970, **85**, 220-227.

Krueger, L. Visual comparisons in a redundant display. *Cognitive Psychology,* 1970, **1**, 341-357.

Lewis, J. L. Semantic processing of unattended messages using dichotic listening. *Journal of Experimental Psychology,* 1970, **85**, 225-228. (a)

Lewis, J. L. Activation of "logogens" in an audio-visual word task. Unpublished doctoral dissertation, University of Oregon, 1970. (b)

MacKay, D. G. Aspects of a theory of comprehension and attention. Unpublished manuscript, University of California at Los Angeles, 1972.

Melton, A. W. The situation with respect to the spacing of repetitions and memory. *Journal of Verbal Learning and Verbal Behavior,* 1970, **9**, 596-606.

Miller, G. A. The magical number seven, plus or minus two: Some limits on our capacity for processing information. *Psychological Review,* 1956, **63**, 81-97.

Miller, G. A. Psycholinguistic approaches to the study of communication. In D. L. Arm (Ed.), *Journeys in science.* Albuquerque: University of New Mexico Press, 1967.

Moray, N. Where is the capacity limited? A survey and a model. *Acta Psychologica,* 1967, **27**, 84-92.

Morin, R. E., DeRosa, D. V., & Stultz, V. Recognition memory and reaction time. *Acta Psychologica*, 1967, 27, 298-305.

Morton, J. Interaction of information in word recognition. *Psychological Review*, 1969, 76, 165-178.

Neisser, U. *Cognitive psychology*. New York: Appleton-Century-Crofts, 1967.

Osgood, C. E., Suci, G. J., & Tannenbaum, P. H. *The measurement of meaning*. Urbana: University of Illinois Press, 1957.

Peterson. L. R., Wampler, R., Kirkpatrick, M., & Saltzman, D. Effect of spacing presentations on retention of paired associates over short intervals. *Journal of Experimental Psychology*, 1963, 66, 206-209.

Pollio, H. R. Composition of associative clusters. *Journal of Experimental Psychology*, 1964, 67, 199-208.

Posner, M. I. Short-term memory systems in human information processing. *Acta Psychologica*, 1967. 27, 267-284.

Posner. M. I. Abstraction and the process of recognition. In G. H. Bower & J. T. Spence (Eds.), *The psychology of learning and motivation*, Vol. 3. New York: Academic Press, 1969. pp. 43-100.

Posner. M. I., & Boies, S. W. Components of attention. *Psychological Review*, 1971, 78, 391-408.

Posner, M. I., Buggie, S., & Summers, J. On the selection of signals. Paper presented at the meeting of the Psychonomics Society, St. Louis, November, 1971.

Posner, M. I., & Keele, S. W. On the genesis of abstract ideas. *Journal of Experimental Psychology*. 1968, 77, 353-363.

Posner, M. I., & Keele, S. W. Time and space as measures of mental operations. Paper presented to the meeting of the American Psychological Association, Miami Beach, September, 1970.

Posner, M. I., & Klein, R. On the function of consciousness. Paper presented to the Fourth Conference on Attention and Performance, Boulder, Colorado, August, 1971.

Posner, M. I., Lewis, J. L., & Conrad, C. Component processes in reading: A performance analysis. In J. F. Kavanaugh & I. G. Mattingley (Eds.), *Language by ear and by eye*. Cambridge. Mass.: M.I.T. Press, in press.

Reed, S. Decision processes in pattern classification. Unpublished doctoral dissertation, University of California at Los Angeles, 1970.

Reicher, G. M. Perceptual recognition as a function of meaningfulness of stimulus material. *Journal of Experimental Psychology*, 1969, 81, 275-280.

Reicher, G. M., & Haller, R. Further studies of the master's eye. Unpublished manuscript, University of Oregon, 1971.

Reitman, J. Rehearsal and short-term memory. *Cognitive Psychology*, 1971, 2, 185-195.

Romney, A. K., & D'andrade, R. G. Cognitive aspects of English kin terms. In A. K. Romney & R. G. D'andrade (Eds.), Transcultural studies in cognition. *American Anthropologist*, 1964, 66, 146-170 .

Schaeffer, B., & Wallace, R. Semantic similarity and the comparison of word meanings. *Journal of Experimental Psychology*, 1969, 82, 343-346.

Shulman, H. G. Encoding and retention of semantic and phonemic information in short-term memory. *Journal of Verbal Learning and Verbal Behavior*, 1970, 9, 449-508.

Simon, H. A. *The sciences of the artificial*. Cambridge: M.I.T. Press, 1969.

Slamecka, N. J. *Human learning and memory*. London: Oxford Press, 1967.

Sperling, G. A. The information available in brief visual presentations. *Psychological Monographs*, 1960, 74, 11, Whole No. 498.

Sternberg, S. Memory scanning: Mental processes revealed by reaction time experiments. In J. Antrobus (Ed.), *Cognition and affect*. Boston: Little, Brown, 1970.

Tomkins, S. S. A theory of memory. In J. Antrobus (Ed.), *Cognition and affect*. Boston: Little, Brown, 1970.

Tversky, B. Pictorial and verbal encoding in a short-term memory task. *Perception & Psychophysics*, 1969, 6, 225-233.

Underwood, B. J. Interference and forgetting. *Psychological Review*, 1957, 64, 49-60.

Underwood, B. J. The 1971 Arrowhead conference. *American Journal of Psychology*, 1971, 84, 442-444.

Warren, R. E. Stimulus encoding and memory. Unpublished doctoral dissertation, University of Oregon, 1970.

Wickelgren, W. A. Multitrace strength theory. In D. A. Norman (Ed.), *Models of memory*. New York: Academic Press, 1970. Pp. 65-102.

Wickens, D. D. Encoding categories of words: An empirical approach to meaning. *Psychological Review*, 1970, 77, 1-15.

3

ENCODING AND STIMULUS SELECTION IN PAIRED-ASSOCIATE VERBAL LEARNING[1]

Jack Richardson
State University of New York at Binghamton

In 1963 Underwood called attention to the fact that subjects often use only part of the nominal stimulus (the stimulus as presented by the experimenter) as the functional stimulus (the stimulus as used by the subject) for learning. Almost all of the research on stimulus selection in verbal learning has appeared since 1963. Since stimulus selection is directly concerned with what is learned, it has implications for a variety of studies. For instance, stimulus selection has been used to interpret the differences between backward and forward recall (Houston, 1964; Nelson, Rowe, Engel, Wheeler, & Garland, 1970; Young, Farrow, Seitz, & Hays, 1966), some effects of formal stimulus similarity (Runquist, 1970), false stimulus recognition (Martin, 1968a), the effects of interpolated learning on recall (Goggin & Martin, 1970; Schneider & Houston, 1968, 1969; Weaver, 1969), the effects of similarity of meaningfulness within compound stimuli (Solso & Trafimow, 1970), and to investigate differences between retardates and normal children (Baumeister & Berry, 1968, 1970; Baumeister, Berry, & Forehand, 1969).

It was also in 1963 that Lawrence's influential article on the stimulus-as-coded appeared. The term *coding* is currently used in a variety of ways and Bower (this volume) gives four major senses of the concept. All of these are operations on the stimulus-as-presented but there is no reason to assume that they are mutually exclusive, for example, stimulus selection may occur and the selected component may then be represented as a list of attributes before entering memory. However, before discussing the place of stimulus selection in encoding, the paradigm will be presented.

[1] The author's research is supported by the National Science Foundation.

THE STIMULUS SELECTION PARADIGM

In studies of stimulus selection, the subjects learn a paired-associate list in which the stimulus items are compounds of two or more components and a different response is consistently paired with each compound. Following learning of the paired-associate list, the components are presented individually and the subjects are asked to recall the response that had been paired with the compound containing that component. Stimulus selection, during learning, is inferred from the differential effectiveness of the components from a compound as cues for recall. The most effective cue is said to be "dominant" or "selected." The components are redundant and relevant so that any component or any combination of components from a compound stimulus is a distinctive cue and may become the functional stimulus. This is a simple paradigm but, as usual, there are further restrictions.

First, if it is assumed that some kind of time sharing is responsible for the learning that occurs to the components, the difficulty of learning when the components are the nominal stimuli must be considered. For example, if the compound consists of a common word and a low meaningful consonant-vowel-consonant trigram, more learning should occur to the word than to the trigram (assuming a single letter is not selected from the trigram) even though an equal amount of time is spent on each (see Richardson, 1971, for a more detailed discussion). Second, it is assumed that the recall reflects the direct learning of the response to the component. This requirement causes some methodological problems. Postman and Greenbloom (1967) pointed out that associations may be formed among the components of a compound during the paired-associate learning. Thus, some of the correct responses at recall may be due to mediation via other components and not to a direct component–response connection. In order to eliminate this possibility, Postman and Greenbloom inferred single-letter selection from a trigram only when the subject recalled the correct response and failed to recall additional letters from the trigram. When they used this double criterion for single-letter selection there was little evidence for selection from trigrams that were easy to pronounce.

The possibility of mediated recall leads directly to the consideration of the components. Verbal components may be single letters, common words, and, although they have not been used, single digits. This verbal material may occupy a rather special place among stimuli, at least with the usual adult subject. Letters of the alphabet, common words, and digits elicit a reliable "reading" response over a comparatively wide range in the physical aspects of the stimuli. Although the reaction time to most classes of stimuli increases as the number of stimuli increase, the latency of the reading response to single digits (Morin & Forrin, 1962), single letters (Morin, Konick, Troxell, & McPherson, 1965), and common words (Fraisse, 1964) may well be exceptions to this rule. Reading a word or letter aloud occurs with a shorter latency than the naming of a drawing of the corresponding object (Fraisse, 1967, 1968) and it requires about 297 milliseconds longer to categorize a word then to read it (Fraisse, Lanati, Régnier, & Wahl 1965). Reading a letter aloud occurs about 100 milliseconds faster than saying the next letter in the alphabet (Richardson, 1967) and reading a word aloud occurs about 225 milliseconds faster than saying a well-learned word response (Richardson, 1968). Grant (1968) has found that words are unusually effective stimuli for conditioning.

This evidence shows that verbal stimuli are well differentiated and that the reading response is an immediate well-practiced response. Letters, digits, and words seem to correspond to nonintegral stimuli (Garner & Felfoldy, 1970) which may be analyzed into parts but that are, in most situations, responded to as patterns rather than as a collection of parts (see Shepard, 1963). It seems possible that the identifying responses for verbal items in a paired–associate task are essentially implicit reading responses. At any rate, the identifying responses for verbal stimuli are well established and the correlated stimuli lead directly to overt responses such as saying the item aloud.

The type of verbal component and the relation among components are important because the use of certain procedures and materials may well result in subjects attempting to integrate the compound and to respond to it as a unit. Single words or word-like sequences of letters can be used as compounds and the letter components should still be differentially effective as cues for recall of the response. However, this would be due, not to component selection, but to the differential effectiveness of the letters in reinstating the compound; that is, the response would be learned with the compound as the functional stimulus, and the effectiveness of the components as cues for recall of the response would depend upon their effectiveness as cues for redintegration of the compound (Horowitz & Prytulak, 1969). If related words (e.g., words from the same category) are used as components of a compound, there is less evidence for selection and this may be due, in this case, to learning the response to the category name rather than directly to the components (Liftik & Leicht, 1968).

It is probably obvious from the above discussion that stimulus selection is considered as the result of an active process that determines the identifying response, or responses, to a stimulus. It is the identifying response, or the corresponding stimuli, that enter into the associative learning.

THE PLACE OF STIMULUS SELECTION IN THE SCHEME OF THINGS

At the empirical level, stimulus selection specifies, to some extent, what is learned. Thus it has direct implications for the effect of many variables on learning and transfer. Also, the selected components must enter into any further encoding that may occur. If, in addition to the empirical aspects, stimulus selection is considered as a type of encoding, there are much broader implications.

First, let us admit that normal adult humans will, given the proper instructions, task, practice, and rewards, do many very wonderful things in the world of memory. They will rehearse, organize, select, mediate, imagine, associate, cluster, categorize, generate, and relate. In fact, this is only a partial list and a complete list probably will be limited only by the imagination and ingenuity of the experimenters concerned with memory. It seems that any theory of memory must assume some common processes underlying these descriptively different operations. If stimulus selection is one type of encoding then there should be some common processes with the other types. Stimulus selection has the advantage of being more directly observable than other types of encoding and the evidence may be of use at the decision points in a theory of memory.

EVIDENCE FROM STUDIES OF STIMULUS SELECTION

A variety of studies have found differential effectiveness of components as cues for recall following paired-associate learning with compounds as stimuli. In order to progress beyond the demonstrational stage, there are three aspects of stimulus selection that should be measured in some fashion. Otherwise, we will continue to find that stimulus selection occurs with a variety of materials, subjects, and conditions but will not be able to make very meaningful comparisons.

The first measure is one of the extent to which components are differentially effective as cues for recall. This will be called *efficiency of cue selection*. The basic concept is that the most efficient selection occurs if subjects learn the response to one component of a compound and effectively ignore the others. Thus, the maximum possible efficiency comes from a control group which learns the paired-associate list with single components as stimuli. A series of studies (Richardson, in press) used, as a measure of efficiency, the percentage correct recall responses to the individual components that would be necessary to give the correct responses to the trigrams: The number of compounds from which one or more of the components produced a correct recall was divided by the total number of correct recalls to the components and the result multiplied by 100. In this case, the compounds were consonant trigrams and the mean efficiency scores for the various conditions varied from about 75 to 95 and the percentage of subjects with efficiency scores of 100 varied from about 30 to 90. The minimum possible efficiency score computed in this fashion decreases as the number of components in the compound increases. It remains to be determined if this method of computing an efficiency score is useful in comparing efficiency when the compounds differ in the number of components.

The second aspect of stimulus selection that should be measured is *consistency of cue selection*. This does not apply to all situations, but in many cases a set of components can be specified by a simple rule that distinguishes the selected component in each compound without distinguishing among the selected components. For example, select the letters in the first position in the trigrams, or select the underscored words. A measure of consistency should specify the extent to which learning conforms to a simple rule of selection without regard to whether learning also occurs to other components. It should also be independent of the fact that different subjects may select different sets of components. In the series of studies with consonant trigrams as compounds (Richardson, in press), the consistency score for each subject was the percentage of all cases in which the recall to the selected component was correct if any component of the compound produced a correct recall response. The number of correct recalls to the selected components was divided by the number of compounds from which one or more of the components produced a correct recall and the result multiplied by 100. The mean consistency scores varied from 85 to 100 and the percentage of subjects with scores of 100 varied from 46 to 100.

The third aspect of stimulus selection that should be measured is more complicated and difficult to handle. If the components of a compound are equally difficult as nominal stimuli for paired-associate learning and the subject learns to only one component in the compound, there is no problem. The subject is perfectly efficient and we may infer that he has focused his attention on the selected component to the exclusion of the other components. However, many subjects recall the correct response to more than one of the components from some compounds and are not perfectly efficient. The *independence* of the learning of the response to two or more components from the same compound is critical to the interpretation of stimulus selection studies. If components from a compound become directly associated or related in some way, then the components may have been integrated rather than selected as functional stimuli. In this case, the major phenomenon is not one of stimulus selection but of integration (see Martin 1971a, p. 325).

Underwood, Ham, and Ekstrand (1962) pointed out that if the correct response is recalled to more than one component of a compound, there is the possibility that the response recall to one component may be mediated by another component. Postman and Greenbloom (1967) inferred single-letter stimulus selection only when the subject recalled the correct response to a letter and failed to recall any additional letters from the compound. This dual criterion seems to insure that only selected letters will be considered but in no way specifies whether the response was learned independently to the excluded components.

If there is a direct connection between two components in the same compound, we expect that one of the components would be a sufficient cue for the other and that response recall to one component might be mediated by the other. The other side of the coin is the same. If the same response is learned to two components, we expect both components to be effective cues for response recall and that one component might be a sufficient cue for the other because the recall is mediated by the common response. Some authors (e.g., Richardson, 1971) have concluded that direct component-component connections are established simply because of plausibility and the fact that components are often sufficient cues for recall of other components of the compound. This evidence does not force the conclusion.

Martin (Wichawut & Martin, 1970; Martin, 1971a,b) has objected to the evidence presented to support the conclusion that direct component–component connections are formed during paired-associate learning and has presented evidence that the component–response associative learning is independent for components within compounds. His recall procedure consists of presenting each individual item from the paired-associate list (both stimulus components and responses) with blanks representing the missing items. The subject attempts to fill in the blanks for each item. Martin finds that, given a stimulus component as a recall cue, the probability of recalling another component from the compound is essentially zero if the correct response is not recalled. On the other hand, if the correct response is recalled, the probability of recalling one or more components from the compound is appreciable and increases with the degree of learning of the paired-associate list. Although there is some evidence which suggests that the generality of Martin's independence results may have some limitations (Richardson, in press), Steiner and Sobel (1968) have presented the only evidence that direct component–component connections do form during paired-associate learning. However, Martin also objects to this evidence (see Martin, 1971b, for a detailed discussion).

If direct component-component connections are formed during paired-associate learning, it does not necessarily follow that the component-response learning is not independent. It also does not necessarily follow that part of the response recall is mediated. Production of mediated recall in the A–B, B–C, A–C paradigm with unrelated materials usually requires extended training on A–B and on B–C.

Stimulus Selection as a Strategy

All the evidence indicates that stimulus selection is the result of a learning strategy that is under the control of the subject. It is assumed to be the result of an active, organized, attentional process. Most of the studies of stimulus selection have presented the stimuli visually with the components of a compound in a constant spatial relation. However, stimulus selection is not only the result of external orienting responses that may eliminate or reduce the stimulation from nonselected components. It also occurs when the letters of trigram stimuli are in a different sequence on each learning trial (Richardson, in press), although the efficiency is slightly reduced. Words are selected as functional stimuli when each word is printed in a distinctive color (Ann Wolfgang, personal communication) and letters are selected from consonant trigrams when the subjects are required to spell the trigrams aloud during learning (Jenkins, 1963). Thus, components may be selected as functional stimuli for learning even though the subject is forced to process all the components in some fashion.

With this conception of stimulus selection, we expect that many, perhaps subtle, variables will determine whether selection occurs and what components are selected. This means that we should be rather cautious about assuming the generality of any particular result of an experiment.

Techniques of Experimenter Control

The learning in the stimulus selection paradigm corresponds to the paired-associate learning paradigm and recall is the attempt to assess the relative control of the response by the components of the stimulus compounds used during learning. With redundant, relevant components, the subjects tend to use a rule of selection that permits consistent identification of the selected components (Richardson, in press). Several techniques have been used to influence or control which components will be selected as the functional stimuli. These techniques may increase or decrease the efficiency of selection depending upon the relative difficulty of learning to the specified set of components and upon the subject's preferences.

One set of techniques specify a set of components in some way so that subjects are more apt to use a particular rule for selection. Among these are instructions (Houston, 1967; Richardson, in press), emphases such as a color (Harrington, 1969; Rabinowitz & Witte, 1967) or underscoring (Richardson, in press), and prior learning that requires the use of a specific type of component as the functional stimulus (Richardson & Chisholm, 1969).

A second set of techniques may provide the basis for a rule of selection but they are also an aid to learning the response to the specified set of components. Among these are prior learning of the responses to a set of components (Richardson & Stanton, in press), a relationship between a set of components and the responses such as identical first letters (Weaver, 1969), mediation between a set of components and the responses (Schulz & Zitzelman, 1970), prior learning of similar responses to one set of components (Houston, 1967), and the relative meaningfulness of the components (e.g., Cohen & Musgrave, 1964).

The use of techniques that result in the more consistent use of a rule of selection, or of the use of associative aids, may facilitate performance during learning and increase the efficiency of selection even though other components are reliable cues for learning. Another group of techniques are variations on the stimulus selection paradigm and determine component control by methods that are, in some respects, similar to those used in concept identification tasks. In these variations, the to-be-selected (relevant) component is always paired with the same response and each relevant component is paired with a different response. The other (irrelevant) components of the compounds are not reliable functional stimuli because of formal similarity relationships (Brown & Sanford, 1968; Richardson & Chisholm, 1969), because different sets of irrelevant components appear on different trials, or because the irrelevant components are paired with different relevant components on different trials (Jacoby & Radtke, 1969, 1970).

Variability

In stimulus selection studies, as in any task, there is variability among subjects in trials to learn, amount recalled, components selected, and so on. However, the concern here is with the within-subject variability, over trials, in the component selected from the possibilities offered by the compound stimulus. The evidence discussed is from a series of studies in which the compound stimuli were consonant trigrams and the responses were single digits (Richardson, in press).

In Experiment I, 24 subjects learned a compound list and all 24 selected the set of letters from the first position in the trigrams, that is, there were more correct recall responses to letters from the first position than to letters from the other two positions. Compared to a control list with single letters as stimuli during learning, the compound list required more trials to learn, the standard deviation of the trials to criterion was larger, the mean consistency score was smaller, and the mean efficiency score was smaller. It was shown (Experiment II) that underscoring one letter in each trigram and instructing the subjects to learn to the underscored letter produced mean trials to criterion, standard deviation of the trials to criterion, mean consistency scores, and mean efficiency scores equivalent to the control. This suggests that the difference in the difficulty of learning lists with compound stimuli and lists with component stimuli is due to the time required for subjects to select the components to be used as functional stimuli from the compounds, that is, the trial-to-trial variation in the components selected from the compounds.

In an attempt to make selection overt during learning (Experiment III), subjects were instructed to learn to one letter of each trigram and to say this letter aloud each time the trigram appeared. There was no restriction on which letters were to be selected nor on changing letters during the learning trials. Thirteen of 24 subjects selected letters from a single position on the first trial and continued to say these letters throughout learning. (Six of the subjects selected letters from the first position, five from the second and two from the third.) The remaining 11 subjects, who selected letters from more than one position of the trigrams on the first trial, all changed some of the letters selected during learning. Five of the 11 were selecting letters from only one position when they reached the criterion of two successive perfect trials, while the other six were still selecting letters from more than one position. The 13 subjects who selected from only one position on the first trial and continued with the same letters throughout learning learned as fast, and their selection was as efficient, as the control group. The other 11 subjects, who changed letters during learning, learned more slowly and their selection was less efficient.

Two other experiments (IV and V) used the same procedure of the subjects saying the selected letters aloud but the sequence of the three letters within a trigram was changed on each trial so that the position of the letters could not be the basis of the selection. Again, the subjects who managed to continue to say the same letters throughout learning (20 of 108 and 23 of 72 for Experiments IV and V, respectively) learned as fast as a control group; the subjects who changed letters during learning required more trials to criterion. In both cases, the efficiency of selection was somewhat less than the control but the subjects who changed letters tended to be less efficient than those who did not change. It may be worth noting that increasing the presentation time per pair from 2 to 3 seconds not only decreased the trials to criterion but also increased the proportion of subjects who selected the same letters throughout learning.

The evidence from these experiments, and it should be noted that they were all with the same material, suggests that subjects who select a set of components at the very beginning of learning and do not change selected components during learning, learn as fast and as efficiently as subjects presented lists with single components as stimuli. The subjects who change components from trial to trial learn more slowly and less efficiently. If there is a simple rule of selection available, the nonvariable subjects use the rule as a basis of selection and some of the variable subjects zero in on a rule as learning continues.

When a first list of trigram stimuli induces subjects to select first, second, or third letters systematically, these selection habits transfer to second-list learning (Richardson & Chisholm, 1969). This suggests that selection may become less variable as subjects learn successive unrelated lists. However, there is no direct evidence on this point.

Effects of Positive and Negative Transfer on Selection

A response may be trained to a component prior to learning the same response (Richardson & Stanton, in press) or a similar response (Houston, 1967) to a compound containing that component. In these situations of positive transfer, the prior learning results in the selection of the pretrained component as the functional stimulus during learning to the compound. These results are so obvious as to be of little interest and, due to Martin's (1968b) encoding variability hypothesis, experimental activity has been focused on the negative transfer paradigm.

Although there is evidence that instructions and prior experience can change the components selected in second-list learning (Houston, 1967; Richardson & Chisholm, 1969; Schneider & Houston, 1968, 1969), there is no evidence that different components are selected simply because of negative transfer (Goggin & Martin, 1970; Houston, 1967; Richardson & Stanton, in press; Weaver, 1969; Williams & Underwood, 1970). There have been different interpretations of Houston's (1967) Experiment III so it will be presented as an example of the generally negative results.

In this experiment the compounds consisted of A and X components (colors and digits). Prior to learning the compound list, the subjects learned a list with the A components as stimuli and with adjective responses that were either unrelated (B) or similar (C') to the corresponding second-list responses. The paradigms were the negative transfer A-B, AX-C and the positive transfer A-C', AX-C. Following learning of the two lists, separate groups of subjects recalled and relearned the C responses with either AX, A, or X as the stimuli. The mean correct recall scores for the A-C' paradigm were 7.00, 5.88, and 2.88 for the AX, A, and X cues, respectively. The corresponding means for the A-B paradigm were 7.13, 4.88, and 4.38. The interaction of paradigm and recall cue was not significant but the analysis included the recall in the AX conditions and, if we assume selection, this condition is not relevant to the effect of the prior learning on the components selected. Assume that the 2 X 2 interaction, eliminating the AX conditions, is significant. This indicates that the two types of prior learning had differential effects on the components selected but in no way indicates whether this was due to a shift in the A-C' condition, to a shift in the A-B condition, or to both. This decision requires knowledge of the selection without the prior learning and this control was included in the experiment. For half the subjects in each paradigm, the digits were the A units and the colors were the X units. For the other half of the subjects, the colors were the A units and digits were the X units. Since the A and X items were the same items over subjects, we could reasonably expect that the recall to A and X items would be equal if there were no prior learning. The difference between the mean correct recall of 5.88 and 2.88 for the A and X components in the positive transfer paradigm gives some basis for concluding that the A-C' training produced increased selection of A components. The difference between the mean correct recall of 4.88 and 4.38 for the A and X units in the negative transfer paradigm offers no support for the hypothesis that the subjects shifted to the X components to avoid negative transfer to the A components. In fact, the small difference is in the wrong direction.

Retaining the same functional stimuli in the second list of a negative transfer paradigm produces more retroactive inhibition than shifting to different functional stimuli for second-list learning. However, it is not clear that using the same functional stimuli in both lists would, in general, interfere more with second-list learning than would a search for a different set of functional stimuli. There is very little, if any, negative transfer with low-meaningful words as stimuli (Martin, 1968b; Martin & Carey, 1971; Weaver, McCann, & Wehr, 1970) and the possibility remains that more complex stimuli would produce positive transfer in the negative transfer paradigm.

The nominal stimuli are the same for both lists in the negative transfer paradigm and the evidence shows that ordinarily the functional stimuli are also the same. Thus, the stimulus identifying responses remain the same for second-list learning and the only basis for a different encoding of the second-list stimuli is some of the list attributes and the identifying responses to the response terms. If encoding occurs according to a rule applied to all the identifying responses from a list, there is some reason for expecting the transfer and retroactive inhibition to be, to some extent, list effects rather than item specific.

Learning and the Amount of Training to the Compound Stimuli

The course of component selection over learning trials was discussed under the heading of *Variability*. In addition to the selection, there is the question of the course of the component-response associative learning over the learning trials on the paired-associate list. It seems reasonable to assume, at this point, that associative learning of the response occurs to whatever component is selected on the trials it is selected. However, it remains possible that little, if any, associative learning occurs before the subject has settled on a strategy of selection. James and Greeno (1967) found that there might be a small amount of learning to the not-finally-selected components very early in learning but that the selector mechanism was essentially completely efficient from that point until the subject attained perfect performance on the list. With overlearning of the paired-associate list, additional components became effective. The relaxation of the selector mechanism with overlearning has been confirmed by Wichawut and Martin (1970) and Martin (1971b). Houston (1967) and Lovelace and Blass (1968) failed to find a significant increase in the effectiveness of the nonselected components with overlearning. Berry, Joubert, and Baumeister (1971) used retarded subjects and trigrams as compounds. They found that the number of single-letter solutions (the recall response was correct to only one of the three letters from the compound) remained relatively constant throughout learning but the number of two-letter solutions increased as number of learning trials increased.

Since selection is viewed as the result of an attentional process under the control of the subject, the efficiency of selection as well as the set of components selected would be expected to vary with conditions. However, there is little indication of what produces relaxation of the selector mechanism with overlearning. Prior training of the response to one component of a compound may block learning that response to other components of the compound (Richardson & Stanton, in press). This shows that relaxation of the selector mechanism during perfect performance on the compound list is not automatic and suggests that some procedures may result in continued selection of the same components.

It should be noted that, although it seems to occur in some situations, there is nothing about stimulus selection as it is presented here that requires selection to be perfectly efficient over any sequence of learning trials. The question about the selector mechanism at any stage of learning is a question about the relative amount of time spent on the components within the compounds; a change in time sharing should produce changes in efficiency.

SUMMARY

Stimulus selection is viewed as the result of an active attentional process that determines the identifying response, or responses, to compound stimuli consisting of unrelated redundant components. It is the identifying responses that enter into any further encoding prior to storage in memory. Since stimulus selection deals with what is learned, it is important for the interpretation of a variety of recall and transfer phenomena. In addition, the evidence may be useful as a relatively overt example of a stimulus transformation prior to associative learning.

REFERENCES

Baumeister, A. A., & Berry, F. M. Context stimuli in verbal paired-associate learning by normal children and retardates. *Psychological Record*, 1968, 18, 185-190.

Baumeister, A. A., & Berry, F. M. Single-letter cue selection in the paired-associate learning of normal children and retardates. *Journal of Experimental Child Psychology*, 1970, 9, 400-410.

Baumeister, A. A., Berry, F. M., & Forehand, R. Effects of secondary cues on rote verbal learning of retardates and normal children. *Journal of Comparative and Physiological Psychology*, 1969, 69, 273-280.

Berry. F. M., Joubert, C. E., & Baumeister, A. A. Single-letter cue selection and degree of paired-associate learning in retardates. *Journal of Experimental Psychology*, 1971, 88, 196-204.

Brown, S. C., & Sanford, J. F. Intralist categorization in paired-associate learning. *Psychonomic Science*, 1968, 10, 345-346.

Cohen, J. C., & Musgrave, B. S. Effect of meaningfulness on cue selection in verbal paired-associate learning. *Journal of Experimental Psychology*, 1964, 68, 284-291.

Fraisse, P. Le temps de réaction verbale: I. Dénomination et lecture. *L'Année Psychologique*, 1964, 64, 21-46.

Fraisse, P. Latency of different verbal responses to the same stimulus. *Quarterly Journal of Experimental Psychology*, 1967, 19, 353-355.

Fraisse, P. Motor and verbal reaction times to words and drawings. *Psychonomic Science*, 1968, 12, 235-236.

Fraisse, P., Lanati, L., Régnier, J., & Wahl, M. Le temps de réaction verbale: II. Réponses spécifiques et catégorielles. *L'Année Psychologique*, 1965, 65, 27-32.

Garner, W. R., & Felfoldy, G. L. Integrality of stimulus dimensions in various types of information processing. *Cognitive Psychology*, 1970, 1, 225-241.

Goggin, J., & Martin, E. Forced stimulus encoding and retroactive interference. *Journal of Experimental Psychology*, 1970, 84, 131-136.

Grant, D. A. Adding communication to the signalling property of the CS in classical conditioning. *Journal of General Psychology*, 1968, 79, 147-175.

Harrington, A. L. Effects of component emphasis on stimulus selection in paired-associate learning. *Journal of Experimental Psychology*, 1969, 79, 412-418.

Horowitz, L. M., & Prytulak, L. S. Redintegrative memory. *Psychological Review*, 1969, 76, 519-531.

Houston, J. P. S-R stimulus selection and strength of R-S association. *Journal of Experimental Psychology*, 1964, 68, 563-566.

Houston, J. P. Stimulus selection as influenced by degrees of learning, attention, prior associations, and experience with the stimulus components. *Journal of Experimental Psychology*, 1967, 73, 509-516.

Jacoby, L. L., & Radtke, R. C. Effects of contiguity and meaningfulness of relevant and irrelevant attributes on concept formation. *Journal of Experimental Psychology*, 1969, 81, 454-459.

Jacoby, L. L., & Radtke, R. C. Effects of meaningfulness of relevant and irrelevant stimuli in a modified concept formation task. *Journal of Experimental Psychology*, 1970, 83, 356-358.

James, C. T., & Greeno, J. G. Stimulus selection at different stages of paired-associate learning. *Journal of Experimental Psychology*, 1967, **74**, 75-83.

Jenkins, J. J. Stimulus "fractionation" in paired-associate learning. *Psychological Reports*, 1963, **13**, 409-410.

Lawrence, D. H. The nature of a stimulus: Some relationships between learning and perception. In S. Koch (Ed.), *Psychology: A study of a science*, Vol. 5. New York: McGraw-Hill, 1963. Pp. 179-212.

Liftik, J., & Leicht, K. L. Effect of number and relatedness of stimulus-term components on paired-associate learning. *Psychonomic Science*, 1968, **13**, 315-316.

Lovelace, E. A., & Blass, E. M. Utilization of stimulus elements in paired-associate learning. *Journal of Experimental Psychology*, 1968, **76**, 596-600.

Martin, E. Recognition and correct responding mediated by first letter of trigram stimuli. *Journal of Verbal Learning and Verbal Behavior*, 1968, **7**, 703-704. (a)

Martin, E. Stimulus meaningfulness and paired-associate transfer: An encoding variability hypothesis. *Psychological Review*, 1968, **75**, 421-441. (b)

Martin, E. Verbal learning theory and independent retrieval phenomena. *Psychological Review*, 1971, **78**, 314-332. (a)

Martin, E. Stimulus component independence. *Journal of Verbal Learning and Verbal Behavior*, 1971, **10**, 715-721. (b)

Martin, E., & Carey, S. T. Retroaction, recovery, and stimulus meaningfulness in the A-B, A-Br paradigm. *American Journal of Psychology*, 1971, **84**, 123-133.

Morin, R. E., & Forrin, B. Mixing of two types of S-R associations in a choice reaction time task. *Journal of Experimental Psychology*, 1962, **64**, 137-141.

Morin, R. E., Konick, A., Troxell, N., & McPherson, S. Information and reaction time for "naming" responses. *Journal of Experimental Psychology*, 1965, **70**, 309-314.

Nelson, D. L., Rowe, F. A., Engel, J. E., Wheeler, J., & Garland, R. M. Backward relative to forward recall as a function of stimulus meaningfulness and formal interstimulus similarity. *Journal of Experimental Psychology*, 1970, **83**, 323-328.

Postman, L., & Greenbloom, R. Conditions of cue selection in the acquisition of paired-associate lists. *Journal of Experimental Psychology*, 1967, **73**, 91-100.

Rabinowitz, F. M., & Witte, K. L. Stimulus selection as a function of letter color. *Journal of Verbal Learning and Verbal Behavior*, 1967, **6**, 167-168.

Richardson, J. Latencies of implicit verbal responses and the effect of the anticipation interval on mediated transfer. *Journal of Verbal Learning and Verbal Behavior*, 1967, **6**, 819-826.

Richardson, J. Latencies of implicit associative responses and positive transfer in paired-associate learning. *Journal of Verbal Learning and Verbal Behavior*, 1968, **7**, 638-646.

Richardson, J. Cue effectiveness and abstraction in paired-associate learning. *Psychological Bulletin*, 1971, **75**, 73-91.

Richardson, J. Stimulus selection in associative learning. In C. P. Duncan, L. Sechrest, & A. W. Melton (Eds.), *Human memory: Festschrift for Benton J. Underwood*. New York: Appleton-Century-Crofts, in press.

Richardson, J., & Chisholm, D. C. Transfer of cue selection based on letter position. *Journal of Experimental Psychology*, 1969, **80**, 299-303.

Richardson, J., & Stanton, S. K. Some effects of learning to a set of components on stimulus selection. *American Journal of Psychology*, in press.

Runquist, W. N. Structural effects of letter identity among stimuli in paired-associate learning. *Journal of Experimental Psychology*, 1970, **84**, 152-163.

Schneider, N. G., & Houston, J. P. Stimulus selection and retroactive inhibition. *Journal of Experimental Psychology*, 1968, **77**, 166-167.

Schneider, N. G., & Houston, J. P. Retroactive inhibition, cue selection, and degree of learning. *American Journal of Psychology*, 1969, **82**, 276-279.

Schulz, R. W., & Zitzelman, P. W. Mediation as a basis for stimulus selection in paired-associate learning. Paper presented at the meeting of the Psychonomic Society, San Antonio, Texas, November, 1970.

Shepard, R. N. Comments on Professor Underwood's paper. In C. N. Cofer & B. S. Musgrave

(Eds.), *Verbal behavior and learning: Problems and processes.* New York: McGraw-Hill, 1963, Pp. 48-70.

Solso, R. L., & Trafimow, E. S. Stimulus competition as a function of varying stimulus meaningfulness. *Psychonomic Science,* 1970, 18, 103-104.

Steiner, T. E., & Sobel, R. Intercomponent association formation during paired-associate training with compound stimuli. *Journal of Experimental Psychology,* 1968, 77, 275-280.

Underwood, B. J. Stimulus selection in verbal learning. In C. N. Cofer & B. S. Musgrave (Eds.), *Verbal behavior and learning: Problems and processes.* New York: McGraw-Hill, 1963. Pp. 33-48.

Underwood, B. J., Ham, M., & Ekstrand, B. Cue selection in paired-associate learning. *Journal of Experimental Psychology,* 1962, 64, 405-409.

Weaver, G. E. Stimulus encoding as a determinant of retroactive inhibition. *Journal of Verbal Learning and Verbal Behavior,* 1969, 8, 807-814.

Weaver, G. E., McCann, R. L., & Wehr, R. J. Stimulus meaningfulness, transfer, and retroactive inhibition in the A-B, A-C paradigm. *Journal of Experimental Psychology,* 1970, 85, 255-257.

Wichawut, C., & Martin, E. Selective stimulus encoding and overlearning in paired-associate learning. *Journal of Experimental Psychology,* 1970, 85, 383-388.

Williams, R. F., & Underwood, B. J. Encoding variability: Tests of the Martin hypothesis. *Journal of Experimental Psychology,* 1970, 86, 317-324.

Young, R. K., Farrow, J. M., Seitz, S., & Hays, M. Backward recall with compound stimuli. *Journal of Experimental Psychology,* 1966, 72, 241-243.

4
STIMULUS ENCODING IN
LEARNING AND TRANSFER[1]

Edwin Martin
University of Michigan

This paper is about how stimuli control performance in a learning task. It is therefore about how learners encode the learning situation in which they are expected to perform. I will begin with a sketch of some relevant background problems and suggestive reasons why stimulus encoding must be viewed as an essential yet an uncertain process; and then, in two additional sections, discuss some evidence that partially characterizes stimulus encoding in learning and transfer tasks.

BACKGROUND COMMENTS

An ever-present feature of performance in a learning task is the apparent variability of that performance. In some learning situations such variability is easily describable, as, for example, in certain paired-associate tasks where the incidence of errors over trials before the last error is nicely modelled by the binomial distribution (e.g., Bower, 1961). In general, however, performance variability is not an easy feature of learning to capture in simple terms.

In the Darwinian century, spontaneous variability of performance was assumed necessary for adaptive modification of behavior. From Bain (1855), Spencer (1872), and Morgan (1904) through Thorndike (1913) to Hull (1930) and Dashiell (1937), such variability was a sine qua non for learning: If R_i is some response less likely than the dominant R_1 in an established response hierarchy, and if in a given new situation R_i optimizes success, then the only escape from the now less optimal R_1 is some sort of performance variability that allows R_i occasionally to occur and thereby to become selectively strengthened. For the foregoing writers, the required

[1] The author's own research was supported by the Advanced Research Projects Agency, Department of Defense, and monitored by the Air Force Office of Scientific Research, under Contract Nos. AF 49 (638)-1736 and AF44620-72-C-0019 with the Human Performance Center, Department of Psychology, University of Michigan.

variability was assumed to be spontaneous, although clearly the range of alternative behaviors was restricted by relevant past experience (e.g., Hull, 1930; Thorndike, 1931).

The attempt of Hull (1943) to handle performance variability is instructive. The organism's competence was represented by the concept of habit. The translation of that competence into behavior was mediated by two distinctly different concepts— one that related competence to performance through motivational variables and one that did no more than name a gratuitous generator of performance variability. Given control over the learner's state of motivation, the former did not provide for variability. The latter (Hull's $_sO_R$), however, ensured variability, and ensured it at all stages of learning. In a sense, modern postulation of a guessing process, as represented by the ubiquitous g parameter, is a refinement of $_sO_R$, and as such is formal acknowledgement of unexplained performance variability, in this case prior to complete mastery.

It is interesting that all early conceptualizations of performance variability centered on the response end of the total information processing system. This is especially clear in the writings of Dodge (1931), who placed considerable weight on the notion of response refractoriness. Carr (1925) and Guthrie (1935), though speaking of variable stimulation, attributed changes in the stimulus situation to the responses emitted by the learner.

Perhaps the single most important advance on the problem of performance variability in a learning task was the introduction (Estes, 1950) and development (e.g., Estes, 1955a,b) of stimulus sampling theory. The essence of this theory is that between the organism and his environment there is an uncertain, probabilistic relation. Whether this relation should be conceptualized in terms of sensory or perceptual variability is not basic to the general idea. What is basic is the notion of functional inconstancy in the face of nominal constancy somewhere at the front end of the total process.

Although it was stimulus sampling theory that highlighted this point, the idea itself has no mean history. Both Höffding (1891) and Köhler (1940) worried over the variable and dynamic relation between the nominal input event and the contact it makes with central information. Variability in attention to component aspects of the stimulus situation was a critical part of Guthrie's (1935) view of how learning and extinction proceed. Spence (1956) also attributed performance variability partly to attentional variability. And the concept of discrepancy between the nominal and functional stimulus as essential and undeniable has been convincingly argued both by Lawrence (1963) and by Underwood (1963). In short, it would seem that the matter of performance variability could be homing on the domain of its solution. It has progressed from an unexplained prerequisite, through an unexplained discrepancy from one or another competence model, toward some conceptualization involving perceptual encoding.

Another line of argument for the centrality of some sort of notion of stimulus encoding revolves around certain failures of verbal learning theories that do not incorporate a stimulus analysis in their assumptions. I have elaborated this argument elsewhere (Martin, 1971a) and will only summarize it here. Theorizing in the learning area has most often focused on three primary concepts—the stimulus, the response, and a conditional relation between them known as an association. The associative interference theory of learning and transfer postulates that learning is S–R association formation and that transfer is extinction of one association due to acquisition of a new, substitute association. It is now clear, however, that no such reciprocally interfering relation between competing associations exists (e.g., DaPolito, 1966). The list differentiation theory postulates an availability organization of responses common to a given task. When the responses are changed, the old class of responses is seen as suppressed and replaced by a new class. But such task-determined organization does not materialize when a specifically organizational test is made (Martin & Mackay, 1970; Dalezman, Engle, & Wickens, 1971). It appears that learned behaviors organize themselves in terms of the stimulus features common to their past occurrence, not in terms of when or in what task they were elicited. Moreover, these two theories each entail two ordered stages, making responses available and forming S–R associations, and hence entail an ordered differential sensitivity to stimulus and response difficulty variables that does not obtain in fact (Greeno, James, & DaPolito, 1971). Thus the two standard verbal learning theories, associative interference theory and list differentiation theory, emphasize, respectively, the concepts of association formation and response integration. That they are inadequate and that neither entails any treatment or elaboration of the stimulus concept may be two closely related facts.

The problem of performance variability and the inadequacy of standard theories that do not incorporate a stimulus analysis are but argumentative convergence on the need for a conceptualization of stimulus encoding. On the other hand, there are many tangible phenomena that seem to require such a conceptualization. I will briefly mention a few general classes of such phenomena; most anyone can think of dozens more.

1. Stimulus selection in paired-associate learning. That learners use as effective cues for responding fewer than all of the components of a compound stimulus is an established fact (Underwood, 1963; Richardson, 1971). That learners differ in which components they tend to utilize is also an established fact (Wichawut & Martin, 1970), as is intrasubject inconsistency (Richardson, in press).

2. Selective cue utilization in concept formation. The 1968 Trabasso and Bower book, *Attention in Learning,* is an extensive theoretical and experimental monograph on selective differential cue utilization in a classification learning task. From this source and elsewhere it is clear that the effects of such experimental variables as cue saliency and numerosity of irrelevant cues on learning require a conceptualization of stimulus encoding that treats the nominal stimulus on some basis other than as an irreducible Gestalt or as an invariant, unmodifiable partial representation.

3. Selective attention. Simple mention of such review papers as those by Haber (1966) on the effects of set on perception and by Treisman (1969) on selective attention should redintegrate a host of phenomena whose demonstrability depends on nonuniform processing of simultaneous sensory information.

4. Differential utilization of representational dimensions in memory tasks. Wickens (this volume) has demonstrated that, for example, semantic dimensions of words are critical to memory for words while syntactic dimensions are irrelevant;

and that within the domain of semantic dimensions, taxonomic categorization is a more salient basis of encoding than is a sense-impression basis. Further, the modality (visual, auditory) of information input is an important dimension, but not nearly so important as is the difference between Spanish and English for bilinguals. Whatever imaging is, moreover, doing it versus not doing it, or receiving stimulus materials that variably permit it, both have huge effects on recallability of information from memory (e.g., Paivio, 1969). Also, recall of words that belong to specific conceptual categories is better when at the time of presentation the relevant categories are made more apparent by blocking the words by categories, as opposed to mixing the words randomly (e.g., Cofer, Bruce, & Reicher, 1966; Bower, Clark, Lesgold, & Winzenz, 1969).

These are but a few topical examples of classes of phenomena that seem inexplicable except in terms of some hypothesis that entails a stimulus encoding process other than complete, nonselective, nonelaborative, nonmodifiable reception and utilization of input information. Bower (this volume) has made this point nicely by outlining and exemplifying a fourfold taxonomy of the senses in which the term "encoding" is used. *Selection*: ". . . explicit selection by the subject of a component of a complex but fractionable stimulus pattern" (p. 86). *Rewriting*: Substituting a single symbol for a longer string of symbols; for example, rewriting triads of binary digits into single octal digits. *Componential description*: "An item presented to the memory system becomes represented in terms of a list of components, attributes, properties, or features . . . . The location of a given item in the feature space may vary from one presentation to another if its interpretive context changes" (p. 87). *Elaboration*: "The input is assumed to give rise to associated operators which qualitatively transform the to-be-remembered item" (p. 88). Bower cites the phenomena of mental imagery and natural language mediation as examples.

These considerations, which are but a modest sampling of the turbulent concern with stimulus encoding, together with the problem of performance variability and the shortcomings of learning theories that depend upon conceptualizations only of associative interaction or response class availability, indicate that stimulus encoding processes must be central to learning and transfer.

STIMULUS ENCODING IN LEARNING

There are many experimental variables pertaining to stimuli that affect the ease and progress of learning. Their effects on learning, however, I believe to be understandable in terms of a single notion, namely, the degree of difficulty the learner experiences in settling on a stable, reliable encoding of the stimuli presented. A given nominal, external event can, in principle, be characterized by a listing of physical attributes or features and the relations among those attributes or features. A learner may attend or register only some of these, and which some of these he attends or registers may be different on Trials n and $n + 1$. Additionally, there are internal states of expectation or remembrance not directly determined by the immediate external stimulus situation that impose rewrite, elaborative, or interpretive transformations on whatever was attended or registered.

These effects, too, may vary between Trial n and Trial $n + 1$. Thus what the functional stimulus is at any given time is uncertain and variable. The learner's task is somehow to arrive at a representation of his circumstances so that his performance satisfies a prescribed criterion.

Shepard (1964) has distinguished two types of stimuli, "those that are reacted to as homogeneous, unitary wholes, and those that tend to be analyzed into perceptually distinct compounds or properties" (p. 80). In discussing this distinction, Shepard writes:

> One way of conceptualizing the distinction advocated here is in terms of uniformity of internal response. With highly analyzable stimuli, the evidence indicates that subjects actually "take in" or "sample" quite different aspects or properties upon different presentation of the same physical stimulus . . . . With unitary stimuli such as homogeneous colors, however, essentially the same internal representation seems to be evoked on each occasion . . . . In this respect, then, analyzable stimuli are psychologically more complex, i.e., they require more elaborate characterizations and they lead to more variable responses in learning and judgment tasks (p. 81).

Shepard's view arises from stimulus scaling research wherein he found that while unitary or unanalyzable stimuli satisfy a Euclidean metric, complex or fractionable stimuli do not, requiring rather a Minkowski ("city block") metric. This distinction is also the basis of Garner's (this volume) concept of dimension integrality, which underlies his analysis of how and under what conditions feature redundancy affects discrimination of multifeatured stimuli.

Stimulus Encoding Variability

Biederman, Dumas, and Lachman (1968) experimentally distinguished the effects on paired-associate learning of two features of a priori association activation by stimuli. A given word that is to be a stimulus in a learning task may, either strongly or weakly, elicit a primary or dominant association. As distinct from that consideration, the same word may elicit in addition other, potentially interfering associations. These other associations may distribute themselves over a likelihood or strength scale in any number of ways so that as a group their potentiality for interference varies. Biederman et al. gave 88 essayists a 500-word, high-frequency vocabulary from which to write a 200-word essay on any topic of their choosing. From the essays produced they constructed paired-associate lists such that four pair types were included: HUN-HTP pairs were those where the response member was a frequent subsequent word to the stimulus member (High Transition Probability, HTP), but also the relation between the stimulus and response was nevertheless highly uncertain (High Uncertainty, HUN) as measured by

$$UN = -\Sigma p(i) \ln p(i),$$

where $p(i)$ was the relative frequency of word i subsequent to the stimulus word in the essays. An example is *never-seen*. The other three pair types were HUN-LTP (e.g., *system-came*), LUN-HTP (e.g., *far-out*), and LUN-LTP (e.g., *door-also*), where the initial H or L stands for High or Low and UN and TP stand for Uncertainty and Transition Probability. Other subjects were then given (within lists) a fixed number of study-test paired-associate trials on these pair types. The resulting mean number of correct responses per item according to pair type indicated that both transition probability (TP) and uncertainty in usage (UN) were separable and significant factors. Biederman et al. concluded that while it is certainly true that stimulus-to-response transition probability is a clear factor in learning, equally clear is the fact that uncertainty in usage is a separately definable and significant factor. My reading of this experimental result is as follows: If an a priori relation exists between stimulus and response (high TP), then the prescribed learning is already partly done, hence the advantage of high TP. As distinct from this, the degree of variability of encoding of the stimulus (UN) determines the rate of progress of learning, that is, determines the difficulty of settling on a stable, reliable stimulus encoding.

An experiment by Butler and Merikle (1970) makes a similar point. They selected 100 consonant-vowel-consonant (CVC) trigrams from the Archer (1960) norms covering the entire range of scaled meaningfulness, then obtained from 100 subjects the first word to each that came to mind as a free associate. From this corpus of free associates, Butler and Merikle calculated two clusters of measures: *meaningfulness*, the usual association value measures of Archer (1960), Glaze (1928), Krueger (1934), and Noble (1961); *variability*, the number of different associates given over subjects and the associative uncertainty as measured by Biederman et al. (1968). The principal result of this phase of their research was that the variability measures correlated negatively with the meaningfulness measures. The next step was to construct paired-associate lists of either CVC-digit or digit-CVC pairs and administer a fixed number of learning trials. Their purpose was to relate number of correct responses to the measures of meaningfulness and variability as they applied to stimulus versus response members of pairs. The result of factor analysis was three distinct factors, meaningfulness, variability, and a general learning factor. When the CVCs were on the response side, the loadings were primarily on the meaningfulness and general learning factors; when on the stimulus side, primarily on the variability and general learning factors. Thus meaningfulness and variability are inversely related measures, but with the latter serving as the distinguishing characteristic of those input events that have a cue function.

It is worth noting that these two reports center on variability of associations to stimuli. This sort of variability is not what one ordinarily thinks of when one thinks of stimulus encoding; rather one tends first to think of variable component selection. My counter to this is that a conceptualization of encoding variability should not be limited to external selectional phenomena, as might be produced by, say, receptor orientation. Instead, it should encompass all effects that entail differential perception or interpretation of a stimulus over several occurrences of that stimulus. It would seem that degree of variability in free association might be an excellent index of variability in perception or interpretation of the association-eliciting stimulus.

A final note on this topic is a particular result (out of an array of results) reported by Abra (1968). Among other conditions, he compared the effects of low- and high-meaningfulness stimuli (with low intralist stimulus similarity) on paired-associate learning by the method of generated responses. During learning, the subject spelled any three-letter response he wished to each stimulus. He was completely free in his choice of responses, except for the restriction of no numbers or proper names. Learning continued until two perfectly consistent trials occurred in succession. What is interesting is the number of "drop-out" errors per stimulus, that is, the number of different responses supplied, en route to criterion, that did not become final criterion responses. For high-meaningfulness stimuli, which we may consider to be more unitary than low-meaningfulness stimuli, the mean number of such responses per stimulus was 1.8; for low-meaningfulness stimuli, 2.7. Thus the more fractionable low-meaningfulness stimuli gave rise to more variability in subject-generated responding than did the high-meaningfulness stimuli. That this result cannot be a matter of more forgetting of generated responses with low-meaningfulness stimuli is clear from the fact that the mean frequency of occurrence of each such generated response was slightly higher for low- than for high-meaningfulness stimuli: Each drop-out error was used 1.5 times for low-meaningfulness stimuli, 1.4 times for high-meaningfulness stimuli.

Although the evidence just outlined does not establish stimulus encoding variability as an undeniably necessary consideration in learning theory, it nevertheless seems to establish a convincing level of cogency. It is worth pointing out, however, that direct evidence of variability of stimulus encoding is probably not attainable. The notion as it now exists indiscriminately groups together several source levels of uncertainty—sensory, receptor orientation, internally directed tuning or attenuation, and "contextual drift" (Bower, this volume) both of the external and the cognitive varieties. Liberman (this volume) treats encoding of acoustic signals into phonemic representations via a speech code while Miller (this volume) considers how one "suburb of the lexicon" might be organized, thus exemplifying in one place a broad range of analyses from perceptual functionalism to mental structuralism, in both of which, and at all levels between, there is inherent some degree of indeterminism.

Stimulus Recognition

If a given experimental stimulus variable relates to ease of learning because that variable is an index of how easy it is for the learner to settle on a stable, reliable encoding of the stimulus, then what we are saying is that from trial to trial the learner, at least at the outset, is varying his encoding of the stimulus. If he varies his encoding of the stimulus from Trial 1 to Trial 2, then we must expect him to fail to recognize that stimulus on Trial 2. If the learner encodes the stimulus one way on Trials 1 through n and then changes his encoding on Trial $n + 1$, we must expect him not only to fail to recognize this de facto old nominal stimulus but also to show no tendency to emit the prescribed response he had been learning.

Earlier (Martin, 1967a), I reported that in a paired-associate learning situation wherein three-consonant (CCC) trigrams and digits were paired and studied silently on study trials but on test trials the learners had both to recognize the study-trials stimuli out of a larger set of always-new but like items (CCCs) and to respond with the first digit response that came to mind, response recall improved steadily over trials *providing the stimuli were recognized.* On those occasions when the learner failed to recognize the stimulus, response recall was at the level of chance guessing.

This result is shown in Figure 1, where $P(CR|R)$ is the proportion correct responses given stimulus recognition and $P(CR|\overline{R})$ is the proportion correct responses given failure of stimulus recognition. The dashed line is the chance level for guessing the correct digit response out of eight possible. In further analyses (see Martin, 1967a) it was shown that this reduction of correct responding to the chance level upon stimulus recognition failure was not a function of how many previous correct responses were emitted. Moreover, in a subsequent analysis of which responses were emitted when the learner falsely recognized a test-trials distractor item (Martin, 1968a), it was discovered that if the distractor item had its first letter in common with a study-trials stimulus, the learner reliably emitted the digit response that went with the study-trials stimulus. In Figure 2 is plotted, with open circles, the proportion times the response that went with a study-trials stimulus was emitted to a falsely recognized distractor stimulus that had the same first letter. This function, though lower absolutely, has the same form as that for correctly recognized study-trials stimuli (the curve with the filled circles, replotted from Fig. 1). Thus, although false recognition of such distractor stimuli declined steadily over trials (the lower curve with open triangles connected by dashes), a component of those stimuli that prompted "false" recognition also produced a "correct" response with increasing likelihood over trials.

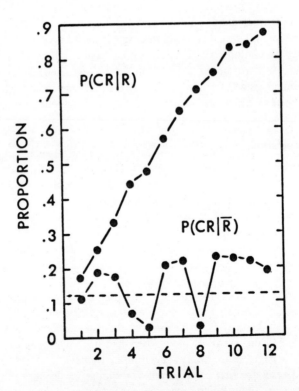

FIG. 1. Proportion correct responses (*CR*) given recognition (*R*) and nonrecognition (*R̄*) of stimuli. (from Martin, 1967a).

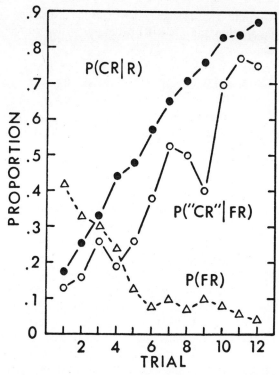

FIG. 2. Proportion correct responses given recognition of stimuli (*CR* |*R*), proportion "correct" responses given false recognition of fillers with same first letter as a learning stimulus ("*CR*" |*FR*), and proportion false recognition of fillers with same first letter as a learning stimulus (*FR*). (from Martin, 1968a).

Altogether, what these results mean is that retrieval of a prescribed response requires a proper reinstatement of a particular functional version of its cuing stimulus. All stimuli were presented auditorily through earphones, so there is no question of the learner not being exposed to the stimuli in their nominal entirety. The facts (*a*) that stimulus nonrecognition occurs even on later learning trials, (*b*) that a single letter from a partially new stimulus (a distractor) can lead to (false?) recognition, (*c*) that such recognition can produce "correct" responding, and (*d*) that correct responding in any case cannot, except by chance, occur when there is no stimulus recognition, add up to the conclusion that stimulus encoding is partial, variable, and a yes-no antecedent to response retrieval.

Research of the foregoing type has been replicated and extended by Martin (1967b) and Royer (1969).

An interesting application of this experimental approach has resolved the old question of why pictorial stimuli produce faster paired-associate learning than do word stimuli. Wicker (1970) has shown that while simple pictures indeed produce faster learning than do the words that describe those pictures, if response recall is conditionalized on stimulus recognition the difference disappears. In demonstrating this phenomenon, he also reaffirmed the well-known result that pictures are easier to recognize than words. The substantial difference in stimulus recognizability between words and pictures thus proved to be the source of the observed difference in response recallability.

All this, of course, returns us to Höffding's (1891) original problem: One cannot get to B unless A makes contact with the specific trace representation a to which b is associated in the mediative schema $A \rightarrow a \rightarrow b \rightarrow B$. What is critical is the conditional probability $P(a|A)$, the likelihood of stimulus recognition. It was Shepard's (1964) point that $P(a|A)$ varies inversely with degree of analyzability of A.

Stimulus Component Interdependence

If a stimulus is a collection of attributes or components over which the learner variously distributes his attention, then one might be curious about possible interrelations among the attributes or components that a stimulus comprises. The question of importance is, given certain specified a priori interrelations before learning begins, does the process of learning change any of these interrelations? More to the immediate point, does learning involve formation of associations (conditional relations) among stimulus components that prior to learning were unassociated? Richardson (1971, p. 78) concluded there is evidence for such intercomponent association formation. I have argued elsewhere, though, that the evidence ordinarily cited is not acceptable (or at least that it is alternatively interpretable), and Wichawut and I have reported experimental results that are a counterexample to at least the inclusive hypothesis that such associations are always formed during learning (Martin, 1971b; Wichawut & Martin, 1970).

The results just alluded to are that after any of several degrees of learning, if a single word from a triad of unrelated words that was a compound stimulus during learning is presented alone and the subject asked to recall both the response and the remaining stimulus components, he can recall neither of the two missing stimulus components unless he can recall the response. If the subject can recall the response, then and only then can he recall also other stimulus components. In Figure 3 are shown the proportion recall of at least one of the two nonpresented stimulus components $(A_j \cup A_k)$ when component A_i was presented for two conditions of analysis, when the response was recalled (B, upper curves) and when the response was not recalled ($\overline{B}$, lower curves). Moreover, additional analyses show that given that a particular stimulus component does elicit the prescribed response, then the two missing, not-presented components are recalled stochastically independently of each other (Martin, 1971b).

What seems to be going on is that components of a compound stimulus form independent and parallel associations with the response member of the pair. Even 16 additional learning trials beyond the once-perfect criterion failed to produce the slightest recall dependency between two components of the same stimulus except via mediation through their common response. While it is clear that additional learning trials result in additional stimulus components becoming effective elicitors of the response (James & Greeno, 1967; Lovelace & Blass, 1968; Martin, 1971b; Wichawut & Martin, 1970), the above results supplement this standard fact with the possibility that stimulus components, whether long standing or newly effective, do

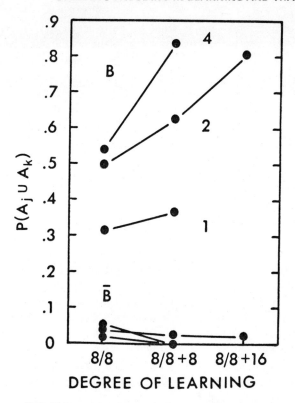

FIG. 3. Proportion times at least one stimulus word ($A_j \cup A_k$) recalled given stimulus word A_i presented and response *was* (B, upper curves) and *was not* ($\overline{B}$ lower curves) recalled, as a function of degree of learning. The numbers 1, 2, and 4 refer to length of anticipation interval, in seconds, during learning. (from Martin, 1971b).

not interrelate among themselves on a direct component-component associative basis.

What to do with this fact is not clear. It suggests, however, that perhaps for every nominal stimulus event there is a level of description such that the features or attributes named in the description are mutually noninteractive; that is, among all the possible ways of characterizing a stimulus event, there is at least one way such that Wichawut independence (as I call it) holds over all the stimulus components listed. Indeed, we might consider a stimulus component to be defined as a collection or subset of features or attributes that in no way determines the effectiveness of any other subset of features or attributes as a cue for the common learned response. If several features are bundled together as an invariant percept, then from a functional point of view they jointly constitute a stimulus component.

Whatever we shall ultimately mean by the word "component," it is nevertheless critical to develop a body of knowledge about interrelations among stimulus parts and how those interrelations change during learning. An important first step should be determination of whether or not or to what degree a known a priori associative relation or organization among stimulus parts is altered during learning. Of particular interest also is the situation wherein the compound stimuli of a paired-associate list are either of low or high intralist similarity. Hintzman (1969) has shown that when such similarity is high, subjects are forced to use all or nearly all of the stimulus parts to discriminate properly the several compound stimuli. But even so, do these parts in fact interassociate with each other during learning? Or is their apparent organization determined only by mediation through their common response?

Summary

However scant the hard evidence, I am inclined to the following view of stimulus encoding in a learning task. A stimulus event, especially when it is serving a cue function, is seldom perceived in exhaustive completeness. The ordinary case is that it is encoded on the basis of fewer than all of its possible components. By "encoding" I mean a sampling of some subset of stimulus components; by "stimulus component" I mean an independent set of attributes or features; and by "independent" I mean that such a set of attributes or features does not condition the likelihood of sampling any other component. At the outset of a learning task, stimulus encoding is variable, which is to say that from trial to trial different components may be attended or perceived. Accumulation of probability of correct responding depends entirely on resampling previously sampled components. As practice continues, more components may become independently effective elicitors of the correct response. In any case, correct responding cannot occur unless a previously associated component is sampled.

How the sampling process might change over learning trials is not clear. I doubt that it remains random. The effects on learning of prior set and instructions are marked. And after all, learning trials are at least just another way to impose a set or to transmit instructions. Moreover, acquired rigidity of perception is a clinical as well as an experimental fact. Accordingly, one might hypothesize that at some point in learning no more components are added to the effective list, the remainder being simply not perceived. Finally, I see no reason to suppose that a once-effective component will ever lose its effectiveness (if sampled) except in the case where it becomes counterconditional for some new, incompatible response (Guthrie, 1935).

STIMULUS ENCODING IN TRANSFER

From the frame of reference of an external observer, learners or subjects often seem to emit erroneous responses. There is a sense, however, in which so categorizing responses is a form of theoretical resignation. An advance is made whenever some of such responses are removed from this category, that is, whenever we can arrive at an explanation of them. An example of this kind of advance is the change in attitude toward false positives in recognition tasks. We no longer view false positives in terms of a general slop factor; instead, we are sensitive to their possible sources, including semantic, phonemic, and orthographic similarities with previously presented information. This is an analytic advance and reflects our suspicion that no behavior or decision comes from nowhere.

If a given response indeed, in the last analysis, comes from a specific somewhere, then it seems reasonable to argue that two different responses cannot, again in the last analysis, come from the exact same somewhere. If R_1 and R_2 are two distinct behaviors and if S_1 is the presumed stimulus for R_1, then any assertion that S_1 can be also the stimulus for R_2 is a mistake. The nature of the mistake is that the external observer, from his frame of reference, sees S_1 as the antecedent both to R_1 and to R_2. The existence of such a mistake means that the external observer has a frame of reference that is different from that of the learner. The learner discriminates S_1 from S_2; the external observer fails in that discrimination and calls both stimuli S_1. My point is that while S_1 and S_2 may be nominally identical from one point of view, they are functionally different from another.

These comments are introductory to what I believe to be a reasonable position regarding stimulus encoding in a transfer situation. If a subject first learns an A–B contingency and later learns an A–D contingency, then either he retains them both in the form of A_B–B and A_D–D or, if he cannot or will not differentiate functional A_B and A_D, he dumps A–B and retains only A–D. A learner cannot retain both A–B and C–D where A and C are identically encoded.

This position in its general form does not specify how it is that A_B and A_D differ in case a learner can remember both A–B and A–D. The possibilities are essentially limitless. In A–B learning the subject might encode the stimulus XPO at a low level, say as the letter sequence X-P-O; while in A–D learning he might associatively elaborate XPO into *eXPOse*. Bower (this volume) would permit the A in A–B to be identical with the A in A–D but "tag" the former as List 1 and the latter as List 2, thus making $A_B = A + T_1$ and $A_D = A + T_2$ where T_i is the list tag. But the basic point, or proposition, remains: Unless A_B and A_D differ, both A–B and A–D cannot be retained.

Selection of a Novel Stimulus Component

A particularly simple way to find out if a learner will develop a new functional encoding in the second task of a transfer paradigm is to add a new redundant component to the stimulus and see to what extent he makes use of it. Merryman and Merryman (1971) did precisely that. In doing so they also examined the role played by the prescribed response in stimulus encoding (a topic we shall take up later). Let the A–B task be learning a list either of eight digit-adjective pairs or eight color-adjective pairs. In the second task, each A stimulus was compounded, with a color if it was a digit in the first task, with a digit if it was color. If X denotes the added component, then the second-task stimuli are denoted AX. For half of the subjects, the adjective responses were correspondingly paired similar adjectives, thus forming an A–B, AX–B′ paradigm. For the other half of the subjects, the same similar adjectives were assigned to the compound stimuli in a scrambled fashion, thus forming an A–B, AX–Br′ paradigm. The Merrymans argued that in the A–B, AX–B′ paradigm the subjects should stick with the original A component of the AX compound, this on the basis of the well-known premise that in the conventional A–B, A–B′ paradigm the subjects retain the first-task B responses as mediators for the similar B′ responses. But in the A–B, AX–Br′ paradigm, the second-task response to a given stimulus bears no similarity to the first-task response for that stimulus, thus forcing the subject to discard somehow the first-task response. The hypothesis is that he does this by shifting his stimulus code to the new X component. If he does this, then on a subsequent test where the A and X components are presented separately and the subject is asked to provide the second-task response to each, he should fail on the X component were he in the A–B, AX–B′ paradigm, but fail on the A component were he in the A–B, AX–Br′ paradigm. The results are shown in Table 1.

TABLE 1

Mean Correct Second-Task Responses
(from Merryman & Merryman, 1971)

Component	Paradigm	
	A–B, AX–B′	A–B, AX–Br′
A	6.05	3.80
X	2.70	4.30

While the word "fail" is not strictly descriptive of the entries 2.70 and 3.80 (out of a maximum of 8), the expected interaction is nevertheless highly significant. Moreover, Houston (1967, Exp. III) has reported a similar result. The conclusion seems to be that learners will capitalize on the opportunity to select a new stimulus component when they run into transfer interference.

Schneider and Houston (1969) have reported an interesting experiment, among the results of which is the following development. Their subjects first learned to a once-perfect criterion a trigram-adjective list, which we may denote A–B. Of the five conditions I want to consider, two involved second tasks of the form C–D or A–D, where the C stimuli were colors. These two paradigms are thus the A–B, A–D negative transfer paradigm and the A–B, C–D control paradigm. In the top and bottom rows of the first column in Table 2 are shown the mean number trials to a once-perfect criterion in the second task. The A–D list took over twice as long to learn as the C–D list. After second-task learning, the A stimuli were presented singly and the subject asked to recall the first-task responses. The results are shown in the top and bottom rows of the second column in Table 2. The B responses were over twice as available in the A–B, C–D paradigm as in the A–B, A–D paradigm. So far, we have the simple facts of negative transfer and retroactive interference.

In the other three conditions I wish to report, Schneider and Houston used as second-task stimuli compounds (AC) of the trigrams (A) and colors (C). In one of these conditions, "Attend C," they told their subjects to pay attention only to the C components (the colors) as they would be the basis of a later test. In another condition, "Attend A," they similarly emphasized the A components (the trigrams). In the third condition, "Free," they left their subjects uninstructed about stimulus components. The transfer and retroaction results for these conditions are also shown in Table 2.

The compound stimuli of the AC–D conditions clearly retarded second-task learning relative to the single-component C–D control condition. Moreover,

TABLE 2

Trials to Criterion in Second Task and Number First-Task Responses
Recalled
(from Schneider & Houston, 1969)

Paradigm	Trials to Criterion Second Task	Number First-Task Responses Recalled
A–B, C–D	5.9	5.6
A–B, AC–D		
Attend C	9.4	5.7
Free	11.3	3.6
Attend A	11.4	3.2
A–B, A–D	12.4	2.6

retardation was greater when the instructional emphasis was on sticking with the old A component (11.4) than when it was on switching to the new C component (9.4). Not only that, but switching to the new C component resulted in considerably less retroactive interference (5.7 correct recalls out of 8) than sticking with the old A component (only 3.2 out of 8). As for the subjects who were free to do what they liked, they seem to have preferred to stick with the old A component; their performance matches closely that of the "Attend A" subjects. This result on freedom was obtained also by Goggin and Martin (1970).

Thus when a transfer task involves an additional stimulus component, learners sometimes will (Merryman & Merryman, 1971) and sometimes will not (Schneider & Houston, 1969) opt to make use of the new cue. If they use the new cue, however, they purchase for themselves less interference between the two tasks, both in second-task learning and on a later test for what is remembered. The way to beat the consequences of a negative transfer assignment is to find or develop functional stimuli that are different for the two tasks. Apparently, learners cannot retain both A–B and C–D when A and C are functionally identical.

Opportunity to Recode the Stimulus

As pointed out in the preceding section, a learner may or may not develop or select a new functional stimulus encoding in the second task of a transfer paradigm. The two studies discussed there demonstrate that a learner can be variously prompted or coerced to recode by the nature of the prescribed response and by instruction, this in the situation where a new alternative stimulus component is provided in second-task learning. When either by his own free will or by prompting or coercion the learner recodes the stimulus in the second task, he avoids retroaction against the contingency he learned in the first task.

But the important learning situation is the one in which no additional cue has been gratuitously supplied by the experimenter and the learner is on his own. What happens then? And how can we find out what happens? One approach, though indirect, has been to vary the integrality of the stimuli on the grounds that stimuli that are more fractionable or analyzable provide more *opportunity* for recoding in the second task of a transfer paradigm. The idea is that with such stimuli transfer and retroaction should be less negative: Recoding a stimulus should be easier the more fractionable or analyzable it is; consequently, transfer interference with second-task learning and retroactive interference against the product of first-task learning should be reduced to the degree that the learner opts to use as his functional encoding in the second task a component (feature set) that is different from what he used in the first task.

In an experiment by Martin and Carey (1971), the A–B, A–Br negative transfer paradigm (in which the first-task B responses are used again in the second task, but are scrambled in their assignments to the A stimuli) was compared with its A–B, C–B control paradigm over two levels of stimulus meaningfulness. The high-meaningfulness stimuli were CVCs of 96 percent Archer (1960) and the low-meaningfulness stimuli were CCCs of 52 percent Witmer (1935). The idea is that the high-meaningfulness stimulus PEG is more integrated or unitized than is the low-meaningfulness stimulus JFN. The former, PEG, is more a single event than is the latter, JFN, which is more like three events. Thus in transfer there is more of an opportunity to recode JFN than to recode PEG. Although clearly too simplistic a view, researchers have tended to think in terms of selection of individual letters. Thus PEG would be the functional stimulus in both the first and the second task; but in the case of JFN, perhaps the letter J would be selected in the first task and N in the second task. At any rate, if the learner recodes the low-meaningfulness stimuli in the second task, then for these stimuli the A–B, A–Br transfer paradigm should be functionally identical with the A–B, C–B control paradigm, where the C stimuli are de facto new items. In other words, negative transfer should be observed primarily with high-meaningfulness stimuli. This is because there is limited opportunity to discriminate functionally an A_{Br} from an A_B, hence the learner's only recourse is to dump the first-task association.

In the Martin and Carey experiment, each task consisted of learning nine trigram-digit pairs, where the trigrams were either low or high in meaningfulness as described above. In Table 3 are shown the mean number of trials to criterion in each of the tasks, and the mean percent transfer based on individual-subject transfer scores (percent transfer from the first to the second task). The interaction between stimulus meaningfulness and transfer paradigm is significant, both when calculated in terms of trials to criterion in the second task and when calculated in terms of individual-subject percent-transfer scores. With low-meaningfulness stimuli, transfer in the A–B, A–Br paradigm closely approximates transfer in the A–B, C–B control paradigm. It is with the high-meaningfulness stimuli that transfer is strikingly negative. This result might be interpreted by saying that low-meaningfulness stimuli provide the opportunity to recode the stimuli in the second task, thereby functionally equating the A–B, A–Br paradigm with its A–B, C–B control paradigm to the extent that recoding in fact occurred.

While this interpretation is not unreasonable, at least on the surface, there are reservations that are instructive. I will begin by passing over the fact that Postman and Stark (1971) could not replicate the critical interaction, and that

TABLE 3

Mean Trials to Criterion and Percent Transfer
(from Martin & Carey, 1971)

Stimulus Meaningfulness	Paradigm	Task 1	Task 2	Percent Transfer
High	C–B	8.4	4.6	42.5
	A–Br	8.2	5.9	22.1
Low	C–B	9.5	6.4	30.3
	A–Br	9.2	5.9	34.3

Martin (1968b) found only weak evidence for such an interaction.[2] More important is the observation mentioned earlier that learners, when free to recode if they like, may or may not recode the stimulus in the second task. This means that with low-meaningfulness stimuli, and to a lesser degree with high-meaningfulness, there is an undetermined amount of "switching" and "staying," both between and within subjects, a fact that makes statistical tests on group means little more than an exercise. Until we understand the conditions under which a learner can be counted upon to spontaneously recode a stimulus when offered the chance, opportunity studies must remain of doubtful value. They must remain of doubtful value also to the extent that we do not know whether it is easier to recode a stimulus, which might involve further stimulus discrimination learning, or to keep the earlier encoding and extinguish the old response. Moreover, which of these two alternatives is the case must depend heavily on task conditions. It is quite likely that recoding in the second task will not occur to the extent that the learner had trouble developing discriminative encodings of the stimuli during first-task learning, this on the two premises that stimulus identification learning is the burdensome part of learning in general and that a learner is loath to discard a learning product he spent considerable effort attaining.

Recoding Stability

In the Martin and Carey (1971) experiment, after second-task learning was completed in the A–B, A–Br paradigm, the subjects were given three spaced tests on each of the A stimuli. They were to respond to each, on each presentation, with the first response that came to mind. In Figure 4 is shown the proportion times when

[2] It is worth noting that none of these interactions has been properly evaluated. For example, Weaver, McCann, and Wehr (1970) report a suggestive but nonsignificant interaction between stimulus meaningfulness and paradigm. Not accounted for, however, is an opposing, cancelling interaction in first-task learning, an interaction presumably due only to sampling error. On re-examination, the weak interaction reported by Martin (1968b) was found also to have a small cancelling interaction in the first task. On the other hand, Postman and Stark (1971) have a *favoring* interaction in the first task. In short, the evidence pro and con the target interaction between stimulus meaningfulness and transfer paradigm so far reported in the literature has been at a rather nonanalytic level.

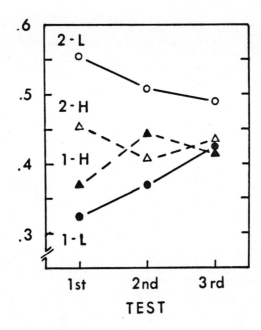

FIG. 4. Proportion first-task (1) and second-task (2) responses recalled over three stimulus presentations, for low-meaningfulness (L) and high-meaningfulness (H) stimuli. (from Martin & Carey, 1971).

the response given was from the first or the second task (1 vs. 2) as a function of test (1st, 2nd, 3rd) for high- and low-meaningfulness (H vs. L). When the stimuli were low meaningfulness, second-task responses predominated in the first test, but the dominance dissipated over successive tests (the converging top and bottom curves). I interpret this as evidence that over successive tests the stimulus encoding bias established by second-task learning was weakened, thereby permitting an increased incidence of sampling of the stimulus component(s) utilized in first-task learning. That this trend is absent with high-meaningfulness stimuli (the middle two curves) prompts me to conclude that low-meaningfulness stimuli are encoded with less stability.

A Components Analysis for Recoding

Up to this point, my case for the idea that stimulus recoding in a negative transfer problem is what may happen, and that if it does negative transfer is avoided, has been largely convergent argument, hopeful interpretation, and proselytization, a trio of modes of "theorizing" not entirely unknown to man. But perhaps a stronger test can be made.

Suppose each stimulus is a compound of three unrelated words, $A = \{A_1 A_2 A_3\}$, and the learning paradigm is A–B, A–D. Suppose further that following the second task we present, in random order, the B and D responses one at a time and ask the subject to respond to each with its compound stimulus. For any given subject, select any B response from first-task learning and record which stimulus components he recalled to that response. Now do the same for its corresponding D response from second-task learning. Proceeding in this way through all the A–B, A–D pairs for all the subjects, one ends up with some number of B-D combinations for which B and D elicited the exact same stimulus components. We shall call such item-subject event-pairs *Stay* events. We shall call *Switch* events those item-subject event-pairs where the corresponding B and D responses elicited entirely different stimulus components. Thus a Stay event may be $B \rightarrow A_1 A_2$ and $D \rightarrow A_1 A_2$, while a Switch event may be $B \rightarrow A_1 A_2$ and $D \rightarrow A_3$. A *Partial* event is one where B (or D) elicits a set of stimulus components that contains at least one but not all of the stimulus components elicited by the corresponding D (or B); for example, $B \rightarrow A_1 A_2$ and $D \rightarrow A_2 A_3$, or $B \rightarrow A_1 A_3$ and $D \rightarrow A_3$.

For each event, of any type, we can now count the number of errors incurred both during first- and during second-task learning for that A–B, A–D pair for that subject. If the hypothesis that stimulus recoding circumvents negative transfer is anything short of foolish, then we should find second-task performance is better for Switch than for Stay events. Just such an experiment has recently been completed in our laboratory by Donald J. Polzella. The mean errors per item-subject in first- and second-task learning for the three event types, Stay, Partial, and Switch, are plotted in Figure 5, where the number of observations per event type are 136, 16, and 72, respectively.

There was an A–B, C–D control paradigm included in the experiment. In this paradigm the subjects had no choice but to switch stimulus encodings. The mean errors per item-subject in first- and second-task learning for this paradigm are also plotted in Figure 5. This function is essentially coincidental with the Switch events from the A–B, A–D paradigm.

The only appropriate comment is that if one accepts backward, response-to-stimulus recall as a valid probe for the effectiveness of stimulus components, then clearly Switch (recode) events are functionally an A–B, C–D paradigm. Negative transfer is traceable to failure to recode the stimulus.

We pointed out earlier that subjects free to do as they like often opt not to recode. This fact is reflected in the frequency of Stay, Partial, and Switch events—136, 16, and 72, respectively.

Response Determination of Stimulus Encoding

Greeno (1970) has argued convincingly, with data, that if learning is to be seen as a two-stage process, then the first stage must be jointly sensitive to both stimulus and response variables. His consequently adopted view is that the first stage entails entry into memory of an integrated unit that jointly represents the stimulus and the response in combination, and that the second stage is development of a functional retrieval route that originates with the nominal stimulus and terminates with the joint representation. Such a view invites, of course, a serious consideration of how the encoded nature of the response might determine, at least in part, the encoded nature of the stimulus. Moreover, in arguing for a distinction between functional

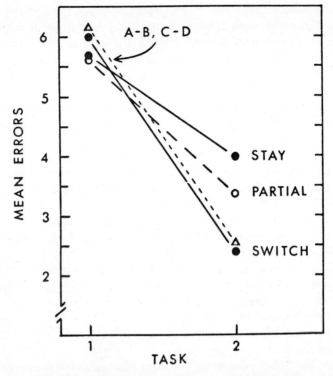

FIG. 5. Mean errors in Tasks 1 and 2 for item-subject events that involved no (Stay), partial, and complete (Switch) stimulus recoding in transfer.

A_B and A_D in the A–B, A–D transfer paradigm, I have proposed elsewhere that because the difference between responses B and D is the most obvious difference between the A–B and the A–D tasks, the responses themselves should be taken as potential determiners of the probability of stimulus recoding in transfer (Martin, 1971a).

Evidence in support of such a contention, however, is not easy to come by. Probably the most definitive is that from the studies of Weaver (1969) and Merryman and Merryman (1971). You might recall from an earlier section in this paper my discussion of the latter report: If the second-task response is semantically similar to the first-task response, learners tend to ignore an added novel stimulus component in second-task learning; this as compared with their switching to the added novel stimulus component when the second-task response is semantically unrelated to the first-task response.

Weaver's (1969) experiment entailed compound stimuli of the form VXK, HFG, with one of these appearing directly above the other. In first-task learning, the response for such a compound stimulus was a word that began with a letter that was the same as the initial letter of one of the stimulus components. For the pair of trigrams just listed, the response was *village*. The presupposition is that the response will determine stimulus selection; thus the response *village* will dictate selection of the letter V (or the trigram VXK) out of the composite VXK, HFG. In second-task learning, the nominal compound stimulus remained the same, but the new response was either *heaven* or *region*. The former response should prompt a stimulus encoding switch away from V (or VXK) toward selection of H (or HFG), while the latter, unrelated response (*region*) should leave the learner to his own untutored devices. The result was that the response-prompted stimulus-recoding condition made second-task learning very much easier. Moreover, when later the compound stimuli were presented and the subjects asked to provide the first-task responses, those subjects in the response-prompted stimulus-recoding condition were better able to retrieve the first-task responses. Such results, together with those of Merryman and Merryman (1971) and Schneider and Houston (1969), can leave little doubt about the a priori reasonable suspicion that expected or prescribed behavior can play a role in determining how the nominal stimulus is encoded. I will certainly notice and remember different things about you according to whether my job is to evaluate you as a suitable spouse for my daughter or to evaluate you as a candidate for director of the Ann Arbor Drum and Kazoo Ensemble, your nominal identity in the two cases notwithstanding.

The proposition that expected or prescribed responses might determine stimulus encodings is one that carries a number of implications, some of which are clinical or therapeutic in nature. An implication of theoretical relevance here, however, is that it provides an alternative explanation of the phenomena Postman has cited as demanding of a list-differentiation or response-suppression theory of transfer and retroaction.

Postman, Stark, and Fraser (1968, Exp. III) had their subjects first learn an A–B list of CVC-adjective pairs and then an A–D list of CVC-adjective pairs. Subsequent to this they imposed two different tests for retroaction of A–D learning against A–B learning. *MMFR(1)*: The D responses from second-task learning were presented along with the A stimuli and the subject was asked to provide the first-task B responses as best he could. *MMFR(2)*: The A stimuli were presented alone and the subject asked to provide both the first- and the second-task responses. The result was that the first-task responses were less forthcoming under the MMFR(1) condition than under the MMFR(2) condition: The presence of the provided second-task responses in MMFR(1) resulted in decreased ability to recall the first-task responses. Postman et al. argued as follows: "The amount of output interference on the immediate test should depend upon the degree to which the set to continue giving, or 'thinking of,' List-2 responses is reinforced by the method of testing" (p. 678). Thus MMFR(1) entails a persisting "set" for second-task responses because in this test the second-task responses are provided by the experimenter. Not so for MMFR(2): The experimenter in not providing, but rather only requesting, the second-task (as well as the first-task) responses did not impose a response-class bias; consequently, there was less retroactive interference under the MMFR(2) test. Postman et al. conclude that retroactive interference "is largely a matter of reduced *response availability* . . . [and that] unlearning results from the operation of a mechanism of response selection under conditions of negative transfer . . . . This mechanism exerts its primary effect on the entire *class* of first-list responses rather than on specific stimulus-response associations" (p. 689, italics added). They argue that "the first-list repertoire has been suppressed" (p. 691).

But there is another explanation. It could easily be the case that the imposed presence of second-task responses in MMFR(1) did no more than bias the learner's subjective encoding of the stimuli toward that of second-task learning. Accordingly, the learner was constrained with respect to retrieval access to the first-task responses. Without such externally imposed biasing, as in MMFR(2), more of the first-list responses could be recalled. The following quote from Postman et al. (1968) is more to the point: "Response-set interference reflects the dominance at the time of recall of the *second-list criteria of selection*" (p. 691, italics added), where instead of reading "criteria" to apply directly to response repertoires it is read to apply to stimulus encodings. In other words, the presence of the second-task responses in the MMFR(1) test condition effectively influenced subjective encoding of the A stimuli, to the end that the retrieval routes for first-task responses were not activated.

It should be completely unsurprising from any theoretical orientation to discover that after A–B, A–D learning multiple-choice matching of the B responses with the A stimuli is superbly better than simple recall of the B responses to the A stimuli. The standard explanation had been one of response availability in the matching test. That there may indeed be an element of response availability is amply attested by those particular transfer conditions in which the A–B, A–Br paradigm yields less negative transfer than does the A–B, A–D paradigm (Martin, 1965). But the question of ordinary response availability in a multiple-choice retroaction test is not so easily settled. Consider an oft-cited experiment by Postman and Stark (1969). After either A–B, C–D or A–B, A–D or A–B, A–Br learning, their subjects were confronted either with a recall test in which the A stimuli were presented and they were to recall the first-task responses or with a multiple-choice matching test in which the subjects had to select one from among four first-list responses as the correct response for a given A stimulus. Consider now the four alternatives on the matching test: For the A–B, C–D and A–B, A–D paradigms, the four alternatives were all from the first task. The mean number of correct matches out of 10 possible were 9.8 and 9.4, respectively, averaged over three test events for each stimulus. Apparently the associations, whether of the forward or backward variety, were not simply lost in the A–B, A–D paradigm in this experiment. The mean number of correct matches (choices of the correct first-list response) for the A–B, A–Br paradigm, however, was only 8.0. Does this mean that associations tend to be broken in this paradigm? Postman and Stark conclude that this "observed retention loss must be attributed entirely to interference with specific associations" (p. 174). The alternative view is that because the response that was correct in second-task learning was one of the alternatives in 35 percent of the tests under this paradigm (the A–B, A–Br, see their p. 170), the subject very simply was faced with a tougher multiple-choice decision. In terms of the thesis of the present paper, such subjects were on some proportion of the tests conned into a second-task recognitive encoding of the stimulus because of the presence of certain responses.[3]

---

[3] Anderson and Watts (1971) have shown that if the second-task response is not one of the alternatives, then no retention loss of first-list responses is observed in the A–B, A–Br paradigm. Moreover, if in the A–B, A–D paradigm the corresponding second-list D response is included as one of alternatives to B, then the A–B, A–D paradigm yields a decrement in multiple-choice performance.

In short, a response availability interpretation of transfer and retroaction experiments at least has a thoroughly viable competitor, namely, an interpretation involving response-determined stimulus encoding.

Summary

What happens in a transfer situation must include possible re-perception (recoding) of the nominal stimulus event common to the old and the new task. What the general conditions are that cause a learner either to recode the stimulus or to stick with his earlier encoding are not clear. He can follow the experimenter's advice when explicitly instructed and he certainly is influenced by the behavior (responses) expected of him. There is evidence that mere opportunity to recode may sometimes produce recoding. Throughout, however, is the recurrent fact that when stimulus recoding is the case there is reduction both of transfer interference and retroactive interference.

FINAL REMARK

This paper was intended to be about how stimuli control performance in learning and transfer tasks. Its principal theoretical orientation involved the ideas of encoding variability, stimulus recognition as necessary for response retrieval, and stimulus recoding as the way to avoid negative transfer.

An immediate response to the contents of this paper might be that we (or at least I) do not know very much about how stimuli control performance in learning and transfer tasks. I submit, however, that the breadth of this ignorance is traceable largely to ignorance of what constitutes a functional encoding. The extant literature has tended to identify functional stimuli with obvious, externally-defined, a priori components of a composite, or with the abstract features or stimulus elements of a mathematically tractable model. Such identification may be acceptable in a few fortuitous cases; but mostly it must be a mistake. How to define or identify or characterize subjective representations is the central problem. Behaviorist functionalism and its later conceptual bedfellow, early information-processing-ism, gave us generalization gradients, Hick's law, and in general a passle of relations between what the experimenter thought the stimulus to be and what the experimenter thought the response to be. That there is a discrepancy between what the experimenter thinks and what the subject thinks has become obvious. Workable theory must account for that difference. Giving the difference a name like "coding" is at least acknowledgement of the problem.

REFERENCES

Abra, J. C. Acquisition and retention of consistent associative responses with varied meaningfulness and similarity of stimuli. *Journal of Verbal Learning and Verbal Behavior,* 1968, 7, 647-652.

Anderson, R. C., & Watts, G. H. Response competition in the forgetting of paired associates. *Journal of Verbal Learning and Verbal Behavior,* 1971, 10, 29-34.

Archer, E. J. A re-evaluation of the meaningfulness of all possible CVC trigrams. *Psychological Monographs,* 1960, 74, Whole No. 497.

Bain, A. *The senses and the intellect.* London: Parker, 1855.

Biederman, I., Dumas, J. S., & Lachman, R. The effects of stimulus uncertainty and S-R transitional probability on paired-associate learning. *Journal of Verbal Learning and Verbal Behavior,* 1968, 7, 864-868.

Bower, G. H. Applications of a model to paired-associate learning. *Psychometrika,* 1961, **26**, 255-280.

Bower, G. H., Clark, M. C., Lesgold, A. M., & Winzenz, D. Hierarchical retrieval schemes in recall of categorized word lists. *Journal of Verbal Learning and Verbal Behavior,* 1969, 8, 323-343.

Butler, B. E., & Merikle, P. M. Uncertainty and meaningfulness in paired-associate learning. *Journal of Verbal Learning and Verbal Behavior,* 1970, 9, 634-641.

Carr, H. A. *Psychology.* New York: Longmans, 1925.

Cofer, C. N., Bruce, D. R., & Reicher, G. M. Clustering in free recall as a function of certain methodological variations. *Journal of Experimental Psychology,* 1966, **71**, 858-877.

Dalezman, J. J., Engle, R., & Wickens, D. D. Organization of PA list responses in RI and PI. Paper presented at meeting of the Midwestern Psychological Association, Detroit, Michigan, 1971.

DaPolito, F. J. Proactive effects with independent retrieval of competing responses. Unpublished doctoral dissertation, Indiana University, 1966.

Dashiell, J. F. *Fundamentals of general psychology.* New York: Houghton, 1937.

Dodge, R. *Conditions and consequences of human variability.* New Haven: Yale University Press, 1931.

Estes, W. K. Toward a statistical theory of learning. *Psychological Review,* 1950, 57, 94-107.

Estes, W. K. Statistical theory of spontaneous recovery and regression. *Psychological Review,* 1955, 62, 145-154. (a)

Estes, W. K. Statistical theory of distributional phenomena in learning. *Psychological Review,* 1955, 62, 369-377. (b)

Glaze, J. A. The association value of nonsense syllables. *Journal of Genetic Psychology,* 1928, 35, 255-269.

Goggin, J., & Martin, E. Forced stimulus encoding and retroactive interference. *Journal of Experimental Psychology,* 1970, 84, 131-136.

Greeno, J. G. How associations are memorized. In D. A. Norman (Ed.), *Models of human memory.* New York: Academic Press, 1970.

Greeno, J. G., James, C. T., & DaPolito, F. J. A cognitive interpretation of negative transfer and forgetting of paired associates. *Journal of Verbal Learning and Verbal Behavior,* 1971, **10**, 331-345.

Guthrie, E. R. *The psychology of learning.* New York: Harper, 1935.

Haber, R. N. Nature of the effect of set on perception. *Psychological Review,* 1966, **73**, 335-351.

Hintzman, D. L. Backward recall as a function of stimulus similarity. *Journal of Verbal Learning and Verbal Behavior,* 1969, 8, 384-387.

Höffding, H. *Outlines of psychology.* (Transl. by M. E. Lowndes) London: Macmillan, 1891.

Houston, J. P. Stimulus selection as influenced by degrees of learning, attention, prior associations, and experience with the stimulus components. *Journal of Experimental Psychology,* 1967, **73**, 509-516.

Hull, C. L. Simple trial-and-error learning: A study in psychological theory. *Psychological Review,* 1930, 37, 241-256.

Hull, C. L. *Principles of behavior.* New York: Appleton-Century-Crofts, 1943.

James, C. T., & Greeno, J. G. Stimulus selection at different stages of paired-associate learning. *Journal of Experimental Psychology,* 1967, 74, 75-83.

Köhler, W. *Dynamics in psychology.* New York: Liveright, 1940.

Krueger, W. C. F. The relative difficulty of nonsense syllables. *Journal of Experimental Psychology,* 1934, 17, 145-153.

Lawrence, D. H. The nature of a stimulus: Some relationships between learning and perception. In S. Koch (Ed.), *Psychology: A study of a science,* Vol. 5. New York: McGraw-Hill, 1963.

Lovelace, E. A., & Blass, E. M. Utilization of stimulus elements in paired-associate learning. *Journal of Experimental Psychology*, 1968, **76**, 596-600.

Martin, E. Transfer of verbal paired associates. *Psychological Review*, 1965, **72**, 327-343.

Martin, E. Stimulus recognition in aural paired-associate learning. *Journal of Verbal Learning and Verbal Behavior*, 1967, **6**, 272-276. (a)

Martin, E. Relation between stimulus recognition and paired-associate learning. *Journal of Experimental Psychology*, 1967, **74**, 500-505. (b)

Martin, E. Recognition and correct responding mediated by first letter of trigram stimuli. *Journal of Verbal Learning and Verbal Behavior*, 1968, **7**, 703-706. (a)

Martin, E. Stimulus meaningfulness and paired-associate transfer: An encoding variability hypothesis. *Psychological Review*, 1968, **75**, 421-441. (b)

Martin, E. Verbal learning theory and independent retrieval phenomena. *Psychological Review*, 1971, **78**, 314-332. (a)

Martin, E. Stimulus component independence. *Journal of Verbal Learning and Verbal Behavior*, 1971, **10**, 715-721. (b)

Martin, E., & Carey, S. T. Retroaction, recovery, and stimulus meaningfulness in the A–B, A–Br paradigm. *American Journal of Psychology*, 1971, **84**, 123-133.

Martin, E., & Mackay, S. A. A test of the list-differentiation hypothesis. *American Journal of Psychology*, 1970, **83**, 311-321.

Merryman, C. T., & Merryman, S. S. Stimulus encoding in the A–B', AX–B and the A–Br', AX–B paradigms. *Journal of Verbal Learning and Verbal Behavior*, 1971, **10**, 681-685.

Morgan, C. L. *Introduction to comparative psychology.* (2nd ed.) New York: Scribner's, 1904.

Noble, C. E. Measurements of association value (*a*), rated associations (*a'*), and scaled meaningfulness (*m'*) for the 2100 CVC combinations of the English alphabet. *Psychological Reports*, 1961, **8**, 487-521 (Monograph Supplement 3-V8).

Paivio, A. Mental imagery in associative learning. *Psychological Review*, 1969, **76**, 241-263.

Postman, L., & Stark, K. Role of response availability in transfer and interference. *Journal of Experimental Psychology*, 1969, **79**, 168-177.

Postman, L., & Stark, K. Encoding variability and transfer. *American Journal of Psychology*, 1971, **84**, 461-472.

Postman, L., Stark, K., & Fraser, J. Temporal changes in interference. *Journal of Verbal Learning and Verbal Behavior*, 1968, **7**, 672-694.

Richardson, J. Cue effectiveness and abstraction in paired-associate learning. *Psychological Bulletin*, 1971, **75**, 73-91.

Richardson, J. Stimulus selection in associative learning. In C. P. Duncan, L. Sechrest, & A. W. Melton (Eds.), *Human memory: Festschrift for Benton J. Underwood.* New York: Appleton-Century-Crofts, in press.

Royer, J. M. Associative recall as a function of stimulus recognition. *American Journal of Psychology*, 1969, **82**, 96-103.

Schneider, N. G., & Houston, J. P. Retroactive inhibition, cue selection, and degree of learning. *American Journal of Psychology*, 1969, **82**, 276-279.

Shepard, R. N. Attention and the metric structure of the stimulus space. *Journal of Mathematical Psychology*, 1964, **1**, 54-87.

Spence, K. W. *Behavior theory and conditioning.* New Haven: Yale University Press, 1956.

Spencer, H. *Principles of psychology.* (2nd ed.) London: Williams & Norgate, 1872.

Thorndike, E. L. *The psychology of learning.* New York: Teachers College, 1913.

Thorndike, E. L. *Human Learning.* New York: Century, 1931.

Trabasso, T., & Bower, G. H. *Attention in learning.* New York: Wiley, 1968.

Treisman, A. M. Strategies and models of selective attention. *Psychological Review*, 1969, **76**, 282-299.

Underwood, B. J. Stimulus selection in verbal learning. In C. N. Cofer & B. S. Musgrave (Eds.), *Verbal behavior and learning: Problems and processes.* New York: McGraw-Hill, 1963, 33-48.

Weaver, G. E. Stimulus encoding as a determinant of retroactive inhibition. *Journal of Verbal Learning and Verbal Behavior*, 1969, **8**, 807-814.

Weaver, G. E., McCann, R. L., & Wehr, R. J. Stimulus meaningfulness, transfer, and retroactive inhibition in the A–B, A–C paradigm. *Journal of Experimental Psychology,* 1970, **85,** 255-257.

Wichawut, C., & Martin, E. Selective stimulus encoding and overlearning in paired-associate learning. *Journal of Experimental Psychology,* 1970, **85,** 383-388.

Wicker, F. W. On the locus of picture-word differences in paired-associate learning. *Journal of Verbal Learning and Verbal Behavior,* 1970, **9,** 52-57.

Witmer, L. R. The association value of three-place consonant syllables. *Journal of Genetic Psychology,* 1935, **47,** 337-360.

5
STIMULUS-SAMPLING THEORY OF ENCODING VARIABILITY[1]

Gordon H. Bower
Stanford University

Judging from an intuitive frequency count, one must infer that encoding (coding or recoding) is a truly central concept in modern theories of memory. My suspicion is that variability of reference accounts in part for the high frequency of the term in theoretical discourse. The concept of encoding is used in many different senses, and it would take a practicing semanticist forty days hard labor to disentangle all its senses and their commonality of reference.

Those contributing to this volume agree that coding is a critical component in any psychological account of behavior. This is because we do not believe in the empty organism nor conceive of the person as a reliable through-put channel. In fact, the empty-organism view is today a barren strawman, held by very few psychologists. Rather, most psychologists today agree that responses of the organism to stimulation are mediated by that organism's cognitive state, which provides a context for and an interpretation of the stimulus as it makes contact with the record of his past experiences. We believe that a most significant aspect of the record of an event is how it comes to be represented in the person's memory.

The representation of an event in memory is significant for later performance. Let us enumerate a few of these reasons.

1. The representation of a set of events determines the proximity metric or psychological distances among those events. The psychological distance between the representations of event A and event B determines performances such as recognition of identity from memory, identification, differentiation, and stimulus generalization between the two events. In practice, of course, the theorist usually

[1] This author's research is supported by a grant, MH 13950-05 from the National Institute of Mental Health.

works in the reverse direction; given an observed pattern of generalization among stimuli, the theorist infers a set of distances between their representations expressed as points in a Euclidean space (Shepard, 1962), and these relations typically imply further generalization effects.

2. The representation of an event in memory also determines the types of other events that will interfere with memory of it. Recall of a given event can be drastically reduced by interpolation of extraneous material that is encoded in a similar manner. A good illustration of this is the research on release from proactive interference by Wickens (this volume); memory declines over a series of tests with items from the same class of materials, but it can be reinstated to a high level by switching to items that are encoded in significantly different ways.

3. The representation of an event in memory also determines the effectiveness of certain kinds of cues for retrieving that event. Tulving and Osler (1968) and Tulving and Thomson (1971) have conjectured that a given cue will serve as a retrieval cue for a to-be-remembered item only if the item is encoded in relation to that cue. A good illustration of this is an experiment on cued recall of ambiguous words by Bobrow and Light (cited in Bower, 1970). Their subjects studied a list of adjective-noun pairs, with the adjective stipulating one particular meaning of the ambiguous noun. A cued recall test followed in which the cue given was appropriate or inappropriate to the studied meaning of the noun. Recall was best when the cues corresponded to the studied noun meaning. The category name *bird*, for example, was a good retrieval cue for the word *cardinal* if it had been studied in the context *chirping cardinal* but not if it had been studied in the context *church cardinal*.

There are doubtless other effects of the memory representation of an event, for example, the usefulness of various representations for verbal problem solving. However, the three mentioned—the proximity structure of events, their interference properties, and retrieval-cue effectiveness—illustrate the significance for memory theorists of the concepts of internal representations and encoding as the process of activating a given internal representation from the nominal input stimulus.

As stated earlier, encoding is used in several different ways by memory theorists. I will indicate briefly what I view as the several main senses of the concept. In brief, they involve coding viewed as *selection,* as *rewriting,* as *componential description,* and as *elaboration.* These several uses of the coding concept will be briefly illustrated.

Coding as stimulus selection. In this usage, the concept of coding refers to explicit selection by the subject of a component of a complex but fractionable stimulus pattern, which selected element is used as the critical element of the entire complex. Examples would be responding to the color but not the shape of concept identification patterns, or selecting the first letter of a trigram to cue the response in paired-associate learning. In the case of concept identification (e.g., Trabasso & Bower, 1968) and discrimination learning (e.g., Sutherland & Mackintosh, 1971), the selection of an attribute or dimension of stimulus variation is done by an observing response or attentional response of some kind. This selection is presumed to be learned and governed by simple reinforcement principles, as "win-stay, lose-shift," and the theories in this area are supported by an extensive array of evidence. Similar cue selection is observed in paired-associate learning. In recognition of such facts, Underwood (1963) and others have distinguished the nominal (full) stimulus from the *functional* (selected fractional) stimulus. The main principles assumed to govern stimulus selection are those of Gibsonian differentiation (Gibson, 1940) along with differential reinforcement. A component is likely to be selected if it enables effective differentiation between the nominal stimulus in question and the others on the list. Richardson (this volume) addresses his paper directly to these issues of stimulus selection.

Coding as rewriting. Rewriting was the sense of coding used initially in Miller's (1956) "Magical Number 7" paper. The explicit example cited was Sydney Smith's experiment on recoding of series of binary digits into octal digits. This required Smith to learn and apply a dictionary in which triplets of binary digits were rewritten (in immediate memory) as octal digits. Thus, 000 was rewritten as 0, 001 as 1, 010 as 2, 011 as 3, and so forth. In this manner, Smith could recode a string of 21 binary digits into 7 octal digits and, by this ruse, increase his immediate memory span for strings of binary digits. Slak (1970) has reported elaborations of these basic results, using a "decimal digit-plus-location to phoneme" dictionary to code three-digit numbers into distinct, pronounceable syllables. These two illustrations are transparent examples of rewriting of the input into another mode, which is then remembered and later decoded to mediate recall of the original string. A less obvious but nonetheless equally compelling illustration of coding is verbal encoding (descriptions) of visual stimulus patterns. A clear example is the verbal encodings of binary sequences studied by Glanzer and Clark (1963). A briefly presented binary sequence was well remembered if it tended to arouse a short verbal description, for example, "alternating 1s and 0s." A more remote illustration of coding as rewriting is Johnson's (this volume) use of the term "code" to denote an abstract name for a sequence of a few letters in the chunked letter strings that Johnson's subjects learned. Johnson does not coordinate his hypothetical codes with the occurrence of actual names to the subject (e.g., "second chunk of first half") although nothing in his theory proscribes such identifications.

Coding as componential description. In this third sense, an item presented to the memory system becomes represented in terms of a list of components, attributes, properties, or features, where the ith entry on the list specifies the value of attribute i for that item. For words, the list of features might include the phonemes in the word, a set of semantic markers characterizing the meaning of the word, semantic categories to which it belongs, its ratings on the Value-Potency-Activity poles of the Semantic Differential Scale, and so forth. Papers by Bower (1967a), and especially Underwood (1969) and Wickens (this volume) should be consulted for illustrative details. The general belief is that presentation of an item leads to a relatively complete analysis or activation of its various features. (Shulman, 1970, has conjectured that acoustic properties become available sooner than semantic components of a briefly presented word that is being committed to memory.) These models represent similarity of two events in terms of geometrical distance between the vectors (points) corresponding to those events. For instance, Wickens assesses the similarity of coding of items in class A versus those in class B by his release-from-PI technique. If the shift from A to B causes no release from PI, then items in the two classes are said to be encoded similarly.

On this view, the location of a given item in the feature space may vary from one presentation to another if its interpretive context changes. Thus the semantic markers representing occurrence of the word *jam* will vary depending on whether the person interprets it as traffic jam or strawberry jam (see Light & Carter-Sobell, 1970).

Coding as elaboration. In this sense of coding, the input is assumed to give rise to associated operators that qualitatively transform the to-be-remembered item. The best illustration of this type of coding is the occurrence of natural language mediators for learning nonsense syllables (see Prytulak, 1971). In such cases, a CVC stimulus is altered in some way to make it into a word—a suffix or prefix is added, a letter is inserted in the middle, a letter is replaced by another, letters are permuted, or a sequence of two or more such elementary operations may be used (as in PYM → PaYMent). Prytulak classified such operations, ranked them in priority or preference of their use, and showed that syllables transformable to a word by a high-priority operation also tend to have a high association value. Regarding learning of a CVC, the basic idea is that the person first searches for a transformation that converts the CVC to a word, and then he remembers the word plus the transformation. At the time of recall, the inverse transformation (e.g., "delete the suffix") is applied to the word to yield the original CVC. Prytulak showed that this hypothesis gave a decent account of the memorability of different CVCs as well as the types of decoding errors subjects made while recalling. So, in this illustration, the word plus transformation serve as a code for the original CVC.

A second illustration of coding as elaboration is that by Bower (in press), Paivio (1969), and others investigating mental imagery as a way of remembering words. Under appropriate instructional conditions, the person can apparently substitute a mental image for a word having the same referent. One might say that the image codes the word. Under circumstances of serial, paired-associate, or free recall learning, this conversion apparently enhances the person's learning rate (Paivio, 1969). Why this happens is still to be explained, despite much effort expended on the issue. One can obtain a similar facilitation of paired-associate and serial learning of unrelated words if the individual words are bound together by meaningful phrases or sentences. In this latter case, we might say that the subject's action phrase "*flower* sprouting out of a *gun*" codes the unrelated word pair *flower-gun,* and that he recalls the pair by redintegrating the phrase from the cue of *flower.*

Having briefly reviewed the several uses of the concept of coding in discussions of memory, I turn now to the main task of my paper. What I hope to do is to provide an abstract theoretical framework within which ideas about encoding and encoding variability of stimulus events achieve a natural representation. Because I am primarily interested in memory, the implications of this theory for recognition memory will be the primary focus of my discussion. Moreover, I will attempt to show also how the theory applies to other mnemonic phenomena such as list differentiation, temporal lag judgments, retrograde amnesia, and to the relations between recall and recognition in paired-associate learning. That is a tall order and I will be satisfied if a fraction of the hypotheses prove viable.

THE THEORY

Review of Martin's Formulation

The theoretical framework to be developed is an amalgamation of the approach of Lawrence (1963) and Martin (1968) with the stimulus sampling theory of Estes (1959). I will show this correspondence, then proceed to theoretical derivations of phenomena within the context of stimulus sampling theory. We begin by some review of Lawrence's and Martin's main concepts.

As in all such theories, the basic idea is that stimulus control of responding is mediated through an encoding process. Both Lawrence and Martin thought of encoding as representable as a response process operating on the nominal stimulus, which process has as output one or another functional stimulus. The output of an encoding operation applied to a stimulus will be a particular "stimulus-as-coded," which term we will abbreviate as s-a-c. Martin's system is schematized in Figure 1, showing a nominal stimulus leading to one of three encoding operations. Regarding the encoding operation, Martin says "r_i-s_i is a central event composed of a perceptual response, r_i, plus the consequent functional encoding, s_i, of the nominal stimulus S" (p. 422). From comments throughout Martin's paper, it is clear that he usually thinks of these perceptual encoding responses as selective focusing on one or another fragment of a verbal stimulus, like the first or third letter of a consonant trigram. This is similar to the observing response theory of selection in discrimination learning (e.g., Zeaman & House, 1963).

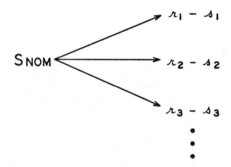

FIG. 1. Illustration of encoding of a nominal stimulus by one of several perceptual-encoding responses, r_i, leading to the stimulus-as-coded, s_i.

Central to Martin's theory is the idea that selection of an encoding response is a probabilistic matter, that we can define a probability-of-selection distribution over the several encoding responses. In fact, his chief auxiliary hypothesis was that this distribution is more variable for low-meaningful than for high-meaningful trigrams. However, it is supposed that this distribution may change with learning so that one (or one of two) encodings is occurring on every trial. In this view, one and only one encoding response can occur at a given moment in time; in fact, during the presentation time of an experimental trial, it is usually assumed that only one encoding occurs.

As in other encoding or attention theories of learning (e.g., Trabasso & Bower, 1968), it is assumed that the s-a-c on a trial controls the response (if any) performed on that trial. Also the s-a-c is the unit that enters into any new associations to overt responses due to the reinforcing events that terminate the trial. These reinforcing events are usually assumed also to affect the selective encoding probabilities in an adaptive manner, enabling differentiation of the present nominal stimulus from other stimuli in the list.

Two further remarks will complete our review of the main concepts. First, the discriminability of two nominal stimuli depends on the identity of their encoding. So long as two stimuli are encoded in the same way, differential responses cannot be attached to them. Similarity of coding causes a cluster of item interactions labelled by names such as "false-alarm recognitions," "stimulus generalization errors," and "inter-item associative interference."

The second remark is related to the foregoing and it concerns recognition of identity from memory. A nominal stimulus will be recognized as a repeat of one seen earlier (will be confused with itself) only if it is encoded in the same way on its two presentations. We may conceive of this as follows: At the first presentation of a nominal stimulus, the s-a-c is marked or tagged as having occurred; then upon the second presentation of the nominal complex, the s-a-c at that time is checked for a tag. If it is tagged, the subject decides that this stimulus occurred earlier in the experiment; if it is not tagged, the subject is likely to guess that he has not seen this stimulus before in the experimental context. This is not a very sophisticated model for the decision process in recognition-memory judgments, but Martin was not concerned with elaborating the model in this respect in his paper. He was more concerned with testing assumptions regarding stimulus-meaningfulness, negative transfer and unlearning in A–B, A–Br paradigms, which elaborations seem to have encountered a few empirical difficulties (see Williams & Underwood, 1970).

Before leaving this review of encoding theory in verbal learning, one should note the fundamental similarity of such theories to the class of two-process theories of discrimination learning and concept identification. The basic concepts and ideas are much the same; encoding responses (Lawrence, 1963; Martin, 1968), mediating responses (Kendler & Kendler, 1962), observing responses (Zeaman & House, 1963), attentional selection (Trabasso & Bower, 1968), and switched-in stimulus analyzers (Sutherland & Mackintosh, 1971) are all theoretical devices for converting a nominal into a functional stimulus that controls performance in an adaptive way. The ideas differ somewhat because of details of the reference experiments. For example, the stimuli in concept identification experiments are typically highly dimensionalized patterns (e.g., geometric figures varying in size, color, and shape), and to each dimension is coordinated a "dimensional encoding process" of some kind. Also the nature of the usual S-R reinforcement contingencies in concept identification enables the subject to "solve" by applying the same encoding operation to each stimulus pattern of the entire set, for example, asking in effect "What size is the nominal stimulus?". The verbal learning applications differ insofar as the usual dimensions of fractionation are the letter positions, and it is rarely the case that one and the same encoding operation (such as "look at the first letter") will suffice to discriminate all the list stimuli that require different responses.

Coordinating Encoding Concepts to Stimulus-Sampling Theory

Stimulus-sampling theory provides a mathematical framework for representing stimulus variability, S–R associations, and the effects of variability on learning and performance. It also provides a natural account of forgetting in terms of spontaneous alterations in the stimulus-encoding process. The main ideas and their coordinating encoding concepts may be enumerated as follows:

1. Each nominal stimulus in the experiment (e.g., presentation to the subject of the trigram XQH) may give rise to a number of possible stimulus elements or components. We let N denote the total number of these potential stimulus elements that could ever be aroused in a given subject by presentations of the item XQH. Herein, each stimulus element will be conceived of as the output of a particular encoding response or encoding operation. That is, the terms, "stimulus element" and "s-a-c" will be taken to have the same referents.

2. For each distinct experimental item, there will be a corresponding set of stimulus elements. The sets corresponding to two nominal stimuli may share common elements (overlap), and these will be the basis for stimulus generalization. For instance, the encoding operation "select first letter" would produce a common element in the stimulus populations corresponding to the trigrams XQH and XZK, and such encoding would produce generalization between the two trigrams.

3. Each stimulus element may be associated in all-or-none fashion to one or more responses or other cognitive elements (ideas or thoughts). Admitting association of ideas retreats from a strict S–R framework, but I think it is needed to handle several facts including, for example, associations from an item to an implicit list marker. Furthermore, admitting that a stimulus element may be simultaneously associated to two or more responses or ideas departs from established convention in stimulus-sampling theory, but I feel it too is a necessary breach. There is simply too much evidence showing that learning a second association to a stimulus need not cause unlearning of an earlier association but rather only edited differentiation or temporary suppression of the earlier response.

4. Performance to a nominal stimulus is dependent upon the associative connections of the elements in the active sample. The response in most cases will be, in effect, a decision made with respect to criteria required by a particular memory test. For instance, for each nominal stimulus, the subject may be asked to decide whether it was presented before in a training series, or whether it appeared in List 1 rather than List 2, or how long ago was an earlier presentation of the item. Theoretical interpretations of particular judgments will be discussed as the theory is applied to the respective contexts.

The assumptions above are the modified framework of stimulus-sampling theory as I shall use it here. Since I believe that people are better at remembering pictures, I offer Figure 2 as a pictorially encoded summary of the main stimulus-sampling ideas. This shows a nominal stimulus going through the encoding process, which is represented as a set of N operators or encoding responses. The probabilities, θ_i, are to be interpreted as the likelihood that operator i will be used, thus leading to activation of s-a-c or stimulus element s_i. These elements comprise the population of potential stimulus elements that could be aroused by presentation of a particular

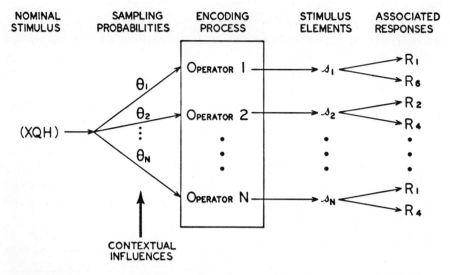

NOMINAL STIMULUS · SAMPLING PROBABILITIES · ENCODING PROCESS · STIMULUS ELEMENTS · ASSOCIATED RESPONSES

FIG. 2. Schematic representation of stimulus encoding and sampling consistent with theoretical assumptions in the text. XQH is the nominal stimulus, θ_i is the probability that encoding operator i is active, and s_i is the stimulus-as-coded by operator i.

item such as the trigram XQH. On the far right are shown illustrative associative connections between the s-a-cs and responses or ideas.

As noted above, a number of sampling schemes are possible, but relatively few are mathematically tractable. The particular sampling scheme that will be used in this paper is called the fixed-sample-size scheme. It is assumed that exactly s encoding operators are active on each trial, resulting in s active stimulus elements whenever a nominal stimulus complex is presented. The s operators that will be active on a given trial are partly described by a theory that is elaborated below as the "contextual drift" hypothesis.

The value of s is a theoretical parameter, but it could be coordinated to the molecular, moment-by-moment processes of stimulus scanning and extraction of descriptions. On that account, s would vary with exposure duration from extremes of tachistoscopic presentations up to slow, 4-second presentations of items. Also if we were to conceive of the encoding operators as selective naming ("there's an X in the first position") or as implicit associations ("looks like Headquarters backwards"), then these operators would be applied *serially* rather than in parallel, and the products or s-a-cs of the s operators would be stored serially in short-term memory. From that short-term "scratchsheet" a response would be made first by a dictionary look-up and retrieval of information associated with the s-a-cs, and then by a deliberative decision based on that retrieved information. From these sorts of considerations, I would expect the parameter s to be in the range 5 to 10 with the usual presentation rates prevalent in verbal learning studies.

Contextual Determination of Encoding

Figure 2 also reveals my assumption that a complex set of contextual factors affect the probability distribution over the encoding operations. I think of "context" in terms of background external and interoceptive stimulation prevailing during presentation of the phasic experimental stimuli. Included here would be internal factors like posture, temperature, room and apparatus cues, and stray noises, as well as internal physiological stimuli such as a dry throat, pounding heartbeat, stomach gurgles, nausea, and boredom. But more significant than any of these is what the subject is thinking about, what his mental set is, at the time the experimental stimulus intrudes. I think of this psychological context as being produced by the free flow of the "stream of consciousness," the internal monologue as the subject describes to himself what is going on around him and comments upon or free associates to his descriptions. These descriptions provide his moment-by-moment conception of the structure of the experimental task, his instructions, the nature of the materials he has been encountering, strategies of encoding and learning he thinks have been helpful, and what he thinks the experiment is really about. The free associations contain thoughts about the experimenter's stupidity, the subject's stupidity, what he ate for lunch, what he will do with his earnings, and similar wool-gatherings.

I will suppose that all of these factors, acting through multiple means, influence the state of the encoding machinery such that some encoding operators become temporarily more probable at the expense of others. In other words, changes in context will effect changes in the encoding process. These changes are of two types, systematic (intentional) and random (unintentional).

Systematic context changes. The simplest way to produce systematic changes in context is for the experimenter to present nonlearning material (as context) alongside the to-be-remembered items. The subject is effectively asked to think of the item in relation to the context material. In recognition memory, if the context word is changed between study and text, recognition of the memory item is worse than if the context remains constant (Light & Carter-Sobell, 1970; Tulving & Thomson, 1971). The loss in recognition is particularly great with polysemous words when different meanings are aroused at study (e.g., strawberry *jam*) versus test (e.g., traffic *jam*). In this instance, the context word is clearly altering the semantic associations to the grapheme. A similar result could doubtless be shown with recognition memory for ambiguous sentences and ambiguous pictures.

A similar biasing of encoding by manipulation of a phasic context occurs with emphasizers that point to selected features of a nominal stimulus (Trabasso, 1963). An example is coloring one letter red in a trigram stimulus or printing an item in red letters in a word-plus-trigram compound stimulus. The emphasized component is now likely to be selected for encoding.

Background context can also be systematically altered as when we test subjects before versus after lunch, in the morning versus at night, in one laboratory room versus another, standing versus sitting, with items printed on white versus blue cards, and so forth (see Bilodeau & Schlosberg, 1951; Strand, 1970). Generally speaking, performance is poorer if learning occurs in one context but is tested in a different context. It is possible to think about this decrement as resulting from altered encoding of the experimental stimuli because the changes in context bring in different encoding operators.

Random contextual drift. From the foregoing remarks about background stimuli and the psychological components of context, it is reasonable to suppose further that there is a slow drift or gradual change in the prevailing context as other items and events occur during a lapse of time. The change in context presumably grows progressively over elapsed time. As the context changes, so does the setting of the encoding operators, thus making active a somewhat different set of s of the N possible operators. This change in context is rarely total; states of the mind recur many times over—a fact developed in intriguing ways in Crovitz's book *"Galton's walk"* (1970). Nonetheless, the average overlap between the contexts at times t and $t + k$ will decrease to some asymptotic proportion as k increases.

Mathematical Development of Fluctuation Theory

The notions of gradual and spontaneous changes in contextual stimulation are essentially those of stimulus fluctuation theory as developed by Estes (1955). He also developed the necessary mathematical concepts and representations of the problem. From our position, we are interested in contextual fluctuation insofar as it affects which s of the N encoding operators will be active at the time a particular nominal stimulus is presented.

To begin derivations, suppose that a particular nominal stimulus like XQH has just been presented in a learning experiment and encoded by s of its N possible operators. Call this moment "time 0" and call the s active operators the "active set" and the remaining $N - s$ operators the "inactive set." We assume that if XQH were to be presented immediately once again, the same s operators would still be active and so the item would be encoded in exactly the same way as before. But suppose instead that other items and other thoughts intervene between the initial presentation of XQH and a later test presentation of it. The change of context may change which encoding operators are active upon the second presentation.

The change in the active set can be formulated as a Poisson process. In each small time-unit of length Δt, there is either no change or exactly one random change; in this latter case, an operator in the active set becomes inactive and is replaced by a formerly inactive operator. The process constitutes a Markov chain. The two states of a given operator are that it is active at time t, which event we will write as A_t, or inactive at time t, written as $\bar{A}_t$. Letting c denote the probability of an interchange in each time unit, the matrix of transition probabilities is:

$$
\begin{array}{cc}
 & \begin{array}{cc} A_{t+1} & \bar{A}_{t+1} \end{array} \\
\begin{array}{c} A_t \\ \\ \bar{A}_t \end{array} &
\left[\begin{array}{cc}
1 - \dfrac{c}{s} & \dfrac{c}{s} \\
\dfrac{c}{N-s} & 1 - \dfrac{c}{N-s}
\end{array} \right]
\end{array}
$$

The entries c/s and $c/(N-s)$ follow from the assumptions that when an interchange occurs (with probability c), an operator is picked at random from the s active operators to be replaced by an operator picked at random from the $N - s$ inactive operators.

Let a_t denote the probability that an operator is in the active state A_t. A difference equation for a_t is

$$a_{t+1} = (1 - \frac{c}{s})a_t + (1 - a_t)\frac{c}{N - s} \tag{1}$$

Equation 1 is a linear difference equation having as solution

$$a_t = \frac{s}{N} - (\frac{s}{N} - a_0)\left[1 - \frac{c}{s} - \frac{c}{N - s} \right]^t. \tag{2}$$

If we let $J = s/N$ and $h = 1 - c/s - c/(N - s)$, then Equation 2 can be rewritten as

$$a_t = J - (J - a_0)h^t. \tag{3}$$

Here J is the proportion of active operators, h is a fraction dependent upon the rate of contextual change, and a_0 is 1 or 0 according to whether the operator in question began in the active or inactive state, respectively, at some arbitrary time 0. Equation 3 describes an exponential growth (or decay) curve starting at a_0 (0 or 1) and asymptoting at J, the unconditional proportion of active operators. It is to be understood that Equation 3 applies separately and independently to each item in the experiment. The initial presentation, or the end of some learning period with each item, defines "time 0" for calculating encoding changes over time before the second or retention-test presentation of that specific item.

Associations to List-Markers

In the following we shall be concerned with applying this fluctuation theory to experiments on recognition memory and on list differentiation. In recognition memory, the model needs some way to tag or mark those s encodings elicited by an initial presentation of a nominal stimulus. The presence of these tags on encodings of later test items is used to decide whether the test item was presented earlier. For a learning theorist, the easiest way to think of these "list tags" or "list markers" is in terms of direct associations between the s-a-cs and a cognitive element (idea, response) called "LIST." It shall be assumed that in a simple recognition-memory experiment, the s active s-a-cs, occasioned by presentation during study of a nominal stimulus item, are each associated fully to LIST upon that occasion. In later applications to list-differentiation experiments, we will postulate conditioning of s-a-cs to appropriate List-1 or List-2 markers which will enable efficient list discriminations.

SIMPLE RECOGNITION MEMORY

General Concepts

An elementary experiment to model is one in which a nominal stimulus is presented once in a block of study items and then is tested later for recognition. The subject is asked to indicate for each test stimulus whether it is one that was in the study list. Usually, 50 percent of the test items are "new" or "distractors," mixed in randomly among the old items.

In any recognition model one is required to handle false positives or false alarms, the subject incorrectly saying "old" to new test items not seen before. In common with most others, we will suppose that these result from stimulus generalization or overlap of the s-a-cs of the new test stimulus with those elicited by other stimuli during study and successfully tagged at that earlier time. We shall assume that for a homogeneous population of study and test items, there is some small probability p that each s-a-c resulting from a new nominal test stimulus may nonetheless have been aroused by earlier stimuli and tagged during study. The parameter p is an index of the amount of overlap of each new stimulus with all other prior stimuli in the experiment; it will be related to the false alarm rate, and will increase with the number of homogeneous training stimuli.

The "Noise" Distribution

When a new test item is presented, a set of s s-a-cs (elements) will be activated, and more or less of these will have been tagged (due to overlap) with an association to the list marker. Let Z_n denote the number of tagged elements activated when a new item is presented. If each element has independent probability p of having been tagged earlier, then Z_n will have the binomial distribution given by

$$Pr\left\{Z_n = x\right\} = \binom{s}{x} p^x(1 - p)^{s - x}. \qquad (4)$$

The mean of Z_n is sp and the variance is $sp(1 - p)$. A significant feature about a binomial distribution is that for moderate values of s, it rapidly approximates the normal distribution with the same mean and variance. That normal approximation to Z_n will be used later.

The "Signal" Distribution

Consider the test presentation of an old item. On its first presentation at time 0, its s active elements became tagged, but over time and interfering items (assumed to be confounded here) these have changed according to the fluctuation process described by Equation 3. Consider that the lag or time between study and test presentation is t units. The proportion of the active sample at time t which will be tagged is $p(t)$, expressed as

$$p(t) = \frac{1}{s} \left[s[J + (1 - J)h^t] + (N - s)pJ(1 - h^t) \right]. \qquad (5)$$

The first part of this expression is the proportion of elements active at time 0 ($a_0 = 1$ in Equation 3) which are still active at time t; the second part of the equation is the proportion of elements that were inactive at time 0, which may have been tagged unintentionally with probability p due to their overlap with other study items, and that have become active by time t ($a_0 = 0$ in Equation 3). Equation 5 can be simplified, since $J(N - s)/s = 1 - J$, to yield

$$p(t) = p^* + (1 - p^*) h^t, \qquad (6)$$

where $p^* = J + (1 - J)p$ is the overall proportion of tagged elements in the population of encodings of a given experimental item. Equation 6 describes a decay curve going from 1 at $t = 0$ to an asymptote of p^*.

Upon test presentation of a target item at lag t, the probability is $p(t)$ that any given s-a-c in the active set is marked. Let $Z_0(t)$ be the number of marked s-a-cs in the active sample provided by an old stimulus at lag t. Then $Z_0(t)$ has the binomial distribution given by

$$Pr\left\{Z_0(t) = x\right\} = \binom{s}{x} [p(t)]^x [1 - p(t)]^{s-x}. \tag{7}$$

An important statistic is the mean or expected value which is

$$\mu_0(t) = s\, p(t) = s\, [p^* + (1 - p^*)\, h^t].$$

This describes an exponentially decaying mean for the binomial distribution given in Equation 7.

The Decision Rules

Yes-no decisions. The most elementary judgment in recognition memory tests is a binary indication of whether the subject thinks the test item was on the study list. In the theory, the test stimulus gives rise to s encoded elements. It will be presumed that the decision is based on the number of tagged elements in the active sample. Figure 3 depicts the theoretical situation, showing the probability distribution of tagged elements for new items and for old items presented at a lag of t before the test.

The test item gives rise to a certain number of tagged active elements and the subject must decide whether that observation came from the Z_n or the $Z_0(t)$ distributions. It is assumed that the subject resolves this decision by selection of a criterion, C, the number of tagged elements required for a positive response. For instance, C might be chosen so as to maintain a constant false alarm rate on tests involving a mixture of new and old items of varying strength. An example criterion is shown in Figure 3.

The location of C with respect to the means $\mu_0(t)$ and μ_n determines the hit rate and false-alarm rate, respectively. Graphically, the false-alarm rate is the area above C in the Z_n distribution. The hit rate for old items presented at lag t is the area above C in the $Z_0(t)$ distribution. This hit rate will be higher the greater the distance between the two means. The distance between the two means, scaled with respect to the standard deviation of the Z_n distribution, is the basic parameter, $d'(t)$:

$$d'(t) = \frac{s[p(t) - p]}{\sqrt{s\, p(1 - p)}}.$$

For moderate values of p, the square-root of $p(1 - p)$ will be near .50. Using this simplifying approximation, the equation for $d'(t)$ will be

$$d'(t) \simeq \sqrt{2s}\,(1-p)\,[J + (1 - J)h^t].$$

(8)

Some comment on Equation 8 is warranted, since it is a basic theorem of the theory regarding recognition performance. The higher $d'(t)$ is, the more discriminating will be the memorial performance. First, the lower is p, the amount of stimulus generalization between old and new items, the greater is d'. Second, the greater is J, the proportion of population elements active upon any one trial, the better the discrimination, due to tagging of more elements during study of old items. Third, the lag t between study and test contributes an exponentially decaying component to $d'(t)$. This exponential decay of $d'(t)$ in recognition memory has been confirmed a number of times (e.g., Wickelgren, 1967; Wickelgren & Norman, 1966). A final comment regarding Equation 8 is that $d'(t)$ is expected to increase with s, the number of active elements. This is a consequence of the statistical law of large numbers, but it can also be appreciated intuitively that a decision will be more discriminating the more evidence (active s-a-cs) examined before the decision is taken.

Rating scales and MOC curves. The simple Yes-No decision can be replaced by a more refined rating scale of 5 to 10 categories. In effect, the subject judges the likelihood that the test item came from the old rather than the new distribution. Such multiple-category decisions can be implemented by multiple criteria or cutpoints placed along the Z-axis of Figure 3.

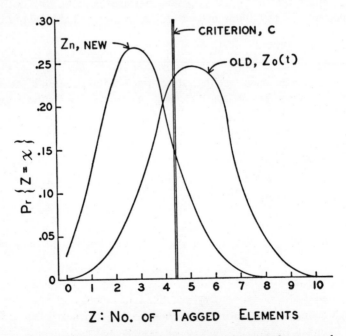

FIG. 3. Probability distributions of tagged elements for new and old test items. The parameter values are $s = 10$, $p_n = .3$, $p_o(t) = .5$, and $C = 4.5$.

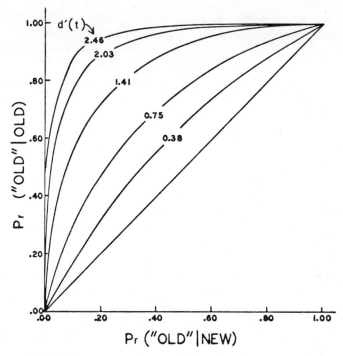

FIG. 4. Memory operating characteristics for differing values of $d'(t)$. The parameter values are $\sqrt{2s}\,(1-p) = 3$, $J = .1$, $h = .8$, and $t = 1$, 2, 4, 8, and 16, respectively, for the five declining curves.

A standard analytic procedure is to calculate the cumulative probability that a new or an old item receives a rating of C_i or higher. A plot of the cumulative probabilities $Pr\,\{Z_o(t) \geqslant C_i\}$ against $Pr\,\{Z_n \geqslant C_i\}$ as i is varied yields the memory operating characteristic (MOC) curve. Figure 4 plots hypothetical MOC curves generated for different values of $d'(t)$.

If Z_n and $Z_o(t)$ are normal or almost normal distributions, then MOC curves will plot as straight lines on normal probability paper. Results confirming normality assumptions for recognition ratings have been reported by Bernbach (1964), Wickelgren and Norman (1966), and many others. Although the present view implies binomial distributions of the Z scores, for moderate values of s and p these are "almost normal" in shape. Also, the pooled population of old items is typically comprised of items of varying strengths tested at varying lags, so one is often pooling many different $Z_o(t)$ variables to obtain a composite Z_o distribution. Of course, the effect of this pooling of variable binomial distributions is to make the average appear even more "normal like" than any individual distribution.

Multiple-choice tests. The theory applies directly to multiple-choice tests of various kinds. The simplest is two-alternative forced choice in which one old item (at lag t) is presented with one new item, and the subject chooses that one he thinks is more likely to be the old item. If we assume that each item is processed independently, then the subject will be comparing one observation sampled from the Z_n distribution to one from the $Z_o(t)$ distribution, choosing as "old" that item leading to the greater number of tagged elements. Therefore, the probability of a correct response in a situation, with no response biases, is

$$p(c) = \sum_{x=1}^{s} Pr\left\{Z_o(t) = x\right\} Pr\left\{Z_n < x\right\} + .5 \sum_{x=0}^{s} Pr\left\{Z_o(t) = x\right\} Pr\left\{Z_n = x\right\}.$$

The first term in $p(c)$ is the probability that Z_o exceeds Z_n; the second term is the probability of a correct guess in case Z_o and Z_n are tied.

These calculations proceed on the assumption that multiple-choice test items are processed and encoded independently, for which there is some good evidence (Kintsch, 1968). This assumption may be slightly in error for meaningful words (see Tulving & Thomson, 1971). The distractor item, serving as a new context, may partially change the encoding of the old stimulus item, thus producing a more radical shift in the encoding-operator probabilities than would be caused by contextual drift acting alone. But the net effect mathematically would be to lower $p(t)$ in Equation 6 by a constant fraction, as in $\beta p(t)$. Since p^* in Equation 6 is a parameter to be estimated anyhow, multiplication by β will be of no consequence. The effect of this new context could be estimated by comparing recognition ratings on each item when a word was studied alone or along with another, and then is later tested alone or together with the same or a new context word. The effect in multiple-choice tests might be to produce lower d' estimates than one observes in comparable Yes-No procedures with simple stimuli.

Experimental Variables and Recognition Memory

Lag between repeated presentations. Any learning theory must predict an increase in recognition memory if the subject receives a second study trial on a given item. This second trial on an item will increase the hit rate on a later test because it provides an opportunity for another set of s elements of the population to be sampled and to become associated to the list marker. How much advantage is added by this second opportunity depends on the change in encoding over the interval between presentations, since the more new codes that are aroused, the more total codes that are tagged.

As a paradigmatic case, consider a continuous Shepard and Teghtsoonian (1961) recognition memory experiment in which a particular target item occurs three times. Let τ denote the lag between the first and second presentations, and let t denote the lag between the second and third presentations. The following function, derivable from the fluctuation theory, gives the expected proportion of tagged elements active at the third presentation of the item:

$$p(\tau,t) = J + (1 - J)h^t + (1 - J)(1 - h^t)[p + (1 - p)J(1 - h^\tau)].$$

If we fix t and concentrate only upon the lag between the first two presentations, it may be seen that the equation simplifies to an exponential function in τ, namely,

$$p(\tau,.) = A + B(1 - h^T),$$

where A and B are constants. Thus, performance on the third test and $d'(t)$ should be an exponentially increasing function of the lag between the first two presentations of the item. Several reports confirming this general relationship are available (e.g., Kintsch, 1966, and Olson, 1968, for correct recognition; Hintzman, 1969a, for recognition latency; Hintzman, 1969b, for judgments of frequency; Rumelhart, 1967, for paired-associate recall). Attempts to conditionalize the third-trial hit rate on a hit or miss on the second trial would appear to be hopelessly complicated by item- and subject-selection artifacts, so one should be overly cautious in interpreting theoretically such conditional probabilities.

Number of trials. We may be sure that repeated exposure to an item eventually drives its recognition probability to 100 percent. This fact is expressed in Equation 9 below for the simple case in which presentations of the item recur exactly at intervals of lag τ. The equation gives the proportion of tagged elements in a sample taken from an item at lag τ after its nth presentation, each separated by lag τ:

$$p(\tau, n) = J + (1 - J)h^T + (1 - J)(1 - h^T) \left[1 - (1 - p)[1 - J(1 - h^T)]^{n - 1} \right]$$

$$= 1 - (1 - p)(1 - \alpha - h^T)(1 - \alpha)^{n - 1}, \tag{9}$$

where $\alpha = J(1 - h^T)$.

It is clear that $p(\tau,n)$ asymptotes at one as n increases, since $(1 - \alpha)$ is a fraction converging to zero as it is raised to higher powers. The rate of learning—the increase in $p(\tau,n)$ as n increases—depends positively on the interpresentation interval, τ. If τ is large, α is large, which implies rapid learning.

Latency of recognition responses. In statistical decision theory, specifically sequential-sampling theory, it is customary to suppose that the *speed* (reciprocal latency) of the decision is faster the more extreme is the evidence in favor of one versus the other response. Murdock (personal communication, 1971) has collected evidence that agrees very well with this supposition. Mathematically, the assumption means that response latency decreases as the distance between the number of tagged elements, Z, and the criterion, C, increases. In equation form, response speed will be

$$s(Z) = \omega | Z - C|,$$

where $s(Z)$ is the speed associated with a given Z score and ω is a conversion constant. This sort of relation would be produced, for example, by a decision mechanism that scans the s encoded stimulus elements sequentially, in random order, accumulating a count of the number of marked versus unmarked elements, and responding as soon as either counter exceeds its criterion of C or $s - C$.

Considering only positive responses to old items (hits) and weighing each value of Z according to its probability, then the average recognition speed will be

$$\bar{s} = \omega\mu_o(t) - \omega C$$

$$= s^* + (s_o - s^*)h^t$$

where $s_o = \omega(s - C)$ and $s^* = \omega(sp^* - C)$. This describes response speed as an exponentially decreasing function of the lag between a first presentation and a test trial.

Hintzman (1969a) has collected recognition latencies that accord with these implications. He used distinct words as test items in a continuous recognition design. With the short (up to 16) lags he used, practically perfect recognition performance was observed, that is, $Pr\{Z > C\} \simeq 1$. Nonetheless, recognition latency varied appreciably with lag, being slower at the longer lags.

Hintzman also varied τ and t in a three-presentation design as discussed above. Just as increasing lag between the first two presentations increases recognition accuracy on the third test (Kintsch, 1966; Olson, 1968), so did it also quicken recognition latencies in Hintzman's experiment. The results are consistent with a strength-like theory that can accomodate variation in recognition latency while recognition accuracy remains constant near 100 percent.

TEMPORAL LAG JUDGMENTS

General Ideas

The general problem to be addressed now is how it is that memory keeps track of *when* an event happened. Stated differently, the issue is how we judge from memory how long ago (or conversely, how recently) it was that a particular event occurred. For example: When was the Cuban missile crisis? When did Goldwater run for U.S. President? When did you first meet your wife or girl friend?

Many events of that kind, both personal and impersonal, are stored along with a calendar date that is retrieved directly. However, for the larger set of our memories we have to reconstruct or infer an approximate calendar date by retrieval of some of the causal context in which the event was located; by judicious searching and self-questioning we eventually stumble across a memory that is temporally dated. In such cases, one essentially calculates the time of an event from associated information.

But suppose that the task and the environment are artificially constrained and impoverished so that no specific, distinctive marking events occur, and the items to be remembered occur independently in no logical or causal sequence. Examples would be the order of arrival of pupils before a class begins, of concert goers at a symphony hall, or in-bound aircraft at Kennedy airport. In laboratory experiments simulating these impoverished conditions (see Hinrichs, 1970) the subject may be exposed to a long series of items such as names, pictures, words, letters, numbers, or nonsense syllables. Each item might appear exactly twice, the two presentations separated by a controlled number of intervening items. The second presentation of a given item is accompanied by a question mark, which is the instructed cue for a test response. To this cue, the subject is required to make a judgment regarding how far back in the sequence had been the first presentation of the test item. The subject's usual response mode is to indicate how many presentations of other items have intervened between the first and second presentations of the test item. This is analogous to an absolute judgment made along a category scale. A different kind of testing situation involves a comparative judgment. Two test items are shown, both of which may have been presented earlier, and the subject decides which of the two items occurred more recently. These have been called "relative recency" judgments (Yntema & Trask, 1963).

Trace-Strength Theory

Absolute judgments of recency. If the strength of a memory trace declines regularly as a function of the number of items interpolated since its presentation, then the strength of the trace at the time of test provides an index of its age. Whether strength is a reliable index of age of the trace depends on how much "noise" from one or another source is in the system. "Noise" in this instance corresponds to variability of strengths for memories of a particular age, and it could be a result of differences across items in degree of learning or rate of decay as well as inherent variability in the trace retrieval process. In any event, an appreciation of variability in the strengths leads one to use of statistical decision criteria for judging a trace at a particular strength to have a particular age.

One is led, in fact, to a model for multiple category judgments such as Thurstone's theory of "successive intervals" scaling (see Torgerson, 1958). Corresponding to each age (or lag) of memory trace is a theoretical distribution of strengths having an average value that decreases with the age of the items. To calculate a response, a number of category boundaries or cutpoints are ordered along the strength scale, such that a particular observation (of trace strength) is assigned to age i if its strength falls between the boundaries for categories i and $i + 1$. This describes the model for lag judgments published by Hinrichs (1970). He successfully fit several sets of data assuming that trace strength decayed exponentially with lag, and estimating a variance parameter for the normal (Gaussian) strength distribution corresponding to each lag. A particularly impressive confirmation of his model involved separation of the memory component from the decision component of the model. That experiment varied the number of judgmental categories used by the subject, 6, 9, or 12, but used the same distribution of actual lags in memory (equiprobability of lags 1 to 9). In each case, the means of the theoretical distributions of strengths at given lags could be fit by the same memory-strength decay function; the number of judgment categories affected only the decision process, that is, the number and location of category boundaries along the strength scale, and not the underlying memory strengths on which the judgments were based.

The present model may be applied similarly to lag-judgment data since it effectively specifies for each item something like a strength that decays as a function of lag. Equation 6 specifies how $p(t)$, the proportion of marked elements in the active set, declines as a function of lag since presentation of a given item. Thus, the judgment of the lag since presentation of an item could be made according to the number of marked elements in the set active at the time of the test presentation. This number will be binomially distributed around a mean of $s\,p(t)$. For moderate values of s and p the binomial approximates the normal distribution used by Hinrichs (1970) in fitting his data. It would thus appear that the encoding variability model, along with the contextual drift hypothesis, might account in principle for Hinrichs' data on temporal lag judgments from memory.

A consequence of implicating memory strength of items in judgments of their recency is that other variables that affect strength may thereby be expected to affect temporal recency judgments. One such variable is frequency of experience. If several repetitions of an item result in a high strength of association between it and its context, then its apparent recency should be enhanced on a later test requiring a recency judgment. The evidence on this implication is conflicting. Peterson (1967) reported no effect of item frequency on recency judgments, whereas Fozard and Yntema (1966) and Morton (1968) reported a strikingly positive influence of frequency on apparent recency. That is, in these latter experiments, more frequent items were judged to be more recent, as predicted by the trace-strength theory. The exact procedural variations producing these conflicting results have not yet been tracked down.

Comparative judgments of recency.   Just as it is possible to have absolute ratings and comparative tests of recognition memory, so is it possible to have ratings and comparative tests of recency judged from memory. Ratings are analogous to absolute judgments, whereas comparative recency judgments involve multiple-choice tests. After being exposed to a continuous stream of items, the subject is tested by having to choose which of two test items has occurred more recently (see Yntema & Trask, 1963). In the general case, each item of the test pair has been presented just once; to establish notation, we suppose that the more recent item was presented at lag n back whereas the more distant item was presented at lag $n + k$ back in the continuous series.

The proposed model applies directly to such comparative judgments. Each test item gives rise to s encodings, some of which are marked by an association to LIST. We assume that the subject chooses as more recent that test item having the greater number of marked elements in its set of active encodings. In case of ties, the subject chooses randomly.

Mathematically, the decision is based on the sign of

$$Y(n, k) = Z_O(n) - Z_O(n + k).$$

The Z_Os are binomial random variables with means of $s\,p(n)$ and $s\,p(n + k)$, respectively, as given by Equation 6. Using the continuous normal approximation to the binomial, it follows that $Y(n, k)$ will be a normally distributed random variable with mean and variance equal to

$$\mu(Y) = s\,[p(n) - p(n + k)]$$

$$= s(1 - p^*)\,h^n\,(1 - h^k),$$

$$\sigma^2(Y) = s\,p(n)\,[1 - p(n)] + s\,p(n + k)\,[1 - p(n + k)].$$

The probability of a correct response, saying that the item at lag n is more recent than the item at lag $n + k$, is given by the likelihood that Y exceeds zero. This is the area above $-\mu(Y)/\sigma(Y)$, which cutoff is approximately $-Qh^n(1 - h^k)$, where Q is a constant.

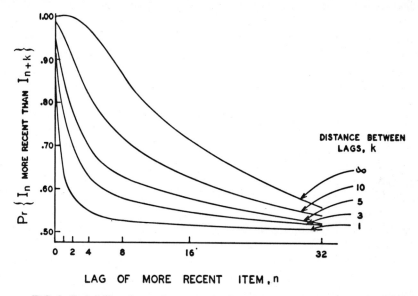

FIG. 5. Probability that an item presented at lag n is judged to have occurred more recently than an item presented at lag $n + k$. Parameters of the curves are $s = 8$, $h = .9$, and $p^* = .1$.

Figure 5 shows this function plotted against n, the shorter lag, with different curves for the parameter k, the distance between the shorter and longer lags. Such curves resemble those reported by Yntema and Trask (1963); the more recent item is better identified the more recent it is (the smaller n is) and the greater is the difference in age, k, between the more and less recent items. The curves in Figure 6 are intuitively reasonable, and reveal something like a Weber-Fechner function for discrimination between times in memory.

LIST DIFFERENTIATION

General Ideas

One of the more recent developments in research on verbal learning and retention is the increasing emphasis on "response set" differentiation and suppression rather than the older concepts of stimulus-specific unlearning, spontaneous recovery, and associative interference (see Martin, 1971; Postman & Stark, 1969). However, along with this increasing use to the concept of list differentiation, there has not been much empirical or theoretical elaboration of the concept itself. The notion of list differentiation has been used without specifying whether it is based on time tags, relative strengths of traces, familiarity, retrieval of other list items, or whatever.

A recent paper by Anderson and me (1972) touches on this topic of list differentiation in the course of theorizing more generally about recognition memory. A critical viewpoint of our theory is that we conceived of list identification as analogous to a paired-associate learning task, in which items as stimuli are becoming associated to list tags or list markers as responses. A list marker or tag denotes a particular subset of list-context elements (thoughts, cognitive events, cues) active at the time a particular item occurs. We elaborated upon what we meant by list-context cues, the set of stimulus events that combine to identify for the subject that time block of item presentations he calls List i, $i = 1,2,3,\ldots$. For instance, one simple list context cue is a subjective count or label, as "first list," "second list," and so on, sustained by the subject throughout presentation of a given list. Thus at the time the item *cat* appears in List 1, the subject may be in a particular state of arousal, may be thinking of his stupidity, that this is the first set of items, and worrying about how well he will be able to remember them. The combination of these several cognitive elements that happened at a particular time (when *cat* was presented) during List 1 serves to identify a list marker.

A further point to be added is that list contexts, conceived as sets of stimulus elements, are not completely disjoint or separate from one another. On the contrary, there will be overlap among the sets of adjacent list-context elements, so that a collection of List i elements (a marker for List i) may later refer ambiguously to Lists $i - 1$ or $i + 1$ as well as to List i, depending on the degree of degradation of information over a retention interval.

Acquisition and Retention of List Identification

We will consider the case in which a given item occurs several times in List 1. List 1 is then followed by a certain number of presentations of items in List 2, and then a list-differentiation test follows. In the test, the subject is shown a mixed series of List 1 and List 2 test items, and has to guess whether each item occurred in List 1 or List 2.

Suppose that the target item occurs n times in List 1, with a constant lag of τ between presentations, and a net lag of length t intervenes between the last presentation of the item in List 1 and its ultimate test after List 2. Let $p(t,n,\tau)$ denote the proportion of stimulus elements (s-a-cs) aroused by such an item during the test that are associated to a List 1 marker. The function implied by the theory, similar to that given previously in Equation 9 for n presentations, is

$$p(t,n,\tau) = J + (1 - J)h^t + (1 - J)(1 - h^t)\left[1 - [1 - J(1 - h^\tau)]^{n-1}\right]$$

$$= r(t) + [1 - r(t)]\, p(n, \tau). \tag{10}$$

In Equation 10, $r(t)$ is defined in the obvious manner as the retention function over an interval of length t since the last presentation of the item.

In order to simplify the following mathematical analyses, I shall revise the response rule of the model to the assumption that the subject chooses or responds "List i" with a probability equal to the proportion of active s-a-cs aroused by a test item that are associated to List i markers. In case an element is sampled that is not associated to either of the available list markers, it is assumed to lead to a guess among the available list-identifying responses. In a two-list discrimination test, for instance, this is equivalent to the assumption that half the potential stimulus elements (s-a-cs) start out associated to List 1 and half to List 2.

With these response axioms, then, the probability of a correct list identification in a two-list experiment for an item presented n times in List 1 and tested at interval t, is

$$c(t,n,\tau) = p(t,n,\tau) + .5 \ [1 - p(t,n,\tau)]$$

$$= .5 + .5r(t) + .5[1 - r(t)] \ p(n,\tau). \tag{11}$$

The terms $r(t)$ and $p(n,\tau)$ were defined in Equation 10. A few curves for $c(t, n, \tau)$ are shown in Figure 6 for differing values of the number of presentations, n, plotted against the retention interval t. List identification increases with the number of times an item occurred in a list and decreases with the retention interval before testing.

A side comment is appropriate here. Equation 11 shows that list identification should improve with the number of repetitions of a word in the list. This seems

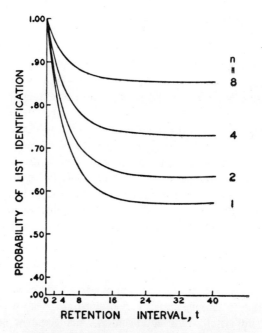

FIG. 6. Probability that an item presented n times in List 1 is correctly identified on a test given at a retention interval of t minutes after presentation of a second list. Parameters are $J = .15$, $\tau = 8$, and $h = .8$.

obvious within the paired-associate framework. However, it appears superficially discrepant from data on list-differentiation reported by Winograd (1968). However, his results may be due to optimal guessing strategies inadvertently introduced by his method of manipulating item frequency. Winograd presented List 1, a set of 25 unrelated nouns, as a unit either 1, 3, or 6 times, followed by List 2 (25 different nouns) presented as a unit for either 1, 3, or 6 times. Different subjects experienced different combinations of trials on List 1 and List 2 before the final test, when all words were shown in mixed order and judged as having been on List 1 or List 2. We will refer to the various condition by a pair of numbers, (i, j), which will denote i trials on List 1 and j trials on List 2.

Most of Winograd's results were consistent with our paired-associate theory; for example, list identification was more accurate in the $(6, 6)$ case than in the $(3, 3)$ case, which was in turn more accurate than in the $(1, 1)$ case. The sole disturbing point is that accuracy in the cases of the unbalanced frequencies, $(1, 3)$ and $(3, 1)$, was a bit higher than in the $(3, 3)$ case. To offer an excuse, this advantage could have arisen from differential guessing in these unbalanced cases as compared to the $(3, 3)$ case. To simplify the argument, imagine that a test word is either associated to a List 1 tag, to a List 2 tag, or to neither. In the last case, the subject must guess a list for the test item. In the $(1, 3)$ and $(3, 1)$ cases, an optimal strategy is to guess that the unknown or uncertain test item belongs to the less frequent list. This is because the item is more likely to have been associated to a list tag if it had been in the more frequent list. Therefore, absence of a list tag on a test word is fairly good evidence that the item was in the less frequent list. This optimal guessing strategy may thus inflate the list-identification scores for the $(1, 3)$ and $(3, 1)$ cases compared to the $(3, 3)$ case for which no optimal guessing strategy exists. This account, by the way, is not very much different from Winograd's, who conceived of identification accuracy as a combined result of the relative strengths and absolute strength of associations between the background contextual cues and the two lists of items.

An alternative experiment that eliminates this guessing bias is to manipulate item frequency within each list independently. In a recent experiment of ours, subjects studied and were later tested on list identification with three lists in each of which some words (unrelated nouns) appeared once, some twice, and some three times. By this method, frequency of pairing a word with a list tag is not confounded with which list is involved. As our theory expects, in that experiment accuracy of list identification increased directly with the frequency with which a word occurred in a list.

Generalization Among List Contexts

Several theoretical devices exist for representing and dealing with the phenomena of generalization among lists. I will illustrate one of the more obvious approaches to this issue. This approach assumes that the sets of list-context elements overlap, and that they overlap more the closer in time are the two lists. In particular, it is assumed that the successive sets of list-context elements, for Lists 1, 2, 3, ..., N, form a continuum of overlapping sets (see Atkinson & Estes, 1963, p. 203). The proportion overlap, or shared elements, between Lists i and $i + k$ is assumed to be ω^k, where ω is a fraction identified as the basic generalization parameter. Figure 7 shows a Venn diagram illustrating the overlapping subsets and their probability measures for three lists given in succession. As is obvious, Lists 1 and 3 have an advantage over List 2 in terms of the number of unique identifying elements. This is simply because these are the ends of the continuum of three sets.

Recall now that a List i marker was defined as a random subset of the context elements prevailing during presentation of List i. To the extent that list contexts share common elements, the random subsets denoted as markers will consist of some elements unique to List i and some elements later found to be shared with adjacent lists. In effect, the test word may retrieve a marker established during presentation of List i, and yet the subject may err in interpreting that marker as referring to List $i - 1$ or $i + 1$ rather than to List i. Let π_{ij} denote the probability that a marker established during presentation of List i refers later to List j, possibly because of overlap of context elements. For the generalization coefficients illustrated in Figure 7, the corresponding values of π_{ij} are as follows:

$$\pi_{11} = \pi_{33} = 1 - \omega + (\omega - \omega^2)\frac{1}{2} + \omega^2\frac{1}{3}$$

$$\pi_{12} = \pi_{32} = (\omega - \omega^2)\frac{1}{2} + \omega^2\frac{1}{3}$$

$$\pi_{13} = \pi_{31} = \omega^2\frac{1}{3} \tag{12}$$

$$\pi_{22} = (1 - \omega)^2 + 2\omega(1 - \omega)\frac{1}{2} + \omega^2\frac{1}{3}$$

$$\pi_{21} = \pi_{23} = (\omega - \omega^2)\frac{1}{2} + \omega^2\frac{1}{3} \cdot$$

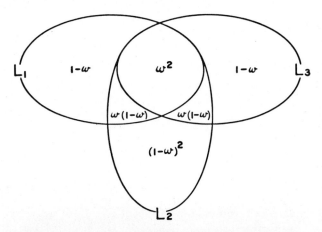

FIG. 7. Venn diagram illustrating overlapping sets of contextual elements for three successive lists, assigning measure ω^k to the proportionate overlap of sets k units apart on the stimulus scale.

The values of π_{ij} in Equation 12 are calculated on the assumption that areas in Figure 7 representing overlap of two or three sets lead to the appropriate list response with probabilities 1/2 or 1/3, respectively.

Consider now applying these ideas to a three-list discrimination situation. Suppose that each list is presented a fixed number of times. Assume too that the time of testing after input, t in Equation 10, is very large, so that $p(t, n, \tau)$ is asymptotic in t. We interpret $p(n, \tau)$ as the probability that an active s-a-c of an item is conditioned to a corresponding list marker. In case the s-a-c is not conditioned to any list marker, it is assumed to produce random guesses among the three lists. Let $d_{ij,n}$ denote the probability that an item presented n times in List i is later judged to have occurred in List j. The equation for $d_{ij,n}$ is

$$d_{ij,\,n} = p(n, \tau)\pi_{ij} + \frac{1}{3}[1 - p(n, \tau)]. \tag{13}$$

Illustrative values of $d_{ij,n}$ are depicted in Figure 8, which gives the expected probability that an item of List 1, 2, or 3 (the parameter of the curves) will be judged to have been in the list indicated on the abscissa. These are list generalization gradients, showing confusion decreasing with distance between the actual and the judged list context. The gradient for responses to List 2 items is predicted to be shallower than for the other lists, reflecting more generalization between it and its adjacent lists. The gradients for Lists 1 and 3 are equal in these graphs because they are calculated on the assumption of a long retention interval after the block of three study lists. Had this test been given immediately following the third study list, then t would have been significantly shorter for List 3 than for List 1 items. Consequently, $p(t, n, \tau)$ would have been larger and the percentage correct for List 3 would have been larger than in List 1.

The worry about these predictions is whether equiprobable guessing is the proper way to describe the person's strategy with nonassociated s-a-cs. If memories decay over time, then an optimal guessing strategy is to guess List 1 for a nonassociated (forgotten?) s-a-c. Such guessing strategies would perturb somewhat the qualitative predictions depicted in Figure 8.

Recognition versus List Discrimination

A basic premise of the theory (see Anderson & Bower, 1972) is that recognition memory and list identification involve similar processes. In recognition, the person decides whether he has seen a test item before in a specified context; in differentiation, he decides in which of several contexts he has seen the test item. The context specified in the yes-no recognition experiment is usually "in this experiment," as when we ask the subject "Did you see the word *dog* earlier in this word series I've shown you in this experiment?" The context specified in the list differentiation experiment is more restricted, involving, for instance, "first" versus "second" temporal blocks within this experiment.

The model supposes that both judgments are mediated (when successful) through retrieval of markers, that is, through retrieval of bundles of cognitive elements referring to temporal contexts. However, our earlier assumptions about overlap and generalization of list-context elements imply that a marker does not

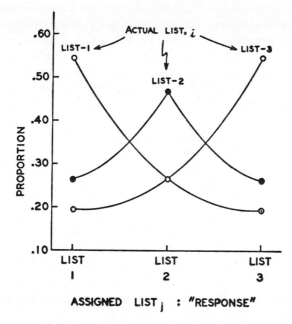

FIG. 8. Values of $d_{ij, n}$, the probability that an item presented in List i is later remembered as having occurred in List j in a three-list experiment.

unambiguously identify a list. Thus, a test word may retrieve an associated marker—leading the subject to judge with assurance that the item has occurred earlier—but yet he may mistakenly assign the item to the wrong list because the marker refers ambiguously to several lists.

Winograd (1968) reported just this sort of difference between recognition and differentiation. Yes-no recognition memory for, say, the (3, 3) condition was around 97 percent at the same time that list discrimination was around 80 percent correct. This corresponds, then, to what our model would expect.

Multiple-List Memberships

The list-differentiation experiments examined heretofore are ones in which each item appears in just one of the several lists presented. But there is no legislation proscribing experiments in which a given item appears in several different lists. Given our assumption that each s-a-c may become associated to several different responses, there is no particular reason to expect any unlearning of a List 1 tag during learning of a List 2 tag for the same item. This is not to rule out the possibility of negative transfer and also list generalization when a given item appears in two or more lists.

Hintzman and Block (1971) have reported relevant data on multilist memberships of the same item. Their subjects judged the *frequency* of occurrence in each list of words that occurred either 0, 2, or 5 times in List 1 *and* in List 2. The average frequency estimate given from subjects' memory increased directly with an item's frequency in the list being judged. But there was also negative transfer insofar as the differentiation of frequencies of 0, 2, 5 was poorer for items in List 2 than for the same items in List 1. The authors also observed clear list-generalization effects: Holding constant the true frequency of the item in the list being judged, its mean judged frequency increased directly with its frequency in the alternate list. This is precisely the result expected if there were some confusion about the list identification of the markers associated to a word.

Another example of apparent negative transfer in list tagging occurs in an experiment by Anderson and Bower (1972). Their subjects were exposed to a sequence of 15 overlapping lists of 16 items, each list drawn from a master set of 32 words. Each list overlapped with each other list in respect to 8 words, but a different set of 8 for each pair of lists. As one might expect, in this confusing situation it is very difficult for the subject to keep track of exactly which lists a given item has been in. Anderson and I tested after each list-input trial for free recall of the master set of 32 words, and this improved continuously over lists as more items were presented and recalled frequently. The subject was also asked to indicate, for his recalled words, which ones were presented on the most recent list of 16 words he had just studied and which ones were not presented in that most recent list (but were members of the master set presented in earlier lists). This is a list differentiation judgment, reflecting the ability to discriminate items that were in the most recent list. This ability to discriminate items in the most recent list declined across lists as items occurred haphazardly in progressively more lists. This result was exactly as expected if there were negative transfer in associating a new list tag to an item that already had several prior list tags associated to it. A fine detail confirming this hypothesis was that an individual item presented in the most recent list was more likely to be later remembered (correctly) as having been in the most recent list the *less* frequently it had occurred in lists prior to the one being judged. Thus, the more prior list-tags associated to a given word presented in the most recent list, the less likely it was to become associated to the tag denoting the most recent list.

This notion of negative transfer in tagging of items in multiple lists may help explain other puzzling phenomena such as negative transfer in part-to-whole or whole-to-part transfer studies of free recall (see Tulving, 1966). A subject pretrained with part of a free-recall list will subsequently learn the whole list more slowly than a control subject pretrained on an irrelevant list before receiving the whole list. The difficulty is largely localized in very poor improvement in recall of *old* (part-list) items (see Bower & Lesgold, 1969). This outcome would be predicted if there were negative transfer in associating a List 2 marker to an item previously associated to List 1, and if whole-list recall were monitored and edited for a List 2 tag associated to the items. Thus, part-list items previously associated to a List 1 tag would acquire List 2 tags more slowly and would thus be edited out from recall.

This outcome hinges critically upon the experimental subject not being aware that all part-list items are contained in the whole list. If he were to be informed of this fact, then there would be no list discrimination problem, and the monitor would recall any candidate item retrieved having either a List 1 or List 2 tag associated to it. Thus, informed subjects should give only positive part-to-whole transfer. This is indeed the case, as has been found by Tulving (personal communication, 1971).

Nontemporal List Cues

My next comment is not on a theoretical point but on a methodology that prevails in research and thinking about list differentiation. The point concerns our common means for specifying what is a list of items. Almost always in current discussions, a list is defined by a time reference, as "all those items presented between a beginning-of-list signal and an end-of-list signal." Other common temporal designations are "first list" or "second list," or the "most recent list," which refer to an implicit temporal order.

Our theory about list tagging of items leads us to a broader view of what constitutes a list. A list tag can be any discriminable cue or marker enabling differentiation of items associated to that cue as opposed to other cues. On this basis, a list would simply be a collection of items that share an association to a distinguishing cue or marker. That distinguishing cue need not be a temporal one. It could be a spatial location (e.g., items shown on the left), a characteristic of the visual or auditory presentation of the items (e.g., words printed in red letters, or words spoken in a female voice), a common verbal context of their presentation (e.g., items paired with the cue *auto* versus those paired with the cue *kitchen*), or a simple numerical but nontemporal contex cue. In this latter case, for instance, one might first show a few items designated as List 2 items, then some List 1 items, then some more List-2 items, then more List 1 items, alternating this way through the two sets.

In these several examples, the subject would be associating the items to a designated list cue according to a paired-associate procedure. That list cue becomes the instructional cue for commencing retrieval of the various list items in a free-recall test. That list cue is also the implicit response term when the subject is later asked whether a stimulus item occurred in a particular list. Asking whether *dog* was presented in that collection of words shown in Location 1 is analogous to asking whether the subject recognizes the pairing *dog*-Location 1, by either forward or backward association.

The import of these remarks is methodological. We may view list differentiation as a special kind of paired-associate learning, and investigate variables other than "time" as list cues. This may give us more flexibility in manipulating experimental variables such as list-cue discriminability, temporal blocking versus randomized presentations of items belonging to several lists, and compound list-cue redundancy.

Tulving has pointed out to the author that such nontemporal list cues nonetheless must still have implicit reference to a temporal span. When an experimenter presents some words in red letters, some in black letters, and later asks for the black word list, he is implicitly adding the differentiating instruction "Those black-letter words seen here since the experiment began," and he excludes such words read in the instructions or prior to the present exposures. Similar arguments, of more of less cogency, can be advanced for other nontemporal list cues. The observation is correct but immaterial to the multiple-list differentiation issues being addressed. For instance, items presented in two locations (two lists) are differentiated from one another only by that property; time of their presentation differentiates them at least from all other items, but serves not at all to differentiate one set from another. In this respect, although time and time-tagging is necessarily implicated in all memories for episodic happenings (e.g., the episode that the word *chair* appeared in Location 1), that time tag need not be the feature distinguishing two experimentally defined sets (lists) of items in memory.

PAIRED-ASSOCIATE LEARNING AND STIMULUS RECOGNITION

General Ideas

Stimulus fluctuation theory was applied earlier by Estes (1959; also Bower, 1967b) to paired-associate recall. I will not review those applications but will address myself briefly to the relationship between stimulus recognition, stimulus-response pair-recognition, response recall when cued with the stimulus, and the confidence rating of the recalled response. All these indices should be closely related in some way (see Adams & Bray, 1970). Stimulus-sampling theory as elaborated herein implies a particular set of relationships.

In applications to paired-associate learning with familiar unitary response terms, the basic idea is that each reinforced (or study) trial associates the correct response to that set of s encodings of the stimulus member active upon presentation of the pair. As time passes after study, there is fluctuation in the contextual determinants of the encoding process, so that a later presentation of the same nominal stimulus may activate a new sample of encodings. The probability that an earlier "conditioned" encoding is reactivated at the time of test is given by the derived retention function, $r(t)$ (see Equation 10). The probability of recall of the correct response is the proportion of elements active in the test-trial sample that is associated to the correct response.

For present purposes, it will be assumed that each s-a-c active during study acquires two simultaneous associations, one to a list marker and one to the paired-associate response term. These distinct associations provide the hypothetical subject with the information necessary to do later stimulus recognition as well as paired-associate response recall. The stimulus will be recognized later if a sufficient number of its active elements are marked, as prescribed in the earlier subsection *The Decision Rules*. Similarly, the stimulus-response pairing shown on a test trial will be recognized as a correct "old" pairing if a sufficient number of the active encodings of the test stimulus are associated to the test response. The stimulus as a cue will lead to recall of the response, we assume, according to the proportion of its active elements associated to that response. The confidence that the person has in his recalled response, we assume, would depend upon the number of active elements associated to both the recalled response and the list marker.

Conditional Relationships

It is not yet obvious how to diagram or conceptualize the pattern of associations among the three terms of the paired-associate, namely, the stimulus, the list context, and the response. The simplest diagram in some ways just assumes that each stimulus-as-coded (s-a-c element) acquires two quite independent connections, one to a list-context marker and another to a response term. Assuming independent forgetting of the two associations then would predict instances of paired-associate recall without list identification as well as list identification without paired-associate recall. Moreover, paired-associate recall would be predicted to be above chance even when stimulus recognition failed. The first and third of these implications are contradicted by the available data (e.g., Bernbach, 1967; Martin, 1967).

An alternative associative diagram supposes that a stimulus plus a list context become jointly associated as a compound unit to the paired-associate response. That is, the diagram would be (S → LIST context) → R. The stimulus would acquire an association to the list context, of course; but only the joint compound, of stimulus plus context, would be conditioned to the paired-associate response term. At the time the S–R pair is studied, the encoded elements of the stimulus would be presumed to become associated to a set of contemporaneous contextual events (a marker), and the stimulus-plus-context as a unit would also become associated to the response term on that study trial.

Several theoretical implications follow from such ideas. First, this approach provides a basis for the learning of different responses to the same nominal stimulus in different contexts. This is clearly needed to handle the subject's ability to learn to say "dog" to *cat* in List 1 but to say "bird" to *cat* in List 2. The list-context cue augments the nominal stimulus and provides the means for such conditional discriminations.

Second, the cue-plus-context viewpoint readily leads to the prediction that paired-associate recall is dependent upon stimulus recognition. Putting matters in the converse way, if the subject fails to recognize the stimulus term (i.e., if insufficient list-context cues are retrieved from the stimulus alone), then recall of the paired-associate response will only be at the chance level.

Third, the cue-plus-context viewpoint would appear to provide a richer framework within which to represent interaction effects among two or more lists learned in succession with the same nominal stimuli. In the A-B, A-C paired-associate paradigm, we may suppose that stimulus A comes to function in two successive compounds, in the $A + L_1$ compound, and then in the $A + L_2$ compound. The diagram in Figure 9 illustrates the state of the system after successful learning of the two lists. Depending on instructional cues, the cue A by itself may retrieve either the List-1 context cues which combine with A to be associated as a unit to response B; or A may retrieve the List-2 context cues, and the two as a unit are associated to response C. Or, given enough time, cue A may retrieve or redintegrate *both* of these compounds in succession, leading to recall of both B and C.

Several remarks are warranted regarding the relations diagrammed in Figure 9. First, in a test following A-B, A-C learning where cue A is presented and the subject tries to recall both B and C (the MMFR test), any response recalled should be assigned to the correct list (as well as to the correct stimulus). This prediction accords with fact; list identification of recalled responses in MMFR tests is usually

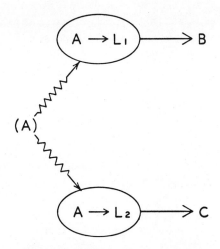

FIG. 9. Schematic representation of possible associative structure existing after learning A–B in the context of List 1 and A–C in the context of List 2. The cue term, A alone, is presumed to redintegrate the A-L₁ or A-L₂ contextual patterns that are conditioned as units to response B or C, respectively.

perfect, as is the assignment of responses to stimuli (if original learning was assured). Second, in retroactive- or proactive-inhibition studies with instructions to retrieve only the first- or second-list response to the cue A alone, the model predicts that the subject will frequently be able to retrieve the wrong response but recognize and reject it as coming from the wrong list. Thus, retrieval of list-context cues provides a means for list editing.

Third, as the comment above indicates, a major component of forgetting in Figure 9 is the branch from cue A alone to redintegration of the "A plus list-context " compound that is associated to the paired-associate response. Loss of access to this link could be caused by fluctuation in the stimulus-encoding process over the retention interval, so that re-presentation of cue A leads predominantly to s-a-cs not associated to a list marker. Another possible reason for loss of access to the "A plus List-1 context" bundle might be unlearning during interpolated A-C learning. The notion is that the ability of A alone to redintegrate the bundle can be lost because of A-C learning in the second list. The present status of such unlearning is much in dispute.

There are several implications of these last remarks. First, a retrieval attempt with cue A alone may fail initially, but then succeed later if sufficient context cues are reinstated by one or another means (e.g., reconstructive free associations). The relevant context cues needed are *not* the name "List 1" or "first list," but rather the things that the subject was thinking about at the time he first learned the A-B pair in List 1. Second, an A-B pair recognition test may succeed where A-B recall has failed following A-C learning. Failure of B recall would be due to inability of A to redintegrate the set of List-1 context cues prevailing at the time A-B was studied. On the other hand, multiple-choice recognition tests or associative matching tests provide reinstatement of some context cues (namely, other items in the list), which is a help to remembering; such recognition tests also require less supporting evidence for a correct response than does recall. Moreover, even though the forward association from A to B may have been unlearned due to A–C interpolation, the pair may still be recognized because the backward association from B to A is still intact. On this latter basis, one would expect interpolation of an A-Br list, composed of the same responses but re-paired with the stimuli, to cause unlearning of both forward and backward associations, and thus to produce a large loss in recognition of the original A-B pair. This pattern seems to accord with the facts of the matter (see Postman & Stark, 1969).

These particular ideas about multiple-list learning can be brought into correspondence with recent theories about response set suppression, differentiation, and recovery. For example, if we equate list-context cues with particular response-selection criteria as well as a train of thoughts, then it is easy to imagine how the List-2 context cues persist for awhile and intrude themselves even when the subject is trying to revive or redintegrate the old context cues of List-1. As time passes after List-2 learning, however, the List-2 context dissipates and the List-1 context becomes easier to redintegrate so that List-1 responses become more available for cued recall. These ideas apply to the loss in A–B recall following C–D learning as well as following A–C learning. These notions are essentially those proposed by Postman and Stark (1969). However, much more conceptual development is needed to decide the explanatory power of these tentative ideas.

CONSOLIDATION AND RETROGRADE AMNESIA

The encoding fluctuation theory would appear to provide a means for interpreting the retrograde effect produced by traumatic brain injuries such as concussions, electroconvulsive shock (ECS), drug-induced convulsions, and coma. The basic facts of trauma-induced amnesia are clear enough: A convulsion, concussion, or similar trauma seems to temporarily obliterate memories for events that happened just before the trauma, with the probability of memory loss increasing with proximity of the event to the trauma. This disruptive effect of convulsion or concussion has been offered as primary evidence in favor of a consolidation hypothesis, which assumes that the amount of long-term memory about an event accumulates over time until some disruptive event stops fixation of memory for that earlier event. This interpretation is not without its competitors (see Lewis & Maher, 1965; Lewis, 1969), and the correct theoretical interpretation is still in doubt. For example, the consolidation hypothesis does not account for the human clinical observation that many memories do return over time, with forgotten events farthest from the trauma being recovered earlier.

An interpretation of retrograde amnesia effects in terms of stimulus fluctuation theory was first suggested by Kohlenburg and Trabasso (1968). Their idea was that stimulus elements active at the time of the trauma or ECS acquire, as a consequence, a low sampling probability for some time after the ECS. This hypothesis can be restated in terms of an encoding-response theory such as proposed here. The basic approach is to conceive of an encoding operation as a response that can be selectively activated or inhibited. A second assumption is that ECS or a similar brain trauma causes inhibition to be attached to those encoding responses active at the time of the ECS or trauma. This is conceived along the lines of the ECS acting like a punishment that suppresses coincident observing responses; but that analogy cannot be taken literally since a painful footshock, which is also a punishment, does not at all have the same amnestic effect as an ECS.

Notice the assumption is that certain *perceptual* encoding responses are inhibited or suppressed by the ECS; the assumption is *not* that inhibition of all behavior has been conditioned to cues coincident with ECS. This latter position is like that of Lewis and Maher (1965), and it has been justly criticized as failing to explain data showing amnesia through preservation of an active but punished response, for example, where a rat shows amnesia for having received a painful shock by continuing to press a lever actively for a water reward. Postulating that certain perceptual responses are inhibited is like claiming that certain stimulus elements in the standard experimental situation have almost zero sampling probabilities.

A third optional assumption is that the suppression or inhibition may dissipate over a long time of several days or weeks, slowly returning all encoding responses to their pre-ECS level of availability. It just is not clear now how much of this recovery from amnesia needs to be allowed for, since the evidence is conflicting.

A few comments are required to relate these assumptions to the ECS studies of retrograde amnesia. Recall that the hypothesis of contextual drift implies a steady turnover of active encoding operators as time passes. Therefore, the probability that an encoding response active at time t before ECS is still active at the time of ECS (and hence becomes inhibited) is the exponential function, $J + (1 - J)h^t$.

A concrete illustration may aid comprehension here. Suppose that over several days a thirsty rat has been trained to drink in a distinctive experimental box. In the diagram in Figure 10, we identify the open dots with stimulus elements of the box associated with drinking in this situation. On a particular day, the rat is placed in the drinking box and after a few minutes receives a painful electric shock to its feet. This, we assume, causes the stimulus elements (s-a-cs) active at that time to become conditioned immediately to an emotional response (anxiety) which would compete with drinking. Elements conditioned to the emotional response are indicated by black filled dots in Figure 10. Then, for half the subjects, ECS is given immediately after the painful footshock experience; for the other subjects, a much longer delay intervenes between the footshock and the ECS.

We assume that encoding responses active at the time of ECS are driven into an inhibitory state. This implies that the s-a-cs (elements) corresponding to those inhibited encodings will have zero sampling probabilities for some time thereafter. For illustrative emphasis, these inhibited s-a-cs are encapsulated by a small circle in the diagram of Figure 10. Figure 10 shows the expected composition of this capsule as a function of the interval between footshock and ECS; the capsule contents in the beginning are in fact the set of encoding responses that were active at the time of ECS.

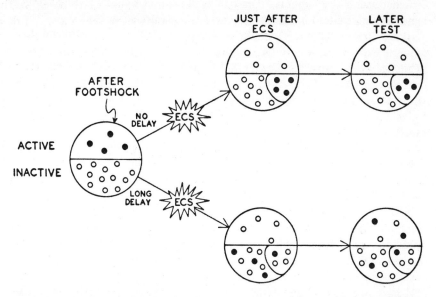

FIG. 10. Diagram of conditioning status of active versus inactive s-a-cs immediately after footshock, then immediately after ECS at zero delay (upper branch) or ECS at a long delay (lower branch), each followed by a test trial much later. Open dots denote stimulus elements associated with drinking; filled dots denote elements associated to the anxiety reaction elicited by footshock. The boundary encircling four elements after ECS represents the inhibition and near-zero sampling probability of those encoding responses present at the time of ECS.

As Figure 10 shows, with a longer delay between footshock and ECS there is more opportunity for change in the active encoding responses. Thus, encoding responses active at the time of footshock, (with s-a-cs leading to an anxiety reaction) are replaced by new ones, and the former ones thus escape being inhibited by the ECS. The differences in the immediate versus delayed ECS become apparent later (shown as the "Later Test" in Figure 10) in terms of the likelihood of the conditioned emotional response in the test situation. Indexing rate of drinking by the proportion of active s-a-cs conditioned to drinking (as opposed to fear), subjects that received ECS immediately show complete amnesia for the footshock experience, whereas those receiving delayed ECS will display emotional responses, inhibit drinking, and generally show obvious memory for the footshock experience.

The difference in retrieval of the footshock experience between these two conditions depends systematically in theory on the delay between footshock and ECS. The fluctuation theory supposes that this will be an exponential function, with more memory of the footshock experience the greater the delay. Furthermore, certain drugs that act as central nervous system stimulants or depressants may shorten or lengthen the consolidation time constant by altering the time rate of stimulus intake and encoding-response fluctuation. Thus, if picrotoxin or strychnine enhances the speed of stimulus sampling and speed of shifting among different encoding operations, then one would expect subjects given such drugs to remember more later for a given delay before ECS (McGaugh, 1966).

It is of interest that this hypothesis supposes that all subjects learn and store the requisite experience; what differs among them is the degree of blocking of retrieval of the learned information. Lewis (1969) has also considered retrieval difficulties as a viable explanation for ECS effects. We can say that the amnesiac rat who drinks without fear would be frightened if he could perceive the situation in the way he had at the time of the painful footshock. But the ECS has made those perceptual modes of operation improbable for the moment.

The issue of whether there is any ultimate recovery, how much and its time course, is a quite independent matter from the assumptions above. The strict consolidation hypothesis expects no recovery of disrupted memories. On the other hand, some of the clinical literature as well as an increasing portion of the experimental literature shows some recovery of the lost memories over time. For instance, with our example of the drinking rat, a rat given immediate ECS after footshock will show no anxiety on a one-day retention test but will show increasing anxiety and suppression of drinking on tests given after several days or weeks (Kohlenberg & Trabasso, 1968).

I have not thought about the encoding-suppression hypothesis long enough to see now how to differentiate it experimentally from the consolidation hypothesis. Possibly some of Lewis' (1969) experiments on "footshock reminders" will prove interpretable within the encoding-retrieval framework while remaining outside the fold of consolidation theory. Perhaps techniques of perceptual alterations (e.g., wearing of prisms, sensory isolation, sensory adaptation) can be brought to bear creatively on the perceptual hypothesis regarding "amnestic" effects of ECS.

CONCLUDING REMARK

I have claimed here that the stimulus sampling theory of Estes, with a few emendations, provides a determinate framework within which to investigate the effects of encoding variability on memory. One purchases the power of stimulus sampling theory at the price of giving up certain cherished complexities and accepting idealized sample schemes, such as equal-sampling probability of all elements. But perhaps the range of phenomena explained by the model is worth the small purchasing price for those believers in encoding-variability theory.

I have made explicit the correspondences and connections between the stimulus sampling approach and Martin's theory of encoding variability. I would argue that the correspondences range as well into some of the other senses of encoding discussed at the outset, namely, coding as selection (or fractionation), as componential description, and as elaboration of the nominal stimulus. In each of these senses, we may investigate variability (across trials) in the full encoding of a given stimulus, and consider each code pattern as a distinct element or s-a-c to which the sampling theory might apply. I will not pursue the argument here, but will leave you with the claim that stimulus-sampling theory will provide a plausible abstract representation of the effects of encoding variability, contextual determination, and time-dependent drift in encoding, no matter what the exact nature of the coding envisaged by the differing approaches. I am not saying that those approaches can now be pre-empted by stimulus-sampling theory; quite the contrary, the bases, varieties, and usages of different encoding systems in memory must continue to be systematically explored. Such investigations identify the stimulus elements, the mechanisms of their selection, and the sampling processes that stimulus-sampling theory refers to in only an abstract and elliptical manner. Thus, I view the hypotheses proposed in this paper as useful when one addresses himself to encoding variability (of whatever sort) of an episode that is to be remembered for later recognition of identity or recognition of its context of earlier occurrence.

REFERENCES

Adams, J. A., & Bray, N. W. A closed-loop theory of paired-associate verbal learning. *Psychological Review*, 1970, 77, 385-405.

Anderson, J. R., & Bower, G. H. Recognition and retrieval processes in free recall. *Psychological Review*, 1972, 79, 97-123.

Atkinson, R. C., & Estes, W. K. Stimulus sampling theory. In R. D. Luce, R. R. Bush, & E. Galanter (Eds.). *Handbook of mathematical psychology*, Vol. 2. New York: Wiley, 1963.

Bernbach, H. A. A decision and forgetting model for recognition memory. Ann Arbor: University of Michigan, Mathematical Psychology Program, Technical Report No. 64-4, 1964.

Bernbach, H. A. Stimulus learning and recognition in paired-associate learning. *Journal of Experimental Psychology*, 1967, 75, 513-519.

Bilodeau, I. McD., & Schlosberg, H. Similarity in stimulating conditions as a variable in retroactive inhibition. *Journal of Experimental Psychology*, 1951, 41, 199-204.

Bower, G. H. A multi-component theory of the memory trace. In K. W. Spence & J. T. Spence (Eds.), *The psychology of learning and motivation*, Vol. 1. New York: Academic Press, 1967. (a)

Bower, G. H. Verbal learning. In H. Helson & W. Bevan (Eds.), *Contemporary approaches to psychology*. Princeton: Van Nostrand, 1967. (b)

Bower, G. H. Organizational factors in memory. *Cognitive Psychology*, 1970, 1, 18-46.

Bower, G. H. Mental imagery and associative learning. In L. Gregg (Ed.), *Cognition in learning and memory*. New York: Wiley, in press.

Bower, G. H., & Lesgold, A. M. Organization as a determinant of part-to-whole transfer in free recall. *Journal of Verbal Learning and Verbal Behavior*, 1969, 8, 501-506.

Crovitz, H. F. *Galton's walk*, New York: Harper, 1970.

Estes, W. K. Statistical theory of spontaneous recovery and regression. *Psychological Review*, 1955, 62, 145-154.

Estes, W. K. The statistical approach to learning theory. In S. Koch (Ed.), *Psychology: A study of a science*, Vol. 2. New York: McGraw-Hill, 1959.

Fozard, J. L., & Yntema, D. B. The effect of repetition on the apparent recency of pictures. *American Psychologist*, 1966, 21, 873 (Abstract).

Gibson, E. J. A systematic application of the concepts of generalization and differentiation to verbal learning. *Psychological Review*, 1940, 47, 196-229.

Glanzer, M. & Clark, W. H. Accuracy of perceptual recall: An analysis of organization. *Journal of Verbal Learning and Verbal Behavior*, 1963, 1, 289-299.

Hinrichs, J. B. A two-process memory strength theory for judgment of recency. *Psychological Review*, 1970, 77, 223-233.

Hintzman, D. L. Recognition time: Effects of recency, frequency, and the spacing of repetitions. *Journal of Experimental Psychology*, 1969, 79, 192-194. (a)

Hintzman, D. L. Apparent frequency as a function of frequency and the spacing of repetitions. *Journal of Experimental Psychology*, 1969, 80, 139-145. (b)

Hintzman, D. L., & Block, R. A. Repetition and memory: Evidence for a multiple-trace hypothesis. *Journal of Experimental Psychology,* 1971, 88, 297-306.

Kendler, H. H., & Kendler, T. S. Vertical and horizontal processes in problem solving. *Psychological Review,* 1962, 69, 1-16.

Kintsch, W. Recognition learning as a function of the length of the retention interval and changes in the retention interval. *Journal of Mathematical Psychology,* 1966, 3, 412-433.

Kintsch, W. An experimental analysis of single-stimulus tests and multiple-choice tests of recognition memory. *Journal of Experimental Psychology,* 1968, 76, 1-6.

Kohlenberg, R. N., & Trabasso, T. Recovery of a conditioned emotional response after one or two electro-convulsive shocks. *Journal of Comparative and Physiological Psychology,* 1968, 65, 270-273.

Lawrence, D. H. The nature of a stimulus: Some relations between learning and perception. In S. Koch (Ed.), *Psychology: A study of a science,* Vol. 5. New York: McGraw-Hill, 1963.

Lewis, D. J. Sources of experimental amnesia. *Psychological Review,* 1969, 76, 461-472.

Lewis, D. J., & Maher, B. A. Neural-consolidation and electro-convulsive shock. *Psychological Review,* 1965, 72, 225-239.

Light, L. L., & Carter-Sobell, L. Effects of changed semantic context on recognition memory. *Journal of Verbal Learning and Verbal Behavior,* 1970, 9, 1-11.

Martin, E. Stimulus recognition in aural paired-associate learning. *Journal of Verbal Learning and Verbal Behavior,* 1967, 6, 272-276.

Martin, E. Stimulus meaningfulness and paired-associate transfer: An encoding variability hypothesis. *Psychological Review,* 1968, 75, 421-441.

Martin, E. Verbal learning theory and independent retrieval phenomena. *Psychological Review,* 1971, 78, 314-332.

McGaugh, J. L. Time-dependent processes in memory storage. *Science,* 1966, 153, 1351-1358.

Miller, G. A. The magical number seven, plus or minus two: Some limits on our capacity for processing information. *Psychological Review,* 1956, 63, 81-97.

Morton, J. Repeated items and decay in memory. *Psychonomic Science,* 1968, 10, 219-220.

Olson, G. M. Learning and retention in a continuous recognition task. Stanford: Stanford University, Institute for Mathematical Studies in the Social Sciences, Technical Report No. 131, 1968.

Paivio, A. Mental imagery in associative learning and memory. *Psychological Review,* 1969, 76, 241-263.

Peterson, L. R. Search and judgment in memory. In B. Kleinmuntz (Ed.), *Concepts and the structure of memory.* New York: Wiley, 1967.

Postman, L., & Stark, K. The role of response availability in transfer and interference. *Journal of Experimental Psychology,* 1969, 79, 168-177.

Prytulak, L. S. Natural language mediation. *Cognitive Psychology,* 1971, 2, 1-56.

Rumelhart, D. E. The effects of interpresentation intervals on performance in a continuous paired-associate task. Stanford: Stanford University, Institute for Mathematical Studies in the Social Sciences, Technical Report No. 116, 1967.

Shepard, R. N. The analysis of proximities: Multidimensional scaling with an unknown distance function. I. *Psychometrika,* 1962, 27, 125-140.

Shepard, R. N., & Teghtsoonian, M. Retention of information under conditions approaching a steady state. *Journal of Experimental Psychology,* 1961, 62, 302-309.

Shulman, H. G. Encoding and retention of semantic and phonemic information in short-term memory. *Journal of Verbal Learning and Verbal Behavior,* 1970, 9, 499-508.

Slak, S. Phonemic recoding of digital information. *Journal of Experimental Psychology,* 1970, 86, 398-406.

Strand, B. Z. Change of context and retroactive inhibition. *Journal of Verbal Learning and Verbal Behavior,* 1970, 9, 202-206.

Sutherland, N. S., & Mackintosh, N. J. *Mechanisms of animal discrimination learning.* New York: Academic Press, 1971.

Torgerson, W. S. *Theory and methods of scaling.* New York: Wiley, 1958.

Trabasso, T. R. Stimulus emphasis and all-or-none learning in concept identification. *Journal of Experimental Psychology*, 1963, 65, 398-406.

Trabasso, T. R., & Bower, G. H. *Attention in learning: Theory and research.* New York: Wiley, 1968.

Tulving, E. Subjective organization and effects of repetition in multitrial free-recall learning. *Journal of Verbal Learning and Verbal Behavior*, 1966, 5, 193-197.

Tulving, E., & Osler, S. Effectiveness of retrieval cues in memory for words. *Journal of Experimental Psychology*, 1968, 77, 593-601.

Tulving, E., & Thomson, D. M. Retrieval processes in recognition memory: Effects of associative context. *Journal of Experimental Psychology*, 1971, 87, 116-124.

Underwood, B. J. Stimulus selection in verbal learning. In C. N. Cofer & B. S. Musgrave (Eds.) *Verbal behavior and learning: Problems and processes.* New York: McGraw-Hill, 1963.

Underwood, B. J. Attributes of memory. *Psychological Review*, 1969, 76, 559-573.

Wickelgren, W. A. Exponential decay and independence from irrelevant associations in short-term memory for serial order. *Journal of Experimental Psychology*, 1967, 73, 165-171.

Wickelgren, W. A., & Norman, D. A. Strength models and serial position in short-term recognition memory. *Journal of Mathematical Psychology*, 1966, 3, 316-347.

Williams, R. F., & Underwood, B. J. Encoding variability: Tests of the Martin hypothesis. *Journal of Experimental Psychology*, 1970, 86, 317-324.

Winograd, E. List differentiation as a function of frequency and retention interval. *Journal of Experimental Psychology Monographs*, 1968, 76 (February, Pt. 2), 1-18.

Yntema, D. B., & Trask, F. P. Recall as a search process. *Journal of Verbal Learning and Verbal Behavior*, 1963, 2, 65-74.

Zeaman, D., & House, B. J. The role of attention in retardate discrimination learning. In N. R. Ellis (Ed.), *Handbook of mental deficiency: Psychological theory and research.* New York: McGraw-Hill, 1963.

6
ORGANIZATION AND THE CONCEPT OF A MEMORY CODE[1]

Neal F. Johnson
The Ohio State University

The present paper is an attempt to examine current conceptions of what is learned in terms of (*a*) previous data that purport to be inconsistent with traditional views, (*b*) current, but different, data that also purport to be inconsistent with traditional views, and (*c*) the general problem of explaining serially-ordered behavior. The major difficulty in dealing with the alternative theoretical treatments of these issues is, and has been, that of defining the alternatives such that they can be meaningfully examined and compared.

The two conceptions of learning to be compared in the present analysis are those usually identified by the terms association and organization. The paper begins with an attempt to define an associationistic theory of what is learned, and to show the difficulty of the task stemming from the vagueness of the position. In fact, there is even an ambiguity as to whether the position is a theory or a methodological commitment. Similarly, it is demonstrated that the early formulations of organization were equally ambiguous, and they also had vague specifications of what is learned.

As an illustration of these ambiguities, the early work on free recall is reviewed in terms of how it was used in the association-organization controversy. The fact that none of those studies provided critical data relevant to the controversy points out the lack of clarity in the positions that were being examined. That review, however, is followed by a description of two experimental situations that might

[1] The work reported here was supported in part by grants MH 08526 and MH 11236 from the National Institute of Mental Health, United States Public Health Service, and by Grant 534.1 from the Office of Science Information Service, National Science Foundation, to the Computer and Information Science Research Center, The Ohio State University.

pose serious problems for an associative interpretation of what is learned. It is these situations, and the problems posed by Lashley (1951), that motivate a consideration of alternatives to association.

An attempt is then made to formulate an organizational theory of what is learned in terms of a coding relationship between responses and their memorial representations. The coding relationship is the basic construct, and organization is defined in terms of the pattern of encoding. A few experiments are then described that relate the concept of coding to learning and illustrate the way coding relationships can be used to produce behavior. In particular, the studies illustrate the way the coding model handles the issues of unitization, the storage of order and item information, and the problem of defining what is learned. Finally, the model is illustrated by applying it to Lashley's (1951) problem of serial order, with emphasis on the way it solves the specific issues he raised.

HOW WE CHARACTERIZE WHAT WE KNOW

Broadly speaking, the field of human learning and memory is concerned with the development of an understanding of how knowledge is acquired. A very simple analysis of the problem is to say that we would like to know exactly why a person can describe or reproduce an experience after it has been encountered, and why, after the experience, there may be marked changes in his behavior in other situations. As such, the emphasis is clearly on the processes of acquisition and utilization of knowledge, and we are content to interpret the outcomes of our experiment in terms of what they mean regarding those processes. However, in our preoccupation with those processes we frequently fail to remember that our conception of them will depend quite critically on our conception of what is learned.

As a result of the combined influence of factors such as the British Associationists, Ebbinghaus, and behaviorism, among others, we have shown an unusual concern over the way learners master the relationship between stimuli and responses or two adjacent responses. In conjunction with that interest we have developed a number of tasks that allow us to examine in detail the conditions under which such learning takes place. Furthermore, that activity has been reinforced by conceptual developments such as the transfer surface reported by Osgood (1949). These developments pointed out that we had been led astray when we studied problems using tasks that could not be easily analyzed into separate stimuli, responses, and their relations. As a consequence, a large portion of what we know about the learning process is based on the way we learn specific stimulus-to-response associations.

The body of knowledge we have about learning based on the way learners acquire individual associations or habits has been labeled S-R psychology, and that approach to the problem has been under vigorous attack for the past few years. Unfortunately, the issues have been clouded by the fact that S-R psychology has been used to refer to two different things. The first meaning is relatively neutral and is simply the methodological point that our experiments are described in terms of stimulus settings and the responses the subjects emit in those settings. This meaning is quite broad and is used by almost everyone who has ever conducted an experiment. The other use of the term is somewhat less neutral and it refers to a commitment to the use of a hypothetical connection between a stimulus and a response as the basic theoretical construct with which to explain the outcomes of our experiments. (See Postman, 1968, for a description of the variety of ways the construct has been used.)

While most individuals who identify themselves as S-R psychologists would embrace the first meaning described above, it would be difficult to find one who would admit adhering rigidly to the second. That fact notwithstanding, there is a strong tendency for many of us to include only statements about stimulus-to-response connections within our discussions, and to say "I don't know what you mean" when others use other types of explanatory constructs. Furthermore, we support our use of the connection as a basis of explanation on the grounds that we do not have experimental outcomes that are not understandable in those terms. That is, why should we give up a conceptual system that serves our purposes perfectly well?

The problem with that argument, of course, is that not only do we interpret our outcomes within the framework of stimulus-to-response connections, but we also formulate our hypotheses, choose our experimental tasks, and design our experiments with that idea in mind. Given that the experiments are deliberately designed to yield data relevant to hypotheses about stimulus-to-response connections, it is not overly surprising that we do not encounter data that cannot be handled within that system.

The recent questions that have been raised regarding S-R psychology have come primarily as a result of experiments which were not conceived within that tradition. However, it should be made clear that it is not the methodological commitment that is being questioned, but rather the theoretical position. Furthermore, the attack on the theoretical position has never been intended to imply: (a) that stimulus-response relationships cannot be learned, (b) that there is something so trivial or unimportant about such relationships that they are not worthy of study, nor (c) that the results of such experiments cannot be described and explained in a meaningful way using only S-R connections as the basis of the explanation. Furthermore, such arguments, if made, would be inconsistent with existing data.

What the attack has attempted to do is question the adequacy of the theory as a basis for explaining what occurs in all learning situations. There seems to be a number of situations to which an S-R analysis does not apply. For example, if the learner's task is to master the material in a philosophy text, the concepts of stimulus, response, and trial do not seem to have any clear-cut referents. At the very minimum there would be a great deal of disagreement as to how these concepts should be applied to the task. The problem, then, is that while we have developed an understanding of the learning process in terms of these constructs, we have not concerned ourselves with the secondary problem of developing procedures for task analysis that allow us to determine how to use the constructs in any given situation.

The solution to this problem, however, is not a wholesale rejection of all traditional formulations of what is learned, but rather the development of alternative conceptions that can include the earlier conceptions as special instances. To a large extent, that has been the type of conceptual change we have encountered during the past decade. That is, not only have there been changes in the areas and topics of research in the field, and some rather fundamental changes in the conceptual framework within which we conceive and interpret the research, but there has also been work on some of the more traditional issues with the results being interpretable within either an associationistic or organizational system (see Postman, 1971).

In 1968, Battig argued that we were becoming somewhat more analytic in our approach to learning, and he supported his point with some data showing a shift across many years in the frequency a particular procedure was used. What might be even more interesting, however, is a plot of the relative frequency with which the words *learn* and *learning* have occurred in the experimental literature as compared to *encode* and *encoding*. There is an increased tendency to view what occurs during study as the encoding of information rather than the learning of items. Similarly, the terms *association* and *habit* seem to be decreasing in frequency while there is an increase in the use of the word *code*. Furthermore, these differences seem to be more than just changes in terminology, because there have been other related changes that are more concrete. For example, there has been an increase in the use of experimental procedures that cannot be readily analyzed into separate stimuli and responses. These would include such tasks as the Brown-Peterson paradigm (Brown, 1958; Peterson & Peterson, 1959), free recall, continuous recognition memory (Shepard & Teghtsoonian, 1961), and tests of memory span. In addition, there has been an increase in the use of dependent variables that do not directly reflect learning rate, such as measures of subjective organization, clustering, and transitional-error probabilities.

THE PROBLEM OF ORGANIZATION

The issue of the role of organization in memory has presented a problem for associative conceptions of what is learned for two reasons. The first is that when a subject imposes an organization on a set of material the output order does not necessarily conform to the order of input. If subjects learned connections between items at the time of input, then these connections should be demonstrated in their behavior by an output order that agrees with the input order. In fact, however, a discrepancy between the two orders exists and it does not seem to be reduced as a function of trials.

The second reason research on organization presents a problem for association theory is that the relationships among items apparent in a subject's output cannot always be reduced to interitem associations. For example, clustering seems to be influenced by nonassociative conceptual relations. Furthermore, as will be noted below, in serial recall where input and output order must agree, there are variations in the extent to which subjects relate adjacent items to one another and the variation cannot be explained very readily in associative terms.

Early Work with Free Recall

One of the first clear demonstrations of organization in which the effect could be quantified, was that reported by Bousfield (1953). He used a free-recall task and demonstrated that input and output orders were not the same. If the items in the list represented instances of several categories, the instances of a given category tended to be recalled together even though they were not presented together. He interpreted his results as indicating the operation of an organizing tendency, and recall level was explained in terms of habit strength and a relatedness increment.

It is difficult to understand Bousfield's use of the term *habit strength* in terms of traditional conceptions, because he does not specify the nature of the habit. That is, he refers to the habit strength added to an item as a result of its occurring within the list, but he does not specify that to which the item is related by the habit. He does indicate that there is a need for stimulus-response constancy for this concept of habit to be applied, so he does seem to be using the term in a traditional sense, but the nature of the stimulus is left undefined.

He defined the relatedness increment as an increment in habit strength added to an item by virtue of the fact that a related item occurred in the list. He seemed to view this strength as the same as habit strength developed through direct reinforcement, with the only difference being the conditions under which it is established. He did not specify what he meant by *related*, but he has been most frequently interpreted as referring to a nonassociative relationship.

The Issue of Nonassociative Relatedness

While at the time of publication of the Bousfield paper there seemed to be little problem with the concept of habit strength, the notion of relatedness increment resulted in some concern. In retrospect, however, the above would indicate as many problems with his use of habit strength. In addition, while he does not specify habit or associative relationships as the basis of relatedness increment, it is clear that that could be the case. Under those circumstances both the concepts of habit strength and relatedness increment could be handled by the same construct (i.e., association). Wood and Underwood (1967) have reported an effect that suggests such an interpretation.

Since the publication of Bousfield's (1953) paper, there have been a number of efforts to account for clustering in free recall in terms of association. Jenkins and Russell (1952) demonstrated that when pairs of stimuli and their primary associates appear in a list, the associated pairs cluster in recall. Cofer (1965) has reviewed a large number of experiments in which efforts were made to manipulate associative relatedness and conceptual relatedness independently of one another. In general, these experiments also demonstrated that associative relatedness is a basis on which subjects will cluster during recall.

A critical point concerning this issue, however, is not whether associatively based clustering can occur, but whether there can be clustering that is not associatively based. The Cofer review suggests that clustering is minimal when associative relatedness is absent, but Marshall (1967) demonstrated a marked independent effect of conceptual relatedness when associative relatedness was controlled at some greater-than-zero level. It appears that some form of associative relationship (as measured by word association techniques) is needed to obtain clustering, but given some minimum level of association the amount of clustering can be augmented by conceptual relationships among the items.

Some Definitions of Relationships

There are several ways that associative relatedness can be defined. Two of the most common are in terms of word association and Cofer's (1965) measure of relatedness. The first measures the relatedness of two items in terms of the frequency that one elicits the other in a word-association test, and the second is the degree to which the two items elicit common associates on a word-association test. Both measures are reasonably well accepted and both yield measures of relatedness that can be used for predicting clustering in free recall.

Categorical or conceptual relations are somewhat more difficult to assess. Generally, these appear to represent logical rather than empirical relationships and, as such, are quite difficult to define and measure. The usual procedure has been to give a group of subjects the label for a logical category and ask them to provide instances. For other types of conceptual relationships, an item can be presented and the subject is asked to supply a response that bears a specified relationship to the presented item (e.g., synonym of *lady*, antonym of *tall*, coordinate of *cow*, superordinate of *cat*, and subordinate of *dog*).

In fact, of course, a large portion of the items elicited in these tests of conceptual relationships are the same items elicited in the word-association tests. Therefore, to insure that the relationships that are utilized are purely conceptual, the only responses that are used are those that occur on the test of conceptual relatedness but not on the test of word association. For that reason, however, it might be more realistic to describe the relationships as nonassociative rather than conceptual.

These considerations suggest that it is possible to draw a distinction between two classes of measured relationships, with one class called associative and the other called conceptual or nonassociative. Unfortunately, that distinction is not very clear. In both cases the measure is the frequency of a response to a stimulus. That, however, is generally accepted as an operational definition of associative strength.

In terms of the procedures used for assessing the relationships, the only difference between those that are labeled associative and those that are labeled conceptual is the nature of the instruction given to the subjects who are used to collect the normative data. In the case of a word-association task the instruction is "give me your first association to . . . ," while for the other type of task the instruction could be something like "give me an instance of . . . ," or "give me a superordinate of . . . ."

It seems clear that the instruction must be part of the stimulus to which the subject responds. If subjects are asked for a first association to a stimulus, that is what subjects give as a response; if subjects are asked for a second or third association, they do it (Rosen & Russell, 1957). Therefore, there is a change in the response when the stimulus word remains the same but the instruction changes. Likewise, the instruction for responses that conform to what has been labeled a conceptual relation also changes the nature of the responses given to a stimulus word. In all these cases we have a word-association task that contains a set of complex stimuli, with each stimulus consisting of an instruction plus a stimulus word.

While this discussion began with a consideration of the various relationships that might exist between words, the preceding would suggest that they all may reduce to just one, namely associative. In every case all we know about the relationship between the stimulus and the response is the response frequency given the stimulus (i.e., associative strength). The conditions differ among themselves considerably in terms of the nature of the stimuli, but the nature of the stimulus is not the relationship. Furthermore, even if it were possible to specify the relationship only in terms of the stimulus we would be faced with arguing that there is a critical distinction between the instruction to give the first word one thinks of when a given word is presented and the instruction to give a synonym of the presented word. At the very minimum we would have to demonstrate that a qualitative distinction exists between those two instructions, but that a qualitative distinction does not exist between the instruction to give a synonym and the instruction to give a subordinate or superordinate of the presented item.

One could reasonably argue, however, that there is a quantitative distinction between the tasks in terms of the difference between the stimulus words alone as stimuli and the stimulus words plus instructions. For example, the stimulus word *tree* may be more similar to the stimulus *give me your first associate to tree* than *tree* is similar to *give me a subordinate of tree*. If that were the case, then the failure to obtain much clustering when only conceptual relations exist among the items in the list (i.e., words that elicit one another on a standard word-association test do not appear) could be explained in terms of changed stimuli. The stimulus complex *give me a subordinate of tree* may elicit *juniper* as a response. However, *tree* and *juniper* may not cluster because it is not *tree* to which *juniper* is related. That is, it is only related to the complex, which did not appear in the free-recall list.

To summarize, it is doubtful whether the early work on alternative explanations of clustering in free recall dealt with issues that could not be construed in terms of associative relationships. Even what appeared to be cases of pure conceptual relatedness ultimately rested on an associative definition of the relationship. The differences among the tasks seemed to be in the nature of the stimulus. If this analysis of the problem is correct, then Cofer (1965, 1966, 1967) would not have to abandon the associative basis for understanding clustering even if he had demonstrated the effect when the word-association strengths among the related items were zero. The results could have been explained in terms of stimulus generalization.

Conditions for Testing the Adequacy of Associative Explanations

Even if conceptual relations were not ultimately reducible to associative definitions, there still would be no need to invoke nonassociative explanations to account for clustering when word-association strength was zero. The variables discussed above all represent preexperimental characteristics of lists, which it is assumed the subjects use to detect word sets that could be included within a single cluster. In terms of the process of learning, and a characterization of what is learned, there is very little information provided by knowing the basis on which subjects detect possible word sets to be clustered during learning. The critical issue is what they learn about these items once they have been detected and how they acquire the information.

For example, suppose items from a conceptual category appeared within a list and there were no interitem associations among the items before learning (as indexed by word-association data). The subjects might learn the list by initially detecting these categories and then forming strong interitem associations among the items from within a category, followed by forming associations between the categories. While nonassociative factors may have influenced the way the subjects decided to organize the list, the relationships they learned were simple interitem associations.

Alternatively, a list might consist of subsets of highly interassociated items, and the subjects could use those associative relationships to detect word sets that could constitute clusters. If, during learning, the subjects established a single memory code to represent all the items in a cluster, and learned only the relationship between each item and its code, then none of the preexperimental associations would be either increased or decreased as a result of the learning experience. If that occurred it would be difficult to explain clustering and organization in associative terms.

The essential point is that if we are to draw conclusions about the process of learning, and what is learned, we must attend primarily to what occurs during learning, and what exists after learning, rather than to preexperimental conditions. Knowledge of preexperimental conditions is of interest only in light of learning and postlearning data. If associative explanations of learning are found to be inadequate, it will have to be because the change from what a subject knows before a learning experience to what he knows after the experience cannot be characterized using only interitem connections.

The Relationship between Organization and Learning

The early work on clustering demonstrated it to be a performance phenomenon that occurred during learning, and the type of lists that most clearly demonstrated clustering (categorized lists) were also lists that subjects learned rapidly. These results, however, do not indicate any direct relationship between learning and organization.

Similarly, much of the work on organization and the learning of serial lists resulted in ambiguous outcomes. For example, studies like that reported by Miller and Selfridge (1950) could be interpreted as indicating that learning is facilitated when subjects are presented with material similar to material they have learned in the past (i.e., positive transfer). Similarly, the effect of redundancy demonstrated in the Miller (1958) study could be interpreted as being the result of a reduction in the amount that needed to be learned.

Correlational data. Some of the first suggestions that organization per se might influence learning directly were correlations reported between learning rate and indices of degree of organization. For example, Tulving (1962) reported an almost perfect correlation between mean recall on a free-recall trial and his measure of subjective organization (SO). In addition, he (Tulving, 1964) reported a substantial, although somewhat lower, correlation between mean free-recall performance for a subject and his SO score (i.e., subjects were the sampling units rather than trials).

When subjects learn sentence materials (Johnson, 1965), the probability that each word in a sentence will be wrong given the immediately preceding word was right (i.e., the transitional-error probability, or TEP) is highly related to the grammatical characteristics of the particular word-to-word transition. The pattern of TEPs for a sentence can be predicted from the grammar, and the extent to which a subject's TEP pattern matches the expected pattern can be indexed by computing a rank-order correlation (rho) between them. With subjects as the sampling unit, the correlation between the rho for each subject and the rate the sentences were learned is about .50. Similarly, Fritzen and Johnson (1969) had subjects learn digit sequences that were organized in terms of simple ascending or descending runs (e.g., 4,3,2,1,8,10,12,14,7,5,3,1,6,7,8,9). The subjects tended to make more errors on the first member of a run than on the others, and the proportion of all errors that occurred on the first member correlated about .70 with overall learning rate.

Peterson (1968) had mentally retarded and normal children learn sequences of five letters each. During the study interval the letters were organized by physically grouping them (e.g., SB JFQ). The extent to which the subjects organize the sequence during learning can be assessed by determining the degree to which transitional errors tend to occur at the between-unit transition, rather than within the units. Peterson's data indicate that that tendency was greater for normal than for retarded children, although the differences in learning rate were not quite as clear. In addition, her results indicated that when the experimenter did not provide an organizational scheme, both the normal and retarded children adopted one of their own. Again, however, the retarded children did not organize to the same extent as did the normals and, across a set of different sequences, the normal children were much more consistent in the type of organization they imposed on the material.

While these results indicate that across trials and subjects there is a substantial relationship between organization and learning, they do not demonstrate a direct influence of one on the other. That is, to demonstrate that a fast learner is a good organizer is not the same as demonstrating that he is a fast learner because he is a good organizer.

Altered organization. More direct data on the relationship between learning and organization have come from an approach to the issue described by Tulving (1966). In the Tulving experiment subjects were asked to learn a free-recall list of unrelated items, followed by the learning of another list that was twice as long as the first. The second list either contained words that had not appeared in the first list, or half of the second list consisted of the first-list words. The data indicated that having previously learned half the second-list words did not result in any positive transfer. Tulving interpreted the results as indicating that the organization adopted for the words in the first list was not appropriate for the second list, and it was the organization of the words that was learned.

Tulving's interpretation of the results are in accord with more recent data that indicate that if the organization the subjects adopt during the first list is usable on the second list, then second-list performance is facilitated (Bower & Lesgold, 1969; Birnbaum, 1968, 1969; DeRosa, Doane, & Russell, 1970). Birnbaum (1968, 1969) had subjects learn categorized second lists, and the first list varied from being either one member of each of 12 different second-list categories to four members from each of three second-list categories. When complete second-list categories appeared on the first list, performance was facilitated. In addition, the DeRosa, Doane, and Russell (1970) data suggest that some second-list facilitation occurs even when the first-list categories are appropriate to the second list, but none of the words are the same.

Bower and Winzenz (1969), in an immediate-memory experiment, induced subjects to organize digit sequences that exceeded their memory span by reading the digits with a particular rhythm. They reported that if a particular sequence was presented more than once recall would increase, but only if the sequence was read with the same rhythm on all occasions. If the rhythm changed from presentation to presentation the recall level remained at the level of once-presented items. In the free-recall experiments using the Tulving (1966) procedure there is some change in the content of the material to be learned from the first list to the second, and that change in content could be responsible, in part, for the lack of positive transfer. The Bower and Winzenz study is of interest because neither content nor order was changed from the first learning experience to the second.

A similar effect has been demonstrated by Johnson and Migdoll (1971). In their experiment subjects memorized two sequences of seven letters each. The sequences were paired-associate response terms and the stimuli were the digits 1 and 2. During the study trials the materials were organized for the subjects by grouping them (e.g., SBJ FQLZ or SB JFQ LZ). In one condition subjects first learned a pair of sequences grouped in one manner (SB JFQ LZ) and then learned the same sequences grouped in the other way (SBJ FQLZ). After second-list learning the subjects were asked to recall the two sequences they had learned on the first list.

In comparison to a condition in which different letter sequences occurred on the second list, the above condition demonstrated no evidence of positive transfer. That is, if subjects first learned SB JFQ LZ the rate at which they would then learn SBJ FQLZ was no faster than if the sequences were entirely different. In addition, when subjects had the same letter sequences on the two lists, but adopted a different organization for the second list, there was significant retroactive inhibition as compared to a rest-control condition. These data, and those reported by Bower and Winzenz (1969), seem to indicate that if a subject does not organize material in the same manner on two occasions he will treat the materials as if they were completely different, even though they were otherwise identical. The organization appears to be a critical part of the response learned by the subject.

These results seem to be somewhat more difficult to interpret in terms of interitem associations than were the earlier findings on clustering. The results from the Tulving technique (Tulving, 1966) could be interpreted associatively to the extent that the interitem associations established during first-list learning were not useful during second-list learning. One implication of that explanation is that the associated items that tended to occur adjacently during first-list learning, should not occur adjacently during second-list learning. The lack of positive transfer would occur because the subjects were not using associations that were available to them.

Birnbaum's (1969) data are consistent with this interpretation. The second lists her subjects learned consisted of several instances of each of several categories. The first lists were either most of the members of a few categories or one member from all of the categories. In the first case the subjects would have a way of detecting and adopting a first-list organization that also could be used on the second list, while that would not be the case if only one member of each category appeared on the first list. When the first list consisted of only one member of each category, second-list learning was quite slow and there was only a small tendency to recall the first-list words in the clusters that had been used during first-list learning. Furthermore, even that small tendency declined during second-list learning. The results from the condition that had intact categories appearing during first-list learning were quite different. Second-list learning was quite fast and these subjects tended to recall the first-list words together as they had during first-list learning. In this experiment, then, rate of second-list learning was related to the opportunity to capitalize on interitem associations established during first-list learning.

The results of the Bower and Winzenz (1969) and Johnson and Migdoll (1971) experiments are less easy to interpret in terms of interitem associations. In both experiments the sequences presented to the subjects on each learning occasion were superficially identical, and an orally produced response that was scored as correct for the first learning occasion also would have been scored as correct on the second. Given that the sequence of responses demanded by the two tasks were identical, there also should be identical associative relationships among the items. Therefore, the subjects' rearrangement of the response terms, which the Birnbaum (1969) data indicated was related to the failure to obtain positive transfer in the Tulving transfer paradigm, cannot be used as an explanation when serial recall is required and no content or order changes are made.

A CODING VIEW OF WHAT IS LEARNED

The concept of the recoding of information was first introduced by Miller (1956a, b). He proposed that when subjects are presented with information sets for retention, one way they can reduce the amount to be remembered is to recode subsets of more than one item into a single higher-order code. His illustration was the act of remembering a string of binary digits in terms of pairs which were recoded into decimal digits. For example, the pair 00 could be remembered as 0, 01 as 1, 10 as 2, and 11 as 3. The sequence 010010110110 could then be remembered as 102312 and that would reduce by 50% the number of items that would have to be held in memory. The collection or subset of response items that are recoded into the same higher-order code is referred to as a *chunk*. The first two binary digits in the above sequence would, together, constitute a chunk because they are represented in memory by the same code. The second and third digits, however, would not constitute a chunk because they are represented by different memory codes.

A yet higher-order recoding scheme could then be introduced that would allow subjects to recode pairs of decimal digits into letters. A 00 pair could be remembered as A, a 01 pair as B, a 02 pair as C, etc., on down to a 32 pair as O, and a 33 pair as P. The above sequence of binary digits could then be remembered as ELG, which would reduce the memory load from 12 binary digits to 3 letters. Schemes such as this allow subjects to increase their immediate memory span for binary digits from 7 or so to as many as 20. This increase supports the hypothesis that subjects can use the schemes to facilitate performance.

This view of coding information is different in two critical ways from that described earlier as a traditional associative view. First, it supposes that there is some single memorial representation for the information within a chunk. An associative view seems to imply a representation in memory of the stimulus, or immediately preceding response, a representation of the response, and finally a representation of the association between them. If another item were added to the sequence one would have to assume a representation in memory of that item as well as an association leading from its immediate predecessor. The coding view, on the other hand, assumes that there is only one representation in memory (the code) regardless of the amount of information or number of items included within the chunk. While there does seem to be a limit to the number of items that a subject can include within a chunk (and, presumably, within a code), it does seem to exceed the response-set size of two imposed by the concept of association.

The second critical distinction between a coding and an associative relationship is that the coding relationship assumes no direct connection between the items. That is, the items within a chunk are related only to the extent that they share a common representation in memory. For example, if subjects learn the response sequence SBJ, the associative view would have to assume that the occurrence of S is the precondition for B, which in turn is the precondition for J. If S or B was forgotten there also should be a loss of J. The coding view of learning assumes only that these items are stored together in memory within a common code. The recall of an item should be dependent upon remembering the code, but should not be influenced by whether other items represented by that code are also remembered.

It is in these two ways, then, that the current view of coding differs from what has been labeled as the associative view. Schematically, the associative relationship can be characterized as:

$$\text{Stimulus} \longrightarrow S \longrightarrow B \longrightarrow J,$$

while the coding relationship would appear as:

$$\text{Stimulus} \longrightarrow \underset{S \quad B \quad J}{\overset{0}{\diagup\mid\diagdown}}$$

In both cases it is assumed that some external stimulus is the initiating event, with the difference being in the relationships among the items in the set.

This view of hierarchical coding has been used as a model for both the general organization of memory (e.g., Mandler, 1968) and the way a particular response item is organized (Johnson, 1968, 1970). In terms of individual responses, a set of statements has been listed elsewhere (Johnson, 1970) that attempts to formalize the way this concept of a code has been used in the past. These statements can be summarized as the following points.

First, the major theoretical property of codes is that they are unitary in the sense that they are single memory devices that can represent a number of individual response items. If they are unitary they should be recovered from memory in an all-or-none manner. Once recovered, all the information they represent should be available for recall. It is from this theoretical property that most of the dependent variables have been derived (e.g., clustering, SO, hesitation, TEPs).

Second, a distinction important to maintain is that between codes and the information that they represent. For example, in a free-recall task with categorized lists, a separation has been made between the recall of the category and the recall of items from the category. Category recall is measured in terms of the probability that a category is represented in a subject's output, regardless of the number of items recalled from that category. Recall of the category members is measured by the mean number of items recalled from a category, given at least one member is recalled. Several investigators (e.g., Shuell, 1968; Cohen, 1966) have demonstrated that these measures are independent and that variables that influence one may not affect the other.

Third, an important implication of the above distinction is that it may be reasonable to view memory codes as if they were opaque containers. That is, if the code and the represented information are distinct, then it should be possible to be in a state of code recall without having any immediate awareness of the information represented by the code. For example, a subject might feel confident that he can remember a free-recall list, because he remembers that it contained instances of birds, fish, trees, and flowers. However, at the time of recall he might discover that when he attempts to decode the category labels into their appropriate instances he is unable to remember the exact items that appeared in the list.

Finally, codes can represent either individual response items or other codes. Hierarchical coding occurs when the codes at one level in the hierarchy are recoded into yet higher-level codes. For example, if a subject were presented a sequence of letters grouped such as SBJ FQL ZNG, he might recode the letters in each group into some code, and then recode the codes for the individual chunks into a code that would represent the entire sequence in memory.

The organization of a sequence can be defined as the pattern of recoding. That is, for a particular sequence a subject could impose a variety of organizations that differ in terms of which items or codes are included together. The sequence SBJFQLZ could be organized by including SBJ in one chunk, FQLZ in another, and then recoding the codes for those two chunks into one high-order code representing the entire sequence. Alternatively, the sequence could be organized into codes for three low-order chunks like SB, JFQ, and LZ, and then the codes for these three chunks could be recoded into a code representing the entire sequence. A third possible organization would be to have the same low-order chunks, but then recode the codes for the first two into a higher-order code. Then that code and the code for LZ could be recoded into the code for the sequence. Clearly, for a serial set of as few as seven items there are many different organizations that could be imposed, and each can be unambiguously defined by the recoding pattern. (This point is detailed in the later section on serial order.)

While the number of different possible organizations for a serial set is large, there are two critical limitations. The first concerns the size of the chunks, or the number of items that can be included within a single code. A number of studies have indicated that performance is optimum when the chunk size is three (Mandler, 1967; McLean & Gregg, 1967; Ryan, 1969) and if subjects are given a choice regarding chunk size they adopt chunks of three and resist chunks of four or larger (Johnson, 1970; McLean & Gregg, 1967). Wickelgren (1964, 1967) has offered data that suggest that the subjects' problem with larger chunks is the retention of intra-chunk order. When free recall is allowed, subjects seem to handle chunks of six and seven elements without trouble.

The second limit on the nature of organization is theoretical. If a code is included as a component of a higher-order code, all the information it represented must be represented by the higher-order code. In addition, any individual response item cannot be represented by more than one code at any level in the organizational hierarchy. For example, if SBJFQLZ is chunked as SB JFQ LZ at the lowest level, with a single code representing each chunk, it would not be possible to recode the sequence at the next level into a code for SBJ and another for FQLZ, because the higher-order code that represented the code for JFQ would also have to represent the codes for J, F, and Q. Similarly, if the sequence is chunked as SBJ F QLZ at the lowest level it could not be recoded as SBJF and FQLZ at the next higher level because F would be represented by more than one code at one organizational level. The decoding of these codes would produce two Fs rather than one. Support for this limit on organization is provided in an experiment by Marmurek (1972) reported below.

GENERATIVE DECISIONS AND THE CONCEPT OF A UNIT

If the item sets that constitute a chunk are represented by a single code in memory, then all the information in the set or chunk should be retrieved at the same time. That should result in the items in a chunk being produced in an all-or-none manner. That is, when a code is recovered it must be decoded into the information it represents before any of the items within the chunk can be produced. To that extent, then, subjects must make chunk-size recall decisions.

Chunks as Decision Units

The issue of chunks as decision units has been examined most recently in the context of a model of the way subjects use organization as a retrieval scheme at the time of recall. Quite simply, the decoding-operation model (Johnson, 1968, 1970) assumes that at the time of recall the subject recovers a code for the entire sequence and decodes it into the items or codes it represents at the next lower level in the hierarchy. The second assumption is that the codes recovered by that decoding step are tagged to indicate their temporal order in the sequence. The subject temporarily stores all the codes except for the one that has temporal priority in the sequence, and then further decodes that code. Again he recovers a set of tagged codes and again he stores all but the one with temporal priority in the sequence, and so on. That procedure would continue until the subject produced a response item at which time he would return to his memory and retrieve the most recently stored code, or the code whose tag indicated it had temporal priority over the others. The same procedure would continue until the entire sequence was produced. The final assumption is that subjects are relatively conservative when they attempt to recall a sequence, and whenever they are uncertain they terminate their recall attempts.

If subjects make recall decisions at chunk boundaries in the sense that it is at those points that codes are decoded, then it is at those points they should discover they are uncertain of some item in the chunk that follows. Therefore, if subjects terminate their recall attempts before completing a sequence it should occur at chunk boundaries. This issue was examined by asking subjects to learn sequences of seven letters as paired-associate responses (Johnson, 1970). The stimuli were digits and each subject learned a two-pair list. Subjects were induced to organize the sequences in a particular manner by having the letters appear in groups during the study trial. For one condition the responses were grouped as SB JFQ LZ and for the other the grouping was SBJ FQLZ. There were 20 learning trials and subjects' responses were scored for the frequency during learning that they terminated a recall attempt at each letter-to-letter transition. The frequency for each transition was divided by the frequency with which the letter before the transition was correct to obtain a transitional-error probability (TEP).

The results of the study indicated that there were clear TEP spikes on the transitions from the last item in one chunk to the first item in the next. The TEPs on the transitions within chunks were relatively low and equal.

If subjects do make all the decoding decisions for a chunk before producing any item from the chunk, and terminate recall if they are uncertain of any item, then the probability of terminating at the beginning of a chunk should be an increasing function of the size of the chunk. That issue was tested using the letter-learning procedure described above (Johnson, 1970). One condition had three letter responses grouped as SB J. Three other conditions also had two-letter first chunks, but the second chunk was either two, three, or four letters long. As the size of the second chunk increased from one to four letters there should be an increasing tendency to stop at the transition from the last letter of the first chunk to the first letter of the second. Furthermore, if all the decisions regarding the second chunk are made at that point there would be no reason to expect any variation across groups at any other transition. The results indicated a marked increase in the TEP on the between-chunk transition as the size of the second chunk increased, but no significant variation for any other transition.

Decisions regarding the items in the first chunk should be made before the subject recalls any items in the sequence. Therefore, if they should be uncertain about an item in the first chunk, the result should be a complete omission of the entire sequence on that recall attempt. In an experiment similar to the one just described, the size of the first chunk was varied from two to four letters (Johnson, 1970). The expected increase in omissions was obtained.

In a related study (Johnson, 1970) one condition had responses organized as SB JFQ LZ while a second condition had their responses grouped as SBJ FQ LZ. The first condition should result in fewer complete omissions during learning than the second because the first chunk is smaller, but it should have resulted in a larger TEP at the beginning of the second chunk because the second chunk was larger. Again, the results were in accord with the expectation.

In addition to the decisions regarding the items within the first chunk, a subject also makes decisions regarding the codes for other chunks in the sequence before producing the first item in the sequence. For example, if a sequence were organized into three chunks of three items each (SBJ FQL ZNG), and the codes for those chunks were integrated into a code for the sequence, then at the time of recall the subject would recover the code for the sequence, followed by the codes for each of the chunks, followed by the codes for the items within the first chunk. If he were uncertain of any of those decoding steps he would terminate his recall attempt before saying anything. Therefore, the rate of complete omission during learning should be a function of the number of chunks in the sequence. However, the model assumes that subjects do not decode the codes for chunks past the first until the time to produce them. Therefore, the number of items they represent should have no effect on the omission rate.

Again, a letter-learning experiment was used which had six conditions (Johnson, 1970). The sequences learned by the six conditions can be characterized as follows: (1) SBJ FQL ZN, (2) SBJ FQLZN, (3) SBJ FQLZ, (4) SBJ FQL, (5) SBJ FQ, and (6) SBJ. All the conditions had three-letter first chunks so that should not differentially affect omission rate. The first two conditions differ only in the number of chunks in the sequence, so the first condition should have a higher omission rate because it has more chunks. Conditions 2 through 5 have the same number of chunks, so the frequency of an omission across 20 learning trials should be the same for these conditions. They do differ in the size of the chunk past the first, but according to the model the second code should not be decoded until after the first chunk has been recalled. If that is the case, then decoding difficulties for the second chunk cannot affect omission rate. Finally, the last condition (6) only has one chunk so its omission rate should be lower than for Condition 5. All of those predictions were supported by the data.

The outcomes of these experiments on chunks as decision units seem to be inconsistent with an associative view of what is learned. If subjects learn sequences in terms of interitem associations, then the decision about a response could not be made until its immediate predecessor had occurred. That is part of the problem of serial order described by Lashley (1951).

Juncture, Timing, and Decision Units in Speech Production

In addition to experiments such as those just described, there also have been many studies in the area of experimental phonetics that demonstrate that subjects make generative decisions only at certain loci. In particular, there are a number of reasons why one could not assume that individual speech sounds (phones) are decided upon only after the immediately preceding phone was produced (beyond the fact that rate of speech precludes such an inefficient procedure). From a logical point of view, it seems necessary to assume that at least short sequences must be preprogrammed in the sense that all the generative decisions must be made at the same time and before anything in the segment is produced.

The relationships between the phenomenal experience of speech, the acoustic signal that partially gives rise to the phenomenal experience, and the motor acts that produce the signal, are complex and in something less than a one-to-one correspondence. When one hears a complex and long utterance the phenomenal experience is that of a sequence of discrete acoustic events, with each one being a phone that can be clearly separated from the ones that precede and follow it. Unfortunately, the physical reality does not match the phenomenal experience. A spectrographic representation of the acoustic signal indicates that it is a continuous flow that cannot be separated into discrete events. Furthermore, if a segment can be identified as corresponding to a particular phone it probably would not look like another segment that presumably was another instance of the same phone. Finally, there are certain phenomenal events for which there are no corresponding acoustic events (see Liberman, Mattingly, & Turvey, this volume).

Timing. Some of the problems that suggest the need for preprogramming stem from difficulties in the mechanics of producing speech. One problem is the fact that the mass of an articulator like the tongue is considerably greater than the mass of other articulators (e.g., the tip of the tongue, or the lips), and they move more slowly. Therefore, if these response components of the total gesture for a phone were initiated at the same time, the acoustic result would be something other than intended.

Another problem, which is related to the first, is the fact that to produce a desired sound it is necessary to have all the articulators in a particular position. However, the previous phone partially determines where the movements for positioning the articulators begin. Consequently, any commonality among recurrences of a particular phone in terms of oral musculature has to be in the position of the articulators at the time of production and not in the responses that put them into those positions.

More important, however, is that depending on the prior position of the articulator, the distance and time of movement might be great or small in comparison to that for another articulator involved in the same total gesture. Therefore, while the differences in the speed with which an articulator moves requires that the components of a gesture start at different times, this problem indicates that differential time of onset for the components is not invariant and changes as the context changes. The fact that some components of the total gesture for phone $N + 1$ might be initiated at the same time as some of the components for phone N indicates that in real time there can be no one-to-one match between the motor activity and the acoustic segments. Clearly, such complex interrelationships among the response components requires some form of preprogramming. (See Lenneberg, 1967, or Lehiste, 1970b, for a more detailed discussion of these empirical issues, and Liberman, Cooper, Shankweiler, and Studdert-Kennedy, 1967, for a discussion of their theoretical implications.)

While the preceding statements were based primarily on logical considerations, there are a number of empirically demonstrated effects that also indicate the need for preprogramming speech segments. In that the speech signal is continuous, and the articulators are moving continuously, the way a phone is produced (as well as its acoustic characteristics) must be influenced by the position of the articulators immediately prior to that phone. In addition, it also must be influenced by the position to which the articulators move immediately after that phone is produced. In fact, in continuous speech phones are so influenced by their environments that it is unlikely that the articulators actually reach their destinations before they are on the move for the next phone (MacNeilage, 1970). Therefore, the destinations would be hypothetical and the perception of a phone would be heavily influenced by its environment.

A study by Öhman (1966) illustrates these contextual effects. He demonstrated that such dependencies exist even in simple vowel-consonant-vowel sequences. The initial vowel influenced the final consonant-to-vowel transition and the final vowel influenced the initial vowel-to-consonant transition. Similarly, Lehiste and Peterson (1960) demonstrated that an initial /l/ in a segment is influenced by the following vowel but a medial /l/ is influenced by both the preceding and following vowels. It seems necessary to assume some form of preprogramming to explain the way a sound to be produced later in a sequence can have an influence on one occurring earlier.

There are at least two ways that such preprogrammed units might be organized. The simplest, and intuitively most appealing way, would be to assume that a segment can be defined as a set of phones that occur in a particular sequence. Under this view the unit of organization would be the phone and the coordinating principle would govern the movement of complexes of articulators from one position to another. As such, the pacing of the segment should be determined by the rate that the units of organization (the phones) were realized. That is, if a certain position complex (or hypothetical position complex) were realized, then the subject would be ready to move on to the next position complex and the only thing that should determine the timing of such movements would be the occurrence of previous items. The important point is that there would be no basis for expecting that the duration of one phone would have an influence on the duration of the next, or any other phone in the segment. The duration of the phones would be influenced only by the time it takes to move from one to the next.

Another view of the organization of a segment would assume that the complex movement of a single articulator is the unit of organization. In this case the number of subcomponents in the segment would be defined in terms of the number of articulators that need programming, rather than the number of phones or movements of each articulator. While this view has somewhat less intuitive appeal than the preceding view, it seems more in accord with the continuity of the motor responses that produce a segment.

Such parallel, but independent, programming of the articulators loses one critical advantage of the preceding view in that it does not provide any mechanism for coordinating the articulators so that they would reach the various target positions at the same time. One possible solution is to assume that the code for the programming is temporal; that is, not only is the pattern of the response preprogrammed, but the exact timing of the program is also predetermined. Therefore, while the behavior of the articulators are independent of one another, there is a temporal coordination such that they are programmed to be in certain positions at fixed points in time. The important implication is that if the time that an articulator reaches a particular position is predetermined it cannot be influenced by what has intervened between the beginning of the segment and that point.

Lehiste (1970a, 1971) has reported data of two sorts that support the idea of temporal programming of the segments. If a subject produces a segment like *skit*, the total duration of the segment and the temporal location of the final phone /t/ should be determined before production begins. If, for any reason, there should be a mistiming of an articulator for the initial consonant cluster the subject would slide into the vowel a little early. However, that should mean that the duration of the vowel, rather than the duration of the segment, would be lengthened, because the temporal location of the /t/ would have been determined already. Similarly, if the initial cluster should be prolonged for any reason there would have to be a shortening of the duration of the vowel. Therefore, the durations of the vowel and consonant cluster should be negatively correlated.

Lehiste's results indicate that when subjects are asked to repeat such segments over and over (more than 100 times in her study) there were small variations in the duration of the phones within the segments. However, rather than extending or reducing the duration of the segments (which would result in a zero correlation between the durations of the phones) the segment durations remained amazingly constant and there were compensating variations in the durations of the other phones. These variations resulted in negative correlations between the durations of phones within the segment.

The other data reported by Lehiste also deals with sequence timing. If individual phones were the units of organization (and the pacing mechanism), the timing for a sequence of phones should be independent of the environment in which the sequence appears. For example, the timing of *speed* should be the same in *speed, speedy,* and *speedily.* Lehiste's data, however, indicate that the timing was markedly influenced by the environment. In fact, the total duration for segments like *speedy* and *steady* were from 20 to 30 percent less than for *speed* and *stead* and the durations of the core sequences, *speed* and *stead*, were reduced by as much as 50 percent by adding the suffixes.

The variations demonstrated in these studies do not seem completely consistent with the concept of the pacing mechanism being the realization of phones. As noted earlier, the pacing mechanism offers no means for explaining the long-range timing constraints evident in these studies. Those constraints can be explained, however, by assuming that part of the preprogramming of a segment involves the exact timing of each of the articulators. That assumption receives particular support from Lehiste's (1970a, 1971) demonstration that subjects adjust the durations of individual phones and hold segment durations constant. That would seem to be exactly the opposite of what one would expect if the realization of phones was the pacing mechanism.

Juncture. While the timing data have their own theoretical importance, they also offer additional support for the concept of preprogrammed speech segments. That is, the spans across which such timing constraints hold must be response sequences for which all the generative decisions were made prior to the production. As such, these segments conform, both theoretically and operationally, to the chunks discussed in the preceding section. An important issue, therefore, is the extent to which these speech segments have similar boundary events. That is, if generative decisions are made at the boundaries, then behavioral effects correlated with these decisions should be evident at those points.

The initial issue concerns what behavioral effects should be expected at the segment boundaries. These can be clarified (and the interdependencies and temporal constraints among the phones within a segment may be explained) by assuming that (a) all the generative decisions for a segment are made at the same point, and (b) that production cannot proceed until the decisions within the set are both complete and compatible with one another. That latter point is the most critical. If the decisions must be complete and compatible with one another before any one of them is carried out, then it is easy to understand how the production of a phone from the middle of a segment can be influenced by both the preceding and the following environments.

It is further assumed, however, that influences of phones on one another are determined by the temporal contiguity of the decisions, rather than the contiguity of the phones themselves. Therefore, while a phone may be influenced by those immediately adjacent to it, it could be equally influenced by one more remote from it provided the decisions for the two phones were made at the same time. It also follows, however, that if the decisions for two adjacent phones are not made at the same time (i.e., one is the last member of one segment or chunk while the other is the first member of the next segment), adjustments in the productive decisions cannot be made to make one compatible with the other. That is, the generative decisions should be independent and the two phones should not influence one another.

These issues were anticipated, in part, by Pike (1947), although there has been more recent work on the problem. His solution to the problem of boundary identification can be most readily understood in terms of these theoretical considerations. He suggested that when highly modifiable sounds occur at boundaries they should not be modified by the adjacent sound that occurs in the other unit. That is, a unit boundary or juncture should be phonologically recognizable by the fact that the constraints that span the immediately preceding items are released at that point.

A number of such boundary signals have been identified (Lehiste, 1962, 1964) and some sounds seem to be more modifiable (and hence, better signals) than others. One illustration of these effects is the Lehiste and Peterson (1960) study, which demonstrated that if /l/ occurs in the middle of a segment it is influenced by both the preceding and the following vowels, but at the end of the segment it is only influenced by the preceding vowel. Similarly, nasal consonants tend to modify the vowels that follow them, but not if they immediately precede a word boundary (Lehiste, 1964). These juncture effects, plus the timing data, indicate these phonological segments (Lehiste, 1962) may represent decision units that are similar to the chunks identified in the letter-learning experiments described in the preceding sections. Of particular interest is the fact that the data also seem to indicate that generative decisions are made at only certain locations, and that the decisions made at a particular point govern more than one item.

ORGANIZATION AS THE RELATIONSHIP BETWEEN CODES AND INFORMATION: STORAGE OF CONTENT AND ORDER

The preceding suggests it might be quite reasonable to view what is learned as a vertical relationship between codes and the represented information, and that such coded information sets can be viewed as decision units. However, the specific relationship between codes and the represented information needs to be clarified as well as the types of information represented by the codes. While it is clear that codes must represent the content of a sequence, the way the order information might be encoded is somewhat less clear. One possibility is to view organization as the interrelationships among codes and that sequential order is determined by those interrelationships.

The Opaque Container Theory of Codes

In one of the experiments described above, the subjects in the various conditions were asked to learn letter sequences that varied in both the number of chunks in the sequence and in the size of the chunks past the first. The results of the experiment indicated that the probability of a complete omission is an increasing function of the number of chunks in the sequence. The fact that the size of those chunks did not also have an effect on omissions was interpreted as indicating that the subjects recalled the codes for those chunks before starting to produce the sequence, but did not decode them at that time. That assumes, however, that a subject can recover a code for a chunk without knowing what or how much information that code represents. That is, it is assumed that the code is opaque and the information it represents is not immediately available to the subject when it is in the coded state. The information becomes available only after the code is decoded.

An important implication of the opaque theory of codes is that any similarity in the content of two chunks cannot be reflected in a similarity between their codes. That is, if a code is opaque and represents information, rather than *being* the information itself, then there is no reason for the code to reflect in any way the nature of the content it represents. Therefore, if any information from within a chunk is changed it should be necessary for the subject to adopt an entirely new code for that chunk.

To examine that possibility, subjects learned a pair of letter sequences like SBJ FQL ZNG following the procedure described above (Johnson, 1969). Following the first-list learning they were asked to learn another list that was identical to the first except that one letter in each of two chunks was changed (e.g., SBJ FQL ZNG changed to SXJ FQL TNG). After learning the second list they were asked to recall the first list.

If a letter was changed within a chunk then a new code for that chunk should be used during second-list learning and the first-list code should be subjected to retroactive inhibition. If the subjects were unable to recall the code for the first-list chunk they should be unable to recall any of the information it represents Therefore, both the changed and unchanged letters should be unavailable at recall The fact that there were no changes in one of the chunks would allow the subjects to use the same code on the two lists for that chunk. Therefore, recall of the unchanged chunk should not be influenced by the second-list learning.

In a large number of experiments in which this procedure has been used (Johnson, 1969, 1970) the loss for the unchanged letters from a chunk with a change has been about 50 percent, relative to a rest control condition (where there is no second list), whereas the loss of the unchanged letters in chunks without changes has been about 10 percent or less. The loss of the two changed letters is usually about 60 percent. These results indicate quite clearly that if one item within a chunk is changed, then there is a loss of nearly all the information.

As a further demonstration of this effect, an experiment (Johnson, 1970) was conducted in which four-item chunks were used and, within a chunk, there were either one, two, or three changed letters in the second list. If codes are opaque, then any change should result in a completely different code, and the degree of loss of the unchanged letters should not be affected by the number of changed letters. Those results were obtained.

Association, Coding, and the Knowledge of Order

One of the advantages of an associative interpretation of what is learned is that it offers a very simple and intuitively appealing account of order information. Response events are properly ordered because each item in a sequence is the strongest associate of its immediate predecessor. In that sense, the knowledge of order is inherent to the concept of association. The concept of a memory code has no such obvious way of explaining order. As noted above, each item represented by a code is directly related to the code, but not directly related to any of the other items. Therefore, the occurrence of these other items should not be part of the subjects' knowledge of order.

One way to account for the knowledge of order is to assume that codes are tagged to indicate their position within an organizational scheme. For example, in the letter-learning experiments the code for a letter could have tags to indicate which sequence, which chunk, and which within-chunk position that item occupies. That would assume three order tags for the code, and the subject's knowledge of the ordinal position of that item should in no way depend upon their knowledge of any other item.

In order to examine that issue an experiment was conducted in which subjects learned a pair of letter sequences followed by the learning of a second pair of sequences, just as in the preceding experiments. However, rather than replacing some items on the second list, the order of some of the items was changed. For one condition the within-chunk order of two items was reversed (e.g., SBJ FQL ZNG changed to SBJ QFL ZGN). For another condition the between-chunk order of two items was changed (e.g., SBJ FQL ZNG changed to SBJ FNL ZQG). In a third condition a letter from one position in one sequence was interchanged with the letter from that same position in the other sequence. For other conditions these changes were made either two at a time or three at a time. For example, changing SBJ FQL ZNG to SBJ FGL ZNQ would involve changing two items of order infor mation for each changed item.

If the subject learns the location of an item by associating it with its neighbors, then changing its location in any way changes its neighbors, and the item should be completely lost from memory. If subjects know the order of items in terms of their tags, then the probability of correct recall should be a function of the number of tags that remain unchanged after second-list learning. That is, the tag view of order information predicts that retroactive inhibition should be an increasing function of the number of tags changed on the second list, while the associative view has no basis for such a prediction.

The results indicated that recall was a decreasing function of the magnitude of the order change on the second list. Furthermore, across a series of recall tests, the subjects were given increasing amounts of information as to where the items should be put. That is, they were given a letter and told in which sequence it had appeared, in which chunk it had appeared, or in which intrachunk position it had appeared. Recall improved only when subjects were given the specific information about what was changed.

These results would be quite difficult to explain using an interitem-association explanation of the knowledge of order. Furthermore, in the studies in which a letter within a chunk was replaced on the second list, there was no evidence that forgetting was a function of the particular letter that was changed. For example, if the middle letter of a chunk were changed, then the stimulus for the first letter would not be affected, nor would the first letter itself be affected. However, the stimulus that elicits the final letter (i.e., the middle letter) would be changed and lost from memory so the last letter should be forgotten as well. Clearly, the first letter in the chunk should be recalled at a higher level than the last. However, the results indicated no differential loss of the first and last letters within these chunks. In addition, if the first two chunks in the sequence had changes but the final one did not, recall of the last chunk was no lower than was recall of the first chunk when it was unchanged. Again, the results seem inconsistent with the view that subjects learn direct relationships between the response items.

Learning as the Identification of Organizational Position

These results and inferences concerning a learner's knowledge of order, along with the intimate relationship between learning and organization, suggests that learning a sequence might be nothing more than learning a unique organizational position for each item. That is, if a subject were to learn the organizational location of each item in a sequence, then the sequence itself should be known even though the subjects were not instructed to learn it.

This point can be illustrated with an experiment by Martin (1972) in which he used a procedure similar to that reported by Keeney (1969). The task was to learn a set of permutations of a fixed sequence, and the set of permutations defined a hierarchical organization for the sequence. For example, if the base sequence was SBJFQ, the four learned permutations might be: (1) JFQSB, (2) SBFQJ, (3) BSJFQ, and (4) SBJQF. The first permutation indicates that the hierarchical structure of the sequence divides it into two major units, (SB) and (JFQ). The second permutation indicates that the second major unit has two immediate constituents, (J) and (FQ). Finally, the third permutation indicates the immediate constituents of the first major unit (SB) are (S) and (B), and the fourth permutation indicates the immediate constituents of (FQ) are (F) and (Q). The important point is that the set of permutations defines a clear hierarchical organization for the sequence, and each letter has a single and unique position within the organization. If a subject learns the set of permutations, the above view predicts that he would have learned the organizational position of each item in the sequence. Consequently, by learning the permutations he should have learned the sequence.

During learning the base sequence appeared along with a digit and the subject's task was to read the letters in the permuted order signified by that particular digit. If SBJFQ (1) appeared as a display the correct response would be to read the letters in the JFQSB order, or if SBJFQ (3) appeared it should elicit BSJFQ as a response. After the subject read the letters in the order he thought correct for the presented digit, a new display appeared, which was the same as the previous one, except it also included the correct permutation of the letters, and the subject was allowed time for study.

The relationship between organizing and learning is of interest in this situation because the task does not demand that subjects learn the base sequence. Each time they are asked to respond they are presented with the base sequence and all they need do is read the letters in the order that is correct for the presented digit. Martin's experiment tested the hypothesis that learning the permutations entails learning the base sequence by having an experimental condition in which subjects were shown only the digit and not the base sequence during the anticipation interval. In order to emit a correct response the subjects would have to recall both the base sequence and the correct permutation, and then read the items from memory rather than the display. As with the standard condition, after anticipation the subjects were shown the base sequence, the digit, and the correct permutation during the study interval. In the control (standard) condition the subjects were shown both the digit and the base sequence during the anticipation interval, and all they had to remember was the correct permutation for the digit. For both conditions the base sequence contained eight letters and the subjects were asked to learn seven permutations signaled by the digits 1 through 7.

The experimental condition imposed a much greater memory demand on the subjects than did the control (standard) condition in that it required recall, at least implicitly, of the base sequence before anticipation. However, as suggested above, if learning the permutations entails learning the sequence, the experimental procedure would not force them to do anything that they would not also do in the control condition. That is, in that they were learning the permutations in the control condition they also would be learning the sequence, even though the task did not otherwise require them to do so.

The results of the study indicate that the rate of learning seven permutations under the two conditions was exactly the same when measured in terms of trials to criterion and mean errors across 10 trials. Clearly, as suggested by the above model, the increased memory load required by the experimental condition did not increase the difficulty of the task.

A second experiment by Marmurek (1972) tested the hypothesis that learning the sequence involves learning a single and unique organizational position for each item. While the preceding study indicated that learning a set of permutations for a sequence entailed learning the sequence, the Marmurek study examined whether that would also be true if the permutations did not identify a unique organizational position for each item. For example, the permutations of SBJFQ listed above indicated that J is the first member of the second major unit (first permutation) and is an immediate constituent of that unit along with FQ (second permutation). However, if the second permutation changed SBJFQ to FQSBJ, rather that SBFQJ, it would indicate that J was the last member of the first unit. Therefore, it would be inconsistent with the first permutation and the result would be that J would not have a single and unique organizational position.

Marmurek's study was similar to Martin's in that subjects were asked to learn seven permutations of an eight-letter base sequence. For one of his conditions the permutations were internally consistent in that they defined a single and unique organizational position for each letter in the base sequence. In the other condition the permutations were internally inconsistent in the manner illustrated above.

The results of the study were quite dramatic. The learning performance of the group with internally consistent permutations was considerably greater than for the other group. In fact, only three subjects in the condition with consistent permutations learned their seven permutations as slowly as did the fastest learner in the condition with inconsistent permutations. From these data it is clear that the introduction of an organizational ambiguity in the form of some items not having unique positions results in a marked decrement in performance. A reasonable interpretation of the Martin and Marmurek experiments is that subjects learn sequences by assigning single and unique organizational positions to each item.

LASHLEY'S SERIAL-ORDER PROBLEM: AN APPLICATION OF THE THEORY

The serial-order problem, as originally construed by Lashley (1951), stemmed primarily from two issues. The first was the problem of rate of response production. If subjects were dependent upon the occurrence of the previous item in the sequence to act as an elicitor of the next item, then in any sequence the interitem latencies should approximate the reaction time to a stimulus. In fact, however, the interitem latencies are so short that the response elements in well-integrated sequences merge together, as has been described in the case of speech production.

The second issue, and the one which seemed to suggest a solution to Lashley's (1951) problem, was that in any well-integrated behavioral sequence there are complex interdependencies among the items that seem to go beyond a simple elicitor-elicited relationship. One illustration of these other dependencies is the concept of a decision unit described above. That is, generative decisions are made at only certain locations, with the result being that the way an item is produced can be influenced by other items that are not immediately adjacent to it. A second illustration of these other dependencies is an organism's ability to reorganize a sequence with no disruption in performance. Lashley pointed out that an insect or animal that loses a leg can immediately reorganize its pattern of stepping to accommodate the loss, and a good translator has no more trouble translating when the word order is different in the two languages than when it is the same. Any construction of the concept of integration in terms of simple elicitor-elicited relationships would have difficulty handling these effects, particularly the spontaneous reorganization of a sequence.

Framework of a Solution

Lashley (1951) suggested a schema solution to the problem, although the details of the schema, and the specific way it would be utilized by a subject, were left more or less unspecified. In this regard, it is interesting to note that he also stated the general nature of the serial-order problem in these terms. That is, he defined the issue as that of identifying a generalized schema that would determine a sequence of acts when the acts themselves, and their direct relations with other acts, did not imply a specific order. The central issue, then, seems to be that of formulating a concept of a generative plan, where the plan itself carries information in addition to the information provided by the acts or responses.

There are at least three attributes such a schema must have in order to overcome the difficulties encountered by most accounts of serial ordering. First, and a point Lashley considered to be vital, is that the functioning of the schema should not depend in any way on sensory control or feedback. As a mechanism, the schema should predetermine both the events and their order, and once activated it should be independent of any further stimulation or input.

The second required attribute is a mechanism for momentarily increasing the availability of the specific response items or acts that appear in the sequence. Lashley suggested that all items might be partially activated before sequence production begins. Clearly, if the response pool is immediately available to the subject before production begins, performance should be facilitated. For example, such facilitation does occur in word-association tasks if the class of the desired response is narrowly defined before the stimulus is presented. Subjects can respond faster if they are asked to give an opposite of a stimulus word than if they are just asked to give their first association.

Finally, the schema must contain all the information necessary to properly order the items in the sequence. Clearly, the subject must know the order information, but if order is an attribute of the response items it would be difficult to account for their ability to reorganize sequences. For example, the Keeney (1969) task described above should be almost impossible to learn if the order information were tied to the response items. While the ordinal position of an item in an overt response was clearly defined and constant for a particular permutation cue, it did change depending upon which permutation cue was presented. If order information were an attribute of the response, each response item would carry several pieces of conflicting order information and subjects would not know which was appropriate for a particular cue. However, if one assumes that order is an attribute of the schema, and that a unique schema was related to each permutation cue, then no conflict should arise. In the Keeney study a cue had only one schema related to it, and each schema defined a single and unique organizational position for each item.

Coding, Organization, and Some Details of the Solution

Feedback.   The coding of what is learned, and the view of order information as code tags, offers one conception of schemas and the way subjects might use them for the efficient production of a response sequence. That model is consistent with the first attribute of schemas described above to the extent that it assumes that responses within a sequence are not directly related to one another. Any relationships that do exist are only indirect and the result of the fact that the items are represented in memory by a common code. As such, the model does not even contain a mechanism for feedback control (feedback control presumes direct relationships between items). In that items are directly related only to their codes, the feedback might reinstate the code, but that would serve no function in that the subject would have already decoded the code and recovered all the available information it represented. In addition, in that it is assumed that codes are tagged for order information, the additional feedback information would not be needed to determine order. Therefore, the model neither needs a feedback mechanism nor does it provide a means for using such information.

Item availability. In that it is assumed that there is a one-to-many relationship between codes and the information they represent, the model does contain a mechanism whereby a subject can make the response items available to himself before production begins (i.e., the second attribute of schemas described above). That is, in that the code for a chunk has to be decoded before any of the information can be produced, all the information in the chunk that is represented by the code should be immediately available to the subject before he begins production. As such, production should involve little more than a read-out of the contents of working memory.

Such prior availability of the response items should facilitate performance in at least two ways. First, in that the items are all available before production begins there should be no need for any delaying memory search during the production of the chunk. Secondly, in that no memory search for items from a chunk is necessary during its production, the subject would be free to do whatever memory searching and decoding is necessary for the next chunk.

This view of the process of production assumes that there are two subprocesses. The first is the decoding of memory codes into the information they represent (and whatever attendant memory searching might be necessary), and the second is the process of reading the recovered information out of memory by the production of an overt response. The model assumes that these two processes can be done in parallel, and that the read-out does not disrupt the searching and decoding in any way.

An overt analogue of this proposal is a case where someone is reading and at the same time thinking of something else. Under these circumstances the comprehension of what is read is almost zero, but the words can be read without error. Similarly, when subjects free recall a categorized list they frequently report an active memory search for the next category as they are producing the instances of its predecessor. These effects are made possible because subjects need not process their own outputs. The only processing to which they must attend is the search and decoding.

Order information. The final issue is for the model to account for order information, and its use, without using feedback as the basis of the account. Furthermore, as indicated above, the ordering mechanism must be a property of the organization or schema rather than the response items. That is, once initiated the organization should contain all the information necessary to sustain itself.

At the outset two points should be noted. First, within the coding model of what is learned the overall organization or schema for the sequence is defined in terms of the pattern of encoding of the item information, or, alternatively, the pattern of immediate constituents. For example, there is a very large number of organizations or schemas that could be imposed on SBJFQ, which, when used, would all generate an overt response that began with S, followed by B, followed by J, followed by F, with Q coming at the end.

The variety of possible organizations can be illustrated with the following structures which were generated from the rather confining constraints that (a) at any level any constituent can have only two immediate constituents and (b) that the first immediate constituent of the sequence must have either two or three ultimate response members. If the circles represent the codes, which are part of the organization, it becomes clear how the pattern of encoding determines the organization.

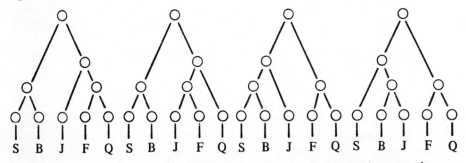

The second point to note is that while there is a distinction between the organization and the overt responses, together they comprise the two components of the total response. Furthermore, they are equally necessary components. That is, the organization is as critical in production as are the overt acts or responses that are used by the experimenter to identify a response occurrence. This point can be illustrated with the distinction between an experimenter's conception of a response and that of a subject. From the experimenter's point of view, if the subject's task is to generate an acceptable letter sequence, any one of the above organizations would be completely adequate to produce SBJFQ, and they would be interchangeable. However, Johnson and Migdoll (1971) have demonstrated that while they would all be adequate from the subject's point of view, they would not be interchangeable. That is, even though two overt sequences are the same, subjects treat them as completely different if their organizations differ in the way illustrated above. Therefore, from the subject's point of view, it is clear that the organization is an integral component of the response.

Within this conception of organization, order information can be defined, at least partially, in terms of the pattern of encoding. That is the case because the encoding pattern alone severely limits the number of possible orders that can occur. The limitation is achieved in two ways. First, at any point within a sequence, the pattern of decoding determines which items will be available to the subject for him to read out of memory. Secondly, for any level in the organizational hierarchy, items that are represented by one code cannot be intermixed with items represented by another code at the same organizational level. All of the items represented by one code must either precede or follow all those represented by another. For these reasons, then, part of the order information for a sequence is an inherent attribute of the sequence's organization.

These considerations can be illustrated using the first organization listed above for the sequence SBJFQ. The first point is an implication of the decoding operation model (Johnson, 1968, 1970). The model assumes that at the time of production the subject would recover a code from memory which represented the entire sequence (top node). He would then decode that code into the code for (SB) and the code for (JFQ). Both those codes would then be stored in the subject's working memory, and they would be immediately available to him for later use. The code for (SB) would then be decoded into the codes for (S) and (B), and those codes would be temporarily stored in working memory. Finally, the subject would need to select an item to produce overtly. At this point, the critical issue is that the model limits his range of choices to the contents of working memory, and the pattern of decoding has confined those contents to the codes for (S), (B), and (FQL). Of these, however, only (S) and (B) would be appropriate to the level at which the subject would be decoding. Therefore, if all the item information were appropriately encoded, and the subject decoded the code for (SB) before the code for (JFQ), the pattern of decoding would limit the possible two-letter combinations that could begin the sequence to two, SB and BS. That would be a reduction of 18 from the 20 that would be possible by combining any one of the five letters with any one of the remaining four.

The second source of order constraint imposed by the organization is an implication of the nature of immediate constituents and their codes, and it can be illustrated by using the same organization. The sequence code has two immediate constituents. The first is a code whose ultimate members are the first two letters, and the second is a code whose ultimate members are the last three letters. The pattern of encoding alone would not indicate whether (SB) preceded (JFQ), or vice versa, but it would limit the possible orders for the sequence to those in which S and B appeared adjacently (although not necessarily in that order) and J, F, and Q appeared adjacently (but, again, not necessarily in that order). Finally, the fact that the immediate constituents of the code for the unit (JFQ) are a code for (J) and a code for (FQ) indicates that of the six possible orders in which J, F, and Q could appear, the orders FJQ and QJF are ruled out.

While these points make it clear that the pattern of encoding limits the number of possible orders for a sequence, it is equally clear that even organizational structures as complete as those listed above still allow a large number of possibilities. As a result, the pattern of encoding would have to be augmented with some additional information, and the concept of order tags as described above seems a reasonable candidate.[2] If the

[2] Estes (this volume) has provided another account of ordering which relies on inhibition as a mechanism. His inhibitors fill the function of order tags within the present model. In this regard, it is interesting to note that his concept of inhibition is highly related to Yngve's (1960) concept of depth. In terms of the decoding-operation model (Johnson, 1970), both mean depth and inhibition appear to be highly correlated with the mean number of items in working memory at any point during the process of generating a sequence. In addition, all three should be negatively related to learning and performance, although the models differ as to the reasons

(*footnote continued next page*)

code for each immediate constituent in the above illustration was tagged for first or second position, then the order for the sequence would be completely defined. That is, the only order information not provided by the pattern of encoding is which of a code's immediate constituents has temporal priority in the sequence. If the code for a constituent was tagged to indicate its temporal position then that single source of ambiguity would be eliminated.

This particular conception of order information has a number of advantages. First, in that much of the order information is an inherent property of the organization, there is a marked reduction in the amount of additional order information subjects need acquire. In that a subject must learn the item information, and the organization is the pattern in which the item information is encoded, that portion of the order determined by the organization should be acquired without any additional cost to the subject. In this sense, the organization provides an augmented efficiency in the storage of order information that is similar to the increased efficiency in the storage of item information described by Miller (1956a).

A related point is that performance should be facilitated by one of the means whereby the organization provides order information. That is, at any point during the production of the sequence the organization limits the number of items immediately available to the subject, and, as noted above, it is from among those items that he must choose the next response in the sequence. If the organization reduces the size of the search set from being any item in the entire sequence down to anywhere from one to three items, there should be a reduction in search time. In addition, that also would reduce the number of different degrees of order information among which the subject would have to discriminate. Clearly, it would be easier to learn to discriminate among three items than to learn to discriminate among the items in a much larger set.

Finally, in that it is assumed that items are tagged for their position within each of the codes that represent them, it is not necessary to assume that order information is stored in terms of relationships among items. For example, a difficult problem for many alternative conceptions of order information is that subjects can place an item in its correct position within a sequence when that is the only item he can remember. If order information was relational, the subject would have to recall at least two items before he could start reconstructing order.

Empirical Support for the Application

This account has relied on two primary mechanisms provided by the theory for explaining why the human information processor is as facile as he is with serially ordered behavior. The first is that a single code can represent many response items, which should result in a subject being able to make many generative decisions at the same time. The second is that much of the order information is an inherent property of the organization. If one knows the pattern of encoding for a

---

for the negative relationship. For Estes the inhibitors are learned associations. Therefore, with increasing inhibition there is an increasing amount to be learned. On the other hand, both Yngve (1960) and the decoding-operation model predict a performance decrement resulting from the increasing demand on working memory. Both Martin (1972) and Marmurek (1972) offer data supporting these negative relationships.

sequence then one should also know both the items in the sequence and most, if not all, of the order information.

The previously described experiments on decision units offer support for the first mechanism. Both the letter-learning experiments and those on speech production indicate that at certain locations subjects make decisions for segments larger than a single item, and that once production is initiated for those chunks the generative process is relatively immune to disruption. For example, once a subject began to produce a difficult chunk, he had no more trouble than for somewhat easier chunks, with the major impact of the difficulty occurring before production began.

The second mechanism is supported by the Martin (1972) and Marmurek (1972) experiments. In the control conditions of those studies the subjects were asked to learn just the pattern of encoding, and there was no demand that they learn any item or order information. In the Martin study the subjects in the experimental condition had the additional task demand that they learn the item and order information, and yet their learning performance did not differ from that of the controls. The subjects appeared to have learned that additional information as a consequence of having learned the encoding pattern.

In the Marmurek study the subjects in the experimental condition were treated in the same way as the controls with the single exception that the encoding pattern did not define an unambiguous organizational position for each item. His results indicated a marked decrement in performance under those conditions. Both these studies seem to suggest that much of the order information for a sequence is carried by the encoding pattern.

One final point that should be mentioned is that, to a degree, these two hypothetical mechanisms are in opposition to one another. It would appear that for maximum efficiency in item production the chunks should be as large as possible so that the decoding of one code would make many items available. However, while that should facilitate item generation it would increase order difficulties. With increasing numbers of items in a subject's working memory there would be an increasing difficulty in identifying a specific item appropriate for a specific position.

In this regard, Wickelgren (1964, 1967) has reported data indicating that as chunk size increases there is an increase in the number of items a subject can recall from immediate memory (at least up to chunk sizes of about five or six). Mandler (1967) has reported data demonstrating similar effects. However, the Wickelgren data also indicate that if ordered recall is required, the optimum chunk size is reduced to about three, and larger sizes result in a performance decrement. These effects seem quite consistent with the assumed functions of the two mechanisms under consideration.

CONCLUSIONS

The major issue examined in the present paper is whether research on the role of organization in memory requires abandonment of traditional associative interpretations of learning. As was noted, experiments conceived within an associative framework will yield data that are interpretable in those terms. An important question, then, is whether results from experiments not conceived within that framework can also be interpreted in associative terms.

The early work on category clustering in free recall appeared, at first, to be inconsistent with traditional associative explanations, yet on close examination it became clear that the alternative explanations that were offered were associative in nature. Furthermore, the types of experiments that were conducted could not yield critical data in that they offered no direct assessment of what was learned.

The research on organization in serial recall is somewhat more difficult to explain in terms of interitem associations, and a coding interpretation has been offered. It was hypothesized that subjects establish codes for representing small response sets in memory, and that the items are directly related to the code but not to one another. That appears to be the critical distinction between the concept of a code and the traditional view of associations.

In terms of human learning and behavior the major value of a coding model (as opposed to an associative model) of what is learned is in its ability to account for the learning and production of well-integrated high-speed behavior sequences. In particular, the model can handle several, if not all, of the specific issues that Lashley (1951) indicated were particularly troublesome for associative models. Among these are: (*a*) a generative plan (schema) that is self sustaining and represents both order and item information; (*b*) a characterization of order information that is not dependent upon a feedback mechanism; (*c*) a means of increasing the availability of response items before they are produced; and (*d*) a means whereby subjects would be able to spontaneously reorganize highly overlearned sequences without experiencing interference.

In this regard, it is interesting to note that the mechanisms that allow the model to account for these issues also imply that the pattern of encoding for a sequence should represent both the item information and much of the order information. That is, the model implies that if subjects encounter a task in which they are required to learn the pattern of encoding for a sequence, but are not required to learn the items or their order, the item and order information would be learned as completely and as efficiently as if the task required such learning. Both the Martin (1972) and the Marmurek (1972) experiments support that implication. These data, along with those of Bower and Winzenz (1969) and Johnson and Migdoll (1971), focus attention on the intimate relationship between organizing and learning, and they support the use of a coding relationship as a basic construct within which to understand learning.

REFERENCES

Battig, W. F. Paired-associate learning. In T. R. Dixon & D. L. Horton (Eds.), *Verbal behavior and general behavior theory*. Englewood Cliffs, N.J.: Prentice-Hall, 1968. Pp. 146-171.

Birnbaum, I. M. Free-recall learning as a function of prior-list organization. *Journal of Verbal Learning and Verbal Behavior*, 1968, 7, 1037-1042.

Birnbaum, I. M. Prior-list organization in part-whole free-recall learning. *Journal of Verbal Learning and Verbal Behavior*, 1969, 8, 836-837.

Bousfield, W. A. The occurrence of clustering in the recall of randomly arranged associates. *Journal of General Psychology*, 1953, 49, 229-240.

Bower, G. H., & Lesgold, A. M. Organization as a determinant of part-to-whole transfer in free recall. *Journal of Verbal Learning and Verbal Behavior*, 1969, 8, 501-506.

Bower, G. H., & Winzenz, D. Group structure, coding, and memory for digit series. *Journal of Experimental Psychology Monograph*, 1969, 80, (May, Pt. 2), 1-17.

Brown, J. Some tests of the decay theory of immediate memory. *Quarterly Journal of Experimental Psychology*, 1958, 10, 12-21.

Cofer, C. N. On some factors in the organizational characteristics of free recall. *American Psychologist*, 1965, 20, 261-272.

Cofer, C. N. Some evidence for coding processes derived from clustering in free recall. *Journal of Verbal Learning and Verbal Behavior*, 1966, 5, 188-192.

Cofer, C. N. Conditions for the use of verbal associations. *Psychological Bulletin*, 1967, 68, 1-12.

Cohen, B. H. Some-or-none characteristics of coding. *Journal of Verbal Learning and Verbal Behavior*, 1966, 5, 182-187.

DeRosa, D. V., Doane, D. S., & Russell, B. The influence of first-list organization on second-list free-recall learning. *Journal of Verbal Learning and Verbal Behavior*, 1970, 9, 269-273.

Fritzen, J. D., & Johnson, N. F. Definiteness of pattern ending and the uniformity of pattern size: Their effects on learning number sequences. *Journal of Verbal Learning and Verbal Behavior*, 1969, 8, 575-580.

Jenkins, J. J., & Russell, W. A. Associative clustering during recall. *Journal of Abnormal and Social Psychology*, 1952, 47, 818-821.

Johnson, N. F. The psychological reality of phrase structure rules. *Journal of Verbal Learning and Verbal Behavior*, 1965, 4, 486-475;

Johnson, N. F. Sequential verbal behavior. In T. R. Dixon & D. L. Horton (Eds.), *Verbal behavior and general behavior theory*. Englewood Cliffs, N.J.: Prentice-Hall, 1968. Pp. 421-450.

Johnson, N. F. Chunking: Associative chaining versus coding. *Journal of Verbal Learning and Verbal Behavior*, 1969, 8, 725-731.

Johnson, N. F. Chunking and organization in the process of recall. In G. H. Bower (Ed.), *The psychology of learning and motivation*, Vol. 4. New York: Academic Press, 1970. Pp. 171-247.

Johnson, N. F., & Migdoll, D. M. Transfer and retroaction under conditions of changed organization. *Cognitive Psychology*, 1971, 2, 229-237.

Keeney, T. J. Permutation transformations on phrase structures in letter sequences. *Journal of Experimental Psychology*, 1969, 82, 28-33.

Lashley, K. S. The problem of serial order in behavior. In L. A. Jeffress (Ed.), *Cerebral mechanisms in behavior*. New York: Wiley, 1951. Pp. 112-136.

Lehiste, I. Acoustic studies of boundary signals. *Proceedings of the Fourth International Congress of Phonetic Sciences*, 1962, 178-187.

Lehiste, I. Juncture. *Proceedings of the Fifth International Congress of Phonetic Sciences*, 1964, 172-200.

Lehiste, I. The temporal organization of higher-level linguistic units. Paper presented at the meeting of the Acoustical Society of America, Atlantic City, April, 1970. (a)

Lehiste, I. The quest for phonetic reality. In A. Bronstein, C. Shaver, & C. Stevens (Eds.), *Essays in honor of Claude M. Wise*. Hannibal, Mo.: Standard Printing Co., 1970. Pp. 25-35. (b)

Lehiste, I. The temporal realization of morphological and syntactic boundaries. *Journal of the Acoustical Society of America*, 1971, 50, 116.

Lehiste, I., & Peterson, G. Some allophones of /1/ in American English. *Journal of the Acoustical Society of America*, 1960, 32, 914.

Lenneberg, E. *Biological foundations of language*. New York: Wiley, 1967.

Liberman, A. M., Cooper, F. S., Shankweiler, D. P., & Studdert-Kennedy, M. Perception of the speech code. *Psychological Review*, 1967, 74, 431-461.

MacNeilage, P. F. Motor control of serial ordering of speech. *Psychological Review*, 1970, 77, 182-196.

Mandler, G. Organization and memory. In K. W. Spence & J. T. Spence (Eds.), *The psychology of learning and motivation*, Vol. 1. New York: Academic Press, 1967, Pp. 327-372.

Mandler, G. Association and organization: Facts, fancies, and theories. In T. R. Dixon & D. L. Horton (Eds.), *Verbal behavior and general behavior theory*. Englewood Cliffs, N.J.: Prentice-Hall, 1968. Pp. 109-120.

Marmurek, H. H. C. The relationship between organizing and learning: On the use of hierarchical organizations. Unpublished master's thesis, The Ohio State University, 1972.

Marshall, G. R. Stimulus characteristics contributing to organization in free recall. *Journal of Verbal Learning and Verbal Behavior*, 1967, 6, 364-374.

Martin, J. R. The relationship between organizing and learning: The role of structural balance and necessity to memorize. Unpublished master's thesis, The Ohio State University, 1972.

McLean, R. S., & Gregg, L. W. Effects of induced chunking on temporal aspects of serial recitation. *Journal of Experimental Psychology*, 1967, 74, 455-459.

Miller, G. A. The magical number seven plus or minus two: Some limits on our capacity for processing information. *Psychological Review*, 1956, 63, 81-97. (a)

Miller, G. A. Human memory and the storage of information. *IRE Transactions on Information Theory*, 1956, IT-2, 129-137. (b)

Miller, G. A. Free recall of redundant strings of letters. *Journal of Experimental Psychology*, 1958, 56, 484-491.

Miller, G. A., & Selfridge, J. Verbal context and the recall of meaningful material. *American Journal of Psychology*, 1950, 63, 176-185.

Öhman, S. E. G. Coarticulation in VCV utterances: Spectrographic measurements. *Journal of the Acoustical Society of America*, 1966, 39, 151-168.

Osgood, C. E. The similarity paradox in human learning: A resolution. *Psychological Review*, 1949, 56, 132-143.

Peterson, J. A. A comparison of normal and mentally retarded children on a paired-associate task using letters with and without a suggested break. Unpublished master's thesis, The Ohio State University, 1968.

Peterson, L. R., & Peterson, M. J. Short-term retention of individual verbal items. *Journal of Experimental Psychology*, 1959, 58, 193-198.

Pike, K. L. Grammatical prerequisites to phonemic analysis. *Word*, 1947, 3, 155-172.

Postman, L. Association and performance in the analysis of verbal learning. In T. R. Dixon & D. L. Horton (Eds.), *Verbal behavior and general behavior theory*. Englewood Cliffs, N.J.: Prentice-Hall, 1968. Pp. 551-571.

Postman, L. Organization and interference. *Psychological Review*, 1971, 78, 290-302.

Rosen, E., & Russell, W. A. Frequency-characteristics of successive word-association. *American Journal of Psychology*, 1957, 70, 120-122.

Ryan, J. Grouping and short-term memory: Different means and patterns of grouping. *Quarterly Journal of Experimental Psychology*, 1969, 21, 137-147.

Shepard, R. N., & Teghtsoonian, M. Retention of information under conditions approaching a steady state. *Journal of Experimental Psychology*, 1961, 62, 302-309.

Shuell, T. J. Retroactive inhibition in free-recall learning of categorized lists. *Journal of Verbal Learning and Verbal Behavior*, 1968, 7, 797-805.

Tulving, E. Subjective organization in free recall of "unrelated" words. *Psychological Review*, 1962, 69, 344-354.

Tulving, E. Intertrial and intratrial retention: Notes toward a theory of free recall verbal learning. *Psychological Review*, 1964, 71, 219-237.

Tulving, E. Subjective organization and the effects of repetition in multitrial free recall learning. *Journal of Verbal Learning and Verbal Behavior*, 1966, 5, 193-197.

Wickelgren, W. A. Size of rehearsal group and short-term memory. *Journal of Experimental Psychology*, 1964, 68, 413-419.

Wickelgren, W. A. Rehearsal grouping and the hierarchical organization of serial position cues in short-term memory. *Quarterly Journal of Experimental Psychology*, 1967, 19, 97-102.

Wood, G., & Underwood, B. J. Implicit responses and conceptual similarity. *Journal of Verbal Learning and Verbal Behavior,* 1967, 6, 1-10.

Yngve, V. H. A model and an hypothesis for language structure. *Proceedings of the American Philosophical Society,* 1960, 104, 444-466.

7

AN ASSOCIATIVE BASIS FOR CODING AND ORGANIZATION IN MEMORY[1]

W. K. Estes
The Rockefeller University

Taking together the facts that a great part of what we know about human memory has grown out of research conducted within the broad aegis of association theory and that research on memory is currently flourishing as never before, one might well be led to ask why some new type of theory should be contemplated. One reason, which becomes abundantly clear on reading a number of the other papers in this volume, is that many phenomena, and particularly those falling on the fringe area between learning and psycholinguistics, seem to call for a theory with much richer conceptual structure than that of traditional associationism.

We will doubtless see continuing attempts to meet the changing demands simply by modifying the basic concepts of association theory. But the resulting multiplicity of memory traces and varieties of connections quickly becomes cumbersome to work with and may be basically ill adapted to deal with phenomena of organization. Further, many investigators have been impressed by the number of conspicuous features of perception and memory not readily handled by extant associative models, which suggest the involvement of some kind of coding process.

Take, for example, current work on memory for strings of letters. When retention is imperfect, the confusion errors that occur are highly systematic. But the patterns of substitution errors are predictable, not from analyses of the stimulus inputs on physical dimensions, but rather from analyses in terms of critical features revealed by linguistic research and theory. Indeed many specific predictions can be made simply on the basis of the phonemes that are shared by pairs of letters.

Thus it is clear that of the information input generated when a letter is heard or read, a great part is discarded in the perceptual processing and what is retained is just sufficient to identify the constituent phonemes (and perhaps a few other

[1] Research reported herein was supported in part by USPHS Grant GM16735 from the National Institute of General Medical Sciences.

acoustic features). What is stored in memory is evidently not a multiplicity of connections between all aspects of the complex input pattern and the response made at the time, but rather a coded representation which suffices to specify at the time of recognition or recall which member of the set of possible patterns occurred.

A new question arises. If concepts of coding are as promising as indicated by some of these findings, why should we not simply scratch association theory and construct a new theory based on concepts of coding and information processing, as suggested, for example, by Johnson (1970)? If there is indeed any reason why we should not, it might lie in the possibility that the conception of coding is useful for dealing with what is remembered but has less to offer with regard to dynamics of forgetting. Perhaps the most promising theory would be one drawing upon both associative and coding models. The present paper is addressed to this possibility.

To show more specifically the considerations which seem to demand a new, hybrid theory, I should like now to review in some detail a particular research topic which has been central to some of the developments briefly alluded to above, namely, experimentation on short-term memory for serial order. The three questions to be addressed are: (a) Just what do we know about short-term memory for order of events? (b) Will any extant theory, based either on associative or on coding principles, handle the range of established phenomena? And (c) if the attempt seems indicated, how might ideas of association and coding be combined into a viable theory that amplifies the advantages of both traditions rather than compounding the limitations?

A starting point for much of the more analytical research on coding in short-term memory has been the familiar experiment on memory span for random strings of digits or letters. Without reviewing the considerable earlier literature, I can assume it well known to readers of the present volume that an individual can substantially increase retention for a digit or character string if the string is subdivided into groups or "chunks" of three to five characters separated by pauses, either upon input or during rehearsal immediately following input. Also I shall assume familiarity with Miller's (1956) paper concerning limitations on immediate memory capacity and the concept of chunking, and with the recent substantial review and augmentation of the literature on this concept by Johnson (1970). The special relevance of this line of research for the present volume is the view, developed in most detail by Johnson, that grouping or chunking of character strings simplifies the learner's task by permitting him to assign codes to the subgroups of a sequence, so that he then need only remember the smaller set of codes which can be decoded on a later occasion in order to reconstruct the entire sequence.

Granting the essential soundness of this general conception of coding as a means of organizing material in memory, I wish to direct interest to the question of precisely where in the chain of events constituting a short-term memory experiment the recoding of information occurs. Further, I should like to elucidate the detailed processes involved and their relation to or bases in associative learning processes.

ORDER AND ITEM INFORMATION IN MEMORY
FOR CHARACTER STRINGS

Empirical Relationships

As a preliminary to discussion of theoretical issues I should like to summarize what I believe we know at present concerning the separate representation and short-term retention of order and item information. There is no question but that the experimenter can at will score the subject's recall protocol either simply on the basis of the number of items of the input string which are included or on the basis of the number of these which occur in their correct serial positions. But whether or not data obtained by the two scoring procedures reflect different memory processes is presently a controversial question (Bjork & Healy, 1970; Conrad, 1964; Johnson, 1970). One of the most directly relevant sources of information should be a picture of the time course of retention loss for the two types of information. To my surprise I have found little information concerning this basic problem in the literature. Quite likely, others are able to fill out my background in this respect but in the meantime I shall summarize principal results of a series of recent studies conducted in my laboratory employing variations on the experimental paradigm employed by Conrad (1967).

In this experimental paradigm each trial consists in the presentation to the subject of a string of four letters followed by a sequence of random numbers and then a recall test. The letters and numbers are presented visually and appear singly all in the same location, specifically a single Binaview cell. In what I shall term the standard procedure, the characters are presented at a rate of 2.5 characters per second, with no perceptible blank interval between characters; the interval between the last letter of the string and the recall test is filled by a random sequence of digits also appearing at the rate of 2.5 characters per second. The subjects are required to pronounce aloud the name of each letter in the string as it appears and also the name of each random digit. This rate of presentation is sufficiently taxing so that verbal rehearsal of the letter string during the retention interval is virtually impossible.

At the end of the retention interval the subject attempts to recall the four letters of the string and enter these in their proper order in the four boxes on an answer card. In the experiment of Conrad (1967) subjects were required to fill in all four boxes on each trial, guessing when necessary. In the first of our experiments that I shall discuss (Estes, 1969), a replication and extension of Conrad's experiment, the procedure differed only in that subjects were instructed to leave a box blank rather than making random guesses if they had no memory for a particular letter.

The four letter strings used by Conrad and in my 1969 study were all drawn without replacement from a set of 10 consonants which may be categorized into three groups (BCPTV, FSX, and MN) having the characteristic that the letters within each of the subsets are more acoustically confusable with each other than with letters outside the subset.

In treating the data I shall define any overt error as an acoustic confusion error if the letter actually presented at a particular position in a string has been replaced in the subject's protocol by another letter belonging to the same subset and a nonconfusion error as one in which the letter presented has been replaced by any letter outside that subset. Also I shall use an orthogonal categorization of transposition versus nontransposition errors, a transposition error being defined as one in which the letter which was presented at a particular position in a string has been replaced in the subject's protocol by a letter which appeared at some other position in the same string. Transposition errors provide our principal means of tracing changes in retention of order information. Confusion errors may reflect imperfect memory for either order or content, but the combined category of nontransposition-confusion errors specifically measures loss of item information.

In our extension of the Conrad experiment[2] seven subjects, all students or affiliates of Rockefeller University, were tested. For each subject a set of 21 four-letter strings was assigned to each of five retention intervals, the recall test being given after 3, 6, 12, 18, or 30 intervening random digit presentations. The different recall intervals were intermixed in a random sequence for each subject. The aspects of the data of immediate interest are presented in Figure 1 in the form of separate retention curves for the four categories of overt errors formed by combining the confusion-nonconfusion (AC, NC) and transposition-nontransposition (T, NT) categories.

In general the retention curve for each type of overt error increases to a peak and then declines, with a clear tendency for the curves for transposition errors within both the confusion and nonconfusion categories to rise more rapidly than the curves for nontransposition errors. Most striking is the sharp early peak for the combined confusion-transposition category. However, within both the confusion and nonconfusion categories considered separately, there is a heavy preponderance of transposition errors, of the order of 2 or 3 to 1, at the shortest retention intervals, shifting gradually over to a slight preponderance of nontransposition errors at the longest intervals. The same trends appeared in an experiment by Bjork and Healy (1970) utilizing the same general procedures but a somewhat different design in terms of confusion sets of letters.

Since it is also the case that the ratio of confusion to nonconfusion errors shifts systematically during the course of retention, from a heavy preponderance of acoustic confusions at the short intervals to a preponderance of nonconfusions at the long intervals, one might wonder whether there is a causal relationship between acoustic confusions and transpositions (as suggested by Conrad, 1964). Some light is shed on this question by a later experiment of mine (Estes, 1970a) which replicated the first experiment in all essentials except that the subjects were not permitted to vocalize the names of the letters or digits as they appeared.[3] In this experiment the ratio of acoustic confusion to nonconfusion errors was constant over retention intervals, but nonetheless within each confusion category the ratio

---

[2] Conducted in collaboration with Elizabeth Bjork, Alice Fenvessy Healy, Owen Floody, and Peter Waser at Rockefeller University.

[3] Instead they were required to say "high" or "low" to each letter according as it fell in the first or second half of the alphabet, and to each digit according as it fell in the first or second half of the digits 0 through 9.

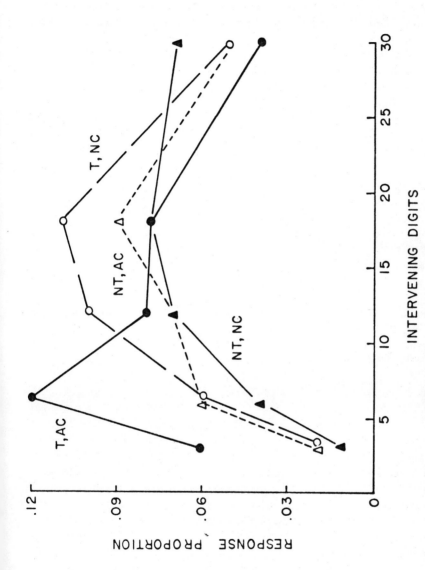

FIG. 1. Proportions of four types of overt errors (T, AC: transposition, acoustic confusion; T, NC: transposition, nonconfusion; NT, AC: nontransposition, acoustic confusion; NT, NC: nontransposition, nonconfusion) as a function of number of random digit presentations between input and recall (from Estes, 1969).

of transpositions to nontranspositions shifted from nearly 2 to 1 at the shortest retention interval to virtual equality at the longest interval.

Although the forgetting of order and item information can be dissociated to a degree by the different time course of retention loss for measures of these two types of information, there is also clear evidence of an intimate relationship between the acoustic confusability of any two letters and the likelihood that a transposition error will occur if they are both present in the same display. This relationship was noted by Conrad (1964), but the study of Bjork and Healy (1970) was much better controlled for purposes of relevant analyses than either Conrad's or my own. Bjork and Healy's data show convincingly, first, that the great majority of acoustic confusion errors involve two letters which were present in the same string; but, secondly, within the small proportion of overt errors occurring at short retention intervals which do not involve transpositions (that is, which reflect loss only of item information), in the great majority of cases the letter substituted for the correct letter in a string belongs to the same acoustic confusion set.

Several experiments utilizing differing materials, procedures, and measures have yielded similarly clear-cut interactions between order versus item information loss and other experimental variables. In an experiment reported by Wickelgren (1965) subjects attempted ordered recall of strings of nine consonants presented auditorily at a rate of three per second. Recall was poorer for strings of acoustically similar consonants (those sharing a common vowel phoneme) than for dissimilar strings, but the difference was attributable entirely to the greater incidence of transposition errors involving acoustically similar letters in the phonemically similar strings; the number of letters recalled correctly without regard to position did not differ significantly for the two types of strings. Up to a point an analogous result was obtained for recall of strings of seven consonant-vowel digrams; transposition errors were significantly more frequent for strings in which all the digrams had a common vowel than in dissimilar strings, but item recall was actually significantly better for the similar strings.

Serial position curves provide especially distinct differences in the retention of item and order information both as a function of position and in the way the serial position curve changes with retention interval. We should perhaps expect the simplest case, from a theoretical standpoint, to arise in data from the letter string experiment. Since the relatively rapid presentation rate and the requirement of pronouncing each character effectively preclude rehearsal, and since each letter string is followed by a sequence of random digits, the factors of selective rehearsal and sensory persistence, which have been implicated as major determiners of the primacy and recency segments of the serial position curve in other short-term memory experiments, are eliminated; and we might expect any remaining position function to reflect more intrinsic processes having to do with the storage and retrieval of information.

The experiment by Bjork and Healy (1970), which employed the standard procedure, yields the serial position functions for transposition and nontransposition errors separately shown in Figure 2. Clearly the increase in errors at the interior positions two and three of the 4-letter string, yielding the familiar bowed curve, is more accentuated in the functions for transposition errors, which represent

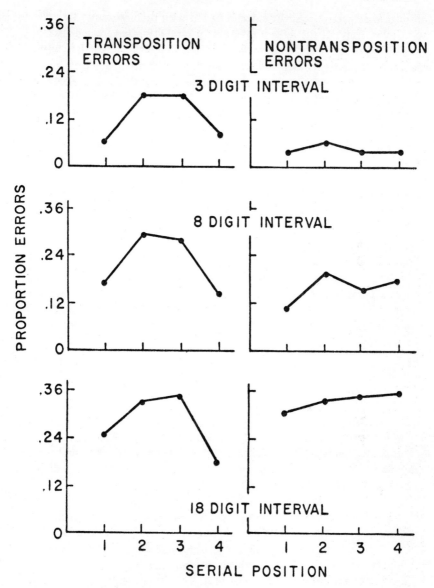

FIG. 2. Serial position curves for transposition (left column) and nontransposition (right column) errors (from Bjork & Healy, 1970).

solely loss of order information, than for nontransposition errors, which represent solely loss of item information. If we obtain a single composite measure of total item information retained by adding correct responses and transposition errors at each position (thus achieving essentially the same result as rescoring the protocols by a free recall criterion), the functions obtained are conspicuously flat: at the shortest retention interval (3 intervening digits), .97, .94, .97, .97, for positions 1 through 4 respectively; slightly declining but with no bow shape, .69, .66, .65, and .64, respectively, at the longest retention interval (18 intervening digits).

Confirmation of the picture for transposition errors, together with a useful additional analysis, is available from a study by Healy (1971) utilizing the same procedures and retention intervals as those of the Bjork and Healy study but employing a single set of four consonants which was randomly repermuted to generate the letter strings for all trials; this set was known to the subjects from the beginning so only transposition errors were possible on recall tests. Whereas in the Bjork and Healy study half of the trials for each subject used letter strings containing two acoustically confusable letters and half used strings including no acoustically confusable letters, the same division was obtained by utilizing independent groups of subjects in the single set experiment. In both experiments the serial position functions were very similar in form for the confusable and nonconfusable strings.

For the experiment involving a vocabulary of only four letters, Healy also constructed distance functions showing the probability that the letter which was entered by the subject at a given position in his recall protocol for a trial was the letter which appeared at the same position in the display (hence a correct response) or was a letter from a position 1, 2, or 3 characters removed in the display (hence a transposition error). These functions, pooled over subjects and conditions at each retention interval are shown in Figure 3. Two aspects of these functions are noteworthy. The first is the orderliness of the gradients, an error which occurs in any position being more likely to represent the intrusion of a letter belonging at a neighboring position than a letter belonging at a more remote position. The second is the conspicuous symmetry with respect to temporal position. The functions at each retention interval for the third panel, in which position 3 is correct, could be folded over and placed on top of the corresponding functions for the second panel, in which position 2 is correct, yielding strikingly close agreement of the superimposed values. Almost the same is true of the fourth panel and the first, the only deviation from symmetry being the slight across the board difference in correct responses at positions 1 and 4.

The possibility that these relationships involving position are of considerable generality is suggested by the closeness with which they are confirmed in another experimental context differing in numerous particulars. A study reported by Fuchs (1969) required subjects to recall strings of four-letter nouns which were presented simultaneously on slides, the subject reading the words aloud, then counting backward for the prescribed interval of 4, 8, or 16 seconds before the recall test. Recall was cued by the appearance of a symbol on the screen indicating the positon on the previous slide from which recall was to be attempted. Serial position curves for transposition errors, which comprised approximately 56% of all errors, were similar in form to those of the letter string studies, whereas errors reflecting only loss of item information yielded a distinctly shallower gradient when recall was tested following a single presentation of the string and entirely flat gradients when recall was not tested until after two or three repetitions of the string. Distance functions for strings having the correct response at different serial positions showed the same conspicuous symmetry as those of Healy's letter string study. Orderly

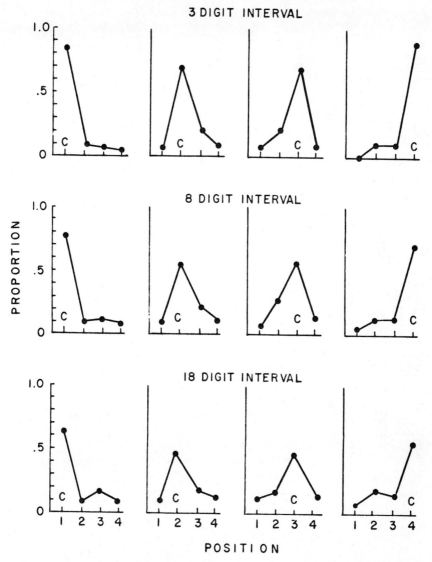

FIG. 3. Distance functions for Healy (1971) study. The point plotted for position *i* of any panel represents the proportion of instances in which the response occurring in the position marked C on the subject's answer card was the letter appearing at position *i* of the string for the given trial.

distance functions have been obtained by Murdock and vom Saal (1967), with three-letter words as items, but their analysis did not provide evidence on symmetry.

It might be remarked that the data of Fuchs's study agree with those of Wickelgren (1967) and Johnson (1970), among others, in exhibiting positional constancy of intrusion errors across strings. That is, when the subject made an error by replacing the word which had appeared at a particular position in a string with a word which had appeared in a preceding string, with significantly greater than chance frequency the incorrect word came from the same serial position as the correct one.

Differences in the handling of order and item information appear also in experiments in which the subject is led to group the elements of a string into subgroups or "chunks." In a study reported by Wickelgren (1967), strings of 8, 9, or 10 digits were presented to subjects at the rate of one per second with instructions to group the digits into chunks of one to five digits under different conditions. Item recall was affected only slightly by size of the rehearsal group, but a measure of order information (the probability that a digit from a string was given at the correct position if recalled at all) increased to maximum at rehearsal group size three and decreased at group sizes four and five.

The massive supply of data showing that under the conditions of this last study recall tends strongly to be organized in terms of the rehearsal groups will doubtless be well covered in other contributions to this volume. For completeness I would like here to mention only a few aspects of these data that will be particularly relevant to the theoretical interpretation of order effects. Contingency functions for recall of successive serial positions in a string show marked discontinuities at subgroup boundaries. That is, if a subject gives a correct recall response for the item at position i of a string, he has a very low probability of making an error at the next position if it falls within the same rehearsal subgroup, but a much higher probability of making an error if the next position falls in a different subgroup (see for example, Johnson, 1970, and Wickelgren, 1969). Secondly, if a particular string is repeated many times at irregular intervals during an experiment with a single subject, the proportion of letters recalled increases steadily over repetitions only if the mode of subgrouping remains constant from one repetition to the next (Bower & Winzenz, 1969). Finally, Johnson (1969, 1970) has shown that in a number of respects a subgroup which the subject has been led to treat as a chunk tends to behave as a unit in recall. In Johnson's basic paradigm, a sequence of three subgroups of three letters each is presented to the subject, then prior to recall a sequence is presented in which one of the subgroups is unchanged but the others undergo changes, either the substitution of a letter from outside the presented string at some position or the interchange of letters at two positions in the subgroup. When recall of the original string is determined by a modified free recall procedure, retention of the unchanged subgroup is characteristically found to be fully as good as that of a control condition in which there was no interpolated presentation but recall of both changed and unchanged letters in the changed subgroup is severely depressed.

Interpretation of Order Effects

The rather substantial body of clear-cut and replicable factual information concerning order effects in short-term memory now available should, it seems, set the stage for a commensurate effort toward theoretical interpretation. Indeed a number of initial efforts, stemming from quite diverse premises, have appeared in the literature and I should like now to review these briefly and to point out what seem to be the strong points and limitations of each.

Coding. The most explicit and empirically documented coding hypothesis appears to be that of Johnson (1969, 1970). He proposes that in short-term memory for a sequence of characters grouped into chunks, the individual assigns a code to each chunk and then need only retain the codes in memory over the retention interval. The code for each chunk is assumed to be unique and to contain all of the item and order information contained in the chunk, yet at the same time to be "opaque" in the sense that even when the individual has recalled the code for a particular chunk, information about the items in the chunk is not available to him until he has carried out decoding operations. Some of the general features of the chunking of material in memory that are expressed in the idea of coding certainly are well established. In particular, Johnson's own research using his retroactive inhibition paradigm provides considerable evidence regarding the independence of retention loss for material in different chunks and for the selective disruption of chunks by interpolated training procedures.

The all-or-none loss of information by chunks which might be taken to be implied by the coding concept does not entirely come off, however, as witness the substantial differences in recall for changed and unchanged letters within altered chunks (Johnson, 1969).

The principal difficulty I find with the coding hypothesis at present is that the specific processes involved in assigning codes and, even more importantly, decoding at the time of recall are largely unspecified and it is difficult to foresee the extent to which they may turn out to differ from those entailed by, say, an associative theory. It seems beyond question that the retention of character strings involves some process that can be characterized as the assignment of codes to subgroups. But I must confess that at present the additional idea that the code includes all of the information in a subgroup and that the individual carries in memory a set of operations adequate fully to recover all of the information in a chunk given only the code seems to me extremely elaborate and possibly even more complex than the phenomena it is supposed to explain. For the moment I am inclined to use freely when convenient the term "code" to refer to the assignment of a tag or label to a subgroup of a character string but to turn primary attention to the possibility of elucidating the detailed processes involved by concepts drawn from more general theories of learning and memory.

Interitem association. A rather simplistic rendition of classical association theory would interpret the memory for a letter string in terms of formation of an association between the first letter and the signal for recall, the second letter with the first, the third letter with the second, and so on. The inadequacy of any scheme of this sort as a general theory of serial order was demonstrated to the satisfaction of most psychologists by Lashley in his 1951 paper. With respect to the type of experiment under consideration, one particularly severe difficulty arises from the consideration that the letters in any particular string would already have strongly established associations as a result of previous experience of the subject outside the laboratory and that a single trial in a short-term memory experiment could do little to alter the strengths of these associations.

One might attempt to rescue the theory by appealing to the same distinction between short- and long-term memory that is seen in many contemporary models. It might be assumed that long-term associations are suppressed by an overall set in a short-term memory experiment and that strong but transient associations are set up as a result of a single presentation. A theory of this sort seems, however, to run into a pyramiding of difficulties as one attempts to apply it to specific phenomena. Firstly, the retention curves in the letter string experiments do not appear to approach zero, or chance levels of responding asymptotically; and to the extent that the associations formed within a trial are not entirely transient, the old problems with the theory reemerge. Secondly, one could not account for the orderly distance gradients for intrusion errors as a function of distance from the serial position of the correct letter, except perhaps by complicating the scheme greatly with the assumption of remote associations between the letter in any serial position and those not only adjacent but in more remote serial positions. It is very difficult, however, to imagine how such a scheme could account for the observed symmetry of the distance functions; or how it would be made to predict that repetitions of the string would lead to improved recall only if the mode of grouping of characters was constant from trial to trial (Bower & Winzenz, 1969); or how it could be made to jibe with Johnson's findings that interference with the middle letter of a three-letter group (in a retroactive inhibition paradigm) produces no more impairment in recall of the first and third letters than interference with the first or the third letter produces in the remaining two (Johnson, 1969, 1970).

Finally, there is considerable reason to doubt whether associations of any sort form or are strengthened between adjacent characters in the type of experiment under consideration. The well known experiments of Thorndike (1931) on "belongingness" yielded negative evidence regarding formation of associations between adjacent members of a list when the individual is not instructed to attend to or rehearse relations between them. Similarly, Lesgold and Bower (1970) studied the relation between learning of a serial list and subsequent learning of paired associates in which stimulus and response members of each pair were successive items from the serial list. Positive transfer was found only when the subjects had been instructed concerning the relationship between the tasks.

Coding on a temporal attribute. A possibility to be considered is that recall for order of a sequence of items is simply a by-product of the individual's ability to remember the times at which the individual items occurred. The idea that each item which is stored in memory is identified by a "time-tag" has recurred frequently in the literature since it was applied by Yntema and Trask (1963) to the interpretation of a study in which subjects were asked at various points during a session to judge which of two words had appeared earlier in the series being presented. More recently, Underwood (1969) has reviewed the evidence for a temporal attribute in the coding of events in memory and has concluded that it can be distinguished from the concept of strength of a memory trace based on recency.

The conception of time tags, in the sense of positioning events on a continuous temporal attribute, seems never to have been elaborated to the point that one can really come to grips with it. Further, on the basis of available information concerning order effects in short-term memory, this theoretical direction does not appear very promising. Surely any reasonable theory of this type would imply that discrimination is easier between two events with a given temporal separation if both occur more recently, with the implication that serial position functions for order information should be skewed in the direction favoring higher proportions of correct responding at the more recent positions, and a similar skewing should appear in distance functions. However, neither of these effects is manifest in the data of the relevant studies cited above. But, although it seems reasonably clear that direct tagging of items of a temporal dimension could not suffice to account for order effects in memory, the possibility should be kept in mind that a representation of this kind may exist in very-short-term memory, the information being recoded in some other form for longer term storage.

Positional coding. A conception of "position tags" seems considerably more workable than that of time tags. An associative mechanism to accomplish this coding is immediately at hand, in that the learner might associate each successive item of a sequence with an ordinal number, 1, 2, 3, ... This process, or at least a formal equivalent, appears to be required for Johnson's (1970) conception of coding, in which full information concerning order of items is embodied in the code for a "chunk," and also in Conrad's (1964, 1965) outline of a model for short-term retention. The associations of items of a string with ordinal numbers would immediately account for a number of the qualitative facts about retention of order information; in particular, the assumption of associations between items and ordinal numbers would yield a direct prediction of the tendency for intrusion errors between strings presented on different trials of a short-term memory experiment to occur at the serial position of the intruding item.

However, a number of questions can be raised about the conception of positional encoding which are not easy to answer. Firstly, how could one account for the orderly distance functions, in which probability of an order error involving any two items within a display is inversely related to the number of intervening items? A rather speculative possibility, suggested by Underwood (1969) among others, is that representations of the items of a string might be projected onto a spatial array at some level of the nervous system, so that the encoding of order information would arise from association of each item with its spatial position rather than with an ordinal number. This assumption would immediately have to be augmented to account for Wickelgren's (1967) finding that, whereas retention of item information is relatively constant over size of rehearsal groups, retention of order information varies according to a distinct nonmonotonic function with a maximum at rehearsal group size three. Evidently the spatial representation would have to be of limited informational capacity with only the categories of end and interior positions being clearly discriminable.

This last observation leads in turn to the question of how the different courses of retention loss for item and order information could be handled. Conrad (1964, 1967) has circumvented this question by denying that there is any separate representation of order and item information in memory at all. He suggests that, in effect, the incoming items of a string are coded with respect to position, as though they are deposited in a series of boxes or slots, and that forgetting is solely a matter of loss of item information. Transposition errors arise, according to Conrad, when the items in some pair of positions have suffered partial loss of information so that in choosing his responses for these slots on the answer card the subject guesses either from the two corresponding responses, or at least from a small subset including these and others auditorily confused with them. However, Conrad's scheme seems quantitatively quite inadequate to account for the observed heavy incidence of transposition errors in short-term memory (e.g., Bjork & Healy, 1970) and, further, provides no hint as to why the observed rate of loss of order information should be distinctly faster than that of item information.

Finally, a question which goes to the heart of a positional encoding interpretation is that of why severe impairment of recall should be observed for the unchanged letters in changed subgroups in Johnson's (1969) experiments on recall of grouped letter sequences.

In summary, an adequate interpretation of retention of order information must account for the high accuracy of recall for order at very short intervals, for the differential rates of loss or order and item information, for grouping effects, together with the sensitivity of retention of order information to disruption by changes at any point within a subgroup, and for the orderly serial position and distance functions with their distinctly different forms and different interactions with retention interval for measures of item and order information. None of the types of theory reviewed seems close to achieving this task. Nonetheless, several of them include ingredients which may be needed in an adequate theory.

A PROVISIONAL ASSOCIATIVE MODEL FOR STIMULUS CODING

Since neither classical association theory nor coding schemes so far developed come close to providing an adequate interpretation of order effects in short-term memory, I should like now to explore the idea of formulating a theory embodying some of the concepts and assumptions of these two hitherto disparate traditions. It is not easy to choose which type of model to make the basis for further development since the ideas of coding seem the more natural for interpreting structural characteristics and those of association theory for interpreting changes as a function of time or trials. Perhaps partly out of habit, but partly also because I can better envisage how to relate the results to other aspects of learning theory, I shall follow the strategy of attempting to revise and augment the concepts of association theory so as to incorporate some of the insights arising from analyses in terms of coding.

Since in the preceding review of empirical phenomena the weakest aspect of association theory appears to be the conception of interitem associations as the basis for organization, this is the point at which I propose to introduce a new conception to bring the associative model more nearly into line with ideas coming from coding theory. The principal new concept to be introduced is that of a *control element*.

Control Elements as the Basis of Associative Structures

Quite generally in the literature of association theory I believe, and certainly in my own interpretations of human learning (Estes, 1970b), it is assumed that as a consequence of an individual's experiencing a sequence of stimuli, for example, letters or words in a short-term memory experiment, representations of these stimuli are set up in his memory system (presumably somewhere in the brain although I shall not speculate as to specific localization). Associations between these stimulus elements, perhaps more aptly termed memory elements, provide the basis for retention.

The new assumption to be explored is that there is available in the memory system also a pool of elements which we may term control elements. Suppose that an individual experiences in close temporal conjunction two elementary stimuli, say two critical features of an auditorily presented letter. Denoting the representations of these two features in the memory system by f_1 and f_2, the resulting associative structure in terms of classical association theory would be simply

$$f_1 - f_2,$$

whereas in the new theory it would be

$$\overset{\textstyle C}{\overset{\displaystyle \diagup \diagdown}{f_1 \quad f_2}}$$

where C denotes a control element. The learning which results from the contiguous occurrence of the two stimuli is conceived in the new theory to be, not the establishment of association between them, but rather of an association of each with a control element. The sense of the term *association* is much the same as in classical theory. If following the establishment of this elementary associative structure, the control element is activated from some motivational source (for example an instruction to recall), the result is the reactivation of the representations of the two associated features in memory and the evocation of the corresponding articulatory responses. A rather similar structure, but without a specific associational mechanism, has been suggested by Lesgold and Bower (1970) in connection with serial list learning.

Even a minimal short-term memory experiment involves a presentation of a sequence of letters each comprising a number of critical features. In representing the memory structure set up by such an input, I wish to assume firstly that a new control element is established at each discontinuity in the input sequence. The discontinuities may result from the input procedure, as those between letters in a string or between words in a sequence, or they may be generated by the subject when he groups or "chunks" subsets of letters together in rehearsal.

As a result of groupings induced either by the input procedure or by the subject's rehearsal strategy, control elements may be established at successively higher levels, generating a hierarchical organization. For example, suppose two letters are presented in sequence, the first letter comprising features f_1 and f_2 and the second letter the features f_3 and f_4. Two first-order control elements, $C_{1,1}$ and $C_{1,2}$, would be established, one for each letter, and a second-order control element, $C_{2,1}$, for the pair of letters, generating the following structure:

$$C_{2,1}$$ syllables or words

$$C_{1,1} \qquad C_{1,2}$$ letters

$$f_1 \qquad f_2 \; f_3 \qquad f_4$$ features

Now activation of either of the first-order control elements would reinstate memory of the particular letter whereas activation of the second-order control element would reinstate memory of the pair of letters.

It will be seen that so far as structural relations are concerned there is a one to one mapping of coding theory onto the association model. Wherever one would speak of the subject's introducing a code for a set of elements, the associative model introduces a control element. For most purposes, in representing the memory representations set up as a result of the input of a single trial in a short-term memory experiment, it will be convenient to simplify the diagram by treating the lower order structures as units. Thus, for example, a short-hand representation of the memory structure for a sequence of four letters would be written

where L_i denotes the representation of the ith letter, C is a control element and M a motivational source which may activate the control element.

When one is presenting a new theory, it is generally best to concentrate on showing how the concepts are to be used, rather than struggling with formal definitions. This is the course I am following with respect to control elements. For the present it will suffice to treat the control element as an abstract construct, on a par with "association," "memory trace," or "habit strength." My general idea is that at the time of input of to-be-remembered items, some element or aspect of the current context serves as a temporary control element. The transient associations with the contextual control element maintain the items in short-term memory by means of a mechanism to be elucidated in the next section. However, the context shifts with the passage of time (see Bower, this volume), and the memory is lost unless control is taken over by a more stable structure. Stability is achieved if some item in long-term memory is activated by the joint effect of its existing associations with some aspect of the context and one or more of the input items. This item establishes new associations with the other input items which are currently in short-term memory, and takes over the control function. Retrieval of the items from memory at a later time will be facilitated to the extent that the permanent control element is associated with cues which constitute part of the context at the time of recall.

Reverberatory Pathways and the Representations
of Order in Immediate Memory

The model as presented up to this point provides a basis for representing retention of item information, but so far has nothing to say about the critical matter of information regarding position or serial order of items. I propose to treat the problem of order in terms of two distinct mechanisms, the first having to do with the short-term representation of order information and its loss as a function of time and the second with the stable representation of order in long-term memory which may be established as a result of rehearsal.

Taking together a variety of sources of evidence, which I shall assume to be familiar to readers of this volume, we can sketch the course of events on a typical trial of a short-term memory experiment: (*a*) A stimulus pattern, say a vocally presented letter, arrives at the sensory apparatus; (*b*) much of the information in the pattern is lost within a matter of milliseconds, but during this brief interval subsystems of the perceptual apparatus which may be termed feature detectors are activated and a representation of the letter is set up in short-term memory in the form of a combination of features, phonemes in the case of a spoken letter; (*c*) by an associative process a representation of the letter in long-term memory is activated and the individual is enabled to identify or label the letter. In terms of the work of Posner (1969; this volume) we can assume that at an early stage in this sequence the subject is able to make a same-different judgment regarding physical similarity of the input letter to one previously presented but that only at the end of the sequence can he name the letter.

Now we arrive at one of the central problems with respect to memory for serial order. If the retrieval times for various letters, words, or other possible items of a sequence were approximately equal, and had negligible variance, then following the presentation of a sequence of items the listener might be expected automatically to generate a sequence of names in the same order, that is, to remember the input order perfectly. However, the assumption of constant times of retrieval from memory is certainly incorrect. In general the items of an input sequence must have substantially varying retrieval times from long-term memory; and, judging by associative reaction time data, latency distributions even for such familiar items as digits or letters of the alphabet have standard deviations which are substantial relative to their means. Thus if a series of letters or words is presented at a rapid rate, as is frequently done in short-term memory experiments, the order in which representations of these items are retrieved from long-term memory cannot be assumed invariably to agree with the input order.

The organism's way out of this difficulty, suggested by much current research on memory, is to maintain a coded representation of the last few items of an input sequence in a short-term memory store for an interval of a few seconds. The labels or other associations activated by these items in long-term memory can, then, be checked for order against the representation of the sequence in short-term memory and the labels or names rehearsed in their proper order before the short-term representation is lost.

The basic concept of the short-term mechanism in the present model is a reverberatory loop which, for a single element in the stimulus sequence, say a feature f_i of a letter L_{ij}, and a contextual control element, might be schematized as follows:

The idea is that once a representation of the feature f_i has been set up in memory and has established a connection with a control element, the reverberatory loop connecting the two produces a recurrent reactivation of the representation of the feature at a rate determined by the refractory phase of the system. This maintenance of the representation of the element in a state of heightened excitability is the basis of short-term retention. Further, if a sequence of stimulus features has become associated with a single control element as a result of the input of a single experimental trial, a similar reverberatory loop is established for each feature, with the consequence that the features will be reactivated in sequence, thus providing for the initial representation of order information in short-term memory.

If the reverberatory loops were completely deterministic, this memory would be permanent. However, it seems reasonable to assume that there is a certain amount of random error in the recurrence times owing to differences in refractory phases among individual elements and to perturbations arising from other concurrent activity in the nervous system. The result of these random variations is that over a period of time the timing of recurrent activations of the individual elements of a sequence will come to deviate sufficiently from the original relationships so that eventually interchanges in order will begin to appear between adjacent elements.

This cyclic reactivation process is assumed to operate in basically the same way at each level at which perceptual processing of a stimulus input produces units that may enter into short-term memory. With the materials ordinarily used in short-term memory experiments, these units would include at least the critical features which identify visually displayed characters, acoustic features (e.g., phonemes) which identify auditorily presented characters, and semantic features or markers in the case of words as units.

Thus the representation of a sequence of items in short-term memory is not like a string of beads, but rather like sequences of indicators on parallel tracks, each track having to do with a different kind of information about any given item. When, for example, a letter is displayed visually, representations of identifying visual features are activated and begin their reactivation cycles in short-term memory; then when the individual, in response to the visual input, pronounces the character and hears his own auditory feedback, representations of acoustic features are activated and in turn begin their reactivation cycles.

The representations arising from different modalities are assumed to be independent, but they will presumably have different rates of reactivation. Further, it seems quite likely that the visual representation is more sensitive to changes in context than auditory representations and consequently that in the former case the reactivation process would damp out more rapidly as a result of shifts in context; to the extent that this is so, there would be less time available following input for the activation of associated control elements in long-term memory in the case of visual than in the case of auditory input.

Even in the case of auditory features, the duration of the short-term process appears on the basis of considerable evidence to be no more than 2 to 3 seconds (Bjork & Healy, 1970; Crowder & Morton, 1969; Estes, 1970a). However, even 2 or 3 seconds is a rather long time on a scale of sensory information processing and short-term memory. If the sequence of letters is presented at the rapid rate characteristic of many short-term memory experiments, often 2 to 3 per second, then for a short time following input of the string the individual, according to the present model, has available in short-term memory information concerning the order in which various identifying visual features of the letters and various phonetic features, for example stop and vowel phonemes, occurred in the input sequence.

According to this conception, loss of order information in short-term memory results entirely from perturbations in timing in the reactivation cycles of representations of various features of the stimulus input. Most importantly, these perturbations lead to interchanges in order of the representations of features of characters in the string which is to be remembered and thus lead to transposition errors in recall. However, it should be noted that, when the interval between a presentation of a string of characters and the recall test is filled with presentations of "noise" characters (as when a string of letters is followed by a sequence of random digits), perturbations in reactivation cycles may also lead to interchanges in ordering of the representations of the characters of the string with characters in the intervening sequence. Depending on the nature of the material, this process may lead to intrusion errors at recall, or to errors of omission if the result of a transposition is to mix into the representation of the string a character of a type which the subject knows could not be admissible.

Since transpositions of characters of the input string and characters in the sequence intervening between the string and the recall test will most frequently involve the later items of the input string, a serial position curve for loss of item information will, on the present assumptions, be predicted to be monotonically decreasing (that is, showing only a primacy effect). On the other hand, as will be shown later in this section, the serial position curve for loss of order information is predicted to be bowed in form and symmetrical.

Concerning the duration of the short-term memory process, I assume that the limits ordinarily observed result primarily from the effects of successive inputs. In most experiments the subject receives the new inputs of successive trials at relatively rapid rates, with the result that the feature detectors and other mechanisms involved in setting up representations of one input string in short-term memory are soon captured by the new input from another string. Doubtless the continuation of reactivation cycles for a particular string depend also on maintenance of the input context, but I shall not attempt to deal with this aspect of the process in the present exposition.

In order to make these ideas specific enough to permit some illustrative calculations with the model, I shall utilize for the present the following set of assumptions.

i. Upon input of a string of items, an associative structure is established, with reverberatory loops connecting the representation of each item to a contextual control element. The structure reactivates the representations cyclically, initially following the input sequence.

ii. Let us denote by h the time between reactivations. Then, for any element of the sequence, during any unit time interval following input, there is some constant probability θ of a perturbation in timing which will result in the next reactivation being advanced or delayed by h time units. Advances and delays are assumed to be equally likely.

iii. Whenever the control element is activated from a motivational source, the articulatory responses corresponding to the items of the string will be made in the order determined by the current timing relationships.

iv. When a perturbation in timing results in an interchange of elements between adjacent items that results in producing unacceptable characters (for example combinations of phonemes that do not constitute letters in a letter string experiment), then the items involved are lost from short-term memory and the corresponding response will not be made on a recall test given at this point. Thus both order and item information are lost as a result of disturbances in timing with, in general, order information being the more sensitive.

Some of the general properties of the model will be fairly readily apparent at an intuitive level from consideration of the assumptions. At the time of input of a string of characters, a representation is established in memory incorporating both order and item information. During a subsequent retention interval, particularly if the interval is filled with other input which contributes perturbations to the timing mechanisms, order information is lost at an exponential rate.

Unlike other models, this one assumes that the loss of order information is primary and the loss of item information is derivative. The rate of loss of information is greater the larger the number of items in the string and the smaller the time intervals between presentations of successive items.[4] Also the rate of loss of order information is directly related to the similarity (communality) between items of the string and, in particular, transpositions are most likely to occur between adjacent similar items.

Within a string, a serial position curve develops in the course of the retention interval which is symmetric, with the highest proportions correct at the initial and terminal positions. The distance functions reproduce at least the main qualitative features exhibited in the data of Healy (1971) and Fuchs (1969), with an orderly decrease in probability of transpositions involving any two items of a string as a function of their distance apart and with these functions being symmetric in the forward and backward directions.

---

[4] A finding by Aaronson, Markowitz, and Shapiro (1971), which appeared after this passage was written, seems especially compatible with the present model. These investigators demonstrated a selective facilitation of retention of order information as the ratio of speech-to-pause time in an auditorily presented digit string was decreased.

To illustrate these last features, I prepared a computer simulation program by translating assumptions *i-iv* as directly as possible into Fortran statements. Boundary conditions were chosen to simulate Healy's (1971) experiment on recall of order of sequences obtained by randomly permuting a single set of four letters. Then sets of 100 hypothetical subjects were tested on the computer simulation with differing values of the perturbation parameter, θ. Theoretical values obtained for serial position curves and distance functions with $\theta = .10$ are shown in Figure 4,

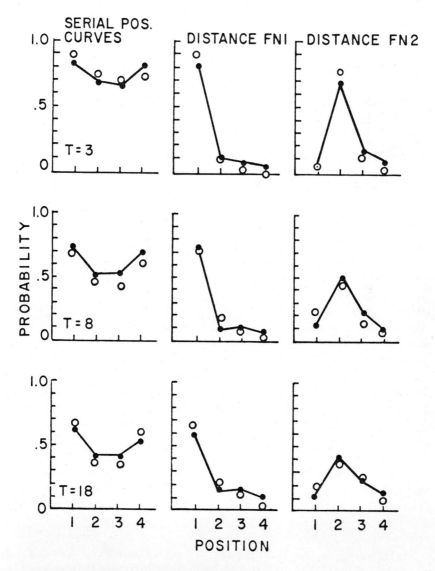

FIG. 4. Serial position and distance functions from Healy (1971) study (connected points) compared with predicted values from reverberatory loop model.

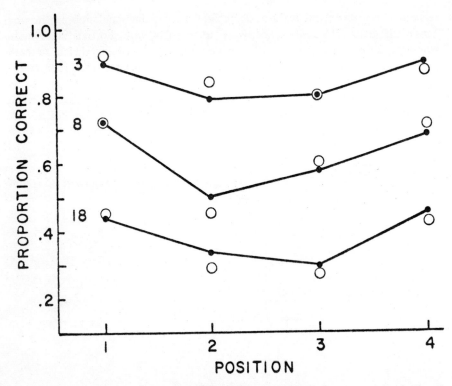

FIG. 5. Serial position curves from Bjork and Healy (1970) study (connected points) compared with predictions from reverberatory loop model.

together with corresponding points plotted for Healy's data.[5] The same program, with a different choice of θ, provides a comparable description of the serial position curves of the study by Bjork and Healy (1970), shown in Figure 5 (distance functions were not available for this study). Even this preliminary and highly simplified version of the model appears to predict the principal quantitative trends in these data reasonably well.

Long-Term Memory for Order

To account for the preservation of order information in long-term memory, we need to take account of the conspicuous fact that the course of retention loss in short-term memory can be arrested at any point if the individual is permitted to

[5] To increase the reliability of the observed values, the distance functions shown in Figure 3 were folded and pooled; thus the middle column in Figure 4 represents the pooled data from the first and fourth columns of Figure 3, and the righthand column of Figure 4 the second and third columns of Figure 3.

rehearse the material currently available in memory; then the rehearsed material can, for all practical purposes, be retained indefinitely. One view of the mechanism of rehearsal that has frequently been mentioned in the literature is the idea that it simply resets the process of short-term retention loss to its starting point; then some additional assumptions having to do with consolidation or the like are required to account for the fact that material may be transferred from short- to long-term memory. I propose to take a different tack and assume instead that the transition to long-term memory is effected by processes intrinsic to rehearsal itself.

One of the most obvious properties of rehearsal is that it involves the actual occurrence of the responses corresponding to the items held in memory. Further, it is clear that in order to order his output properly, the individual must inhibit response tendencies to later items in a sequence until the responses to earlier items have been emitted.

The assumption I wish to entertain is that the inhibitory tendencies which are required to properly shape the response output become established in memory and account for the long term preservation of order information. Thus, if rehearsal is permitted immediately following input of, say, a four-letter string in a short-term memory experiment, the diagram for the associative structure generated would be augmented by the inhibitory connections established at the time of rehearsal as illustrated in the following schema.

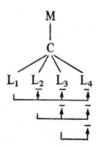

Each of the arrows terminating in a minus sign denotes an inhibitory connection which is activated when the originating response is evoked and temporarily inhibits the response tendency associated with the terminal item.

The process envisaged is that upon activation of the control element, excitatory inputs occur to all of the associated items, bringing them into an active memory state. However, owing to the inhibitory connections, the responses associated with items 2, 3, and 4 are inhibited until the response of item 1 occurs, at which time inhibitory input from it to the other items ceases so that response to the second item is released, and so on along the chain.

Some general properties are reasonably apparent. Firstly, taking the combined short- and long-term model as now formulated, it is clear that order information is completely lost from short-term memory if rehearsal is completely prevented for a long enough interval. If at any point in the process rehearsal is permitted, the order information still retained is crystallized, so to speak, by the establishment of inhibitory connections and thus is preserved in long-term memory. Secondly, it will be clear that, unlike a model based on a chain of interitem associations, the present model preserves order information in a form which is not unduly sensitive to disturbances of particular items. If, for example, for some reason the second or third item of a four-letter string were lost from memory, the order relationships among the remaining items would still be preserved. This property seems quite desirable in the light of some of Johnson's (1970) findings.

Further, I think it can be shown that the present schema leads directly to an interpretation of phenomena of "chunking." Consider, for example, the representation in memory of a string of six letters. If the letters are not grouped, six associative connections must be established with a control element, together with 15 inhibitory links; if they are grouped in 3s, eight associative plus seven inhibitory connections are required. In the latter case the final structure is

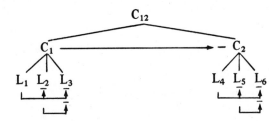

Proceeding similarly, we can compute the numbers of associative and inhibitory connections required for a 4-2 grouping, generating the table

Grouping	Number of Associative Connections	Number of Inhibitory Connections	Total Connections
6	6	15	21
3-3	8	7	15
4-2	8	8	16

Applying the same analysis to a string of 12 letters, we obtain

Grouping	Number of Associative Connections	Number of Inhibitory Connections	Total Connections
12	12	66	78
6-6	14	31	45
4-4-4	15	21	36
3-3-3-3	16	18	34
2-2-2-2-2-2	18	21	39

Further elaboration of the theory is needed to relate the "total connections" measure to recall score. However, on the assumption that all connections are formed with equal probabilities, which seems a reasonable idea to start with, we should predict that the recall scores for the different groupings will be inversely related to the total number of connections.

On this assumption, the illustrative results look quite plausible. For both 6- and 12-character strings, the model predicts maximal recall with a chunk size of 3, but with little difference between chunk sizes 3 and 4, in agreement with the data of Wickelgren (1967) on size of rehearsal group. It should be emphasized that the predictions depend on there being opportunity for rehearsal. If rehearsal were precluded, as in some of the experiments on short-term memory discussed in previous sections, inhibitory connections would not be involved in recall, and performance would depend on the total number of associative connections required and on the temporal spacing of the characters.

The preceding sketch of the model was somewhat elliptical, in the interest of a simple initial exposition. I should like now to make explicit some of the assumptions bearing on the more detailed working of the system.[6] It will be convenient to spell these out in relation to a three-level structure, which will bring out some problems not apparent in the simpler examples. Thus let us consider the structure

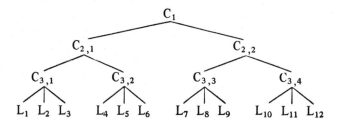

where inhibitory connections have been omitted to reduce clutter. The additional assumptions I should like to mention are as follows:

v. Inhibitory relations obtain only laterally at each level, and only among the associative connections branching off from any one control element. Thus, when the full structure is established, activation of $C_{2,1}$ inhibits $C_{2,2}$; activation of $C_{3,1}$ inhibits $C_{3,2}$ (but not $C_{3,3}$); L_1 inhibits L_2 and L_3 (but not L_4).

vi. Inhibition of a control element means that the activity of retrieving it from long-term memory is suppressed.

vii. When a control element C_j is activated, it continues to deliver excitatory input to its subordinates for some interval Δt. At the end of the interval C_j becomes refractory; control reverts to the next higher level, and any active control element at that level can excite its least inhibited subordinate.

Thus, referring to the diagram, if C_1 is activated, $C_{2,1}$ is activated and starts delivering excitatory input to the C_3 level; $C_{3,1}$ is activated and starts delivering excitatory input to the response level; L_2 and L_3 are inhibited by L_1, so the response corresponding to L_1 occurs and its branch goes into its refractory period; $C_{3,1}$ is still active, and L_2 inhibits L_3 so L_2 response occurs next, then L_3; as soon as $C_{3,1}$ goes refractory $C_{2,1}$, which is still active, excites $C_{3,2}$, and generates a

[6]A helpful critique of the original draft of this section by George A. Miller led to this effort toward clarification.

cycle similar to that for $C_{3,1}$; when $C_{2,1}$ becomes refractory C_1 can now excite $C_{2,2}$, and the process proceeds as on the first main branch; finally, the L_{12} response occurs, C_1 becomes refractory, and after a sufficient interval the system is ready to restart.

Considerable quantitative or computer analysis will be needed to explicate the workings of the system fully. However, I think it is fairly apparent from inspection of the diagram, in the light of the assumptions presented above, that the model can account in a simple and straightforward way, not only for the efficiency of chunking, but for many of the more detailed properties of memory for sequences. Examples in this category would be the greater probability of transposition errors involving items within a chunk than items in a different chunk, and the increase in transition error probabilities (Bower & Winzenz, 1969; Johnson, 1970) at chunk boundaries. Also, the model can readily predict Johnson's finding that disturbance of memory for order within one chunk, as produced by means of a retroactive inhibition paradigm, may leave retention of order information for the other chunks unaffected.

The items represented in the model need not, of course, be letters. For a rather different realization, we might consider the studies of repeating light sequences by Restle and Brown (1970). In their situation, the subject faces a row of six lights, with a response button under each. The lights are illuminated in some sequence, then the subject attempts to reproduce the sequence by pressing the buttons in the proper order. One of the basic patterns used by Restle and Brown was the sequence 1235433234, where digits denote positions of the lights. On the assumption that the breaks between runs would serve as discontinuities, we might expect the representation of the sequence in memory to take the form

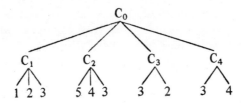

with inhibitory connections among the elements being added as the sequence is repeatedly rehearsed. Like Restle and Brown, we should expect errors to occur more often at the boundaries between control elements than within the subgroups. To account for the observation that the most frequent errors are continuations of runs (for example, "4" after "1,2,3") we should have to go beyond the basic machinery of the model and assume, as Restle and Brown do in effect, that subjects associate labels, "up" and "down" or the equivalent, with the subgroups.

I shall try to avoid going too far overboard in making claims for a new model that has not yet been extensively tested in detail, but I cannot refrain from pointing out how simply it appears to handle some of the general classical problems of serial order in behavior. For example, the difficulty which bothered Lashley (1951), that a serial association model could not allow for the high speeds observed in the response sequences of typists or pianists, does not arise in the present model. Since we do not assume that each response in a sequence constitutes the stimulus for the next, the reaction times of responses to the successive items of a sequence do not set a limit on the speed with which the responses can follow one another. If several stimuli are associated with a single control element, the responses corresponding to the stimuli can occur in sequence at a rate limited only by the effector apparatus, since any response of the sequence can occur as soon as the inhibitory input preventing its occurrence has been released by the evocation of its predecessor.

Similarly the difficulties with association theory which led to Wickelgren's (1969) theory of context-sensitive coding are by-passed entirely in the present model since associations are conceived to be formed between items and control elements rather than between successive items. Thus, in the present theory there is no special problem raised by the observation that the letter *b* can uniformly have the letter *o* as its successor when an individual is pronouncing or spelling the word *boy* whereas it equally uniformly has *e* as its successor when he pronounces or spells *bet*. An interpretation in terms of a model relying on simple, interitem associations would represent the two sequences as *b-o-y* and *b-e-t*. If both sequences were learned, the letter *b* would have to be associated simultaneously with *o* and *e*, and some additional machinery would be required to dictate which association would be activated. In the present theory the associative structure providing a basis for long-term memory of each of these two words consists in a control element having associative connections to each of the three appropriate letters, together with the three necessary inhibitory connections of the first letter with the second and third and the second letter with the third. When either word is called for in speech or writing, some aspect of the context activates one of these control elements, and thus leads to output of the corresponding word. The common initial letter *b* would generate ambiguity only if the individual were specifically asked to produce a three-letter word beginning with *b*, as in working a crossword puzzle; then the control elements for both *boy* and *bet*, and possibly other alternatives, might be activated simultaneously and the response would be indeterminate.

As may be almost too obvious to require mention, the model outlined here should be applicable to a much wider range of phenomena than those growing out of short-term memory experiments, with or without rehearsal; for example, the problem of interpreting forward and backward associations in paired-associate learning, some of the transfer phenomena in verbal learning discussed by Martin (1968) in terms of an encoding hypothesis, and phenomena of clustering in free recall.

RELATIONSHIPS TO OTHER MODELS FOR MEMORY

Any new model for human memory, or any of its aspects, which appears on the contemporary scene immediately invites comparison with the rather extensively developed theories of Atkinson and Shiffrin (1968), Norman and Rumelhart (1970), and Wickelgren (1970), all of which deal in considerable detail with numerous phenomena of both short and long-term retention. The most important way in which the theory presented here differs from all of the others is in the shift of attention from a primary concern with retention of items to a primary concern with memory for order of events.

All of the other models can generate predictions concerning, for example, serial position curves for sequentially presented items. However, the primacy and recency effects which generate the bowed serial position curve in those models result from different time parameters in functions describing storage and decay of item information. Thus in the model of Norman and Rumelhart the primacy effect arises from the greater time available for feature extraction from the early elements of a list and the recency effect from the smaller amount of time for decay of the last items. I have tried to go beyond the other models in seeking specific mechanisms to account for the preservation of input order in very-short-term memory, for the nature of the errors that arise as the memory deteriorates, and for the critical role of rehearsal in the transition from short-term to long-term memory.

The model I propose could well be considered either complementary or supplementary to the more general systems developed by Atkinson and Shiffrin or Norman and Rumelhart. With respect to the former, my short-term reverberatory loop model would bridge the gap between input of material and the setting up of a rehearsal buffer on the part of the subject. The concept of control element in the present theory appears to correspond quite closely to that of "image" in Shiffrin's (1970) recent extension of the Atkinson-Shiffrin model to the treatment of memory search processes. The principal concern of Atkinson and Shiffrin's theory is the description of information flow from input to retrieval and its relation to the control processes utilized by the subject. With respect to transitions from short- to long-term memory, my theory would supplement theirs by specifying just how the rehearsal process acts to establish long-term memory for sequences of items.

At least in its short-term aspect, my concept of control element also has a counterpart in the "contextual cues" of Norman and Rumelhart's system. The conception of feature extraction as developed by Norman and Rumelhart seems very promising as a basis for the first stage in stimulus coding. However, I suggest that the additional assumption of a reactivation process may be needed to account for the maintenance of temporal relationships, both among features of a given character and among characters of a sequence, in short-term memory.

Although at a first glance my work may seem most similar to that of Wickelgren (1970), in that we both have set out to revise and retain the most valuable features of association theory, it turns out that in detail my model differs more from Wickelgren's than from any of the others mentioned. Rather than revising the basic associative structure, Wickelgren has proceeded by multiplying the number and variety of associative traces that are laid down at the time of a learning experience and by adding processes of consolidation and comparative judgment. Wickelgren's conception of multiple traces and response decisions on the basis of strengths of traces has provided quantitative accounts of a number of aspects of recognition memory. However, I think that perhaps something more than an assemblage of trace strengths may be needed to deal with problems of coding and organization. About the phenomena with which I have been concerned, Wickelgren remarks, "Essentially nothing is known about the relation between event and order memory"

(Wickelgren, 1970, p. 92). That is precisely the gap in present theories of memory which I would like to fill.

REFERENCES

Aaronson, D., Markowitz, N., & Shapiro, H. Perception and immediate recall of normal and "compressed" auditory sequences. *Perception & Psychophysics,* 1971, 9, 338–344.

Atkinson, R. C., & Shiffrin, R. M. Human memory: A proposed system and its control processes. In K. W. Spence & J. T. Spence (Eds.), *The psychology of learning and motivation,* Vol. 2. New York: Academic Press, 1968. Pp. 89-195.

Bjork, E. L., & Healy, A. F. Intra-item and extra-item sources of acoustic confusion in short-term memory. In *Communications in Mathematical Psychology,* Rockefeller University Technical Reports, April, 1970.

Bower, G. H., & Winzenz, D. Group structure, coding and memory for digit series. *Journal of Experimental Psychology, Monograph Supplement,* 1969, 80, May, Pt. 2, 1-17.

Conrad, R. Acoustic confusions in immediate memory. *British Journal of Psychology,* 1964, 55, 75-84.

Conrad, R. Order error in immediate recall of sequences. *Journal of Verbal Learning and Verbal Behavior,* 1965, 4, 161-169.

Conrad, R. Interference or decay over short retention intervals? *Journal of Verbal Learning and Verbal Behavior,* 1967, 6, 49-54.

Crowder, R. G., & Morton, J. Precategorical acoustic storage (PAS). *Perception & Psychophysics,* 1969, 5, 365-373.

Estes, W. K. Evaluation of some models for acoustic confusion effects in short term memory. In *Communications in Mathematical Psychology,* Rockefeller University Technical Reports, October, 1969.

Estes, W. K. On the source of acoustic confusions in short term memory for letter strings. In *Communications in Mathematical Psychology,* Rockefeller University Technical Reports, April, 1970. (a)

Estes, W. K. *Learning theory and mental development.* New York: Academic Press, 1970. (b)

Fuchs, A. H. Recall for order and content of serial word lists. *Journal of Experimental Psychology,* 1969, 82, 14-21.

Healy, A. F. Short-term memory of consonant order. In *Communications in Mathematical Psychology,* Rockefeller University Technical Reports, October, 1971.

Johnson, N. F. Chunking: Associative chaining versus coding. *Journal of Verbal Learning and Verbal Behavior,* 1969, 8, 725-731.

Johnson, N. F. The role of chunking and organization in the process of recall. In G. H. Bower (Ed.), *The psychology of learning and motivation,* Vol. 4. New York: Academic Press, 1970. Pp. 171-247.

Lashley, K. S. The problem of serial order in behavior. In L. A. Jeffress (Ed.), *Cerebral mechanisms in behavior.* New York: Wiley, 1951.

Lesgold, A. M., & Bower, G. H. Inefficiency of serial knowledge for associative responding. *Journal of Verbal Learning and Verbal Behavior,* 1970, 9, 456-466.

Martin, E. Stimulus meaningfulness and paired-associate transfer: An encoding variability hypothesis. *Psychological Review,* 1968, 75, 421-441.

Miller, G. A. The magical number seven, plus or minus two: Some limits on our capacity for processing information. *Psychological Review,* 1956, 63, 81-97.

Murdock, B. B., Jr., & vom Saal, W. Transpositions in short-term memory. *Journal of Experimental Psychology,* 1967, 74, 137-143.

Norman, D. A., & Rumelhart, D. E. A system for perception and memory. In D. A. Norman (Ed.), *Models of human memory.* New York: Academic Press, 1970. Pp. 19-64.

Posner, M. I. Abstraction and the process of recognition. In G. H. Bower & J. T. Spence (Eds.), *The psychology of learning and motivation,* Vol. 3. New York: Academic Press, 1969. Pp. 43-100.

Restle, F., & Brown, E. R. Serial pattern learning. *Journal of Experimental Psychology*, 1970, 83, 120-125.

Shiffrin, R. M. Memory search. In D. A. Norman (Ed.), *Models of human memory*. New York: Academic Press, 1970. Pp. 375-447.

Thorndike, E. L. *Human learning*. New York: Century, 1931.

Underwood, B. J. Attributes of memory. *Psychological Review*, 1969, 76, 559-573.

Wickelgren, W. A. Short-term memory for phonemically similar lists. *American Journal of Psychology*, 1965, 78, 567-574.

Wickelgren, W. A. Rehearsal grouping and the hierarchical organization of serial position cues in short-term memory. *Quarterly Journal of Experimental Psychology*, 1967, 19, 97-102.

Wickelgren, W. A. Context-sensitive coding, associative memory, and serial order in (speech) behavior. *Psychological Review*, 1969, 76, 1-15.

Wickelgren, W. A. Multitrace strength theory. In D. A. Norman (Ed.), *Models of human memory*. New York: Academic Press, 1970. Pp. 65-102.

Yntema, D. B., & Trask, F. P. Recall as a search process. *Journal of Verbal Learning and Verbal Behavior*, 1963, 2, 65-74.

8
CHARACTERISTICS OF WORD ENCODING[1]

Delos D. Wickens
The Ohio State University

During the past decade there has been a growing consensus of opinion concerning the way in which people respond to the symbolic information that is contained in words. This consensus would seem to hold that final word meaning results from the encoding of a word along a number of dimensions. Perhaps the first in the group representing this point of view was Osgood (Osgood, Suci, & Tannenbaum, 1957) who presented the conception that certain classes of word meanings could be represented by a point in three dimensional space, where the axes of the space were the connotative characteristics of Evaluation, Potency, and Activity. This basic idea—that elements or attributes or components combine in some way to eventuate in the unique meaning of a word—has become more popular in recent years. The view seems to be represented in papers by Bower (1967), Morton (1970), Norman and Rumelhart (1970), Underwood (1969), and Wickens (1970). These papers agree, in one way or another, that a word's meaning is the vector whose value is determined by a number of components.

The hypothesis that word meaning is a bundle of attributes contains certain empirically testable assumptions or implications, and among them are the following: (*a*) Psychologically prominent attributes of words can be identified. (*b*) Most, if not all, words have multiple component values. (*c*) Component values can exist independently of the word itself. Undoubtedly there are more predictions that are derivable from modern word identification theory, but the contents of the present paper will attempt to react only to the three implications just mentioned.

The first section (Identification of Encoding Features) will address itself to the statement that psychologically prominent attributes of words can be identified, and will present research that explores, and possibly quantifies, potential (or actual)

[1] Much of the research reported in this paper was supported in part by a grant, OEG-5-9-450276 from USOE.

encoding dimensions. It will report the considerable body of research that extends and adds information to the material presented in the paper by Wickens (1970). It will also cover the as yet very sparse developmental work on the subject of encoding, that is, research that has attempted to identify attributes used by children of different ages in attaching meaning to words.

The second section (The Question of Multiple Encoding) will address itself to the statement that most, if not all, words have multiple component values. It will present research that attempts to determine whether more than one of the dimensions identified in the first section are used *coincidently* in retrieval from memory.

The third section (The Existence of Component Values Independent of the Word Itself) will address itself to the statement that component values can exist independently of the word itself. It is based upon the possibility that information processing of different attributes may follow differing temporal courses, and it attempts to determine whether there is any evidence for semantic encoding prior to the occurrence of the naming process.

Many methods are available for the identification of dimensions along which words are encoded. They include false positives in recognition memory, clustering in free recall, sorting, rating, and reports of tip-of-the-tongue phenomena. The research presented in the first two sections of this paper is based upon another method: performance in a particular adaptation of the Brown-Peterson short-term memory situation; the adaptation uses amount of release from proactive inhibition as an index of encoding.

Historically, this method grew out of the Keppel and Underwood (1962) paper on proactive inhibition in short-term memory, which showed that the Peterson and Peterson (1959) paradigm was subject to proactive interfering effects. Later Wickens, Born, and Allen (1963) presented data to indicate that proactive inhibition was specific to the class of material being presented. Their experiment built up interference for consonant trigrams or three-digit numbers, then switched the class of material—trigrams to numbers, and vice versa. There was a marked improvement in performance (virtually a complete recovery of performance) when, on a given trial, there was a shift from material of one sort to that of another. Since the present volume is primarily concerned with meaningful material, the release effect is illustrated, in Figure 1, with material from a study similar to the Wickens, Born, and Allen research, but one that used words and numbers rather than trigrams and numbers. The figure is drawn from an article by Reutener (1972). Note that the dotted line for the experimental group represents results of shifts on Trial 4 both from words to numbers and from numbers to words (the shift effect was symmetrical). The control group was given numbers for the entire series of four trials when the experimental group commenced with words; it received words for four trials when the experimental group began with numbers. Quite clearly, the interference effect was specific to the class of material being presented and was not apparent for material of a different type, as seen by comparing Trial 3 and Trial 4 performance in the experimental group. The implication of these data for other subject matter is that one may investigate many psychologically different classes of materials by use of the shift technique. The Wickens et al. (1963) research became

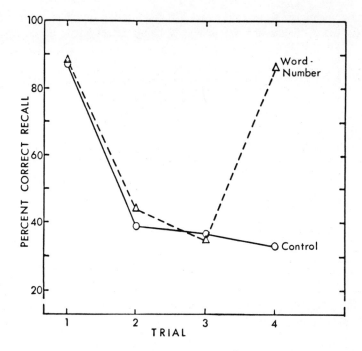

FIG. 1. Illustration of release from PI in the instance of shifting between the classes of spelled-out numbers and common words. (after Reutener, 1972).

the first of a series of experiments using the release from proactive inhibition as a technique for identifying features of symbolic information.

The majority of the research presented in the first two sections was done at the Ohio State University Laboratory, or has stemmed from work done there and therefore rests upon common general procedures. The basic procedure commences with the presentation of a triad of words that may be considered to be members of a common class—by various definitions of class, which will become clear as the specific experiments are described. The triad appears; a rehearsal preventative or distractor task follows for 20 seconds; a recall is requested; 30 seconds after an item has been presented, another item of the same class follows, and so on for three trials. The control group continues in the same fashion on the fourth trial; but for the experimental group, the fourth-trial triad consists of materials drawn from some different class. The terms "experimental" and "control" never refer to materials, but always to the presence of shift on Trial 4 (experimental group) or the absence of any shift at all (control group). There are always, of course, two experimental groups and two control groups, since for both experimentals and controls half of the subjects must begin trials with one class of material while the other half commences with the other class. It is arranged so that the control group's fourth-trial triads are always the same as those for the experimental group. The particular triads are, of course, counterbalanced across trials so that each triad occurs equally often in each trial, and an effort is made to use a large number of words of a given class so as to produce a representative sample of items. Whenever any class other than word frequency is being investigated, the average word frequency of one class is matched with that of the other. The usual number of subjects per subgroup in these experiments is 48, leading, since one shifts in both directions, to 96 experimental and 96 control subjects. The subjects are never informed of the presence of classes or of the planned shift in class; they are told only that the experiment concerns their memory for words and their performance on the distractor task.

All items are presented by means of a Carousel projector, using a vertical array, with each item staggered one space to the right of the item above, as:

BOOK

CHAIR

DOCTOR

Since, in all but one clearly designated instance shift effects were symmetrical, the graphs of the experiments combine results for shifts in both directions (e.g., numbers to words and words to numbers) in the dashed graph line for the experimental group. The graphs, then, represent all 96 subjects for the experimental group and all 96 of the controls.

IDENTIFICATION OF ENCODING FEATURES

The identification of the psychologically prominent aspects by which people encode words is the general topic of this section, and identification in college-student adult subjects will be its first consideration.

Identification and Quantification of Encoding Dimensions in Adults

Well over twenty experiments contribute data on this subject, and an attempt has been made to quantify, in some relative fashion, the amount of release obtained from differing materials. Figure 3, which will be referenced frequently in the exposition of the studies, presents graphically a summary of the experiments, but Figure 2 should be studied first. It demonstrates the typical results for experimental and control groups in the typical procedure outlined above, along with an explanation of the method of quantification used in the experiments represented in Figure 3.

It can be seen in Figure 2 that recall is excellent on Trial 1, but declines steadily across the first three trials for both the control and experimental groups; for the control group it continues to decline through Trial 4. In the experimental group, when there is a shift to a new class of psychologically differentiated materials on Trial 4, there is a marked improvement in performance. The phrase, "release from proactive inhibition (PI)" refers to this shift, and the percentage of release is calculated by determining the relationship between the improvement of the experimental groups on Trial 4, arrow X, and the total decline of the control groups, arrow Y; that is, X divided by Y, expressed in percentage terms.

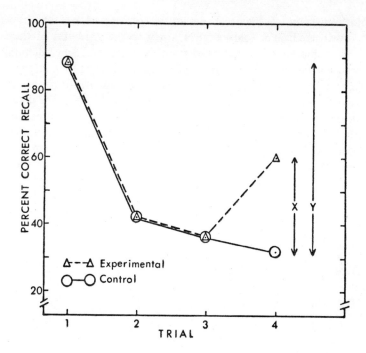

FIG. 2. Schematic presentation of the method used in quantifying release from PI, the percentage release being given by X/Y × 100.

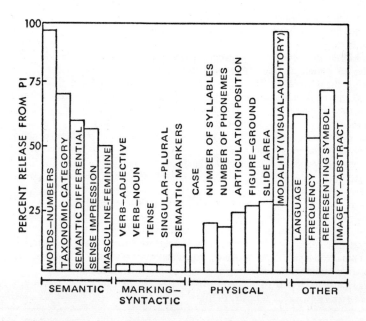

FIG. 3. Percent release from PI as a function of various shifts as described in Table 1.

The block diagram of Figure 3 shows the percent release for the various attributes investigated; and Table 1 gives a key to the attributes of the figure, together with examples of the triads used for each attribute. Figure 3 demonstrates clearly that manipulations of some dimensions are quite effective in releasing from PI, while manipulations of other dimensions are essentially ineffective. A value of approximately 20 percent is needed for significance at the .05 level. The divided line at the bottom of Figure 3 suggests a categorization of attributes, and this categorization will be discussed along with aspects of the contributing experiments that need some elaboration. Most of the studies represented in Figure 3 need no discussion in this type of paper. They are simple applications of the procedures

TABLE 1

Description of the Attributes Referred to in Figure 3

1. Words to numbers, as *book, chair, doctor* to *three, nine, one* (Reutener, 1972).
2. Taxonomic categories, as *door, window, cellar* to *bread, carrots, potatoes* (Goggin & Wickens, 1971; cf. also Loess, 1967).
3. Semantic Differential (shift in polarity), as *hate, fire, kill* to *able, mother, wise* (Wickens & Clark, 1968).
4. Sense impression, as *dome, knob, wheel* to *rice, teeth, bandage* (Wickens, Reutener, & Eggemeier, unpublished).
5. Masculine to feminine, as *queen, nylons, cow* to *butler, rooster, tuxedo* (Ickes, unpublished).
6. Verbs to adjectives (Wickens, Clark, Hill, & Wittlinger, 1968).
7. Verbs to nouns as *roam, destroy, listen* to *earth, house, pony* (Wickens, Shearer & Timmons, unpublished).
8. Tense, as *ride, dig, take* to *wrote, stood, ran* (Wickens, Shearer & Timmons, unpublished).
9. Singular to plural, as *oxen, feet, men* to *child, tooth, mouse.* (Wickens, Shearer, & Timmons, unpublished).
10. Semantically marked to unmarked, as *foul, dim, bland* to *long, clean, sane* (Deese & Wickens, unpublished).
11. Upper case to lower case nouns (Shearer & Wickens, unpublished).
12. One- to two-syllable nouns, as *bread, Maine, nose* to *rifle, spider, airplane* (Baldwin, 1969).
13. Number of phonemes in one syllable words (two or three phonemes to four or five), as *dumb, hay, eel* to *branch, wrist, month* (Baldwin, 1969).
14. Articulation (closed-front to open-back), as *splint, pig, sea* to *fork, gauze, swan* (Baldwin, 1969).
15. Figure-ground, CCCs white on black to black on white (Reutener, 1972).
16. Illuminated area of the slide background, large area to small (Turvey & Egan, 1969).
17. Modality of presentation, auditory to visual (Wittlinger, 1967; Rubin, 1967).
18. Language of common words with bilinguals, English to Spanish (Goggin & Wickens, 1971).
19. Thorndike-Lorge high- to low-frequency nouns and verbs (Swanson & Wickens, 1970).
20. Representing symbol, as 397 to *eight, five, two* (Reutener, 1972).
21. Imagery (abstract words to concrete words), as *advantage, boredom, position* to *palace, acrobat, factory* (Wickens & Engle, 1970).

Note.—All shifts were made in both directions, but for the sake of saving space, only one direction is indicated. With one exception (modality, see text) shift direction seems to be symmetrical.

previously outlined to the attributes listed; they have been published or are on their way to publication.[2]

Semantic. The first five blocks (reading from the left of Figure 3) represent attributes that are clearly of a semantic type, for they deal with the meaning and nature of the concepts represented by the symbols used. The diagram demonstrates that the effect is quite powerful for such measures as words to numbers, taxonomic class, the Semantic Differential, sense impression, and masculine-feminine. That such attributes as these would prove to be dominant features in the experimental situation seems inevitable; for, in a sense, they must be the core of what language is all about.

Marked-syntactic. The next grouping is labeled "Marked-Syntactic." The clearly syntactic items of this grouping (verb-adjective, noun-verb, tense, and number) give no evidence at all of being uniquely encoded.

A further word about the noun-verb data is in order. After an original experiment with triads of single words produced negative results, a second experiment was conducted, one in which a triad of three- or four-word *sentences* was presented with the to-be-recalled words underlined (e.g., we *roam* the earth; *destroy* the town; he *rode* the pony). The subjects read each sentence aloud, repeated the underlined words, and then commenced the distractor task. It was assumed that this method would force the subjects to encode the word syntactically and that this effect would persist through the recall period. Once again, however, just as in the simpler experiment, there was no increment of performance on the shift trial.

It could be argued that, in the above situation, the subjects attended only to the underlined words, while parroting the sentence. A third experiment was then conducted in which the sentence triads were presented without any denotation of what words were to be recalled. Again the sentences were read aloud and were replaced with the three target words, either all nouns or all verbs. This method also proved ineffective in producing a release from PI. It should be added that only single function words (according to dictionary definition) were employed, and if, in the experimenter's opinion, a certain noun had acquired verb characteristics (or vice versa) through slang usage, it too was eliminated from the materials.

The final dimension in the Marked-Syntactic category, semantic marking, approaches significance, but probably not because of the effectiveness of marking per se. As an inspection of the sample triads in Table 1 suggests, the unmarked words represent "desirable" and the marked words "undesirable" characteristics. Subsequent to the completion of the original experiment on this dimension, another group of subjects rated all the triads on three scales: good-bad, active-passive, and strong-weak. For every scale, the unmarked word triads were

[2] Some of the experiments cited in this article are only on their way to publication and cannot be specifically referenced. I should like to express appreciation to the many students who have contributed both to the conduct and discussion of these studies. They are: Roger Baldwin, Laird Cermak, Sandra Clark, Thomas Eggemeier, Randall Engle, Francis Hill, Robert Ickes, Donald Reutener, Michael Turvey, William Shearer, James Swanson, Margaret Timmons, and Roy Wittlinger.

significantly more positive than were the marked. Clearly, the marked and unmarked classes were confounded with a semantic factor, and it is likely that the presence of the semantic factor accounted for the amount of release obtained.

The data on the Marked-Syntactic dimension as a whole indicates that, when an individual sees or hears sets of unrelated words, he does not encode them according to their syntactical characteristics—at least not in any way that enhances memory on the shift trial.

Physical. The next general category of the diagram is classified as Physical, and, in the experimental situation of the procedures described, its items seem to have only a moderate range of effectiveness. It is worth noting, however, that, although such manipulations of attributes as case, syllables, phonemes, articulation, and figure-ground had no statistically significant effect, the experimental group was always superior to the control group. These physical variables, then, seem to have some psychological importance. The moderate effectiveness of the physical manipulations suggests that the individual is somewhat sensitive to the manner in which verbal information is presented, but much less sensitive than he is to the semantic characteristics of the materials. It is not possible from the data to determine whether the effect we do obtain arises from a few subjects using the physical cues quite well, or from all subjects showing a small degree of use. However an awareness of the physical change does not seem to be a critical factor; Reutener (1972) quizzed his subjects subsequent to the experiment in his work on figure-ground shift and found no difference in magnitude of release between those who reported an awareness as opposed to unawareness of the physical change.

Results for the modality variable (auditory presentation to visual and vice versa) are somewhat conflicting and need elaboration and further consideration. The modality bar in Figure 3 has two horizontal lines and refers to two experiments. The lower space (up to about 20 percent) represents a study by Wittlinger (1967); he obtained no significant release effect. The entire bar (about 100 percent) shows the high release obtained by Rubin (1967) at the University of Michigan. Rubin used a technique of presentation different from Wittlinger's in that he showed one item at a time in the same location, rather than three items at a time. To further confound the question, Hopkins, Edwards, and Gavelek (1971), in three independent experiments, obtained good release (about 65 percent) when they shifted from visual to auditory, but found absolutely no release when they shifted in the other direction. Their experiments employed the same technique as did Rubin's, that is, successive presentation, although the rate was 1 word per second, as compared with Rubin's 1 word per .5 second. The results they obtained represent the only experiment in this paper where an asymmetrical shift occurs. At the present time it is impossible to account for the discrepant results following modality shifts.

Other. The "Other" category simply includes studies which do not fit clearly into the first three classifications. One of these is research that investigates the Language dimension (Goggin & Wickens, 1971). It was conducted at the University of Texas at El Paso and used Spanish-English bilinguals as subjects. The diagram block in Figure 3 shows quite clearly that an encoding characteristic of a word is the language in which it is presented. An additional item of interest in this study relates to fluency. The subjects were required to rate themselves as to fluency in each language. Only students who rated themselves as having a fair amount of skill in both Spanish and English were chosen as subjects, but, among these, there were some who rated themselves as being highly proficient and others who indicated a moderate disparity in competence. When the data for these two groups were compared, it was found that those who felt equally fluent in each language showed a release of nearly 100 percent; those who considered themselves more competent in one language than another showed about 40-percent release. An interpretation of this finding is that the nonequal group may have been translating the words (or some of the words) and thereby lessening the effect of the experimental variable on the shift.

The bar for Frequency represents a study where the shift was from low to high frequency words and vice versa (Swanson & Wickens, 1970). Words were chosen from Thorndike-Lorge and were either AA for the high frequency class or below 15 per million for the low frequency items. The low frequency words were also chosen to be ones that would be well within the vocabulary of the usual college student. That the choices were appropriate is suggested by the fact that the overall level of performance on the high- and low-frequency words did not differ. The semantic content of the two sets of words was broad, and both nouns and verbs were used (but of course not mixed within triad sets). The release effect of shifting frequency, while not as gargantuan as changing from words to numbers, is still considerable. Apparently, we do encode verbal information according to overall frequency. Perhaps the reader will have already reacted to the low frequency "gargantuan" in the preceding sentence.

The Representing Symbol bar is drawn from the experiment by Reutener (1972) in which there was a shift between a three-digit number expressed in arabic numerals and three completely spelled out numbers. The effect of this shift was relatively high—a somewhat surprising finding since the situation might be considered similar to those classified as "physical" and most of those were not effective. The Representing Symbol situation was not classified as Physical because the modification is in the symbol carrying the information rather than in the accompanying physical properties. Perhaps this difference accounts for the difference in effect.[3]

The final bar, Imagery, indicates the effect of shifting from concrete or high-imagery words to abstract or low-imagery ones (Wickens & Engle, 1970). The words were drawn from the Paivio, Yuille, and Madigan (1968) norms, and were matched for frequency and for m value. The shift effect was slight, and its ineffectiveness offers little support for the view that concrete words tend to be encoded differently than are abstract words. The negative finding in this paradigm, of course, does not deny the fact that the creation of images can be a facilitating mechanism for memory, but it does suggest that the average college student, given 2 seconds in which to encode three words for memory, does not seem to make use of the imagery mechanism to encode concrete words in a fashion different from that he uses for abstract ones. One should mention that, subsequent to the first trial, performance on the concrete words was superior to that with abstract words. It is

---

[3] Although one cannot calculate the magnitude of release from PI from the experiments by Brodie and Lippman (1970a, b), they too report consistent release for this type of shift.

noteworthy that, although this familiar superiority for memory of the concrete words was found, there was no evidence for a differential encoding of the two classes of words as measured by the PI-release procedure.

Conclusion. Aside from identifying potential encoding dimensions, some of which are salient and others of which appear to be nonexistent in the release paradigm, the studies taken all together seem to have something to say about the richness of information processing in the adult human. Except in the modality shift experiments, the subjects were not informed of the manipulations which were to be employed; they knew only that they were to try to remember the symbols presented to them. Thus, they were not set to encode in a particular way, but were simply behaving in their normal fashion for the act of perceiving words. If we may assume that, at any given time, an individual acts as do the separate groups in these experiments, one is impressed with the sheer amount of information that is processed in 2 seconds available for encoding the three items. In that brief time, the subjects (or at least some subjects) pick up information about the various physical characteristics of the presentation method, about the language of the message, the extra-experimental frequency of the words experienced, and most of all, about the semantic content with its connotative and denotative components. Many of these characteristics are irrelevant to the task, which is simply to remember the three words for 20 seconds. So why should the subject record a word's frequency, or whether it was seen or heard, or the figure-ground contrast of its presentation, and perhaps much more? One can only conclude that the human adult has the potential for using, and perhaps uses, a multiple information processing system in the brief durations that the symbolic data are made available to him.

Developmental Characteristics of Encoding

All of the previously described researches have used college students as subjects, and are, therefore, tapping into the encoding structure after years of practice have trained the language skills to a high level. It is of obvious concern, from an educational viewpoint, to observe the ontogenetic development of encoding features.

In a study by Pender (1969), the release from PI paradigm was used to investigate encoding in children of second- and of sixth-grade levels. The attributes measured were rhyming, taxonomic category, and the three dimensions of the Semantic Differential. The choice of the second and sixth grade was based upon previous research by DiVesta (1966), who, using a rating technique, found that although the Evaluative dimension was clearly present by the second grade, the Activity and Potency dimensions did not emerge as independent attributes until the fifth to the seventh grades. At the earlier age levels, Activity and Potency were represented by a general Dynamism factor.

Pender's procedures were essentially the same as those described in the earlier sections of this chapter except that the materials were presented auditorily—for the obvious reason of avoiding the reading differences between the grade levels. The usual control groups were employed and shifts were made in both directions. Four trials were presented prior to the shift trial, this being the same number used by Wickens and Clark (1968) in their Semantic Differential study.

Pender's rhyming items consisted of words sharing sounds with *glue* (e.g., *blue, shoe*) or with *hair* (e.g., *care, fair*). For the Semantic Differential, the words were chosen from the Heise (1965) norms, with the further restriction that they be in the first five thousand in frequency for second-grade children, according to the Rindsland (1945) count. The taxonomic shifts employed were animals to body parts and vegetables to clothing.

The writer has converted Pender's results into the type of percentage figures described in Figure 2 with respect to the research with college students. For the second-grade children, the percent PI release for rhyming was 84 percent; for taxonomic category, 75 percent; for Evaluative dimension of the Semantic Differential, 64 percent. There was no effect for either Activity or Potency. With the sixth-grade children, the percent of release for rhyming stood at 85 percent; for taxonomic category, at 80 percent; for the Evaluative dimension, at 64 percent. Potency was ineffective. Although the Activity effect was not significant in the Pender sixth-grade analysis, there actually was a release effect of about 25 percent. Pender also included a college level group for rhyme and found its release to be 60 percent, or about 15 percent less on this dimension than was true for her younger groups. She suggests that college students are less sensitive to this rather formal dimension than are children. A diagram representation of the Pender results appears in Figure 4.

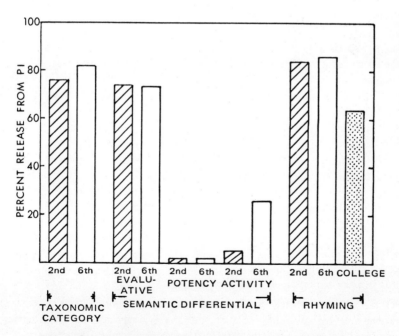

FIG. 4. Percent release from PI as a function of chronological age and type of attribute. (after Pender, 1969).

The processes tapped by the PI release technique in the Semantic Differential seem to parallel those reached by the rating technique of DiVesta (1966), but to become apparent only at a later chronological age. In the memory processes involved in the Brown-Peterson task, encoding by the Evaluative dimension appears to be an "automatic" process (in the sense used by Posner, this volume), even at the youngest age measured (second grade), although encoding by either Activity or Potency was not present at all at that level. According to the DiVesta rating data, Activity and Potency have become relatively independent dimensions by the sixth-grade level, indicating that encoding in these ways is achievable. The PI release technique gives only slight evidence for Activity encoding and none for Potency with sixth-grade children. By college age, however, all of these dimensions are powerful as measured by the release from PI method (Wickens & Clark, 1968).

One effect of increased language experience may be the moving of the individual from an optional encoding situation (evidenced by rating and sorting) to an automatic, and even obligatory, encoding which becomes the basis for the PI release phenomena. This developmental trend may have something to say about communication between adults and children. An encoding dimension of a word that is automatic for the adult, a dimension that adds a particular flavor to the word in question, may not be achieved by a child; hence a lack of communication arises.

THE QUESTION OF MULTIPLE ENCODING

The original hypothesis of this paper stated that word meaning is a bundle of attributes, and its second implication was that most, if not all, words have multiple-component values. At the end of the section on identification and quantification of encoding in adults, it was suggested that the profile of attribute sensitivity obtained in the many different experiments reported might be applicable to the processes which go on in an individual subject. Obviously this suggestion is highly speculative, and it remains to be demonstrated experimentally that more than a single attribute is normally encoded in one experience with a word, and used in recall.

Both Bregman (1968) and Shulman (1970) have shown that, in a particular forced situation, subjects can encode several attributes of a symbol. The basic design of their experiments was to present a word or a series of words and then to ask the subject whether a test word sounded like, had a similar meaning to, or looked like, a word previously presented. It was found that subjects would respond appropriately in this situation, even though they did not know in advance which attribute was to be tested. The particular situation required that the subjects know that they were to be tested on a set of identified dimensions, and there remains the question whether such advance preparation is essential for the achievement of multiple encoding. Such preparation is probably not essential, but certainly a direct investigation of the question of multiple encoding is in order.

Several already-reported studies using the release from PI method have given some evidence for multiple encoding, but the evidence has not been extremely strong. The Goggin and Wickens (1971) research on Spanish-English language shift employed two classes of words: kinds of food, and parts of a house. Thus it was possible to shift on language alone, on taxonomic category alone, or on both language and taxonomic category. The results for these three kinds of shifts are shown in Figure 5. Significance tests showed all shift groups to be superior to the control, and the double shift (both language and category) to be superior to language alone but not to category alone. However, the effect of the double shift is probably stronger than these data imply, since, it will be recalled, a language shift leads to about 100-percent release for those who are fluent in both tongues. For some people, therefore, the language shift alone reached the ceiling, as measured by Trial 1 performance, and there was little or no room left for the additional category effect.

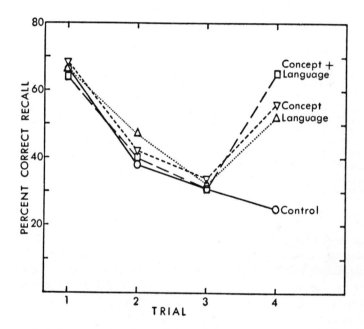

FIG. 5. Percent release from PI for single shifts of the attributes of taxonomic category or language and for the combination of the two. (after Goggin & Wickens, 1971).

In the previously mentioned research by Hopkins, Edwards, and Gavelek (1971), the authors included a study in which they shifted category alone (musical instruments and four-footed animals), modality alone, or both modality and category. As earlier noted, the visual to auditory shift was the only modality shift they found to be effective, so only shifts in that direction will be considered. The modality shifts and category shifts were about equally effective at approximately 65 percent, whereas the dual shift led to a release of about 100 percent. The evidence for dual encoding seems to be fairly strong in this experiment.

A doctoral dissertation by Eggemeier (1971) represents another direct attack upon the problem of multiple encoding by means of a PI release technique. For the first three trials, the experimenter used words that differed as much as possible, in one direction, from the mean rating score on the Evaluative and the Activity dimensions of the Heise (1965) Semantic Differential norms; for the fourth or shift trial, he used words from the other side of the mean, either for both dimensions (Evaluative and Activity) or for only one of these dimensions. In short, there was a double shift for one set of groups and a single shift for the other set. The question asked was whether both dimensions of the Semantic Differential could be encoded *and used* by the subject. Table 2 shows the procedural arrangement for two of the four sets of groups in the experiment. The other two followed the same pattern.

TABLE 2

Arrangement of Groups in the Single- and Double-Shift Experiment
(Eggemeier, 1971)

Condition	First Three Trials		Fourth Trial	
	Activity	Evaluation	Activity	Evaluation
Control	+	+	+	+
Single shift	−	+	+	+
Single shift	+	−	+	+
Double shift	−	−	+	+
Control	−	+	−	+
Single shift	+	+	−	+
Single shift	−	−	−	+
Double shift	+	−	−	+

The results for the overall experiment are presented in Figure 6. All three groups differed from each other at the .05 level on the shift trial. One could argue that these results cannot, as yet, be accepted as unqualified evidence for the use of two dimensions; for it could be assumed that a given subject used only one dimension, and, if he was in the single dimension group, had only a .5 probability of choosing a dimension that would be shifted. The double group, on the other hand, carried a 1.0 probability. If both groups used only a single dimension, the single shift groups would be expected to show a bimodal distribution of scores on the shift trial, the scores being composed of those who chose the to-be-shifted dimension and those who did not. The distributions of scores on Trial 4 are shown in Figure 7. There was no evidence of a bimodal distribution for the single-shift groups, nor for a difference in variance between the double and single groups. The effect of the double shift was simply to displace the distribution to the right. In some manner, the double shift aided performance in a fashion that appeared to be continuous.

One cannot claim, from the data of the Eggemeier experiment, that multiple encoding operates equally well for all attributes. The universality of the double-shift opportunity is complicated by the fact that, although the double-shift group always excelled the single-shift groups, the effect was not significant for two of the four conditions. In both of the two nonsignificant instances, the shift items on Trial 4 included the Evaluative Positive. An internal analysis of the data of the entire experiment suggests that even though both dimensions of the word had probably been encoded, the Evaluative Positive dimension was used exclusively in retrieval on

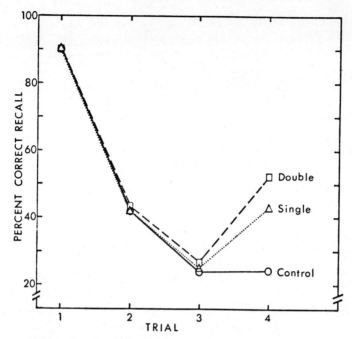

FIG. 6. Percent release from PI for single shifts on the Evaluative or the Activity dimension of the Semantic Differential and for the combination of the two. (after Eggemeier, 1971).

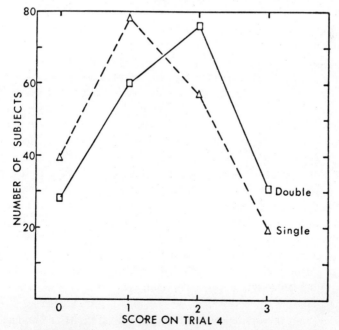

FIG. 7. Distribution of scores of the single- and double-shift groups on the critical shift trial in the Semantic Differential study. (after Eggemeier, 1971).

Trial 4. This description of the process agrees with the suggestion by Shiffrin (1970) that a biasing of search sets at the time of retrieval may occur. In other words, although the advantage afforded by multiple encoding may be available to the subject, he does not always use it. If this interpretation is correct, further research is required to determine the conditions under which the subject will not utilize multiple encoding in retrieval.

An unpublished study by Wickens and Morisano used a slightly different approach to the subject of multiple encoding. The experiment commenced by presenting the category names of the Battig and Montague (1969) norms on IBM cards to 75 subjects and then asking them to sort the cards into piles of "items which go together." When the data were tabulated, it was found that, as one could readily predict, the association of categories across subjects ranged from 0 to 100 percent. The next step was to select a pair of categories with 100-percent association value, for example, *fruits* and *vegetables*. Another category, *flowers,* was selected because it was associated with *fruits* about 50 percent of the time. Finally, the category of professions was chosen because the subjects had never placed it in the same pile as *fruits,* that is, a zero association. A release from PI experiment was constructed with triads from these three categories. In each of the categories, only high priority items (Battig and Montague norms) were used. There were four groups in the experiment. The Trial 4 item-set for all groups was always selected from the fruit category, and the four groups differed only in the classes of items used in the first three trials. For one group, the class was *vegetables* (100 percent); for another, it was *flowers* (50 percent); for another it was *professions* (0); and the control group had *fruits* across all four items. All groups, then, were presented with the same materials on Trial 4, but they differed from each other in their experimental histories.

The results of this study are shown in Figure 8. Statistical analysis indicates that the *vegetable* group did not differ significantly from the control group although there seemed to be some slight evidence of release. *Flowers* showed the next amount of release and differed significantly from both the control and the *vegetable* groups. Highest of all in release was the group for *professions,* but it was not significantly above that for *flowers.* Despite lack of certain statistically significant differences, the groups line up in the order that a multiple encoding interpretation would predict.

A highly intellectualized interpretation of the results—and one probably not paralleled by the subjects' conscious perceptions—might be as follows. *Fruits* are encoded as something (*a*) nonhuman, (*b*) to eat, (*c*) that comes from the ground, and (*d*) that tends to be a dessert course. *Vegetables* are encoded as something (*a*) nonhuman, (*b*) to eat, (*c*) that comes from the ground, and (*d*) that tends to occur with the entree. *Flowers* are encoded as something (*a*) nonhuman, (*b*) decorative, (*c*) that comes from the ground, and (*d*) that is often fragrant. *Professions* are encoded as (*a*) human activities, (*b*) that produce a living, and (*c*) that have certain other characteristics.

It is possible that the overlap of *fruits* and *vegetables* in the non-human, edible, ground-grown dimensions is a predominating characteristic leading to an almost

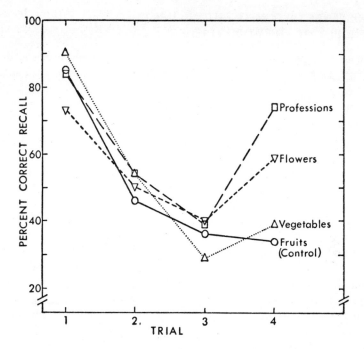

FIG. 8. Percent release from PI as a function of degree of similarity of taxonomic categories.

identical total encoding, so that a slight difference between the two in general flavor or in the position they hold in the prandial parade leads to little distinctiveness between them in the memory task. In conceptual similarity, there is little overlap between *fruits* and *flowers* no overlap between *professions* and *fruits*.

Another possibility, following the Collins and Quillian (1969) view of cognitive storage economy, is that the major memory retrieval cue is stored only at the superordinate node of "something to eat." *Flowers* and *professions,* then, would be differentiated at retrieval from *fruits* and *vegetables,* but the latter and the former two would be treated alike. This analysis handles the data quite well, if one accepts the null hypothesis and assumes no difference in performance between the fruit and vegetable groups, and also none between the flowers and professions groups. If one does not accept the null hypothesis, then additional attributes, differentiating *flowers* and *professions* and *fruits* from *vegetables,* must be encoded and be a part of the retrieval set.

It should be noted parenthetically that the Wickens and Morisano experiment places a restriction on the statements concerning the magnitude of release from PI when taxonomic categories are changed. Obviously, the magnitude will depend on degree of relatedness of the categories at least as measured by the sorting technique.

THE EXISTENCE OF COMPONENT VALUES
INDEPENDENT OF THE WORD ITSELF

The material presented in the earlier section on the multiplicity of encoding and in the last section on the probability of simultaneous or nearly simultaneous multiple encoding, cannot but suggest that the semantic processing operation occurs with abundance and great speed. It also suggests the possibility that a certain amount of processing may be done without the individual being aware of the fact that he *is* processing, and that he may actually encode some dimensions of a word before the name of the word is identified.

As we have noted earlier in this paper, many modern theories of word perception seem to imply the above-named possibilities, in that they speak of attributes developing and then eventuating in the naming process or the vector that is the word. Posner (this volume) refers to encoding that takes place prior to conscious processing. All in all, there has been enough positive material implying the rapid and nonconscious encoding of words to motivate several experiments investigating the possibility that attributes of words are identifiable before the word-name itself enters consciousness. Admittedly, these experiments seem to be a departure from the rules of common sense—or perhaps one should say the dictates of phenomenology—but they are certainly plausible empirical predictions from much modern theory.

The general design of the unpublished experiments by Wickens, Shearer, and Eggemeier has been to present words tachistoscopically at durations too brief to result in identification and then, after a masking stimulus, to present a different word at a suprathreshold level. Subjects were asked to judge whether or not the fully-seen word had some similarity to the semantic experience produced by the tachistoscopically exposed "unseen" word. The task was really quite simple: The subjects guessed whether or not the word they saw briefly was in some way or another similar to the word they saw fully. The requirements placed upon the subjects would seem to be unreal, yet college students were quite willing to cooperate in the experiment. One half of the time, the second or "match" word really did (according to the experimenter's judgment) share some attribute with the "target" word, and half of the time it did not do so.

More specifically, the procedure was as follows: extremely brief presentation of the target word; presentation of a broken-letter mask for 1.5 seconds; presentation of the match word for 5.0 seconds. There were four experimental groups, each receiving a presentation time that was, under the imposed viewing conditions, typically too short to result in target identification. These times were 50, 60, 70, and 80 milliseconds. One control group received a 2.0-second exposure of the target word and was used to check whether the subjects, given a full view of the target word, would judge that the selected match words did indeed match and the selected nonmatching ones did not match; in short, did the subjects of this control group agree with the experimenter's judgments? Prior to the beginning of the experiment, the subjects were told, quite truthfully, that for half the words there would be a match, and for half there would not, so that optimal performance would be associated with 50 percent "yeses" and 50 percent "noes."

In addition to the four experimental short-presentation groups and the 2.0-second control group, a response-bias control group was used to determine whether there was a built-in tendency to say "yes" or "no" to the match words *qua* words, and whether such a tendency, if present, happened to agree with the target-match pairing. Response bias could probably have occurred if, for example, the target word *mother* and the match word *peace* had been employed. If a typical college student saw only the single word *peace* and was asked to give a "yes" or "no" answer to it, he would undoubtedly say "yes." This would lead to a spurious matching on this attribute. To measure response bias to the match words, anagrams of the actual target word were presented for 50 milliseconds and were followed by the mask and matching words with a judgment request, just as in the other groups.

In the first experiment, seven different categories (dimensions, attributes) were selected, with a sample of 12 words per category, making 84 words. The Semantic Differential as a whole was represented by two words from each of the two ends of the three dimensions. The 84 words were presented to the four experimental short-presentation groups and to the two control groups, once with a half "yes" and half "no" proportion, and then a second time with the previous matches becoming nonmatches and vice versa. An identification of the dimensions and samples of the specific items are shown in Table 3.

The results of the experiment for all six groups are shown in Table 4 by statements of the percentage agreement between the subjects' judgments and correct matching as judged by the experimenter. There are at least 900 responses

TABLE 3

Selected Examples of Target Words and Comparison Words for Different Dimensions
(Wickens, Shearer, & Eggemeier, unpublished)

Similarity Dimension	Target Word	Comparison Word	
		Match	Nonmatch
Semantic Differential (Activity −)	Sleep	Egg	Join
Semantic Differential (Activity +)	Sailor	Football	Decrease
Semantic Differential (Potency −)	Flowers	Delight	Wagon
Semantic Differential (Potency +)	Law	Building	Name
Semantic Differential (Evaluation −)	Fire	Hate	Suggest
Semantic Differential (Evaluation +)	Religious	Peace	Mark
Taxonomic category	Chair	Desk	Atom
Synonyms	Empty	Vacant	Snow
Sense impression	Wheel	Ball	Queen
Rhyme	Source	Horse	Market
Pleasant	Caress	Sunshine	Oven
Unpleasant	Anger	Suicide	Passage

represented in each cell. In instances where subjects identified the target word (as they were constantly encouraged to do throughout the experiment), their responses were, of course, not included.

The first group to be examined should be the 2.0-second control, since it indicates how valid were the materials for testing the hypothesis of semantic preprocessing. It is apparent that the materials were appropriately selected, for in all cases there was a significant agreement between the experimenter's scoring and the subject's matching responses. It is also clear that success was not equal in all dimensions. It seems odd that the similarity in a dimension so apparently salient as rhyme was so poorly recognized. Possibly, the subjects were set for semantic rather than phonetic identifications. In the table as a whole, the percentages in the row established by the 2.0-second control group set the ceiling for the effect, and the ceiling is definitely not 100 percent.

The next group to be considered is the anagram control, which was used to determine whether or not there was a response bias. The response bias controls were not conducted for all dimensions, since a number of them could be established as being close to 50 percent on the basis of results of the experimental groups with exposures of 50 or 60 milliseconds. Table 4 indicates that response bias could have been operating for the pleasant, and possibly for the unpleasant, dimension, so it must be concluded that the experiment offers no evidence in these dimensions either for or against preprocessing prior to the word naming process.

Next under consideration will be the results for the short-presentation experimental groups. As indicated in Table 4, a percentage of 53.7 is required for significance at the .05 level. It should be remembered that the percentages for the short-exposure groups should, in all cases, be compared with the ceilings established for appropriate material by the 2.0-second control group where full viewing was

TABLE 4

Percent Correct Matches for Seven Dimensions of Similarity
(Wickens, Shearer, & Eggemeier, Unpublished)

| Group | Dimension Tested | | | | | | |
	Semantic Differential	Taxonomic Category	Synonymity	Sense Impression	Rhyme	Pleasant	Unpleasant
50 Milliseconds	53.4	52.0	47.2	49.2	51.0	51.3	53.7
60 Milliseconds	53.7	50.6	52.7	49.1	49.9	51.3	53.7
70 Milliseconds	53.3	52.1	49.9	47.9	49.2	54.6	54.3
80 Milliseconds	58.5	54.6	56.1	51.8	49.3	53.3	56.1
Anagram control	51.3					54.2	53.6
2.0-Second control	62.7	86.1	88.5	74.1	56.9	55.6	66.8

Note.—53.7 is significant at the .05 level.

possible. The data offer some evidence for encoding prior to awareness of the word itself along the Semantic Differential and on the dimensions of Synonymity and Taxonomic Category. The data for Synonymity and Taxonomic Category are rather nicely regular, with longer exposures producing better matching, and indicate that these attributes appeared rather late in the preprocessing stage. The Semantic Differential is less orderly, but is indeed quite suggestive of a preprocessing at an early temporal stage.

A certain amount of credibility is lent to the data by the performance on the Sense Impression and on the Rhyming dimensions. These two dimensions remain close to 50 percent for all presentation intervals. The major significance of these data bears upon the question of the recognition criterion for the subject. It could be argued that the better-than-chance performance on other dimensions might arise from a high criterion set by the subject for guessing the target word. Certainly this flaw must have characterized some of the subception research of the 1950s when pornographic words were employed as target items. None of the words of the studies reported here was of this sort for any of the dimensions, and the essentially negative results for Rhyme and Sense Impression argue against a high criterion notion. There is no reason to believe that there should be a high criterion for other dimensions and not for Rhyme and Sense Impression.

A second study simply investigated the various dimensions of the Semantic Differential more extensively. It was a companion piece to the previous experiments, and used 10 target items from each end of the Semantic Differential. The words were selected from the Heise (1965) monograph. The results for this experiment are shown in Table 5. The Potency-negative data seem to have been confounded with response bias, and thus cannot be evaluated with respect to preprocessing. The Activity-negative and Potency-positive experimental groups gave no evidence of excelling the anagram control at any presentation time duration, but Activity-positive and the Evaluative scale (positive and negative) seem to have done

TABLE 5

Percent Correct Matches in a Detailed Study of the Semantic Differential
(Wickens, Shearer, & Eggemeier, unpublished)

Group	Semantic Differential Dimension					
	Activity −	Activity +	Potency −	Potency +	Evaluative −	Evaluative +
50 Milliseconds	50.3	55.6	52.1	50.6	52.4	55.0
60 Milliseconds	49.8	57.6	57.5	51.5	53.2	53.3
70 Milliseconds	48.7	56.6	52.0	50.7	57.0	57.1
80 Milliseconds	49.2	54.3	55.4	49.1	52.8	57.3
Anagram control	48.8	49.2	56.4	52.9	49.8	49.7
2.0-Second control	61.8	66.2	73.9	61.0	81.6	73.3

Note.−54.3 is significant at the .05 level.

so. It would have been more convincing if the data were more orderly in the sense of a progressively increasing proportion of agreements with increasing target duration. The data for the Evaluative dimension would also have been neater had the 50-millisecond group been at the 50-percent level, although one might assume that 50 milliseconds was not a short enough time to prevent some encoding for this dimension. Were it not for the anagram control data, one might suspect the results on these attributes of Activity and Evaluation of being influenced by response bias.

It is interesting to note that the two dimensions of the Semantic Differential that gave suggestive evidence for preprocessing are the two dimensions that seemed to produce release from PI in the Pender (1969) experiment with children. Pender found clear evidence for encoding by the Evaluative dimension, even with her second-grade children, and some evidence for encoding by Activity at the sixth-grade level. The data on synonym and taxonomic categories in the first experiment reported in this section need to be evaluated in greater detail to determine whether their apparent effectiveness could be attributed to the same primitive type of connotative encoding.

Admittedly, the conclusions that can be drawn from the results of our experiments must be tentative. None of the data are conclusively strong, but there is perhaps strength enough to lead to an also-tentative description of the temporal course of the encoding process: (a) The attributes of words do not come into being simultaneously, and the total meaning of a word accumulates across time. (b) Certain attributes can be triggered prior to name identification, while others occur simultaneously with the naming process or wait upon it.

A rather inadequate analogy likens the process of dealing with words to a wave with a leading edge, a crest, and a trailing edge. The crest is the naming of the unique word; the leading edge is the preprocessing of some attributes, as suggested by the two experiments just described; and the trailing edge is evidenced by false recognition of words that are related semantically or associatively to words that occurred earlier in a list (Underwood, 1965).

As has been noted, contemporary word perception theory has, more than a few times, seemed to assume some sort of preprocessing. In addition, there has been, from time to time, other support for the suggestion that we process some information without awareness of the full stimulus situation. In the simple activity of sound localization, we experience directly only the location of the sound and not the comparison of the dichotic differences that make localization possible. In the Sternberg (1969) task, the subject responds without awareness of making comparisons or engaging in an exhaustive search. These are just two, out of a number of experimental situations, that have indicated that the psychological processes responsible for behavior need not be a part of conscious experience.

SUMMARY

The original hypothesis that word meaning is a bundle of attributes carries three testable implications and it has been the purpose of this paper to present experimental data and speculation relating to all three.

There is no question but that the problems raised by the third implication that component values can exist independently of the word itself have not yet been solved. No final statement can be made, but the two experiments on the preprocessing of words offer some evidence for differential semantic preprocessing prior to the naming stage. In addition, there were mentioned some theoretical approaches of other authors and some experimental data of other fields, all of which point to at least a possibility of psychological processes that can affect behavior even though not clearly a part of conscious experience.

The experimental and theoretical conclusions in relation to the first and second expectations—that psychologically prominent attributes of words can be identified, and that most if not all words have multiple component values—are far more clear. The picture of encoding presented by the data on release from PI is that the individual is sensitive to (encodes) a large number of the aspects of words, but is also insensitive to certain other aspects. He is particularly reactive to semantic attributes of words, mildly reactive to the method of their physical presentation, and essentially impervious to their syntactical characteristics.

This order of priorities seems to be a most adaptive one. The purpose of language is communication, and therefore it deals with the meaning of symbols. That the message is carried by a two-syllable rather than a four-syllable word or by upper rather than lower case letters may be of little relevance to the communication process. Regarding syntactic factors, they are of little importance in dealing with single words, and hence are not dimensions of word encoding. But, in any highly verbal culture, such as our own, semantic encoding is obligatory, and continued usage plus the typical demand for high speed in communication, eventuates in the automatic encoding of certain aspects of the semantic content. The release from PI paradigm seems to deal primarily with the automatically encoded materials.

The release data point to a multiplicity of encoding, but the use of multiple codes for memory retrieval does not, of necessity, follow. In some of the experiments that have been reported there was indeed evidence for the advantage in recall arising from availability of a dual rather than a single encoding dimension. One of the experiments, however, suggests that such a high priority may be given to one of two dimensions that the other dimension is disregarded and only a single attribute is used in the recall situation.

The final picture seems to be one that represents the initial encoding, particularly the semantic, to be rich and multiple—as it would need to be for distinguishing between words and nuances of words. However, not all dimensions are used in the recall process, for the presence of certain salient characteristics may mitigate against the simultaneous use of others, despite potential helpfulness. The experiments on the preprocessing of words give some evidence, but not strong evidence, for differential semantic processing prior to the naming stage.

REFERENCES

Baldwin, R. B. Release from PI and the physical aspects of words. Unpublished master's thesis, The Ohio State University, 1969.

Battig, W. F., & Montague, W. E. Category norms for verbal items in 56 categories: A replication and extension of the Connecticut category norms. *Journal of Experimental Psychology Monograph,* 1969, 80, (June, Pt. 2), 1-46.

Bower, G. H. A multicomponent theory of the memory trace. In K. W. Spence & J. T. Spence (Eds.), *The psychology of learning and motivation,* Vol. 1. New York: Academic Press, 1967. Pp. 229-325.

Bregman, A. S. Forgetting curves with semantic, phonetic, graphic, and contiguity cues. *Journal of Experimental Psychology,* 1968, 78, 539-546.

Brodie, D. A., & Lippman, L. G. Effects of shifts in visual, semantic and acoustic-semantic stimulus attributes in STM tasks. *Psychonomic Science,* 1970. 20, 335-337. (a)

Brodie, D. A., & Lippman, L. G. Symbolic and size shifts in short-term memory tasks. *Psychonomic Science,* 1970, 20, 361-362. (b)

Collins, A. M., & Quillian, M. R. Retrieval time from semantic memory. *Journal of Verbal Learning and Verbal Behavior,* 1969, 8, 240-247.

DiVesta, F. J. A normative study of 220 concepts rated on the semantic differential by children in grades 2 through 7. *The Journal of Genetic Psychology,* 1966, 109, 205-229.

Eggemeier, F. T. Multidimensional encoding in short-term memory. Unpublished doctoral dissertation, The Ohio State University, 1971.

Goggin, J., & Wickens, D. D. Proactive interference and language change in short-term memory. *Journal of Verbal Learning and Verbal Behavior,* 1971, 10, 453-458.

Heise, D. R. Semantic Differential profiles for 1000 most frequent English words. *Psychological Monographs,* 1965, 79, Whole No. 601.

Hopkins, R. H., Edwards, R. E., & Gavelek, J. R. Presentation modality as an encoding variable in short-term memory. *Journal of Experimental Psychology,* 1971, 90, 319-325.

Keppel, G., & Underwood, B. J. Proactive inhibition in short-term retention of single items. *Journal of Verbal Learning and Verbal Behavior,* 1962, 1, 153-161.

Loess, H. Short-term memory, word class and sequence of items. *Journal of Experimental Psychology,* 1967, 74, 556-561.

Morton, J. A functional model for memory. In D. A. Norman (Ed.), *Models of human memory.* New York: Academic Press, 1970. Pp. 203-254.

Norman, D. A., & Rumelhart, D. E. A system for perception and memory. In D. A. Norman (Ed.), *Models of human memory.* New York: Academic Press, 1970. Pp. 19-64.

Osgood, C. E., Suci, G. J., & Tannenbaum, P. H. *The measurement of meaning.* Urbana: University of Illinois Press, 1957.

Paivio, A., Yuille, J. C., & Madigan, S. A. Concreteness, imagery, and meaningfulness values for 925 nouns. *Journal of Experimental Psychology Monograph,* 1968, 76, (January, Pt. 2), 1-21.

Pender, N. J. A developmental study of conceptual, semantic differential, and acoustical dimensions as encoding categories in short-term memory. Final Report of Project #9-E-070, U. S. Department of Health, Education, and Welfare, Northwestern University, 1969.

Peterson, L. R., & Peterson, M. J. Short-term retention of individual verbal items. *Journal of Experimental Psychology,* 1959, 58, 193-198.

Reutener, D. B. Class shift, symbolic shift, and background shift in short-term memory. *Journal of Experimental Psychology,* 1972, 93, 90-94.

Rinsland, H. D. *A basic vocabulary of elementary school children.* New York: Macmillan Company, 1945.

Rubin, S. M. Proactive and retroactive inhibition in short-term memory as a function of sensory modality. Unpublished manuscript, Human Performance Center, University of Michigan, 1967.

Shiffrin, R. M. Forgetting: Trace erosion or retrieval failure? *Science,* 1970, 168, 1601-1603.

Shulman, H. G. Encoding and retention of semantic and phonemic information in short-term memory. *Journal of Verbal Learning and Verbal Behavior,* 1970, 9, 499-508.

Sternberg, S. Memory scanning: Mental processes revealed by reaction time experiments. *American Scientist,* 1969, 57, 421-457.

Swanson, J. M., & Wickens, D. D. Preprocessing on the basis of frequency of occurrence. *Quarterly Journal of Experimental Psychology*, 1970, **22**, 378-383.

Turvey, M. T., & Egan, J. Contextual change and release from proactive interference in short-term memory. *Journal of Experimental Psychology*, 1969, **81**, 396-397.

Underwood, B. J. False recognition produced by implicit verbal responses. *Journal of Experimental Psychology*, 1965, **70**, 122-129.

Underwood, B. J. Attributes of memory. *Psychological Review*, 1969, **76**, 559-573.

Wickens, D. D. Encoding categories of words: An empirical approach to meaning. *Psychological Review*, 1970, **77**, 1-15.

Wickens, D. D., Born, D. G., & Allen, C. K. Proactive inhibition and item similarity in short-term memory. *Journal of Verbal Learning and Verbal Behavior*, 1963, **2**, 440-445.

Wickens, D. D., & Clark, S. E. Osgood dimensions as an encoding category in short-term memory. *Journal of Experimental Psychology*, 1968, **78**, 580-584.

Wickens, D. D., Clark, S. E., Hill, F. A., & Wittlinger, R. P. Grammatical class as an encoding category in short-term memory. *Journal of Experimental Psychology*, 1968, **78**, 599-604.

Wickens, D. D., & Engle, R. W. Imagery and abstractness in short-term memory. *Journal of Experimental Psychology*, 1970, **84**, 268-272.

Wittlinger, R. P. Phasic arousal in short-term memory. Unpublished doctoral dissertation, The Ohio State University, 1967.

9
THEORETICAL IMPLICATIONS OF DIRECTED FORGETTING[1]

Robert A. Bjork
University of Michigan

We sometimes speak of "good encodings" or "long-term encodings" of to-be-remembered items as if those terms denoted particular encodings that were "good" or "long-term" in some absolute sense. It is largely a relative matter, however, whether a particular encoding of a to-be-remembered item in terms of certain features or associations will result in the long-term storage and reliable retrieval of that item. A particular encoding of a particular item in a particular context by a particular person may uniquely characterize that item, but the same encoding of the same item in a different context, or by a different person having a different verbal history, may lead instead to confusion and interference with other similarly-encoded items in memory. And the goodness of an encoding is not invariant with time either: An encoding that is good at some particular time may become not so good at some later time as a result of subsequent inputs to memory.

There is no doubt that the effective utilization of one's memory depends in a critical way on one's ability to discriminate specific items-as-coded from other items-as-coded. The problem of understanding the nature of coding processes in memory is completely intertwined with the problem of understanding the mechanisms by which items in memory are differentiated (or not differentiated) from other items in memory. This paper is concerned with one aspect of the general problem of how items and sets of items are differentiated in memory. The aspect of concern is how current to-be-remembered information is discriminated from past to-be-forgotten information. In other words, how do we update our memories?

[1] The author's research reported herein was supported by the Advanced Research Projects Agency, Department of Defense, monitored by the Air Force Office of Scientific Research under contracts No. AF(638)-1736 and AF44-620-72-C-0019 with the Human Performance Center, Department of Psychology, University of Michigan.

That we need to update our memories is clear: We would degenerate to a proactive-interference-induced state of total confusion otherwise.

THE DIRECTED-FORGETTING PARADIGM

One promising approach to the problem of understanding how we keep our memories current, and the approach of interest in this paper, is through research on directed forgetting. The directed-forgetting paradigm involves the use of signals to subjects to forget particular items they have been presented. The various phenomena exhibited by subjects in such experiments have implications not only as to the mechanisms by which subjects are able to take advantage of signals to forget some items in order to facilitate their processing of other items, but also as to the general problem of how items are differentiated in memory.

Much of the interest in the directed-forgetting paradigm has been motivated by the feeling that it reveals some curious and previously unappreciated abilities. In my opinion, however, the paradigm is important not primarily because it raises new questions or illustrates surprising capacities, but rather because it has the potential of contributing new leverage on some old and important problems in the study of memory. There is no doubt that the effects of a cue to forget can be quite amazing in some situations, but to anyone who has kept up with the growing literature on directed forgetting it should be apparent that the issues involved are not unique—they are clearly related to those involved in other lines of research. An adequate analysis of directed forgetting will involve interference mechanisms, rehearsal processes, mechanisms by which lists and sets of items are differentiated, the relative roles of storage and retrieval in producing memory failures, and other factors.

From a subject's standpoint in an experiment on directed forgetting, a cue to forget is not such a strange event. The cue simply informs him that he is free to forget the cued material, that his memory for that material will not be tested. Intentional forgetting is a frequent event in one's everyday life; it is probably, in fact, more frequent than is intentional remembering. We overhear conservations, we see things in newspapers and store windows, we add up numbers, we dial phone numbers, we pay attention to advertisements, and so on—nearly all of which we have no use for beyond the point at which we attended to them. To the degree that we have any intentions at all with respect to that information, we intend to forget it rather than remember it.

A number of different procedures, motivated by different purposes and interests, have been employed in research on directed forgetting. In order to provide background for the theoretical questions of main interest, the procedural variations and basic results in research on directed forgetting are reviewed below.

PROCEDURAL VARIATIONS IN DIRECTED FORGETTING

Although experiments on directed forgetting differ in many ways in terms of what types of materials, tests of performance, and timing of events are involved, their primary differences fall on two dimensions: (*a*) whether subjects are cued to forget or remember sets of items or are cued item-by-item, and (*b*) the temporal position of the cue relative to the to-be-remembered items (R-items) and the to-be-forgotten items (F-items).

Cuing of Item Sets

Sets of items (defined, for example, by type of item, color of item, or temporal grouping) are presented and subjects are cued to forget one of the sets. It is assumed in the following (as has been true in every published case) that the number of sets is limited to two.

Intraserial cuing. Subjects are presented a series of items one by one and are cued at some point in the series to forget the items presented prior to the signal. Such experiments are designed (by including lists without any forget-signals, for example) so that subjects can not anticipate when or whether a forget cue (F-cue) will occur; they must, therefore, attempt to memorize each item as it is presented. The sets of items before and after the F-cue may be defined only by being prior or subsequent to the cue, respectively, or they may differ in type of item, input modality, or some such. The procedure has been used in paired-associate probe experiments (e.g., Bjork, 1970a), free recall experiments (Bruce & Papay, 1970), continuous paired-associate experiments (e.g., Elmes, 1969a, b; Elmes, Adams, & Roediger, 1970), ordered recall tasks (e.g., Block, 1971), and in other situations.

Postinput cuing. Rather than present the F-cue prior to the R-items, the cue is delayed until after the input of both item sets. That is, subjects are presented a postinput cue to forget one of the sets. This procedure has been used extensively by Epstein and his co-workers (Epstein, 1969, 1970; Epstein, Massaro, & Wilder, 1972; Shebilske, Wilder, & Epstein, 1971). In their experiments, the task is to learn two successive short lists (typically, six items) differentiated by temporal grouping, item type, or input modality, and the postinput cue specifies whether one or both of the lists is to be recalled. The procedure has also been used by Reed (1970) in a modification of the Brown-Peterson short-term memory paradigm (e.g., Peterson & Peterson, 1959).

Preinput cuing. A possible procedure that has not been used in published reports on cued forgetting would involve cuing subjects prior to the presentation of two sets of items to forget (not learn) one of the sets. Such a procedure does occur in incidental learning paradigms and in standard memory paradigms, as, for example, when subjects are required to shadow but not recall a list of distractor items in the Brown-Peterson paradigm.

It is possible, of course, to conduct experiments that involve combinations of the procedures outlined above. An example is an experiment by Bjork (1970a, Exp. III), in which both intraserial and postcuing were used.

Item-by-Item Cuing

In these procedures, subjects are cued whether to remember or to forget each item in turn.

Cuing at onset. In some cases, the cue to remember or to forget an item is coincident with the onset of the item. Such a procedure has been used by Weiner and Reed (1969) and by Roediger and Crowder (1972). In their experiments, subjects were cued simultaneously with the presentation of a consonant trigram at the start of a Brown-Peterson trial whether to remember or forget the trigram. Subjects are typically required to say each item aloud in such experiments to insure that they attend to F-items.

Cuing after offset. In other cases, the cue to remember or to forget an item is delayed until after the offset of the item. This procedure has been used in experiments employing modifications of the Brown-Peterson paradigm by Bjork, LaBerge, and LeGrande (1968), Turvey and Wittlinger (1969), Pollatsek (1969), and Block (1971). Woodward and Bjork (1971), Davis and Okada (1971), and Bugelski (1970) have used the procedure in free recall experiments. With this procedure, the delay from the offset of an item to the cue to forget or remember the item is an important variable and has been manipulated in several of the studies mentioned above.

Implicit Cuing

The procedures of primary interest to this paper are procedures that involve explicit cues to forget, but it is worth pointing out that many memory paradigms involve implicit F-cues. In many paradigms (the standard Brown-Peterson paradigm, for example), there is an implicit cue to forget at the end of each trial. Also, as mentioned earlier, memory paradigms often require subjects to attend to, but not remember, distractor items of some kind.

The foregoing organization of experimental procedures in research on directed forgetting is presented for organizational purposes. It is not difficult to think of possible experiments that do not fit neatly within the organization, but nearly all experiments to date are exemplars of one or more of the procedures described above.

BASIC PHENOMENA

Two kinds of data are of primary interest in research on directed forgetting: (*a*) the effects of an F-cue on items to be remembered, and (*b*) the effects of an F-cue on items to be forgotten. In the former case, one is interested in the extent to which performance on R-items is facilitated by the F-cue in comparison with cases in which there is no such cue. Knowledge of the extent to which an F-cue reduces interference owing to F-items on the recall of R-items in various situations is relevant to a number of issues, especially issues having to do with interference mechanisms in memory. In the latter case, one is interested in the extent to which F-items remain in memory as measured directly, by recall or recognition tests, or indirectly, by intrusion rates, transfer effects, subsequent repetitions of F-items, and so forth. Knowledge of what happens to F-items under various cuing circumstances is relevant to questions about interference processes, effects of rehearsal, differences between recall and recognition, and other issues.

The following review of the basic results deriving from research on cued forgetting is selective, and some specific results relevant to questions considered later in the paper are introduced there and are not reviewed in this section.

Effects of F-Cues on R-Items

Depending on the situation, the effectiveness of an F-cue can vary from completely effective to completely ineffective in eliminating interference owing to F-items on the recall of R-items. The effectiveness of an F-cue can be judged by noting where performance on the R-items falls between two controls, one in which there are no F-items and the other in which there is no F-cue. If performance is as good as when there are no F-items, the F-cue is completely effective, and if performance is no better than when there is no F-cue, the cue is completely ineffective.

Except for certain special cases, a cue to forget has been demonstrated to be completely effective when the cue follows the items to be forgotten and precedes the items to be remembered (intraserial cuing). The proactive interference attributable to the first set on the recall of the second set that would normally obtain if there were no F-cue can be completely eliminated by the F-cue. Two examples of this result are shown in Figures 1 and 2. The data shown in Figure 1

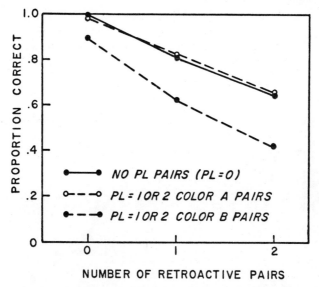

FIG. 1. Proactive interference resulting from to-be-forgotten (color A) pairs versus proactive interference resulting from to-be-remembered (color B) pairs (after Bjork, 1970a).

are from an experiment by Bjork (1970a, Exp. I). Subjects were presented lists of consonant-vowel-consonant (CVC) trigrams paired with words. The lists varied in number of pairs and each list was followed by a single probe test of one of the pairs. Some of the lists contained a signal to subjects to forget the pairs presented prior to the signal. The signal consisted of a change from color A to color B (green to yellow or yellow to green) in the background on which the pairs were shown.[2]

[2] It turns out to matter very little what the cue to forget is, as long as it is salient Color changes, tones, changes in spatial position, the word "forget," and other cues have been used with apparently equal efficacy.

In Figure 1, performance when there were no proactive pairs is contrasted with performance when there were one or two proactive color A (F-cued) pairs and when there were one or two color B (to-be-remembered) pairs. It is clear from Figure 1 that the F-cue, in effect, truncated the color A items from the list as far as their interference with the recall of color B pairs is concerned.

The second example is an experiment by Block (1971). In his experiment, subjects were presented lists of six words. On some trials two lists were presented and subjects were cued at the end of the first list to either forget the first list, in which case their recall of the second list was tested (F2 trials), or to remember the first list, in which case they were cued at the end of the trial to recall either the first list (P1 trials) or the second list (P2 trials). On other trials, subjects were presented single lists corresponding to either a first list (C1 trials), in which case they could not anticipate that they would be required to recall the list after it was presented, or to a second list (C2 trials), in which case they could anticipate (by virtue of a cue presented at the start of the list) that they would be required to recall the list after it was presented.

Block's results are shown in Figure 2. The fact that performance is about as good in the F2 case as in the C2 case indicates once again that the F-cue was very effective. The average correct-recall proportions were .41, .58, and .60 in the P2, F2, and C2 cases, respectively.

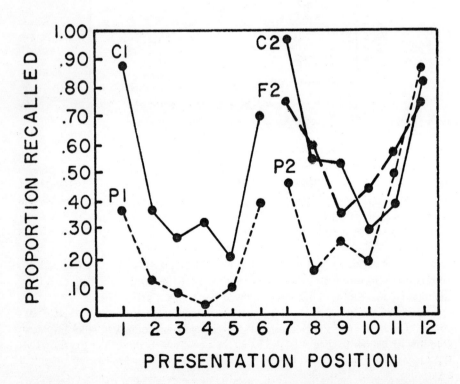

FIG. 2. Mean proportion recalled as a function of presentation position (after Block, 1971).

Similar findings have been obtained by Bruce and Papay (1970) with a free-recall paradigm, and by Bjork, Abramowitz, and Krantz (1970) with a memory-search paradigm. In the latter case, response latency rather than recall probability was shown to be unaffected by F-items. Elmes and his co-workers (e.g., Elmes, 1969a, b; Elmes et al. 1970; Elmes & Wilkinson, 1971) have also found that an F-cue facilitates performance on R-items subsequent to the cue in continuous paired-associate tasks. Whether F-cues in their experiments were completely effective in eliminating proactive interference owing to pairs prior to the signal is difficult to judge, because their experimental designs did not include the control condition in which there are no pairs corresponding to the F-pairs in the F-cue condition.

Postinput cues to forget are not as effective in reducing interference owing to F-items as are cues that precede the items to be remembered. The difference in effectiveness between intraserial cuing and postinput cuing is illustrated by the results of an experiment by Bjork (1970a, Exp. III). In Bjork's experiment, a single trial consisted of the following sequence of events: Two CVC-word paired associates were shown on a yellow background, there was a first instruction, two CVC-word pairs were shown on a green background, there was a second instruction, and the trial concluded with a single probe test (on a white background) of one of the pairs. Five different list types were generated by the following combinations of first and second instructions: RY:RG (remember yellow, remember green), RY:FG (remember yellow, forget green), RY:FY (remember yellow, forget yellow), FY:RG (forget yellow, remember green), and FY:FG (forget yellow, forget green). The last condition was included so that a "forget yellow" first instruction would not predict a "remember green" second instruction. Following FY:FG lists, the probe test was replaced with a presentation of "no test."

The results of the experiment are shown in Figure 3. The difference in performance on tests of the green pairs in the RY:FY and FY:RG conditions demonstrates the differential effectiveness of an F-cue presented prior to the R-pairs and an F-cue presented subsequent to the R-pairs. That is, the only difference between the RY:FY and FY:RG conditions is the location of the FY instruction.

With a postinput cuing procedure, one can attempt to attenuate either proactive interference or retroactive interference by cuing subjects to forget either the first or second set, respectively. In Figure 3, it appears that the postinput cues did attenuate both proactive and retroactive interference somewhat. There is some question, however, whether postinput cues are effective at all. There are other cases in which facilitation of R-item recall owing to a postinput F-cue has been demonstrated (e.g., Epstein, 1969, 1970; Reed, 1970, Exp. II; Shebilske et al., 1971), but there are also cases resulting in no facilitation (e.g., Reed, 1970, Exp. III; Block, 1971, Exp. I).

One problem in deciding the question is that performance in a postinput F-condition can be compared with one of two different control conditions. An experiment by Reed (1970, Exp. III) serves to illustrate clearly the two different types of controls, because both were included in the design. Reed's study employed a variation of the Brown-Peterson paradigm. In the conditions of interest, subjects were shown two three-consonant (CCC) trigrams, there was an interpolated activity,

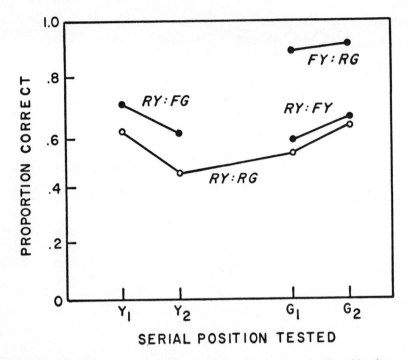

FIG. 3. Proportion correct responses as a function of instructional combination (after Bjork, 1970a).

and the trial concluded with a recall test. In one such condition, a cue to forget the second trigram was presented immediately after the second trigram was presented; in another condition there was no F-cue, but the recall cue at the end of the trial instructed subjects to recall only the first trigram; and in a third condition, there was no F-cue and the cue at the end of the trial specified that both CCCs were to be recalled, in the order first CCC, second CCC. The probability of correct recall of the first CCC was .68, .67, and .52, respectively, for the three conditions specified above. Thus, if the appropriate control is the condition where both trigrams were recalled, then the F-cue did facilitate performance. On the other hand, if the appropriate control is the condition where the recall cue required recall of only the first CCC, then the F-cue did not facilitate performance.

   An argument can be made for or against either type of control condition. The condition in which complete recall is required can be criticized on the grounds that comparisons between such a condition and an F-condition confound differences in amount to be recalled and conditions. Use of the other control condition can be criticized on the grounds that the control condition itself constitutes a kind of F-condition in which the F-cue is administered at the time of recall, hence using such a control constitutes a comparison between F-conditions differing only in the delay of the F-cue.

   It is not clear which control is the more appropriate; in fact, the choice may be completely theory-specific. It is clear that one's conclusion with regard to the effectiveness of a postinput F-cue is heavily dependent on which control is used. Whether the individual studies listed above found or did not find facilitation with postinput cuing is heavily correlated with the type of control employed.

In the experiments reviewed thus far, the F-items and R-items have been temporally blocked. It is of obvious interest whether such temporal blocking is a necessary condition for an F-cue to be effective in facilitating performance on R-items. The answer to the question depends on the cuing procedure. If F-items and R-items are intermingled during presentation and postcuing is used, there is no facilitation even when performance is contrasted with a recall-everything control (Epstein, 1969). If R-items and F-items are intermingled during presentation, but are cued item by item, there is substantial facilitation. The latter result was demonstrated by Woodward and Bjork (1971) and was replicated by Davis and Okada (1971).

An interesting case in which an implicit F-cue seems not to be very effective is the standard Brown-Peterson paradigm. The fact that there is substantial proactive interference from trial to trial in such experiments, even though there is an implicit cue to forget at the end of each trial, is well documented (see Wickens, this volume). It may be that an item can be processed to a point after which a cue to forget the item has little effect. Thus, after a subject has studied an item during its presentation, attempted to retain the item during an interfering activity, and endeavored to retrieve the item at the time of recall, it may be too late to administer an F-cue. Some support for such a notion derives from an experiment by Turvey and Wittlinger (1969). In their experiment, an F-cue administered at the time an item was presented resulted in a significant attenuation of the proactive interference attributable to that item, as measured by recall performance on the next item. They also found that a cue to forget (not recall) an item at the start of its recall period did not significantly attenuate proactive interference traceable to that item.

Effects of F-Cues on F-Items

The fate of F-items, in terms of the nature of their existence or nonexistence in memory has been evaluated by a number of different techniques. As mentioned earlier, some of those techniques involve direct measures of F-item recall and recognition, other techniques involve indirect measures, such as intrusion rates and transfer effects.

Recall of F-items. Several different procedures have been used to assess recall of F-items. The most straightforward procedure, but possibly the most problematical as well, was introduced by Weiner and Reed (1969). They simply cued subjects at the onset of an item in a Brown-Peterson paradigm whether to forget the item or remember the item, and required them to attempt to recall the item in either case. A second procedure (Bjork, 1970a; Bruce & Papay, 1970; Davis & Okada, 1971) involves testing recall of F-items on the last trial or two of the experiment, by which time subjects presumably believe F-cues and are always trying to forget F-items; since the experiment proper is over, destroying their faith in an F-cue by testing F-items can do little harm. A third procedure, similar to the second, involves a delayed recall test of all items presented during the course of the experimental session (e.g., Woodward & Bjork, 1971). A final procedure, used by Reitman, Malin, Bjork, and Higman (1971), involves practicing subjects on trials during which F-items are never tested, and then informing them that during the subsequent trials there will be infrequent tests of F-items, that such tests will be designated by a special signal, and that their best strategy is to attempt always to forget F-items.

The reasons for wanting to test F-items, and the problems in doing so, are both obvious. In my opinion, the best of the four procedures mentioned above is the last one mentioned. With the Weiner and Reed (1969) procedure, subjects are told to forget items they know they will have to recall, and hence one can never be sure that they are attempting to forget when instructed to do so, or, for that matter, whether they are recalling F-items when instructed to do so. The second procedure has the problem of not generating very much data on the recall of F-items, and, in addition, the test of F-items is a surprise to the subject, which may in turn, through delay or disruption of his recall attempt, result in impaired performance. The third procedure is useful, but a delayed attempt to recall all items shown during the experiment does not provide a reasonable measure of the status of the F-items during any one trial of the experiment. With the Reitman et al. (1971) procedure, F-items can be tested on a number of different individual trials during the experiment, the tests of F-items do not come as a surprise, and if performance on the normal trials is characteristic of performance in an equivalent experiment not involving tests of F-items, one has some evidence that subjects were consistently trying to forget F-items.

The complete pattern of results from the different experiments and procedures in which F-item recall has been tested is very complex. The following summary statements convey some of the general findings.

1. In those experiments where it is possible to test for the recall of F-items without informing subjects that such a test is occurring, recall of F-items is negligible. Such tests are possible and have been included in paired-associate probe experiments (Bjork, 1970a; Reitman et al., 1971), but are not possible in the other (nonprobe) experiments that have been employed in research on directed forgetting.

2. When subjects are aware that F-items are to be tested, recall depends on the experimental paradigm, and on the delay from the presentation of an F-item to the cue to recall the item. With the Weiner and Reed (1969) procedure, and with the paired-associate probe procedure, F-item performance varies from about 90 percent of performance on comparable R-items at very short retention intervals (2 or 3 seconds) to about 40 to 50 percent at long retention intervals. In free recall, when cuing is item by item, intentional recall of F-items is only about 10 to 15 percent of the level of recall for R-items.

3. The experiment by Reitman et al. (1971) provides evidence that F-items can interfere both proactively and retroactively with each other even though they do not interfere with the recall of R-items. In their experiment, lists of paired associates were presented and at the end of each list a single pair from the list was tested. Some of the lists contained a signal to forget the pairs prior to the signal. On tests of R-pairs, recall averaged .75, .73, .76, and .72 when there were 0, 1, 2, or 3 F-pairs in the list, respectively. On tests of F-pairs, when there were 0, 1, or 2 F-pairs preceding the tested F-pair in the list, recall averaged .55, .49, and .24,

respectively; when there were 0, 1, or 2 F-pairs succeeding the tested F-pair in the list, recall averaged .55, .33, and .27, respectively. Thus, recall of R-pairs was not influenced by the number of F-pairs in the list, but recall of F-pairs was influenced heavily by both the number of other proactive F-pairs in the list and by the number of other retroactive pairs in the list.

Recognition of F-items. The results of experiments including tests for the recognition of F-items are particularly interesting. In three experiments (Block, 1971; Elmes et al., 1970; Gross, Barresi, & Smith, 1970), the delayed recognition of F-items was not significantly different than the delayed recognition of R-items. Block's data are shown in Figure 4. The F2 curve is the delayed recognition probability for items that had been presented in a first list on trials where there was a first list, a cue to forget the first list, a second list, and a cue to recall the second list. The P2 curve is for items presented in a first list on trials where there was a first list, a cue to remember the first list, a second list, and a cue to recall the second list. The C2 value is the false positive rate for words that had not been presented during the experiment.

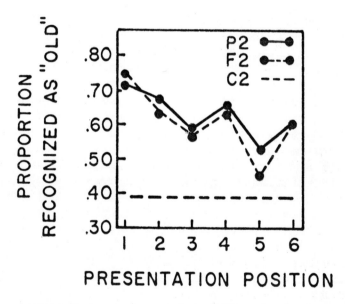

FIG. 4. Mean proportion recognized as "old" as a function of presentation position (after Block, 1971).

In contrast to the results just mentioned, Davis and Okada (1971) found a clear difference between the immediate recognition of F-cued words and R-cued words following a free-recall list in which the words were cued word by word.

An unpublished experiment conducted by Paul Winchester at the University of Michigan suggests that there are situations in which the recall of F-items may be clearly inferior to the recall of R-items, whereas the recognition of F-items is equal to the recognition of R-items. Winchester employed a paired-associate probe design and found that the delayed recognition of F-pairs did not differ from delayed recognition of comparable R-pairs, even though the delayed recall of F-pairs was about one-half the level of recall of R-pairs.

Intrusion of F-items. The rate at which F-items are intruded during the recall of R-items has been analyzed in a number of exeriments. In general, in those conditions where an F-cue is effective in eliminating interference attributable to F-items, intrusions are very infrequent. In conditions where an F-cue is less effective, intrusions are more frequent. Supporting data for this generalization have been reported by Bjork (1970a, Exp. III) and Block (1971, Exp. I). Reitman et al. (1971) have also shown that when F-items are tested, the frequency of intrusions of other F-items is much higher than is the frequency of F-item intrusions when R-items are tested. Of the intrusions of response members from other pairs in the tested list, only 6 percent were from F-pairs when an R-pair was tested, whereas 75 percent were from F-pairs when an F-pair was tested.

Repetition of F-items. Another method that has been used to indirectly assess F-items is to re-present an F-item subsequent to its initial presentation and to contrast the effects of that repetition with an appropriate control. An example of one such procedure is found in Reed (1970). In a modified Brown-Peterson design, Reed examined the recall of CCC items following a second presentation as a function of whether they had been F-cued or R-cued following their first presentation. It turned out that the probability of recall of initially F-cued items (.86) was as good as the recall of initially R-cued items (.86).

Weiner and Reed (1969) also obtained a similarly striking equality of performance following the repetition of R-items and F-items, but the extent to which inferences can be drawn from repetition results is quite limited. Such procedures depend on the assumption that performance following a repetition of an item is a reliable indicator of the status of the item in memory prior to the repetition. That such an assumption is not tenable is indicated clearly by research on the effects of spacing of repetitions in memory. The fact that two spaced presentations of an item usually result in clearly superior performance following the second presentation in comparison to performance following two massed presentations, even though recall of an item at the time of a second spaced presentation is clearly inferior to recall of an item at the time of a second massed presentation, indicates that recall after a repetition is an imperfect indicator of the representation of an item in memory prior to the repetition (for discussions of this issue, see Bjork, 1970b, and Melton, 1970).

Pupillary responses to F-cues. An intriguing result has been obtained by Johnson (1971), who monitored subjects' pupillary reactions during an experiment involving F-cues. Johnson presented a series of five-word lists, some of which contained an F-cue inserted between two adjacent words in the list. The subjects were required to recall all five words in lists containing no F-cue, and they were required to recall the postsignal words in lists containing an F-cue. For the no-cue lists, Johnson found the characteristic gradual increase in pupil size during list input (the "loading" function), and the characteristic gradual decrease in pupil size during recall (the "unloading" function). The terms "loading" and "unloading" are due to Kahneman and Beatty (1966), and are meant to reflect the covariation of pupil size and memory load. During lists with an F-cue, Johnson found an increase in pupil size during the presentation of precue words, a momentary further increase in response to the onset of the F-cue, a decrease following the F-cue, and a standard loading and unloading pattern during the presentation and recall of the postcue words. Thus, on the surface at least, Johnson's results imply that the F-cue in his experiment functionally deleted the to-be-forgotten words from the subject's memory load.

MECHANISMS OF DIRECTED FORGETTING

Subjects might invoke a number of different information-processing mechanisms, singly or in combination, when they are cued that certain items need no longer be remembered. Three possibilities (Bjork et al., 1968) are (a) active erasure or dumping of F-items from short-term memory, (b) differential rehearsal of R-items following the cue, and (c) differential grouping of R-items to functionally separate them in memory from F-items. A fourth possibility (Weiner, 1968; Weiner & Reed, 1969) is active inhibition of the retrieval of F-items (repression) at the time of recall. Finally, in those procedures where a postinput F-cue reduces the amount to be recalled, Epstein (1969, 1970) has proposed that the F-cue facilitates retrieval by eliminating output interference owing to circulation of yet-to-be-recalled items during the prior recall of other items.

Only two of the five possibilities mentioned above are considered seriously in this section: the differential rehearsal and differential grouping mechanisms. The active erasure notion is a dramatic and interesting possibility, but it is untenable in view of the ample evidence that F-items exist unerased in memory. The retrieval-inhibition mechanism is less easily discounted, but the full pattern of results on tests of recall and recognition argues against it, and the mechanism is somewhat specific to Weiner and Reed's (1969) procedure, which is problematical for the reasons discussed earlier. Epstein's output interference notion is both reasonable and supported by considerable data, but the notion is specific to comparisons between F-conditions and R-conditions in which the amount to be recalled differs. Such procedures are a kind of special case in research on directed forgetting and, although interesting in their own right, are not considered in this section (see Epstein, in press, for a thorough consideration of such procedures).

A Two-Process Theory

According to a theory proposed by Bjork (1970a), subjects take advantage of an F-cue in two ways: (a) They devote all further rehearsal, mnemonic, and integrative activities exclusively to R-items, and (b) they differentially group, organize, or code R-items in a way that functionally segregates them from F-items in memory. Neither mechanism alone is sufficient to account for existing results in research on directed forgetting, and to some extent the mechanisms coimply each other. That is, efficient selective rehearsal of R-items in memory depends on their being differentiated as a set, and the differentiation of R-items as a set may depend on their being rehearsed together.

According to the theory, whether an F-cue is effective in attenuating interference owing to F-items in a particular situation is determined by the extent to which the situation permits differential rehearsal of R-items and the differentiation of R-items as a set. For example, an F-cue in the following case should be quite effective: Present set A; cue to forget A; present set B; recall set B. The cue to forget set A occurs before set B is presented, and set A and set B are blocked temporally. Thus, the situation permits differential rehearsal of set B following the F-cue, and set A and set B are not difficult to differentiate. In such a situation, as reviewed earlier, an F-cue is typically completely effective in eliminating interference owing to F-items. If set A and set B were made highly similar and confusable, and if rehearsal opportunities were minimized, an F-cue should not be completely effective. The results of experiments by Bjork et al. (1968) and Block (1971, Exp. I) support this interpretation. In Block's experiment, for example, an F-cue was not completely effective when the F-items and R-items were highly similar.

An F-cue in the following case should not be very effective: Present set A; present set B; cue to forget set A or set B; test recall of remaining set. In such a case, subjects must attempt to rehearse both lists during input because the F-cue does not occur until after input. That an F-cue in such a condition is less effective than an F-cue in the preceding condition is demonstrated in the results shown in Figure 3 (Bjork, 1970a, Exp. III). When set A and set B are intermingled rather than temporally blocked, a postinput F-cue is completely ineffective (Epstein, 1969), and when rehearsal following the F-cue is prevented by a distractor activity, a postinput F-cue is also ineffective (Reed, 1970, Exp. III; Block, 1971, Exp. I). Both results make sense in terms of the theory.

In general, the theory predicts the basic effects of an F-cue on the recall of R-items quite well. With respect to the effects of an F-cue on F-items, the theory in the general form postulated above lacks the specificity to make clearcut predictions. The overall evidence that F-items exist in memory at the time of R-item recall, even in those cases where the F-items are noninterfering, is in accord with the theory, because the theory asserts that F-items are not absent from memory, but are segregated in some manner.

A Modest Elaboration of the Theory

Although the theory as stated is promising, it is also unsatisfying in that it is not specific enough to yield predictions with respect to certain phenomena. The following assertions are an attempt to further specify the theory.

1. We come equipped with a short-term memory system and a long-term memory system, and both systems have the general properties typically attributed to them as far as capacity, format of storage, rate of forgetting, and likelihood of retrieval are concerned.

2. Rehearsal is a control process consisting of activities such as rote cycling of items, and efforts to associate items. Rehearsal schemes operate primarily on the contents of short-term memory, though items may be entered into a rehearsal scheme from long-term memory. A rehearsal scheme is a rehearsal routine over a particular set of items, but it is to be thought of as more flexible, variable, and changeable than a fixed-capacity buffer.

3. The time an item remains in short-term memory and the extent to which it is stored in long-term memory are straightforward increasing functions of rehearsal.

The entry of an item into long-term memory, as measured by a recognition test, requires very little rehearsal; any additional rehearsal of the item may improve recognition memory somewhat, but its principal effect is on retrievability in recall.

4. Long-term memory can be thought of as a large structure having many different storage locations or regions. When items in a particular rehearsal scheme are entered into long-term memory, they are entered at the same storage location.

5. When a subject is presented an F-cue, he starts a new rehearsal scheme involving only R-items, to the degree it is possible to do so. The new rehearsal scheme automatically opens up a new storage area in long-term memory into which any items entered into it from the new rehersal scheme are stored. Finally, when a new rehearsal scheme is started, any items in the prior rehearsal scheme are lost from short-term memory at the rapid rate characteristic of unrehearsed items.

Some Predictions of the Elaborated Theory

It should be clear that the foregoing specification of the theory retains the differential rehearsal and differential grouping mechanisms. Thus, the theory's predictions of the effects of an F-cue on R-items are essentially the same as those of the original theory discussed above. The elaborated theory does make some predictions not derivable from the original theory with regard to the effects of F-cues on F-items.

Recall of F-items. According to the theory, F-items should be retrievable from long-term memory to the extent that they were rehearsed, and they should be differentiated from R-items in storage to the degree that an experimental situation does not require them to be rehearsed together with R-items.

One experiment providing considerable detail on the recall of F-items is the paired-associate experiment carried out by Reitman et al. (1971). The basic features of their data on the recall of F-items are predicted quite well by the model. They found much better performance on informed tests of F-items than on uninformed tests of F-items; on the uninformed tests, performance was essentially zero. This is explicable in the theory in terms of subjects searching the wrong storage area on uninformed tests. On trials when a single F-pair was presented and, following a variable number of R-pairs, was tested, performance was very sensitive to the number of R-pairs. When there was only one R-pair, the probability of correct recall on the test of the F-item was .75. When there were 2, 3, or 4 R-pairs, the probability of correct recall was .34, .19, and .09, respectively. In terms of the theory, the F-item is no longer rehearsed once the F-cue occurs, and is, therefore, lost from short-term memory at a rapid rate. The .75, .34, .19, and .09 values represent that loss rate. That performance on the F-item appears headed toward zero as the number of R-items increases indicates a very low likelihood that the F-item is retrievable from long-term memory, which should be the case according to the theory, because the item was rehearsed very little before the F-cue occurred.

The results of a test of F-item recall by Bruce and Papay (1970) can be interpreted similarly. In their experiment, a cue to forget was administered after the first 15 words in a free-recall list. After 20 more R-words, subjects were asked to recall both

R-words and F-words. Recall of the F-word presented just prior to the F-cue was only about 5 percent, whereas recall of the first F-word in the list was about 25 percent.

Intrusions of F-words. The general finding that the less effective an F-cue is in attenuating F-item interference during R-item recall the greater the frequency of F-item intrusions is consistent with the theory. Forget-items should not interfere with R-item recall to the extent that they are differentiated (are stored in a different memory area) from R-items. Thus, frequency of intrusion of F-items and amount of interference owing to F-items should be closely related.

The findings of Reitman et al. (1971) that F-items interfered with the recall of other F-items even though they did not interfere with the recall of R-items, and that the frequency of intrusions of other F-items when an F-item was tested was much greater than the frequency of intrusions of F-items when an R-item was tested, are also consistent with the set differentiation notion in the theory.

Recognition of F-items. The theory assumes that the principal effects of rehearsal are on retrieval from long-term memory rather than on storage in long-term memory. Thus, even though R-items are rehearsed more and are better recalled than F-items in a particular experimental situation, the likelihood that R-items and F-items are stored in long-term memory may not differ substantially, and recognition performance on tests of F-items may approximate recognition performance on R-items. As reviewed earlier, Elmes et al. (1970), Gross et al. (1970), and Block (1971)—Block's data are in Figure 4—found near equality of recognition of R-items and F-items.

Davis and Okada (1971) found substantially better recognition of R-items than of F-items. In their experiment, however, words in a free-recall list were F-cued or R-cued word by word. With such a cuing procedure, subjects need not rehearse a word seriously until, and if, an R-cue is presented after the word. Many F-words might not be given even the minimal rehearsal required to enter them in long-term memory.

THE UPDATING OF MEMORY

There are some properties of the theory that merit comment, especially those having to do with possible mechanisms involved in the updating of memory. Much of what is assumed in the theory is not novel, but there are several aspects of the theory that have implications with respect to the problem of how we keep (or fail to keep) our memories current. Those properties and implications are discussed below.

Role of Short-Term Memory

Almost by definition, short-term memory is critical to the updating of memory. At any one point in time, the contents of short-term memory consist of information that is in fact current or is related in some important way to information that is current. When information is lost from short-term memory it is assumed to be completely lost and, hence, incapable of providing proactive interference with the storage or handling of subsequent information within the short-term memory system.

Interaction Between Short-Term Memory and Long-Term Memory

A very important property of the theory is that short-term memory and long-term memory are assumed to interact in a structural and organizational way. The notion that both the length of time an item resides in short-term memory and the extent to which the item is stored in long-term memory are rehearsal-dependent is familiar, but the theory assumes in addition that how items are grouped or differentiated in long-term memory is a function of rehearsal, and that, conversely, the pre-existing structure of information in long-term memory influences rehearsal schemes.

According to this view, rehearsal processes are important to the updating of memory in two different ways. Because rehearsal is assumed to be a control process of great flexibility, and one that can maintain items in short-term memory, it provides a means of keeping available those items that are most current or important. And since starting a new rehearsal scheme is assumed in the theory to lead to differentiated storage in long-term memory of the information involved in that rehearsal scheme, rehearsal provides a means to segregate relatively current from relatively old information in long-term memory.

Role of Set Differentiation in Long-Term Memory

Probably the most important and least well defined notion in the theory is that subjects are able to differentially group two sets of items in memory in a way that prevents interference between the sets. The total evidence suggesting such a mechanism is formidable, but the basis on which an arbitrary set of items is differentiated in memory from other sets of items is not clear at all. Assuming such a mechanism exists, it is still not clear how sets of relatively up-to-date information would be identified as such. If it is the case, however, that rehearsal operates primarily on retrieval rather than on storage, and that information in long-term memory becomes less retrievable with time, it is possible that the degree to which information is retrievable would provide a basis (even though somewhat fallible) for identifying relatively current information. The fact that such a system would not be perfect does not argue against it: Subjects are not perfect either.

SUMMARY AND CONCLUSIONS

This paper is based on the argument that the problem of understanding coding processes in memory is intertwined with the problem of understanding how items are differentiated in memory, and that one promising approach to the latter problem is through research on directed forgetting. More specifically, research on directed forgetting is particularly relevant to one very important aspect of differentiating items in memory: the processes by which current to-be-remembered information is discriminated from to-be-forgotten information. That is, how do we keep our memories current?

The directed-forgetting paradigm involves the use of signals to subjects that they can forget some or all of the items they have been presented. The principal procedural variations in research on directed forgetting differ (*a*) in whether subjects are cued to forget individual items or sets of items defined in some way, and (*b*) in the temporal position of the cue to forget (F-cue) with respect to the to-be-remembered and to-be-forgotten items.

The effectiveness of an F-cue can be judged both in terms of whether subjects can take advantage of the cue to facilitate their processing of to-be-remembered items, and in terms of whether subjects lose access to the to-be-forgotten items. The degree to which an F-cue is effective, in either sense, depends on the particular procedural variation employed and on the way in which performance is tested. As a function of the situation, a cue can vary from completely effective to completely ineffective in eliminating interference owing to to-be-forgotten items on the recall of to-be-remembered items. Also, as a function of the situation and whether performance is assessed by a recall test, a cued-recall test, or a recognition test, to-be-forgotten information can vary from completely unavailable to completely as available as comparable to-be-remembered information.

The implications of the full pattern of results in research on directed forgetting can be summarized by the following statements. (*a*) Whether items are differentiable in memory depends on whether they were rehearsed differentially and on whether they were organized (grouped) differentially. (*b*) Whether such differential rehearsal and organization is achieved depends on the interaction of short-term memory and long-term memory, which, in turn, depends on situational factors such as rate of presentation, similarity of materials, and so forth; in particular, the nature of rehearsal processes in short-term memory influences the structural organization of information stored in long-term memory, and the structure of long-term memory influences the nature of rehearsal processes in short-term memory. (*c*) The retrieval of an item from long-term memory depends heavily on the degree to which that item was rehearsed and interrelated with other times in long-term memory; the existence of an item in long-term memory as measured by a recognition test requires neither extensive rehearsal nor association with other items in long-term memory. (*d*) Finally, the processes by which items become nonretrievable are interrelated with the processes by which items become noninterfering.

REFERENCES

Bjork, R. A. Positive forgetting: The noninterference of items intentionally forgotten. *Journal of Verbal Learning and Verbal Behavior,* 1970, 9, 255-268. (a)

Bjork, R. A. Repetition and rehearsal mechanisms in models of short-term memory. In D. A. Norman (Ed.), *Models of human memory.* New York: Academic Press, 1970. (b)

Bjork, R. A., Abramowitz, R. L., & Krantz, D. H. Selective high-speed scanning of item-sets in memory. Paper presented at the Midwest Mathematical Psychology Meetings, Bloomington, Indiana, April, 1970.

Bjork, R. A., LaBerge, D., & LeGrande, R. The modification of short-term memory through instructions to forget. *Psychonomic Science,* 1968, 10, 55-56.

Block, R. A. Effects of instructions to forget in short-term memory. *Journal of Experimental Psychology,* 1971, 89, 1-9.

Bruce, D., & Papay, J. P. Primacy effect in single-trial free recall. *Journal of Verbal Learning and Verbal Behavior*, 1970, 9, 473-486.

Bugelski, B. R. Words and things and images. *American Psychologist*, 1970, 25, 1002-1012.

Davis, J. C., & Okada, R. Recognition and recall of positively-forgotten items. *Journal of Experimental Psychology*, 1971, 89, 181-186.

Elmes, D. G. Role of prior recalls and storage load in short-term memory. *Journal of Experimental Psychology*, 1969, 79, 468-472. (a)

Elmes, D. G. Supplementary report: Cueing to forget in short-term memory. *Journal of Experimental Psychology*, 1969, 80, 561-562. (b)

Elmes, D. G., Adams, C., & Roediger, H. L. Cued forgetting in short-term memory: Response selection. *Journal of Experimental Psychology*, 1970, 86, 103-107.

Elmes, D. G., & Wilkinson, W. C. Cued forgetting in free recall: Grouping on the basis of relevance and category membership. *Journal of Experimental Psychology*, 1971, 87, 438-440.

Epstein, W. Poststimulus output specification and differential retrieval from short-term memory. *Journal of Experimental Psychology*, 1969, 82, 168-174.

Epstein, W. Facilitation of retrieval resulting from postinput exclusion of part of the input. *Journal of Experimental Psychology*, 1970, 86, 190-195.

Epstein, W. Mechanisms of directed forgetting. In G. H. Bower (Ed.), *The Psychology of Learning and motivation*, Vol. 6, New York: Academic Press, in press.

Epstein, W., Massaro, D. W., & Wilder, L. Selective search in directed forgetting. *Journal of Experimental Psychology*, 1972, in press.

Gross, A. E., Baresi, J., & Smith, E. E. Voluntary forgetting of a shared memory load. *Psychonomic Science*, 1970, 20, 73-75.

Johnson, D. A. Pupillary responses during a short term memory task: Cognitive processing, arousal, or both? *Journal of Experimental Psychology*, 1971, 90, 311-318.

Kahneman, D., & Beatty, J. Pupil diameter and load on memory. *Science*, 1966, 154, 1583-1585.

Melton, A. W. The situation with respect to the spacing of repetitions and memory. *Journal of Verbal Learning and Verbal Behavior*, 1970, 9, 596-606.

Peterson, L. R., & Peterson, M. J. Short-term retention of individual verbal items. *Journal of Experimental Psychology*, 1959, 58, 193-198.

Pollatsek, A. W. Rehearsal, interference, and spacing of practice in short-term memory. Ann Arbor: University of Michigan, Human Performance Center, Technical Report No. 16, 1969.

Reed, H. Studies of the interference process in short-term memory. *Journal of Experimental Psychology*, 1970, 84, 452-457.

Reitman, W., Malin, J. T., Bjork, R. A., & Higman, B. Strategy control and directed forgetting. Ann Arbor: University of Michigan, Mental Health Research Institute, Information Processing Working Paper No. 17, 1971.

Roediger, H. L., & Crowder, R. G. Instructed forgetting: Rehearsal control or retrieval inhibition (repression)? *Cognitive Psychology*, 1972, 3, 255-267.

Shebilske, W., Wilder, L., & Epstein, W. Forget instructions: The effect of selective rehearsal and categorical distinctiveness. *Journal of Experimental Psychology*, 1971, 89, 372-378.

Turvey, M. T. & Wittlinger, R. P. Attenuation of proactive interference in short-term memory as a function of cuing to forget. *Journal of Experimental Psychology*, 1969, 80, 295-298.

Weiner, B. Motivated forgetting and the study of repression. *Journal of Personality*, 1968, 36, 213-234.

Weiner, B., & Reed, H. Effects on the instructional sets to remember and to forget on short-term retention: Studies of rehearsal control and retrieval inhibition (repression). *Journal of Experimental Psychology*, 1969, 79, 226-232.

Woodward, A. E., & Bjork, R. A. Forgetting and remembering in free recall: Intentional and unintentional. *Journal of Experimental Psychology*, 1971, 89, 109-116.

10

HOW GOOD CAN MEMORY BE?[1]

Earl Hunt and Tom Love
University of Washington

Most of our scientific knowledge of memory has come from the study of the capabilities of haphazardly chosen subjects. We can add to this a smaller, although still sizeable, body of literature concerning memory pathologies. Only very occasionally do psychologists study the gifted memorizer. Such individuals are difficult to locate, both because they are by definition rare and because fine memory, unlike great athletic or acting ability, seldom results in personal publicity for the individual possessing it. The only detailed study of a mnemonic "superstar" of which we have knowledge is Luria's (1968) semiclinical account of a man studied in the Soviet Union before World War II. Since 1945 our views on memory have changed greatly. How would an outstanding memorizer appear if his examiners had our more modern theories of memory in mind?

In the winter of 1971 we discovered that a man known slightly to us, whom we shall call VP, gave exhibitions in which he played up to seven simultaneous chess matches, blindfolded. A newspaper article described an exhibition in which he simultaneously played chess, bridge, and read a book. We later found that VP could play as many as 60 correspondence games without consulting written records. While

[1] This research has been supported in part by the U.S. Air Force, Office of Scientific Research, Air Systems Command, under Grant No. 70-1944 and in part by the National Science Foundation, Grant No. GB 25979. Earl Hunt was principal investigator on each project.

The authors regard their contribution as co-equal, and have listed their names alphabetically without implication of seniority.

Our first and foremost acknowledgement is, of course, to our subject, VP, whose cooperation has made this research possible. We would also like to acknowledge the contributions and comments of our colleague, Nancy Frost, in all phases of our work. Psychometric testing was supervised by Clifford Lunneborg and the eidetic imagery studies were suggested by Davida Teller. Beth Nyblade conducted the auditory STM study.

this is impressive to the uninitiated, it is in itself not evidence of extraordinary memory, since championship chess players are very emotionally involved in their games, much as scientists become enmeshed in the literature of their field. Further investigation showed, however, that VP does in fact have a memory capacity that rivals that of Luria's famous mnemonist. In this paper we shall report a systematic study of this unusual individual. After giving a few biographical facts about VP, we shall report studies substantiating the anecdotes about his remarkable memory capabilities, showing that they are not limited to chess, and indicating, although not clearly, how his performance is achieved. Finally we shall join VP in speculating as to how he acquired his ability.

BIOGRAPHICAL DATA[2]

VP was born in Latvia in 1935. By a fascinating coincidence, he spent his early life in a city close to the town where Luria's subject was raised. He was an only child in an intellectual home. He plays competitive games very well, but has never been interested in athletics. He began to read at the age of three and a half, and soon progressed to adult books that he found about the house. At the age of five he had memorized the street map of Riga, a city of about 500,000, railroad time schedules, and bus schedules. At ten he memorized 150 poems for a contest. He began to play chess at the age of eight. Prior to that he had played Mah Jong, sometimes playing all four hands of a solitary game. He is bilingual in English and Latvian, is fluent in German and Russian and has a reading knowledge of virtually all the modern European languages except Greek and Hungarian.

VP and his family lived in Displaced Persons camps in Germany from 1945 until 1950. During this period he went to a school which did not have texts or teaching aids. As a result, a great deal of stress was placed upon note taking and rote memorization. He soon mastered the strategy of learning generalizations from which he could reconstruct the original material essentially verbatim. This skill may have greatly influenced his subsequent use of memory.

Considering the unsettled times of his childhood, VP does not have an unusual medical history. At age ten he was hospitalized for four months for a ruptured appendix, during which time he contracted measles and pneumonia. He reports having had a very stringent diet (molding cheese) while in DP camps, but, to the casual observer, he is not physically marked by this experience. Interestingly, considering the considerable body of evidence concerning pathologies of memory associated with alcoholism (Talland, 1965), VP did drink heavily as a young adult although he has virtually abstained since about age 20. He does not smoke or take drugs.

In conventional terms, VP could be described as an economic underachiever. He is a store clerk. On the other hand, if you take the view that his principal interest is

---

[2] Most of our biographical information was obtained from discussions with VP and, in some cases, with his wife. Aside from questions of professional ethics, we are speaking of a man who, although not a close acquaintance, is certainly a friend. We have not provided a public dossier of VP's life nor do we feel that we ought to do so.

competitive chess and that his economic role is an unfortunate necessity, he is doing quite well. VP had some graduate study at the University of Washington, in history, but did not complete his degree.

Luria reported that his subject had a personality which was strongly affected by his vivid memory. VP has reported that if he has a quarrel in which he acts stupidly, he recalls it almost verbatim, so that he cannot forget and thus, can see his own role in a better light. On the other hand, it appears to us that if memory has been a problem in his personal life, it is not nearly as great a one as was the case for Luria's subject.

PSYCHOMETRIC PROFILE

VP scored 167 (I.Q. 136) on the short form of the Wechsler Adult Intelligence Scale. His highest scores were on digit span, digit symbol, and information, and his three lowest scores were object assembly, picture completion, and picture arrangement.[3] Note that the high scores are on memory-related tests. Picture completion and picture arrangement are obviously not memory-related. VP himself denies high mechanical competence. To quote him, "I even have difficulty putting lead in a pencil." VP's approach to taking the Wechsler Tests was exactly like his approach to our experimental tasks. The examiner was struck by his systematic behavior. Prior to each subtest he inquired carefully about the nature of the test, the way it was to be scored, the time limits, and whether or not the scoring was on the basis of speed or accuracy. He adjusted his performance accordingly. He gave complete, elaborate answers to information items. For instance, upon being asked the boiling point of water he replied with the correct answer on three different temperature scales.

VP took Raven's (1958) progressive matrices test, in which the subject is given a matrix of figures in which he is to detect a relationship. It is a concept identification test, very similar to the letter completion tasks simulated by Simon and Kotovsky (1963), who pointed out the importance of short-term memory in such tasks. He scored in the 95+ percentile for his age group.

VP was given five short tasks designed to measure Guilford's (1967) factors of intelligence. The tests used have been documented by French (1963). On the picture-number test, a test of associative rote memory which requires paired-associate learning of a picture-number pair, he scored 19 out of 21 correct on each part of a two-part test. In a second test of associative memory, the object-number test, the subject examines 20 word-number pairs, and then produces the number when the word is presented. VP performed perfectly.

On a test of originality, the symbol production test, in which the task is to produce symbols to represent given activities and objects, he correctly portrayed 25 of 31 symbols. He required 10 minutes to do this, as opposed to the normally allowed time of 5 minutes.

---

[3] The tests and the manner of their administration are described in the *Counselor's Manual* (1971) of the Washington Pre-College testing program conducted by the University of Washington.

VP's most striking non-memory performance was on a test designed to measure Guilford's perceptual speed factor. Guilford (1967, pp. 186-189) describes perceptual speed (factors ESU, EFU) as the ability to note differences between figures or semantic units very rapidly. Typical figural tests for perceptual speed require the subject to locate small picture inserts within an aerial photograph, or to detect matches or mismatches between aircraft outlines. The factor is found in children and adults. In the test used the subject is asked to inspect pairs of multidigit numbers (e.g., 6410739___ 6410739) and indicate as rapidly as possible whether they are the same or different. There are 48 items in each of two parts of the test. VP correctly answered 38 items of the first part and 40 of the second. We gave the same test to 69 students enrolled in a University of Washington undergraduate course in psychology. The range of scores in this group was from 11 to 39, with a median of 23.

Finally, VP was given the Cube Comparison Test, which is a test of spatial orientation ability. In this test two drawings of projections of cubes are presented to the subject, each drawing showing faces of a cube as seen from different projections. There is a design on each face of every cube, but the subject is told to assume that no design appears on two faces of a single cube. The subject's task is to decide whether the two drawings could be different projections of the same cube, seen from different orientations. There are 21 pairs of drawings on each part of the two-part test. The test is scored by subtracting the number of errors (incorrect same-different judgments) from the number of correct judgments. VP scored 12 on the first part of the test and 15 on the second part.

In summary, the psychometric tests reveal an intelligent but not exceptional individual with a good memory for items presented 5 minutes or so before testing and with the ability to notice perceptual details rapidly. One would not predict his reputation for memory feats on the basis of these results. The experimental results, however, give quite a different picture.

SUBSTANTIATING EXPERIMENTS

Studies with the Atkinson-Shiffrin "Keeping Track" Task

This is a continuous paired-associates task used by Atkinson and Shiffrin (1968) to test their model of short- and long-term memory. Our first experiment was a modification of Atkinson and Shiffrin's Experiment 1. The subject sat in front of a computer controlled cathode ray display tube on which a sequence of study and test trials was displayed. On a study trial a CVC nonsense syllable was presented, paired with a number. On a test trial the CVC alone was presented and the subject was required to indicate the last number paired with the CVC. Immediately following the response, a new study trial was presented, using the same CVC and a new response. Thus a typical sequence might be

STUDY	JAQ	23
TEST	ROQ	
STUDY	ROQ	95
TEST	CUH	
STUDY	CUH	47
TEST	JAQ	

with a response required on each test trial. The lag is defined as the number of study-test pairs intervening between a test trial involving a CVC and the preceding study trial. Thus the last test trial in the example has a lag of two.

In our first experiment self-pacing was permitted, that is, the study trials lasted as long as the subject wished. The following three conditions were used: (*a*) Four CVC stimuli paired with 75 possible responses; (*b*) Six CVC stimuli paired with 100 possible responses; (*c*) Eight CVC stimuli paired with 150 possible responses. There are 150 trials in each condition. The test took about an hour in each condition. VP made *no* errors in any of the above conditions. This is far above the performance level reported by Atkinson and Shiffrin using a very similar procedure. We also have data from subjects in another experiment in our laboratory using exactly the same apparatus and procedure as in condition *a*. These subjects were University of Washington students selected for having either high or low scores on the verbal or quantitative aptitude tests of the Washington Pre-College Aptitude Tests (see footnote 3). Figure 1 shows the number of items correct as a function of lag for 39

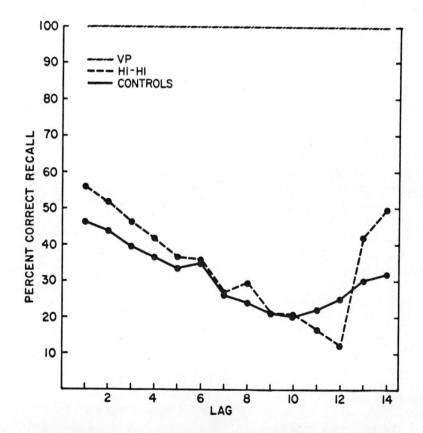

FIG. 1. Percent correct recall in the Atkinson and Shiffrin (1968) task, as a function of lag, for VP, 12 subjects high on both verbal and quantitative aptitude scores (Hi-Hi), and 39 unselected college subjects (Controls).

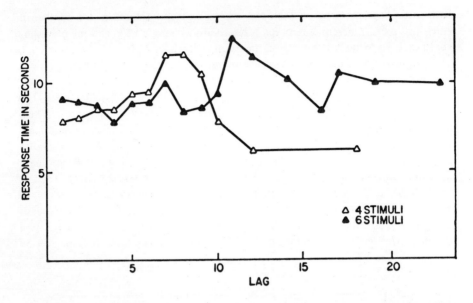

FIG. 2. Response latency as a function of lag for VP in the Atkinson and Shiffrin (1968) task, with 4 and 6 different stimulus trigrams.

subjects, without regard to group, and for 12 students who were high on both the verbal and quantitative aptitude scores on the test. VP's data are plotted as a horizontal line at 100 percent for all lags. It is obvious from these figures that VP is grossly superior to the most talented control subjects on this task.

Conditions *a* and *b* were then repeated with study trials limited to 3 seconds. VP made a perfect score in condition *a* and five errors (out of 150 trials) in condition *b*. The five errors were made on the first six pairings, that is, on the items for the six study trials needed prior to the first test trial.

In these conditions the maximum lag was 18 in the four-stimulus case, and more in the other conditions. Atkinson and Shiffrin's subjects, who were much more practiced than VP or our own control subjects, were responding at chance level at this lag.

Obviously, it is impossible to apply Atkinson and Shiffrin's analytic techniques to obtain estimates of VP's memory parameters, since he provides no error data. We have noticed an interesting effect. Our apparatus permits us to time the latency of responding on a test trial. Figure 2 plots latency as a function of lag. VP's latencies *increase* as lag, and presumably memory load, increase up to a point, and then *decrease* to about 7 seconds. This is not consistent with the hypothesis that short-term memory (STM) buffers are searched and then long-term memory (LTM) is searched. Neither is it consistent with the hypothesis that buffers and LTM are searched in parallel. It is more as if VP somehow recognized a long-lag item and went directly to a search of LTM. Long latencies would be associated with items that might be in either LTM or STM.

Recall for Stories

VP was asked to read Bartlett's (1932) "The War of the Ghosts," as well as a number of other stories.[4] We shall report data only for the Bartlett story, as distortions in it are well known. The passage was read through twice, and VP was then asked to count backwards by sevens from 253 to 0. Specific portions of the story were then reconstructed at 1 minute after completing the counting task, 15 minutes, 30 minutes, 45 minutes, and the entire story reconstructed after 1 hour. By far the most interesting result of the experiment was the fact that VP reproduced the original story nearly verbatim. After six weeks VP was asked to rewrite the story once again. He had no previous knowledge that he was going to be asked to do this. This reproduction was almost identical to the one he wrote after only 1 hour.

TABLE 1

Number of Nouns and Verbs Recalled from "The War of the Ghosts" by VP and the Best Subject of 10 Control Subjects

	VP Data		Best of 10 Controls	
	Nouns	Verbs	Nouns	Verbs
Words in story	49	68	49	68
1-hour recall	33	40	27	26
6-week recall	30	39	16	21
Words in both recalls	26	28	15	14

We have tried this procedure with two control groups, five computer science graduate students and five University of Washington students hired to serve as subjects through the University of Washington employment agency. As one would expect, there were wide individual differences. The best control subject was a member of the second group. Table 1 shows a count of verbs and nouns in the original story, in the story the first time it was reproduced by VP and the control subject, and a similar comparison for reproduction after 6 weeks. VP's recall is much better and, unlike the recall of the other good memorizer, shows virtually no drop over the 6-week retention period. A count of nouns and verbs does not really give a picture of VP's capabilities. So that the reader may gain some idea of the quality of this man's recall, we have reproduced, as an appendix, the original story and VP's recall of it 1 hour and 6 weeks later. Note that his recall is not verbatim, nor is it absolutely perfect. Nevertheless, it is very impressive.

Eidetic Imagery

Recent reports (Luria, 1968; Stollmeyer & Psotka, 1970) on individuals with outstanding memories have emphasized their strong visual imagery. VP, however,

---

[4] In one case we asked him to read and recall the librettos of obscure operas we had found in a book in the University library. Unfortunately, some years before, VP had decided he would like to read the librettos of operas and, of course, he remembered them.

denies relying primarily on visual cues although he does report using some interesting visual codings at times. For example, when he did the Atkinson and Shiffrin task he associated pictures on a wall with each of the CVC trigram stimuli, and visualized the current response as hanging on the wall below the appropriate picture. We do not see why VP would be motivated to deny visual imagery if, indeed, he does use it. Nevertheless, we felt it necessary to test his imagery ability.

We then gave VP the only memory task on which he has ever failed in any sense. This is a task devised by Julesz (1971) as an "unfakable test of eidetic imagery." Julesz has shown that stereoscopic patterns can be formed from binocular vision of two apparently random fields of gray dots. Stollmeyer and Psotka (1970) found that an eidetic imager whom they studied could form a stereoscopic image if one pattern was presented at one time, followed by another pattern as much as 24 hours later. Since the unfused patterns are not meaningful, there is no possibility for nonvisual recoding. Similarly, since the stereoscopic image cannot be detected from either pattern alone, one cannot identify the image without fusing the image visually if they are presented simultaneously to each eye, or in memory if one image is presented before the other. VP was unable to form the stereoscopic image when pictures were presented serially to both eyes with a 60-second interval. Thus he did not pass the unfakable test for eidetic imagery. Note, however, that the "unfakable" test is, in a sense, too hard. Stereoscopic vision is a matter of degree. It may be that the memory task requires exceptionally good stereoscopic vision as well as eidetic imagery. In this case a true eidetic imager without strong stereoscopic vision could fail the test. Using a stereoscope in the conventional way, VP was able to see the stereoscopic images, but with great difficulty.

Haber (1969) has developed an easier test for eidetic imagery, in which the subject is presented with two pictures, in sequence, which can be fused to make a third picture which is not predictable from the other two. We used two pictures, ostensibly of a cloud and a boat, which, when fused, appear as a Santa Claus face. VP was unable to fuse the two pictures in memory. However, we are rather suspicious of this result since VP did not see Santa Claus when presented with the two pictures simultaneously. This, of course, is consistent with the idea that he is not a very strong imager.

Number Matrices

Following Luria's (1968) procedure, we asked VP to memorize matrices consisting of eight rows of six numbers. The matrices were typed on a card. Data will be reported for Matrices A and B, shown in Figure 3. Matrix A is typed with columns aligned, in the normal fashion. Matrix B is "staggered," so that it is difficult to read. VP was asked to study the matrices. When he was ready, the matrices were removed and he was asked to recall all or various parts of the matrices. Recall was perfect for both matrices. When asked to recall matrix A two weeks later, he transposed two numbers, but made no other errors.

Table 2 shows the times VP required to read or recall various parts of the matrices. Note that there is no consistent difference in time to recall from either matrix. On the other hand, except for row by row reading, Matrix A (normal) can be read much more rapidly than Matrix B (staggered). We regard this as strong

(A)
NORMAL MATRIX

```
1 6 4 3 5 9
2 6 6 5 5 9
4 1 3 2 6 4
9 6 2 4 0 4
0 3 7 4 2 8
5 1 9 7 2 3
5 4 8 4 6 5
6 5 1 3 0 0
```

(B)
STAGGERED MATRIX

```
2 4 27 8 5
3 1 059 1
41 326 8
3 6 2 26 9
7 58 3 9 1
4 2 9 90 1
9 20 28 8
8 8 175 7
```

FIG. 3 Number matrices used for matrix recall study.

TABLE 2

Recall and Reading Speed (Seconds) for Various Number-Matrix Tasks

Test	Matrix Recall		Matrix Reading	
	Normal	Staggered	Normal	Staggered
Study time	246.	508.[a]		
Recall time	51.7	29.2	19.4	18.7
Row 6	5.7	7.6	3.4	2.4
Row 3	7.0	4.7	1.9	2.0
Column 4	26.7	22.8	3.0	10.0
Row 6 backwards	8.4	8.2	2.7	2.1
Column 1	10.6	11.0	3.1	3.6
Column 2 up	14.7	23.2	2.7	4.1
Diagonally from upper left	18.4	21.3	2.1	3.6
Diagonally up from column 6, row 7	33.7	32.0	3.1	3.6
Diagonally down from column 1, row 3	26.0	19.5	2.0	3.8
Diagonally up from column 6, row 6	19.2	24.0	2.6	2.8
Number at column, row				
4,4	5.4	5.2	1.3	1.9
2,2	.8	1.4	1.0	1.0
3,5	7.1	6.8	0.5	2.4
6,1	3.3	3.4	0.7	1.0
1,3	2.3	3.5	0.9	0.4
5,6	5.3	5.9	2.2	1.3
1,8	2.2	0.9	0.9	0.5
2,7	7.7	2.0	0.7	1.0
3,4	6.5	2.6	0.7	1.7
4,5	5.7	4.8	1.0	2.0

[a]VP misunderstood instructions and thought he was supposed to remember locations of blanks.

evidence against the proposition that VP relies on unusual visual memory. If he were "reading from memory" his recall times for the matrices ought to resemble his reading times, which they do not. Further evidence against the visual hypothesis is found in the mnemonics used in this task. The mnemonics were devices for recoding by row; for example, storing a row as a date, then asking himself what he was doing on that day. This indicates to us more than visual memory was used.

We also tested VP on the matrix which Luria used to test the memory of his subject. Both VP and Luria's subject recalled the matrix perfectly. Table 3 shows the time each mnemonist required to study and recall the matrix. Although VP took twice as long in the study phase, his recall is similar to the recall of Luria's subject.

TABLE 3

Times (Minutes) Required for VP and
Luria's Subject to Study and Recall
Matrix of Digits

	VP	Luria's Subject
Study time	6.5	ca. 3.0
Recall in seconds		
Entire matrix	41.5	40
Third column	58.1	80
Second column	39.4	25
Second column bottom to top	39.7	30

Legal Versus Illegal Chess Positions

If a person is an eidetic imager, he ought to reproduce a chess board by seeing it "in his mind." If he is coding chess, he ought to rely upon the role of the pieces. For example, from reading Luria's report we would not expect his subject to differ in his ability to recall a meaningful or nonsensical chess position. On the other hand, DeGroot's study (1965) of chess masters indicates that they are very aware of the meaning of the pieces and that they key their memory for a board upon that meaning. In VP's case we have an outstanding chess player who is also an outstanding memorizer. We therefore asked whether he had a similar memory for legal and illegal positions. VP was shown a chessboard on which a number of chessmen had been placed. The number of chessmen on the board varied from trial to trial. On some trials the pieces were arranged in a conceivable configuration, on other trials the pieces were arranged in illegal positions; for example, two black bishops on black squares. The experimenter arranged the board out of VP's sight, then signalled him to turn and look at the board. VP studied the board until he felt he could recall it correctly. The time he required to do this was recorded with a stop watch. When VP was ready, he turned away and recalled the location of each piece on the board. His recall was always perfect. He differed markedly, however, in the time he required to memorize legal and illegal positions. This is demonstrated in Figure 4, which shows the time VP required to memorize a position as a function of

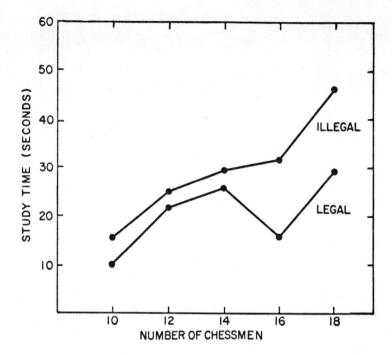

FIG. 4. Study times required by VP to become confident of his ability to recall chess displays; number of chessmen and legal and illegal chess positions are the independent variables.

the number of pieces on the board. He always required more time to memorize an illegal position than a legal position with the same number of pieces. This fact is in accord with a remark VP made in explaining how to play blindfold chess. He said he does not visualize the board, but rather remembers the function of each piece in the game.

High and Low Imagery

Paivio (1971) found consistent differences in the recall of English nominalizations as a function of the degree to which the nominalization could be visualized. Easily visualized nominalizations, such as *snarling tigers*, were easier to recall than low imagery items, such as *rising honors*. VP was given a similar free recall test. The first study was modeled after Paivio's Experiment II. A list of 30 nominalizations, taken equally from Paivio's high, low, and intermediate imagery lists, was presented item by item on the computer display screen. Each item was displayed for 3 seconds. VP was then given 5 minutes to recall the list. The results are shown on the top graph of Figure 5. Although VP was considerably above Paivio's averages, as shown in the figure, he did not do as well as we expected. Like Paivio's subjects, he could recall high imagery items better than low imagery items.

In another experiment (Experiment III) reported in the same paper, Paivio found that the imagery effect obtained only if the nominalization was the subject of the verb. Thus a high imagery effect would be obtained for a phrase such as

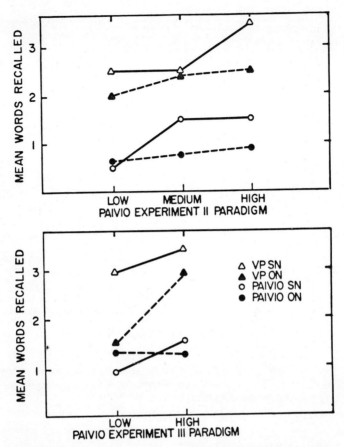

FIG. 5. Mean recall scores for high- and low-imagery subject nominalizations (SN) and object nominalizations (ON) for Paivio's (1971) subjects and VP.

growling lions but not for *fighting windmills.* Using the same procedure as before, VP was asked to recall Paivio's lists which counterbalanced high and low imagery against subject and object nominalizations. To maintain comparability with Paivio, 3 minutes were allowed for recall. The bottom part of Figure 5 shows the results. VP did better than Paivio's subjects and, unlike them, was sensitive to imagery in both subject and object nominalizations.

Digit Span

Digit span is often used as an indicator of the capacity of short-term memory (STM). If digits are presented one at a time at a relatively rapid rate (too fast to be grouped or recoded) college-level subjects have a span of about eight decimal digits (Miller, 1956). Occasionally individuals can recall more. If the number of digits that can be recalled without recoding does, in fact, reflect the capacity of STM, then one ought not to be able to improve digit span with practice if the presentation rate is rapid (Kleinberg & Kaufman, 1971). One of the hypotheses that we entertained about VP was that he had an unusually large STM. Informal studies, however, indicated that his memory span for rapidly presented digits was not unusually large. VP himself, however, told us that he believed he could improve his digit span with practice, by grouping the digits and by creating associations to the digits—even if digits were presented at a 1-per-second rate. He demonstrated this in a digit span experiment.

Strings of digits were presented, one at a time at a constant location, on the computer controlled CRT. There was a 1-second interval between the onset of presentation of each digit and the onset of presentation of the next digit. After n digits had been presented VP was asked to recall the series. If he correctly recalled two strings of digits in a row the process was repeated with $n + 1$ digits, until a number, n^*, was reached such that VP was unable to recall two consecutive sequences. A trial terminated at this point, and $n^* - 1$ was recorded as the digit span on that trial.

Figure 6 shows VP's digit span over successive trials. It clearly increased, in spite of the rapid presentation rate.

We then asked whether other people could also learn to increase their digit spans at a high presentation rate. Five University of Washington undergraduates served as paid subjects in an experiment in which they tried to increase their digit spans over 11 trials. The first three trials were conducted in the same manner as VP's trials. On Trials 4 and 5 each subject was offered $2.00 a digit for each digit by which he could increase his digit span. After Trial 5 the subject was given the following

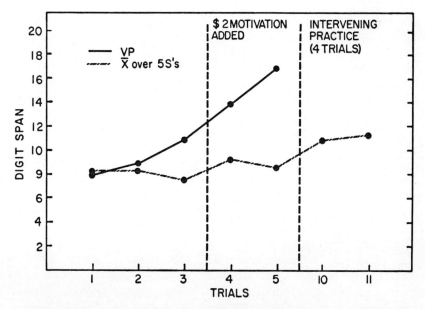

FIG. 6. Digit span performance of VP over successive trials and of experimental subjects over trials and with additional incentive for performance.

instructions: (a) Pay strict attention to the number of digits you will expect on each presentation. (b) Group the digits into groups of 3 to 5 digits, depending on the length of the sequence. (c) Decide prior to seeing the first digit how you will group digits. (d) Make verbal associations with each group of 3 to 5 digits, for example, regard them as weights, dates, or anything that a number might represent. The more unusual the association the more helpful it will be. (e) If possible, make associations between the groupings.

These instructions were a statement of the strategy which VP described to us. In order to allow subjects to practice these techniques, we conducted four practice trials with a 6-second interdigit interval. (Previous work in our laboratory had shown that subjects could, indeed, learn to increase their digit span at a 6-second presentation rate.) After the four practice trials subjects were again presented with digit sequences at the 1-per-second rate for two trials. As before, the subjects were paid for increases. The lower curve of Figure 6 shows the results. The graphic picture is confirmed by statistical analysis. Both reward introduction and training resulted in significant increases in digit span. On the other hand, VP showed much greater improvement in performance over trials than did any individual subject. While normal subjects can increase their digit spans using VP's techniques, they are not nearly so adept at creating chunks of information as he is.

Searching Short-Term Memory

Sternberg (1966) developed a method of measuring the time required to make comparisons between items held in short-term memory. The subject first hears a presentation set of from 1 to 6 digits. A probe digit is then presented in a brief visual exposure. The subject's task is to say whether or not the probe digit was included in the presentation set. Sternberg found that the time required to determine whether or not the probe digit was in the presentation set is a linear function of the number of digits in the presentation set, s. Reaction times are nearly identical for cases in which the probe digit is or is not in the presentation set. This is taken as evidence that the subject makes an exhaustive serial search through his memory of the presentation set in order to identify the probe digit. The rate of increase of reaction time as a function of s is then interpreted as the time required to make each comparison.

VP served as a subject in a study whose procedure was modeled after Sternberg's. Two seconds after auditory presentation of the presentation set, the probe digit was presented in a tachistoscope. VP indicated whether or not it had been included in the presentation set by pressing one of two buttons. Figure 7 shows his response latency as a function of s. For comparison, Figure 7 also shows the latencies reported by Sternberg. It is apparent that although VP and Sternberg's subjects took about the same time to identify a single digit, VP's reaction time is almost independent of increases in s. This suggests that VP is able to process all members of the presentation in parallel. Figure 7 also shows the time calculated by Sternberg as the maximum time that subjects would require to process all members of the presentation set in parallel. VP is well below this time.

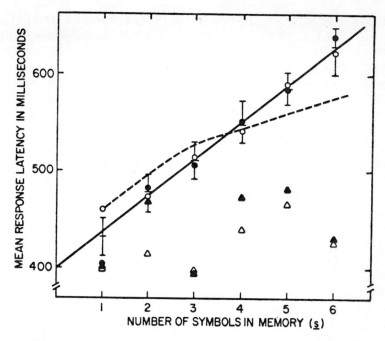

FIG. 7. Response latency as a function of the number of items in the memory set, using Sternberg's (1966) experimental procedure. Triangles are data for VP, circles and estimates of ±1 SD are from Sternberg's report. Positive responses are filled-in points, negative responses are open points. The dotted line indicates Sternberg's estimate of the upper limit of parallel processing.

Auditory Short-Term Memory

The procedure developed by Peterson and Peterson (1959) and Brown (1958) has become almost classical in the study of short-term memory. In this paradigm the subject is presented an item auditorily, then asked to engage in a distractor task which prevents rehearsal until recall is required. Forgetting can be shown in a matter of seconds.

To test VP using the Brown-Peterson paradigm tape recordings were made of 49 CCC-number pairs, with numbers ranging from 001 to 999. Trigrams and numbers were chosen randomly, with the restriction that each CCC trigram contained three different letters and no two consecutive trigrams shared a letter. A taped trial consisted of four beats of a 120 beats-per-minute metronome, followed by pronunciation of a CCC trigram, and then a three-digit number. VP counted backwards by threes from the number, accompanying the metronome, until a green light in front of him came on, indicating that he was to recall the trigram. The recall signal came on at a variable time, from 3 to 18 seconds following the trigram.

Figure 8 shows VP's results for this task. For comparison the other curve shows the results from 12 of the subjects who had been selected for being high on the verbal and the quantitative tests of the Washington pre-college test battery. It is clear that VP's recall over time deteriorates much less than does the recall of the other subjects. Indeed, we hesitate to say that he shows any reliable loss in recall at all.

In the conference discussion of this paper, Melton suggested that VP's data looked like the data from the first trial for a "typical" subject in the Peterson and Peterson paradigm, since the correlation of duration of retention interval and amount of forgetting in this situation only appears after several trials have introduced proactive interference. Fortunately this can be checked. We were at the time conducting another experiment using the identical tapes and equipment as were used in the trials with VP. The subjects in this study were University of Washington sophomores recruited from an introductory course. Figure 9 compares VP's data to that obtained by averaging over subjects only the data from the first trial of each session. (Thus for this purpose it is as if we conducted a between-subjects design, with different groups of subjects having a single CCC-number trial with different retention intervals.) The figure shows that there is a striking comparability between VP's data and the first-trial data of the undergraduate subjects. However, when the data from all the trials of the undergraduates are examined, the rapid decrement in recall is found. The usual interpretation of this phenomenon is that the presence of forgetting in the Brown-Peterson paradigm depends on the presence of proactive interference from previous items. If this is so, then VP has been able to eliminate the proactive interference effects.

VP regarded the task as a rather silly one, in marked contrast to his usual attitude of cooperation and interest. He did remark that because he knows a great

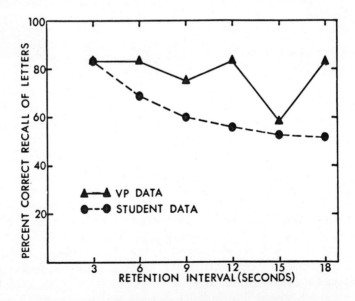

FIG. 8. Recall of 3-consonant trigrams as a function of lag for VP, and for 12 selected subjects from the University of Washington in a replication of the Peterson and Peterson (1959) study.

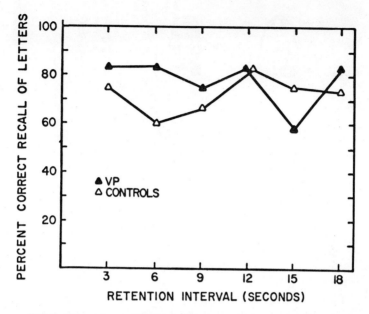

FIG. 9. Comparison of VP's performance with control subjects' performance on their first trial, that is, with no proactive interference from prior items.

many languages, he can usually associate a word with almost all trigrams. If he did this consistently he would have converted the task into one of remembering only a single chunk of information. Both the conversion of a trigram to a single chunk and the use of different languages to generate these chunks would minimize proactive interference and lead to a near-zero slope of the forgetting function.

Visual Clustering Study

The next study was an attempt to see if we could untangle the types of coding that VP uses. A free-recall paradigm was used to examine VP's clustering along semantic and visual categories. Frost (1971) developed a set of 16 line drawings that can be clustered on the basis of meaningful categories (e.g., wearing apparel) or visual orientation (e.g., long axis vertical, horizontal, or tilted to left or right). Six of the stimuli are shown in Figure 10. Frost's task requires that the subject free-recall the drawings after viewing them once. Recall is then scored for semantic or visual clustering. Ordinarily subjects cluster on a visual basis unless they have previously been led to believe that they will be given a recall test.

VP and six control subjects (graduates and undergraduates working in the laboratory) were presented with Frost's stimuli at the rapid rate of 1 per second. An interfering task was then introduced to prohibit rehearsal. For the control subjects this was a number cancelling task, to limit rehearsal and avoid STM effects in recall. For VP we felt something more difficult was in order, so he did the Atkinson-Shiffrin task for an hour. Following their respective interfering tasks, VP and the control subjects were given an unannounced free recall trial.

FIG. 10. An example of Frost's (1971) stimuli with
orientation and semantic categorization.

Free recall was scored for both semantic and visual repetitions, and two indices
were calculated for each subject. First was the ratio of observed to total possible
semantic repetitions for his recall protocol. The second index was the ratio of
observed visual to maximum possible visual repetitions for the same list of recalled
items. These indices, which give no weight to the total number of words recalled,
allowed a fair comparison of the type of clustering used by VP and control subjects.

The results were simple and dramatic. The control subjects consistently clustered
by visual orientation. VP's clustering scores indicated only chance visual organization, but a high degree of semantic organization. In fact, if the scoring procedure
is modified to allow for his interpretation of the stimuli,[5] his semantic clustering
was perfect.

This study again emphasized a point that has been driven home to us. VP is
amazingly efficient with verbal mnemonics.

VP'S COMMENTS ON LURIA'S SUBJECT,
HIMSELF, AND MEMORY

Luria's (1968) commentary on "S" is, insofar as we know, the only report of a
person with a memory capacity approaching that of VP. It is natural to compare
VP's abilities to that of "S," for whom Luria gave a semiclinical case report. Rather
than do this ourselves, we asked VP to read Luria's *Mind of a Mnemonist* and then
discuss it with us. The resulting interview turned into a general discussion of
memory which we found quite illuminating. We now present some excerpts from
the interview, in which VP comments on memory. The only editing we have done is
to correct syntactical errors which normally occur in spoken speech and to
compress some sections of the interview. For each excerpt we indicate the general
topic of the conversation at the time.

[5] A picture, which Frost called a train, VP called a jukebox; a picture she called a handbag,
he called a box. In both cases either name would be appropriate.

(On early school experience)

VP: There may be a direct causal connection between (memory) and the kind of school system that was set up in Europe at the time (the 1930s) and particularly the internal cultural school system that the Jewish minorities had (for "S"), or the kind of education I endured. I am not sure that you find this in American schools, since American schools emphasize peer group acceptance. Why did I (develop memory)? Tom (TL) has used the words "rote learning." This is particularly (apparent) in any number of biographies of (Jews) who were sent to the Hedder at age three, and who spent ten hours a day there. They couldn't daydream, couldn't laugh. They had to study the scriptures. This gave them a head start. That head start would also explain to a degree that later in life you think of (your ability) as pure memory. Most people (find) that memory alone is rather useless. You have to apply it. This man ("S") never did and, well, I have a handicap that way.

(On selectivity of memory, a topic to which he returns later)

VP: Many of the things that ("S") associates are from his early childhood. I could never recall the country lanes I walked down. I do recall that when I remember a place through which I walked, I remember it exactly, but I was able to forget (most things). That is what we acquire later in life, selectivity (in memory).

(Talking about memory and chess)

VP: It is possible that there are many books or encyclopedic works (about chess) which could be memorized, but that does not necessarily make you the best player in the world.

(On synesthesia, which Luria stressed as important to "S")

VP: I can't think of even one example (of synesthesia in my own experience). I suppose if I thought long enough one might come to mind, but, no, not as a rule. . .

(On commenting that he does not have an unusual ability to remember faces. In fact, he had failed to recognize EH's wife on meeting her at the store where he works, although he had met her socially on two or three occasions.)

VP: It's really applications of memory that are of importance in the learning process. That politician, Mr. Nixon, would certainly remember your wife by name and face, no matter what the circumstances in which he met her.

(On responding to a question from TL, who asked if VP felt he could do everything Luria reported "S" could do)

VP: Well, with one exception maybe. The exception I would make is being able to recall conversations from as long as fourteen years before. Fourteen years (from now) I will have ceased to care what experiment you are writing about, and I will have forgotten it. I think that the *conscious decision* (emphasized in his voice) that a test is over and done with has something to do with it. I am going to forget it! If it were something that impressed me as a life and death matter, I should not forget it. I would recall it fourteen years later, but not as a matter of course.

EH: What was your telephone number in a house previous to your present house?

VP: You have me.

VP: . . .I recall some addresses. I've forgotten some where if I had to I could go back and pick out the house. . . .I think that all of us, as we grow older, become more selective. Young kids cannot make a distinction between what is important and what should not be retained. . . .As we grow older we get more selective. We simply get the idea that there isn't storeroom enough back here (pointing to head) to crank it all in. Therefore we must touch things over lightly and forget them.

(On education again, with more remarks about selectivity)
VP: Where I went to school there were other kids like me who memorized not only 150 poems—some of them memorized novels . . . fiction, chapter by chapter, word for word. It was not a great feat of memory . . . I never thought of it that way. They liked it and it came easily. Now if you had a piece of fiction or escapist literature today they would not bother.
EH: Suppose we set out to find people like you, adults with exceptional memories. Where should we look?
VP: I think that it would be best to look some place where they still do it (educate) the way they used to. Maybe by this time you have to go to (orthodox synagogues) in Brooklyn. . . .This (orthodox Jews) is one group I think of which would probably send its kids off into rote religious learning very early. If you deprive them of some of the normal childhood experiences . . . they might not feel deprived . . . they would be exposed to things very early in life before they could say, "Well, this is not important, so I'll be selective about it."

(On personality and memory)
VP: Here's another point I want to touch on. All of us have come across this in the literature . . . boys who will simply not take this kind of discipline (enforced rote learning) . . . they are too much in love with the outdoors and baseball games and what have you. Here you have somebody who is not going to have a good memory, insofar as you can cultivate it. You have to be a rather passive individual. In other words, you have to accept the rules of the game. If somebody says to you, "Study scriptures" or "Study this matrix" or "Study whatever," you have to study it without any conflict. . . .Whereas, if you are going to be, let's say, a businessman, and somebody said to you, "Study this matrix," instead of studying the matrix you start looking for ways to turn the matrix to your advantage. . . . Being in the stock market, studying charts, yes. But aside from that (businessmen do not memorize for memorizing's sake).

In the remainder of the interview VP kept returning to his three major points. These were that memorization must begin in early childhood, that outstanding memory can only be obtained by being a rather passive individual who, in his words, "accepts the rules of the game," and that adults, and particularly dynamic adults, fail to memorize because their minds are actively operating on the information in front of them, *not* just to recode it, which the good memorizer does, but rather to change the situation to their own advantage. It would be fair to say that VP distinguishes strongly between a recorder and a manipulator of situations. He clearly regards himself as one of the former.

DISCUSSION

How does VP do what he does? In answering this question we have a few facts and more speculations. Some of the speculations challenge current theories of long-term memory organization. Others raise questions about our educational system.

We are quite confident VP is not an eidetic imager. In fact, visual imagery seems to be less important in his memory than in the memory of most people. He makes very heavy use of linguistic associations, both at a nonsense and a meaningful level. To do this he must understand what he is trying to remember, at least in the sense that he can tie newly presented material into previously acquired memories. This is apparent if one reads his reproductions of "The War of the Ghosts." Although his reproductions are close to the original version, there are a significant number of changes of tense and rephrasings. There are a few changes of meaning, but they are minor. It is more as if he were reconstructing the story from its main ideas than if he were reading a visual image of a page, as an eidetic imager would do. It might be objected that "The War of the Ghosts" lends itself to more normal visual imagery, since one could image it as a sort of mental moving picture. We do not think that VP did this, both because he did not tell us that he did and because he also had a very good recall for a comparably long passage from B. F. Skinner's *Science and Human Behavior* (1953). We do not see how Skinner's discussion could be imaged.

As VP has repeatedly stressed, one must concentrate to memorize. In more formal terms, VP is much better than most people in creating stimulus codes. There is a conscious effort involved. If he can, VP studies the information he is to remember for a longer time than the average person will spend. When we watched him playing blindfolded chess matches, we could see that, although he was acting with considerable flair, he was also working very hard. He would make "casual" jokes while thinking about his next move, but the veins on his forehead were standing out. The fact that he could joke while calculating moves indicates that he has an ability that most of us do not have: he can do a number of mental tasks in parallel. This would perhaps account for his phenomenal performance of the Brown-Peterson task. Unlike most subjects, he seems to be able to repeat numbers backwards while processing information in memory. Similarly, on the Sternberg task his data, unlike that of most persons, indicate a parallel search.

The data from the perceptual speed test demonstrate that VP is unusually rapid at noticing small details between stimuli. One can make out a logical case that this should be an important ability in recoding. The perceptual speed test, however, is not a diagnostic for good memory. We gave the test to 69 students in an introductory psychology course, in an attempt to find people who might be like VP. We found several people who had perceptual speed test scores which approximated his, but further testing indicated that they did not have particularly good memories. In fact, the psychometric tests do not seem capable of making any clear distinction between VP and other bright subjects. We suspect that there is a "memorizing" ability which is simply outside the range of the relatively standard psychometric instruments we have used.

In the face of all this evidence, we are inclined to believe that VP acquired his memory ability by a combination of two factors. One, which is quite probably innate, is his ability to notice details rapidly. Roughly, this ability is reflected by a high score on tests of Guilford's perceptual speed factor. This, alone, is probably not enough to produce the outstanding memorizer. We suggest believing VP himself, in assigning great importance to early learning. In his preschool and grade school years VP was placed in a situation where the ability to recite facts as opposed to the ability to do things or talk to people, was highly valued. Thus he may well have learned to sharpen his perceptual abilities, because memory was valued for its own sake. Perhaps this explains why we do not find a great many VPs in our current society. We do not reward knowledge as such, we reward knowledge indirectly, when it is used to manipulate the environment. Even in academia our highest rewards go to a scientist who produces a new theory, not to one who memorizes old experimental results. Given this, is it any wonder that our children learn, early in life, that the amount of effort which VP invests in memory is usually an unwise investment? Therefore they do not practice memorizing as he did, and they simply fail to acquire the skill.

This hypothesis has led us to the next stage of our research. Can we identify other mnemonists? More particularly, can we predict where they will be found? At this time we have no answer, but we shall certainly make the search.

APPENDIX

"The War of the Ghosts" (Original Story)

One night two young men from Egulac went down to the river to hunt seals, and while they were there it became foggy and calm. Then they heard war-cries, and they thought: "Maybe this is a war-party." They escaped to the shore, and hid behind a log. Now canoes came up, and they heard the noise of paddles, and saw one canoe coming up to them. There were five men in the canoe, and they said:

"What do you think? We wish to take you along. We are going up the river to make war on the people."

One of the young men said: "I have no arrows."

"Arrows are in the canoe," they said.

"I will not go along. I might be killed. My relatives do not know where I have gone. But you," he said, turning to the other, "may go with them."

So one of the young men went, but the other returned home.

And the warriors went on up the river to a town on the other side of Kalama. The people came down to the water, and they began to fight, and many were killed. But presently the young man heard one of the warriors say: "Quick, let us go home: that Indian has been hit." Now he thought: "Oh, they are ghosts." He did not feel sick, but they said he had been shot.

So the canoes went back to Egulac, and the young man went ashore to his house, and made a fire. And he told everybody and said: "Behold I accompanied the ghosts, and we went to fight. Many of our fellows were killed, and many of those who attacked us were killed. They said I was hit, and I did not feel sick."

He told it all, and then became quiet. When the sun rose he fell down. Something black came out of his mouth. His face became contorted. The people jumped up and cried.

He was dead.

VP's Reproduction of "The War of the Ghosts"
One Hour after Reading

One night two young men from Egulac went down to the river to hunt seals. While they were there, it became foggy and calm. They came ashore quietly and hid behind a log. Soon they heard canoes approaching and the sound of paddling. One canoe with five men in it came ashore and spoke:

"What do you think? We are going up the river to make war on the people. Come with us."

One young man said: "We have no arrows."

"There are arrows in the boat," said the war party.

"I will not go. I may be killed. My relatives will not know where I have gone. But he will go with you."

So one young man stayed behind and the other went upriver with the war party to the other side of Kalama to make war on the people. When the people heard them coming they came down to the river to fight with them, and they fought.

Soon the young man heard somebody say: "Let us return. That Indian has been hit."

"Maybe they are ghosts," thought the young man.

The voices insisted that he was wounded, and they returned although he felt fully well.

He went from the river up to his house, lit a fire, and sat outside the house. He told his people: "I was with a war party, and we went upriver, and we fought, and many of them, and many of us were killed. Maybe they were ghosts. They said I was wounded, but I don't feel anything (i.e., wounded)."

When the sun rose, something black came out of his mouth. His face contorted, and he fell over.

He was dead.

VP's Reproduction of "The War of the Ghosts"
Six Weeks after Reading

One night, two young men from Egliac went down to the river to hunt seals. While they were there, it became foggy and calm. Soon they heard the sound of paddles approaching, and they thought: "Maybe it's a war party." They fled ashore and hid behind a log. Soon, one of the (unspecified number of) canoes came ashore, with five men in it, and one of them said: "What you think? Let us go upriver and make war against the people."

"I will not go," said one of the young men. "I might be killed. My family does not know where I have gone." "But he," said he, turning to the other young man, "will go with you." So one of the young men returned to village and the other accompanied the party.

The party went upriver to a point beyond Kalama, and when the people saw them approaching, they came down to the river, and they fought. In the heat of the battle, the young man heard somebody say: "Quick, let us go home. That Indian has been wounded."

"They must be ghosts," thought the young man, who felt no pain or injury. However, the party returned, and he walked from the river up to his village, where he lit a fire outside of his hut, and awaited the sunrise.

"We went with a war party to make war on the people upriver," he told his people who had gathered around, "and many were killed on both sides. I was told that I was injured, but I feel alright. Maybe they were ghosts."

He told it all to the villagers. When the sun came up, a contortion came over his face. Something black came out of his mouth, and he fell over.

He was dead.

REFERENCES

Atkinson, R. C., & Shiffrin, R. M. Human memory: A proposed system and its control processes. In K. W. Spence & J. T. Spence (Eds.), *The psychology of learning and motivation,* Vol. 2. New York: Academic Press, 1968. Pp. 89-195.

Bartlett, F. C. *Remembering: A study in experimental and social psychology.* London: Cambridge University Press, 1932.

Brown, J. Some tests of the decay theory of immediate memory. *Quarterly Journal of Experimental Psychology.* 1958, **10**, 12-21.

Counselor's Manual 1971. Washington Pre-college Testing Program. Seattle: University of Washington, 1971.

DeGroot, A. D. *Thought and choice in chess.* The Hague: Mouton, 1965.

French, J. (Ed.) *Kit of reference tests for cognitive factors. 1963 Revision.* Princeton, N.J.: Educational Testing Service, 1963.

Frost, N. A. H. Clustering by visual and semantic codes in long-term memory. Unpublished doctoral dissertation, University of Oregon, 1971.

Guilford, J. P. *The nature of human intelligence.* New York: McGraw-Hill, 1967.

Haber, R. N. Eidetic images. *Scientific American,* 1969, **220**, 36-44.

Julesz, B. *Foundations of cyclopean perception.* Chicago: University of Chicago Press, 1971.

Kleinberg, J., & Kaufman, H. Constancy in short-term memory: Bits and chunks. *Journal of Experimental Psychology,* 1971, **90**, 326-333.

Luria, A. R. *The mind of a mnemonist.* New York: Basic Books, 1968.

Miller, G. A. The magical number seven, plus or minus two: Some limits on our capacity for processing information. *Psychological Review,* 1956, **63**, 81-97.

Paivio, A. Imagery and deep structure in the recall of English nominalizations. *Journal of Verbal Learning and Verbal Behavior,* 1971, **10**, 1-12.

Peterson, L. R., & Peterson, M. J. Short term retention of individual items. *Journal of Experimental Psychology,* 1959, **58**, 193-198.

Raven, J. C. *Advanced progressive matrices I and II.* New York: The Psychological Corporation, 1958.

Simon, H. A., & Kotovsky, K. Human acquisition of concepts for serial patterns. *Psychological Review,* 1963, **70**, 534-546.

Skinner, B. F. *Science and human behavior.* New York: The Macmillan Company, 1953.

Sternberg, S. High speed scanning in human memory. *Science,* 1966, **153**, 652-654.

Stollmeyer, C. F., & Psotka, J. The detailed texture of eidetic imagers. *Nature,* 1970, **225**, 346-349.

Talland, G. A. *Deranged memory.* New York: Academic Press, 1965.

11
INFORMATION INTEGRATION AND FORM OF ENCODING[1]

Wendell R. Garner
Yale University

The problem of concern in this paper is perceptual discrimination, rather broadly defined. In terms of experimental task, two or more alternative stimuli are presented to the experimental subject, ordinarily one at a time, and the performance rules specified by the experimenter provide one correct response for each possible stimulus. Such tasks are called various things depending on the number of stimuli, the nature of the response, and the performance measure used. In different experimental contexts we would refer to our experiments as simple discrimination, identification, absolute judgment, speeded classification, choice reaction time, and probably others as well. While a variety of performance measures can be used, they usually fall into the class of either accuracy or speed measurement.

The issue of concern in this paper is the role of stimulus redundancy in affecting performance in such tasks. Suppose that we have a given performance level, and that this performance level is less than could be obtained from the experimental subject if stimulus conditions were improved. In other words, the task is not limited by the output or processing capabilities of the subject; we know that performance can be improved. We introduce redundancy into the set of stimuli used, and then ask the perfectly reasonable question whether redundancy improves perceptual discrimination.

The earliest research on this topic, which I reviewed a decade ago (Garner, 1962), led to the conclusion that only chaos reigns with regard to the role of redundancy in perceptual discrimination. There seemed little rhyme or reason to the different results obtained in different experiments, some showing marked

[1] Preparation of this article was supported in part by Grant MH 14229 from the National Institute of Mental Health to Yale University.

improvement in performance when stimuli were made redundant, others showing little or no improvement at all. There was very much a quality of: Now you see it, now you don't. I will not review the contradictory results at this time, even though the number of contradictions is actually fascinating to somebody who is looking for order rather than chaos. Rather I will try to show that there is some order in the many apparently discrepant results. Seeing this order depends on our recognizing two basic factors:

1. There are different kinds of redundancy. Information theory provided us with a measure of amount of redundancy, and perhaps with the incentive to manipulate it experimentally. But measures of amount of redundancy do not differentiate among kinds of redundancy which are functionally quite different for the organism. As we shall see, at a minimum it is necessary to distinguish between redundancy whose primary function is simply to repeat the stimulus, and redundancy which adds new dimensions of variation to the set of stimuli. Even further, we will have to distinguish between dimensional redundancy that does simply add dimensions of variation, and dimensional redundancy that provides a combination which changes the nature of the stimuli themselves in a more fundamental way.

2. There are different ways in which performance can be limited. As we have noted, there must be less than optimum performance before there is any reason to expect redundancy to improve performance. But, as modern research on information processing is making eminently clear, there are many different stages between the stimulus input and the final response output, and each of these stages may be the limiting factor. Perhaps stages is not the best term to use to differentiate these various internal processes, and form of encoding is probably preferable, because it connotes less an orderly sequence, and it is not at all clear that these various forms of encoding do exist in a neatly chained sequence.

The most important point about these two distinctions is that they interact. The effectiveness of different kinds of redundancy in improving perceptual discrimination performance depends on the processing stage that is limiting performance. Clearly such a state of affairs means there is no conclusion we can draw which will state that one kind of redundancy is effective in improving performance while another is not; or that performance limitations caused by one form of encoding can be removed or ameliorated with redundancy, while other types of performance limitation cannot be helped with redundancy. The situation is considerably more complicated than that.

What I shall do here is list six different ways in which redundancy can aid performance. There are probably more—certainly the number of logical possibilities is great—but these are the ones that seem reasonable at the moment. Perhaps these six are not all different either, but this analysis will at least provide a start in solving a problem with a level of complexity appropriate to the nature of the problem.

Parenthetically, one difficulty in trying to sort out various ways in which redundancy can aid performance is that performance obviously can be limited by more than one form of encoding at the same time. We will need more experiments that are aimed at sorting out these different kinds of redundancy and the different reasons for its need.

REDUNDANCY THAT INCREASES DETECTION OPPORTUNITY

Certainly one of the simplest forms of redundancy is straightforward repetition of the stimulus in time or space. Such repetition redundancy frequently, but not always, produces an increase in discrimination accuracy.

As an example, Eriksen and Lappin (1965) required discrimination among three letters (A, T, and U) presented tachistoscopically at a constant distance from a visual fixation point, with a duration and contrast low enough to produce errors of identification. On a given trial just one of the three possible letters occurred, but these were on different trials either 1, 2, 4, or 6 identical letters spaced on the circumference of an imaginary circle whose center was the fixation point. (This procedure assured approximately equal perceptual accuracy for each letter position.) The accuracy of discrimination increased as the number of simultaneously presented letters increased, accuracy of discrimination being 54, 63, 72, and 74 percent for the 1, 2, 4, or 6 simultaneous stimuli.

Keeley and Doherty (1968) replicated this experiment with 1 or 4 simultaneous letters and obtained essentially identical results. They also presented the same letter four times in succession with an interstimulus interval of several seconds, and got an equally good improvement in performance.

Some data from our own laboratory are shown in Figure 1 (Garner & Flowers, 1969). For these data the stimulus elements were either Xs or Os, and for a given series of trials there were either 4 or 2 simultaneous and identical stimulus elements. When there were four, they were spaced around a visual fixation point as the corners of a square. When just two simultaneous stimuli were used, in some conditions they were presented in a fixed position either above or below the fixation point, and in one condition were randomly placed above or below the fixation point. These variations were used to get some idea whether the random

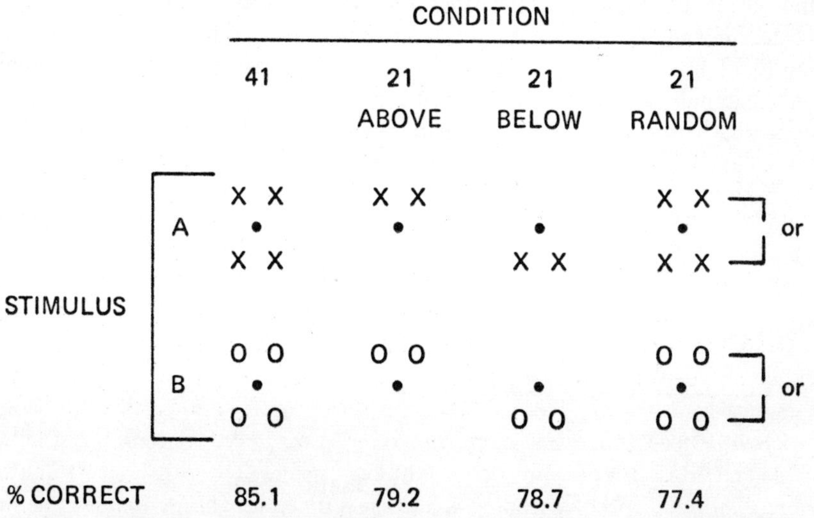

FIG. 1. Percent correct responses for multielement stimuli used by Garner and Flowers (1969). (The dot shows location of fixation point.)

position fluctuations which were an essential part of both the Eriksen and Lappin experiment and the Keeley and Doherty experiment were necessary for the improvement in discrimination with repeated stimuli to occur. These data show that four identical stimuli gave better discrimination performance than two with all conditions of presentation. Thus we have little doubt about the validity of this result, at least with letters as stimulus elements.

Simple repetition redundancy does not lead to an improved performance, however, unless some care is taken to ensure that each element is equally visible. In all the experiments reported so far this condition was ensured with the use of a fixation point. Garner and Lee (1962), however, presented 2, 4, or 9 stimulus elements. Combinations of Xs and Os were used, and the subject was required to discriminate four alternative patterns of elements. These patterns were always known to the subject in advance. They found no improvement in discrimination as the number of stimulus elements per presentation was increased. The explanation for this failure is quite simple. The subjects knew where the stimuli would appear, and they changed their fixation so as to see stimulus positions which would give them maximum information to discriminate the four patterns. Clearly this result shows that foveal vision is far better than multiple stimulus elements, so there is some doubt about how generally useful such redundancy is in the free situation. As one last example, Pollack (1958) has shown that repetition of words heard in noise improved discrimination of the words. In other words, accuracy of perceptual discrimination is improved with spatial or temporal repetition for many types of stimuli.

Can speed of discrimination also be improved? Under some circumstances, the answer is also yes. Table 1 shows some data from our laboratory on this point (Flowers & Garner, 1971). The task for the subject was to discriminate the lateral position of dots on hand-held cards. In some conditions there was just a single dot on each card, and in others there were two dots, but the two dots were on the same side of the card. These dots were either black, thus giving high contrast, or yellow, thus giving low contrast. Still further, the two alternative positions were either easy to discriminate, or difficult to discriminate by virtue of being closer together. The results of interest here concern whether two dots gave better discrimination than one, and under what conditions. When contrast was high and position discriminability easy, performance was good and there was no substantial improvement in

TABLE 1

Mean Sorting Times (Seconds) for Six Conditions Involving Repetition
Redundancy for State- and Process-Limited Tasks
*Decks of 36 Cards Were Sorted into Two Categories Defined by
Lateral Position of Dots.*
(from Flowers & Garner, 1971).

Number of dots	1	2	1	2	1	2
Color of dots	Black	Black	Black	Black	Light	Light
Position dis-criminability	Easy	Easy	Difficult	Difficult	Easy	Easy
Sorting times	21.3	21.0	25.0	24.6	25.6	24.1
Difference		.3		.4		1.5

discrimination speed when the second dot was added. When contrast was high but the discrimination was difficult, performance was poorer, but still there was no substantial improvement in discrimination speed when the second dot was added. However, when the basic discrimination task was easy, but contrast was decreased, then adding the second dot did improve discriminability. Furthermore, since the sorting time required for the low-contrast stimuli was about the same as that for the difficult discriminability task, we know that the possibilities for improvement were equal in both cases. Therefore the fact that improvement with repetition redundancy occurred only when the need for it was due to low stimulus contrast has considerable importance.

State Versus Process Limitation

Clearly these results, as well as others we will discuss later, require a distinction between different factors that produce a need for performance improvement. In regard to this problem, Garner (1970) had previously pointed out that failure of performance can be due to a state limitation or to a process limitation. The distinction relates to the nature of the assigned task. In a discrimination experiment, the experimenter defines the informational dimension to be processed, that is to say, the stimulus dimension which is to be correlated with the responses the subject uses. If the subject must discriminate among three letters, or between two positions, then letters or spatial position constitute the process dimensions, the dimensions which correspond to the task assignment. Failure of perfect discrimination which occurs because the process dimension or dimensions produce poor discrimination (the letters look too much alike, or the alternative positions are too close together) is failure due to a process limitation.

State limitation occurs when an energy dimension limits performance, but is not itself the dimension pertinent to the assigned information processing task. In simple cases it is due to inadequate energy or contrast, or too much noise, factors that do not act upon discrimination directly, but rather prevent adequate representation of the physical stimulus in the organism. I have used the term state limitation because it has broader implications than necessary in the present context, and certainly for present purposes we could talk about energic limitations, referring the limiting factor to a stimulus parameter rather than to an organismic property. But of course they must go together, since a given energy limitation can be just as well considered an inadequacy of the state of the organism.

Experiments have not usually distinguished between these two ways in which discrimination performance can be impaired. In studies on the effect of redundancy, some level of inadequate performance is necessary in order that improvement may be shown. But to impair the energic nature of the input is quite different from degrading the process dimension itself.

The necessity for the distinction is most clearly shown by the Flowers and Garner (1971) experiment on speed of discrimination. When performance was impaired by making the discrimination task difficult, performance was process limited and there was no improvement in performance with repetition redundancy. When, however, performance was degraded by the use of light dots, thus decreasing the contrast, performance was state limited, and under this circumstance it was improved with repetition redundancy.

The importance of the role of state limitation and the necessity to distinguish it from process limitation can most easily be seen by noting the effect of stimulus repetition in a detection task, where the dimension of discrimination is itself the energic dimension which determines adequacy of the input. Green and Swets (1966) have reviewed much of this literature, and the results of various experiments consistently show improvement in detection with repetition of the stimulus. This fact alone should make us suspect that apparent improvement in discrimination of a process variable may be due not at all to improvement in the discrimination process itself, but may be due to improvement in perceptibility or detectability of the stimulus. The distinction might not have been important. However, research results now make clear that the distinction is very necessary, and this fact should remind us not to make our operational distinctions too simplistic. Having less than optimum performance is not alone sufficient to determine whether repetition redundancy will improve performance. It matters how the inadequate performance was obtained.

Conclusion

Simple repetition redundancy improves discrimination performance if the need for improvement is due to state limitation in the organism, or complementarily, to an inadequate stimulus energy. It does not improve performance if the need for improvement is due to inadequate discrimination on the informational continuum, that is, process limitation. Basically, the mode of operation of repetition redundancy is that it increases detection opportunity, thus providing a discrimination gain indirectly.

REDUNDANCY THAT IMPROVES DIMENSIONAL DISCRIMINABILITY

Can redundancy improve discrimination when the need for improvement is due to process limitation rather than state limitation? The answer unequivocally is yes, and the rest of this paper is concerned with such cases. However, there are many ways in which process limitation can occur, and just as many kinds of redundancy necessary to improve performance.

Certainly the simplest way in which a process limitation can occur is that the two or more levels on the informational dimension are not far enough apart, that is, they are not sufficiently discriminable. If dimensional redundancy, where a new dimension is added to the stimulus and covaries with levels on the original stimulus, is used, discriminability may be improved and thus performance may be improved as well. There is clear evidence that under some circumstances dimensional redundancy improves discrimination performance by directly improving discriminability between the levels of the dimensions. However, once again the conditions for obtaining improvement are very specific, and some additional concepts about redundancy and perceptual dimensions are necessary.

We have already seen in Table 1 that repetition redundancy did not improve speed of discrimination when the need for the improvement was due to a process limitation—and in that case the process limitation certainly was due simply to an inadequate difference between the two levels on the dimension to be processed. Thus repetition redundancy is ineffective with process limitation.

Table 2 demonstrates that a still further distinction must be made. The data illustrated there (Garner & Felfoldy, 1970) are from an experiment involving speed of card sorting into two categories, and dimensions to be discriminated were value and chroma (Munsell terms) of visual stimuli. Table 2A shows the results of the experiment when these two dimensions were varied in a single color chip, either each dimension varying alone, both varying in correlated (i.e., redundant) manner, or both dimensions varying orthogonally although sorting was done by just one dimension. Even in the correlated case the subjects were instructed to sort the stimuli by one or the other dimension. The results of this experiment are unambiguous: The addition of a redundant stimulus dimension increased the speed of discrimination. Furthermore, the addition of a stimulus dimension orthogonal to the dimension to be discriminated produced interference in discrimination.

TABLE 2

Mean Sorting Times for Stimuli Varying in One, Two
Correlated, and Two Orthogonal Dimensions
Decks of 32 cards were sorted into two categories
defined by levels on one dimension.
(from Garner & Felfoldy, 1970)

	Type of Stimulus Set		
Dimension Sorted	One Dimension	Correlated Dimensions	Orthogonal Dimensions
A. Value and Chroma in a Single Stimulus Chip			
Value	15.09	13.73	18.55
Chroma	14.22	13.24	17.49
B. Value and Chroma in Two Separate Chips			
Value	15.85	15.69	15.78
Chroma	15.57	15.09	15.10

Table 2B shows the results of the same experiment when the two dimensions were varied, either redundantly or orthogonally, in separate color chips. The results in this case are equally unambiguous: The addition of a new stimulus dimension did not improve discrimination when it was done redundantly, nor did it interfere with discrimination when it was done orthogonally. Thus dimensional redundancy will aid when there is limited discriminability, but only under certain circumstances.

Further evidence that it matters exactly how the redundant dimension is presented comes from an experiment by Lockhead (1966b). Eriksen and Hake (1955) had shown that absolute judgments of 20 alternative visual stimuli improved when stimulus dimensions of hue, brightness, and size covaried redundantly rather than varying as single dimensions. In fact, this was the first experiment to give such an unequivocal result, and it has become the base experiment against which results of others are compared. To return to Lockhead, however, he showed that there was no gain in accuracy of absolute judgments of 10 stimuli when hue and brightness were varied in a correlated fashion but on spatially separated color chips on the same card. Thus dimensional redundancy does not guarantee that discrimination limitations will be offset; the dimensions must somehow vary in the same stimulus. To complicate this picture further, however, Lockhead also showed that if the two stimulus dimensions were varied redundantly but were presented in separate color chips presented successively, there was a gain in discrimination accuracy. We will return to this result later.

One other experiment (Lockhead, 1966a) needs mentioning now, however. It involved absolute judgments of 10 alternative stimuli. Lockhead covaried the length of a line and its vertical position, and found that discrimination accuracy improved when a redundant dimension was added. This experiment was done under conditions of very brief exposure and low contrast, however, so that almost certainly state limitation existed as well as process limitation. Thus this experiment alone did not clarify the fact that dimensional redundancy does not aid discrimination when the only discrimination inadequacy is due to a state limitation.

Dimensional Integrality

The results from these various experiments showing that dimensional redundancy aids discrimination when it is process limited, and in a way which makes it fairly clear that the limitation is on interstimulus discriminability, have led to the concept of dimensional integrality. Lockhead (1966a) first used this term to try to explain the results of an experiment on the effects of dimensional redundancy on discrimination. Garner (1970) suggested a dichotomy between integral and separable dimensions, although Garner and Felfoldy (1970) elaborated the concept by recognizing that there probably are degrees of integrality, rather than there being a simple dichotomy. Garner (1970) argued further that the concept has considerable generality, one which helps its operational definition. As was shown in Table 2, dimensions which improve performance when used redundantly also impair performance when used orthogonally, and conversely, dimensions which do not improve performance when used redundantly do not impair performance when used orthogonally. Still further, these relations coincide with a series of experiments reviewed by Garner (1970) showing that integral dimensions are those which produce a Euclidean metric in direct distance judgments, and separable dimensions are those which produce a city-block metric. But this is not the place to elaborate on that history. The important point here is that dimensional redundancy aids discrimination performance when the limitation is on discriminability, but only when the redundant dimensions are integral.

More on State and Process

When talking about state versus process limitations in the context of repetition redundancy, the distinction is fairly simple, and refers primarily to whether the limitation is getting enough energy to the receptor organ, or whether the limitation is in the processing of information after each stimulus clearly has gotten into the organism. In that context, if there is no question that the stimulus on each occasion has been seen or heard, then the only limitation must be process.

There is a broader context to the distinction, however, as originally made by Garner and Morton (1969). The distinction makes clearer why we used the term "state" in reference to the organism rather than the term "energy" in reference to the stimulus. Our original distinction was concerned with the problem of perceptual independence, and the many meanings which the term can have. State independence refers to the condition in which the existence of errors for two or more dimensions, without regard to their direction, is correlated. An organism can be in a poor state for discriminating, and this may be due to alertness level, for example, rather than stimulus energy level. Process independence, however, refers to the condition in which the two or more dimensions lead to direct correlations of the appropriate responses. If two stimulus dimensions are correlated, then correlation of errors of responses to these two dimensions, at whatever level of encoding it occurs, constitutes nonindependence of process.

The importance of the point here is that truly independent dimensions in the process sense are those which here we are calling separable—they do not interact. Thus process independence is not a desirable condition for effectiveness of dimensional redundancy when the need lies in a lack of discriminability. Nevertheless, noncorrelation of errors is a necessary condition in a logical sense for two stimulus dimensions to lead to improved performance. Thus it is clear that many distinctions concerning the term "perceptual independence" are necessary, as Garner and Morton argued. Perhaps it is true, as these authors also argued, that the search for sources and loci of interaction (form or level of encoding) is a more profitable approach than to ask the hopefully universal question about perceptual independence. At least that is the approach in this paper.

One last comment on state versus process limitations. The distinction can be made with experiments other than those on redundancy, or even multidimensional discrimination experiments more generally. Garner, Kaplan, and Creelman (1966) investigated absolute judgments of visual size with variations in stimulus duration and contrast, as well as variations in range of stimulus sizes. Their results showed that within limits, the effects of the energy variables of duration and contrast were interchangeable with the effects of the process variable of stimulus range. Nevertheless, there were conditions of contrast and duration above which the interchange did not operate: No increase in an energy variable produced an increase in accuracy of absolute judgments, although the range of stimulus sizes continued to have an effect. Thus even with single dimensional judgments there is an operational distinction between state and process limitation. In ordinary language, this result shows that beyond some limit the energic variables which offset state limitations can have no further effect—each single stimulus can be seen very well. But when this condition holds, process limitations (the range, or size of interstimulus differences) still affect performance.

Conclusion

If the limitation on discrimination performance is a process limitation, specifically a limit on discrimination between the two or more levels on the dimension to be discriminated, then performance can be improved with dimensional redundancy, but the dimensions must be integral. In some way they must produce a new set of stimulus values with a greater perceptual distance between them. Dimensional redundancy with nonintegral dimensions will not provide improvement, nor will repetition redundancy provide improvement. In fact, it is conceivable that repetition redundancy is simply a special case of dimensional redundancy with separable dimensions.

REDUNDANCY THAT PRODUCES A NEW DIMENSION

The situation just discussed can be thought of as one in which two dimensions combine to provide a new dimension with greater discriminability between the levels. The perceived distance between levels has been increased by the dimensional combination, but there is no sense that the new dimension is different in kind from the two separate dimensions. Rather, the appropriate analogy is one of a vector combination in a two-dimensional space, an analogy which fits very comfortably with the fact of a Euclidean distance metric in the two-dimensional space.

There is a closely related consequence of dimensional redundancy, but one which is probably psychologically quite different. That is where two dimensions combine so as to produce a new derived dimension which is psychologically much more effective for discrimination purposes. At the moment we will only assume that such a dimensional redefinition occurs, without inquiring further about the locus of effectiveness.

The special case which most clearly illustrates this effect of dimensional redundancy is the combination of two spatial dimensions to provide a new dimension of form. Figure 2 illustrates a set of stimuli used by Weintraub (1971) pertinent to this problem. His experimental task was absolute judgment of 15 rectangular stimuli, chosen from various combinations of heights and widths. Some of his experimental results are shown at the bottom of the figure. The average information transmissions obtained when the stimuli varied just in height or just in width was 2.26 bits. If height and width are varied in a correlated fashion along the main diagonal, we can consider that the experimental subject is presented with two correlated or redundant dimensions. Alternatively, we can consider that he has been presented with a new single dimension of size, since all stimuli are squares and vary only in area. The experimental result which Weintraub obtained showed less information transmission than when just height or width was varied alone. Clearly there was no gain with these redundant dimensions. Equally clearly, it seems unreasonable to explain this lack of gain as being due to separability of the dimensions, as discussed in the previous section, since squares are perceptually unitary by their very nature. So some additional explanation is required, and it is that this particular combination of dimensions simply produces a psychologically new dimension which is no better than either of the two dimensions which were combined.

However, when Weintraub used the secondary diagonal to produce 15 stimuli, those stimuli all had equal area but now varied in form. Under these conditions, information transmission jumped to 2.65, a substantial improvement. As a last

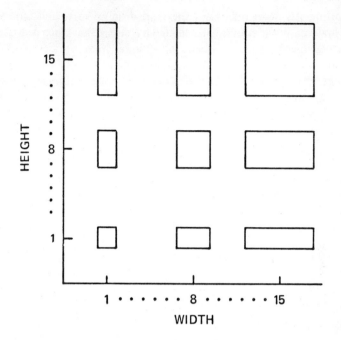

INFORMATION TRANSMISSIONS (BITS) FOR:

ROWS OR COLUMNS (AVERAGE): 2.26
REDUNDANT MAIN DIAGONAL (SQUARES): 2.04
REDUNDANT SECONDARY DIAGONAL (EQUAL AREA): 2.65
REDUNDANT RANDOM RECTANGLES: 2.67

FIG. 2. Rectangles used by Weintraub (1971) in absolute judgment task, and information transmissions for four different methods of selecting 15 stimuli.

condition, Weintraub selected a random set of 15 rectangles, which varied in both form and size but not in a regular fashion. Information transmission obtained with this condition was about the same as that obtained when just form varied.

If it seems unreasonable to explain the lack of gain obtained with stimuli varying in area as being due to the nature of the dimensions which were combined, it is equally unreasonable to explain the gain obtained with stimuli varying in form as due to the properties of the combined dimensions. Rather, we should conclude that form is a perceptually easier dimension to discriminate than area, and that while we have performed logical operations of dimensional combination in producing either form or area variation, the psychological reality is that judgments are being made by a subject of two meaningfully different single stimulus dimensions (form or area), one of which is more discriminable than the other.

Further evidence on this advantage of form as the discriminable dimension has been provided by Felfoldy, working at Yale, but with results not yet published. He used the card-sorting task, with just two alternative stimuli. When the stimuli varied in form, sorting was faster than when they varied only in area and form was held constant. However, this result is mildly limited by the fact that area provided just as fast a sorting speed as form when the stimuli were squares for the area classification.

Still further evidence on the strong psychological value of form as a dimension is provided by Lockhead (1970), with stimuli illustrated in Figure 3. For the single dimensional case, a single line varied in tilt (between 1.5 and 30 degrees from the horizontal) and occurred in one of four possible locations. For one redundancy condition, four lines appeared in each stimulus, but all had the same tilt. (This condition is one of repetition redundancy.) There was little improvement in accuracy of judgment with this form of redundancy. However, when the four lines were not all of the same tilt—thus providing a kind of form configuration for each of the 20 stimuli—accuracy of identification went to 100 percent, and there was the strong suggestion that considerably more stimuli could have been handled. Thus

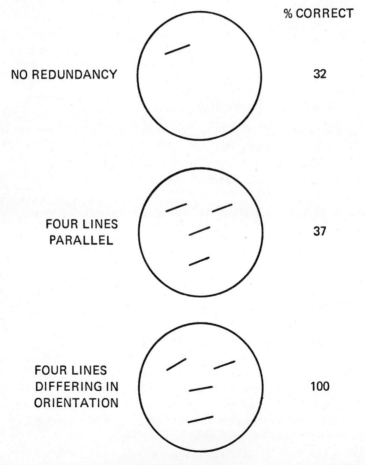

FIG. 3. Percent correct identification of 20 alternative stimuli, for nonredundant and two types of redundant stimuli (Lockhead, 1970).

once again when dimensional covariation occurs but the combination produces a form dimension, accuracy of perceptual discrimination becomes very great.

Conclusion

When two or more stimulus dimensions are correlated, it is possible that the new set of stimuli produced are not perceived in a multidimensional sense at all. Rather a new and psychologically meaningful dimension is perceived. If this new dimension is a visual form, it is very effective for information processing purposes. It is possible that form is unique in this respect, but it certainly seems very likely that some auditory dimensions could be covaried so as to produce a new set of stimuli differing more as speech sounds than as simple auditory dimensions.

REDUNDANCY THAT IMPROVES THE MEMORY CODE

In the preceding section, the question was begged of why a dimension like form is better for perceptual discrimination than one like size. However, one very real possibility is that memory for form is better than memory for size. We need to be reminded that in any experiment involving single stimulus presentation with a response requirement of identification of the single stimulus (whether a two-stim-ulus sorting task, or an absolute judgment task), the subject must remember what the set of alternative stimuli is, as well as what the correct differentiating responses for these stimuli are. Usually the labelling problem per se is not critical in discrimination experiments (at least experimenters try to minimize the effect of this aspect of the task), but the ability to remember the alternative stimuli in the set may be the essence of the problem. If I were required to make my best guess as to why form is such a good psychological dimension, this factor of memory would be my choice. In this section, however, I will present some general evidence that suggests that the adequacy of the memory code is an important factor in perceptual discrimination tasks, and that the adequacy of the memory code can be improved with redundancy.

The Eriksen and Hake (1955) experiment mentioned earlier, in which hue, size, and brightness were varied redundantly in an experiment requiring absolute judgments of 20 stimuli, seems at first glance simply to be evidence for redundancy which improves perceptual discrimination. Since a redundancy gain was obtained, then the dimensions were integral. It is possible, however, that the real improvement was obtained because the redundant dimensions made it easier for the subject to remember the set of alternatives, and possibly also their numeric designations. The reasons for suggesting this possibility are the following: First, with all three dimensions correlated, the information transmission obtained was 4.11 bits. This is a value considerably greater than has been obtained in any such experiment involving a single stimulus dimension, so if correlating three dimensions is effectively producing a new dimension with greater interstimulus discriminability, it is doing so with truly great effect.

Second, the interstimulus discriminability, level by level, was already very great with each stimulus dimension used alone, since the full range of possible values was used. In other words, the stimuli were not deliberately spaced close together to produce a need for redundancy so that a gain could be obtained. Rather, each dimension was used in such a way that essentially the maximum possible information transmission per dimension was obtained.

In this connection, Garner and Creelman (1964) showed, using equivalent values of hue and size, that shortening the exposure duration did not affect the information transmission per dimension, nor did it prevent the gain in information transmission when the two dimensions were used redundantly. Thus the spacings used between stimuli and the performance levels obtained were well beyond the levels at which interchanging effects with energic (state limiting) factors could occur. To quote these authors, "such tasks are of *judgmental* discrimination rather than perceptual discrimination." In present terms, the limiting factor is the memory image, not interstimulus discrimination.

Third, we presently have inadequate evidence that the three stimulus dimensions of hue, brightness, and size are integral dimensions, and the evidence is clear that dimensions must be integral for them to improve discriminability. Biederman and Checkosky (1970) used dimensions of size and brightness in a discrete reaction time experiment and showed only a very slight improvement in reaction time when the two dimensions were used redundantly. Similar small effects of redundancy on speeded classification have been found for color and form at Yale (unpublished data from Gottwald and Garner). Thus it is not entirely clear just what the integrality status of these dimensions is. Intuitively it seems reasonable that they should be integral, but the evidence is weak that they are.

Lockhead (1970) provides some further, although not conclusive, evidence on the role of integrality in making redundancy effective with absolute judgments. Table 3 presents some information transmissions obtained with three pairs of variables, used alone, in linear pairings, or in "sawtooth" pairings. With linear pairings, values on the two dimensions increased together throughout the range of values used. With sawtooth pairings, stimuli were selected to give maximum interstimulus differences in the two-dimensional space, and this was accomplished by selecting values from one dimension to go with successive values on the other in an up-and-down, or sawtooth fashion. Results with the dimensions of hue and

TABLE 3

Information Transmissions (Bits) for Three Pairs of
Variables in Lockhead (1970) Study
*Ten levels of each dimension were used. With linear
pairings, pairs 1,1; 2,2; . . . 10,10 were used. With
sawtooth pairings, pairs 1,3; 2,6; 3,9; 4,1; 5,4;
6,7; 7,10; 8,2; 9,5; 10,8 were used.*

Experiment	Dimensions Alone		Dimensions Paired	
A.	Hue	Lightness	Linear	Sawtooth
	1.80	1.59	1.99	2.50
B.	Lightness	Loudness	Linear	Sawtooth
	1.65	1.45	1.68	2.29
C.	Roughness	Hue	Linear	Sawtooth
	2.15	2.31	2.65	3.05

lightness in a single stimulus showed some gain with the linear pairing (thus they might be presumed to be integral), but showed a great gain with the sawtooth pairings. When lightness and loudness were used as dimensions, there was no gain when they were paired linearly. This is the result one would expect, because if ever two dimensions were nonintegral, those involving different modalities are. However, when sawtooth pairing was used, once again great gain in information transmission was obtained. Thus integral dimensions clearly are not necessary to obtain a gain with redundant dimensions in at least some absolute judgment tasks. The third pair of dimensions were again from two modalities, roughness of papers and hue. With these dimensions, gains were obtained both with linear and with sawtooth pairings.

This experiment leaves a great deal unknown. If nonintegral dimensions can produce a gain in information processing performance in absolute judgment, why did not spatially separated dimensions accomplish the effect (Lockhead, 1966b)? Perhaps they would have if sawtooth pairings had been used. But however unclear the final picture is at this point, what is clear is that there are conditions which will not produce a redundancy gain with speeded classification of just two stimulus levels, but which will produce a redundancy gain when absolute judgment is used, and with widely spaced stimulus values. Clearly different processes, or stages of encoding, are involved, and must be separated. This picture is further complicated by the fact that a single discrimination task may involve limitations of discriminability and also limitations of memory. In such cases, improvement in performance with redundancy may well be due to improvement with respect to both factors.

Almost certainly memory factors will be important only for tasks involving identification or discrimination among fairly large numbers of stimulus alternatives. Absolute judgment provides such a task, and it is with this task that large gains in discrimination with redundant dimensions have most often been found. In fact, the small effects of redundancy on speeded classification with dimensions which have given large effects with absolute judgments (such as color and form, or size and brightness) may be due entirely to the fact that only discriminability is involved when just two stimuli are used, although the memory factor will be involved for larger sets of alternative stimuli. Later we will note this same problem with respect to the role of verbal encoding.

Conclusion

Dimensional redundancy will improve discrimination if the limiting factor is the subject's ability to retain a stable memory code for the stimuli. The optimum form of such redundancy is one in which the memory spaces for each dimension are not linearly correlated. The redundant dimensions need not be integral to accomplish this purpose.

REDUNDANCY THAT IMPROVES NUMERIC PROCESSING

In a judgmental situation involving the use of a numeric judgment continuum, the most obvious way in which redundant stimulus dimensions can improve performance is for the subject to make a numeric estimate of each dimension separately and then to average them. Such numeric averaging requires that there be at least three judgment categories for effectiveness, since averaging with two judgment categories and then recoding to just two alternatives cannot produce improvement under any circumstances (Garner & Morton, 1969). However, with three or more categories such numeric averaging and recoding to the original number of categories will produce a gain in discrimination or judgmental accuracy if errors of judgment are uncorrelated, that is, if there is process and state (if appropriate) independence.

Is there any situation in which numeric averaging is known to be operating? The experiment which directly establishes such a possibility has not been done, probably because its outcome seems so inevitable. However, consider the results of the experiment by Lockhead (1966b) in which a gain in accuracy of absolute judgment was not obtained when hue and brightness were presented spatially separated, but was obtained when they were presented successively. The most likely explanation for this result is that subjects were able to do a rough numeric averaging when the stimuli were presented successively (the interstimulus interval was half a second). Thus this particular discrepancy in results almost certainly means that different encoding operations are involved in spatial and temporal separation of stimulus dimensions, each in turn different from what happens when the dimensions are combined into a single stimulus.

Another discrepancy in results of this same kind occurs in an experiment by Keeley and Doherty (1968), some of whose results were mentioned earlier. Table 4 shows the results of their experiments. In one case, the stimuli were the letters A, T, and U, and as previously mentioned, with these stimuli there was a gain in accuracy with repetition redundancy, whether the stimuli were presented all at once in four locations, or whether they were presented successively (with several seconds between stimuli). As noted earlier, these stimuli are almost certainly state limited, thus comfortably fit the paradigm in which repetition redundancy helps perceptual discrimination when the need for improvement is due to a state limitation.

In another case, however, Keeley and Doherty's stimuli were Landolt rings, with a gap in one of four positions: up, down, right, or left. With such stimuli, when four

TABLE 4

Comparisons (Percent Correct) of Simultaneous and Successive
Repetition Redundancy for Landolt Rings (Four Orientations)
and Letters (A, T, and U)
(from Keeley & Doherty, 1968)

Stimuli	One Stimulus	Four Simultaneous Stimuli	Four Successive Stimuli
Landolt rings	52	50	73
Letters	51	68	70

are presented simultaneously there is no gain in discrimination accuracy. I have argued elsewhere (Garner, 1970) that this lack of gain with repetition redundancy is due to the fact that such stimuli are more process limited than state limited, which is to say that telling one stimulus from another with small gaps is what makes the task difficult, not seeing the stimulus in the first place. So far the results and argument are consistent with other known facts. The additional result, however, is that with *successive* presentation of the Landolt rings, there is an improvement in discrimination. What is the explanation? As with the same discrepant result in Lockhead's (1966b) experiment, it seems likely that some form of numeric averaging is occurring with successive presentation, but does not seem to occur with simultaneous presentation.

It is possible that there are at least two kinds of information integration occurring, not just one. Numeric averaging in the sense discussed here is one of these. Doherty and Keeley (1969) suggest, however, that the subject in such experiments is accumulating evidence, not numerically averaging, and that he acts much as a Bayesian predictor in making use of this accumulated evidence. Perhaps, therefore, this section should have included a discussion of both numeric averaging and evidence accumulation as separate issues. Or perhaps the broader term, numeric combination, should have been used to cover both cases.

Conclusion

Redundancy can improve discrimination performance if some form of numeric combination (either averaging or evidence accumulation) is possible. For this purpose, dimensional redundancy is at least adequate, although integrality of stimulus dimensions is an irrelevant consideration. Furthermore, with at least some stimuli repetition redundancy is effective if repetition is over time and not space. Independence of judgmental errors is critical for such a gain to occur, and possibly repetition of stimuli over time is what produces such independence.

REDUNDANCY THAT IMPROVES VERBAL ENCODING

We have seen that redundancy can improve performance in a perceptual discrimination task by increasing opportunity for stimulus detection, by improving dimensional discriminability, by providing a psychologically better dimension, by improving the memory code, and by improving numeric processing. A need for closure requires that we consider redundancy that improves verbal encoding, yet straightforward evidence concerning redundancy that does improve discrimination performance by improving verbal encoding is not available.

One type of experiment does seem relevant to the question at a first glance: Several experiments (Tulving & Gold, 1963; Tulving, Mandler, & Baumal, 1964; Morton, 1964; Pollack, 1964; Stowe, Harris, & Hampton, 1963) presented words as stimuli either visually tachistoscopically, or as in the last reference, auditorily in noise for perceptual recognition. In all cases, redundant information was provided by presenting sentence context for the words before the words themselves were presented, and in all cases accuracy of word recognition improved with the addition of contextual information. This consistent finding might be interpreted as redundancy (the context) improving the adequacy of verbal encoding. However, there are two aspects of these experiments which make such a straightforward interpretation unsatisfactory.

First, the two forms of information—direct stimulus presentation and context—are entirely different, thus cannot possibly operate symmetrically. The need for improved performance is clearly a state limitation in the case of the direct presentation. If context alone is the source of information, then the need for improved performance is due simply to inadequate amount of information in its technical sense. Second, it is likely that the context improves recognition accuracy by a mechanism which is not at all unique to the use of words as stimuli. Most likely, the context provides a smaller message set for the observer, and thus improves accuracy of recognition. But as Egeth and Smith (1967) have shown, decreasing the number of alternative pictures also improves identification accuracy for pictures. In fact, the point of their particular experiment was to demonstrate that if the set of alternatives is made smaller by showing the subject the alternative pictures rather than verbal labels for them, as Lawrence and Coles (1954) had done earlier with no improved identification, then performance would improve. In other words, Egeth and Smith were showing that verbal processes were inadequate in improving performance. Thus with regard to the question of adequacy of verbal encoding, these experiments show that words as stimuli can show improved identification if the subject is given additional information in the form of verbal context, but provide little evidence concerning the role of verbal encoding in the identification process.

An experiment which comes closer to showing that the accuracy or adequacy of the verbal encoding is influenced by verbal context was done by Ladefoged and Broadbent (1957). Four test words were synthetically produced which when presented alone were identified modally as *bit, bet, bat,* and *but.* When these test words were preceded by a voice which served the purpose of establishing the use of formant frequencies by the particular speaker, there were changes in modal identification; but also to some extent there was an increased accuracy of identification in the sense of there being greater group agreement on what the test word was. This accuracy effect was not large, however.

Why is there so little evidence that redundancy aids verbal encoding? Probably because redundancy is primarily valuable in helping perceptual discrimination, and because the evidence indicates that availability of verbal labels does not improve perceptual discrimination. E. J. Gibson's (1969) book reviews the literature on this question and concludes that verbal processes are not really important in discrimination, but just in memory. Some more recent evidence on the lack of importance of verbal labelling in discrimination is given by Taylor (1969). His experimental task required subjects to judge whether two stimuli were the same or different, and reaction time was measured. He used colors and forms as stimulus dimensions, and in each case he used some stimuli which had readily available common labels (letters of the alphabet or colors such as red) and other stimuli which had no common labels. His results showed that the availability of a label did not produce a faster reaction time.

Some conjecture about the possible role of verbal encoding in perceptual discrimination seems necessary, however. If in some discrimination tasks the critical factor is the adequacy of the memory code, and if verbal processes are important in perceptual memory, then it seems more than reasonable that good verbal codes should aid discrimination in such tasks. There is little evidence that directly bears on this point, however. Certainly for the adequacy of the memory set to be a critical factor requires a fairly large number of stimuli, as with an absolute judgment task. Most experiments, such as that by Taylor (1969), use two stimuli presented in rapid succession or even simultaneously. Under such conditions, verbal processes will be unimportant. They might be important with larger memory sets, however.

A recent experiment by Chapanis and Overbey (1971) gives some evidence that accurate verbal encoding does improve discrimination in the absolute judgment paradigm, even with little training in the judgmental task, if the appropriate labels are used. They used three-dimensional color stimuli, with stimuli selected to match color names which were known to have high intersubject agreement in their use. Their subjects could, by the end of 10 trials, identify 36 such colors with essentially perfect accuracy. In bits of information, their subjects performed at a level of 5.17 bits of information transmission. The extent of advantage in this experiment because of the optimum verbal code is not clear, however, since multidimensional stimuli do provide much greater judgment accuracy that unidimensional stimuli, and no control condition was used in which there was equal multidimentional variability in the stimuli, but with a nonoptimum verbal code. Even assuming that the optimum verbal code was important, unfortunately for our purposes, there is no evidence in this experiment on how to use redundancy to improve the verbal code.

Conclusion

There is little evidence that redundancy improves perceptual discrimination by improving the process of verbal encoding, and probably the reason is that verbal encoding processes have little to do with perceptual discrimination. Words, of course, can be used as stimuli, but the factors governing the role of redundancy in improving discrimination of such stimuli are the same as for other types of stimulus material. For example, if state limitations produce the need for redundancy, then repetition redundancy will improve performance as noted earlier. It seems possible, however, that the set of stimuli to be held in memory should be remembered more easily if good verbal labels are available, and in that case redundancy which makes verbal labelling easier should improve performance.

SUMMARY

The question concerning the effect of redundancy on perceptual discrimination is far from being unitary, and its answer lies in differentiating the kinds of redundancy, as well as the processes whose failure produce the need for redundancy. It seems fair to say that for almost any kind of redundancy there is a circumstance under which it will improve discrimination performance. Conversely, for almost any kind of need for improvement in performance, there is a kind of redundancy which will improve it.

Considering these factors jointly, six different ways in which redundancy can improve performance are differentiated: by increasing detection opportunity, improving dimensional discriminability, producing a new dimension, improving the memory code, improving numeric processing, or improving verbal encoding.

REFERENCES

Biederman, I., & Checkosky, S. F. Processing redundant information. *Journal of Experimental Psychology*, 1970, 83, 486-490.

Chapanis, A., & Overbey, C. M. Absolute judgments of colors using natural color names. *Perception & Psychophysics*, 1971, 9, 356-360.

Doherty, M. E., & Keeley, S. M. A Bayesian prediction of four-look recognition performance from one-look data. *Perception & Psychophysics*, 1969, 5, 362-364.

Egeth, H., & Smith, E. E. Perceptual selectivity in a visual recognition task. *Journal of Experimental Psychology*, 1967, 74, 543-549.

Eriksen, C. W., & Hake, H. W. Multidimensional stimulus differences and accuracy of discrimination. *Journal of Experimental Psychology*, 1955, 50, 153-160.

Eriksen, C. W., & Lappin, J. S. Internal perceptual system noise and redundancy in simultaneous inputs in form identification. *Psychonomic Science*, 1965, 2, 351-352.

Flowers, J. H., & Garner, W. R. The effect of stimulus element redundancy on speed of discrimination as a function of state and process limitation. *Perception & Psychophysics*, 1971, 9, 158-160.

Garner, W. R. *Uncertainty and structure as psychological concepts.* New York: Wiley, 1962.

Garner, W. R. The stimulus in information processing. *American Psychologist*, 1970, 25, 350-358.

Garner, W. R. & Creelman, C. D. Effect of redundancy and duration on absolute judgments of visual stimuli. *Journal of Experimental Psychology*, 1964, 67, 168-172.

Garner, W. R., & Felfoldy, G. L. Integrality of stimulus dimensions in various types of information processing. *Cognitive Psychology*, 1970, 1, 225-241.

Garner, W. R., & Flowers, J. H. The effect of redundant stimulus elements on visual discrimination as a function of element heterogeneity, equal discriminability, and position uncertainty. *Perception & Psychophysics*, 1969, 6, 216-220.

Garner, W. R., Kaplan, G., & Creelman, C. D. Effect of stimulus range, duration, and contrast on absolute judgments of visual size. *Perceptual and Motor Skills*, 1966, 22, 635-644.

Garner, W. R., & Lee, W. An analysis of redundancy in perceptual discrimination. *Perceptual and Motor Skills*, 1962, 15, 367-388.

Garner, W. R., & Morton, J. Perceptual independence: Definitions, models, and experimental paradigms. *Psychological Bulletin*, 1969, 72, 233-259.

Gibson, E. J. *Principles of perceptual learning and development.* New York: Appleton-Century-Crofts, 1969.

Green, D. M., & Swets, J. A. *Signal detection theory and psychophysics.* New York: Wiley, 1966.

Keeley, S. M., & Doherty, M. E. Simultaneous and successive presentations of single-featured and multi-featured visual forms: Implications for the parallel processing hypothesis. *Perception & Psychophysics*, 1968, 4, 296-298.

Ladefoged, P., & Broadbent, D. E. Information conveyed by vowels. *Journal of the Acoustical Society of America*, 1957, 29, 98-104.

Lawrence, D. H., & Coles, G. R. Accuracy of recognition with alternatives before and after the stimulus. *Journal of Experimental Psychology*, 1954, 47, 208-214.

Lockhead, G. R. Effects of dimensional redundancy on visual discrimination. *Journal of Experimental Psychology*, 1966, 72, 95-104. (a)

Lockhead, G. R. Visual discrimination and methods of presenting redundant stimuli. *Proceedings of the 74th Annual Convention of the American Psychological Association,* 1966, 67-68. (b)

Lockhead, G. R. Identification and the form of multidimensional discrimination space. *Journal of Experimental Psychology,* 1970, 85, 1-10.

Morton, J. The effects of context on the visual duration threshold for words. *British Journal of Psychology,* 1964, 55, 165-180.

Pollack, I. Message procedures for unfavorable communication conditions. *Journal of the Acoustical Society of America,* 1958, 30, 196-201.

Pollack, I. Interaction of two sources of verbal context in word identification. *Language and Speech,* 1964, 7, 1-12.

Stowe, A. N., Harris, W. P., & Hampton, D. B. Signal and context components of word-recognition behavior. *Journal of the Acoustical Society of America,* 1963, 35, 639-644.

Taylor, R. L. Comparison of short-term memory and visual sensory analysis as sources of information. *Journal of Experimental Psychology,* 1969, 81, 515-522.

Tulving, E., & Gold, C. Stimulus information and contextual information as determinants of tachistoscopic recognition of words. *Journal of Experimental Psychology,* 1963, 66, 319-327.

Tulving, E., Mandler, G., & Baumal, R. Interaction of two sources of information in tachistoscopic word recognition. *Canadian Journal of Psychology,* 1964, 18, 62-71.

Weintraub, D. J. Rectangle discriminability: Perceptual relativity and the law of Prägnanz. *Journal of Experimental Psychology,* 1971, 88, 1-11.

12
REPRESENTATION OF PHYSICAL SPACE[1]

Fred Attneave
University of Oregon

Although spatial relationships are better perceived with two eyes than with one, it is obvious that very good impressions of a tridimensional world may be obtained from a photograph or from a monocular view of one's surroundings. How this happens—how an observer is able to perceive a three-space given a flat picture on the retina—has intrigued a great many people. Let me begin by reviewing briefly three different theoretical approaches to the problem.

THREE THEORIES OF SPACE PERCEPTION

What has been most prevalent, and apparently continues to be most widely accepted at the present time, is some version of a cue theory. The first enumeration of the "cues" that a painter may use to create impressions of depth was by Leonardo da Vinci, and the list of so-called monocular cues given in most textbooks today is for the most part attributable to Leonardo. This includes such familiar factors as relative size, interposition, linear perspective, light and shade, and aerial perspective. It is supposed that the observer arrives at a tridimensional perception by interpreting these features of the flat stimulus array. This sort of theory has typically been empirical in orientation, holding that the observer utilizes stimulus features that have been associated with particular depth or distance relationships in his past experience. Helmholtz emphasized the interpretive aspect of the process; he believed that processes of an essentially rational nature—Brunswik's (1954) term "ratiomorphic" is an apposite one—are carried out at an unconscious level. Cue theories may vary, however, in the amount of unconscious reasoning that they attribute to the observer. A multiple regression model of the kind that Brunswik sometimes entertained assumes a very simple and

[1] This paper is based on research supported in part by the Air Force Office of Scientific Research, Grant 973-66, and in part by the Advanced Research Projects Agency of the Department of Defense, Contract F44620-67C-0099.

more or less stereotyped process of cue combination. In contrast are the highly complicated sequential decision-making processes, often iterative in character, that Minsky (e.g., 1960) and his students postulate in their efforts to simulate human perceptual processes with digital computers.

James J. Gibson (e.g., 1950) has proposed an alternative theory that holds that spatial perceptions are directly and rigidly determined by certain "higher-order variables" in the proximal stimulus array. It may be worth pointing out that the traditional monocular cues have always taken the form of higher-order variables; in no case does any such cue correspond to the stimulation of a single cone or optic nerve fiber. However, Gibson has made a tremendous contribution in going on to identify certain particular variables of this type, like texture gradients and retinal flow patterns, which are without question of great importance. Moreover, for better or worse, Gibson takes an explicit stand on an issue about which cue theories are either vague or different from one version to another: He maintains that a stimulus variable, once abstracted, determines the corresponding perception by a direct stimulus-response (S-R) connection, requiring no further information processing or unconscious inference. This position leads one to look in the stimulus array for relational variables that are not implausibly complex, and that stand in one-to-one relationship to perceptual variables of slant, distance, and the like. Some of Gibson's efforts along this line have met with a good deal of success, as noted, but he has avoided coming to grips with the problem of how different variables are combined in the perceptual process, particularly when they are mutually contradictory; he simply dismisses any such conflict situations as irrelevant to real-life situations.

A third theory had its inception in the work of Ernst Mach (1959), who almost a century ago discussed at some length the role of an economy principle in perception. The Gestalt psychologists proposed that a similar principle of Prägnanz accounts for the organization of tridimensional space: that of the innumerable physical situations that are hypothetically consistent with the prevailing stimulation, the perceptual system chooses the one that is best. For most practical purposes "best" can be taken to mean "simplest"; thus Hochberg (1964, p. 87) has rephrased the idea in the more Machian terms of a "minimum principle": "that our nervous systems organize the perceived world in whatever way will keep changes and differences to a *minimum*." Now, a Prägnanz theory differs from either of the others considered in quite a fundamental respect, by proposing that the perceptual process is, in a very real sense, controlled by its end-state; in other words, it is a teleological theory, as Koffka (1935) clearly and explicitly recognized. At that time most psychologists had a strong tendency to dismiss explanations in terms of final causes as inherently unscientific and unnaturalistic, citing such horrible examples as the argument that the sheep has heavy wool to provide man with warm clothes. Subsequently there has appeared a whole new discipline called cybernetics, which might well be defined as the science of teleological systems, and which has fully explicated the sense in which final causes are operative in such homely mechanisms as flush toilets and the governors of motors. Actually, there was never anything particularly mystical about the physical examples of Prägnanz suggested by the Gestalt psychologists, for example, the familiar soap bubble, which assumes a shape such as to minimize the surface area enclosing a fixed volume. However, we have become acquainted more recently with a class of mechanisms often referred to as hill-climbing machines, which operate to maximize or minimize certain variables by processes that are not necessarily as diffuse as the interplay of forces governing the final shape of the soap bubble.

During the 1950s Hochberg and his associates (Hochberg & McAlister, 1953; Hochberg & Brooks, 1960) revived the Prägnanz or minimum principle in the form given above, and showed, in a series of well-known experiments, that among the various projections of a single, regular, solid object of constant complexity, like a cube, the ones most often perceived in depth were those most complex in the picture plane, which were therefore most simplified in three-space. They were able to devise rather simple measures of picture-plane complexity that would predict with very great accuracy the proportion of the time that such a projection would be seen in depth. Equally important (and rendered no less impressive by the fact that he now considers himself a cue theorist!) were Hochberg's demonstrations that many of the factors traditionally cited as monocular depth cues, and virtually all the higher-order variables discussed by Gibson, may be subsumed under a Prägnanz theory. An extremely obvious example is the Gibsonian projection of a tile floor, as in Figure 1A. According to a Prägnanz theory, the surface should be seen at a slant such that the slopes of lines and the angles and distances between lines in tridimensional space will tend to be equalized. This is approximately what does occur, albeit with some regression toward the frontal plane. To cite just one more example, let us consider one of the traditional monocular cues, that of interposition. Some years ago Ratoosh (1949) raised the very sensible question of how this cue is to be characterized in terms of the proximal stimulus configuration (since interposition is not really a cue at all, but rather what is perceived). His conclusion, elaborating a suggestion from Helmholtz, was that it consisted of a local configuration like that enclosed by the dotted line in Figure 1B. When a T-pattern like this occurs, the continuous contour is seen as belonging to a nearer object and

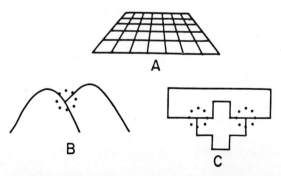

FIG. 1. A. A perspective gradient. B. A conventional example of "interposition"; it appears that the left mountain occludes a portion of the right one. C. A case of apparent interposition not attributable to local contour configurations.

the discontinuous contour to a farther object. Shortly thereafter Chapanis and McCleary (1953) showed many counter examples to this principle, as in Figure 1C. If this is seen as a cross in front of a rectangle, as it almost invariably is, Ratoosh's rule is violated. The perceived organization, however, is the one that would be expected from a Prägnanz principle, being considerably simpler than the alternative of seeing a rectangle with a nick out of it in front of a figure with an indeterminate top.

All I am trying to indicate at the moment is that a Prägnanz theory has considerable attractiveness in terms of economy, predictive power, and plausibility, and that it entails no inherently unscientific assumptions that should lead us to dismiss it without careful consideration. To say whether or not it is correct is a more difficult matter, as we shall presently see.

SOME EXPERIMENTS ON PERCEIVED ORIENTATION

Several years ago Robert Frost and I began a series of experiments that were designed primarily to investigate the predictive power of a Prägnanz theory. The first of these has been published (Attneave & Frost, 1969), but I shall describe the results briefly, as a background for the others. In a specially designed apparatus employing Polaroid filters and a half-silvered mirror, we presented observers with line drawings like those shown in Figure 2. The stimulus figure was viewed monocularly; apparently hinged to its central vertex was a binocularly viewed stick, the angle of which with the frontal plane could be set by the observer with an external wheel. The observer's task was always to set the stick at a slant such that it appeared collinear with one of the edges of the perceived "box" in tridimensional space. The setting thus constituted a judgment of the slant of that edge relative to the frontal plane. People found this an easy and natural thing to do.

Consider now the three conditions illustrated in Figure 2. The picture-plane angles between lines are the same across all three conditions for corresponding figures. Within a given figure, these angles are necessarily unequal to one another in

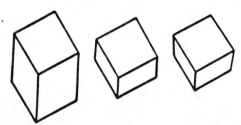

CONDITION 1   CONDITION 2   CONDITION 3

FIG. 2. Illustration of the three kinds of box-like figures studied by Attneave and Frost (1969). Hypothetically, all three parallelepipeds are in the same tridimensional orientation, but see text for specifications of Conditions 1, 2, and 3.

the picture-plane, but by a Prägnanz principle we would expect the observer to see a tridimensional object oriented in a manner tending to make the angles equal and right angles in three-space. If the observer were a perfect geometer, and saw the angles as all equal tridimensionally, he would have to judge the slant of any particular edge equal to

$$\phi = \sin^{-1}\sqrt{\cot\alpha\cot\beta},$$

in which α and β are the central angles on either side of the line being judged. In Condition 1, however, the lines are all of equal *length* in the picture-plane; likewise lines representing opposite edges are equal in slope. These equalities should tend to keep the figure flat in the picture-plane, since taking the figure into depth could only render the lengths and slopes unequal. In Condition 2, lengths are unequal in the picture plane, and are equalized in exactly the same tridimensional orientation at which angles become equal. Finally, in Condition 3, a consistent inequality of slopes—what is commonly called "linear perspective"—is likewise introduced.

The results, pooled over four observers, are shown in Figure 3. The functions steadily improve as the number of variables equated at the same hypothetical slant is increased; the linear correlation coefficient goes from .97 in Condition 1 to .99 in Condition 3. Likewise, the slope of the best fitting straight line increases from .34 to .59 with the addition of the length variable, and to .63 with the further addition of linear perspective. The fact that the slope is still so far from unity, even with all three variables working together, somewhat puzzled us, however. At first we thought that the fairly obvious surface texture of the drawings might have been working against impressions of depth, but later experiments in which the lines were made to fluoresce under black light gave very similar results, forcing us to conclude that some inherent tendency of regression to the frontal plane was in operation. Gogel (1965) has found this in quite different situations, and has called it "the equidistance tendency." Eventually it occurred to us that this tendency of the observer to equalize distances from himself has exactly the same formal status, under a Prägnanz interpretation, as the tendencies to equalize angles, lengths, and slopes that we were investigating.

A disadvantage of our original design was that the effective variables were always either redundant or contradictory, never independent. Frost and I were therefore led to conduct the study that I shall refer to as Experiment II, though it was done later than some others to which I shall return. In this we regressed to somewhat simpler materials (as one so often finds himself doing in research), employing parallelograms, which tend to be seen as tilted in depth. Parallelograms vary in shape on exactly two dimensions, which are most easily characterized in terms of angles between sides and proportional lengths of sides. Likewise, the tridimensional orientation of a plane has exactly two degrees of freedom: the axis of rotation and the amount of rotation from the frontal plane. Therefore, if a parallelogram tends to be seen in depth as a figure with equal sides and equal angles, that is, as a square, it contains just the requisite amount of information (in the logon sense) to determine the orientation geometrically consistent with these equalities.

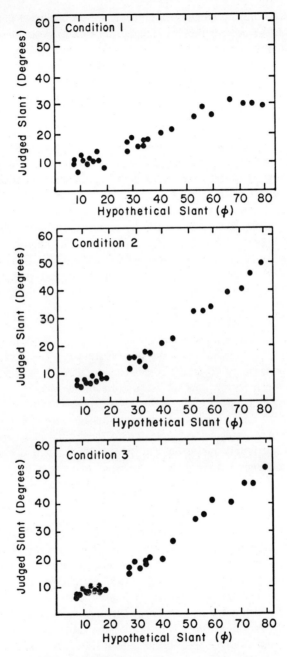

FIG. 3. Judged slant as a function of hypothetical slant. In Condition 1, angles are equalized at the hypothetical value and lengths and slopes are equal in the frontal plane; in Condition 2, angles and lengths are equalized at the hypothetical value and slopes are equal in the frontal plane; in Condition 3, angles, lengths, and slopes are all equalized at the hypothetical value.

The parallelograms judged by our four observers are all shown in Figure 4. Those in Block A are diamonds with equal sides and variable angles, that is, orthogonal projections of a square rotated about a diagonal axis. Those in Block D are rectangles, that is, projections of a square rotated about an axis parallel to its sides. In Blocks B and C the axes of rotation (relative to the hypothetical square) are intermediate in steps of 15°. By this variation we hoped to evaluate the relative efficacy of angular differences and length differences in determining impressions of depth. Over the six columns the tilt of the axis of rotation, relative to the gravitational frame of reference, is varied. The axis is always vertical in column one and horizontal in column four; the others are intermediate in 30° steps. Over the rows within each block the amount of hypothetical slant relative to the frontal plane is varied from 15° to 75°, in 20° steps.

We thought it likely that the rectangles and the diamonds, being more regular in the frontal plane than the intermediate figures, might therefore show more tendency to remain in the frontal plane, and that this tendency might be still

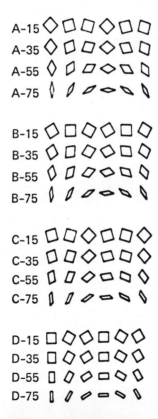

FIG. 4. The complete set of parallelograms used by Attneave and Frost in Experiment II. See text for an explanation of the variables involved.

greater in the rectangles and diamonds of columns one and four, which bear simple relationships to vertical and horizontal reference axes (see Attneave, 1968).

The parallelograms were constructed of fluorescent thread on a dark ground and displayed under black light. In this experiment the binocularly viewed stick appeared pivoted at the middle of the plane figure, and the observer was required to make an orthogonality judgment rather than a collinearity judgment as before, that is, to set the stick perpendicular to the plane in the perceived depth orientation of the latter. In Experiment I the apparatus had allowed the observer to control only one dimension of movement of the stick, toward and away from the frontal plane at a fixed tilt, but before the present experiment it was modified to allow him full control over both dimensions. Just above the observer's knees there was a control stick, the movement of which produced precisely corresponding movements of the stick in his visual field.

At the beginning of each trial the pivoted stick was not illuminated, and the observer saw only the parallelogram in isolation. First he reported whether he saw any depth at all in the figure. If he said that it remained flat in the frontal plane, this response was recorded and the trial was terminated. Only if he reported some depth was the pivoted stick illuminated and then set by the observer perpendicular to the perceived orientation of the surface.

First let us consider the frequency of "no depth" judgments for the various parallelograms; these are listed in Table 1. The maximum number possible in each cell is 8, since four observers had two trials on each figure. As we had anticipated,

TABLE 1

Distribution of No-Depth Judgments in Experiment II

Axis of Rotation Re Figure	Hypothetical Slant	Axis of Rotation Re Gravity					
		1 (Vertical)	2	3	4 (Horizontal)	5	6
A (Diamonds)	15	3	4	1	0	1	3
	35	3	3	1	0	1	1
	55	0	0	1	0	0	0
	75	1	0	0	0	0	0
B	15	2	4	4	3	0	5
	35	0	2	1	0	0	0
	55	0	0	1	0	0	2
	75	0	0	0	0	0	0
C	15	5	2	5	4	1	3
	35	2	0	3	1	0	2
	55	0	0	2	1	0	0
	75	0	0	0	0	0	0
D (Rectangles)	15	7	5	3	7	2	3
	35	7	2	1	6	1	5
	55	8	3	4	7	1	4
	75	7	5	2	6	4	5

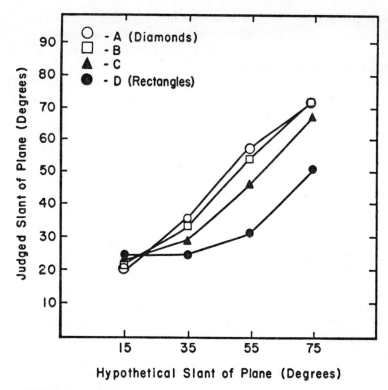

FIG. 5. Judged versus hypothetical slant for the four classes of parallelograms in Experiment II.

the figures most resistant to going into depth were those of Block D, the rectangles, particularly those with horizontal and vertical sides (columns 1 and 4). Contrary to our expectations, the diamonds of Block A were seen in depth about as often as the intermediate figures of Blocks B and C. There may be a slight tendency, for what reason we do not know, for tall diamonds to go into depth less readily than wide ones.

Results from the remaining trials, which involved non-zero judgments of slant, were averaged (over observers and over the columns of Figure 4) and plotted against hypothetical slant in Figure 5. For the figures of Blocks A and B, the diamonds and near-diamonds, the functions are practically linear and have a surprisingly high slope, about .85. The C function shows considerable curvilinearity, and the D function, for the rectangles, shows even more. Whatever may be the reason for the curvilinearity, we can say immediately and with some confidence that angular differences produce judgments much nearer the hypothetical slant values than do differences of length.

In some sense the impressions of depth obtained from parallelograms are never quite as strong or compelling as those obtained from box-like figures of the type used in Experiment I. We were therefore surprised that the functions for the A and B figures of the present experiment were steeper in slope than the best functions ever obtained with the "boxes." It seemed possible that the difference might be between orthogonality and collinearity judgments, or between judgments of planes and judgments of lines. In the following experiment, therefore, we obtained judgments of both types on box-like figures.

In this study, which I shall call Experiment III, the stimulus materials were like those of Experiment I except that only 10 well-spaced values of hypothetical slant were studied. As in Experiment II, the stimuli were presented under black light, and the observer was able to move the response stick in any desired direction. Surrounding the central vertex, to which the stick was apparently pivoted, there were three "sides" and three "edges" (see Figure 2). For each edge there was a corresponding side to which it was hypothetically perpendicular. On separate trials we had the observer set the stick collinear with each edge studied, and orthogonal to each corresponding side; if the side and the edge had been perceived as perpendicular, these settings would necessarily have been identical within the limits of response error. In Figure 6 the mean settings of four observers for edges and corresponding sides are plotted against hypothetical slant. It is essential to note that for edges the frontal plane is at the zero point of the ordinate in each graph, whereas for sides it is at the $90°$ point of the ordinate. Thus the uniformly higher stick settings for sides than for edges result merely from the fact that both sides and edges show regression toward the frontal plane. In addition, however, the functions for sides are uniformly steeper than those for edges, indicating that the former are actually being judged "better." The divergence is greater on the right, where edges are high in hypothetical slant and sides are near the frontal plane. Under Condition 2 (which is perhaps most nearly comparable, though by no means exactly comparable, to Experiment II) we obtain a function for sides which, though somewhat curvilinear, is not grossly out of line with the results of the previous, simpler study.

I can only hazard a guess as to why orthogonality judgments of surfaces are better, relative to the hypothetical values, than collinearity judgments of lines. It may be that the stimulus features to which the observer gives his greatest attention vary with the task, and hence that particular inequalities (or equalities) of length and angle are differentially weighted from one situation to the other. If any such attentional explanation is correct, it makes no easier the problem that we shall consider in the following section.

S-R or Prägnanz?

Let us return to the simpler case of Experiment II, and take a careful look at the function for Block D (rectangles) in Figure 5. The curvilinearity of this and the adjacent C function suggests a Gibsonian rather than a Prägnanz interpretation; that is, that the depth perception corresponds more closely to a simple picture-plane variable, the relative length of the sides of the rectangle, than to some tridimensional end-state. As a line is rotated out of the frontal plane, its projected or retinal length shrinks by a cosine factor, very slowly at first, more rapidly as it goes farther into depth. May not the curvilinearity of the rectangle function indicate merely that the observer is basing his judgment directly on the length of the shorter side relative to that of the longer? Plotting judged slant against the ratio of lengths, as in the lower

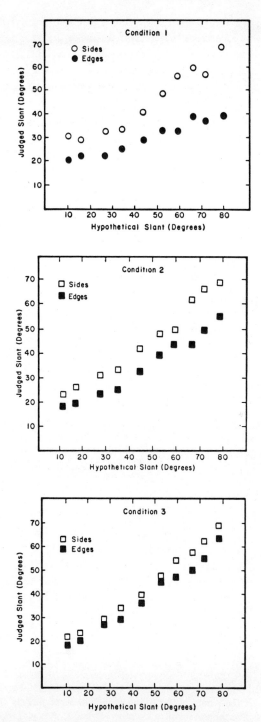

FIG. 6. Judged versus hypothetical slant for sides and angles of box-like figures in Experiment III. The three conditions differ as in Experiment I and Figure 3.

curve in Figure 7, we find some improvement but also a good deal of residual curvature in the same direction. However, if we make the Fechnerian assumption that a change in length is more important the shorter the line, and take the logarithm of the length ratio (i.e., the difference between the log lengths) as in the upper curve in Figure 7, we obtain a function that is very nearly linear.

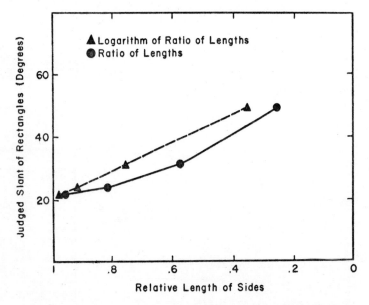

FIG. 7. Judged slant of rectangles (Experiment II) versus relative length of sides. For the function plotted with circles, relative length is defined simply as the ratio of short to long side. For the function plotted with triangles, the abscissa is $1 + \log_{10} \dfrac{\text{short side}}{\text{long side}}$.

We have other data that bear on the same point. If the reader will look back at Figure 3, he may notice that the function for Condition 2 shows at least a suggestion of curvature that is not evident in Condition 1. Since the curvature was slight, and of dubious significance, Frost and I paid little attention to it at first. Subsequently, however, we did several experiments similar to Experiment I that show the same effect with great reliability. I shall call these Experiments IV, V and VI, although chronologically they immediately followed Experiment I.[2] When we

---

[2] In Experiment IV ($N = 4$) and Experiment V ($N = 4$) conditions were the same as in Attneave and Frost (1969): Stimuli were presented under white (fluorescent) illumination, and the observer controlled only the depth dimension of the response stick. Experiment VI ($N = 6$) was similar except that the stimuli were drawn with fluorescent threads and exposed under black light to make surface texture invisible. As noted earlier, Experiment III ($N = 4$) employed black light and allowed the observer to control the response stick in both tilt and depth. None of these variations made much difference.

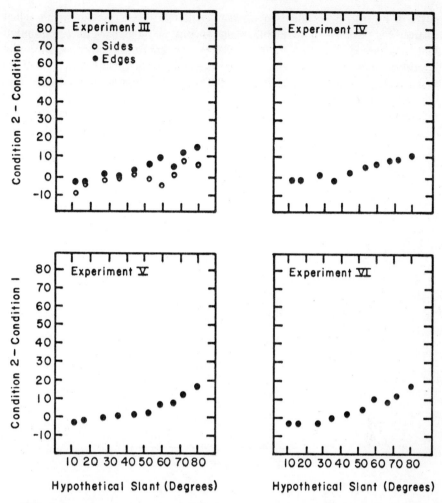

FIG. 8. Data from four experiments, showing increment in perceived slant attributable to variation of lengths, over and above that attributable to variation of angles.

became interested in this point, we went back to the data from these and from Experiment III (all of which, incidentally, employed the same 10 hypothetical slant values) and subtracted Condition 1 judgments from Condition 2 judgments on a point-for-point basis. These difference functions, shown in Figure 8, represent the incremental effect of variations in length, over and above the variations in angle with which they are hypothetically consistent and redundant. They all show a similar upward curvature, indicating (like the function for rectangles in Figure 5) an increasing rate of change with increasing hypothetical slant. Without proliferating graphs, or engaging in a fruitless discussion of differences, I can say in summary that something in the ball park bounded by the two curves in Figure 7 is generally adequate to rectify these functions.

There is little here, then, to discourage the Gibsonian hypothesis that the observer was responding to picture-plane lengths in some fairly direct manner. Before deciding that a Prägnanz theory has been disconfirmed, however, let us see in more detail what its implications might be. Consider first the very simple model shown in Figure 9A, which pertains to the rectangles of Experiment II. Let the orientation of the baseline represent the frontal plane, and its length the side of a hypothetical square. As one side of the square is rotated out of the frontal plane by 15, 35, 55, and 75 degrees, its distant end casts the indicated projections onto the

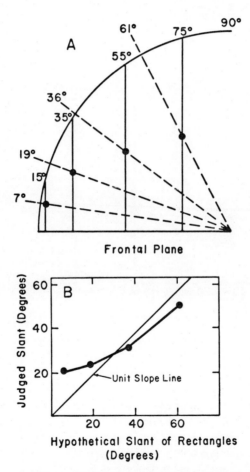

FIG. 9. First model of regression to frontal plane. A. According to this model, a 50 percent regression would cause a hypothetical slant of 75° to be perceived as 61°, and so on as indicated by the relationships between solid and dashed lines about the arc. B. Judgments of rectangles from Experiment II are plotted against the predictions of this model.

frontal plane (vertical lines). Given any such projection (as the short side of a rectangle) it is geometrically permissible for the observer to locate the distant end of the line anywhere on the vertical (see Figure 9A) connecting the hypothetical value with the frontal plane. Suppose, arbitrarily, that regression to the frontal plane takes the form of splitting this difference exactly in half; that is, that the distant end of the line is seen exactly halfway between the frontal plane and its hypothetical location, as indicated by the heavy dots. If we now extend lines through these dots from the origin and determine the angles that they make with the frontal plane, we find that the 15° line regresses to 7°; likewise, there is regression from 35° to 19°, from 55° to 36°, and from 75° to 61°. In Figure 9B the judged slants of rectangles are plotted against these regressed values. The result is about comparable to that obtained in the lower curve in Figure 7: Linearity is improved, but there is still some residual curvature.

The model shown in Figure 10A is only slightly more complex. Here we assume a system that is simultaneously trying to minimize distances from the frontal plane on one hand, and differences between the logarithms of tridimensional lengths on the other, and that a compromise is reached at some equilibrium point described by the equation

$$d = -\log_{10} x$$

where d is the distance behind the frontal plane at which the far point of the shorter side will be perceived, and x is the tridimensional length of the shorter side. Note that the right side of the equation is simply the log ratio of *perceived* lengths at equilibrium. This tradeoff function is quite arbitrary; it merely represents the simplest way of keeping both variables within the same range, that is, between zero and one. Note well that the variables entering into this equation are end-state variables, pertaining to the figure as perceived in three-space. The equilibrium points are shown graphically in Figure 10A, and the actual judgments on rectangles are plotted against them in Figure 10B. The resulting function is at least as good as that of the upper curve in Figure 7, which also used logarithms but on picture-plane lengths. The fact that the function crosses the unit slope line at 42° is indicative of an additional tendency, which I have not commented on before, for judgments to regress toward the middle of the response range. This tendency may be found in nearly all our results, and is of course very common in judgmental situations more generally.

I do not not expect anyone to take seriously the details of this model. It shows merely that a simple and plausible version of a Prägnanz theory can account for the curvilinearity of the length variable quite as well as an S-R theory can.

However, once having opened the Pandora's box of picture-plane variables versus end-state variables, Frost and I felt some compulsion to see how well the former might work in the cases of angular inequality on which we had data. What we have called hypothetical slant in Experiment I and similar studies is calculated from angles by the equation

$$\phi = \sin^{-1}\sqrt{\cot\alpha\cot\beta}.$$

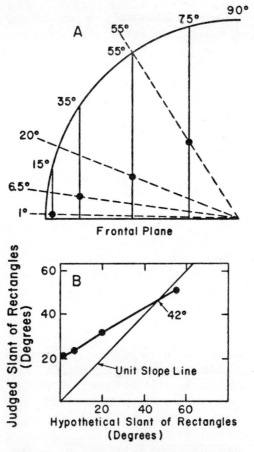

FIG. 10. Second model of regression to frontal plane. The far point of the shorter side will be perceived at some distance d behind the frontal plane. Taking as a unit of distance the length of the longer side (i.e., the radius of the arc in the upper drawing) the model supposes that an equilibrium or compromise between equating lengths and keeping lines in the frontal plane will be reached when the equation $d = \log_{10}$ (tridimensional length of shorter side) is satisfied. Part A, the distance of the heavy circles from the frontal plane are equilibrium values of d and the dashed radial lines through them show the corresponding (regressed) slants. The latter constitute the abscissa values of Part B.

This may be thought of as a complicated way of averaging α and β; what if the observer were merely basing his judgment on a simple mean or sum of these two angles, or, what would be exactly the same thing, on the complementary angle opposite the line being judged? We proceeded to plot judged slant against this complementary angle for the Condition 1 data of Experiments III, IV, V, and VI, in

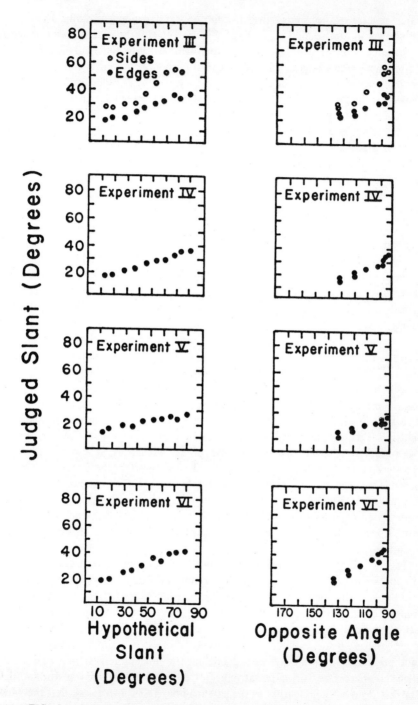

FIG. 11. Judged slant data from four experiments, as predicted from hypothetical slant (an end-state variable), on the left, and from opposite angle (a picture-plane variable), on the right.

which angular relationships constitute the only independent variable. These graphs are shown in the second column of Figure 11, side by side with plots against hypothetical slant. The judgments of Experiment III show some curvilinearity when plotted against raw angle. This is greater in the case of the orthogonality judgments on sides, where the angle in question is merely one of those projected by the side. (However, the same judgments of sides are also rather irregular when plotted against hypothetical slant.) In the other three experiments, this simple picture-plane variable serves as a remarkably good linear predictor of the judgments; to say that it is worse than hypothetical slant (or better) is clearly out of the question in view of the range and variability of the present data. It is, however, difficult to find a rational interpretation for the fact that these functions, considered as straight lines, appear to intercept the baseline in the 160° to 170° region; if they have their origin at 180°, as they rationally ought to, they cannot be linear.

The experiments that we have done are by no means ideal for the present comparisons, which are of course after-the-fact. An additional study employing a number of carefully chosen values near the low end of the hypothetical slant continuum might clarify the matter. It is only when the edge approaches the frontal plane that the projected opposite angle is free to vary over a wide range with hypothetical slant held constant. (The easiest way to see this is by squinting at a cube.)

The purest and simplest case that we have of perceived slant determined by angles is that of the diamonds in Experiment II. Whereas we saw in Figure 5 that the function for diamonds is quite reasonably linear when plotted against hypothetical slant, we see in Figure 12 that it is decidedly nonlinear when plotted against one of the picture-plane angles of the diamond. I must admit, however, to have got myself into a bit of a trap here. If the reasoning illustrated in Figure 9 (which seems rather more applicable than that of Figure 10, which employs logarithms) were extended to the case of the diamonds, it too would predict curvature (though to a lesser degree) of judged versus hypothetical slant. The most plausible answer to this objection, and the one most consistent with the data themselves, is simply that the tendency to equalize angles is stronger than the tendency to equalize lengths (in opposition to the equidistance tendency), and that the 50 percent regression arbitrarily assumed in Figure 9 is much too great in the case of angles.

The foregoing comparisons show, if nothing more, the extraordinary difficulty of experimentally confirming or disconfirming a Prägnanz theory as opposed to its alternatives. Although the further experimentation suggested earlier may be worth doing, I doubt at this point that any experiment of the present kind is going to settle the issue in a decisive way. One basic difficulty is that the list of "higher order" picture-plane variables is potentially endless; if a simple variable is not a good predictor, it can always be argued that the perceptual system is abstracting a more complex one, or, alternatively, introducing a further transformation to straighten out a curvilinearity, as the case may be. This is not to say that the issue is inherently unresolvable, but merely that we have not, up to the present time, designed an experiment likely to resolve it. Meanwhile, my frustration is tempered by the fact that Frost and I have been led, by considerations based on a Prägnanz

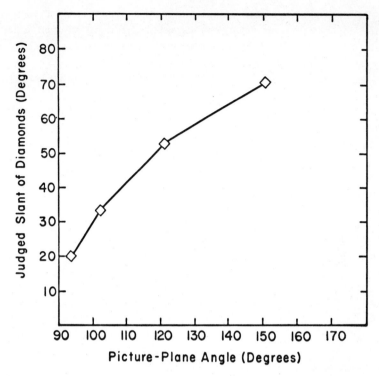

FIG. 12. Judged slant of diamonds (Experiment II) as a function of (obtuse) picture-plane angle between sides. See Figure 5, function **A** (Diamonds).

theory, to investigate some variables that nobody had paid much attention to before, but that turn out to be very powerful determinants of perceived spatial relationships.

THE NATURE OF SPATIAL REPRESENTATION

Now, just what do we mean when we say that an observer *perceives* the location of an object, or the slant of a surface? We must mean at least that he is *representing* certain information about spatial relationships in the outside world. But what is the nature of the representation, in terms of the formal properties of the system that it involves? Is it more like a table or a graph, a descriptive sentence or a picture? Is it digital or analog, or a combination of both? Some representations, of which the identity of an object is an obvious and important example, would appear to be digital by their very nature. However, I am moderately well convinced, along with Mach and his successors the Gestalt psychologists, that we represent space in an essentially analog manner; that there exists some medium, some sand-box in the head (to use a metaphor that I hope is free of neurological overtones) in which a *model* of the outside world is constructed from sensory information.

Before trying to justify this position, let me point out that we are now looking at an issue rather different from the one considered up to now, and that there is no particular incompatibility between the notion of an analog space and any one of the three theories of space perception suggested earlier. Higher-order variables or cues abstracted from the visual input would function, with or without the aid of certain ratiomorphic processes, to determine the locations of surfaces and objects in the model. A little more needs to be said, however, about a Prägnanz system, which would make more integral use of the analog space. A crude illustration will be adequate to suggest how it might do so. Suppose we prepare a photographic transparency of Figure 1A, the Gibsonian tile floor, and mount it rigidly in front of a point source of light. We now hand a cardboard screen to a human operator, and tell him to move it about in the path of the light coming through the transparency until he finds an orientation at which the image on the screen becomes a gridwork of equal squares. He can attain this objective by a rather simple heuristic of continuing whatever he is doing as long as it improves matters, and trying something else when it does not. When he reaches his goal, the slant of the screen will correspond exactly to the slant of the floor of which the transparency is a picture; in other words, he has been guided to discover the inverse of the original perspective transformation. To incorporate the function of the human operator into a perceptual system, we might postulate a mechanism that reads momentary tridimensional values of length, slope, angle, and the like out of the spatial representational medium and computes from them an integrated measure of "goodness" or simplicity that is fed back as a "hot-cold" signal guiding the tridimensional representation to the simplest state consistent with the constraints of the input, at which the system would achieve stability. This mechanism would constitute the altimeter of a hill-climbing system. The measures integrated into the feedback signal might include not only such factors as we have considered earlier, that is, (a) homogeneity of angles, lengths, and slopes in the tridimensional model, and (b) coplanarity or equidistance of components, but also (c) simplicity of relationships to a Cartesian reference framework (Attneave, 1968; Olson & Attneave, 1970) and (d) goodness-of-match between the model and stored schemata (Oldfield, 1954; Attneave, 1957). Note that the continuous analog medium would serve an important function in such a system in providing the hill-climber with a smooth terrain on which to operate. An equivalent digital system involving search through descriptor lists would be less economical, to say the least, unless the lists were themselves structured in an essentially analog manner.

The notion of an analog spatial model is supported, in the first place, by a combination of phenomenological and epistemological considerations that are reasonably consistent with experimental data on spatial constancies. It is an inescapable fact that, if we perceive a tridimensional world, this world-as-perceived has got to be inside the head, linked to the outside world by Morse code signals from a receptor-surface the state of which is clearly not isomorphic with distal events. Perceived space is to a remarkable degree, though not completely, *isotropic*: To a good first approximation, a yardstick looks about a yard long regardless of its tridimensional orientation. This approximate equivalence among extents that combine in countless ways the three spatial dimensions argues strongly against separate and arbitrary coding of the three dimensions. They must be represented in terms that maintain a common metric, and permit tradeoffs fairly consistent with the laws of geometry.

Let us next look, in passing, at the problem of object identification. What makes this problem so difficult (if, for example, one wishes to build a machine or program a computer to recognize objects) is that the system must give an invariant response over a very great many spatial transformations or aspects of the object. Oddly and interestingly, there appears to have been little interaction between people interested in the spatial constancies of size and shape and those interested in object recognition. But James Gibson has argued for a long time that the elements on which object identification is based are essentially tridimensional rather than bidimensional, for example, surfaces and edges rather than lines and angles. This idea makes a great deal of sense. The task of an object recognizer (of, say, the Pandemonium type) would be tremendously simplified if it could take its input from a tridimensional model of the outside world, rather than from the retina more directly.

Striking evidence for the analog representation of tridimensional space has recently been found by Shepard and Metzler (1971). They displayed, in pairs, pictures of solid objects constructed by joining cubes, and asked subjects whether one object could be rotated into the other. When the objects were the same in this sense, the subjects' reaction time was a very precise linear function of the difference in orientation, with an intercept at about 1 second and a slope of 16 milliseconds per degree of rotation. This is consistent with the hypothesis that a subject's image underwent a continuous rotation in real time in his representational space, and quite inconsistent with the hypothesis that he was matching on the basis of invariant descriptors. Moreover, the reaction-time function was almost exactly the same whether the rotation was in depth or in the picture-plane, indicating a high degree of isotropy among the dimensions of the image space. Elsewhere, Shepard and Chipman (1970) have argued convincingly for a modified version of Gestalt isomorphism that avoids most of the implausibilities associated with that doctrine in the past.

Equally intriguing is a pair of studies that Corbin (1942) did for his doctoral dissertation with Woodworth. In the first, he found that when rows and columns of dots are displayed in an obviously nonfrontal plane, perceptual grouping depends more on the physical proximity than on the retinal proximity of the dots. A subsequent experiment by Rock and Brosgole (1964), employing somewhat better controls, verified this finding. Corbin's second study was based on the principle, discovered by Korte, that the time interval for optimal apparent movement increases with interstimulus distance. As before, Corbin dissociated distal from proximal separation by having the screen viewed at various slants. He found that the optimal interstimulus interval consistently corresponded to physical rather than to retinal distance.

If this widely ignored result can be taken seriously, it argues very strongly indeed for an approximately isotropic analog representation of physical space. Corbin's conditions do leave some room for alternative interpretations. When the screen on which his stimuli appeared was slanted (about a vertical axis) its retinal width decreased correspondingly; therefore the important variable might have been retinal distance relative to retinal frame of reference. Moreover, the stimuli were themselves horizontally oriented bars, which likewise shrank retinally with slant.

Currently, Gene Block and I are trying to see whether Corbin's result can be replicated with this loophole closed. We have our lights mounted on movable posts above the surface of a table, so that their only background is the general background of the dimly lighted room. Our initial results agree well enough with Corbin's: Although we are finding that retinal separation has some importance (a lesser importance than physical separation), this may indicate nothing more than imperfect depth perception under the conditions of our experiment. We plan further studies on the Corbin effect in which retinal and physical separation will be dissociated by varying the distance from the observer of pairs of lights in the frontal plane.

A few years ago Benson and I (Attneave & Benson, 1969) did a study that shows an interesting cross-modal effect. We had the subject place his fingers on six vibrators mounted in a T-formation, and learn letters as paired associates to the tactual stimuli. The hands were then shifted to give an entirely different pairing of vibrators and fingers. Subjects who were asked to give the same responses to the same vibrators did slightly better than those asked to give the same responses to the same fingers; both groups showed very efficient transfer. We found further, however, that blindfolding the subjects significantly impaired their ability to give responses that were invariant with respect to the vibrators. This result, together with the subjects' reports of their subjective experience, strongly suggests that they were mapping tactual information into a space that was primarily visual, or otherwise common to both modalities.

Here, as well as in the Shepard and Metzler study, it is evident that we are dealing with imagery, or with images in interplay with percepts. It seems extremely likely to me that visual images, whether constructed from long-term memory or from another modality, occupy the same representational space as visual percepts. If this is true, however, the representational space must have some properties beyond any that we have yet considered: It must be capable of functioning as a working model of the outside world, in which vicarious locomotion and vicarious manipulation are possible. I invite the reader to solve the following problem without external aids, keeping track as well as he can of his own conscious processes all the while: A big wooden cube, painted red, is sawed into three equal slices on each of its three dimensions, thus becoming a lot of little cubes. How many of these little cubes will have 3, 2, 1, and 0 red sides, respectively? It appears that nearly everybody solves this problem by a process of manipulating and observing spatial imagery, with more or less verbal accompaniment. Presumably any such manipulation must be preceded by a transformation of information from digital (i.e., verbal) into analog form, and terminated by a transformation the other way about, essentially a counting operation.

It is remarkable how often we map nonspatial variables onto spatial ones in order to think about them efficiently. The popularity of representing numbers as extents in graphs of various sorts, particularly those showing functional relationships between variables, is familiar to everyone, and Hadamard (1945) has remarked on the prevalence of spatial imagery in the problem solving activity of creative mathematicians. Whenever one is interested in the way objects are ordered by some transitive relation (taller than, louder than, richer than, etc.), there is a strong tendency to map the objects into space, substituting "above" or "to the right of" for the original relation. Logically, "to the right of" has no advantage whatever over "brighter than"; its advantage is rather in the availability of a modeling medium in the head. Like considerations apply to Venn diagrams, which provide an immediate analog solution to simple logic problems, and to tree and lattice structures, in terms of which quite complex logical relationships may be represented.

Let me make one more phenomenological observation, for whatever it is worth. Any particular space that is imagined appears in consciousness as a scene, as if the observer had a determinate position and body orientation in the space itself. (In reading a novel, I have occasionally had the experience, at once annoying and ludicrous, of a door closed in my face by a character on whose heels I was attempting to pass from one room to another.) A remarkable property of the system is its ability to maintain what is loosely called orientation, the ability to maintain fairly accurate representations of the locations of fixed objects, in terms of body coordinates, over varying points of view of the observer. I have often done a casual experiment that takes this form: I say to a friend, "Imagine yourself standing in front of the Library, about to enter. Now, from that position, point at the Law School." Most people will point without hesitation in the general direction that *would* be correct if they were in the position indicated. "The Law School" was almost certainly not present in consciousness when the observer assumed his imaginary position, but its location, relative to his body, seems immediately available on demand.

Now, I am acutely aware that the mere postulation of an analog system for spatial representation, however plausible in a general way, does not begin to answer the questions raised in the foregoing discussion. For several years now I have been groping, unsuccessfully so far, for a model of sufficient specificity and power to qualify as a genuine theory. Although I wish deliberately to avoid neurologizing, let me specifically disclaim the assumption that an analog model of tridimensional space must require a tridimensional neural mass in which effigies are formed out of firing neurons, or DC potential variations, or otherwise. One alternative possibility that might be more promising is the following, which entails at once an internalization of Gibsonian texture and a generalization of Gogel's (1964, 1965) S'/θ variable. Suppose that depth information were utilized to figure the entire visual field with a uniform metric unit, as if, say, closely-packed 1-inch circles were drawn on all the surfaces in the outside world and projected as corresponding ellipses in the retinal image. (It is conceivable that projective fields of adjustable size and shape in the cortex might subserve a comparable function.) A one-to-one correspondence would exist between the length of the major axis of an ellipse and distance from the observer; likewise between the eccentricity of the ellipse and the slant of the surface relative to the line of regard. The sizes and shapes of ellipses would thus represent distance and slant, in an analog manner immediately reflecting the isotropy of physical space. This approach has some attractive aspects, but as yet neither it nor any of its alternatives has been developed into a satisfactory theory.

REFERENCES

Attneave, F. Transfer of experience with a class-schema to identification-learning of patterns and shapes. *Journal of Experimental Psychology*, 1957, **54**, 81-88.

Attneave, F. Triangles as ambiguous figures. *American Journal of Psychology*, 1968, **81**, 447-453.

Attneave, F., & Benson, B. Spatial coding of tactual stimulation. *Journal of Experimental Psychology*, 1969, **81**, 216-222.

Attneave, F., & Frost, R. The determination of perceived tridimensional orientation by minimum criteria. *Perception & Psychophysics*, 1969, **6**, 391-396.

Brunswik, E. "Ratiomorphic" models of perception and thinking. *Proceedings of the XIV International Congress of Psychology*, Montreal, 1954.

Chapanis, A., & McCleary, R. A. Interposition as a cue for the perception of relative distance. *Journal of General Psychology*, 1953, **48**, 113-132.

Corbin, H. H. The perception of grouping and apparent movement in visual depth. *Archives of Psychology*, 1942, No. 273.

Gibson, J. J. *The perception of the visual world*. Cambridge: Houghton-Mifflin, 1950.

Gogel, W. Size cue to visually perceived distance. *Psychological Bulletin*, 1964, **62**, 217-235.

Gogel, W. Equidistance tendency and its consequences. *Psychological Bulletin*, 1965, **64**, 153-163.

Hadamard, J. *The psychology of invention in the mathematical field*. London: Oxford, 1945.

Hochberg, J. *Perception*. New York: Prentice-Hall, 1964.

Hochberg, J., & Brooks, V. The psychophysics of form: Reversible-perspective drawings of spatial objects. *American Journal of Psychology*, 1960, **73**, 337-354.

Hochberg, J., & McAlister, E. A quantitative approach to figural "goodness." *Journal of Experimental Psychology*, 1953, **46**, 361-364.

Koffka, K. *Principles of Gestalt psychology*. New York: Harcourt-Brace, 1935.

Mach, E. *The analysis of sensations*. New York: Dover, 1959.

Minsky, M. Steps toward artificial intelligence. *Proceedings of the Institute of Radio Engineering*, 1960, **49**, 8-30.

Oldfield, R. C. Memory mechanisms and the theory of schemata. *British Journal of Psychology*, 1954, **45**, 14-23.

Olson, R. K., & Attneave, F. What variables produce similarity grouping? *American Journal of Psychology*, 1970, **83**, 1-21.

Ratoosh, P. On interposition as a cue for the perception of distance. *Proceedings of the National Academy of Sciences*, Washington, 1949, **35**, 257-259.

Rock, I., & Brosgole, L. Grouping based on phenomenal proximity. *Journal of Experimental Psychology*, 1964, **68**, 531-538.

Shepard, R. N., & Chipman, S. Second-order isomorphism of internal representations: Shapes of states. *Cognitive Psychology*, 1970, **1**, 1-17.

Shepard, R. N., & Metzler, J. Mental rotation of three-dimensional objects. *Science*, 1971, **171**, 701-703.

13

LANGUAGE CODES AND MEMORY CODES[1]

Alvin M. Liberman[2], Ignatius G. Mattingly[3], and Michael T. Turvey[4]
Haskins Laboratories

When people recall linguistic information, they commonly produce utterances different in form from those originally presented. Except in special cases where the information does not exceed the immediate memory span, or where rote memory is for some reason required, recall is always a paraphrase.

There are at least two ways we can look at paraphrase in memory. If we set rote recall as the ideal, then paraphrase is seen as so much error, regardless of the accuracy with which it might have captured the sense of the original message. The part of recall that exactly matches the message is then thought to be a kind of residue, untouched by the processes of forgetting; other parts, if any, are intrusions and therefore incorrect. In this view, paraphrase occurs because memory fails. Alternatively, we can see paraphrase, not as a result of forgetting, but rather as an essential condition or correlate of the processes by which we normally communicate and remember. This view, which we adopt, takes account of what seems to us quite evident: If linguistic communications could only be stored in the form in which they were presented, we should presumably be making inefficient use of our capacity for storage and retrieval; the information must be restructured if that which is communicated to us by language is to be well remembered. Thus,

[1] The preparation of this paper, as well as much of the research on which it is based, was aided by grants from the National Institute of Child Health and Human Development and the Office of Naval Research. The authors are indebted for many useful criticisms and suggestions to Franklin S. Cooper of the Haskins Laboratories and Mark Y. Liberman of the United States Army.

[2] Also University of Connecticut and Yale University.
[3] Also University of Connecticut.
[4] Also University of Connecticut.

the changes that are reflected in paraphrase include those that the separate processes of communication and memory require. Seen this way, the ubiquitous fact of paraphrase means that language is best transmitted in one form and stored in another.

The dual representation of linguistic information that is implied by paraphrase is important, then, if we are to store information that has been received and to transmit information that has been stored. We take it that such duality implies, in turn, a process of recoding that is somehow constrained by a grammar. Thus, the capacity for paraphrase reflects the fundamental grammatical characteristics of language. We should say, therefore, that efficient memory for linguistic information depends, to a considerable extent, on grammar.

To illustrate this point of view, we might imagine languages that lack a significant number of the grammatical devices that all natural languages have. We should suppose that the possibilities for recoding and paraphrase would, as a consequence, be limited, and that the users of such languages would not remember linguistic information very well. Pidgins appear to be grammatically impoverished and, indeed, to permit of little paraphrase, but, unfortunately for our purposes, speakers of pidgins also speak some natural language, so they can convert back and forth between the natural language and the pidgin. Sign language of the deaf, on the other hand, might conceivably provide an interesting test. At the present time we know very little about the grammatical characteristics of sign, but it may prove to have recoding (and hence paraphrase) possibilities that are, by comparison with natural languages, somewhat restricted.[5] If so, one could indeed hope to determine the effects of such restriction on the ability to remember.

In natural languages we cannot explore in that controlled way the causes and consequences of paraphrase, since all such languages must be assumed to be very similar in degree of grammatical complexity. Let us, therefore, learn what we can by looking at the several levels or representations of information that we normally find in language and at the grammatical components that convert between them.

At the one extreme is the acoustic level, where the information is in a form appropriate for transmission. As we shall see, this acoustic representation is not the whole sound as such, but rather a pattern of specifiable events, the acoustic cues. By a complexly encoded connection, the acoustic cues reflect the "features" that characterize the articulatory gestures and so the phonetically distinct configurations of the vocal tract. These features are a full level removed from the sound in the structure of language; when properly combined, they are roughly equivalent to the segments of the phonetic representation.

Only some fifteen or twenty features are needed to describe the phonetics of all human languages (Chomsky & Halle, 1968). Any particular language uses only a dozen or so features from the total ensemble, and at any particular moment in the stream only six or eight features are likely to be significant. The small number of features and the complex relation between sound and feature reflect the properties of the vocal tract and the ear and also, as we will show, the mismatch between these organ systems and the requirements of the phonetic message.

---

[5] The possibilities for paraphrase in sign language are, in fact, being investigated by Edward Klima and Ursula Bellugi.

At the other end of the linguistic structure is the semantic representation in which the information is ultimately stored. Because of its relative inaccessibility, we cannot speak with confidence about the shape of the information at this level, but we can be sure it is different from the acoustic. We should suppose, as many students do, that the semantic information is also to be described in terms of features. But if the indefinitely many aspects of experience are to be represented, then the available inventory of semantic features must be very large, much larger surely than the dozen or so phonetic features that will be used as the ultimate vehicles. Though particular semantic sets may comprise many features, it is conceivable that the structure of a set might be quite simple. At all events, the characteristics of the semantic representation can be assumed to reflect properties of long-term memory, just as the very different characteristics of the acoustic and phonetic representations reflect the properties of components most directly concerned with transmission.

The gap between the acoustic and semantic levels is bridged by grammar. But the conversion from the one level to the other is not accomplished in a single step, nor is it done in a simple way. Let us illustrate the point with a view of language like the one developed by the generative grammarians (see Chomsky, 1965). On that view there are three levels—deep structure, surface structure, and phonetic representation—in addition to the two—acoustic and semantic—we have already talked about. As in the distinction between acoustic and semantic levels, the information at every level has a different structure. At the level of deep structure, for example, a string such as *The man sings. The man married the girl. The girl is pretty.* becomes at the surface *The man who sings married the pretty girl.* The restructuring from one level to the next is governed by the appropriate component of the grammar. Thus, the five levels or streams of information we have identified would be connected by four sets of grammatical rules: from deep structure to the semantic level by the semantic rules; in the other direction, to surface structure, by syntactic rules; then to phonetic representation by phonologic rules; and finally to the acoustic signal by the rules of speech.[6] It should be emphasized that none of these conversions is straightforward or trivial, requiring only the substitution of one segment or representation for another. Nor is it simply a matter of putting segments together to form larger units, as in the organization of words into phrases and sentences, or of phonetic segments into syllables and breath groups. Rather, each grammatical conversion is a true restructuring of the information in which the number of segments, and often their order, is changed, sometimes drastically. In the context of this volume it is appropriate to describe the conversions from one linguistic level to another as recodings and to speak of the grammatical rules that govern them as codes.

---

[6] In generative grammar, as in all others, the conversion between phonetic representation and acoustic signal is not presumed to be grammatical. As we have argued elsewhere, however, and as will to some extent become apparent in this paper, this conversion is a complex recoding, similar in formal characteristics to the recodings of syntax and phonology (Mattingly & Liberman, 1969; Liberman, 1970).

Paraphrase of the kind we implied in our opening remarks would presumably occur most freely in the syntactic and semantic codes. But the speech code, at the other end of the linguistic structure, also provides for a kind of paraphrase. At all events it is, as we hope to show, an essential component of the process that makes possible the more obvious forms of paraphrase, as well as the efficient memory they always accompany.

Grammar is, then, a set of complex codes that relates transmitted sound and stored meaning. It also suggests what it is that the recoding processes must somehow accomplish. Looking at these processes from the speaker's viewpoint, we see, for example, that the semantic features must be replaced by phonological features in preparation for transmission. In this conversion an utterance that is, at the semantic level, a single unit comprising many features of meaning becomes, phonologically, a number of units composed of a very few features, the phonologic units and features being in themselves meaningless. Again, the semantic representation of an utterance in coherent discourse will typically contain multiple references to the same topic. This amounts to a kind of redundancy that serves, perhaps, to protect the semantic representation from noise in long-term memory. In the acoustic representation, however, to preserve such repetitions would unduly prolong discourse. To take again the example we used earlier, we do not say, *The man sings. The man married the girl. The girl is pretty.* But rather, *The man who sings married the pretty girl.* The syntactic rules describe the ways in which such redundant references are deleted. At the acoustic and phonetic levels, redundancy of a very different kind may be desirable. Given the long strings of empty elements that exist there, the rules of the phonologic component predict certain lawful phonetic patterns in particular contexts and, by this kind of redundancy, help to keep the phonetic events in their proper order.

But our present knowledge of the grammar does not provide much more than a general framework within which to think about the problem of recoding in memory. It does not, for example, deal directly with the central problem of paraphrase. If a speaker-hearer has gone from sound to meaning by some set of grammatical rules, what is to prevent his going in the opposite direction by the inverse operations, thus producing a rote rendition of the originally presented information? In this connection we should say on behalf of the grammar that it is not an algorithm for automatically recoding in one direction or the other, but rather a description of the relationships that must hold between the semantic representation, at the one end, and the corresponding acoustic representation at the other. To account for paraphrase, we must suppose that the speaker synthesizes the acoustic representation, given the corresponding semantic representation, while the listener must synthesize an approximately equivalent semantic representation, given the corresponding acoustic representation. Because the grammar only constrains these acts of synthesis in very general ways, there is considerable freedom in the actual process of recoding; we assume that such freedom is essential if linguistic information is to be well remembered.

For students of memory, grammatical codes are unsatisfactory in yet another, if closely related, respect: Though they may account for an otherwise arbitrary-appearing relation between streams of information at different levels of the linguistic structure, they do not describe the actual processes by which the human being recodes from the one level to the other, nor does the grammarian intend that they should. Indeed, it is an open question whether even the levels that the grammar assumes—for example, deep structure—have counterparts of some kind in the recoding process.

We might do well, then to concentrate our attention on just one aspect of grammar, the speech code that relates the acoustic and phonetic representations, because we may then avoid some of the difficulties we encounter in the "higher" or "deeper" reaches of the language. The acoustic and phonetic levels have been accessible to psychological (and physiological) experiment, as a result of which we are able to talk about "real" processes and "real" levels, yet the conversion we find there resembles grammatical codes more generally, and can be shown, in a functional as well as a formal sense, to be an integral part of language. We will, therefore, examine in some detail the characteristics of the speech code, having in mind that it reflects some of the important characteristics of the broader class of language codes, and that it may, therefore, serve well as a basis for comparison with memory codes. It is the more appropriate that we should deal with the speech code, because it comprises the conversion from an acoustic signal appropriate for transmission to a phonetic representation appropriate for storage in short-term memory.

CHARACTERISTICS OF THE SPEECH CODE

Clarity of the Signal

It is an interesting and important fact about the speech code that the physical signal is a poor one. We can see that this is so by looking at a spectrographic representation of the speech signal like the one in Figure 1. This is a picture of the phrase, *to catch pink salmon.* As always in a spectrogram, frequency is on the vertical axis, time on the horizontal; relative intensity is represented by the density or blackness of the marks. The relatively darker bands are resonances of the vocal tract, the so-called formants. We know that the lowest two or three of these formants contain almost all of the linguistic information; yet, as we can see, the acoustic energy is not narrowly concentrated there, but tends rather to be smeared across the spectrum; moreover, there is at least one higher formant at about 3600 cycles per second that never varies and thus carries no linguistic information at all. This is to say that the linguistically important cues constitute a relatively small part of the total physical energy. To appreciate to what extent this is so, we might contrast speech with the printed alphabet, where the important parts of the signal stand out clearly from the background. We might also contrast a spectrogram of the real speech of Figure 1 with a synthetic spectrogram like the one in Figure 2, which produces intelligible speech though the formants are unnaturally narrow and sharply defined.

In fact, the speech signal is worse than we have so far said or than we can immediately see just by looking at a spectrogram, for, paradoxically, the formants are most indeterminate at precisely those points where the information they carry is most important. It is, we know, the rapid changes in the frequency position of

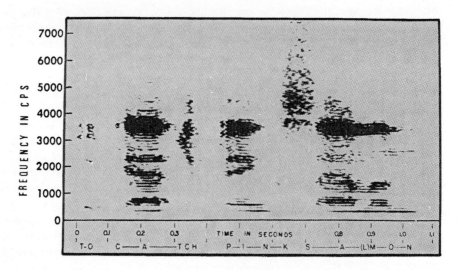

FIG. 1. Spectrogram of *to catch pink salmon,* natural speech.

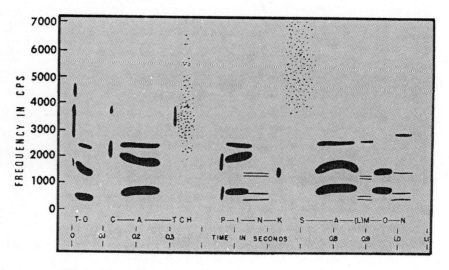

FIG. 2. Schematic spectrogram for synthesis of *to catch pink salmon.*

the formants (the formant transitions) that contain the essential cues for most of the consonants. In the case of the stop consonants, these changes occur in 50 milliseconds or less, and they sometimes extend over ranges as great as 600 cycles per second. Such signals scatter energy and are therefore difficult to specify or to track. Moreover, the difficulty is greatest at the point where they begin, though that is the most important part of the transition for the listener who wants to know the phonetic identity of sound.

The physical indeterminacy of the signal is an interesting aspect of the speech code because it implies a need for processors specialized for the purpose of extracting the essential acoustic parameters. The output of these processors might be a cleaned-up description of the signal, not unlike the simplified synthetic spectrogram of Figure 2. But such an output, it is important to understand, would be auditory, not phonetic. The signal would only have been clarified; it would not have been decoded.

Complexity of the Code

Like the other parts of the grammatical code, the conversion from speech sound to phonetic message is complex. Invoking a distinction we have previously found useful in this connection, we should say that the conversion is truly a code and not a cipher (Liberman, Cooper, Shankweiler, & Studdert-Kennedy, 1967; Studdert-Kennedy, in press). If the sounds of speech were a simple cipher, there would be a unit sound for each phonetic segment. Something approximating such a cipher does indeed exist in one of the written forms of language, namely, alphabets, where each phonological segment is represented by a discrete optical shape.[7] But speech is not an alphabet or cipher in that sense. In the interconversion between acoustic signal and phonetic message the information is radically restructured so that successive segments of the message are carried simultaneously—that is, in parallel—on exactly the same parts of the acoustic signal. As a result, the segmentation of the signal does not correspond to the segmentation of the message; and the part of the acoustic signal that carries information about a particular phonetic segment varies drastically in shape according to context.

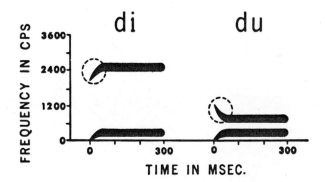

FIG. 3.   Schematic spectrogram for the syllables [di] and [du].

In Figure 3 we see schematic spectrograms that produce the syllables [di] and [du] and illustrate several aspects of the speech code. To synthesize the vowels [i] and [u], at least in slow articulation, we need only the steady-state formants, that is, the parts of the pattern to the right of the formant transitions. These acoustic segments correspond in simple fashion to the perceived phonetic segments: They

---

[7]Alphabets commonly make contact with the language at a level somewhat more abstract than the phonetic. Thus, in English the letters often represent what some linguists would call morphophonemes, as for example in the use of "s" for what is phonetically the [s] of *cats* and the [z] of *dogs.* In the terminology of generative grammar, the level so represented corresponds roughly to the phonologic.

provide sufficient cues for the vowels; they carry information about no other segments; and, though the fact is not illustrated here, they are, in slow articulation, the same in all message contexts. For the slowly articulated vowels, then, the relation between sound and message is a simple cipher. The stop consonants, on the other hand, are complexly encoded, even in slow articulation. To see in what sense this is so, we should examine the formant transitions, the rapid changes in formant frequency at the beginning (left) of the pattern. Transitions of the first (lower) formant are cues for manner and voicing; in this case they tell the listener that the consonants are members of the class of voiced stops [b,d,g]. For our present purposes, the transitions of the second (higher) formant are of greater interest. These are the parts of the pattern enclosed in the broken circles in Figure 3. Such transitions are, in general, cues for the perceived "place" distinctions among the consonants. In the patterns of Figure 3 they tell the listener that the stop is [d] in both cases. Plainly, the transition cues for [d] are very different in the two vowel contexts: The one with [i] is a rising transition relatively high in the spectrum, the one with [u] a falling transition low in the spectrum. It is less obvious, perhaps, but equally true that there is no isolable acoustic segment corresponding to the message segment [d]: At every instant, the second-formant transition carries information about both the consonant and the vowel. This kind of parallel transmission reflects the fact that the consonant is truly encoded into the vowel; this is, we would emphasize, the central characteristic of the speech code.

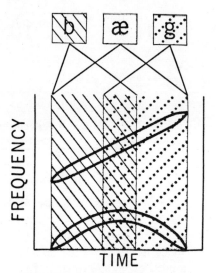

FIG. 4. Schematic spectrogram showing effects of coarticulation in the syllable [bæg].

The next figure, Figure 4, shows more clearly than the last the more complex kind of parallel transmission that frequently occurs in speech. If converted to sound, the schematic spectrogram shown there is sufficient to produce an approximation to the syllable [bæg]. The point of the figure is to show where information about the phonetic segments is to be found in the acoustic signal.

Limiting our attention again to the second formant, we see that information about the vowel extends from the beginning of the utterance to the end. This is so because a change in the vowel—from [bæg] to [big], for example—will require a change in the entire formant, not merely somewhere in its middle section. Information about the first consonant, [b], extends through the first two-thirds of the whole temporal extent of the formant. This can be established by showing that a change in the first segment of the message—from [bæg] to [gæg], for example—will require a change in the signal from the beginning of the sound to the point, approximately two-thirds of the way along the formant, that we see marked in the figure. A similar statement and similar test apply also to the last consonant, [g]. In general, every part of the second formant carries information about at least two segments of the message; and there is a part of that formant, in the middle, into which all three message segments have been simultaneously encoded. We see, perhaps more easily than in Figure 1, that the lack of correspondence in segmentation is not trivial. It is not the case that there are simple extensions connecting an otherwise segmented signal, as in the case of cursive writing, or that there are regions of acoustic overlap separating acoustic sections that at some point correspond to the segments of the message. There is no correspondence in segmentation because several segments of the message have been, in a very strict sense, encoded into the same segment of the signal.

Transparency of the Code

We have just seen that not all phonetic segments are necessarily encoded in the speech signal to the same degree. In even the slowest articulations, all of the consonants, except the fricatives,[8] are encoded. But the vowels (and the fricatives) can be, and sometimes are, represented in the acoustic signal quite straightforwardly, one acoustic segment for each phonetic segment. It is as if there were in the speech stream occasionally transparent stretches. We might expect that these stretches, in which the phonetic elements are not restructured in the sound, could be treated as if there were a cipher. There is, thus, a kind of intermittency in the difficulty of decoding the acoustic signal. We may wonder whether that characteristic of the speech code serves a significant purpose, such as providing the decoding machinery with frequent opportunities to get back on the track when and if things go wrong. It is, in any case, an important characteristic to note, as we will see later in the paper, because of the correspondence between what we might call degree of encoding and evidence for special processing.

Lawfulness of the Code

Given an encoded relation between two streams or levels of information such as we described in the preceding section, we should ask whether the conversion from the one to the other is made lawfully, by the application of rules, or, alternatively, in some purely arbitrary way. To say that the conversion is by rule is to say that it can be rationalized, that there is, in linguistic terms, a grammar. If the connection is arbitrary, then there is, in effect, a code book; to decode a signal, one looks it up in the book.

[8] For a fuller discussion of this point, see Liberman, Cooper, Shankweiler, & Studdert-Kennedy, 1967.

The speech code is, as we will see, not arbitrary, yet it might appear so to an intelligent but inarticulate cryptanalyst from Mars. Suppose that such a creature, knowing nothing about speech, were given many samples of utterances (in acoustic or visible form), each paired with its decoded or plain-text phonetic equivalents. Let us suppose further, as seems to us quite reasonable, that he would finally conclude that the code could not be rationalized, that it could only be dealt with by reference to a code book. Such a conclusion would, of course, be uninteresting. From the point of view of one who knows that human beings readily decode spoken utterances, the code-book solution would also seem implausible, since the number of entries in the book would have to be so very large. Having in mind the example of [bæg] that we developed earlier, we see that the number of entries would, at the least, be as great as the number of syllables. But, in fact, the number would be very much larger than that, because coding influences sometimes extend across syllable boundaries (Öhman, 1966), and because the acoustic shape of the signal changes drastically with such factors as rate of speaking and phonetic stress (Lindblom, 1963; Lisker & Abramson, 1967).

At all events, our Martian would surely have concluded, to the contrary, that the speech code was lawful if anyone had described for him, even in the most general terms, the processes by which the sounds are produced. Taking the syllable [bæg], which we illustrated earlier, as our example, one might have offered a description about as follows. The phonetic segments of the syllables are taken apart into their constituent features, such as place of production, manner of production, and condition of voicing. These features are represented, we must suppose, as neural signals that will become, ultimately, the commands to the muscles of articulation. Before they become the final commands, however, the neural signals are organized so as to produce the greatest possible overlap in activity of the independent muscles to which the separate features are assigned. There may also occur at this stage some reorganization of the commands so as to insure cooperative activity of the several muscle groups, especially when they all act on the same organ, as is the case with the muscle groups that control the gestures of the tongue. But so far the features, or rather their neural equivalents, have only been organized; they can still be found as largely independent entities, which is to say that they have not yet been thoroughly encoded. In the next stage the neural commands (in the final common paths) cause muscular contraction, but this conversion is, from our standpoint, straightforward and need not detain us. It is in the final conversions, from muscle contraction to vocal tract shape to sound, that the output is radically restructured and that true encoding occurs. For it is there that the independent but overlapping activity of independent muscle groups becomes merged as they are reflected in the acoustic signal. In the case of [bæg], the movement of the lips that represents a feature of the initial consonant is overlapped with the shaping of the tongue appropriate for the next vowel segment. In the conversion to sound, the number of dimensions is reduced, with the result that the simultaneous activity of lips and tongue affect exactly the same parameter of the acoustic signal, for example, the second formant. We, and our Martian, see then how it is that the consonant and the vowel are encoded.

The foregoing account is intended merely to show that a very crude model can, in general, account for the complexly encoded relation between the speech signal and the phonetic message. That model rationalizes the relation between these two levels of the language, much as the linguists' syntactic model rationalizes the relation between deep and surface structure. For that reason, and because of certain formal similarities we have described elsewhere (Mattingly & Liberman, 1969), we should say of our speech model that it is, like syntax, a grammar. It differs from syntax in that the grammar of speech is a model of a flesh-and-blood process, not, as in the case of syntax, a set of rules with no describable physiological correlates. Because the grammar of speech corresponds to an actual process, we are led to believe that it is important, not just to the scientist who would understand the code, but also to the ordinary listener who needs that same kind of understanding, albeit tacitly, if he is to perform appropriately the complex task of perceiving speech. We assume that the listener decodes the speech signal by reference to the grammar, that is, by reference to a general model of the articulatory process. This assumption has been called the motor theory of speech perception.

Efficiency of the Code

The complexity of the speech code is not a fluke of nature that man must somehow cope with, but is rather an essential condition for the efficiency of speech, both in production and in perception, serving as a necessary link between an acoustic representation appropriate for transmission and a phonetic representation appropriate for storage in short-term memory. Consider production first. As we have already had occasion to say, the constituent features of the phonetic segments are assigned to more or less independent sets of articulators, whose activity is then overlapped to a very great extent. In the most extreme case, all the muscle movements required to communicate the entire syllable would occur simultaneously; in the more usual case, the activity corresponding to the several features is broadly smeared through the syllable. In either case the result is that phonetic segments are realized in articulation at rates higher than the rate at which any single muscle can change its state. The co-articulation that characterizes so much of speech production and causes the complications of the speech code seems well designed to permit relatively slow moving muscles to transmit phonetic segments at high rates (Cooper, 1966).

The efficiency of the code on the side of perception is equally clear. Consider, first, that the temporal resolving power of the ear must set an upper limit on the rate at which we can perceive successive acoustic events. Beyond that limit the successive sounds merge into a buzz and become unidentifiable. If speech were a cipher on the phonetic message, that is, if each segment of the message were represented by a unit sound, then the limit would be determined directly by the rate at which the phonetic segments were transmitted. But given that the message segments are, in fact, encoded into acoustic segments of roughly syllabic size, the limit is set, not by the number of phonetic segments per unit time, but by the number of syllables. This represents a considerable gain in the rate at which message segments can be perceived.

The efficient encoding described above results from a kind of parallel transmission in which information about successive segments is transmitted simultaneously on the same part of the signal. We should note that there is another, very different kind of parallel transmisssion in speech: Cues for the features of the same segment are carried simultaneously on *different* parts of the signal. Recalling the patterns of Figure 4, we note that the cues for place of production are in the second-formant transition, while the first-formant transition carries the cues for the manner and voicing. This is an apparently less complicated arrangement than the parallel transmission produced by the encoding of the consonant into the vowel, because it takes advantage of the ear's ability to resolve two very different frequency levels. We should point out, however, that the listener is not at all aware of the two frequency levels, as he is in listening to a chord that is made up of two pitches, but rather hears the stop, with all its features, in a unitary way.

The speech code is apparently designed to increase efficiency in yet another aspect of speech perception: It makes possible a considerable gain in our ability to identify the order in which the message segments occur. Recent research by Warren, Obusek, Farmer, and Warren (1969) has shown that the sequential order of nonspeech signals can be correctly identified only when these segments have durations several times greater than the average that must be assigned to the message segments in speech. If speech were a cipher, that is, if there were an invariant sound for each unit of the message, then it would have to be transmitted at relatively low rates if we were to know that the word *task,* for example, was not *taks* or *sakt* or *kats.* But in the speech code, the order of the segments is not necessarily signalled, as we might suppose, by the temporal order in which the acoustic cues occur. Recalling what we said earlier about the context-conditioned variation in the cues, we should note now that each acoustic cue is clearly marked by these variations for the position of the signalled segment in the message. In the case of the transition cues for [d] that we described earlier, for example, we should find that in initial and final positions—for example in [dæg] and [gæd]—the cues were mirror images. In listening to speech we somehow hear through the context-conditioned variation in order to arrive at the canonical form of the segment, in this case [d]. But we might guess that we also use the context-determined shape of the cue to decide where in the sequence the signaled segment occurred. In any case, the order of the segments we hear may be to a large extent inferred—quite exactly synthesized, created, or constructed—from cues in a way that has little or nothing to do with the order of their occurrence in time. Given what appears to be a relatively poor ability to identify the order of acoustic events from temporal cues, this aspect of the speech code would significantly increase the rate at which we can accurately perceive the message.

The speech code is efficient, too, in that it converts between a high-information-cost acoustic signal appropriate for transmission and a low-information-cost phonetic string appropriate for storage in some short-term memory. Indeed, the difference in information rate between the two levels of the speech code is staggering. To transmit the signal in acoustic form and in high fidelity costs about 70,000 bits per second; for reasonable intelligibility we need about 40,000 bits per second. Assuming a frequency-volley theory of hearing through most of the speech range, we should suppose that a great deal of nervous tissue would have to be devoted to the storage of even relatively short stretches. By recoding into a phonetic representation, we reduce the cost to less than 40 bits per second, thus effecting a saving of about 1000 times by comparison with the acoustic form and of roughly half that by comparison with what we might assume a reduced auditory (but not phonetic) representation to be. We must emphasize, however, that this large saving is realized only if each phonetic feature is represented by a unitary pattern of nervous activity, one such pattern for each feature, with no additional or extraneous "auditory" information clinging to the edges. As we will see in the next section, the highly encoded aspects of speech do tend to become highly digitized in that sense.

Naturalness of the Code

It is testimony to the naturalness of the speech code that all members of our species acquire it readily and use it with ease. While it is surely true that a child reared in total isolation would not produce phonetically intelligible speech, it is equally true that in normal circumstances he comes to do that without formal tuition. Indeed, given a normal child in a normal environment, it would be difficult to contrive methods that would effectively prevent him from acquiring speech.

It is also relevant that, as we pointed out earlier, there is a universal phonetics. A relatively few phonetic features suffice, given the various combinations into which they are entered, to account for most of the phonetic segments, and in particular those that carry the heaviest information load, in the languages of the world. For example, stops and vowels, the segments with which we have been exclusively concerned in this paper, are universal, as is the co-articulated consonant-vowel syllable that we have used to illustrate the speech code. Such phonetic universals are the more interesting because they often require precise control of articulation; hence they are not to be dismissed with the airy observation that since all men have similar vocal tracts, they can be expected to make similar noises.

Because the speech code is complex but easy, we should suppose that man has access to special devices for encoding and decoding it. There is now a great deal of evidence that such specialized processors do exist in man, apparently by virtue of his membership in the species. As a consequence, speech requires no conscious or special effort; the speech code is well matched to man and is, in precisely that sense, natural.

The existence of special speech processors is strongly suggested by the fact that the encoded sounds of speech are perceived in a special mode. It is obvious—indeed so obvious that everyone takes it for granted—that we do not and cannot hear the encoded parts of the speech signal in auditory terms. The first segment of the syllables [ba], [da], [ga] have no identifiable auditory characteristics; they are unique linguistic events. It is as if they were the abstract output of a device specialized to extract them, and only them, from the acoustic signal. This abstract non-auditory perception is characteristic of encoded speech, not of a class of acoustic events such as the second-formant transitions that are sufficient to distinguish [ba], [da], [ga], for when these transition cues are extracted from synthetic speech patterns and presented alone, they sound just like the "chirps" or glissandi that auditory psychophysics would lead us to expect. Nor is this abstract perception characteristic of the relatively unencoded parts of the speech signal: The steady-state noises of the fricatives, [s] and [ʃ], for example, can be heard as noises; moreover, one can easily judge that the noise of [s] is higher in pitch than the noise of [ʃ].

A corollary characteristic of this kind of abstract perception, measured quite carefully by a variety of techniques, is one that has been called "categorical perception" (see Studdert-Kennedy, Liberman, Harris, & Cooper, 1970, for a review; Haggard, 1970, 1971b; Pisoni, 1971; Vinegrad, 1970). In listening to the encoded segments of speech we tend to hear them only as categories, not as a perceived continuum that can be more or less arbitrarily divided into regions. This occurs even when, with synthetic speech, we produce stimuli that lie at intermediate points along the acoustic continuum that contains the relevant cues. In its extreme form, which is rather closely approximated in the case of the stops, categorical perception creates a situation, very different from the usual psychophysical case, in which the listener can discriminate stimuli as different no better than he can identify them absolutely.

That the categorical perception of the stops is not simply a characteristic of the way we process a certain class of acoustic stimuli—in this case the rapid frequency modulation that constitutes the (second-formant transition) acoustic cue—has been shown in a recent study (Mattingly, Liberman, Syrdal, & Halwes, 1971). It was found there that, when listened to in isolation, the second-formant transitions (the chirps we referred to earlier) are not perceived categorically.

Nor can it be said that categorical perception is simply a consequence of our tendency to attach phonetic labels to the elements of speech and then to forget what the elements sounded like. If that were the case, we should expect to find categorical perception of the unencoded steady-state vowels, but, in fact, we do not, certainly not to the same extent (Fry, Abramson, Eimas, & Liberman, 1962; Eimas, 1963; Stevens, Liberman, Öhman, & Studdert-Kennedy, 1969; Pisoni, 1971; Fujisaki & Kawashima, 1969). Moreover, categorical perception of the encoded segments has recently been found to be reflected within 100 milliseconds in cortical evoked potentials (Dorman, 1971).

In the case of the encoded stops, then, it appears that the listener has no auditory image of the signal available to him, but only the output of a specialized processor that has stripped the signal of all normal sensory information and represented each phonetic segment (or feature) categorically by a unitary neural event. Such unitary neural representations would presumably be easy to store, and also to combine, permute, and otherwise shuffle around in the further processing that converts between sound and meaning.

But perception of vowels is, as we noted, not so nearly categorical. The listener discriminates many more stimuli than he can absolutely identify, just as he does with nonspeech; accordingly, we should suppose that, as with nonspeech, he hears the signal in auditory terms. Such an auditory image would be important in the perception of the pitch and duration cues that figure in the prosodic aspects of speech; moreover, it would be essential that the auditory image be held for some seconds, since the listener must often wait to the end of a phrase or sentence in order to know what linguistic value to assign to the particular pitch and duration cues he heard earlier.

Finally, we should note about categorical perception that, according to a recent study (Eimas, Siqueland, Jusczyk, & Vigorito, 1971) it is present in infants at the age of four weeks. These infants discriminated synthetic [ba] and [pa]; moreover, and more significantly, they discriminated better, other things equal, between pairs of stimuli that straddled the adult phonetic boundary than between pairs that lay entirely within the phonetic category. In other words, the infants perceived the voicing feature categorically. From this we should conclude that the voicing feature is real, not only physiologically, but in a very deep biological sense.

Other, perhaps more direct, evidence for the existence of specialized speech processors comes from a number of recent experiments that overload perceptual mechanisms by putting competing signals simultaneously into the two ears (Broadbent & Gregory, 1964; Bryden, 1963; Kimura, 1961, 1964, 1967; Shankweiler & Studdert-Kennedy, 1967; Studdert-Kennedy & Shankweiler, 1970). The general finding with speech signals, including nonsense syllables that differ, say, only in the initial consonant, is that stimuli presented to the right ear are better heard than those presented to the left; with complex nonspeech sounds the opposite result, a left-ear advantage, is found. Since there is reason to believe, especially in the case of competing and dichotically presented stimuli, that the contralateral cerebral representation is the stronger, these results have been taken to mean that speech, including its purely phonetic aspects, needs to be processed in the left hemisphere, nonspeech in the right. The fact that phonetic perception goes on in a particular part of the brain is surely consistent with the view that it is carried out by a special processor.

The case for a special processor to decode speech is considerably strengthened by the finding that the right-ear advantage depends on the encodedness of the signal. For example, stop consonants typically show a larger and more consistent right-ear advantage than unencoded vowels (Shankweiler & Studdert-Kennedy, 1967; Studdert-Kennedy & Shankweiler, 1970). Other recent studies have confirmed that finding and have explored even more analytically the conditions of the right-ear (left hemisphere) advantage for speech (Darwin, 1969, 1971; Haggard, 1971a; Haggard, Ambler, & Callow, 1969; Haggard & Parkinson, 1971; Kirstein & Shankweiler, 1969; Spellacy & Blumstein, 1970). The results, which are too numerous and complicated to present here even in summary form, tend to support the conclusion that processing is forced into the left hemisphere (for most subjects) when phonetic decoding, as contrasted with phonetic deciphering or with processing of nonspeech, must be carried out.

Having referred in the discussion of categorical perception to the evidence that the phonetic segments (or, rather, their features) may be assumed to be represented by unitary neural events, we should here point to an incidental result of the dichotic experiments that is very relevant to that assumption. In three experiments (Halwes, 1969; Studdert-Kennedy & Shankweiler, 1970; Yoder, personal communication) it has been found that listeners tend significantly often to extract one feature (e.g., place of production) from the input to one ear and another feature (e.g., voicing) from the other and combine them to hear a segment that was not presented to either ear. Thus, given [ba] to the left ear, say, and [ka] to the right, listeners will, when they err, far more often report [pa] (place feature from the left ear, voicing from the right) or [ga] (place feature from the right ear, voicing from the left) than [da] or [ta]. We take this as conclusive evidence that the features are singular and unitary in the sense that they are independent of the context in which they occur and also that, so far from being abstract inventions of the linguist, they have, in fact, a hard reality in physiological and psychological processes.

The technique of overloading the perceptual machinery by dichotic presentation has led to the discovery of yet another effect that seems, so far, to testify to the existence of a special speech processor (Studdert-Kennedy, Shankweiler, & Shulman, 1970). The finding, a kind of backward masking that has been called the "lag" effect, is that when syllables contrasting in the initial stop consonant are presented dichotically and offset in time, the second (or lagging) syllable is more accurately perceived. When such syllables are presented monotically, the first (or leading) stimulus has the advantage. In the dichotic case, the effect is surely central; in the monotic case there is presumably a large peripheral component. At all events, it is now known that, as in the case of the right-ear advantage, the lag effect is greater for the encoded stops than for the unencoded vowels (Kirstein, 1971; Porter, Shankweiler, & Liberman, 1969); it has also been found that highly encoded stops show a more consistent effect than the relatively less encoded liquids and semi-vowels (Porter, 1971). Also relevant is the finding that synthetic stops that differ only in the second-formant transitions show a lag effect, but that the second-formant transitions alone (the chirps) do not (Porter, 1971). Such results support the conclusion that this effect, too, may be specific to the special processing of speech.[9]

In sum, there is now a great deal of evidence to support the assertion that man has ready access to physiological devices that are specialized for the purpose of decoding the speech signal and recovering the phonetic message. Those devices make it possible for the human being to deal with the speech code easily and without conscious awareness of the process or its complexity. The code is thus a natural one.

Resistance to Distortion

Everyone who has even worked with speech knows that the signal holds up well against various kinds of distortion. In the case of sentences, a great deal of this resistance depends on syntactic and semantic constraints, which are, of course, irrelevant to our concern here. But in the perception of nonsense syllables, too, the message often survives attempts to perturb it. This is due largely to the presence in the signal of several kinds of redundancy. One arises from the phonotactic rules of the language: Not all sequences of speech sounds are allowable. That constraint is presumably owing, though only in part, to limitations having to do with the possibilities of co-articulation. In any case, it introduces redundancy and may serve as an error-correcting device. The other kind of redundancy arises from the fact that most phonetic distinctions are cued by more than one acoustic difference. Perception of place of production of the stop consonants, for example, is normally determined by transitions of the second formant, transitions of the third formant, and by the frequency position of a burst of noise. Each of these cues is more or less sufficient, and they are highly independent of each other. If one is wiped out, the others remain.

[9] One experimental result appears so far not to fit with that conclusion: Syllables that differed in a linguistically irrelevant pitch contour nevertheless gave a lag effect (Darwin, in press).

There is one other way in which speech resists distortion that may be the most interesting of all, because it implies for speech a special biological status. We refer here to the fact that speech remains intelligible even when it is removed about as completely as it can from its normal, naturalistic context. In the synthetic patterns so much used by us and others, we can, and often do, play fast and loose with the nature of the vocal tract excitation and with such normally fixed characteristics of the formants as their number, bandwidth, and relative intensity. Such departures from the norm, resulting in the most extreme cases in highly schematic representations, remain intelligible. These patterns are more than mere cartoons, since certain specific cues must be retained. As Mattingly (1972) has pointed out, speech might be said in this respect to be like the sign stimuli that the ethologist talks about. Quite crude and unnatural models such as Tinbergen's (1951) dummy sticklebacks, elicit responses provided only that the model preserves the significant characters of the original display. As Manning (1969) says, "sign stimuli will usually be involved where it is important never to miss making a response to the stimulus" (p. 39). More generally, sign stimuli are often found when the correct transmission of information is crucial for the survival of the individual or the species. Speech may have been used in this way by early man.

How to Tell Speech from Nonspeech

For anyone who uses the speech code, and especially for the very young child who is in the process of acquiring it, it is necessary to distinguish the sounds of speech from other acoustic stimuli. How does he do this? The easy, and probably wrong, answer is that he listens for certain acoustic stigmata that mark the speech signal. One thinks, for example, of the nature of the vocal-tract excitation or of certain general characteristics of the formants. If the listener could identify speech on the basis of such relatively fixed markers, he would presumably decide at a low level of the perceptual system whether a particular signal was speech or not and, on the basis of that decision, send it to the appropriate processors. But we saw in the preceding section that speech remains speech even when the signal is reduced to an extremely schematic form. We suspect, therefore, that the distinction between speech and nonspeech is not made at some early stage on the basis of general acoustic characteristics.

More compelling support for that suspicion is to be found in a recent unpublished experiment by T. Rand. To one ear he presented all of the first formant, including the transitions, together with the steady-state parts of the second and third formants; when presented alone, these patterns sound vaguely like [da]. To the other ear, with proper time relationships carefully preserved, were presented the 50 millisecond second-formant and third-formant transitions; alone, these sound like the chirps we have referred to before. But when these patterns were presented together, that is, dichotically, listeners clearly heard [ba], [da], or [ga] (depending on the nature of the second-formant and third-formant transitions) in one ear and, simultaneously, nonspeech chirps in the other. Thus, it appears that the same acoustic events, the second-formant or third-formant transitions, can be processed simultaneously as speech and nonspeech. We should suppose, then, that the incoming signal goes indiscriminately to speech and nonspeech processors. If the speech processors succeed in extracting phonetic features, then the signal is speech; if they fail, then the signal is processed only as nonspeech. We wonder if this is a characteristic of all so-called sign stimuli.

Security of the Code

The speech code is available to all humans, but probably to no other species. There is now evidence that animals other than man, including even his nearest primate relatives, do not produce phonetic strings and their encoded acoustic correlates (Lieberman, 1968; Lieberman, Klatt, & Wilson, 1969; Lieberman, 1971; Lieberman, Crelin, & Klatt, in press). This is due, at least in part, to gross differences in vocal-tract anatomy between man and all other animals. (It is clear that speech in man is not simply an overlaid function, carried out by peripheral structures that evolved in connection with other more fundamental biological processes; rather, some important characteristics of the human vocal tract must be supposed to have developed in evolution specifically in connection with speech.) We should think that animals other than man lack also the mechanisms of neurological control necessary for the organization and coordination of the gestures of speech, but hard evidence for this is lacking. Unfortunately, we know nothing at all about how animals other than man perceive speech. Presumably, they lack the special processor necessary to decode the speech signal. If so, the perception of speech must be different from ours. They should not hear categorically, for instance, and they should not hear the [di]-[du] patterns of Figure 3 as two-segment syllables which have the first segment in common. Thus, we should suppose that animals other than man can neither produce nor correctly perceive the speech code. If all our enemies were animals other than man, cryptanalysts would have nothing to do, or else they might have the excessively difficult task of breaking an animal code for which man has no natural key.

Subcodes

Our discussion so far has, perhaps, left the impression that there is only one speech code. In one sense this is true, for it appears that there is a universal ensemble of phonetic features defined by the communicative possibilities of the vocal tract and the neural speech processor. But the subset of phonetic features that are actually used varies from language to language. Each language thus has its own phonetic subcode. A given phonetic feature, however, will be articulated and perceived in the same way in every language in which it is used. Thus, we should be very surprised, for instance, to find a language in which the perception of place for stops was not categorical. If, as the results of Eimas et al. (1971) lead us to suppose, a child is born with an intuitive knowledge of the universal phonetics, part of his task in learning his native language is to identify the features of its phonetic subcode and to forget the others. These unused features cannot be entirely lost, however, since people do learn how to speak and understand more than one language. But there is some evidence that bilinguals listening to their second language do not necessarily use the same speech cues as native speakers of the language do (Haggard, 1971b).

Secondary Codes

A speaker-hearer can become aware of certain aspects of the linguistic process, in particular its phonological and phonetic characteristics. This awareness can then be exploited to develop secondary codes, which may be thought of as additional pseudolinguistic rules added to those of the language. A simple example is a children's "secret language," such as Pig Latin, in which a rule for metathesis and insertion applies to each word. We should suppose that to speak or understand Pig Latin fluently would require not only the unconscious knowlege of the linguistic structure of English that all native speakers have, but also a conscious awareness of a particular aspect of this structure—the phonological segmentation—and a considerable amount of practice. There is evidence, indeed, that speakers of English who lack a conscious awareness of phonological segmentation do not master Pig Latin, despite the triviality of its rules (Savin, 1972). The pseudolinguistic character of Pig Latin explains why even a speaker of English who does not know Pig Latin would not mistake it for a natural foreign language, and why one continues to feel a sense of artificiality in speaking it long after he has mastered the trick.

Systems of versification are more important kinds of secondary codes. For a literate society the function of verse is primarily esthetic, but for preliterate societies, verse is a means of transmitting verbal information of cultural importance with a minimum of paraphrase. The rules of verse are, in effect, an addition to the phonology that requires that recalled material not only should preserve the semantic values of the original, but should also conform to a specific, rule-determined phonetic pattern. Thus in Latin epic poetry, a line of verse is divided into six feet, each of which must have one of several patterns of long and short syllables. The requirement to conform to this pattern excludes almost all possible renditions other than the correct one, and makes memorization easier and recall more accurate. Since versification rules are in general more elaborate than those of Pig Latin, a greater degree of linguistic awareness is necessary to compose verse. This more complex skill has thus traditionally been the specialized occupation of a few members of a society, though a passive form of the skill, permitting the listener to distinguish "correct" from "incorrect" lines without scanning them syllable by syllable, has been possible for a much larger number of people.

Writing, like versification, is also a secondary code for transmitting verbal information accurately, and the two activities have more in common than might at first appear. The reader is given a visually coded representation of the message, and this representation, whether ideographic, syllabic, or alphabetic, provides very incomplete information about the linguistic structure and semantic content of the message. The skilled reader, however, does not need complete information, and ordinarily does not even need all of the partial information given by the graphic patterns, but rather just enough to exclude most of the other messages which might fit the context. Being competent in his language, knowing the rules of the writing system, and having some degree of linguistic awareness, he can reproduce the writer's message in reasonably faithful fashion. (Since the specific awareness required is awareness of phonological segmentation, it is not surprising that Savin's group of English speakers who cannot learn Pig Latin also have great difficulty in learning to read.)

The reader's reproduction is not, as a rule, verbatim; he makes small deviations that are acceptable paraphrases of the original, and overlooks or, better, unconsciously corrects misprints. This suggests that reading is an active process of construction constrained by the partial information on the printed page, just as remembering verse is an active process of construction, constrained, though much less narrowly, by the rules of versification. As Bartlett (1932) noted for the more general case, the processes of perception and recall of verbal material are not essentially different.

For our purposes, the significant fact about pseudolinguistic secondary codes is that, while being less natural than the grammatical codes of language, they are nevertheless far from being wholly unnatural. They are more or less artificial systems based on those aspects of natural linguistic activities that can most readily be brought to consciousness: the levels of phonology and phonetics. All children do not acquire secondary codes maturationally, but every society contains some individuals who, if given the opportunity, can develop sufficient linguistic awareness to learn them, just as every society has its potential dancers, musicians, and mathematicians.

LANGUAGE, SPEECH, AND RESEARCH ON MEMORY

What we have said about the speech code may be relevant to research on memory in two ways: Most directly, because work on memory for linguistic information, to which we shall presently turn, naturally includes the speech code as one stage of processing; and, rather indirectly, because the characteristics of the speech code provide an interesting basis for comparison with the kinds of code that students of memory talk about. In this section of the paper we will develop that relevance, summarizing where necessary the appropriate parts of the earlier discussion.

The Speech Code in Memory Research

Acoustic, auditory, and phonetic representations. When a psychologist deals with memory for language, especially when the information is presented as speech sounds, he would do well to distinguish the several forms that the information can take, even while it remains in the domain of speech. There is, first, the acoustic form in which the signal is transmitted. This is characterized by a poor signal-to-noise ratio and a very high bit rate. The second form, found at an early stage of processing in the nervous system, is auditory. This neural representation of the information maps in a relatively straightforward way onto the acoustic signal. Of course, the acoustic and auditory forms are not identical. In addition to the fact that one is mechanical and the other neural, it is surely true that some information has been lost in the conversion. Moreover, as we pointed out earlier in the paper, it is likely that the signal has been sharpened and clarified in certain ways. If so, we should assume that the task was carried out by devices not unlike the feature detectors the neurophysiologist and psychologist now investigate and that apparently operate in visual perception, as they do in hearing, to increase contrast and extract certain components of the pattern. But we should emphasize that the conversion from acoustic to auditory form, even when done by the kind of device we just assumed, does not decode the signal, however much it may improve it. The relation of the auditory to the acoustic form remains simple, and the bit rate, though conceivably a good deal lower at this neural stage than in the sound itself, is still very high. To arrive at the phonetic representation, the third form that the information takes, requires the specialized decoding processes we talked about earlier in the paper. The result of that decoding is a small number of unitary neural patterns, corresponding to phonetic features, that combine to make the somewhat greater number of patterns that constitute the phonetic segments; arranged in their proper order, these segments become the message conveyed by the speech code. The phonetic representations are, of course, far more economical in terms of bits than the auditory ones. They also appear to have special standing as unitary physiological and biological realities. In general, then, they are well suited for storage in some kind of short-term memory until enough have accumulated to be recoded once more with what we must suppose is a further gain in economy.

Even when language is presented orthographically to the subjects' eyes, the information seems to be recoded into phonetic form. One of the most recent and also most interesting treatments of this matter is to be found in a paper by Conrad (1972). He concludes, on the basis of considerable evidence, that while it is possible to hold the alphabetic shapes as visual information in short-term memory—deaf-mute children seem to do just that—the information can be stored (and dealt with) more efficiently in phonetic form. We suppose that this is so because the representations of the phonetic segments are quite naturally available in the nervous system in a way, and in a form, that representations of the various alphabetic shapes are not. Given the complexities of the conversion from acoustic or auditory form to phonetic, and the advantages for storage of the phonetic segments, we should insist that this is an important distinction.

Storage and transmission in man and machine. We have emphasized that in spoken language the information must be in one form (acoustic) for transmission and in a very different form (phonetic or semantic) for storage, and that the conversion from the one to the other is a complex recoding. But there is no logical requirement that this be so. If all the components of the language system had been designed from scratch and with the same end in view, the complex speech code might have been unnecessary. Suppose the designer had decided to make do with a small number of empty segments, like the phones we have been talking about, that have to be transmitted in rapid succession. The engineer might then have built articulators able to produce such sequences simply—alphabetically or by a cipher—and ears that could perceive them. Or if he had, for some reason, started with sluggish articulators and an ear that could not resolve rapid-fire sequences of discrete acoustic signals, he might have used a larger inventory of segments transmitted at a lower rate. In either case the information would not have had to be restructured in order to make it differentially suitable for transmission and storage; there might have been, at most, a trivial conversion by means of a simple cipher.

Indeed, that is very much the situation when computers "talk" to each other. The fact that the human being cannot behave so simply, but must rather use a complex code to convert between transmitted sound and stored message, reflects the conflicting design features of components that presumably developed separately and in connection with different biological functions. As we noted in an earlier part of the paper, certain structures such as the vocal tract that evolved originally in connection with nonlinguistic functions have undergone important modifications that are clearly related to speech. But these adaptations apparently go only so far as to make possible the further matching of components brought about by devices such as those that underlie the speech code.

It is obvious enough that the ear evolved long before speech made its appearance, so we are not surprised, when we approach the problem from that point of view, to discover that not all of its characteristics are ideally suited to the perception of speech. But when we consider speech production and find that certain design features do not mesh with the characteristics of the ear, we are led to wonder if there are not aspects of the process—in particular, those closer to the semantic and cognitive levels—that had independently reached a high state of evolutionary development before the appearance of language as such, and had then to be imposed on the best available components to make a smoothly functioning system. Indeed, Mattingly (1972) has explicitly proposed that language has two sources, an intellect capable of semantic representation and a system of "social releasers" consisting of articulated sounds, and that grammar evolved as an interface between these two very different mechanisms.

In the alphabet, man has invented a transmission vehicle for language far simpler than speech, a secondary code in the sense discussed earlier. It is a straightforward cipher on the phonological structure, one optical shape for each phonological segment, and has a superb signal-to-noise ratio. We should suppose that it is precisely the kind of transmission vehicle that an engineer might have devised. That alphabetic representations are, indeed, good engineering solutions is shown by the relative ease with which engineers have been able to build optical character readers. However, the simple arrangements that are so easy for machines can be hard for human beings. Reading comes late in the child's development; it must be taught; and many fail to learn. Speech, on the other hand, bears a complex relation to language, as we have seen, and has so far defeated the best efforts of engineers to build a device that will perceive it. Yet this complex code is mastered by children at an early age, some significant proficiency being present at four weeks; it requires no tuition; and everyone who can hear manages to perceive speech quite well.

The relevance of all this to the psychology of memory is an obvious and generally observed caution; namely, that we be careful about explaining human beings in terms of processes and concepts that work well in intelligent and remembering machines. We nevertheless make the point because we have in speech a telling object lesson. The speech code is an extremely complex contrivance, apparently designed to make the best of a bad fit between the requirement that phonetic segments be transmitted at a rapid rate and the inability of the mouth and the ear to meet that requirement in any simple way. Yet the physiological devices that correct this mismatch are so much a part of our being that speech works more easily and naturally for human beings than any other arrangement, including those that are clearly simpler.

More and less encoded elements of speech. In describing the characteristics of the speech code we several times pointed to differences between stop consonants and vowels. The basic difference has to do with the relation between signal and message: Stop consonants are always highly encoded in production, so their perception requires a decoding process; vowels can be, and sometimes are, represented by encipherment in the speech signal, so they might be perceived in a different and simpler way. We are not surprised, then, that stops and vowels differ in their tendencies toward categorical perception as they do also in the magnitude of the right-ear advantage and the lag effect.

An implication of this characteristic of the speech code for research in immediate memory has appeared in a study by Crowder (1971), which suggests that vowels produce a "recency" effect, but stops do not. Crowder and Morton (1969) had found that if a list of spoken words is presented to a subject, there is an improvement in recall for the last few items on the list, but no such recency effect is found if the list is presented visually. To explain this modal difference, Crowder and Morton suggested that the spoken items are held for several seconds in an "echoic" register in "precategorical" or raw sensory form. At the time of recall these items are still available to the subject in all their original sensory richness and are therefore easily remembered. When presented visually, the items are held in an "iconic" store for only a fraction of a second. In his more recent experiment Crowder has found that for lists of stop-vowel syllables, the auditory recency effect appears if the syllables on the list contrast only in their vowels, but is absent if they contrast only in their stops. If Crowder and Morton's interpretation of their 1969 result is correct, at least in general terms, then the difference in recency effect between stops and vowels is exactly what we should expect. As we have seen in this paper, the special process that decodes the stops strips away all auditory information and presents to immediate perception a categorical linguistic event the listener can be aware of only as [b, d, g, p, t, or k]. Thus, there is for these segments no auditory, precategorical form that is available to consciousness for a time long enough to produce a recency effect. The relatively unencoded vowels, on the other hand, are capable of being perceived in a different way. Perception is more nearly continuous than categorical; the listener can make relatively fine discriminations within phonetic classes because the auditory characteristics of the signal can be preserved for a while. (For a relevant model and supporting data, see Fujisaki & Kawashima, 1969.) In the experiment by Crowder, we may suppose that these same auditory characteristics of the vowel, held for several seconds in an echoic sensory register, provide the subject with the rich, precategorical information that enables him to recall the most recently presented items with relative ease.

It is a characteristic of the speech code, and indeed of language in general, that not all elements are psychologically and physiologically equivalent. Some (e.g., the stops) are more deeply linguistic than others (e.g., the vowels); they require special processing and can be expected to behave in different ways when memory codes are used.

Speech as a special process. Much of what we said about the speech code was to show that it is complex in a special way, and that it is normally processed by a correspondingly special device. When we examine the formal aspects of this code, we see resemblances of various kinds to the other grammatical codes of phonology and syntax, which is to say that speech is an integral part of a larger system called language, but we do not readily find parallels in other kinds of perception. We know very little about how the speech processor works, so we cannot compare it very directly with other kinds processors that the human being presumably uses. But knowing that the task it must do appears to be different in important ways from the tasks that confront other processors, and knowing, too, that the speech processor is in one part of the brain while nonspeech processors are in another, we should assume that speech processing may be different from other kinds. We might suppose, therefore, that the mechanisms underlying memory for linguistic information may be different from those used in other kinds of memory such as, for example, visual or spatial.

Speech appears to be specialized, not only by comparison with other perceptual or cognitive systems of the human being, but also by comparison with any of the systems so far found in other animals. While there may be some question about just how many of the so-called "higher" cognitive and linguistic processes monkeys are capable of, it seems beyond dispute that the speech code is unique to man. To the extent, then, that this code is used in memory processes, as in short-term memory, we must be especially careful about generalizing results across species.

Speech and Memory Codes Compared

It will be recalled that we began by adopting the view that paraphrase has more to do with the processes by which we remember than with those by which we forget. In this vein we proposed that when people are presented with long stretches of sensible language, they normally use the devices of grammar to recode the information from the form in which it was transmitted into a form suitable for storage. On the occasion of recall they code it back into another transmittable form that may resemble the input only in meaning. Thus, grammar becomes an essential part of normal memory processes and of memory codes. We therefore directed our attention to grammatical codes, taking these to be the rules by which conversions are carried out from one linguistic level to another. To spell out the essential features of such codes, we chose to deal in detail with just one, the speech code. It can be argued, persuasively we think, that the speech code is similar to other grammatical codes, so its characteristics can be used, within reasonable limits, to represent those of grammar generally. But speech has the advantage in this connection that it has been more accessible to psychological investigation than the other grammatical codes. As a result, there are experimental data that permit us to characterize speech in ways that provide a useful basis for comparison with the codes that have come from the more conventional research on verbal memory. In this final section we turn briefly to those more conventional memory codes and to a comparison between them and the speech code.

We will apply the same terminology to this discussion of conventional memory research that we applied to our discussion of grammatical codes. That is, the term code is reserved for the rules that convert from one representation of the information to another. In our analysis of the speech code we took the acoustic and phonetic levels as our two representations and inferred the properties of the speech code from the relation between the two.

In the most familiar type of experiment the materials the subject is required to remember are not the longer segments of language, such as sentences or discourses, but rather lists of words or nonsense syllables. Typically in such an experiment, the subject is required to reproduce the information exactly as it was presented to him, and his response is counted as an error if he does not. Under those circumstances it is difficult, if not impossible, for the subject to employ his linguistic coding devices to their fullest extent, or in their most normal way. However, it is quite evident that the subject in this situation nevertheless uses codes; moreover, he uses them for the same general purpose to which, we have argued, language is so often put, which is to enable him to store the information in a form different from that in which it was presented. Given the task of remembering unfamiliar sequences such as consonant trigrams, the subject may employ, sometimes to the experimenter's chagrin, some form of linguistic mediation (Montague, Adams, & Kiess, 1966). That is, he converts the consonant sequence into a sentence or proposition, which he then stores along with a rule for future recovery of the consonant string. In a recent examination of how people remember nonsense syllables, Prytulak (1971) concluded that such mediation is the rule rather than the exception. Reviewing the literature on memory for verbal materials, Tulving and Madigan (1970) describe two kinds of conversions: One is the substitution of an alternative symbol for the input stimulus together with a conversion rule; the other is the storage of ancillary information along with the to-be-remembered item. Most generally, it appears that when a subject is required to remember exactly lists of unrelated words, paired-associates, or digit strings, he tries to impart pattern to the material, to restructure it in terms of familiar relationships. Or he resorts, at least in some situations, to the kind of "chunking" that Miller (1956) first described and that has become a staple of memory theory (Mandler, 1967). Or he converts the verbal items into visual images (Paivio, 1969; Bower, 1970). At all events, we find that, as Bower (1970) has pointed out, bare-bones rote memorization is tried only as a last resort, if at all.

The subject converts to-be-remembered material that is unrelated and relatively meaningless into an interconnected, meaningful sequence of verbal items or images for storage. What can be said about the rules relating the two levels? In particular, how do the conversions between the two levels compare with those that occur in the speech code, and thus, indirectly, in language in general? The differences would appear to be greater than the similarities. Many of these conversions that we have cited are more properly described as simple ciphers than as codes, in the sense that we have used these terms earlier, since there is in these cases no restructuring of the information but only a rather straightforward substitution of one representation for another. Moreover, memory codes of this type are arbitrary and idiosyncratic, the connection between the two forms of the information having arisen often out of the accidents of the subject's life history; such rules as there may be (for example, to convert each letter of the consonant trigram to a word beginning with that letter) do not truly rationalize the code but rather fall back, in the end, on a key that is, in effect, a code book. As often as not, the memory codes are also relatively unnatural: They require conscious effort, and, on occasion, are felt by the subject to be difficult and demanding. In regard to efficiency, it is hard to make a comparison; relatively arbitrary and unnatural codes can nevertheless be highly efficient given enough practice and the right combination of skills in the user.

In memory experiments that permit the kind of remembering characterized by paraphrase, we would expect to find that memory codes would be much like language codes, and we should expect them to have characteristics similar to those of the code we know as speech. The conversions would be complex recodings, not simple substitutions; they would be capable of being rationalized; and they would, of course, be highly efficient for the uses to which they were being put. But we would probably find their most obvious characteristic to be that of naturalness. People do not ordinarily contrive mnemonic aids by which to remember the gist of conversations or of books, nor do they necessarily devise elaborate schemes for recalling stories and the like, yet they are reasonably adept at such things. They remember without making an effort to commit a message to memory; more important, they do not have to be taught how to do this sort of remembering.

It is, of course, exceedingly difficult to do scientific work in situations that permit the free use of these very natural language codes. Proper controls and measures are hard to arrange. Worse yet, the kinds of paraphrase that inevitably occur in long discourses will span many sentences and imply recoding processes so complex that we hardly know how to talk about them. But it is nonetheless important that we try to understand what we can of the natural language codes, even if our interest is primarily in rote learning and memory. Suppose, as we do, that the more arbitrary and idiosyncratic ciphers of the rote learning experiments are devices to mold unrelated materials into forms suitable for storage within the framework of the natural language code. If so, then our understanding of the rote learning ciphers will advance more surely as we know more about the natural bases from which they derive and to which they must, presumably, be anchored.

REFERENCES

Bartlett, F. C. *Remembering*. Cambridge: Cambridge University Press, 1932.

Bower, G. H. Organizational factors in memory. *Cognitive Psychology*, 1970, 1, 18-46.

Broadbent, D. E., & Gregory, M. Accuracy of recognition for speech presented to the right and left ears. *Quarterly Journal of Experimental Psychology*, 1964, 16, 359-360.

Bryden, M. P. Ear preference in auditory perception. *Journal of Experimental Psychology*, 1963, 65, 103-105.

Chomsky, N. *Aspects of the theory of syntax*. Cambridge, Mass.: M.I.T. Press, 1965.

Chomsky, N., & Halle, M. *The sound pattern of English*. New York: Harper, 1968.

Conrad, R. Speech and reading. In J. F. Kavanagh & I. G. Mattingly (Eds.), *Language by ear and by eye*. Cambridge, Mass.: M.I.T. Press, 1972.

Cooper, F. S. Describing the speech process in motor command terms. *Journal of the Acoustical Society of America*, 1966, 39, 1221 (Abstract). (Text: In *Status report on speech research S/R-5/6*. New York: Haskins Laboratories, 1966.)

Crowder, R. G. The sound of vowels and consonants in immediate memory. *Journal of Verbal Learning and Verbal Behavior*, 1971, 10, 587-596.

Crowder, R. G. & Morton, J. Precategorical acoustic storage (PAS). *Perception & Psychophysics*, 1969, 5, 365-373.

Darwin, C. J. Auditory perception and cerebral dominance. Unpublished doctoral dissertation, University of Cambridge, 1969.

Darwin, C. J. Ear differences in the recall of fricatives and vowels. *Quarterly Journal of Experimental Psychology,* 1971, **23**, 46-62.

Darwin, C. J. Dichotic backward masking of complex sounds. *Quarterly Journal of Experimental Psychology* (in press).

Dorman, M. Auditory evoked potential correlates of speech perception. Unpublished doctoral dissertation, University of Connecticut, 1971.

Eimas, P. D. The relation between identification and discrimination along speech and nonspeech continua. *Language and Speech,* 1963, **3**, 206-217.

Eimas, P. D., Siqueland, E. R., Jusczyk, P., & Vigorito, J. Speech perception in infants. *Science,* 1971, **171**, 303-306.

Fry, D. B., Abramson, A. S., Eimas, P. D., & Liberman, A. M. The identification and discrimination of synthetic vowels. *Language and Speech,* 1962, **5**, 171-189.

Fujisaki, H., & Kawashima, T. On the modes and mechanisms of speech perception. In *Annual Report No. 1.* Tokyo: University of Tokyo, Division of Electrical Engineering, Engineering Research Institute, 1969.

Haggard, M. P. Theoretical issues in speech perception. In *Speech synthesis and perception 4.* Cambridge: University of Cambridge Psychological Laboratory, 1970.

Haggard, M. P. Encoding and the REA for speech signals. *Quarterly Journal of Experimental Psychology,* 1971, **23**, 34-45. (a)

Haggard, M. P. New demonstrations of categorical perception. In *Speech synthesis and perception 5.* Cambridge: University of Cambridge Psychological Laboratory, 1971. (b)

Haggard, M. P., Ambler, S., & Callow, M. Pitch as a voicing cue. *Journal of the Acoustical Society of America,* 1969, **47**, 613-617.

Haggard, M. P., & Parkinson, A. M. Stimulus and task factors as determinants of ear advantages. *Quarterly Journal of Experimental Psychology,* 1971, **23**, 168-177.

Halwes, T. Effects of dichotic fusion on the perception of speech. Unpublished doctoral dissertation, University of Minnesota, 1969. (Reproduced as *Supplement to status report of speech research.* New York: Haskins Laboratories, 1969.)

Kimura, D. Cerebral dominance and perception of verbal stimuli. *Canadian Journal of Psychology,* 1961, **15**, 166-171.

Kimura, D. Left-right differences in the perception of melodies. *Quarterly Journal of Experimental Psychology,* 1964, **16**, 355-358.

Kimura, D. Functional asymmetry of the brain in dichotic listening. *Cortex,* 1967, **3**, 163-178.

Kirstein, E. Temporal factors in the perception of dichotically presented stop consonants and vowels. Unpublished doctoral dissertation, University of Connecticut, 1971. (Reproduced in *Status report on speech research S/R-24.* New Haven: Haskins Laboratories, 1971.)

Kirstein, E., & Shankweiler, D. P. Selective listening for dichotically presented consonants and vowels. Paper presented at the meeting of the Eastern Psychological Association, Philadelphia, April, 1969. (Text: In *Status report on speech research SR-17/18.* New York: Haskins Laboratories, 1969.)

Liberman, A. M. The grammars of speech and language. *Cognitive Psychology,* 1970, **1**, 301-323.

Liberman, A. M., Cooper, F. S., Shankweiler, D. P., & Studdert-Kennedy, M. Perception of the speech code. *Psychological Review,* 1967, **74**, 431-461.

Lieberman, P. Primate vocalizations and human linguistic ability. *Journal of the Acoustical Society of America,* 1968, **44**, 1574-1584.

Lieberman, P. On the speech of Neanderthal man. *Linguistic Inquiry,* 1971, **2**, 203-222.

Lieberman, P., Crelin, E. S., & Klatt, D. H. Phonetic ability and related anatomy of the newborn and adult human, Neanderthal man, and the chimpanzee. *American Anthropologist* (in press).

Lieberman, P., Klatt, D. H., & Wilson, W. A. Vocal tract limitations on the vowel repertoires of rhesus monkeys and other nonhuman primates. *Science,* 1969, **164**, 1185-1187.

Lindblom, B. Spectrographic study of vowel reduction. *Journal of the Acoustical Society of America,* 1963, **35**, 1773-1781.

Lisker, L., & Abramson, A. S. Some effects of context on voice onset time in English stops. *Language and Speech*, 1967, 10, 1-28.

Mandler, G. Organization and memory. In K. W. Spence & J. T. Spence (Eds.), *The psychology of learning and motivation*, Vol. 1. New York: Academic Press, 1967.

Manning, A. *An introduction to animal behavior.* Reading, Mass.: Addison-Wesley, 1969.

Mattingly, I. G. Speech cues and sign stimuli. *American Scientist*, 1972, 60, 327-337.

Mattingly, I. G., & Liberman, A. M. The speech code and the physiology of language. In K. N. Leibovic (Ed.), *Information processing in the nervous system*. New York: Springer Verlag, 1969.

Mattingly, I. G., Liberman, A. M., Syrdal, A. K., & Halwes, T. Discrimination in speech and nonspeech modes. *Cognitive Psychology*, 1971, 2, 131-157.

Miller, G. A. The magical number seven, plus or minus two: Some limits on our capacity for processing information. *Psychological Review*, 1956, 63, 81-97.

Montague, W. E., Adams, J. A., & Kiess, H. O. Forgetting and natural language mediation. *Journal of Experimental Psychology*, 1966, 72, 829-833.

Öhman, S. E. G. Coarticulation in VCV utterances: Spectrographic measurements. *Journal of the Acoustical Society of America*, 1966, 39, 151-168.

Paivio, A. Mental imagery in associative learning and memory. *Psychological Review*, 1969, 76, 241-263.

Pisoni, D. On the nature of categorical perception of speech sounds. Unpublished doctoral dissertation, University of Michigan, 1971.

Porter, R. J. Effects of a delayed channel on the perception of dichotically presented speech and nonspeech sounds. Unpublished doctoral dissertation, University of Connecticut, 1971.

Porter, R., Shankweiler, D. P., & Liberman, A. M. Differential effects of binaural time differences in perception of stop consonants and vowels. Paper presented at meeting of the American Psychological Association, Washington, D.C., September, 1969.

Prytulak, L. S. Natural language mediation. *Cognitive Psychology*, 1971, 2, 1-56.

Savin, H. What the child knows about speech when he starts learning to read. In J. F. Kavanagh & I. G. Mattingly (Eds.), *Language by ear and by eye*. Cambridge, Mass.: M.I.T. Press, 1972.

Shankweiler, D., & Studdert-Kennedy, M. Identification of consonants and vowels presented to left and right ears. *Quarterly Journal of Experimental Psychology*, 1967, 19, 59-63.

Spellacy, F., & Blumstein, S. The influence of language set on ear preference in phoneme recognition. *Cortex*, 1970, 6, 430-439.

Stevens, K. N., Liberman, A. M., Öhman, S. E. G., & Studdert-Kennedy, M. Cross language study of vowel preception. *Language and Speech*, 1969, 12, 1-23.

Studdert-Kennedy, M. The perception of speech. In T. A. Sebeok (Ed.), *Current trends in linguistics*. The Hague: Mouton, (in press).

Studdert-Kennedy, M., Liberman, A. M., Harris, K. S., & Cooper, F. S. Motor theory of speech perception: A reply to Lane's critical review. *Psychological Review*, 1970, 77, 234-249.

Studdert-Kennedy, M., & Shankweiler, D. Hemispheric specialization for speech perception. *Journal of the Acoustical Society of America*, 1970, 48, 579-594.

Studdert-Kennedy, M., Shankweiler, D., & Shulman, S. Opposed effects of a delayed channel on perception of dichotically and monotically presented CV syllables. *Journal of the Acoustical Society of America*, 1970, 48, 599-602.

Tinbergen, N. *The study of instinct.* Oxford: Clarendon Press, 1951.

Tulving, E., & Madigan, S. A. Memory and verbal learning. *Annual Review of Psychology*, 1970, 21, 437-484.

Vinegrad, M. A direct magnitude scaling method to investigate categorical versus continuous modes of speech perception. In *Status report on speech research SR-21/22*. New Haven: Haskins Laboratories, 1970.

Warren, R. M., Obusek, C. J., Farmer, R. M., & Warren, R. T. Auditory sequence: Confusions of patterns other than speech or music. *Science*, 1969, 164, 586-587.

14

ENGLISH VERBS OF MOTION:
A CASE STUDY IN SEMANTICS AI
LEXICAL MEMORY[1]

George A. Miller
The Rockefeller University
and
The Institute for Advanced Study

It is a psychological commonplace that we do not take experience neat, but select, categorize, label, and elaborate it before we store it away in memory. Language plays a dual role in this process of packaging experience. On the one hand, we use language to characterize our experience, and store the linguistically coded version along with whatever iconic storage we can muster for the raw experience itself. And, on the other hand, the symbols of language must themselves be stored in memory, presumably also in some coded form easily retrievable for later use in producing and interpreting speech.

These two ways in which language and memory interact seem at first glance quite different, but as one probes more deeply into the working of the human memory, the differences tend to become obscured. It is usually not the precise words we happen to use in characterizing an experience that are stored and later recalled. Rather, it is some prelinguistic, conceptual representation that we seem to remember—something nonverbal, but with an affinity for verbal expression, couched in the dimensions of verbal thought. At the time of recall we are usually able to retrieve the information via various verbal clues and express it in many alternative linguistic forms. Thus we are led to consider the theoretical possibility that what we remember is not the particular words that we used to code our experience, but the concepts underlying those words. And that possibility, of course, has the effect of transforming the first interaction of language and memory into an application of the second.

[1] The preparation of this manuscript was supported in part by a grant from the Department of Defense, Advanced Research Projects Agency (DAHC 15) to The Rockefeller University and by a grant from the Sloan Foundation to The Institute for Advanced Study. Carol Wilkinson collected the sorting data given in Tables 2 and 4.

If this line of argument is valid, then the organization of long-term lexical memory poses a central problem for any psychologist interested in how linguistic coding can contribute to the storage and retrieval of information in human memory. As a first step, therefore, we should turn to the lexicographers, linguists, semanticists, and philosophers who study such matters and ask them what the underlying dimensions of the lexicon are. Indeed, there is much in their writings that psychologists should ponder, and most of the dimensions to be illustrated here are borrowed from the linguistic and semantic literature. Our present effort, therefore, can be viewed as an attempt to build on foundations already laid for lexico-semantic analysis.

Serious discussions of meaning most often divide the problem into two parts, and two separate but related theories have been considered: the theory of reference, which deals with such concepts as reference, naming, truth, and extension, and the theory of meaning, which deals with such concepts as significance, intension, synonymity, and analyticity. The consequence of this distinction is that the meanings of most words are divided theoretically into two parts, one part having to do with the extralinguistic things and events (including speech events) to which a word can refer, and the other being the semantic relations of the word to other words and phrases in the language.

A language user must know both parts of a word's meaning, of course. For example, in order to use *red* correctly he must know both that *red* refers to a perceptual aspect common to fresh blood and ripe tomatoes, and also that *red* is one of a related set of color names that can function grammatically as nouns or adjectives. However, not all words have referents, and those that do can often be used correctly by speakers who have never perceived the referents: One can talk about Alaska without having been there, and even those who have been to the equator have perceived nothing tangible for *equator* to refer to. Otherwise said, a blind man could understand the sense of *red* even though he might never have himself perceived the particular visual quality that the word refers to. Philosophers have disagreed as to whether or not the theory of meaning could be reduced to the theory of reference, but for our present purposes we shall accept the distinction as valid and useful psychologically.

The organization of long-term lexical memory must reflect both the senses and the referents of the words we use, but we shall confine ourselves here to the senses of words, especially insofar as those senses can be captured in verbal paraphrases and definitions, and leave aside questions of reference (and imagery of referents) for future consideration. The characterization of lexical memory is a large and difficult subject, and one could scarcely hope to deal with every aspect of it simultaneously. A decision to concentrate first on sense rather than reference still leaves several fascinating psychological questions for us to study. Indeed, many of the most important psychological properties of language seem to be more closely related to similarities of sense than to similarities of reference. That is to say, an intelligent but nonverbal organism might learn to recognize referential similarities, yet without any knowledge of the semantic relations among different words such an organism would be unlikely to form the abstractions, generalizations, and predications that are so natural and obvious to a language user. An analysis of intraverbal relations may not provide a sufficient account of lexical memory, but it must constitute a part of any such account.

There are, of course, many precedents for the strategy we shall follow. If one wished to be critical of the psychological value of this previous work, one might look less at its frequent neglect of reference and truth and more at the fact that most such analyses have not been self-consciously psychological, and that they have usually been more illustrative than comprehensive.

A bridge from the structure inherent in the lexicon to the psychological processes inherent in verbal thought must span a larger gap than one might at first suppose. A description of what a person knows tells us very little about the uses he can or will make of that knowledge. It would be unfair, therefore, to fault a linguist or semanticist for not being a psychologist; the most we might ask is that he be willing to accept responsibility for the psychological implications of his semantic analyses. If, for example, he analyzes the meanings of words into components (or "markers"), he should tell us whether, along with Jakobson (1936), Chomsky (1965), Katz (1966), and some others, he regards these components as mental concepts or not, and, if not, just what psychological status should be assigned to them: habits, unconscious inferences, associations, conditioned reflexes, or whatever. Because the linguistic value of componential analysis in particular languages may seem to be undiminished by leaving this psychological question unanswered, many a linguist has made a virtue of inscrutability, leaving it to psychologists to interpret his results however they can.

With respect to comprehensiveness, surely something more might be done to integrate the brilliant insights so far achieved and to apply them to a representative sample of the lexicon. One of the central problems of linguistic semantics is taxonomic, but it is difficult to evaluate a taxomic principle of classification without applying it to a comprehensive sample of the objects one is trying to systematize. It would take several lifetimes, of course, to systematize the whole lexicon, so it is not surprising that most analyses have concentrated on a small number of examples carefully chosen to support some particular insight of the moment.

In the present work we have attempted to steer a middle course. We have chosen a group of 217 related words that seem to illustrate several conceptual dimensions and have tried to explore the hypothesis that these dimensions comprise a harmonious and organic system of concepts and conceptual relations. In this way we hope to obtain a glimpse of what a truly comprehensive analysis could yield without being overwhelmed by the enormous task of exploring every nook and cranny of the subjective lexicon.

In selecting a particular suburb of the lexicon for this exploration we were guided by several considerations. The first question was whether or not to respect syntactic categories. A single morpheme can play various syntactic roles in different words—*critic, critique, criticise, critical, critically,* for example—and there is obviously some common semantic thread running through them that one might wish to pursue without regard to morphology or syntax. However, we decided to respect syntactic categories for two reasons: (*a*) the analysis seemed more complicated if a context for comparison could not be syntactically well defined, and (b) there is psychological evidence from word-association studies that syntactic categories do play an important role in the organization of lexical memory (Fillenbaum & Jones, 1965).

Having decided to stay within a particular syntactic category, therefore, the next question was which category to select. There is some reason to think that prepositions are a veritable treasure chest of concepts purified by centuries of use, but this "minor" syntactic category seemed too limited and specialized for our purposes. Nouns and verbs carry the major burden of communication in our language, so the choice had to be made between them. Of these two, verbs are by all odds the more challenging. A considerable amount of work has already been done with nouns—kin terms being the best studied example (Goodenough, 1956; Lounsbury, 1956; Wallace & Atkins, 1962; Hammel, 1965)—and various principles of nominal classification are already known. Verbs, on the other hand, seem to be the real motor behind the critically important process of predication, and several theoretical discussions of the syntactic role of the verb have generated hypotheses worthy of more extensive exploration. Therefore, we chose verbs because the rewards, as well as the risks, seemed higher.

Finally, having settled on verbs, the scope was limited further to verbs of motion. Physical motion is an important concept, and one that we have generalized freely into nonphysical contexts, yet not so vague that its lexical boundaries are indeterminate. (The criteria for inclusion in the set are discussed below.) The choice of a particular subcategory of verbs, motion in this case, was the critical step in defining the study, since there is always a danger of choosing some set of verbs that does not comprise a true semantic field. One might, for example, define a set of verbs that describe things one can do in an office, for example, *work, sit, read, talk, pace, smoke, breathe, sleep, eat, think, draw.* Although the criterion for inclusion in the set might be clear, such a group of words would not comprise a coherent semantic domain and their analysis could tell us little about the organization of lexical memory. One might as well define a class of verbs spelled with six letters. There seems to be no good way (other than intuition) to avoid heterogeneous collections a priori, and the only evidence that motion verbs comprise a more homogeneous domain than office verbs must derive from the intrinsic credibility of the semantic analysis itself.

The strategy, therefore, was to use motion verbs as a case study in semantic analysis, and to attempt to find a set of semantic components inherent in their meanings that could eventually be refined by further linguistic analysis and whose psychological validity as concepts could be tested by experimentation. The hope is that the semantic components revealed by such analysis might eventually be shown to include some of the primitive concepts we use to encode experience generally.

CRITERION FOR MOTION VERBS

Nothing is more common in our environment than the movement of people and things; in order to characterize that environment, a language must have a rich supply of words for indicating how an object that is at place P_1 at time T_1 comes to be at place P_2 at some subsequent time T_2. The words that serve this purpose most directly are the verbs of motion.

In order to suggest the resources of the English language for describing changes of location, we constructed an extensive list of motion verbs. The criterion for inclusion was a subjective judgment that the verb, in at least one of its senses, describes motion from one place to another.

A strong test is whether the verb can take a measure phrase that describes the extent of the motion, as will such verbs as *He walked five miles,* and *He carried the package fifty feet.* A permissive criterion was used, so that *The stain was absorbed an inch into the wood,* and *They were admitted six feet into the room* were judged acceptable even though the judgment could be questioned. The intent was to include as wide a variety of motion verbs as possible.

The test based on a measure phrase, even when liberally interpreted, still excludes several verbs that seem intuitively to describe motion from one place to another. For example, *arrives, assembles, attends, collects, departs, embarks, empties, escapes, gathers, interposes, lands, lays, leaves, places, puts, replaces, scatters, sets, starts, stops, substitutes, trips, tucks, vacates,* and *visits* do not readily accept measure phrases, yet they do seem to describe motions from one place to another. That is to say, they will (in some of their senses) accept phrases involving various constructions based on *here* and *there*: *He arrived here from there* (or *from elsewhere*), *They assembled here from there, He collected them here from there, He departed from here to there,* where various substitutions for *here* and *there* will convert these into plausible sentences. On the basis of this weaker criterion, and in order to include as many different examples as possible, therefore, these verbs are also included as verbs of motion.

The list of motion verbs that passed one or the other (or both) of these criteria is given alphabetically in Table 1.

There are, of course, many other English verbs that describe movement. For example, there are all the various contact verbs that describe ways of touching something: *touches, contacts, meets, hits, strikes, slaps, pounds, thumps, bumps, bangs, collides, pummels, jabs, scrapes, scratches.* These are excluded from Table 1 because they do not seem to satisfy the criterion of change of location. Similarly, there are verbs describing bodily movements: *shrugs, swallows, breathes, coughs, sits, stands, gestures, smiles, yawns,* and so on, and many others that are also excluded by this criterion. Indeed, motion or movement is a component of many verb meanings, but there are also many exceptions, such as psychological verbs like *admires, thinks, fears, likes, sees, hears, remembers, feels;* or the performative verbs that signal a speaker's intentions like *promises, warns, appoints, criticises, informs, assures, nominates, proposes;* or the ubiquitous "little" verbs like *is, has, can, may, will, becomes;* and many others. Thus, it is not possible in English to define the syntactic category of verbs in terms of a semantic component of movement or action, since English has both stative verbs (which describe states and are constrained in taking the progressive form) and verbs of action (which describe actions, processes, or events and occur freely in the progressive form). Verbs of motion comprise a limited subset of the verbs of action, and are characterized by the fact that they describe something traveling from one place to another.

TABLE 1

Verbs of Motion

absorbs	empties	lengthens	rides	substitutes
accompanies	enters	lifts	rises	swims
admits	escapes	limps	rolls	swings
advances	exits	lowers	rotates	swoops
ambles	expands	lumbers	rows	takes
approaches	extends	marches	runs	throws
arrives	falls	meanders	sails	thrusts
ascends	fills	minces	saunters	tilts
assembles	flaps	motors	scatters	tiptoes
attends	flees	mounts	scrambles	toddles
attracts	flexes	moves	scurries	tosses
bears	flies	nears	sends	totters
bounces	flings	nods	separates	tours
bounds	flips	opens	sets	tows
brings	floats	oscillates	shakes	travels
broadens	follows	overruns	shifts	traverses
canters	gallops	paces	shoves	treads
carries	gathers	parallels	shrinks	trips
charges	goes	passes	shuts	trots
clambers	grows	penetrates	sinks	trundles
climbs	halts	pivots	skates	tucks
closes	hands	places	skips	tumbles
collects	hikes	plunges	slides	turns
comes	hops	pounces	slinks	twirls
continues	hurls	precedes	slips	twists
crawls	hurries	proceeds	slithers	undulates
creeps	immigrates	progresses	soars	vacates
crosses	inches	projects	speeds	vaults
dances	injects	propels	spins	visits
deepens	inserts	pulls	spirals	voyages
departs	interposes	pursues	spreads	wades
depresses	invades	pushes	springs	walks
descends	jerks	puts	sprints	wanders
diffuses	jogs	races	squirms	waves
dives	journeys	raises	staggers	weaves
drags	jumps	rambles	starts	whirls
drifts	kicks	recedes	steps	widens
drives	lands	releases	stops	wings
drops	launches	removes	straggles	withdraws
ejects	lays	replaces	strays	wobbles
elevates	leads	retreats	strides	worms
embarks	leaps	returns	strolls	wriggles
emigrates	leaves	revolves	stumbles	zigzags
emits				zooms

The list in Table 1 is incomplete (and some of the verbs included may not be motion verbs at all), but at least it serves to illustrate the diversity of motion verbs in English. Moreover, the diversity is not haphazard. Even a hasty scan through the list leaves one with an impression that these verbs comprise a complex, interrelated system of concepts. For example, we find pairs of verbs like *opens* and *shuts,* which have the same antonymous relation as their corresponding adjectival forms; we find such pairs as *raises* and *lowers, comes* and *goes,* and *advances* and *retreats,* which describe motions in opposite directions; we find *starts* and *stops,* which contrast the beginning and the finishing of motion; we find *races* and *crawls,* which differ in the velocity of motion; we find *walks* and *rides,* which differ in the instrumentality that is implied; we find *walks-swims-flies,* which contrast with respect to the medium through which the motion occurs; we find *rises* and *raises,* which differ with respect to whether the subject or the object of the verb is moved. Such pairs suggest that the motion verbs are not just an unrelated set of names for unrelated kinds of motion, but that there are underlying dimensions along which contrasts are drawn. The challenge is to identify these dimensional components of the verbs we use to describe motion and to find some way to bring order into them.

POSITIONAL CHANGE: REFLEXIVE AND OBJECTIVE MOTION

Our choice of "motion" to characterize these verbs suggests that *moves* might be taken as the generic concept in the system. We shall begin, therefore, by examining the definition of *moves.* For our present purposes, *moves* means that something changes position. Thus, we assume that *changes* is an even more generic concept than *moves,* and that in this case the change is specified as being one in spatial location.

How should we phrase a definition of *moves?* The form we choose is important, because we shall rely on similarities among definitions as our primary indicators of similarities in meaning. Since the term "definition" is not only rather ambiguous, but has been pre-empted for various technical uses by different authors, we must be as explicit as possible about what we shall count as a definition in our analysis. For our present purposes, therefore, we shall regard as a definition any paraphrase that can be used to replace the word we are defining in at least some of its uses. (We shall sharpen this idea subsequently.)

Following this line, therefore, we can define *moves* by the substitutable phrase *changes position,* or *changes location.* For example, in the sentence *Arthur moved* we can replace the verb by the definition and obtain *Arthur changed position.* This definition is not wholly satisfactory, however, because it does not give a suitable definition for transitive uses of *moves: Arthur moved the chair* cannot be paraphrased grammatically as *Arthur changed position the chair.* A better definition of *moves,* therefore, is given by the phrase *changes the position or location of,* in which case *Arthur moved the chair* would become *Arthur changed the position or location of the chair.*

But now the intransitive use, *Arthur moved,* would become *Arthur changed the position or location of,* which is hardly satisfactory, either. Although this may seem a minor difficulty, it brings us face to face with an important feature of many motion verbs. In the intransitive use, *Arthur moved,* it is Arthur's movement that is referred to; in the transitive use, *Arthur moved the chair,* it is the chair's movement that is referred to. The two uses are obviously similar in meaning and both are quite different from the senses of *moves* in *He moved us to tears* or *He moved to adjourn;*

the motion verb *shifts*, for example, shares the first two senses of moves, but not the latter two. It seems reasonable, therefore, to look for a way to paraphrase both the transitive and intransitive uses as similarly as possible.

The task is to find a phrase that can be substituted for *moves (X)*, where *X* is the direct object of the verb and the parentheses indicate that *X* can be omitted for intransitive uses. The simplest solution is to adopt the paraphrase, *changes the position or location of X*, with the understanding that *X* is either the direct object or, if no object noun is given, *X* is a reflexive pronoun (in the example above, *himself*).

This definition solves the immediate problem, but the point to note is that motion verbs can describe the movement of either the subject noun or the object noun. We will call the case in which the subject noun moves itself "reflexive," and the case in which it is the object noun that moves "objective." As we shall see, this reflexive-objective distinction is quite useful for categorizing motion verbs.

THE CAUSATIVE COMPONENT AND THE AGENTIVE ROLE

Our definition of *moves* (or *shifts*) is still incomplete, however, because it ignores a causative (or "ergative") component (Lakoff, 1965; Lyons, 1968, p. 350 ff). Native speakers of English will understand the sentence *Arthur moved (shifted) the chair* to mean *He caused a change in the position or location of the chair*. That is to say, the transitive use of *moves* must be defined in terms of at least two generic concepts, *changes* and *causes*. Each of these components should be paraphrased in such a way that they can be combined to define *moves* as a transitive verb. This requirement places special restrictions on the paraphrases we can use; we shall, therefore, refer to this special kind of paraphrase as "componential paraphrase."

Whether or not the intransitive use of *moves* also contains a causative component, however, is less clear. According to the dual-purpose definition suggested above, the sentence *Arthur moved* would have to be paraphrased by *Arthur caused a change in the position or location of himself* or, more colloquially, *Arthur caused his position or location to change*. But is causation really needed here? Surely Arthur can move without causing himself to move. That is to say, there seem to be two possible interpretations of *Arthur moved*, one being that Arthur moved himself (where the cause is inherently expressed), the other being that something else moved Arthur (where a cause is merely assumed).

A brief digression on role structure may be helpful at this point, since semantic relations are most conveniently described in terms of roles (Fillmore, 1968; Langendoen, 1970). The individual who carries out the action of the verb plays the role of agent; the person or thing directly affected plays the role of patient; any object that the agent uses plays the role of instrument. A variety of other roles are needed to characterize various verbs, but these three are probably the most general. For example, in the sentence *John carried the apples to school in a bag*, the grammatical subject, *John*, is the semantic agent; the direct object, *apples*, is the patient; *bag* is the instrument; and a locative phrase, *to school*, plays a role that might be called goal. Note that when the same sentence is transformed, as in *The apples were carried to school in a bag by John,* the grammatical function of these nouns may change, but their semantic roles remain unchanged. Note also that some of the roles can be omitted: *John carried the apples to school, John carried the apples in a bag, John carried the apples, The apples were carried to school in a bag, The apples were carried in a bag, The apples were carried to school, The apples were carried.*

The predicate phrase in the sentence *John carried the apples* could be replaced by some such paraphrases as *caused the apples to go with him* or *made the apples change location with him,* which indicates that the causative component is involved in the meaning of *carries.* When the agent is deleted, as in *The apples were carried,* the causative component seems to have vanished. The apples did not spontaneously cause their own change of location. The causative component seems intimately linked to the agentive role. In this case, however, the causative component of the verb *carries* has not vanished: The passive sentence with the agent deleted is understood to mean *The apples were carried by someone,* where an indefinite someone is the agent.

But the difficulty goes even deeper. Consider the sentence, *John rotated the wheel.* Here it is clear that the agent caused the patient to move. But when the agent is deleted in the sentence, *The wheel rotated,* there is not even an understood agent to whom the cause can be attributed. Thus, *rotates* seems to have two different but closely related senses, 'one with the causative component and the other without it. (Alternatively, one might speculate that a causative component expresses a relation between an action by the agent and an action by the patient, so that if one of these terms is missing, the relation is vacuous, although the causative component of the verb persists unchanged; after all, wheels do not rotate without some cause, even though we may not know, or wish to say, what it was.)

If we return now to the intransitive use of *moves,* we see that it shares this ambiguity. It is not clear whether Arthur should be interpreted as the agent in *Arthur moved,* with the sense that Arthur moved himself, or as the patient, with the sense that something else (he floated downstream, perhaps) moved Arthur. It would seem that two definitions of *moves* are required, one having the causative component when the subject is the agent of the verb, the other omitting the causative component when the subject is not the agent. (Alternatively, one might assume a single definition of *moves,* and regard the causative relation as vacuous when the agentive term is missing.)

Although the theoretical issues involved here are clearly important, they tend to distract us from our main goal of sketching the broad outlines of this semantic domain. Hereafter, therefore, we shall, unless otherwise noted, adopt the arbitrary convention of interpreting only sentences with a human agent explicitly present as subject of the verb. Including examples of uses with the agent deleted merely complicates our larger task, so it seems justifiable, at least initially, to examine only the semantic relations among these verbs as they are used with human agents as their grammatical subjects.

Although this convention will enable us to avoid some of the problems implicit in the causative component, the direction our analysis of *moves* has taken has now led into other difficulties.

THE GENERIC CONCEPT

If, as we suggested, the verb *moves* is considered to be generic for the whole class of motion verbs, then all those verbs should contain all the semantic components that *moves* contains, plus additional components to specify various ways of moving. In particular, since our definition of *moves* (with a human agent) includes a causative component, all definitions based on *moves* would also include a causative component. If *moves* is the generic concept, therefore, all motion verbs would have to have a causative component, and this is clearly not the case.

For example, there are motion verbs like *admits* in which the causative component must be replaced by a permissive component. It would be wrong to interpret *He admitted the visitors* by any such paraphrase as *He caused the visitors to go in.* We require the permissive *allows* (or *lets*): *He allowed the visitors to go in.* Similarly, there is a sense of *releases* that can be paraphrased as *allows to go,* without the directional preposition.[2]

Or, again, there are motion verbs like *accompanies* in which the causative component is missing. *He accompanied the girl* means that they changed location together; it certainly does not mean that he caused the girl to change her location. Inasmuch as he moves with the girl, we might say that *accompanies* means that he *causes himself to change location with her,* but even this is too strong. He might simply have allowed himself to be carried along with her in some conveyance. Since either a causative or permissive situation might be inferred, we must conclude that *accompanies,* although transitive, is neutral with respect to causation.

If verbs like *admits* and *accompanies* (and many others) are to be defined in terms of *moves,* and if *moves* in turn is defined to mean *causes to change position or location,* we will be in serious trouble. *Moves* is too complex a concept with which to begin the analysis.

So we must look elsewhere. When one searches the list of motion verbs in Table 1 for instances that express change of location as simply as possible, unencumbered by any other semantic components, the intransitive verb *travels* seems to fit the description as well as any, and better than most. *He travels* means simply that he goes from one place to another; it leaves open the question of whether he causes or merely allows his location to change, and it says nothing about where or how far he goes, how long it takes, or what else happens to him. We shall, therefore, take *travels* as the generic concept underlying the motion verbs and define it to mean simply *changes location*, where the noncausative sense of *changes* is intended. Since it is not used transitively, the reflexive-objective distinction that is required for *moves* is not a problem for *travels.*

The difficulty with *travels,* however, is that, although it is beautifully abstract, it is not frequent in ordinary usage; paraphrases incorporating it often sound

---

[2] This example may be unconvincing because, as Philip N. Johnson-Laird has pointed out to me, the permissive component can be defined in terms of the causative component if we allow a negative component. Consider, for example, *He holds X,* where *holds* is intended in the sense of *prevents from going. Prevents,* in turn, means *causes not.* Thus, a paraphrase for *He holds X* would be *He causes X not to go.* Now, *releases* is an antonym of *holds,* so *He releases X* would be paraphrased as *He doesn't hold X,* or, more fully, as *He doesn't cause X not to go.* In short, the permissive *allows X* can be paraphrased by the causative *doesn't cause X not.*

suspiciously stilted. For example, beginning with *travels* as *changes location,* we might next define *moves (X)* as *causes X to travel; admits X* as *lets X travel in; accompanies* as *travels with; walks* as *travels on foot.* This is indeed the line we intend to take, but it is difficult to ignore the fact that *Arthur caused the chair to travel* is a strange paraphrase for *Arthur moved the chair.* It is not literally wrong, but it is certainly misleading; it suggests absurd imagery of Arthur sending the chair on a voyage to Europe, or similar irrelevant connotations based on the most frequent usage of *travels* in ordinary language.

The simple solution, of course, is to use *travels* in the definitions wherever its peripheral connotations are not misleading, and to replace it by its own definition, *changes position or location,* wherever it seems awkward or misleading.

Another solution, somewhat more complicated, is to invent a new symbol for the generic concept. Although the method of definition by paraphrase would seem to restrict the analysis to concepts for which words already exist in the language, it is possible to take certain liberties if we explain carefully what is intended. For example, we might wish to use the motion verbs *comes* and *goes* in our paraphrases. As in the case of *moves,* however, we find that *comes* and *goes* have other semantic components beyond the simple concept of positional change. When a speaker says *John came,* we understand him to mean that John traveled to location P and that the speaker himself was also at P; when he says *John went,* we understand him to mean that John traveled to P and that the speaker was not at P. That is to say, *comes* and *goes* have a deictic component; the traveling is toward or away from the speaker (Fillmore, 1966; Lyons, 1968, p. 275 ff). A similar deictic component characterizes *brings* and *takes.*

If we could ignore this deictic component, however, many of our paraphrases would be more acceptable if either *comes* or *goes* could be substituted for *travels.* So we can simply create a synthetic concept, *comes/goes,* to indicate a change of location without reference to the location of the speaker. Either *comes* or *goes* can be substituted for *comes/goes* in forming the paraphrase; if only one is acceptable, then we know that the verb being defined also has a deictic component.

We have now suggested two strategies for avoiding awkwardnesses associated with the generic verb *travels* as it is used in defining other motion verbs by paraphrase. Either we can substitute its own definition, *changes location,* or we can substitute *comes/goes,* with a choice of either *comes* or *goes* in the wording of the paraphrase. These strategies are, however, matters of detail. The generic concept, common to all motion verbs by virtue of the way our list was constructed, is the concept of positional change. *Travels, changes location,* and *comes/goes* are merely notational variants for this central concept.

We are now ready to use this generic concept in paraphrasing motion verbs. First, however, some general comments on method and theory seem appropriate at this point.

THE METHOD OF INCOMPLETE DEFINITIONS

Travels is most frequently used with a human noun as its subject, and it is ordinarily understood to mean something more than a change of location. It usually means that the person took a trip to visit some undisclosed places, probably at a considerable distance. Thus, in addition to the generic definition of *travels* as *changes location or position,* we have another sense of *travels* that is similar to *journeys, tours,* and *voyages.* Since the additional semantic components of these verbs have little generality for the rest of the lexicon, we shall not try here to improve on what can be found in any good dictionary. In this sense, of course, the definitions we are considering are incomplete, and deliberately so.

Our effort here is to put together verbs having similar but not necessarily identical meanings. Words can have similar meanings without being synonyms, and we need some way to characterize that shared part of their meanings on which our judgment of similarity depends. This feature of the present analysis is sufficiently important to justify giving it a name, so we shall speak of this procedure as the method of incomplete definitions. An incomplete definition is a substitutable phrase that has a more general meaning than the word it replaces. Otherwise said, the word defined implies the incomplete definition, but the incomplete definition does not imply the word defined. To use an example discussed by Gleitman and Gleitman (1970, p. 96), to be a garbage-man implies that you remove garbage, but to remove garbage does not imply that you are a garbage-man. Thus, *man who removes garbage* is an incomplete definition of *garbage-man,* incomplete in that the occupational aspect (at least) is missing.

Moreover, two words that imply the same incomplete definition can be said to be similar in meaning to that extent; they may actually be synonyms, but in most cases they will not. For example, to define a *dog* as a *warm-blooded animal* is to give an incomplete definition; a thing cannot be a dog without being a warm-blooded animal, but it can be a warm-blooded animal without being a dog. An elephant is also a warm-blooded animal, so to that extent *dog* and *elephant* are similar in meaning, although it is obvious that they are not synonyms. Similarly, to define *journeys* as *changes location* is to give an incomplete definition; you cannot journey without changing your location, but you can change your location without journeying. Since *travels* shares this incomplete definition, it is similar to *journeys.* Or, again, to define *attends* as *comes/goes to* is to give an incomplete definition; you cannot (in the intended sense of the verb) attend something without going to it, but you can go to something, such as the library, without attending it. Since *visits* shares this incomplete definition, to that extent *attends* and *visits* are similar in meaning. And so on.

If we were setting out to construct an ideal dictionary, we could not be content with incomplete definitions. Our present purposes are quite different, however. We are searching here for abstract concepts that characterize our judgments of similarity and difference among the meanings of a set of related words. In the beginning, at least, we need not push the analysis beyond the most general features, and we can leave open the possibility that there may be residual semantic components, some of which may be highly specific to individual words or small sets of words, which are not caught in our net. In this respect, an incomplete definition contrasts with the "minimal definition" of Bendix (1966), which is intended to be "a statement of semantic components that are sufficient to distinguish the meaning paradigmatically from the meanings of all other forms in the language" (p. 2).

How incomplete an incomplete definition can be and still be of any value is a matter of individual judgment, guided by the judge's appreciation of the semantic domain he is attempting to characterize. We want to make our definitions as complete as possible, of course, compatible with the requirement that the semantic components used are as general as possible, that is, that the semantic distinctions are also needed elsewhere in the lexicon, but the method leaves us free to stop short of complete definitions whenever it seems advisable.

We have spoken rather loosely of incomplete definitions being paraphrases that are "substitutable" for the words they define. Some comment on this terminology is necessary, since our procedure differs somewhat from the substitution technique that is widely used (cf. Nida, 1964) to determine synonyms having identical or overlapping distributions. If an incomplete definition really is incomplete, it will not be synonymous with the word it replaces, so such substitutions cannot leave meaning invariant. The paraphrase will ordinarily have a more general meaning than the word it substitutes for, and its substitution for the word it defines may even alter the truth value of simple declarative sentences; for example, *All elephants have trunks* may be true, but *All warm-blooded animals have trunks* is surely false.

In complex sentences, of course, replacing a verb by its paraphrase can lead to odd results even when the two are fully synonymous. Fodor (1970) has pointed out that a paraphrase having two verbs can exhibit degrees of syntactic freedom unavailable to a single verb. Suppose, for purposes of illustration, that we take *causes X to change location* to be fully synonymous with one of the senses of *moves X,* and consider the following example. In the sentence *He moved the chair by falling* it is reasonably clear that he fell against the chair and caused it to move. When we substitute the definition, however, we obtain *He caused the chair to change location by falling,* where it is no longer clear whether he fell or the chair fell. Since the instrumental adverbial phrase *by falling* can now attach to either of the verbs, the substitution has introduced ambiguity.

Difficulties can also arise in complex sentences when, conversely, we substitute a verb for its paraphrase, even when they are synonymous. For example, the sentence *I caused the chair to change its location and its color* contains our paraphrase definition for *moves X,* but if we substitute the verb for its paraphrase directly we obtain the questionable result *I moved the chair and its color,* where this operation on the surface structure of the sentence has inadvertently removed an implicit second occurrence of change in the underlying structure of the sentence.

This last example, therefore, should lead us to think of substitution as being made in some underlying structure, not the surface structure of the sentence. In this respect, substitution might appear to be a special case of either a "lexical rule" (Chomsky, 1965) or a "lexical transformation" (Lakoff, 1971; McCawley, 1968b), both of which are proposed descriptions of how particular lexical items might be inserted into the underlying structure of a sentence. There is an important difference, however. Lexical rules and transformations may introduce ambiguity in some contexts, but they should never reduce ambiguity.

Yet this is effectively what happens when we substitute a particular word for its incomplete definition—the meaning becomes more specific.

There is nothing mysterious here, of course. It is not difficult to avoid complex contexts in testing our proposed paraphrases. Our present goal is not to provide a complete theory of the semantic interpretation of sentences. A relatively weak notion of substitutability in simple declarative sentences having no negative or quantifiers is all that we require. Our claim is merely that the method of incomplete definitions can help us to gain an overview of a semantic field, and that for this purpose it is not necessary to have complete definitions substitutable without change of meaning in all conceivable contexts.

The method of incomplete definitions is most useful when one is dealing with many words together, as in the present case. With rare exceptions, it will not be the method of choice when one is examining some small set of closely related words in great depth and detail. The virtue of the method is that it enables us to converge gradually toward complete definitions of the words we are studying. We can even leave open the possibility that complete definitions are not feasible, at least within the scope of componential paraphrase and lacking all referential components of meaning. The guiding criterion, of course, must always be that the semantic components we identify leave us with groups of words that seem intuitively similar in meaning. As long as this criterion is met, the method enables us to keep our attention focused on the larger dimensions of the problem without becoming entangled in the numerous and often baffling details associated with particular words. In particular, the method of incomplete definitions suggests one way to formulate the important but all too fuzzy notion of "semantic domains"; a semantic domain is any set of words implied by an incomplete definition.

SOME RELATIONS TO INTERPRETIVE AND GENERATIVE SEMANTICS

Although our goal does not commit us to the development of a semantic theory adequate to explain how the meanings of sentences depend on the meanings of their constituent words and phrases, the relation of our approach to theories which do have this more ambitious goal is probably worthy of at least a brief discussion.

Any incomplete definition leaves an unresolved residuum that may or may not contain further semantic components, or referential information, or affective connotations, or whatever. In general, we have tried to terminate our definitions prior to the introduction of components having little systematic value for the rest of the lexicon. In that respect, the semantic components in an incomplete definition resemble the "semantic markers" of Katz and Fodor (1963), and the residuals resemble their "distinguishers." This resemblance, however, should not be mistaken for equivalence. As Bolinger (1965) has pointed out, the duality between semantic markers and distinguishers does not appear to correspond to any clear division in natural language, and it is a difficult distinction to maintain, because many distinguishers can be converted into strings of markers.

For our present purposes, the undefined residuum of meaning may or may not correspond to a distinguisher; our goals are more modest, so the question can be left open. Bolinger suggests that the marker-distinguisher duality might be usefully identified with a duality between "knowledge of one's language" and "knowledge of the world." Clearly, componential paraphrase cannot express referential relations, so if a word is understood in terms of one's knowledge of the world, such information must remain forever residual in our incomplete definitions. But whether the residuum contains anything more than referential information is a question for which we require no general answer.

Not only does the residuum of an incomplete definition differ from Katz and Fodor's distinguisher, but the semantic components we shall use also differ from their semantic markers. The general spirit of the enterprise is similar, but the details are different. In both cases, a mental concept inherent in a word, and shared with similar words, is what a marker or component attempts to capture, but Katz and Fodor represent the concept by an abstract mark (which for notational and mnemonic convenience is usually an English word, but need not be), whereas the method of incomplete definitions represents it by a particular word or phrase that can serve as a segment of an incomplete paraphrastic definition. Katz and Fodor were concerned to provide a lexical base for the operation of their projection rules, so that strings of semantic markers and projection rules together could generate a semantic interpretation or "reading" for a grammatical sentence. The method of incomplete definitions is concerned only with judgments of semantic similarity, and knowledge of grammar is presumed only insofar as it is needed for generating grammatically acceptable paraphrases from strings of paraphrased components. The more limited goals of the present work enable us to leave difficult questions of sentence interpretation unanswered.

If the present program were carried to its obvious conclusion, a sentence would be (incompletely) interpreted by another, much longer sentence that contained componential paraphrases of the words in the original sentence. The longer sentence would have a more general meaning and it would contain a relatively small vocabulary of standard phrases. Any projection rules for combining the paraphrased components into a grammatical sentence would, presumably, be a kind of transfer grammar based on the general grammar of English. Whether such a program is feasible and, if so, whether there would be any value in carrying it out, are debatable questions, so no claims are here advanced that even this modest version of a general semantic theory is intended. It is far easier to understand incomplete definitions than to define complete understanding.

We have, therefore, tried to steer a middle course between the interpretive semanticists who agree with Katz (1966) and Chomsky (1965) that a semantic theory should explain how the underlying syntactic structure of a sentence is interpreted, and those generative semanticists (Lakoff, 1971; McCawley, 1968a, b; Postal, 1970) who argue that the distinction between semantics and syntax is improperly conceived and both should be replaced by a single system of transformations that convert semantic representations of sentences into their surface forms. Insofar as the semantic components we have tried to paraphrase resemble semantic markers in interpretive theory, some kind of projection rules might be devised to combine our (incomplete) definitions into (incomplete) interpretations for whole sentences. On the other hand, the free combination of predicate-raising transformations and lexical insertion rules that have played a central role in arguments for a generative theory might help us to regularize the various paraphrase combinations that comprise our incomplete definitions.

For our present purposes, the important idea is that lexical entries are semantically decomposable, and that possibility is admitted in both theories. It makes little difference for our analysis whether, say, *causes X to change location* and *moves X* (in one of its senses) are to be interpreted identically by some (presyntactic) lexical component of the grammar, or whether *moves X* is a surface verb generated by a lexical insertion transformation in order to replace *causes (changes location) X*, which was derived in turn by a predicate-raising transformation applied to *causes (X changes location)*, which would otherwise generate the surface phrase *causes X to change location*.

In either case, however, it should be noted again that lexical insertion rules are not appropriate with incomplete definitions, because it is an important generalization that such insertions should not decrease ambiguity. Inasmuch as a word implies its incomplete definition, but its incomplete definition does not imply the word, the meanings of the two are different. Therefore, it will not generally be the case that a word can be inserted for its complete definition by the application of a lexical rule or transformation without making the meaning more specific. The insertion would have to add any residual aspects of the word that were lacking in the incomplete definition, and such additions would violate the convention that these rules must not decrease ambiguity.

Until the theoretical differences at issue between interpretive and generative semanticists have been clarified it will remain difficult to know which theory, if either, a psychologist should embrace. Meanwhile, and fortunately, it appears possible to make some headway with the relatively simpler problem of semantic similarities, to which we now return.

MOTION VERBS OF TRAVELING

Since *travels* is our generic concept, all motion verbs are, in that sense, verbs of traveling. There are, however, many other verbs that share with *travels*, in some of their senses, the simplicity of intransitivity. That is to say, they do not have a causative component, and the need for a distinction between reflexive and objective motion does not arise. We shall refer to these as the motion verbs of traveling, or, if that leads to any confusion, the simple motion verbs of traveling.

Two major types of semantic components can be recognized in the simple motion verbs of traveling. One component is related to whether the traveling is done on land, air, or water. The other is related to whether a conveyance is used. We shall refer to these as the medium component and the instrumental component, respectively.

The verbs *flies, sails, soars, spirals, swoops, wings, drifts, floats,* and *zooms* have senses that can be paraphrased as *travels through the air*, where *wings* seem to include an instrumental component as well. The verbs *drifts, floats, rows, sails, swims,* and *wades* have senses that can be paraphrased as *travels through the water,* where *rows* and *sails* have an additional instrumental component leading to the paraphrases *travels through the water by boat,* and *wades* would be *travels through the water on foot.* The great majority of the verbs that describe different ways of traveling, however, are concerned with travel on land.

Verbs admitting the paraphrase *travels on land* can be (very unequally) subdivided by an instrumental component that distinguishes travel by foot and travel by conveyance. *Drives, motors,* and *rides* have senses that can be replaced by the phrase *travels on land by vehicle,* but there are many more verbs that fall in the category of *travels on land by foot.* Indeed, when one looks closely at this latter class, it appears that the paraphrase *by foot* is too crude to suit all of them. *By foot* can replace *walks* and *runs* and the many variants thereof, but *clambers, crawls, creeps,* and *scrambles* have senses in which the instrumental components must be phrased *on hands and feet. Canters, gallops,* and *trots* are generally used to describe how horses travel, and in that sense should probably be paraphrased by *travels on land on all four feet.* And there are even motion verbs *slithers, squirms, worms,* and *wriggles* for which the appropriate phrasing of the instrumental component is unclear—perhaps, *travels on land on the belly?* And what kind of travel is *tumbles?*

Even with these verbs removed, however, the *travels-on-land-by-foot* paraphrase still characterizes more than thirty verbs that describe ways of walking and running. Apparently pedestrian pursuits are so important to us that we have grown a rich crop of verbs for talking about them. Finer distinctions among them would require additional semantic components. How, for example, should we distinguish *walks* from *runs*? The usual distinction is a rather clumsy one: When we run, both feet come off the ground at some point during the stride, whereas in walking one foot or the other is always on the ground. This difference is certainly precise enough, but it does not lend itself easily to componential paraphrase, and it probably has no applicability elsewhere in the lexicon. Rather than try to force it into the paraphrase form, therefore, we shall stop with the incomplete definition, *travels on land by foot,* and simply list the many verbs it seems to define: *ambles, charges, dances, gallops, hikes, jogs, limps, lumbers, marches, meanders, minces, paces, rambles, runs, saunters, skates, skips, slides, slinks, slips, sprints, staggers, steps, straggles, strays, strides, strolls, stumbles, tiptoes, toddles, totters, treads, trips, trots, walks, wanders, weaves, wobbles.* It is obvious that these verbs are not all synonyms, but so is it obvious that they are similar in meaning at least insofar as they share the same incomplete definition.

THE METHOD OF SORTING APPLIED TO TRAVELING VERBS

Since the method of incomplete definitions does not differentiate among this set of *travel-on-land-by-foot* verbs, ten of them were selected for study by the method of sorting (Miller, 1969). The ten were selected to conform roughly to a hierarchical structure:

goes	*travels* (away from speaker)
rides	*travels by conveyance*
swims	*travels through water*
walks	*travels on land by foot*
strolls	(walks in a leisurely manner)
tiptoes	(walks on the toes)
runs	*travels on land by foot*
sprints	(runs at top speed)
jogs	(runs at a slow, steady pace)
trots	(runs at a slow, steady pace; or quadripedal)

The indicated classification into walking and running verbs is not justified on the basis of our definitions, of course, but it seemed so obvious intuitively that we wanted to determine whether naive language users would share our opinion.

Ten sentences were formed by using these verbs in the frame: *John Verbs to school*. The sentences were typed individually on separate filing cards (3 × 5 inches). The deck of 10 cards was handed to a judge with instructions to sort them into piles "on the basis of similarity of meaning." No constraints were placed on the number of piles to be used and no suggestions were given as to the basis of classification other than the deliberately vague phrase about "similarity of meaning." The task was performed by 64 subjects, all young adults whose first language was American English.

When the task was completed, the piles were noted and a co-occurrence matrix for each subject was constructed in the following way. The matrix had 10 rows and 10 columns, one each for each of the 10 words. Thus, cell (i,j) of the matrix represented the pair of words i and j. If the subject put words i and j into the same pile, thus indicating that he judged them to be similar in meaning, a 1 was entered in that cell; otherwise a 0. A diagonal cell, (i,i), was 1 if word i was placed in a pile by itself; otherwise it was 0. The co-occurrence matrices for all the judges were then added together to obtain the data matrix shown in Table 2. (Since word i cannot go with word j unless word j also goes with word i, the matrix is necessarily symmetric, so only half of it need be given.)

The entries in Table 2 indicate the number of people who put each pair of words together as being similar in meaning. For example, out of the 64 subjects, 55 judged that *walks* and *strolls* were sufficiently similar to be placed together in the same pile. If one assumes that when two words are more similar, more people will put them together, then the entries in Table 2 can be regarded as measures of the semantic proximities among the ten verbs.

There are many ways to process such data matrices in order to reveal the structure underlying them, but this matrix is small and the pattern in the data is sufficiently clear that an elaborate analysis seems unnecessary. One can see immediately that the major clusters are *walks-strolls-tiptoes* and *runs-sprints-jogs-trots,* which a majority of the subjects respected. About 16 percent of the subjects, however, formed a *walks-strolls-tiptoes-runs-sprints-jogs-trots* cluster, which corresponds to our *travels-on-land-by-foot* paraphrase. Apparently some of the subjects also formed a *goes-rides* or a *goes-rides-swims* cluster, presumably on

TABLE 2

Co-occurrences Obtained When 64 Judges Sorted Traveling Verbs for Similarity of Meaning

	GOES	RIDES	SWIMS	WALKS	STROLLS	TIPTOES	RUNS	SPRINTS	JOGS	TROTS
GOES	53									
RIDES	6	50								
SWIMS	5	10	48							
WALKS	6	2	4	4						
STROLLS	5	1	3	55	4					
TIPTOES	2	.	2	21	25	32				
RUNS	1	1	5	11	10	10	2			
SPRINTS	2	1	4	12	10	12	53	6		
JOGS	2	2	5	12	10	11	44	38	2	
TROTS	4	3	7	13	10	12	38	35	54	1

the grounds that these were left over after the major clusters had been formed, but the diagonal entries indicate that most subjects resisted this solution and simply left these three verbs in isolation. The fact that a few judges put *swims* with the verbs of running suggests that there may be a an "effort," "exercise," or "sport" component in their subjective lexicons. In general, however, the data indicate that people will solve the sorting problem on the basis of semantic components, that is, that the concepts we are analyzing have some psychological validity.

The method of sorting, therefore, both confirms the hypothesis that seven of these verbs share a *travels-on-land-by-foot* paraphrase, and also confirms the intuitive impression that there are still other classificatory distinctions between verbs of walking and verbs of running, distinctions finer than those we have captured by the method of incomplete definitions.

MOTION VERBS OF VELOCITY

We should consider the possibility that the difference between *walks* and *runs* might be captured by a velocity component, that is, that we might paraphrase *walks* as *travels on land by foot* and paraphrase *runs* as *travels rapidly on land by foot*. The difficulties become apparent, however, in such sentences as *To jog is to run slowly*, which could hardly be paraphrased by *To jog is to travel rapidly on land by foot slowly*. Sometimes we must invoke the rule that explicit expressions can replace inherent components (e.g., in *walks on the bottom of the sea* the inherent *on land* component is explicitly replaced), but even this replacement rule will not suffice here. Velocity is a relative matter.

Although a velocity component does not distinguish satisfactorily between *walks* and *runs*, some simple motion verbs of traveling do seem to incorporate a component that can be captured by such definitions as *travels rapidly* or *travels slowly*:

Rapidly: *hurries, races, scurries, speeds, sprints*
Slowly: *ambles, crawls, creeps, inches, saunters*

In general, however, velocity does not seem to play a major role in differentiating among the motion verbs.

We turn next to more complicated motion verbs, where the causative component with all its complexities must be included in our analysis.

DIRECTIONAL MOTION VERBS

Travels says nothing about the direction in which the traveling occurs, but other motion verbs do. For example, *admits* implies something about traveling into, and *accompanies* implies something about traveling with, where the prepositions *into* and *with* indicate directions inherent in these verbs. Similarly, the deictic component of *comes* and *goes* is directional, indicating motion toward or away from the speaker. In short, many motion verbs can be defined by a generic verb (*travels, changes location,* or *comes/goes*) plus a preposition to indicate the direction of the motion (Gruber, 1965; Binnick, 1968).

Motion verbs, being verbs of action, are dynamic rather than static, so any prepositions inherent in them must be understood as indicating a directional rather than a locative role. The opposition of directional and locative is illustrated by the difference between *He pointed into the house* and *He pointed in the house*, where *into* would normally be understood to indicate the direction he pointed, and *in* would normally be understood to indicate his location when he was pointing. When we paraphrase *He enters* as *He comes/goes in*, therefore, the preposition *in*, which is usually locative, must be understood as directional, that is, *in* indicates the direction of his traveling not the location of his traveling. Hence, we refer to these as the directional motion verbs.

Many directional motion verbs involve a causative component, however, either in the reflexive or objective senses. This fact complicates the analysis sufficiently that we must consider two different paraphrase formulas, one for replacing directional motion verbs when the causative component is reflexive, and another when the causative component is objective. The general paradigm will be that sentences of the form *He Verb (X)* can be replaced by paraphrases generated according to formula.

When the motion verb is reflexive, we shall use the formula:

He comes/goes Prep (X)

For example, the transitive motion verb in the sentence *He accompanied the man* can be replaced by *came/went with;* the intransitive motion verb in the sentence *He exited* can be replaced by *came/went out;* and so on. This formula permits us to leave open the question of whether the causative component is present or not, for example, whether *He returned* means either *he caused himself to come/go back* or simply *came/went back* involuntarily.

When the motion verb is objective, however, it must be used transitively and we shall assume that the causative component is present. Thus, *He Verb X* must be paraphrased by a slightly more complex formula:

He made X come/go Prep (him)

For example, the motion verb in *He raised his hand* can be replaced by rewriting the sentence according to the formula *He made his hand come/go up,* and *He carried the package* can be written as *He made the package come/go with him.*

In Table 3 the results of applying these formulas to a sample of motion verbs are summarized. The first column gives the various prepositions that indicate the directional component, the second column gives the verb of reflexive motion corresponding to those prepositions, and the third column gives the causative verbs of objective motion. The symbol (+) following some entries in the third column indicates that the pronoun *him* must be included in the definition.

The entries in Table 3 should be self-explanatory. Other verbs could have been added to the table. The second column could provide places for *dives, escapes, immigrates, overruns, precedes, recedes, undulates, vacates.* The third column could accommodate *absorbs, bears, emits, extends, scatters, shakes, twirls, twists, whirls.* Apparently, motion verbs with inherent directionality are quite common in English.

The replacement rule—explicit specifications can replace inherent components—applies to some of these verbs, but not to all. For example, if no other direction is specified, it is assumed that *climbs* means to *travel upward;* it is perfectly possible, however, to *climb across,* or *climb into;* or even to *climb down,* in which case the inherent direction is overridden. This is not the case for *ascends,* however; *ascend across* is to *travel upward across, ascend into* is to *travel upward into,* and *ascend down* is flatly contradictory. Since there is no general way to distinguish verbs that allow replacement from those which do not, this would seem to be a raw fact that we have to learn about each particular verb.

To review: We have isolated a subset of motion verbs in English that have a directional component and have classified them according to appropriate directional prepositions. And we have further subdivided these directional motion verbs into subgroups according to whether the agent himself moves (or moves himself) or causes something else to move in the indicated direction. Componential paraphrases constructed according to the formula given above provide incomplete definitions for each of these verbs.

Further analysis (cf. Gruber, 1965) will undoubtedly necessitate revisions of this scheme, but it seems to provide a first-order classification for an important subset of the motion verbs.

THE METHOD OF SORTING APPLIED TO DIRECTIONAL MOTION VERBS

Directional motion verbs comprise a sufficiently large subclass of motion verbs that it seemed desirable to check our analysis against the judgments of others.

TABLE 3

Classification of Directional Motion Verbs

Directional Preposition	Reflexive Motion: *He came/went Prep (X)*	Objective Motion: *He made X come/go Prep (him)*
to	He ATTENDED the meetings He VISITED the meetings	
toward	He APPROACHED the door	He ATTRACTED many listeners (+)
together		He ASSEMBLED the pieces He COLLECTED the pieces He GATHERED the pieces
with	He ACCOMPANIED the man	He BROUGHT/TOOK the book (+) He CARRIED the book (+)
away	He LEFT He EMBARKED He EMIGRATED He FLED	He REMOVED the dish
away from	He LEFT her	He SHOVED her (+)
in	He ENTERED	He INSERTED the needle He INJECTED the serum
into	He ENTERED the room He INVADED the room	
through	He PENETRATED the barrier	
out	He EXITED He WITHDREW	He EJECTED the man He WITHDREW the needle
out of	He LEFT the room	
forward	He ADVANCED He PROGRESSED	He ADVANCED the pawn He DROVE the car
back	He RETURNED	He RETURNED the gift He REPLACED the book
backward	He RETREATED	
back and forth	He ZIGZAGGED He OSCILLATED	He WAVED the flag He FLEXED his arms
around	He TURNED the corner He PIVOTED He REVOLTED	He TURNED the crank He PIVOTED his hips He ROTATED the wheel He SPUN the wheel

(Continued)

TABLE 3 – Cont'd

Directional Preposition	Reflexive Motion: *He came/went Prep (X)*	Objective Motion: *He made X come/go Prep (him)*
ahead of	He LED the man	He FOLLOWED the man (+) He DROVE the sheep (+) He PUSHED the car (+)
behind	He FOLLOWED the man	He LED the man (+) He PULLED the car (+) He TOWED the car (+)
after	He PURSUED the man	
by	He PASSED the door	
on	He CONTINUED He PROCEEDED	
upward	He ROSE (through the water) He CLIMBED the hill He ASCENDED the stairs He MOUNTED the stairs	He RAISED the baton He ELEVATED the baton He LIFTED the baton
downward	He SANK (through the water) He DESCENDED the stairs He DROPPED He FELL	He LOWERED the baton He DEPRESSED the pedal He DROPPED the book He FELLED the tree
up and down		He FLAPPED his arms He BOUNCED the ball He NODDED his head
across	He CROSSED the street He TRAVERSED the mountains	
over	He LEAPED the fence He JUMPED the fence He VAULTED the fence	

Therefore, another sorting study was conducted, this time using a sample of 18 directional motion verbs. The procedure was identical to that used for sorting traveling verbs; sentence-frames were typed on the cards as follows:

He approached X.   *He assembled X.*
He visited X.   *He collected X.*
                            He gathered X.

He pivoted.   *He rotated X.*
He turned.   *He spun X.*

He descended X.   He dropped X.
He fell.   He lowered X.
He sank.

He exited.   He ejected X.
He left.   He withdrew X.

The judges were told that X stood for a noun phrase, and that they could substitute *something* for it if they wanted to think of it that way.

The results are summarized as a co-occurrence matrix in Table 4. The four directional components, *to, around, down, out,* appear quite clearly as clusters in Table 4. Moreover, within each cluster there is evidence for differentiation between reflexive and objective motion. The reflexive-objective differentiation is strongest for the *to* cluster: *approaches* and *visits* were clustered together with *assembles, collects,* and *gathers* by only one or two judges. Since the directional prepositions are really *toward* and *to* for *approaches* and *visits* (hence a certain reluctance to put them in the same pile), and *together* for the objective motion verbs *assembles-collects-gathers,* the tendency to keep them apart may reflect the directional component as well as the reflexive-objective (or causative) component. The results are cleaner, therefore, in the case of the *around* and *down* clusters. The *out* cluster is slightly flawed by some uncertainty about *ejects X,* which was left ungrouped by almost half the judges; some judges thought of it in terms of a pilot ejecting himself from the cockpit of his plane. Except for *ejects,* which may have been less familiar than the other verbs, the results generally support the analysis given in Table 3.

It should be noted, however, that the directional component is far more salient than the reflexive-objective (or causative) component, and might be said to dominate it hierarchically (Miller, 1969, p. 176). There are only 93 co-occurrences in Table 4 where verbs having different directional components were combined (e.g., *approaches* X and *exits* combine *to* and *out*), and 28 of these were for *ejects.* Of those 93, however, 72 respected the reflexive-objective dichotomy (e.g., *approaches* X and *exits* are both reflexive) and 19 violated it (e.g., *approaches* X is reflexive and *spins* X is objective). Thus, there is some evidence, independent of directionality, that judges were sensitive to the reflexive-objective component, but the overall picture one gets is that people group first on the basis of directionality, and only later on the basis of reflexive vs. objective.

The fact that the sorting studies did give evidence compatible with the componential analysis indicates that people do judge "similarity of meaning" in terms of shared semantic components, and strengthens our claim that such an analysis can reveal the underlying concepts people use to organize, store, and talk about their experience.

LOCATIVE MOTION VERBS

Related to the directional motion verbs in Table 3 is a small but important set of motion verbs that have an objective causative component, but the directional

TABLE 4

Co-occurrences Obtained When 52 Judges Sorted Directional Motion Verbs for Similarity of Meaning

	APPROACHES X	VISITS X	ASSEMBLES X	COLLECTS X	GATHERS X	PIVOTS	TURNS	ROTATES X	SPINS X	DESCENDS X	FALLS	SINKS	DROPS X	LOWERS X	EXITS	LEAVES	EJECTS X	WITHDRAWS X
APPROACHES X	23																	
VISITS X	26	23																
ASSEMBLES X	1	2	10															
COLLECTS X	1	1	38	1														
GATHERS X	1	2	40	50	.													
PIVOTS	.	.	.	.	.	2												
TURNS	.	.	.	.	.	48	2											
ROTATES X	.	.	2	1	1	29	29	3										
SPINS X	1	.	2	1	1	30	28	47	2									
DESCENDS X	2	2	.	.	.	.	.	.		8								
FALLS	.	.	.	.	.	.	.	.		28	8							
SINKS	.	.	.	.	.	.	.	.		31	41	7						
DROPS X	.	.	2	1	1	.	.	1	1	22	19	16	13					
LOWERS X	.	1	1	1	.	.	.	1	1	28	16	18	30	9				
EXITS	3	1	1	1	1	1	2	.	1	2	1	.	1	2	4			
LEAVES	2	2	.	.	.	1	2	.	.	1	.	.	.	.	42	1		
EJECTS X	1	1	2	1	1	.	.	2	2	2	2	1	8	5	4	8	24	
WITHDRAWS X	2	1	2	2	1	.	.	1	1	.	.	.	1	5	22	24	17	9

component is replaced by an obligatory, explicit, locative phrase. The best example is *puts. He put the book* means that *He caused the book to change location,* but the sentence is incomplete without some such locative phrase as *on the shelf, in his case, against the lamp, beside the typewriter.* As used, therefore, these verbs combine an inherent causative with an explicit locative component; direction is not an inherent component of these verbs. Other motion verbs having senses resembling *puts* in this respect are *sets, lays, tucks,* and *hands.* The verb *places* is normally used in the same way as *puts,* except for the connotation of more precise location; but *places* can be used without a locative phrase—*He placed the book very carefully.* (*Interposes* and *substitutes* seem to resemble *places* in this respect.) This whole group can be referred to as the locative motion verbs.

The appropriate paraphrase for the locative motion verbs would seem to be *makes X come/go (to a particular location),* where the parenthetical phrase can be omitted when the location is specified explicitly by a locative phrase. Insofar as our analysis captures their meaning, therefore, *puts X* and *moves X* both take the paraphrase *makes X come/go* or *makes X change location;* the difference between them lies in the fact that the role structure of *puts* makes a locative phrase obligatory, whereas the role structure of *moves* does not.

Binnick (1968) has suggested that *puts* might be considered to be the "locative causative" of *be.* That is to say, a possible paraphrase for *He put the book on the shelf* might be *He caused the book to be on the shelf.* One implication is that the generic concept *come/go* or *travel* might be paraphrased somehow in terms of *be in a (new) location,* rather than *changes location.* We will not pursue this suggestion here, since it leads outside the domain of motion verbs.

INCHOATIVE MOTION VERBS

We have seen that some verbs incorporate inherent prepositions. Others incorporate adjectives. Probably the clearest examples of the latter are the inchoative verbs. We should, therefore, consider adding an inchoative component to our analysis.

Inchoative verbs express the idea that something comes to be in a state describable by an adjective, as, for example, *The sky darkened* means that *The sky became darker* (Lakoff, 1965). Some motion verbs exhibit this property: *The door opened,* for example, means *The door became open.* Other examples from Table 1 that satisfy this inchoative formula include *closes, shuts, fills, empties, broadens, deepens, diffuses, lengthens, nears, separates, shrinks,* and *widens.* For these verbs, the inherent adjective is obvious. For such verbs as *expands, grows,* and *spreads,* an inchoative paraphrase might be *becomes larger,* although here the verb and adjective are different morphemes.

Unfortunately, this group of verbs seems semantically quite diverse. Since the method of incomplete definitions should yield groups of words that are semantically similar, the diversity indicates that this group of inchoative verbs requires further analysis.

Indeed, some of these verbs may not be motion verbs at all. *Broadens, deepens, diffuses, lengthens, shrinks, widens,* as well as *expands, grows, spreads,* might be said to describe changes of size, rather than changes of location. These verbs were included in Table 1 because (*a*) changes in the size of something seem to presuppose movement of its boundaries, and (*b*) they satisfied the strong test of taking a measure phrase, although this latter fact could mean simply that changes in size are as measurable as changes in location. The semantic properties of these verbs might be clarified by considering them in a different context.

There are other reasons for questioning whether *fills* and *empties* belong to the subgroup of inchoative motion verbs. For most motion verbs the entity that is conceived as moving is either the agent or the patient of the verb. *Fills* and *empties,* however, have the unusual property that it is the instrument that moves. Since the instrument can be deleted, the motion component of these verbs may be missing. For example, the sentence *He filled the basin with water* requires some such paraphrase as *He caused water to come/go into the basin until it became full,* which has causative, motion, directional, and inchoative components, and where it is obvious that the water is moving, not the agent or the basin. When the instrument is deleted, however, as in *He filled the basin* or *The basin filled,* the motion component is no longer evident; these sentences can be paraphrased as *He caused the basin to become full* and *The basin became full,* respectively, which involve only inchoative or causative components. Whether *empties* and *fills* should be included with other motion verbs, or whether they, too, might better be considered in relation to a different semantic domain, is at least debatable.

The verbs *nears* and *separates* appear semantically similar, and can be considered together. The transitive use of *separates* will submit to a causative-inchoative paraphrase: *He separated the X from the Y* means roughly *He caused the X to become separate from the Y by changing their locations,* and intransitive uses such as *They separated* could be *They became separate by changing their locations.* The verb *nears,* on the other hand, is only used intransitively: *He neared the house* can be paraphrased as *He became near (to) the house by changing his location.* Although these incomplete definitions incorporating an inchoative component are plausible, they are certainly awkward stylistically. It should be noted, therefore, that the verb *nears* may incorporate the preposition *near,* rather than the adjective *near,* in which case the definition *comes/goes near* would win it a distinguished place among the directional verbs of motion in Table 3. According to this interpretation, the fact that *nears* also fits the inchoative formula would be merely coincidental. Moreover, the preposition *near* suggests the preposition *apart.* The intransitive *separates* could also be defined as a directional motion verb by the paraphrase *comes/goes apart,* and the transitive *separates X (from Y)* could be *causes X to come/go apart (from Y).* Thus, there are reasons for omitting *nears* and *separates* from the list of inchoative motion verbs.

Most of the above list of verbs satisfying the inchoative formula can, therefore, be eliminated from the class of inchoative motion verbs on the grounds either that they are not true motion verbs, or that they are not really inchoative. In that case, the only examples left are *opens, closes,* and *shuts.* This shortened list at least has the virtue of greater semantic homogeneity.

He opened his eyes can be paraphrased as *He caused his eyes to become open,* which makes the causative and inchoative components obvious, but leaves the motion component implicit in the generic concept *become.* However, motion can be introduced by using the more specific *come/go* instead of *become.* (It is interesting to note that it is not really his eyes that move, but his eyelids; boxes, books, envelopes, and containers generally share this characteristic. When doors, shutters, screens, windows, and barriers generally are opened, however, it is the patient or direct object of the verb that moves.) Setting aside the fact that there seems to be an affinity between *come* and *open* and between *go* and *shut,* the general formula for these three verbs, therefore, is that *He Verb X* can be paraphrased as *He made X come/go Adj,* which resembles the formula for objective directional motion verbs (column three in Table 3), except that *Adj* has replaced *Prep.*

Thus, there does seem to be some place for a motional version of the inchoative component in our present analysis, although its scope is rather limited. In a sense, this limitation may be a blessing, since the inchoative formula merely serves to shift the semantic analysis of verbs into the domain of adjectives without really furthering the analysis. Of course, the directional component similarly shifts the analysis into the domain of prepositions, but that is a smaller and more highly structured domain. Turning a verb into an adjective, however, does little to limit the scope of the problem.

CHANGE OF MOTION VERBS

There are motion verbs, of which *arrives* and *departs* are good examples, that signify a change of state, yet cannot be easily paraphrased as, say, *becomes present* or *becomes absent.* We use *arrives* to express the idea that a person was traveling (was in a state of motion) until he came to his destination, and we use *departs* to express the idea that he was at a given location (was not in a state of motion) until he started traveling away from it. The simplest paraphrases for these concepts seem to be *finished traveling* and *began traveling away.* Thus, *Arthur arrived* would become *Arthur finished traveling; Arthur arrived in Princeton* would become *Arthur finished traveling in Princeton; Arthur departed* would become *Arthur began traveling away; Arthur departed from New York* would become *Arthur began traveling away from New York;* and so on.

In this way we can introduce a change-of-motion component, paraphrased *begins* and *finishes.* There are senses of *starts* and *stops* that also require this interpretation. *He started from New York* is very similar to *He departed from New York* (although it may lack the locative preposition *away* we have included for departs). *Stops* may seem to be the very opposite of a motion verb, yet it is frequently used as an antonym for *goes,* in which sense it is similar to *arrives* in that both signify that the traveling is finished, at least temporarily.

In addition to *arrives* and *stops, halts* and *lands* have senses that share the *finishes traveling* paraphrase. And, in addition to *departs* and *starts, goes* and *leaves* have senses that share the *begins traveling* paraphrase. *Throws, jumps,* and *launches* also have senses that share the *begins traveling* paraphrase, but they are more complicated; we shall consider them further in our discussion of pro-pellent motion verbs.

PROPELLENT MOTION VERBS

Consider next the causative motion verb *propels.* The sentence *He propelled the ball* says all that *He moved the ball* says (in both cases he caused the ball to change location) plus something more. *He propelled it* is ordinarily understood to mean that he provided the force that caused its motion. *Propels* thus seems to be doubly causative: He caused the force that caused the motion. If we substitute for *propels* X the definition *applies force to move X,* and substitute for *moves X* the definition *causes X to change location,* then together we obtain for *propels X* the paraphrase *applies force to cause X to change location.* The verbs *drags, jerks, projects, launches, rolls, sends, swings, thrusts,* and *trundles* have senses that share this definition of *propels. Projects* and *launches* (and in some uses, *sends*) have an additional change-of-motion component, however, and so should be paraphrased as *applies force to cause X to begin changing location.*

Given this definition of *propels,* we can identify a further group of motion verbs that contain additional components to indicate various ways of propelling things. The additional components seem to be directional, instrumental, change-of-motion, or reflexive-objective. From Table 3 we can identify such directional motion verbs as *shoves, ejects, drives,* and *pushes* that can be defined in terms of *propels.* Thus, *shoves X* can be defined as *propels X away from him,* or *applies force to make X come/go away from him. Ejects X* can be defined as *propels X out* or *applies force to make X come/go out. Drives X* can be defined as *applies force to make X come/go forward.* And *pushes X* can be defined either as *shoves* was defined, or to mean *propels X ahead of him.*

An instrumental component is apparent in such propellent motion verbs as *kicks. He kicked the ball* is understood to mean that *he propelled the ball by foot,* where *foot* is the instrument. Similarly, *flings, flips, hurls, throws,* and *tosses* are ordinarily used in the sense of *propels by hand,* where *hand* is the instrument. But these verbs seem to have two additional components: One is related to the medium through which the patient travels—through space, or through the air. For example, *He threw the ball* would be defined to mean *He propelled the ball through the air by hand,* or *He applied force by hand to make the ball come/go through the air.* The second additional component is the change-of-motion component that reflects the fact that the ball starts traveling: *He applied force by hand to make the ball begin traveling through the air.* In *throws,* therefore, we can find two causative components (*applied force to make*), a change-of-motion component (*begin*), an instrumental component (*by hand*), and a medium component (*through the air*), in addition to the general motion component (*traveling*).

Throws would seem to be a cognitively complex package of semantic components, and if this analysis is correct, one might be inclined to wonder how children are able to master it so early. There is little reason to believe, however, that cognitively simple verbs must be learned first, and some reason to believe the contrary (Anglin, 1970). The act of throwing is apparently an intuitively simple referent. The more abstract verb *propels* is more difficult for children to learn for a variety of reasons: It seems reasonable to suppose that considerable lexical learning must occur before the simple referential act of throwing can be seen as taking a verb that is so multiply differentiated from other motion verbs. There appears to be no necessary correlation between the complexity of a referent and the complexity of the word that refers to it.

The reflexive-objective distinction is also useful for characterizing propellent motion verbs. All of those mentioned above are used primarily to describe objective motion, but there are also reflexive instances; *jumps,* for example, or *bounds, hops, leaps, pounces, springs, vaults.* All of these carry the sense that the agent propelled himself.

Jumps is a particularly complicated package of concepts. In Table 3 *jumps* is defined to mean *comes/goes over* in such sentences as *He jumps the fence.* Thus, *jumps* can have a directional component when no other direction than *over* is specified; if he *jumps down,* or *off,* or *onto,* or *away from* something, however, the inherent direction, *over,* is replaced explicitly. If we now consider *jumps* as a reflexive propellent motion verb, however, the definition becomes much more complex; then *He jumps the fence* is paraphrased as *He applies force to cause himself to come/go over the fence.* Even this is incomplete, however, because it omits the medium, instrumental, and change-of-motion components. A full componential paraphrase of *He jumps the fence,* therefore, would be *He applies force with his legs to make himself begin traveling through the air over the fence.*

This definition of *jumps* involves an objective causative component (*applies force*), a reflexive causative component (*to make himself*), a change-of-motion component (*begin*), an instrumental component (*with his legs*), a medium component (*through the air*), and a directional component (*over*), in addition to the generic concept (*traveling*). All in all, *jumps* is a very good review of the major semantic components we have used in our analysis (only the inchoative, deictic, velocity, and permissive components are missing), and serves as another example of how a cognitively complex verb can be used to refer to an intuitively simple act.

REVIEW

We have now surveyed a set of motion verbs characterized by the property of describing movement from one location to another. By the method of incomplete definitions we have found that, in addition to the generic concept of positional change, most of these verbs express other concepts that enable users of English to differentiate among various kinds of motion. We have referred to these inherent concepts as semantic components, and we have identified several of them that seem to be shared by groups of verbs, though in various combinations.

If a verb does not inherently contain one of these concepts, the concept can frequently be stated explicitly by adding a standard phrase. If a verb does contain the component, the phrase can be incorporated as part of its definition; to add the phrase explicitly to such a verb introduces redundancy (e.g., *He walked on foot*). Thus, the (incomplete) definition takes the form of a componential paraphrase of the verb built up from appropriate phrases expressing its inherent semantic components. An attempt has been made to formulate these componential paraphrases in such a manner that, if the definition of verb V_1 contains paraphrases of all of the components in the definition of verb V_2 plus some further components, then V_2 can be used in the definition of V_1 by conjoining V_2 with the appropriate additional phrases that express the additional inherent components of V_1.

The semantic components that are used, and their suggested paraphrases are:

motion	*travels, changes location, comes/goes*
reflexive-objective	reflexive pronoun—direct object
causative	*causes to, makes*
permissive	*allows to, lets*
propellent	*applies force to*
directional	directional preposition
medium	*on land, through the air, water*
instrumental	*by foot, by boat,* etc.
inchoative	adjective
change-of-motion	*begins, finishes*
deictic	*toward* or *away from speaker*
velocity	*slowly, rapidly*

Many of these components are needed in the definition of other verbs as well, and could be expected to recur in the analysis of other semantic domains.

The definitions generated in this manner are incomplete, of course, and leave open the possibility that many of these verbs contain further components of an idiosyncratic or referential nature that are not easily expressed by componential paraphrase.

Not all possible combinations of these components were needed in order to paraphrase the motion verbs included in Table 1. The 20 different combinations that did occur (and for which examples can be found in the preceding pages) are indicated in Figure 1 as nodes, where the paraphrase formulas are written out. The lines connecting the definitions signify that all of the concepts contained in the paraphrase at the top of the line are included in the paraphrase at the bottom of the line. Thus, Figure 1 can be taken as our hypothesis as to the semantic structure underlying motion verbs in English.

In effect, therefore, our analysis of 217 motion verbs has generated 20 different classes organized in terms of 12 primitive concepts.

SOME PSYCHOLOGICAL IMPLICATIONS

Psychologists interested in understanding verbal learning and verbal memory have, for methodological reasons, concentrated largely on performances requiring verbatim recall. They know, of course, that instances of verbatim recall are relatively rare in the lives of most people. Learning is usually conceptual, and success is evidenced by the learner's ability to generate a more or less accurate paraphrase "in his own words." But it is easier to be objective in scoring verbatim recall than in scoring paraphrased recall. Lacking any accepted theory

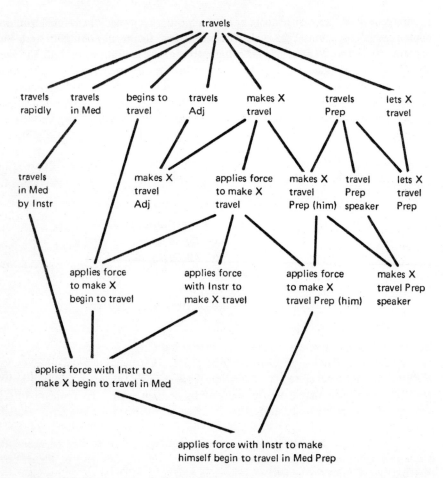

FIG. 1. Relations among paraphrase combinations proposed as incomplete definitions for English motion verbs. If two definitions are connected by a line, the one below includes all the semantic components of the one above, plus others.

of paraphrase or synonomy, psychologists who aspire to scientific precision have been forced to use formal identity as their criterion for a learner's performance. One possible implication of the present analysis, therefore, is to suggest methods of dealing with paraphrase in evaluating performance on conceptual learning tasks. The analysis is only suggestive, of course, not definitive, but at least it indicates a possible direction to pursue.

This implication is, however, quite indirect, since our analysis has not treated the learning process at all. Rather, it has been concerned with the possible structural organization of lexical memory. Processes involved in the acquisition of this memorial organization have not been discussed, nor have we treated the question of how this memory might be affected by or involved in the learning of new materials. In the light of current distinctions between short-term and long-term memory, of course, one might be inclined to view the analysis as relevant for the study of long-term memory. But even this apparently obvious categorization can be misleading.

Suppose you were asked to remember a word, say, *boat*. What would you do? You have, in one sense, known and remembered the word *boat* ever since you were a child, and will probably continue to remember it until you die. The only sense you might make of such a request would be to associate *boat* with some special situation, cue, or contingency designated by the person who made the request. That is to say, laboratory studies of short-term and long-term remembering create demands for special retrieval procedures to be instituted; they do not ordinarily add a new element to the basic memory structure they exploit. Studies of this basic structure, therefore, are necessarily different from studies of short-term or long-term retrieval strategies. The present analysis tells us neither about the acquisition of basic lexical memory nor its utilization in experimental studies of short- or long-term verbal learning.

Indeed, the present analysis does not even tell us anything about mental processes whereby basic lexical information of this kind could be used to produce or comprehend intelligible, grammatical utterances. The result has been a structural description of how one suburb of the lexicon might be organized, but it says nothing about any mechanisms whereby such a structure could be realized or exploited. Lacking such mechanistic hypotheses, attempts to go directly from this description of semantic components to performance measures in psychological experiments (e.g., reaction time, error rates, confusions) must proceed with great caution.

An analogy may be helpful. Suppose we were studying, not an individual, but a business organization, and that we had access only to the filing system that the organization used. How much could we conclude about the way the firm transacted its business on the basis of an analysis of the principles underlying the way it filed and retrieved its correspondence? A little, perhaps, but not much. We would need many other kinds of data before we could claim to understand how the business functioned. The situation is similar for the lexical filing system used by individuals. It may give us some hints about the kinds of processes he can execute, but the functional generalizations we base on such studies must be seasoned with much scepticism.

Experimental investigation of performance in the laboratory is a powerful tool, however, and should not be abandoned in an excess of caution over the possibility of anomalous results. Various ways of testing the psychological validity of the present analysis can be imagined. The most direct would be to ask people for their paraphrases of expressions involving these verbs (cf. Gleitman & Gleitman, 1970). Sorting studies, like the two described here, also seem appropriate. Confusions in recall or recognition might conform to the hypothetical groupings of verbs, and concept learning experiments are certainly feasible.

There is a need, however, for innovative techniques designed explicitly to study the lexical organization of these verbs. For example, it would be valuable to have experimental methods to investigate the effects of negation. In sentences like *Arthur didn't throw the ball,* which components of *throw* is the negative understood to deny? Or, again, it would be valuable to have methods to explore the range of generalization and metaphor that are acceptable for various classes of verbs. Do *throw a party, throw a race, throw an image, throw on clothes, throw* in troops, throw out leftovers, throw away an opportunity, throw off the trial, and throw together a dinner share any semantic components with one another and with throw the ball? And how would throw the lake, throw the anger, throw a technology, and throw a notation be interpreted, that is, what components of throw would be overriden in order to paraphrase such combinations?

The analysis of motion verbs into semantic components lends itself to logographic representation. Perhaps such pictures would be easier to learn to read, or perhaps such a notation would have cognitive advantages over an alphabetic representation. Are there experimental methods adequate to investigate such questions?

Appropriate experiments might do better than merely lend support to the conclusion that the analysis given here represents something more than one chap's introspections. However, failure to find effects of the components on performance might mean either that the theoretical analysis was incorrect, or that semantic components do not function as concepts, or that the experiments were inappropriate or poorly done. In short, it is not obvious what conclusions could be drawn from negative results. Such risks are not peculiar to semantic research, however, so perhaps the dangers should not be overemphasized.

The possibility of large individual differences should also be kept in mind (cf. Pfafflin, 1961; Quirk & Svartvik, 1966; Stolz, 1967; Gleitman & Gleitman, 1970). Although it seems unlikely that these verbs could be used successfully in linguistic communication if there were major disagreements about such general components of meaning, there still might be large differences in how people, even those who speak the same dialect, represent these concepts in memory. Certainly we know from many years of testing intelligence that there are major differences among individuals in size of vocabulary. But, lacking any comprehensive and explicit hypothesis about the memory mechanisms involved, it is impossible to know what other kinds of individual variability one might find on particular performance tests.

One might expect some differences in the organization of lexical memory to correlate with dialect differences. In its broadest definition, of course, individual differences should also encompass differences in language, where we know there would be differences in lexical memory. Another line of attack, therefore, would be to study other languages, to see whether they contain a semantic domain corresponding to English motion verbs and, if so, whether the same components of meaning could be identified, although perhaps assembled differently into word-packages. Any evidence that some or all of the semantic components were universal would have important psychological implications.

Finally, a particularly interesting attack might be mounted along developmental lines. The most obvious conclusion to draw from our observation that some of the simplest referents seem to have some of the most complex componential representations—throws or jumps, for example—would be that children must learn first the referential component of a word's meaning and only later acquire the multiple differentiations that an adult recognizes in the senses of these words. Thus, one might expect to find a slow and extended growth of intraverbal concepts long after the child seemed to be using word-packages of these concepts appropriately. On the other hand, the explosive growth of vocabulary that begins in the third year might be more easily understood if the child had acquired a conceptual framework into which new words could be fitted and remembered as they occurred during these early years. In either case, it could be informative to attempt to trace the growth of these semantic components in the language of young children (cf. Parisi & Antinucci, 1970).

It is possible, therefore, to imagine several alternative lines of investigation that might enrich our understanding of the psychological basis for the lexical organization described here. Nevertheless, the need for some comprehensive hypothesis relating lexical memory to sentence production and comprehension, and to short-term and long-term retrieval, in terms of testable mechanisms for processing information remains a central problem for psycholinguistic research.

Of course, it would not be difficult to devise a coding procedure for lexical entries based on the semantic components we have identified, and to imagine rapid search procedures for exploiting that code. There are many ways this might be done; we have little reason to think that the brain does it one way rather than another. Even without an explicit coding and retrieval system in mind, however, it is obvious that semantic components such as those described here could serve to organize lexical memory so that it would be relatively easy to move from one lexical entry to closely related entries, or to express a multicomponent idea even when we are unable to think of the precise word that contains the desired components. If each sense of each word were entered in lexical memory as an independent, self-contained entity, such judgments of semantic similarity and paraphrase constructions would, of course, be extremely difficult to explain.

Theoretically, one might regard the relation between a verb and its componential paraphrase as an example of "chunking" (Miller, 1956). In rote memorization experiments it is a common strategy for subjects to group items, to use some special symbol to represent the group, and to remember the symbol from which the items can later be reconstructed, rather than to recall the individual items directly. Some similar cognitive strategy might be involved in using, say, *moves X* as a symbol representing the longer string of words, *causes X to change location.* However, such an interpretation puts too much weight on the particular words we happen to have chosen for our paraphrases. It is more plausible to think that *moves X* is one symbol for a package of concepts, and that *causes X to change location* is another more explicit symbol for a closely related package of concepts. That is to say, it is the underlying concepts, not particular words, that are chunked or packaged in such symbols.

Moreover, such terms as "chunk" or "package" do not suggest the highly organized structure of these conceptual compounds. In order to represent this structure adequately we would need some explicit theory of conceptual organization along the lines suggested by Quillian (1968) or Schank (1969, 1971). For example, Schank suggests that the causality component should be considered as a particular kind of relation between two other concepts, one representing what the agent does and the other representing what happens to the patient. The sentence *Arthur moved the chair* involves a concept of Arthur doing something, a concept of the chair changing location, and the concept of causality that relates the first event to the second. (Such an interpretation would account for the uncertainty one feels about precisely what is being denied in the sentence *Arthur didn't move the chair.*) Since it relates two events, the causality component differs from, say, the motion component, which relates an object and its location. Moreover, the causative and permissive components are somehow linked, and so are the directional (prepositional incorporation) and inchoative (adjectival incorporation), the directional and deictic, and the causative-permissive and the reflexive-objective components, and so on. There is considerable structure underlying the paraphrase combinations we have used.

Considerations of this sort make it obvious that the conceptual compounds underlying these words cannot be adequately represented by an unstructured list of semantic components. To develop a conceptual organization relating all the semantic components we have used for motion verbs seems perfectly feasible, although it would entail a deeper analysis than we have undertaken here. Some theory along these lines seems necessary, however, if we hope to understand how these conceptual compounds are used in thinking.

It is tempting to speculate that thinking might go on preverbally at some very abstract level, where the elements of thought would be concepts and relations corresponding to various semantic components. Once these abstract elements were structurally related in a complex idea, the semantic compound could then be translated into particular words or componential paraphrases, and this translation might either provide a deep structure that, by appropriate syntactic transformations, would generate the sentences we use to express our ideas, or it might generate those sentences more directly. Conversely, in speech perception the process would be reversed, with the abstract concepts underlying the various semantic components (in appropriate configurations, of course) being the output of the perceptual process.

There are, however, several reasons to question this view that we must think before we speak and hear before we understand. Although such use of the linguistic machinery is conceivable when a language user is being especially cautious, it is certainly not necessary. The most telling counterargument is that we so often speak before we understand fully what we are saying, and we so often understand what a person means even when he expresses it imperfectly.

A more conservative view, therefore, seems preferable. Thinking can proceed in terms of relatively specific words or in abstract or concrete imagery; thinking is not confined to a realm of general concepts like location, change, causation, and direction. The semantic components and their paraphrase relations comprise only one of many ways whereby we can move on in thought to related ideas or related expressions. The very fact that the thought-to-words progression during speaking must be reversed in speech perception indicates that the operations involved must (in some sense) be reversible, which opens up a much larger and less structured domain over which our mechanistic speculations can range.

REFERENCES

Anglin, J. M. *The growth of word meaning.* Cambridge, Mass.: The M.I.T. Press, 1970.

Bendix, E. H. *Componential analysis of general vocabulary.* The Hague: Mouton, 1966.

Binnick, R. On the nature of the "Lexical Item." In B. J. Darden, C-J. N. Bailey, & A. Davison (Eds.), *Papers from the Fourth Regional Meeting, Chicago Linguistic Society.* Chicago: Department of Linguistics, University of Chicago, 1968. Pp. 1-13.

Bolinger, D. The atomization of meaning. *Language,* 1965, 41, 555-573.

Chomsky, N. *Aspects of the theory of syntax.* Cambridge, Mass.: The M.I.T. Press, 1965.

Fillenbaum, S., & Jones, L. V. Grammatical contingencies in word association. *Journal of Verbal Learning and Verbal Behavior,* 1965, 4, 248-255.

Fillmore, C. J. Deictic categories in the semantics of "come." *Foundations of Language,* 1966, 2, 219-226.

Fillmore, C. J. The case for case. In E. Back & R. Harms (Eds.), *Universals in linguistic theory.* New York: Holt, Rinehart & Winston, 1968. Pp. 1-81.

Fodor, J. A. Three reasons for not deriving "kill" from "cause to die." *Linguistic Inquiry,* 1970, 1, 429-438.

Gleitman, L. R., & Gleitman, H. *Phrase and paraphrase: Some innovative uses of language.* New York: Norton, 1970.

Goodenough, W. H. Componential analysis and the study of meaning. *Language,* 1956, 32, 195-216.

Gruber, J. S. Studies in lexical relations. Unpublished doctoral dissertation, Massachusetts Institute of Technology, 1965.

Hammel, E. A. (Ed.) *Formal semantic analysis.* Special publication of *American Anthropologist,* 1965, No. 5, Part 2, 1-316.

Jakobson, R. Beitrag zur allgemeinen Kasuslehre. *Travaux du Cercle Linguistique de Prague,* 1936, 6, 240-288.

Katz, J. J. *The philosophy of language.* New York: Harper and Row, 1966.

Katz, J. J., & Fodor, J. A. The structure of a semantic theory. *Language,* 1963, 39, 170-210.

Lakoff, G. *On the nature of syntactic irregularity.* Report NSF-16, Harvard Computation Laboratory, 1965. (Reprinted as *Irregularity in syntax.* New York: Holt, Rinehart, & Winston, 1970.)

Lakoff, G. On generative semantics. In D. Steinberg & L. Jakobovits (Eds.), *Semantics: An interdisciplinary reader in philosophy, linguistics, and psychology.* Cambridge: Cambridge University Press, 1971. Pp. 232-296.

Langendoen, D. T. *Essentials of English grammar.* New York: Holt, Rinehart & Winston, 1970.

Lounsbury, F. G. A semantic analysis of Pawnee kinship usage. *Language,* 1956, 32, 158-194.

Lyons, J. *Introduction to theoretical linguistics.* Cambridge: Cambridge University Press, 1968.

McCawley, J. D. The role of semantics in a grammar. In E. Bach & R. T. Harms (Eds.), *Universals in linguistic theory.* New York: Holt, Rinehart, & Winston, 1968. Pp. 124-169. (a)

McCawley, J. D. Lexical insertion in a transformational grammar without deep structure. In B. J. Darden, C-J. N. Bailey, & A. Davison (Eds.), *Papers from the Fourth Regional Meeting, Chicago Linguistic Society.* Chicago: Department of Linguistics, University of Chicago, 1968. Pp. 71-80. (b)

Miller, G. A. Human memory and the storage of information. *IRE Transactions on Information Theory.* IT-2, 1956, 129-137.

Miller, G. A. A psychological method to investigate verbal concepts. *Journal of Mathematical Psychology,* 1969, 6, 169-191.

Nida, E. A. *Toward a science of translating.* Leiden: E. J. Brill, 1964.

Parisi, D., & Antinucci, F. Lexical competence. In G. B. Flores d'Arcais & W. J. M. Levelt (Eds.), *Advances in psycholinguistics.* Amsterdam: North-Holland, 1970. Pp. 197-210.

Pfafflin, S. M. Grammatical judgments of computer-generated word sequences. Mimeographed paper. Murray Hill, N. J.: Bell Telephone Laboratories, 1961.

Postal, P. The surface verb "remind." *Linguistic Inquiry,* 1970, **1**, 37-120.

Quillian, M. R. Semantic memory. In M. Minsky (Ed.), *Semantic information processing.* Cambridge, Mass.: The M.I.T. Press, 1968. Pp. 216-270.

Quirk, R., & Svartvik, J. *Investigating linguistic acceptability.* The Hague: Mouton, 1966.

Schank, R. C. A conceptual dependency representation for a computer-oriented semantics. Stanford A. I. Memo 83, Computer Science Department, Stanford University, 1969.

Schank, R. C. Intention, memory, and computer understanding. Stanford A. I. Memo 140, Computer Science Department, Stanford University, 1971.

Stolz, W. S. A study of the ability to decode grammatically novel sentences. *Journal of Verbal Learning and Verbal Behavior,* 1967, **6**, 867-873.

Wallace, A. F. C., & Atkins, J. The meaning of kinship terms. In T. Gladwin & W. C. Sturtevant (Eds.), *Anthropology and human behavior.* Washington: Anthropological Society of Washington, 1962. Pp. 1-12.

15

A THEORETICAL EXPLORATION OF MECHANISMS FOR CODING THE STIMULUS[1]

Allen Newell
Carnegie-Mellon University

This paper explores the problem of developing an explicit model for how stimulus encoding occurs. It is primarily a theoretical exercise, attempting to extend current work in problem solving (Newell & Simon, 1972) to incorporate perceptual mechanisms and control structures to permit stimulus encoding. The set of conditions that we impose on the total model—in terms of sufficiency of the mechanisms and the detail of their interactions—makes it unlikely that an initial formulation will be successful. And indeed this is the case: The model remains incomplete in a number of significant ways and we can only examine a minute part of its behavior within the confines of this paper. Thus, we have called the paper a theoretical exploration.

This work stems from the view that to study coding in human information processing requires a model of the total process, a model that specifies exactly how coding operations take place. The general strategy in experimental psychology runs to the opposite side, namely, that one should posit a model by stating only a few general properties of the system. When well done, this leads to some implications for behavior that can then be tested. The net effect is slowly to close in on a mechanism, catching it in a conjunctive net of properties, each one

[1] I would like to acknowledge fully the contribution to this effort of a Protocol Workshop held at Carnegie-Mellon University during Spring 1971, and especially Michelene Chase, David Klahr, Donald Waterman, and Richard Young, who all worked extensively on the series-completion protocol discussed herein, developing production systems that were the starting point of this research. The work here is a direct continuation of joint research with H. A. Simon and draws in detail on material in Newell and Simon (1972). The research was supported in part by the National Institute of Mental Health (NH-07722) and in part by the Advanced Research Projects Agency of the Department of Defense (F44620-70-C0107) which is monitored by the Air Force Office of Scientific Research.

established experimentally. Often the objects of most interest, here the coding operations, remain extraordinarily ill specified.

Let me make the point concretely by noting a few examples. All of these represent studies that I feel are successful and have given us both new information and provocative ideas about mechanisms. No straw men are intended.

Consider first the well known study of memory by Atkinson and Shiffrin (1968). Specific models of memory are proposed from which can be computed experimental results to be compared with extensive data. Still, I am left with an uncomfortable feeling. A central part of their story is the notion of control processes, which allow the subject to perform according to different strategies. But these control processes receive no representation in the theory. They are used informally to rationalize the application of specific models to specific situations. In some sense a specific representation of control mechanism is not needed to get on with the study. Still, it remains an incomplete paper from which I find it hard to move on.

Consider next a study by N. F. Johnson (1970; this volume) concerned with coding processes in memory, namely, those that lead to chunking stimuli in various ways. Again, he provides a quite specific model for part of the process, that is, the control process for decoding a stimulus to give a response. This is enough for him to justify the relevance of his response measure and to argue for a number of effects. Still, the process he is studying, coding and chunking, is nowhere specified. He argues to a few properties of it, for example, whether a code (i.e., the internal representation of a part of the stimulus) is like an opaque container, and this is enough of a characterization to set up some experimental tests; but my greatest disappointment is that he proposes no theory of the operations of coding of verbal stimuli.

The McLean and Gregg (1967) study of induced chunking in serial learning offers an almost identical example from my point of view. It evokes a specific view of processing mechanisms and finds an ingenious way of revealing some effects of these processes in an experimental task. But what I want is a model of how the subject says the alphabet backwards, not simply that the backwards recitation can be used to reveal that the organization into chunks is really there.

One last example will suffice. Much recent work has occurred on imagery. One segment of this work is concerned with imagery as a mediator in various verbal learning tasks (e.g., Paivio, 1969; Bower, in press). It is a peculiar feature of all this work that it proposes no theory or model of imagery at all. In fact, if you ask how one knows that the mediator is imagery, rather than something else, the only link is in the semantics of the instructions to the subject, plus the experimenter's participatory conviction that imagery is involved. The problem is not the old saw about operationality. In fact, from one point of view, there is no problem at all. Strong effects are being produced and progress made. Still, if I were going to work on imagery, I would want a theory of imagery to stand at the center of my work, not a symbolic place-holder for which I had only enough intuitive grasp, along with a few explicitly stated properties, to guide further experimentation.

I trust the point is made. No criticism is directed at efforts that make progress, as all the above do. One can still wish for something different. One can also suspect that the reason why so many studies have this characteristic (this flaw?) is because of an accepted style of operation in psychology.

In all events, if I am going to study coding processes, I have to have a model of the coding operations themselves. I will, on balance, prefer to start with a grossly imperfect but complete model, hoping to improve it eventually; rather than start with an abstract but experimentally verified characterization, hoping to specify it further eventually. These may be looked at simply as different approximating sequences toward the same scientific end. They do dictate quite different approaches, as the present paper exemplifies.

Thus, the goal of this paper is to provide at least one explicit set of mechanisms for coding the stimulus. We could enunciate the fundamental operations that seem to be required and from there construct a system that seems consonant with what is known generally about the information processing capabilities of humans. We will, instead, follow a somewhat different course and extend an existing model of human information processing. Consequently, we will start with an expositon of this model in the next section, and after this pose the issue of stimulus encoding. To make progress will require adopting a concrete task, which we do in a subsequent section. This permits us to define the extension to the system, which will be a perceptual mechanism, and to look briefly at its behavior. In the final section we sum up the exploration.

THE BASIC MODEL

The basic model comes from the theory of problem solving that has developed from a study of small symbolic well-defined tasks (cryptarithmetic, chess, and elementary symbolic logic). The theory is set forth most completely in Newell and Simon (1972), but various earlier specialized versions and summaries exist (Newell, 1967; Newell, 1968; Simon & Newell, 1971).

The Elements of the Theory

Let me recapitulate briefly the elements of the theory. We will follow this up with a particular instantiation of the theory for a specific subject on a specific occasion. This latter will give us the requisite level of detail to pose the task of this paper. Since full detail will be provided later, this initial statement can gloss over a number of details.

Structurally, the subject is an information processing system (IPS) consisting of a processor containing a short-term memory (STM), which has access to a long-term memory (LTM). The processor also has access to the external environment, which may be viewed as an external memory (EM).[2] The processor contains the mechanisms for elementary processes, for perception, for motor behavior, and for the evocation of conditional sequences of elementary processes.

---

[2] Due account is taken for the initiation of action from the external environment, a feature not prominent in the task environments studied.

The basic representation of information is in terms of symbols and symbolic expressions. Symbolic expressions are structures composed of discrete collections of symbol tokens, linked by relations (e.g., the *next* relation, where at most one symbol token immediately follows a given token, as in a list). Symbols, as realized in symbol tokens in symbolic expressions, designate other structures, as structures of symbolic expressions, of elementary processes, and of the results of elementary processes. "X designates Y" is short hand for "X permits access to Y or to a representation of Y by some set of elementary information processes."

All action of the system takes place via the execution of elementary processes, which take their operands in STM. The only information available on which to base behavior is that in STM; other information (either in LTM or EM) must be brought into STM before it can effect behavior. At this level the system is serial in nature: Only one elementary information process is executed at a time and has available to it the contents of STM as produced by the prior elementary processes. Seriality here does not imply seriality either of perception or of accessing of LTM.

Problem solving takes place as search in a problem space, each element of which represents a possible state of knowledge about the problem. A problem space is defined by (*a*) a representation of the possible states of knowledge (e.g., a language, such that each expression in the language constitutes a possible state of knowledge) and (*b*) a set of operators for moving from one element of the problem space to another, thus acquiring new knowledge or abandoning old knowledge. Central to the theory is the assertion that the problem space can be specified in finite terms for particular subjects and particular tasks. Not all the knowledge that a subject has is represented by his position in the problem space (e.g., knowledge about his path through the space).

The problem space is not represented in extension in the IPS (i.e., in the subject). However, it exists potentially, because at least one particular knowledge state is represented explicitly in the IPS (namely, the subject's current location in the space) and the IPS has processes corresponding to all the operators of the space, hence can generate other elements of the problem space. The language of knowledge states, then, is representable in the symbolic expressions that form the basic representation of the IPS. Further, the current knowledge state must exist in some form in the memories of the subject, namely, in STM, LTM, and EM.

The program of the subject appears to be well represented by a production system.[3] This is a scheme of the form:

$$C_1 \rightarrow A_1$$

$$C_2 \rightarrow A_2$$

$$\cdots$$

$$C_n \rightarrow A_n$$

[3] Production systems constitute a family of computational and logical systems much studied in computer science (see Minsky, 1967; Hopcroft & Ullman, 1969). Members differ considerably in the details of the conditions, actions, control structure, and the data types on which they work.

Each of the lines consists of a condition (C_i) and an action (A_i), and is called a production. The ordered list of productions is called a production system. The system operates by continually selecting for execution the first action from the top whose condition is satisfied. Since the actions modify the information on which the conditons are based, the same action need not (and in general will not) be evoked on successive cycles of the system.

The conditions operate on the current knowledge state. (That is what makes current and knowledge: It determines the immediately next action of the subject.) Actually, the conditions are limited to that part of the knowledge that is in STM.[4] (That is what gives the STM its special role and makes knowledge in EM or LTM indirect.)

The actions may be operations of the problem space or sequences of such operations:

$$C_i \rightarrow Q_1 \; Q_2 \ldots Q_m$$

In this latter case the sequence is executed unconditionally, except that termination of the sequence is possible after any operation. Depending on how the problem space is defined, the actions may or may not include additional operators (e.g., those involved in attention control).

To provide a complete model for a subject's problem solving requires specifying the problem space and the production system. It also requires giving the details of the memory structures and the symbolic representation, which is implied indirectly in the first two items. On the other hand, strategies and methods of problem solving are to be represented by the contents of production systems, and are not given as separate desiderata.

The work mentioned earlier (e.g., Newell & Simon, 1972) attempts to fill out the gross picture just given, as well as show that the behavior of human subjects can be described successfully by means of such a theory when the details are filled in. We are not concerned here with recapitulating that story, but in shedding light on the encoding of knowledge.

However, we will set out in the next section a specific version of the general theory. This will provide a detailed set of mechanisms for all the parts that have been described above only in general terms. We will use a version in a problem solving task called cryptarithmetic, not because it is well adapted to the study of stimulus encoding, which it is not, but because it represents well the current level of analysis.

A Production System for S2 on CROSS + ROADS = DANGER

We wish to model a subject (S2) behaving on the cryptarithmetic task, CROSS + ROADS = DANGER. For those not familiar with the task, Figure 1 gives the instructions. The protocol for this subject is discussed in detail in Newell and Simon (1972, Ch. 7); he is the subject for which we have detailed eye-movement records. The production system to be presented here corresponds to that presented

[4] There is a question about the status of the immediate perceived EM.

```
  C R O S S
+ R O A D S
-----------
D A N G E R
```

The above expression is a simple arithmetic sum in disguise. Each letter represents a digit, that is, 0, 1, 2, . . . , or 9. Each letter is a distinct digit. For example, C and A may not represent the same digit.

What digits should be assigned to the letters such that when the letters are replaced by their corresponding digits, the above expression is a true arithmetic sum?

FIG. 1. Instructions for cryptarithmetic task.

in the book, but differs in the underlying language for production systems, the representation of knowledge elements, and some details of the immediate processor.

The elements that constitute knowledge are linear expressions. For instance (NEW D = 1) is to be read, "D = 1 and this is new information." (GOAL * PC COL.2) is to be read, "The goal of applying the operator PC to column 2 and this goal current." In general, English terms are used in knowledge elements, for example, GOAL, NEW, and =. In the model all such terms acquire their significance (i.e., their meaning, their semantics, their operational character) entirely by participation in productions. For example, elements containing the term GOAL are goal-like precisely to the extent that there are productions that respond to elements containing the term GOAL (by matching on their conditions) and manipulate them in goal-like ways, such as permitting subgoals, resuming superordinate goals, organizing behavior to attain goals, and so on.

STM consists of a list of knowledge elements, that is, a list of symbolic expressions. It is of limited capacity in this regard, holding (in the example run shown later) seven elements.[5] STM holds the seven most recent expressions: they are pushed into the front of the memory and disappear off the end.

Figure 2 gives the full definition of the production systems for S2. The expressions in the figure are interpreted by a production system program (called PSG, for production system, version G). The system is written in a system building system called L*(F) (for L*, version F), which is a homegrown system (Newell, McCracken, Robertson, & Freeman, 1971) though nothing has to be known about L* for this paper.

There are eight problem space operators. Three of them (FC, FNC and FLA) function to direct attention; essentially they obtain operands. Three others (PC, AV

---

[5] The behavior of the system in problem solving appears to depend only weakly on the exact assumptions about the size of STM and whether it is constant or somewhat fluctuating in size. This is because STM is indeed a buffer memory, which is mostly filled with junk anyway. The general problem solving methods used by a subject avoid critical dependence on the size of STM. With respect to memory errors, which are rare events, the dependence on STM characteristics is not well understood for humans and is not represented in the system.

and TD) do the main work.[6] Finally, two operators (RA, RV) are devoted to recall of information in LTM.

A complete model of the subject's behavior would include a representation of the display (essentially as given in Figure 1) and programs for each operator. In fact, the model makes a distinction between the control structure for evoking the operators and the internal structure of the operators themselves. Consequently, the system of Figure 2 goes down only to the evocation of operators. It then asks for an exogenous specification of the output of the operator within the context in which it was evoked. This shows up in Figure 2 by the fact that all operators are defined as (OPR CALL). OPR identifies the symbol as designating an operator. CALL calls to the terminal running the system to obtain the required output of the operator. The user provides the behavior of each of the operators by typing in these requested outputs.

There are good reasons to run a model of problem solving this way. To model the operators requires a more detailed model of the immediate processor and perceptual mechanisms than the theory of problem solving is prepared to provide. Perhaps more important, in mapping the output of the system on the behavior of a subject there must be a way to correct the system when it commits errors (often called "putting the simulation back on the track"). If this is not done, the accumulation of a few errors causes the system and the behavior to diverge completely and bear no further resemblance to each other, even though the model may be perfect from then on. This follows from the memory-dependent character of cognitive behavior, which tends to magnify small differences. One technique to correct for errors is to force the behavior of the operators so as to keep the system on the track (though stringent limits bound how much a model can be steered in this way). Error scores can then be generated by examining the number of arbitrary outputs required of the operators. Ultimately, the system does not run either in pure CALL mode or in automatic. Rather, programs are used for the regular and predictable parts of the operators, and CALLs are used only when the output cannot be predicted. However, the system of Figure 2 calls for all operator outputs.

The condition sides of productions are written in terms of classes of expressions, which also serve to define completely the forms of knowledge elements. The classes assumed in the example are given after the operators in Figure 2.[7] The operational significance of these classes is determined by how they occur in the condition sides of the productions given later in the figure (A few classes, e.g., ⟨GOAL⟩, never occur per se in condition, but merely serve to show the form of expressions.)

The productions themselves are divided into two functional groups, the Gs and the PDs. The Gs are concerned with the manipulation of the goal system. The PDs are concerned with the task of cryptarithmetic. The production system itself, PS1,

---

[6] Other descriptions include a fourth operator, GN, which generates the values of a letter. The bit of behavior we are simulating does not happen to evoke GN, so it is absent from the system described here.

[7] The angle-bracket notation for class names is purely mnemonic and is not interpreted by the system.

```
00100   ; CY15F: CRYPTARITHMETIC PRODUCTION SYSTEM
00200   ;         FOR S2, TRY 15 (BOOK VERSION) ON CROSS+ROADS=DANGER
00300   ;         REQUIRES PSGF, U1F, DICTF, UTILF
00400   ;
00500   DEFINE.SYMBOLS!
00600   ;
00700   CY.CONTEXT SET.CONTEXT!
00800   ;
00900   ; MAKE NAMES AVAILABLE FOR USE IN CY.CONTEXT
01000   TD* TD CHANGE.NAMES!
01100   ;
01200   DEFINE.PROCESSES!
01300   ;
01400   ; NOTICING OPERATORS:
01500   ;   SET VALUES OF VARIABLES AND (POSSIBLY) PRODUCE <NTC-EXP>
01600   ;
01700   FC: (OPR CALL)  ; FIND COLUMN CONTAINING LETTER <L> (=> <COL>)
01750
01800   FNC: (OPR CALL) ; FIND NEXT UNPROCESSED COLUMN (=> <COL>)
01900   FLA· (OPR CALL) ; FIND LETTER ABOVE LINE IN COLUMN <COL>(=> <L>)
02000   ;
02100   ; STM OPERATORS:
02200   ;   PRODUCE NEW ELEMENTS OR MODIFY EXISTING ELEMENTS IN STM
02300   ;
02400   PC: (OPR CALL) ; PROCESS COLUMN <COL> (=> <EXP>, <GOAL>)
02500   AV: (OPR CALL) ; ASSIGN VARIABLE <VAR> (=> <EXP>, <GOAL>)
02600   TD: (OPR CALL) ; TEST DIGIT <D> FOR LETTER <L> (=> <EXP>,<GOAL>)
02700   RA: (OPR CALL) ; RECALL ANTECEDENT OF <EXP> (=> <EXP>,<COL>)
02800   RV: (OPR CALL) ; RECALL VARIABLE <VAR> (=> <D>)
02900   ;
03000   DEFINE.SYMBOLS!
03100   ; DEFINE CLASSES FOR USE IN PRODUCTION CONDITIONS
03200   ;
03300   ; CLASSES FOR CRYPTARITHMETIC KNOWLEDGE
03400   ;
03500   <D>:   (CLASS 0 1 2 3 4 5 6 7 8 9)
03600   <L>:   (CLASS A C D E G N O R S)
03700   <C>:   (CLASS C1 C2 C3 C4 C5 C6)
03800   <COL>: (CLASS COL.1 COL.2 COL.3 COL.4 COL.5 COL.6)
03900   <VAR>: (CLASS <L> <C>)
04000   <OBJ>: (CLASS <L> <D>)
04100   <EQ>:  (CLASS = <-->)
04200   <IEQ>: (CLASS > < >= <= )
04300   <REL>: (CLASS <EQ> <IEQ>)
04400   <TAG>: (CLASS NEW OLD NOT)
04500   <EXP>: (CLASS (<VAR> <REL> <OBJ>) (<TAG> <VAR> <REL> <OBJ>))
04600   ;
04700   ; CLASSES FOR GOAL EXPRESSIONS
04800   ;
04900   <G>:   (CLASS GOAL OLDG)
05000   <SIG>: (CLASS * % + -)
05100   <END>: (CLASS + -)
05200   <COND>: (CLASS -COND +COND)
05300   <SIG-EXP>: (<SIG> <COND>)
05400   <COND-EXP>: (COND <COND> <END>)
05500   <GOAL-TYPE>: (CLASS USE GET CHECK RECALL SOLVE <OPR>)
05600   <GOAL-SPEC>: (CLASS <COL> <VAR> <OBJ>
05700                      (<VAR> <COL>) (<COL> <VAR>) (<VAR> <OBJ>))
05800   <GOAL>: (CLASS (<G> && <SIG-EXP> <GOAL-TYPE>)
05900                  (<G> && <SIG-EXP> <GOAL-TYPE> && <GOAL-SPEC>))
06000   ;
06100   <OPR>: (CLASS PC AV TD RA RV)
06200   <NTC>: (CLASS FNC FC FLA)
06300   <NTC-COND>: (CLASS MORE END)
06400   <NTC-EXP>: (CLASS (<NTC-COND> <NTC>) (OLD <NTC-COND> <NTC>))
```

(Continued)

```
06500   ;
06600   <KNOWLEDGE-ELEMENT>: (CLASS <GOAL> <EXP> <COND-EXP> <NTC-EXP>)
06700   ;
06800   ; TOTAL PRODUCTION SYSTEM
06900   ;
07000   PS1: (GS1 PS2 GS2)
07100   ;
07200   ; PRODUCTION SYSTEM FOR MANIPULATING GOALS
07300   ;
07400   GS1: (G1 G3 G10 G9 G5 G6 G7 G8 G4)
07500   GS2: (G2 G11)
07600   ;
07700   G1:  ((GOAL <END>) --> (GOAL ==> OLDG))
07800   G2:  ((GOAL *) ABS AND (GOAL %) --> (% ==> *))
07900   G3:  ((GOAL *) AND (GOAL *) --> (* ===> %))
08000   G4:  ((GOAL * <OPR>) --> <OPR>)
08100   G5:  ((GOAL * <COND>) AND (OLDG <END>) --> (<COND> ==>)
08200        (COND <COND> <END>))
08300   G6:  ((COND +COND +) AND (GOAL *) --> (COND ==> OLD COND)
08400        (* ===> +))
08500   G7:  ((COND -COND -) AND (GOAL *) --> (COND ==> OLD COND)
08600        (* ===> -))
08700   G8:  ((COND) AND (GOAL *) --> (COND ==> OLD COND))
08800   G9:  ((MORE) AND (GOAL *) --> (* ===> %))
08900   G10: ((MORE <NTC>) AND (END <NTC>) --> (MORE ==> OLD MORE))
09000   G11: ((GOAL %) ABS AND (GOAL *) ABS AND (GOAL <END> SOLVE) ABS
09100        --> (GOAL * SOLVE))
09200   ;
09300   ; PRODUCTION SYSTEM FOR TASK
09400   ;
09500   PS2: (PD5 PD3 PD4 PD2 PD6 PD7 PD9 PD10 PD11 PD12 PD1 PD8)
09600   ;
09700   PD1:  ((NEW <L> = <D>) --> FC (GOAL * USE <COL>))
09800   PD2:  ((NEW <L> <-- <D>) --> (GOAL * PC))
09900   PD3:  ((GOAL * USE <COL>) --> (USE ==> PC))
10000   PD4:  ((GOAL * GET <VAR>) --> FC (GET ==> PC <COL>))
10100   PD5:  ((GOAL * USE <COL>) AND (OLDG - PC <COL>) -->
10200         FLA (USE <COL> ==> AV <COL> <L>))
10300   PD6:  ((NEW <L> <IEQ> <D>) --> (GOAL * AV <L>))
10400   PD7:  ((NOT <L> <-- <D>) --> (GOAL * AV <L>))
10500   PD8:  ((GOAL * SOLVE) --> FNC (* ==> %) (GOAL * USE <COL>))
10600   PD9:  ((NEW <L> = <OBJ>) AND (<G> <SIG> TD <L> <OBJ>) ABS -->
10700         (GOAL * TD <L> <OBJ>))
10800   PD10: ((NOT <L> = <D>) --> RA (NOT && <EXP>))
10900   PD11: ((GOAL * CHECK <VAR>) --> RA (NEW && <EXP>))
11000   PD12: ((GOAL * RECALL <VAR>) --> RA (<VAR> ==> <VAR> <COL>) RV)
11100   ;
11200   STM: (NIL NIL NIL NIL NIL NIL NIL)
11300   ;
11400   "CY15F LOADED (NOTE: DIGITS ARE CHARS)" RETURN.TO.TTY!
11500
11600
11700
```

FIG. 2. Specifications for S2 on CROSS+ROADS=DANGER.

is a single list of productions, but is given as three sublists—the productions of GS1
followed by those of PS2 followed by those of GS2. Seen as a single-ordered list of
productions, goal manipulation productions come first (i.e., have priority), except
for the few in GS2 that provide a backup action in case none of the task
productions is triggered by the current STM contents.

The detailed set of conventions for production are given in the appendix. The easiest way to understand them is to consider simple examples of a particular production applied to STM. Afterwards we will comment on some of the psychologically relevant aspects. First, we describe the system in its own terms.

Figure 3 shows PD2 applied to a STM holding only a single expression.[8] Since this is matched by the condition form of PD2, the action is executed. The match consists of an identity between the constants NEW and ←, and class inclusion for s as a letter (the class ⟨L⟩) and 1 as a digit (the class ⟨D⟩). The system prints out that the condition of PD2 is satisfied (TRUE). This action consists of an expression, which then enters the STM. Since, the STM only contains a single element, this forces the prior element out of STM, as shown by the print out of STM after the action.

```
stm: ((new s <-- 1))
pd2 try.pd!
PD2: ((NEW <L> <-- <D>) --> (GOAL * PC))
PD2 TRUE
STM: ((GOAL * PC))
```

FIG. 3. Entering new element into STM; fixed size of STM.

Figure 4 shows PD1 applied to a STM of three elements. The middle element matches PD1, thus evoking the action. Because this element, (NEW R = 5), was attended to by the evoked condition, it is moved to the front of STM. Thus, a continuous reshuffling of STM occurs according to what items are attended to (which amounts to an automatic rehearsal mechanism). The action of PD1 consists of two elements. The first is FC. This operator produces the column that is to be attended to. However, as explained above, instead of executing a program for FC, the system calls to the terminal for an answer. It prints out the context in which this answer is to be provided, namely the elements that were recognized by the condition of PD1, including the values for variables and class names (that ⟨D⟩ is 5 and ⟨L⟩ is R). All other elements in STM are essentially out of reach by the actions

[8] The user's input is in lower case, the system's output in upper case. The system does not distinguish upper and lower case (e.g., stm = STM). try.pd is an executive routine and the ! means to execute the preceding routine (here try.pd) immediately.

```
stm: ((new s <-- 1)(new r = 5)(goal * solve))
pd1 try.pd!
PD1: ((NEW <L> = <D>) --> FC (GOAL * USE <COL>))
PD1  TRUE
     (NEW R = 5)
     (<D> 5 <L> R)
     OUTPUT FOR FC = (<col> == col.1)
!z,z
STM: ((GOAL * USE COL.1) (NEW R = 5) (NEW S <-- 1))
```

FIG. 4. Call on terminal for operator output; assignment of value to class names; sequence of actions.

(though another example later will qualify this statement). The answer, as typed in by the user (in lower case), indicates that the symbol ⟨COL⟩ is to have the value COL. 1.[9] ⟨COL⟩ is a class name as well, but in the context of a production it can have associated with it the particular member of the class under consideration. The second element of the PD1 action is an element to be entered into STM, just as in the first example. However, this element contains a symbol that has an assigned value, so that the element is correspondingly instantiated.

```
stm: ((oldg - pc col.3)(goal * use col.3))
pd5 try.pd!
PD5: ((GOAL * USE <COL>) AND
      (OLDG - PC <COL>) --> FLA (USE <COL> ==> AV <COL> <L>))
PD5   TRUE

      (GOAL * USE COL.3)
      (<COL> COL.3)
      OUTPUT FOR FLA = (<l> == r)
l.z,z
STM: ((GOAL * AV COL.3 R) (OLDG - PC COL.3))
```

FIG. 5. Conjunction of conditions.

Figure 5 shows a STM in which PD5 can be evoked. The condition of PD5 consists of a conjunction (AND) of two expressions both of which have to be found in STM. The order in STM is not important, as the example shows. However, the first element of the conditions serves to determine the value of ⟨COL⟩, which is then used in the match of second element (notice that (OLDG - PC COL. 3) was skipped over). The two elements matched by the condition of PD5 must be distinct; once the first one is matched it is excluded as a candidate for further matches. The action of PD5 is not to put a new element into STM, but to modify the one that is there. First, the attention-directing operator FLA is executed, leading to specifying ⟨L⟩ to be R. Then, in the first element of STM, (GOAL * USE COL. 1), the symbol sequence "USE COL. 1" is identified and replaced by "AV COL. 1 R."

```
stm: ((goal * pc)(goal * solve))
g3 try.pd!
G3: ((GOAL*) AND (GOAL *) --> (* ===> %))
G3   TRUE
STM: ((GOAL * PC) (GOAL % SOLVE))
```

FIG. 6. Each condition element matches distinct element; modification of existing element.

Figure 6 shows the operation of G3, the goal production that assures that only one goal is current at a time. STM contains two current goals (each contains *). The condition side of G2 identifies both of these, because the match need only account for the symbols in the condition element. Thus (GOAL *) will match any goal element with the signal *. Since, as noted above, each element of a condition must

[9] The lz, z is a signal to return control from the user to the system A signal is required because the system has given the user indefinite control.

match a distinct element of STM, the second (GOAL *), though identical to the first, matches the second element of that form in STM. The action of G3 is to replace the signal for current (*) with the signal for interrupted (%). Note that this takes place in the second element in STM, as designated by = = ⇒ (instead of = ⇒ which operates on the first element).

Figure 7 shows the operation of G2, the goal production that assures that there is a current goal. It also consists of a conjunction of two condition elements. The first, however, requires the absence (ABS) of an element of the stated form, in this case the absence of a goal with the signal *. The second element identifies this most recently interrupted goal (the one with %): If there are several % goals in the STM, then the first one is taken. Thus, the order of elements in STM is consequential, since an element toward the front can shield an element further back from being picked up. The action of G2 is to replace % by * in the second element identified. (Since the first element does not exist, the second is at the front of STM; hence = ⇒ is appropriate rather than = = ⇒).

```
stm: ((goal - pc)(goal % solve))
g2 try.pd!
G2: ((GOAL *) ABS AND (GOAL %) --> (% ==> *))
G2   TRUE
STM: ((GOAL * SOLVE) (GOAL - PC))
```

FIG. 7. Absence of element condition.

G2 does not handle all situations that lack a current goal. If there is no interrupted goal in the STM (no goal with %), then G2 will not be evoked. However, G11 will then be evoked. It responds to an absence of a current goal, an absence of any interrupted goal, and an absence of a goal saying the problem is all over (⟨END⟩ being either of the terminating signals, + or −). Its action is to put the top goal (GOAL * SOLVE) back into STM. This production is one type of LTM retrieval, since it says that the top goal is remembered whether or not it remains in STM.

```
stm: ((goal * pc)(goal % solve)(new s <-- 1)(oldg + av col.1 s)
     (oldg - pc col.4 r)(oldg - pc col.1)(old cond -cond -))
g4 try.pd!
G4: ((GOAL * <OPR>) --> <OPR>)
G4   TRUE
     (GOAL * PC)
     (<OPR> PC)
     OUTPUT FOR PC = (* ==> +)(ntc (new s <-- 1))
                     (new ==> old)(new r = 2)
Iz,z
STM: ((NEW R = 2) (OLD S <-- 1) (GOAL + PC) (GOAL % SOLVE) (OLDG +
AV COL.1 S) (OLDG - PC  COL.4 R) (OLDG - PC COL.1))
```

FIG. 8. Complex output of operator; use of NTC.

A final example is given in Figure 8, which reveals something of the nature of the interaction between operators and productions. The STM is taken from the illustrative run shown later and contains a number of miscellaneous elements as well as those relevant to the current action. The current goal is to apply PC and this evokes goal production G4, leading to the call on the terminal. The output of PC, supplied by the user, provides several things. First, it changes the signal of the goal to +, since it is producing a new item of information. Second, in producing this item it makes use of the element (NEW S ←− 1), and this must be changed to (OLD S ←− 1). If PC were realized by a production system itself, then its productions would both find this element in STM and modify it. A secondary effect would be to bring the element up toward the front of STM. Thus, to simulate this the action element (NTC(NEW S ←− 1)) notices (NEW S ←− 1) in STM and brings it forward; then the action (NEW = ⇒ OLD) makes the change. Finally, the new knowledge element, (NEW R = 2) is produced. This example shows that the result of an operator, when called for, can be any sequence of actions that is legitimate for production.

The foregoing examples cover most of the types of actions possible. The full set is listed in the appendix. We show a couple of pages of running trace from this system in Figure 9, so its total behavior can be followed through. The important thing to observe is the level of detail at which the system operates. We will not compare this trace with the subject's behavior, though for orientation Figure 10 gives the bit of protocol covered by the sequence of Figure 9.

```
ps1 ps!
8.  STM: (NIL NIL NIL NIL NIL NIL NIL)
G11   TRUE
1.  STM: ((GOAL * SOLVE) NIL NIL NIL NIL NIL NIL)
PD8   TRUE
         (GOAL * SOLVE)
         (NIL)
         OUTPUT FOR FNC = (<col> == col.1)
!z,z
5.  STM: ((GOAL * USE COL.1) (GOAL % SOLVE) NIL NIL NIL NIL NIL)
PD3   TRUE
6.  STM: ((GOAL * PC COL.1) (GOAL % SOLVE) NIL NIL NIL NIL NIL)
G4   TRUE
         (GOAL * PC COL.1)
         (<OPR> PC)
         OUTPUT FOR PC = (* ==> % -cond) (goal * get s) (goal * get r)
!z,z
18.  STM: ((GOAL * GET R) (GOAL * GET S) (GOAL % -COND PC COL.1) (GOAL % SOLVE) NIL NIL NIL)
G3   TRUE
11.  STM: ((GOAL * GET R) (GOAL % GET S) (GOAL % -COND PC COL.1) (GOAL % SOLVE) NIL NIL NIL)
PD4   TRUE
         (GOAL * GET R)
         (<VAR> R)
         OUTPUT FOR FC = (<col> == col.4)
!z,z
14.  STM: ((GOAL * PC COL.4 R) (GOAL % GET S) (GOAL % -COND PC COL.1) (GOAL % SOLVE) NIL NIL NIL)
G4   TRUE
         (GOAL * PC COL.4 R)
         (<OPR> PC)
         OUTPUT FOR PC = (* ==> -)
!z,z
16.  STM: ((GOAL - PC COL.4 R) (GOAL % GET S) (GOAL % -COND PC COL.1) (GOAL % SOLVE) NIL NIL NIL)
G1   TRUE
17.  STM: ((OLDG - PC COL.4 R) (GOAL % GET S) (GOAL % -COND PC COL.1) (GOAL % SOLVE) NIL NIL NIL)
G2   TRUE
18.  STM: ((GOAL * GET S) (OLDG - PC COL.4 R) (GOAL % -COND PC COL.1) (GOAL % SOLVE) NIL NIL NIL)
PD4   TRUE
         (GOAL * GET S)
         (<VAR> S)
         OUTPUT FOR FC = (<col> == col.2)
!z,z
21. STM: ((GOAL * PC COL.2 S) (OLDG - PC COL.4 R) (GOAL % -COND PC COL.1) (GOAL % SOLVE) NIL NIL
NIL)
G4   TRUE
         (GOAL * PC COL.2 S)
```

(Continued)

```
        (<OPR> PC)
        OUTPUT FOR PC = (& ==> -)
|z,z
23. STM: ((GOAL - PC COL.2 S) (OLDG - PC COL.4 R) (GOAL % -COND PC COL.1) (GOAL % SOLVE) NIL NIL
NIL)
G1   TRUE
24. STM:  ((OLDG - PC COL.2 S) (OLDG - PC COL.4 R) (GOAL % -COND PC COL.1) (GOAL % SOLVE) NIL
NIL NIL)
G2   TRUE
25.  STM: ((GOAL * -COND PC COL.1) (OLDG - PC COL.2 S) (OLDG - PC COL.4 R) (GOAL % SOLVE) NIL
NIL NIL)
G5   TRUE
27. STM: ((COND -COND -) (GOAL * PC COL.1) (OLDG - PC COL.2 S) (OLDG - PC COL.4 R) (GOAL %
SOLVE) NIL NIL)
G7   TRUE
29. STM: ((OLD COND -COND -) (GOAL - PC COL.1) (OLDG - PC COL.2 S) (OLDG - PC COL.4 R) (GOAL %
SOLVE) NIL NIL)
G1   TRUE
30. STM: ((OLDG - PC COL.1) (OLD COND -COND -) (OLDG - PC COL.2 S) (OLDG - PC COL.4 R) (GOAL %
SOLVE) NIL NIL)
G2   TRUE
31. STM: ((GOAL * SOLVE) (OLDG - PC COL.1) (OLD COND -COND -) (OLDG - PC COL.2 S) (OLDG - PC
COL.4 R) NIL NIL)
PD8  TRUE
        (GOAL * SOLVE)
        (NIL)
        OUTPUT FOR FNC = (<col> == col.1)
|z,z
35. STM: ((GOAL * USE COL.1) (GOAL & SOLVE) (OLDG - PC COL.1) (OLD COND -COND -) (OLDG - PC
COL.2 S) (OLDG - PC COL.4 R) NIL)
PD5  TRUE
        (GOAL * USE COL.1)
        (<COL> COL.1)
        OUTPUT FOR FLA = (<I> == s)
|z,z
38.  STM: ((GOAL * AV COL.1 S) (OLDG - PC COL.1) (GOAL % SOLVE) (OLD COND -COND -) (OLDG - PC
COL.2 S) (OLDG - PC COL.4 R) NIL)
G4   TRUE
        (GOAL * AV COL.1 S)
        (<OPR> AV)
        OUTPUT FOR AV = (* ==> %)(goal * get r)
|z,z
41.  STM: ((GOAL * GET R) (GOAL % AV COL.1 S) (OLDG - PC COL.1) (GOAL % SOLVE) (OLD COND -COND -)
(OLDG - PC COL.2 S) (OLDG - PC COL.4 R))
PD4  TRUE
        (GOAL * GET R)
        (<VAR> R)
        OUTPUT FOR FC = (<col> == col.4)
|z,z
44. STM: ((GOAL * PC COL.4 R) (GOAL & AV COL.1 S) (OLDG - PC COL.1) (GOAL % SOLVE) (OLD COND
-COND -) (OLDG - PC COL.2 S) (OLDG - PC COL.4 R))
G4   TRUE
        (GOAL * PC COL.4 R)
        (<OPR> PC)
        OUTPUT FOR PC = (* ==> -)
|z,z
46. STM: ((GOAL - PC COL.4 R) (GOAL / AV COL.1 S) (OLDG - PC COL.1) (GOAL % SOLVE) (OLD COND
-COND -) (OLDG - PC COL.2 S) (OLDG - PC COL.4 R))
G1   TRUE
47. STM: ((OLDG - PC COL.4 R) (GOAL & AV COL.1 S) (OLDG - PC COL.1) (GOAL % SOLVE) (OLD COND
-COND -) (OLDG - PC COL.2 S) (OLDG - PC COL.4 R))
G2   TRUE
48. STM: ((GOAL * AV COL.1 S) (OLDG - PC COL.4 R) (OLDG - PC COL.1) (GOAL % SOLVE) (OLD COND
-COND -) (OLDG - PC COL.2 S) (OLDG - PC COL.4 R))
G4   TRUE
        (GOAL * AV COL.1 S)
        (<OPR> AV)
        OUTPUT FOR AV = (* ==> +)(new s <-- 1)
|z,z
51. STM: ((NEW S <-- 1) (GOAL + AV COL.1 S) (OLDG - PC COL.4 R) (OLDG - PC COL.1) (GOAL %
SOLVE) (OLD COND -COND -) (OLDG - PC COL.2 S))
G1   TRUE
52.  STM: ((OLDG + AV COL.1 S) (NEW S <-- 1) (OLDG - PC COL.4 R) (OLDG - PC COL.1) (GOAL %
SOLVE) (OLD COND -COND -) (OLDG - PC COL.2 S))
PD2  TRUE
53.  STM: ((GOAL * PC) (NEW S <-- 1) (OLDG + AV COL.1 S) (OLDG - PC COL.4 R) (OLDG - PC COL.1)
(GOAL % SOLVE) (OLD COND -COND -))
G4   TRUE
        (GOAL * PC)

      (<OPR> PC)
      OUTPUT FOR PC = (* ==> +)(ntc (new s <-- 1))(new ==> old)(new r = 2)
```

                                                                      (Continued)

```
|z,z
58.  STM: ((NEW R = 2) (OLD S <-- 1) (GOAL + PC) (OLDG + AV COL.1 S) (OLDG - PC COL.4 R) (OLDG -
PC COL>1) (GOAL % SOLVE))
G1   TRUE
59.  STM: ((OLDG + PC) (NEW R = 2) (OLD S <-- 1) (OLDG + AV COL.1 S) (OLDG - PC COL.4 R) (OLDG -
PC COL.1) (GOAL % SOLVE))
PD9  TRUE
60.  STM: ((GOAL * TD R 2) (NEW R = 2) (OLDG + PC) (OLD S <-- 1) (OLDG + AV COL.1 S) (OLDG - PC
COL.4 R) (OLDG - PC COL.1))
G4   TRUE
        (GOAL * TD R 2)
        (<OPR> TD)
        OUTPUT FOR TD = (* ==> +)
```

FIG. 9 Trace of PS of Figure 2.

Phrase number	Time (secs)	Eye-movement Aggregation	Verbalization	STM number
B0	0	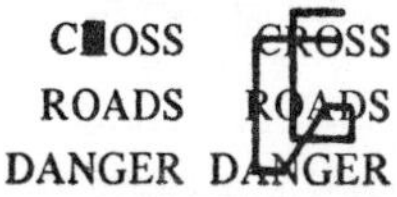 CROSS CROSS ROADS ROADS DANGER DANGER		0
B1	6	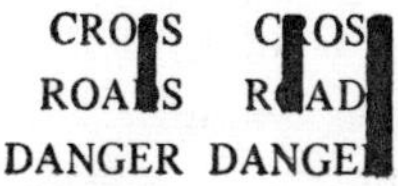 CROSS CROSS ROADS ROAD DANGER DANGE	CROSS Plus ROADS is DANGER	1
B2	10	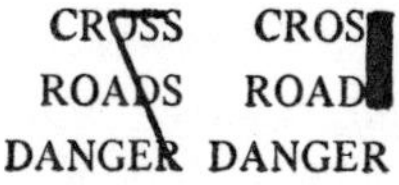 CROSS CROS ROADS ROAD DANGER DANGER	Exp: Please talk.	(none)
B3	12	 CROSS ROADS DANGER	Yes.	
B4	14	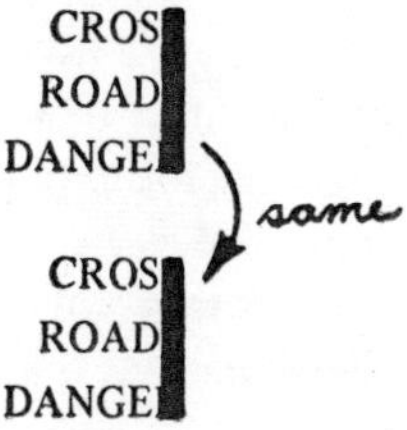 CROS ROAD DANGE	S plus S has to equal R.	6
B5	18	CROS ROAD DANGE	And R will have to equal two S.	
B6	24	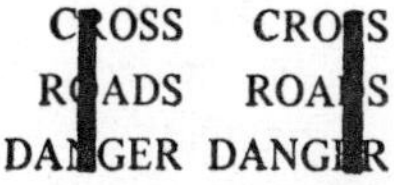 CROSS CROS ROADS ROAD DANGER DANGER	And S plus D also has to equal E.	14
B7	28	 CROSS CROS ROADS ROAD DANGER DANGER	So I'll let S equal . .	31

same

(Continued)

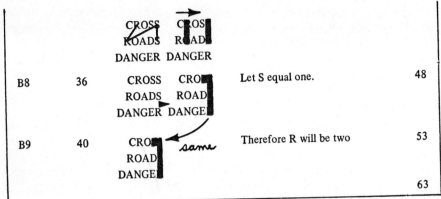

B8	36	CROSS CROS ROADS ROAD DANGER DANGE	Let S equal one.	48
B9	40	CRO ROAD DANGE *same*	Therefore R will be two	53
				63

FIG. 10. Protocol of S2 corresponding to trace in Figure 9.

Psychologically Relevant Features

We can now summarize and comment on a number of the psychologically relevant features of this system, both PSG, the production system, and CY15, the particular system for S2 on CROSS + ROADS = DANGER.

1. The system is serial, executing one action at a time.

2. In gross outline the memory structure is the classical one (Miller, 1956; Waugh & Norman, 1965) of an STM consisting of a limited number of chunks (here symbolic expressions) and an LTM. No account has been taken of any of the indications that the memory structure might be more complex (e.g., Wickelgren, 1970; Broadbent, 1970). The problem solving behavior on which the model is based gives no hint that more complexity is required.

3. The representation of STM is complete and explicit. The number of chunks is a parameter of the system. The depth of detail that can be examined in each chunk is determined by the content of the production conditions.

4. There is no complete representation of LTM. A production is a retrieval on LTM; thus, the set of productions represents the content of LTM with the conditions of the production being the accessing paths. In addition, the ability to construct embedded expressions provides a second form of LTM. But there is no assertion that these constitute the only forms of LTM.

5. There is no direct representation of the writing of new information into LTM. Thus, the model does not handle learning situations that call for modification of LTM.[10]

6. The productions represent a kind of S-R connection between a stimulus, as represented by elements in STM, and a response, as stored in LTM as an element on the action side of a production. However, productions are substantially more complex than classical S-Rs. The link between S and R is made via a match operation that permits identification and instantiation of variables as well as tests for class membership. The actions permit modification of existing elements, as well as the addition of new ones, and in this latter case (the one more like the classical R) instantiation of variables is permitted, as determined by prior conditions or actions.

---

[10] Currently, this is a key theoretical issue. It is not at all clear how LTM acquisition is to take place.

7. There is no representation of the EM, the perceptual mechanism, or the details of the immediate processor. Thus, the model is primarily about the control structure of behavior at the problem solving level.

8. Rehearsal occurs automatically in STM if something is attended to. This is a movement of the attended-to element in STM, not the creation of a copy. Strategies of rehearsal, therefore, are attempts to attend to something, possibly without concern for what processing occurs.

9. There is a highly particular matching system in PSG, the rules of which are summarized in the appendix. Much of the variation in versions of the production system have been in details of this matching scheme. Almost no psychological information is available on which to make direct determination of these details. Several central issues can be identified in information processing terms, but for none of these can the psychological consequences be given: (*a*) The productions deal with information they do not already know in full detail. That is, elements are identified by only partial information. What form should this indirectness take? The use of variables (the class names) is one form. Matching only the symbols in the condition element, not all the ones in STM element, is another (it lets an entire expression be picked up by one part of it, as in the (GOAL *) conditions). Not matching in sequential order is yet another (providing something somewhere does respond to the order). (*b*) What role does order in STM play? In the current system order is revealed in part by the masking of old elements by recent ones, which is a function of the match. This interacts strongly with the more general question of how STM should be structured (as a circulating memory, as a stack (as here), as an unorganized set of cells, as a constructed set of embedded expressions, etc.). (*c*) Should an STM element be able to satisfy more than one element in a condition? The current systems insists on exclusiveness and without it many additional condition elements would be required to force exclusiveness. But should there be some mechanism to permit a designated condition element to be matched to any element in STM independent of other matches? Exclusiveness implies serial dependence in conditions, so that (A AND B) is not the same condition as (B AND A). (*d*) How deep can the match search in an expression? The current system searches recursively; earlier versions did not, and in fact CY15 demands only a single level of search. That is, no embedded expressions such as (GOAL * (NEW ⟨L⟩ = (OLD ⟨D⟩))) occur on the condition side of productions. (*e*) What kind of processing can be done during a match? The current match permits a variable to be defined in one element and used in match elsewhere in the same element or in a following element. This enlarges the class of conditions that can be discriminated. Earlier matches permitted only class inclusion to be recognized (e.g., the system could match (⟨L⟩ = ⟨L⟩) but could not discriminate (R = R) from (R = D). Note that we are talking about what goes on in the match, not what is ultimately possible in the total system by the action of a sequence of productions. The current use of variables introduces a second form of serial dependence in condition elements.

10. Although it may have escaped the reader's notice, an additional "very immediate memory" is required to make the system operate. The actions of a condition make use of variable assignments determined during the match (e.g., the use of ⟨COL⟩ in Figure 4). This means that these assignments must be remembered

from the moment that they are made (in the match) until they are used (in the action). This may be a matter of a few hundred milliseconds up to a second, depending on the time span allotted to a production (a matter discussed below). The STM cannot be used for this memory in any simple way, since if these assignments were put into STM as an element, then another production would have to recognize them again for the action element to deal with. There is a temptation to identify this very-immediate-memory with some of the iconic stores. All that is established, of course, is a functional requirement. Conceivably it can be dispensed with, but the contortions required are not yet clear.

11. There is no general way to designate directly the various elements of STM, as by a naming or addressing scheme. The actions obtain access to the elements via their position in the condition of the match (which is essentially mirrored in terms of position in the front of the STM, though it need not be with slight variants of the shuffle scheme used for rehearsal). Non-matched STM elements do not exist for the actions (though subsearches can be made using the NTC mechanism). This leads to some awkwardness, e.g., in having separate modification operators ($= \Rightarrow$, $= = \Rightarrow$, $= = = \Rightarrow$) corresponding to first, second, and third elements. However, the alternative of an additional naming device raises conceptual problems of how to use it and what it would mean in terms of implied mechanism.

12. Operators do not have arguments in the usual sense, as PC(COL.3) or FC(R). This latter form of operand designation is equivalent to a closed subroutine organization, in which the internal processes of the operator have access only to the arguments. Operators do have access to a context, ultimately bounded by STM. But they are more like open subroutines, which do their work in the same workspace as everyone else, having access to contextually embedding information, as well as leaving around their temporary internal working data, possibly to be responded to by other productions. Thus an operator, such as PC, should be viewed as if it were simply another collection of productions written in line with the main set. This raises problems about the maintenance of control within PC until it is finished, but these are to be solved by matching the productions of PC dependent on elements placed in STM by PC (such as goal elements).

This lack of clean subroutine hierarchy appears to have both positive and negative consequences. On the systems side, it makes it difficult to construct production systems that accomplish specific tasks. The programmer (so to speak) cannot easily control what processing occurs, as he can when working in a standard programming system. On the psychological side, the lack of hierarchy accords well with a single level of awareness and with the sort of supervisory awareness that appears to be a concomitant of much conscious processing (e.g., observing the on-going processing). It also accords well with the potential for distraction that appears to characterize much human processing. In all cases, unfortunately, no good empirical characterizations exist that permit more than informal comparison.

13. When to copy a data structure and when to use the same data structure that occurs in a different context is a general systems problem. It is unresolved here as well. Identity of structure is required at some level, yet if the identical structure is used in two places, a modification at one place communicates (so to speak) simultaneous modification to the other place. This is both a powerful device and a

source of confusion and error. The issues are not clear from an information processing viewpoint, much less from a psychological one.

14. The productions represent the basic action cycle of the cognitive system. Thus, the time associated with a production must be somewhere in the 50–100 millisecond range. It is unclear whether the times typically generated in a Sternberg type of experiment, which are around 30 milliseconds per symbol examined, are to be taken as per-production or as indicating something about the search of a single production through STM. Typical internal processing acts, such as going down the alphabet, seem to require of the order of 200 milliseconds per item. But these would seem to require several productions per item. The counts shown in Figure 9 are obtained by adding 1 for each action element. They underestimate the time involved (i.e., do not multiply them by 100 milliseconds per production to get the time), since the time of the operators are not included. For instance, the subject actually takes 8 seconds to perform the simple addition of S + S with (S ← − 1) to get (R = 2), which only gets a count of 1 in the figure.

15. Although the implementation of the selection of the next production is clearly a serial affair in PSG, it undoubtedly corresponds to some parallel process.[11] The little production systems, such as CY15, are to be considered embedded in a very large set of productions (10^8 ?), that is, of the order of LTM. There may be context mechanisms that in fact select out a small production system for the control of local behavior, but the theory does not yet contain any hint of these.

In general the notion of parallel matching poses no difficulties, with two exceptions. First, the ordering of the productions imposes a global constraint, which could make parallel processing difficult. However, the functional aspect of the ordering appears to be such that specific productions shield general (back-up) versions of related productions. Thus, the ordering is only effective in little strands, which may prove tolerable. Second, with a complex match, involving variable identification and subsequent use within the match itself, the problems of carrying out an indefinite set of such processes simultaneously pose some difficulties. The imaginable sort of broadcast, content-addressed memories work with the matching of constants, that is, with locally definite patterns. With enough local logic, of course, almost anything is possible, but there may still be a strong interaction between the amount of parallelism and the sophistication of the matching process.

16. The system has a system of goals, meaning thereby a set of symbols that control processing in the service of ends to be achieved, permitting the creation of subgoals and the interruption of goal activity with its resumption at a later time.[12] The goal stack is not a separate memory, but is part of STM, with the various goal elements coexisting with other knowledge elements and taking up capacity. The production system for handling the goals (GS1) could be considered hardware relative to the production system for cryptarithmetic (PS2). There are additional

---

[11] As a side note, there is no dissonance (much less conflict) in a system being both highly serial and highly parallel at the same time (though not, of course, in the same respects).

[12] See Newell and Simon (1972, Ch. 14) for a discussion of the essential features of a goal system.

advantages to handling the goal stack in STM (besides avoiding the assumption of a distinct memory), namely, that STM contains knowledge of old goals, even after they have been popped off the goal stack by succeeding or failing. This feature is actually used in PD5 and PD9.

ON ENCODING THE STIMULUS

With the context provided by the model of information processing just described we can turn to the formulation of the problem of encoding the stimulus. It is worth noting, right at the start, that despite the somewhat recent emergence of coding as a significant theme in the main stream of psychology, the problem is not at all special. As soon as one proposes to design an information processing system to accomplish any of the tasks studied, say, in the psychology of learning, then the issue of representing the stimulus and the encoding operations to map the stimulus into its internal representation are forced to center stage. Only by approaching the problems of psychology by descriptive models that deal only in abstract features of behavior can the issues of encoding be avoided.[13]

Three things would seem to be involved in the encoding of a stimulus: the act of encoding, the representation of the code, and the act of decoding. However, it is only in a pure communication system that matters are so simple, where the only use made of the code is to decode it at the other end of the line. In a cognitive system, all manner of processing is accomplished in terms of the internal representation (i.e., the code): It is analyzed for significant features, problem solving methods are selected for it, these methods manipulate and modify it, determination of whether the task is accomplished is made by further processing of it, and so on. Thus, the act of decoding must be extended to an indefinite notion of use of the internal representation.

Let us consider, then, the first two items: the act of encoding and the code. In some sense the most important of these is the code. As indicated above, it is the code that influences all the processing that follows. Conversely, it is the code that is most easy to determine experimentally, since its characteristics are evidenced in many sorts of behavior. In agreement with this, most studies of coding have been devoted to establishing either that coding per se was present (a somewhat redundant exercise given the present viewpoint) or the nature of the code in a specific task environment.

The reasons for concern with the mechanisms of encoding, rather than just with the final code, are at least three-fold. First is the general presumption, stated at the beginning of the paper, that if one is to study coding one should have a model of the encoding process. Second, and a partial justification of the first, is the presumption that knowing how codes are formed will tell something about which

---

[13] Actually, constructing discrete symbolic simulations of the human contains its own dangers in masking the question of encoding. The stimulus must be represented in a discrete symbolic form for use in such simulations, hence it must in fact be encoded (relative to the actual stimulus faced by the human). It is possible to unwittingly perform a significant part of the stimulus encoding performed by the human in setting up the "stimulus" in the model.

codes eventually get formed and under what conditions. We will find out why we appear to be so sensitive to repetitions and alternations in the most diverse guises, when familiar patterns dominate over ruley patterns and vice-versa, when an established pattern inhibits another pattern from being seen, and so on. Third, coding is such a central feature of human information processing that it is necessary to have some model of it in order to develop a model of the immediate processor.

Encoding is not equivalent to all information processing, as the above remarks on the use of codes was meant to indicate. Yet, encoding is equivalent to the generation of internal representations. As such, the processes of encoding are not to be inferred from viewing the collection of different internal representations in use by humans. That collection is too diverse and its sources too multifold to permit such inferences.[14] The story of any major representation for an individual (such as how an astronaut encoded the stimulus of the approaching moon) involves chapters on learning, education, calculation, perception, conversation, and so on.

We wish to focus on the coding events that happen immediately when a stimulus is presented. An act of encoding happens there, since the subject cannot deal with the stimulus at all without producing such an encoding. This encoding may be the product of an indefinite amount of past processing and experience embedded in a current operating context of some depth. It still must be effected with only a modest amount of processing and with only a modest amount of understanding of the stimulus. These limitations follow from the decision to look at the leading edge of encoding: There is not time to do much processing or to develop much understanding; additionally, to do so would imply operating on the encoded stimulus, which would put the processing beyond the point of our interest.

This focus may be viewed as primarily tactical, to produce a scientific problem of manageable size. However, there are more substantial reasons. Changes of representation during the course of processing appear to be rare (though by no means absent). Certainly, in the problem solving tasks studied in Newell and Simon (1972) the problem representation remained fixed for most subjects. Furthermore, these representations were quite close to the problem-as-presented. Thus, the major part of stimulus encoding may occur in the instant, so to speak, when the new situation is presented. Building up a representation may require the extensive chapters mentioned above, but it may only become effective if it can be assimilated into an encoding operation that takes place in short order.[15]

Concern with the immediate processing of the new stimulus implies contact with perceptual mechanisms. Indeed, perception may be conveniently defined as the initial encoding of the stimulus, the one that cannot be fractionated further by the

---

[14] Indeed, what is surprising is the need to demonstrate that encoding is present, which has been the clear attempt in much of the psychological literature on coding. That is, it would be surprising, except for the prior position of stimulus-response psychology that ignored the encoding problem, except in rather carefully framed ways (such as the methodological issues of the nature of the functional stimulus).

[15] We do not put aside the processes involved in change of representation as uninteresting. Indeed, they seem both crucial and fascinating. Being rare events and under subject control, they are somewhat harder to capture experimentally than initial encodings, which are time locked to the presentation of a new stimulus.

behaving subject by normal means. However, the study of encoding mechanisms cannot be limited to perception, as it is usually defined and studied, since many of the issues of encoding involve the participation of conceptual information and conceptual processing.

Existing Proposals for the Mechanisms of Coding

We asserted above that the coding literature generally addresses itself to the existence and nature of the code, and not to the mechanisms of encoding. There are, however, a few studies that provide concrete proposals.

The work of EPAM (Elementary Perceiver and Memorizer) provides a detailed model of the encoding of verbal stimuli (Feigenbaum, 1961; Simon and Feigenbaum, 1964). If a presented stimulus can yield a familiar sequence of features, then it is encoded as a recognized chunk. The discrimination net used by EPAM is the mechanism of encoding and the growth of this net is a model of how new encodings become possible. Although the original work did not emphasize the encoding aspects, current work on how people perceive and remember complex chess positions constitutes a direct study of encoding (Chase & Simon, in press).

EPAM is a model of perception, the net being a mechanism that is evoked prior to STM, which receives the coded chunks as they are recognized. Thus, EPAM places the encoding operation in the perceptual mechanism and places the modification of the encoding in the relatively slow process of storage in LTM. The encodings permitted by EPAM are essentially structureless, they are whatever familiar patterns have been stored away. Some structure can be imposed on the patterns by suitable constraint in the learning mechanism. This has been done in the chess perception situation, where the patterns to be learned on the chess board are generated by relations that have chess-functional significance (e.g., who defends whom). Still, EPAM does not provide a model for the encoding of novel structured situations.

A variety of programs dealing with tasks involving the creation of conceptual structures do provide proposals for the mechanisms for encoding novel structure: classical discrete attribute-value concepts (Hunt, 1962; Johnson, 1964); binary choice experiments (Feldman, 1961; Feldman, Tonge, & Kanter, 1963);[16] and sequence extrapolation tasks (Simon & Kotovsky, 1963). Let us consider the latter example briefly; it will include the lessons from the others.

The task is to predict the next members in a sequence whose initial terms are given, or A B B C C D D − −. Simon and Kotovsky (1963) put forward a theory whose essential element was the representation that a subject would develop for the series, that is, an encoding of the stimulus. For the above series the encoding would be (Alphabet; Ml = A) [Say(M1), Next(M1), Say(M1)], which can be read: the alphabet is the standard alphabet; the initial value of pointer M1 is the letter A; say

---

[16] It is necessary to reach back to early work of an information processing sort to obtain suggestions about encoding mechanisms. Although some recent work in binary sequence prediction has emphasized strongly the structured aspects (e.g., Myers, 1970), it has done so by focussing on the codes themselves, that is, the run structure. This is a good illustration of the point made earlier about the character of the literature, even when working in a generalized information processing framework.

M1; move M1 to the next member in the alphabet; say M1; now repeat the sequence in brackets. The interpretation rules we have just indicated in concrete form tell how to use the representation. The subject presumably can manipulate such a representation rather freely. For example, he could answer such questions as: Will W ever occur in the sequence? What letters occur in the sequence only once?

In addition, Simon and Kotovsky provided a program for how the subject would induct the sequence from the given data. He would first attempt to discover a period in the given data (here 2) and the alphabet (here the standard alphabet). Then he would set up a hypothesis in the form of the specifications for each term in the cycle, as, $[x_1 \ x_2]$, where each x_1 is an expression that ends in the production of the given member of the sequence. Matching these against successive cycles of the given data would show that x_1 has to be Say(M1) (where M1 is a variable pointer into the alphabet) and x_2 has to be Next(M1), Say(M1).

The important aspect of Simon and Kotovsky's proposal for the encoding of the stimulus (the sequence) is that it is conceptual, that is, it occurs in the subject by deliberate acts of investigation and hypothecation in time periods of the order of tens of seconds. The initial encoding of the sequence is taken as we have represented it in the text, as a sequence of distinct letters. The additional structure is sufficiently disguised that the subject requires cognitive investigation to uncover it. This is in marked contrast with EPAM, in which the subject becomes aware only of the recognized chunks in the stimulus.

The other examples of work on concept formation generally concur.[17] The behavior model is at the processing level of many trials (covering tens to hundreds of seconds), thus being behavior at the cognitive level. The basic mechanisms are those of hypothesis and test, where sometimes the hypothesis is a form, whose details can be filled in by matching to the available data about exemplars. Most of these models, in common with the work of Simon and Kotovsky, do not incorporate a detailed model of the immediate processor and of STM, although they sometimes reflect short-term-memory load in a gross way. For example, Simon and Kotovsky measure the difficulty of a concept by the number of independent pointers, M1, M2, . . . that have to be maintained.

What is Provided by the Existing System

Let us now consider the present system, as exemplified by the production system in Figure 2, to see what it provides in the way of encoding mechanisms and what it is missing.

First, in line with the view already expressed of the ubiquity of encoding, as equivalent with internal representation, the theory provides a clear formulation of

---

[17] It is worth noting that a number of studies have appeared dealing with coding of sequences (Leewenberg, 1969; Restle, 1970; Vitz & Todd, 1969), similar to the Simon and Kotovsky study. None of these, except that of Simon and Kotovsky, provide proposals about the encoding mechanisms. However, in an as yet unpublished paper Simon (1972) analyzes all of these schemes and shows their fundamental similarity in terms of the code. Thus, we can assume, perhaps, similarity of the encoding procedures.

the encoding used by the subject for the task (here cryptarithmetic). The problem space is, in fact, exactly a statement of how the subject encodes the task: the basic concepts he uses; the way he can form them into larger concepts; and the operations he has for creating new instances of these concepts and responding to the instances he already has. Although we have not detailed it here, it is shown in great detail in Newell and Simon (1972) that the problem space is not determined by the task, but represents a construction by the subject. Thus, different subjects can have different problem spaces and, as one would expect, problem solving is strongly affected by the problem space used by a subject.

However, no theory is put forth about how a subject comes to have a specific problem space or what mechanisms determined it from the given information about the task (i.e., the stimulus). If we examine the model in Figure 2, we see that it finesses completely the input side from the environment, dealing only with the cognitive behavior on the internal representation in STM. Even if we extend the model to include specific processes for the operators (and substantial detail is given on these in the Newell and Simon book), it would still say nothing about the encoding of the perceived stimulus.

However, the theory does provide: (a) the form of the encoding, namely, the knowledge elements in STM; (b) the ways encoded knowledge can be read, namely, the types of conditions; and (c) the cognitive operations that manipulate encoded knowledge, namely, the types of actions that are possible. These provide a frame into which a complete theory of encoding must fit. Moreover, the theory provides an essentially complete set of mechanisms for the encoding that goes on at the cognitive level, as revealed by the various studies of concept attainment described above. For these encodings operate on representations that already exist in STM, producing other encodings in STM.

To clarify exactly what is provided by the theory as initially given, let us consider a simpler example than the sequence extrapolation. The task of N. F. Johnson (1970; this volume), already mentioned at the beginning of the paper, is a good example of a direct study of encoding. The subject is asked to perform a paired-associate task in which the stimuli are digits and the responses are sequences of consonants, as 1–QKFH. However, the consonant sequences are presented (in the various experimental conditions) with different spacing; X QK FH versus X QKF H versus XQ KF H, and so on. The underlying hypothesis is that the subject will encode the stimuli in the obvious fashion indicated by the spacing and that this will be revealed by the existence of errors in the responses, given some assumptions about the way the decoding occurs to make the response.

The theory at hand provides for a direct translation of a number of the features of this task, while remaining silent on some others. Figure 11 gives a small system that contains the natural encoding corresponding to Johnson's theory plus a set of productions for decoding this representation to yield the response. The example contains a single memorized paired associate, 1–X QK FH, since all that is important is to illustrate the scheme. It is represented as a production (PJ20), with the stimulus on the condition side and the encoded response as the action. The productions PJ1 to PJ4 decode the response by putting the subelements into STM directly (and marking the original sequence to show that it has been processed). The

```
00100    ; NJ: PERFORMANCE SYSTEM FOR NEAL JOHNSON CHUNKING TASK
00200    ;      (IDENTICAL TO NJ.A83)
00300    ;
00400    DEFINE.PROCESSES!
00500    ;
00600    SAY: (OPR <ITEM>eL PRVL)
00700    ;
00800    DEFINE.SYMBOLS!
00900    ;
01000    <D>: (CLASS 0 1 2 3 4 5 6 7 8 9)
01100    <K>: (CLASS B C D F G H J K L M N P Q R S T V W X Y Z)
01200    ;
01300    <ITEM>: (VAR)
01400    X0: (VAR)
01500    X1: (VAR)
01600    X2: (VAR)
01700    X3: (VAR)
01800    X4: (VAR)
01900    ;
02000    PJ4: ((SEQ X1 X2 X3 X4) --> (SEQ ==> OLD SEQ)
02100         X4 X3 X2 X1)
02200    ;
02300    PJ3: ((SEQ X1 X2 X3) --> (SEQ ==> OLD SEQ)
02400         X3 X2 X1)
02500    ;
02600    PJ2: ((SEQ X1 X2) --> (SEQ ==> OLD SEQ)
02700         X2 X1)
02800    ;
02900    PJ1: ((SEQ X1) --> (SEQ ==> OLD SEQ) X1)
03000    ;
03100    PJ10: (<ITEM> == <K> --> SAY EMBED (<ITEM> ==> SAID <ITEM>))
03200    ;
03300    PJ20: ((SR 1) -->
03400          (SEQ X (SEQ Q K) (SEQ F H)))
03500    ;
03600    PS2: (PJ4 PJ3 PJ2 PJ1)
03700    PS1: (PJ10 PS2 PJ20)
03800    ;
03900    STM: (NIL NIL NIL NIL NIL NIL NIL)
04000    TOP.GOAL: (SR 1)
04100    ;
04200    "NJ.A83 LOADED" RETURN.TO.TTY!
04300
04400
04500
04600
```

FIG. 11. Products system for the decoding and responding part of Neal Johnson task.

final production, PJ10, generates a response whenever a letter (⟨K⟩) shows up in STM, by evoking the operator SAY. The other two actions in PJ10 mark the letter occurrence as having been uttered, by converting a letter, say X, first into (X) and then into (SAID X).

Figure 12 shows the operation of this system, in which the responses are printed as ⟨ITEM⟩: X, ⟨ITEM⟩: Q, and so on. The matter of interest here is what is and what is not represented. The code and the details of the decoding are represented, including the information in STM at any instant. The act of encoding from the stimulus into the nested set of elements is not represented. In additon, the act of learning, in which productions such as PJ20 are created, is not represented. With the lack of the learning and encoding, the response measure used by Johnson (the probability of error at a given transition) falls through. Instead, the model reveals the internal coding by means of the pause structure in the response, assuming that the subject does not totally decode the response before uttering the letters, but does so as he goes.

Suppose the subject were asked to respond by giving the letters in pairs, that is, XQ KF H (a task that Johnson did not ask of his subjects). Two (nonexclusive) strategies are open to the subject, assuming he has no further access to the stimulus display. He can attempt a different decoding strategy, in which he accumulates at least two letters before he utters them. He can undertake to relearn the response in the new organization, so he can respond using the same simple decoding strategy. Within the present system both the more complex responding strategy and the recoding of the stimulus can be represented. Thus, Figure 13 gives the additonal productions required for the pairwise responding and Figure 14 shows a run with the same paired associate as used in Figure 12. We have taken the action of PJ10 and made it into an operator, SAY-NOTE. Thus the main production is PJ11, which notes two letters and says them both. However, more is required. For one thing, a single letter left over at the end must be said. PJ14 takes care of this response. It is necessary to add to this something to recognize the end of sequence,

```
8.  STM: ((SR 1) NIL NIL NIL NIL NIL NIL)
PJ20  TRUE

1.  STM: ((SEQ X (SEQ Q K) (SEQ F H)) (SR 1) NIL NIL NIL NIL NIL)
PJ3  TRUE

5.  STM: (X (SEQ Q K) (SEQ F H) (OLD SEQ X (SEQ Q K) (SEQ F H)) (SR 1) NIL NIL)
PJ10  TRUE

<ITEM>: X
8.  STM: ((SAID X) (SEQ Q K) (SEQ F H) (OLD SEQ X (SEQ Q K) (SEQ F H)) (SR 1) NIL NIL)
PJ2  TRUE

11.  STM: (Q K (OLD SEQ Q K) (SAID X) (SEQ F H) (OLD SEQ X (OLD SEQ Q K) (SEQ F H)) (SR 1))
PJ10  TRUE

<ITEM>: Q
14.  STM: ((SAID Q) K (OLD SEQ Q K) (SAID X) (SEQ F H) (OLD SEQ X (OLD SEQ Q K) (SEQ F H)) (SR
1))
PJ10  TRUE

<ITEM>: K
17.  STM: ((SAID K) (SAID Q) (OLD SEQ Q K) (SAID X) (SEQ F H) (OLD SEQ X (OLD SEQ Q K) (SEQ F
H)) (SR 1))
PJ2  TRUE

20.  STM: (F H (OLD SEQ F H) (SAID K) (SAID Q) (OLD SEQ Q K) (SAID X))
PJ10  TRUE

<ITEM>: F
23.  STM: ((SAID F) H (OLD SEQ F H) (SAID K) (SAID Q) (OLD SEQ Q K) (SAID X))
PJ10  TRUE

<ITEM>: H
26.  STM: ((SAID H) (SAID F) (OLD SEQ F H) (SAID K) (SAID Q) (OLD SEQ Q K) (SAID X))
END: NO PD TRUE
```

FIG. 12. Basic operation of NJ system.

```
00100   ; NJ2: VARIATION ON NEAL JOHNSON'S CHUNKING TASK:
00200   ;       RESPOND IN PAIRS INDEPENDENT OF HOW LIST GIVEN.
00300   ;       E.G.: IN:  1 - A BC D EFG
00400   ;             OUT:      AB CD EF G
00500   ;
00600   ;       (IDENTICAL TO NJ2.A03)
00700   ;       ASSUMES NJ ALREADY LOADED
00800   ;
00900   DEFINE.PROCESSES!
01000   ;
01100   SAY-NOTE: (ACTION SAY EMBED (<ITEM> ==> SAID <ITEM>))
01200   ;
01300   DEFINE.SYMBOLS!
01400   ;
01500   PJ0: ((OLD SEQ) AND (SEQ) ABS AND (END SEQ) ABS --> (END SEQ))
01600   ;
01700   PJ11: (<ITEM> == <K> AND X0 == <K> --> SAY-NOTE (<ITEM> == X0)
01800         (NTC <ITEM>) SAY-NOTE)
01900   PJ12: (<K> --> EMBED (<K> ==> HOLD <K>))
02000   PJ13: ((HOLD X0) AND <K> --> (HOLD ==> OLD HOLD) X0)
02100   PJ14: ((HOLD <ITEM>) AND (END SEQ) --> (HOLD ==> SAID) SAY)
02200   ;
02300   PS2: (PJ4 PJ3 PJ2 PJ1 PJ0)
02400   PS3: (PJ13 PJ11 PJ14 PJ12)
02500   PS4: (PS3 PS2 PJ20)
02600   ;
02700   "NJ2.A03 LOADED" RETURN.TO.TTY!
02800
02900
03000
03100
```

FIG. 13. Modification of MJ to respond to a coded stimulus in pairs.

to avoid inadvertent responding with an earlier single letter (e.g., at 5 in Figure 14). PJ10 takes care of this by putting in an (END SEQ) marker, which corresponds to the explicit awareness in STM that no more decoding is possible.

More important, if several chunks must be decoded to obtain a pair of letters, the order of the letters can be lost. To assure the correct order the system must temporarily reencode the letter in (HOLD ⟨K⟩), use this code to reestablish the order, and then decode it again for responding with PJ11. This encoding and decoding can be followed in Figure 14, for example, at 5-12 for the letter X. Thus, already with simple coding tasks additional phenomena arise when an explicit and operational control system is required.

Figure 15 shows another set of productions to be added to those of Figure 11 to create a new internal representation in pairs, rather than simple responding in pairs. Some, but not all, of the productions used in the other version (Figure 13) also occur in this one: analogs of P11 and P14, one to take care of pairs and the other to take care of the possibility of a single letter at the end. The same HOLD mechanism for keeping order is also used. But in addition there needs to be a production (PJ15*) to grow the representation as the groups are put together.

Figure 16 gives a run of this system, which ends up with the new element in STM. The relearning of the paired associate is not represented, just as it was not in the original version (Figure 11). However, this type of recoding corresponds to the

```
8.   STM: ((SR 1) NIL NIL NIL NIL NIL NIL)
PJ28   TRUE

1.   STM: ((SEQ X (SEQ Q K) (SEQ F H)) (SR 1) NIL NIL NIL NIL NIL)
PJ3   TRUE

5.   STM: (X (SEQ Q K) (SEQ F H) (OLD SEQ X (SEQ Q K) (SEQ F H)) (SR 1) NIL NIL)
PJ12   TRUE

7.   STM: ((HOLD X) (SEQ Q K) (SEQ F H) (OLD SEQ X (SEQ Q K) (SEQ F H)) (SR 1) NIL NIL)
PJ2   TRUE

10.  STM: (Q K (OLD SEQ Q K) (HOLD X) (SEQ F H) (OLD SEQ X (OLD SEQ Q K) (SEQ F H)) (SR 1))
PJ13   TRUE

12.  STM: (X (OLD HOLD X) Q K (OLD SEQ Q K) (SEQ F H) (OLD SEQ X (OLD SEQ Q K) (SEQ F H)))
PJ11   TRUE

<ITEM>: X
<ITEM>: Q
22.  STM: ((SAID Q) (SAID X) (OLD HOLD X) K (OLD SEQ Q K) (SEQ F H) (OLD SEQ X (OLD SEQ Q K)
(SEQ F H)))
PJ12   TRUE

24.  STM: ((HOLD K) (SAID Q) (SAID X) (OLD HOLD X) (OLD SEQ Q K) (SEQ F H) (OLD SEQ X (OLD SEQ
Q K) (SEQ F H)))
PJ2   TRUE

27.  STM: (F H (OLD SEQ F H) (HOLD K) (SAID Q) (SAID X) (OLD HOLD X))
PJ13   TRUE

29.  STM: (K (OLD HOLD K) F H (OLD SEQ F H) (SAID Q) (SAID X))
PJ11   TRUE

<ITEM>: K
<ITEM>: F
39.  STM: ((SAID F) (SAID K) (OLD HOLD K) H (OLD SEQ F H) (SAID Q) (SAID X))
PJ12   TRUE

41.  STM: ((HOLD H) (SAID F) (SAID K) (OLD HOLD K) (OLD SEQ F H) (SAID Q) (SAID X))
PJ8   TRUE

42.  STM: ((END SEQ) (OLD SEQ F H) (HOLD H) (SAID F) (SAID K) (OLD HOLD K) (SAID Q))
PJ14   TRUE

<ITEM>: H
47.  STM: ((SAID H) (END SEQ) (OLD SEQ F H) (SAID F) (SAID K) (OLD HOLD K) (SAID Q))
END: NO PD TRUE
```

FIG. 14. Behavior of NJ2.

cognitive encoding postulated by the Simon and Kotovsky (1963) model and by the other concept attainment schemes.

The two deficiencies of the present scheme—the lack of a perceptual mechanism and the lack of a production-learning mechanism—stem from entirely different sources. As mentioned earlier, the question of learning appears to be rather deep. We will not attempt to deal with it further here, but will simply select situations to work with that do not require it. The lack of a perceptual mechanism is due to the problem solving tasks not requiring one. Thus, we will attempt in the remainder of the paper to define the design issues for a perceptual mechanism for the production system and to construct an initial experimental version.

```
00100    ; NJR: 2ND VARIATION ON NEAL JOHNSON'S CHUNKING TASK:
00200    ;        RECODE IN PAIRS INDEPENDENT OF HOW LIST GIVEN.
00300    ;        E.G.:  IN:  1 - A BC D EFG
00400    ;             CODE: (SEQ A (SEQ B C) D (SEQ E F G))
00500    ;           RECODE: (SEQ (SEQ A B) (SEQ C D) (SEQ E F) G)
00600    ;           NO OUTPUT TO THE EXTERNAL ENVIRONMENT
00700    ;
00800    ;        (IDENTICAL TO NJR.A02)
00900    ;        ASSUMES NJ
01000    ;        INDEPENDENDENT OF NJ2, BUT USES SAME NAMES WHERE SAME
01100    ;
01200    DEFINE.SYMBOLS!
01300    ;
01400    PJ0: ((OLD SEQ) AND (SEQ) ABS AND (END SEQ) ABS --> (END SEQ))
01500    ;
01600    PJ1*: ((GROUP X0) AND (NEW SEQ) --> (GROUP ==> OLD GROUP)
01700          (SEQ ===> SEQ X0))
01800    PJ2*: ((GROUP X0) AND (NEW SEQ X1) --> (GROUP ==> OLD GROUP)
01900          (X1 ===> X1 X0))
02000    PJ3*: ((GROUP X0) AND (NEW SEQ X2 X1) --> (GROUP ==> OLD GROUP)
02100          (X1 ===> X1 X0))
02200    PJ4*: ((GROUP X0) AND (NEW SEQ X3 X2 X1) -->
02300          (GROUP ==> OLD GROUP) (X1 ===> X1 X0))
02400    ;
02500    PJ11*: (X1 == <K> AND X2 == <K> --> (NTC X2) EMBED (NTC X1)
02600           EMBED (GROUP (SEQ X1 X2)))
02700    PJ12: (<K> --> EMBED (<K> ==> HOLD <K>))
02800    PJ13: ((HOLD X0) AND <K> --> (HOLD ==> OLD HOLD) X0)
02900    PJ14*: ((HOLD X1) AND (END SEQ) --> (HOLD ==> OLD HOLD)
03000           (GROUP X1))
03100    PJ15*: ((GROUP) AND (NEW SEQ) ABS --> (NEW SEQ))
03200    ;
03300    PS2: (PJ4 PJ3 PJ2 PJ1 PJ0)
03400    PS2*: (PJ4* PJ3* PJ2* PJ1*)
03500    PS3: (PJ13 PJ11* PJ14* PJ15* PJ12)
03600    PS4: (PS3 PS2* PS2 PJ20)
03700    ;
03800    "NJR.A02 LOADED" RETURN.TO.TTY!
03900
04000
04100
```

FIG. 15. Modification of NJ to recode stimulus in pairs.

A TASK FOR EXTENDING THE MODEL

To guide the development of a perceptual mechanism we need a specific task. This should be one that involves both perceptual and cognitive processing and in which the encoding performed by the subject is highly apparent. The data should be on single individuals, so that evidence as to the details of the response are not lost by aggregative data analysis.

The following series completion task used by Klahr (Klahr & Wallace, 1970) appears suitable. The subject sees a display (from a slide projector) consisting of a linear array of pictures of schematic bottles. Each bottle has two attributes: color, with values of blue, green, red, and yellow; and orientation, with values of up, down, left, and right (taking the neck of the bottle as the head of a vector). The subject's task is to say what bottle will occur as the next element to the right of the linear array.

```
8.  STM: ((SR 1) NIL NIL NIL NIL NIL NIL NIL)
PJ28  TRUE


1.  STM: ((SEQ X (SEQ Q K) (SEQ F H)) (SR 1) NIL NIL NIL NIL NIL NIL)
PJ3  TRUE


5.  STM: (X (SEQ Q K) (SEQ F H) (OLD SEQ X (SEQ Q K) (SEQ F H)) (SR 1) NIL NIL NIL)
PJ12  TRUE


7.  STM: ((HOLD X) (SEQ Q K) (SEQ F H) (OLD SEQ X (SEQ Q K) (SEQ F H)) (SR 1) NIL NIL NIL)
PJ2  TRUE


10. STM: (Q K (OLD SEQ Q K) (HOLD X) (SEQ F H) (OLD SEQ X (OLD SEQ Q K) (SEQ F H)) (SR 1) NIL)
PJ13  TRUE


12. STM: (X (OLD HOLD X) Q K (OLD SEQ Q K) (SEQ F H) (OLD SEQ X (OLD SEQ Q K) (SEQ F H)) (SR
1))
PJ11*  TRUE


17. STM: ((GROUP (SEQ X Q)) (X) (Q) (OLD HOLD X) K (OLD SEQ Q K) (SEQ F H) (OLD SEQ X (OLD
SEQ Q K) (SEQ F H)))
PJ15*  TRUE


18. STM: ((NEW SEQ) (GROUP (SEQ X Q)) (X) (Q) (OLD HOLD X) K (OLD SEQ Q K) (SEQ F H))
PJ12  TRUE


20. STM: ((HOLD K) (NEW SEQ) (GROUP (SEQ X Q)) (X) (Q) (OLD HOLD X) (OLD SEQ Q K) (SEQ F H))
PJ1*  TRUE


22. STM: ((OLD GROUP (SEQ X Q)) (NEW SEQ (SEQ X Q)) (HOLD K) (X) (Q) (OLD HOLD X) (OLD SEQ Q
K) (SEQ F H))
PJ2  TRUE


25. STM: (F H (OLD SEQ F H) (OLD GROUP (SEQ X Q)) (NEW SEQ (SEQ X Q)) (HOLD K) (X) (Q))
PJ13  TRUE


27. STM: (K (OLD HOLD K) F H (OLD SEQ F H) (OLD GROUP (SEQ X Q)) (NEW SEQ (SEQ X Q)) (X))
PJ11*  TRUE


32. STM: ((GROUP (SEQ K F)) (K) (F) (OLD HOLD K) H (OLD SEQ F H) (OLD GROUP (SEQ X Q)) (NEW
SEQ (SEQ X Q)))
PJ12  TRUE


34. STM: ((HOLD H) (GROUP (SEQ K F)) (K) (F) (OLD HOLD K) (OLD SEQ F H) (OLD GROUP (SEQ X Q))
(NEW SEQ (SEQ X Q)))
PJ2*  TRUE


36. STM: ((OLD GROUP (SEQ K F)) (NEW SEQ (SEQ X Q) (SEQ K F)) (HOLD H) (K) (F) (OLD HOLD K)
(OLD SEQ F H) (OLD GROUP (SEQ X Q)))
PJ8  TRUE


37. STM: ((END SEQ) (OLD SEQ F H) (OLD GROUP (SEQ K F)) (NEW SEQ (SEQ X Q) (SEQ K F)) (HOLD
H) (K) (F) (OLD HOLD K))
PJ14*  TRUE


39. STM: ((GROUP H) (OLD HOLD H) (END SEQ) (OLD SEQ F H) (OLD GROUP (SEQ K F)) (NEW SEQ (SEQ
X Q) (SEQ K F)) (K) (F))
PJ3*  TRUE


41. STM: ((OLD GROUP H) (NEW SEQ (SEQ X Q) (SEQ K F) H) (OLD HOLD H) (END SEQ) (OLD SEQ F H)
(OLD GROUP (SEQ K F)) (K) (F))
END: NO PD TRUE
```

FIG. 16. Behavior of NJR.

```
Series completion task (Klahr)
Protocol of run with subject LM, 20 Oct 78
.
16-th problem in a series of 23.
.
P15
.
.        GN┐ YL┐ GN┐ RD┐ ┌BL RD┐
.
.
.
         GN  YL  GN  RD  BL  RD
         RT  DN  RT  UP  LF  UP
.
         (BTL GN RT) (BTL YL DN) (BTL GN RT) (BTL RD UP) (BTL BL LF)
         (BTL RD UP)
.
B1       Ah, alternating, up down..
B2       I mean horizontal, vertical..
B3       type of pattern.
B4       Two greens surrounding a blue.
B5       Ah, two greens are laying on their side
B6       and then you've got two reds surrounding..
B7       or rather two greens surrounding a yellow..
B8       and the two reds surrounding a blue.
B9       And the blue..
B10      The reds are upright,
B11      as opposed to the greens,
B12      which are on their sides.
B13      Ah, since they are alternating,
B14      I would expect the next bottle to be laying on its
         side.
B15      Ah, since they're facing the same direction..
B16      No, there's a sequence,
B17      and then there's a second sequence.
B18      I would expect this..
B19      There's a three-patterned sequence,
B20      like a.. ah.. bottle surrounding..
B21      two green surrounding a yellow
B22      both facing..
B23      the two green surrounding..
B24      the two surrounding colors facing in the same direction.
B25      I would expect another pattern like this.
B26      This time they should be facing..
B27      ah.. again towards the..
B28      Well, I'm not quite sure which direction they would
         be facing.
B29      I suppose they would be facing again towards the ah..
B30      A bottle laying on its side facing the right.
B31      Ah this time it should be yellow,
B32      since yellow has not surrounded a color yet.
B33      Next slide.
```

FIG. 17. Protocol of Subject LM on series completion task.

Figure 17 shows an example task along with the protocol of a male college undergraduate.[18] The colors of the bottles appear as labels here; actually they were bright colors on the slides. We have given two additional representations of the display, which will occur in this paper. The task (P15) was one of 23 tasks given

[18] Klahr developed the task for work with children, but is also using it with adults. The protocol is from work by Michelene Chase, and I wish to thank her for letting me use it.

during a single session to the subject. It yielded one of the most complex protocols (but it is also the only task that shows all colors and orientations on a single display).

The basic feature of this task that recommends it for our purposes is its combination of perceptual and conceptual aspects. The subject perceives the display of bottles in some way. For example (at B1-B2), he sees the line in Figure 17 as an alternation of vertical and horizontal objects (thus abstracting from the distinction between up-down and right-left respectively). Also (B4), he sees patterns in which two colors "surround" another. But besides these perceptual organizations he symbolizes the stimulus so as to be able to reason about it (and talk about it, as well). For example, in B32 he makes a clear inference involving the nonoccurrence of a given color in the prior part of the sequence. These reasonings are sufficiently similar to the sort of problem solving analyzed by means of production systems so that we might expect a similar analysis to apply to it.

An interesting feature of the subject's behavior is that his first utterance in each task is a description of the display. A useful hypothesis is that this represents the way he perceives the display and constitutes the starting point for further processing. Verification of this hypothesis depends mostly on the analysis of subsequent behavior after the initial statement. Here, we will simply assume it, and take the initial descriptions as evidence for initial perceptions. Figure 18 gives for each of the 23 tasks the display and the initial statements that were made by the subject LM.[19]

As the figure shows, the subject engages in a rich variety of descriptions. To give some idea of this we present in Table 1 a grammar of the constructs used by the subject. We take E as the class of encodings. It can be any of 12 different expressions. In these expressions, E occurs recursively, since the subpattern also may be described. We have written these classes as E1 and E2 simply to make identification possible in the descriptive phrase given to the right of each type of encoding. Also, at the far right, we give the number of occurrences of the expression in the subjects utterances (as encoded in Table 3, to be described).

A noteworthy feature is the elaboration on the notion of direction. In the stimulus itself there are simply four directions and four colors. The subject, however, imposes several distinct structures on this. One is to describe LF and RT as horizontal (HZ) and UP and DN as vertical (VT). The language the subject uses for this appears confusing, since he uses words like "upright" to mean vertical and "down" to sometimes mean horizontal and sometime DN. Table 2 gives the translations. The reality of this extra level of organization is not in doubt. For example, in P17 the subject categorizes the bottles first as being horizontal or vertical and then, within this, as pointing in a particular direction (see Figure 18).

Besides the use of horizontal and vertical, the subject also describes directions in relative terms, as facing inward, or opposite, and even as being symmetric. Nothing like this elaboration occurs with colors, though there is some indirect indication that BL and GN are much more alike than are any of the other colors. For example,

---

[19] We do not reproduce all of the protocols, since we will be concerned in this paper only with these first parts.

TABLE 1

Grammar for Empirical Description of LM's Initial Utterances

Pattern	Description	Number of occurrences
E: SEQUENCE	No pattern to the sequence	3
E1 + E2 + . . .	E1 followed by E2 followed by . . .	15
[E1]	A repetition of E1	
[E1 + E2]	E.g., an alternation of E1 and E2	
E1 « E2 »	E1 surrounds E2	4
N E1	A sequence of N E1's	24
where N = 1, 2, . . . ALL		
E1 & E2	E1 and E2, independently	5
E1 ⊃ E2	Every E1 implies E2	6
E1 AT L	An E1 located at L	1
where L = . . . MIDDLE . . .		
CHANGE DIM	E differs along dimension DIM	2
where DIM = DIRECTION, COLOR		
SAME DIM-PATTERN	E is the same pattern with respect to dimension DIM	3
COLOR-VALUE:		23
RD	Red	2
YL	Yellow	5
GN	Green	7
BL	Blue	9
DIRECTION-VALUE:		43
ABSOLUTE-DIRECTIONS:	Defined independently of unit	34
HZ	Horizontal	15
LF	Left	4
RT	Right	1
VT	Vertical	13
UP	Up	0
DN	Down	1
RELATIVE-DIRECTIONS:	Defined relative to unit	7
IN	Inward toward middle of unit	4
OUT	Outward from middle of unit	2
OPPOSITE	Opposite to other unit	1
PATTERNED-DIRECTIONS:	Patterns on sequence of directions	2
SYMMETRIC	Symmetric about middle	1
BROKEN	Not symmetric or same	1

Series completion task (Klahr)
Protocol of run with subject LM, 28 Oct 78

Excerpt of first utterances for each task.
Appears to indicate initial perceptual view of stimulus.

...
P1   RD RD RD GN GN GN
        RT RT RT DN DN DN

.
B1   Three red bottles,
B2   three green bottles.
...
P2   GN BL GN BL GN BL
        UP UP UP LF LF LF

.
B1   Three bottles upright again
B2   followed by three that are not..
B3   that are horizontal.
...
P3   YL BL YL BL YL BL
        DN RT DN RT DN RT

.
B1   Alternating bottles,
B2   upright down.
B3   They're yellow, blue.
...
P4   BL BL YL YL BL BL
        UP UP UP RT RT RT

.
B1   Ah, two blue bottles,
B2   a yellow bottle,
B3   and a yellow bottle on its side.
...
P5   RD RD BL BL RD RD
        LF RT RT LF RT LF

.
B1   Ah, bottles facing opposite
B2   ah, then facing inward,
B3   changing colors.
...
P6   YL YL GN GN YL YL
        RT RT DN DN RT RT

.
B1   Green surrounded by two pair of yellow.
...
P7   BL GN BL BL GN BL
        UP UP UP DN DN DN

.
B1   Ah, sequence.
B2   Ah, now you've got one blue,
        (continues to enumerate each bottle's color)
...
P8   GN RD GN GN RD GN
        LF DN LF DN LF DN

.
B1   Alternating.
B2   Ah green always on its..
...
P9   YL RD YL YL RD YL
        DN DN LF LF DN DN

.
B1   Ah
B2   you have two yellow in the middle
B3   all..
...
P10   GN RD GN GN RD GN
        RT LF RT RT LF RT

.
B1   Ah.. green always facing towards the right.
B2   Red is always facing towards the left.
...
P11   RD BL RD GN YL GN
        RT RT RT LF LF LF

.
B1   Ah.. three facing inward
B2   and then three facing it again.
...
P12   BL GN BL YL RD YL
        DN LF DN LF DN LF

(Continued)

```
.
B1        Ah.. alternating up and laying on its side
...
P12B      GN  BL  GN  BL  GN  BL
          UP  RT  UP  LF  DN  LF

.
B1        Ah alternating.
B2        Ah blue green.
...
P13       RD  YL  RD  GN  BL  GN
          LF  LF  UP  UP  LF  LF

.
B1        Ah, you have a sequence
B2        such that the pattern is two surrounding,
B3        two laying on their side facing left,
B4        surrounding two going upright
...
P14       RD  YL  RD  BL  GN  BL
          DN  UP  DN  DN  UP  DN

.
B1        All upright.
...
P15       GN  YL  GN  RD  BL  RD
          RT  DN  RT  UP  LF  UP

.
B1        Ah, alternating, up down..
B2        I mean horizontal, vertical..
B3        type of pattern.
...
P16       YL  RD  GN  YL  RD  GN
          LF  LF  LF  UP  UP  UP

.
B1        Ah three laying on its side.
B2        three standing up.
B3        Both in the same pattern..
...
P16B      BL  BL  BL  RD  RD  RD
          LF  DN  RT  LF  DN  RT

.
B3        All right, you have blue surrounded by blue..
B4        They're going in opposite directions,
B5        such that it's a symmetric type of situation.
...
P17       BL  YL  RD  BL  YL
          LF  DN  LF  DN  LF

.
B1        You have ah same sort of situation..
B2        You have an all horizontal bottles facing toward the
          left
B3        and the vertical bottles are down.
...
P19       BL  GN  YL  BL  GN  YL
          LF  UP  LF  LF  UP  LF

.
B1        Ah, it's all bottles horizontal are facing towards the
          left.
...
P20       YL  BL  RD  YL  BL  RD  YL  BL  RD
          DN  UP  DN  RT  LF  RT  DN  UP  DN

.
B1        Ah.. you have patterns of three horizontal..
B2        I mean vertical..
B3        surrounding a block of three horizontal
B4        and then another ah block of three vertical again.
...
P20B      GN  RD  GN  YL  BL  YL  GN  RD  GN
          LF  UP  DN  LF  UP  DN  LF  UP  DN

.
B1        All right, you have patterns broken up
B2        such that there's a horizontal bottle
B3        and two vertical bottles
B4        facing in the opposite directions,
...
P21       BL  GN  YL  BL  GN  YL
          UP  DN  LF  UP  DN  LF

.
B1        Ah.. alternating bottles,
B2        two upright.
...
(End tasks)
```

FIG. 18. First utterances of Subject LM on all tasks.

TABLE 2

Words Used with Special Meaning by LM

Word	Translation	Occurrences
upright	vertical (VT)	P2 P3 P13* P14 P21
up	vertical (VT)	P12 P16*
down	down (DN)	P17
down	horizontal (HZ)	P3
side, on side	horizontal (HZ)	P4 P8 P12 P13 P16

*Ambiguous whether signifies VT or UP

TABLE 3

Initial Patterns Uttered by LM

P1	3RD + 3GN
P2	3VT + 3(CHANGE DIRECTION) // HZ
P3	[VT + HZ] / [YL + BL]
P4	2BL + 1YL + 1YL&HZ ...
P5	OUT + (IN + IN&(CHANGE COLOR))
P6	2YL 《 2GN 》
P7	SEQUENCE / 1BL + 1GN + 1BL + 1BL + 1GN + 1BL
P8	[HZ + VT] / GN ⊃ HZ ...
P9	2YL LOC MIDDLE ...
P10	(GN ⊃ RT) & (RD ⊃ LF)
P11	3IN + 3IN
P12	[VT + HZ]
P12B	[VT + HZ] / [BL + GN]
P13	SEQUENCE / 2(HZ&LF) 《 VT 》
P14	ALL VT
P15	[HZ + VT]
P16	3HZ + 3VT // (SAME COLOR-PATTERN)
P16B	BL 《 BL 》 ... / OUT / SYMMETRIC
P17	SEQUENCE / (HZ ⊃ LF)&(VT ⊃ DN)
P19	HZ ⊃ LF
P20	3(SAME COLOR-PATTERN) / 3VT 《 3HZ 》
P20B	N(SAME DIR-PATTERN) // BROKEN / HZ + 2VT // OPPOSITE
P21	[2VT + HZ]

Note:

...	Description not completed
E1/E2	E2 is a refinement or addition of E1
E1//E2	E2 is a refinement of a subpattern of E1

in P7, where the subject does not pick up any perceptual grouping at all, the entire sequence apparently looks like identical objects to a first approximation (note that UP and DN both go into VT).

Table 3 gives a quite faithful rendition of the subject's initial utterances in terms of the grammar. The subject's particular description is only one out of many possible encodings permitted by the grammar. The subject himself sometimes provides more than one code, as in P2 where he first codes the second group of three bottles as not the same direction as the first three, and then specifies this further as being horizontal. We use the slash to indicate subsequent encodings, the single slash (/) indicating a refinement of the whole and the double slash (/ /) indicating a refinement of one of the subunits. Also, the subject sometimes does not complete an encoding, which we indicate with three dots (. . .). This is not the same as the abstraction that occurs in all encodings. Here, the subject simply ignores all bottles after a given point. The usual reason is that the encoding fails (e.g., at P8 where only the first two GNs are horizontal).

It must be remembered that the responses catalogued in Table 3 are the results of at least two encoding processes, a perceptual-conceptual process that leads to the subject seeing the object with a given perceptual structure, and the selection of descriptive phrases to be uttered in the linguistic response. There is a close dependence between these. For instance, one cannot (as in P9) talk of two yellows in the middle, without distinguishing the relation of middle. But one can (still in P9) group the entire sequence into (VT VT) (HZ HZ) (VT VT) and choose only to mention the (HZ HZ) group in the middle. However, they are still distinct processes and one may want to represent them separately in a model of the subject.

The role of the task and the behavioral data presented is to provide a concrete situation against which to extend our model and to define a perceptual system. Ultimately, of course, we wish to model this subject's behavior in detail, much as we have done with the cryptarithmetic task. But initially, as will be seen, we must be content to use it more as a foil and a guide.

A PERCEPTUAL MECHANISM

Our task, then, is to construct a (visual) perceptual system that fits with our production system and that produces the symbolized views of the stimulus as shown in Figure 18. Several conditions of this problem are not completely specified. What is a perceptual system? What is it to "fit with" a production system? What aspects of the production system must be invariant—PSG, PSG + GS1, PSG + GS1 + some parts of PS2? What is it to have a view of the display corresponding to the subject's initial statements? Still we should be able to recognize a plausible solution when we find one. Before describing a particular design, let us try to clarify these issues.

We may stipulate the overall structure shown in Figure 19. The perceptual mechanism sits between the STM and the external environment (the display, viewed as an external memory). At a particular moment the environment is in some possible state, that is, there is a particular display of colored oriented bottles. The perceptual mechanism is also in some possible state, which has been determined

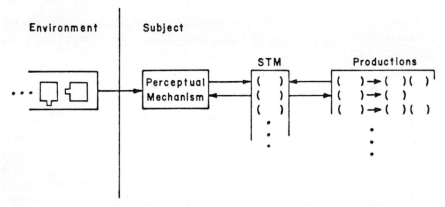

FIG. 19. Overall structure of the system.

partly by prior acts of perception, partly by instructions flowing from the STM to the perceptual mechanism, and partly by longer term adaptations and learnings. The momentary states of the display and the perceptual mechanism jointly determine the output delivered to the STM out of a set of possible outputs whose form is jointly determined by the structure of the perceptual mechanism and the STM.

Basic Issues

Much must be specified to determine an operational perceptual mechanism. The following list of considerations will narrow that specification and make the remainder of the design task more concrete. These considerations are responsive only in part to the known facts of visual functioning. Much remains open, though undoubtedly there are many existing studies that could determine matters further.

The discrete nature of perception. Vision, in tasks with a static display, operates by a sequence of discrete fixations. The duration of a fixation is 200–700 milliseconds, which is of the order of the duration of a production, though on the upper side. There is evidence for units of perceptual attention both larger (groups of fixations) and smaller (attention movement within the field obtained from a single fixation). In any attempt to deal with the detail of a perceptual field (e.g., find all items of a given sort, read all words of test) there are fewer fixations than acts of directed perception. Thus, the functional unit can not be identified with the fixation, defined in terms of constancy of gaze direction. We can take each perceptual act to produce, ultimately, a symbolic structure (or a modification of a symbolic structure) in STM. This discrete nature of perception would be required by the discrete nature of the rest of the processing system, in any event.

The information taken from the display. The display, as a physical structure, is an infinite source of information. The perceptual mechanism selects (extracts, measures, abstracts, . . .) from this source a set of aspects on each perceptual act. It seems safe to consider this a discrete set of features. Although some pattern recognition schemes operate with spatial elements directly (template schemes), almost all reasonable recognition schemes involve the extraction of features at some stage. The set of features is fixed in the short run (i.e., the few hundred seconds of the experiment).

The locus of recognition. One extreme position is that the features themselves are symbolized (i.e., there are sensations) and made available in STM (i.e., to awareness). The recognition process then goes on in STM, so that further abstraction and classification occurs via productions. This makes all encoding conceptual, as that term was used earlier. It is an untenable position. At the other extreme, all recognition occurs within the perceptual mechanism, and only the final symbolized result becomes available in STM. This is not so much untenable as ambiguous, since it is not clear when to withhold the appellation of "recognition process" in describing the processing accomplished by productions. The following seem clear: (*a*) A recognition apparatus does reside in the perceptual mechanism. (*b*) Features can be symbolized and made objects of awareness (i.e., become elements in STM; e.g., we regularly discuss sensations). (*c*) Inferences to new perceptual objects are also possible, especially in situations where perception is difficult. (*d*) Conceptual recoding occurs routinely. The question of the back-flow from conceptually constructed perceptual objects to their subsequent perception is somewhat more open, though there is no doubt that perception itself can be affected by conceptual operations (e.g., setting expectations by verbal instructions).

The momentary state of the perceptual mechanism. Perception is selective, taking out of the display only certain information. The perceptual act is complex, consisting of an alternation of saccade and fixation, and within this additional attentional saccades and fixations. Thus, the specifications for the momentary state are correspondingly complex. Actually, the distinction between an eye movement system and a within-fixation system may not be functional at the level at which our model operates. The perceptual system may be defined in terms of perceptual acts that operate out of a memory (an iconic buffer), this memory being refreshed under local control by succeeding fixations of the eyes. In any event, it is problematical whether we must always continue to distinguish two systems of saccades and fixations, or simply operate with a single system.

There does not appear to be much vision during the saccade itself, and the saccade appears to be determined (in direction and angular extent) prior to take off. Thus, the momentary state can be divided into two parts: that for perception at a fixation and that for the next saccade. However, the saccade itself appears often to be determined by the characteristics of the perceptual object sought, that is, it has the characteristics of a search operation. In this respect it makes sense to consider the perceptual act as consisting of a saccade followed by intake at the subsequent fixation. In fact, often the appropriate unit appears to be a series of saccades and minimal fixations that end up in a fixation directed at the desired perceptual field. These sequences are often seen even in gross eye movements, in which a long saccade is followed quickly by a very short, obviously corrective, saccade. But the existence of a continuous distribution of saccade lengths down to saccades of several minutes of arc also fits the same view.

There is ample evidence for the role of peripheral vision in general and it obviously plays a strong role in defining the next saccade. However, there seems to be little data at the level of detail required for our model.

We can at least list the items that should be considered in defining the perceptual state. *At fixation:* the direction of gaze; vergence; light adaptation; the features to be noticed; ordering of features and/or conditional cutoffs; the set of recognizable objects; expectations for perceptual objects to be recognized; the grain of perception, i.e., the level of detail. *At saccade:* the direction of the current gaze; the perceptual target desired; knowledge of the peripheral field. The list is not very operational and it is unclear how to make it so prior to setting out a particular perceptual mechanism.

Determinants of the perceptual state. Operation of the perceptual system implies that changes take place in the perceptual state from within the system itself. But in addition, all of the state variables (i.e., the items on the above list) must be subject to determination by systems outside the perceptual system itself, that is, either by the display or by the remainder of the IPS. The key design issue is to specify, for each aspect of the momentary state, who determines it and with what time constant. The timing issue is critical. For example light adaptation is relatively slow and can be generally disregarded as a state variable in our task. New objects can be added to the stock of recognizables at rates consonant with the write operation into LTM (indeed such recognition later is a test of LTM retention). This is the control mechanism used in EPAM, as noted earlier. But what aspects can be set by symbolic expressions in STM? This is instruction on the time scale of a single perceptual act. Certainly, the next saccade is instructable, as in the verbal command "Look right!" or the perception of an arrow that points. But are short run, instantaneous expectations set for each saccade? Are the features to be noticed set or ordered for each fixation, or does the cognitive system simply take what the perceptual system gives it, after telling it the rough direction in which to look? These and many other finer grained questions about who determines what appear not be be specifiable in terms of existing knowledge.

What is symbolized from a perception. After a perceptual act has taken place what is included in the symbolic expression or expressions produced in STM? Is there a recollection of the instructions given to the perceptual system? If there is some set of expectations, either of perceptual features or objects, is there knowledge of what was expected as well as what was found? If additional information is obtained about the object, is it remembered what was expected as well as what was observed, or is it all combined in a single result? Are the features used to recognize an object remembered, as well as the object? And so on.

Summary. We have listed a number of considerations that enter into the specification of a perceptual system, though the list is not yet systematic. Our purpose in doing so is to make evident the range of design options. The particular system described in the next section results from one set of design decisions covering all the above issues. We do not understand this design space yet, nor the consequences of many of the specifications. Consequently, the presented perceptual system is simply a first cut.

LKE: A Particular Perceptual Mechanism

Given the background of the previous sections, we simply present the details of a particular subsystem, called LKE (for the Eth version of a system for looking). This system augments the basic production system, PSG, described in an earlier section. The display for the series completion task is one dimensional, and can be

conveniently modeled as a list. Figure 20 shows the display with the eyes located
(⟩⟩) at the first bottle from the left, which has three features: the shape BTL, the
color RD, and the orientation RT. LKE assumes a single system of saccades and
fixations, which therefore have a finer grain than gross eye movements. The interior
logic design of the perceptual system is not modeled, so we talk indifferently of the
eyes and of the locus of perceptual attention.

Initiation of perception may be under the control of either STM or the
environment, though in a self-paced task such as series completion almost all of the
initiation will come from STM. Thus there are perceptual operators, analogous to
the operators in the cryptarithmetic task. LKE has two perceptual operators,
LOOK.FOR and LOOK.AT. Each requires additional instructions from STM.
LOOK.FOR requires a direction for the eye-movement (RIGHT, LEFT or STAY)
and a perceptual object to guide the search in a display. For example, a typical
instruction in STM might be: (LOOK.FOR RIGHT (OBJ BTL)). This is an
instruction to look to the right for an object with the shape of a bottle (BTL). The
operator LOOK.AT assumes that the eyes are already located at a proper place. It
requires only that a perceptual object be given in its instruction, for example,
(LOOK.AT (OBJ BTL RD)).

The result of a perceptual operation is the construction in STM of one or more
symbolic structures giving what has been observed. For example, one might get
(OBS (OBJ BTL RD RT)), which is to say that an object that was a red bottle
pointing to the right was observed. Or one might get (NOBS (OBJ BTL)), which is
to say that no object that was a bottle was found.

Perception often leaves open the possibility that additional observations may be
possible. Thus, when doing (LOOK.FOR RIGHT (OBJ BTL)) in the situation of
Figure 20, there are three more bottles that could be observed. LOOK.FOR will
observe the first one, but if it were executed again it would obtain yet another
observation. At some stage no more observations are possible. This is symbolized in
an additional structure, (END LOOK.FOR). Thus the system creates positive
knowledge of termination.

DSP1: (EDGE >> (BTL RD RT) (BTL RD RT) (BTL RD RT) (BTL GN DN) (BTL GN DN) (BTL GN DN) EDGE)

FIG. 20. Display for task P1.

The features detectable by the perceptual system form a structured system of
successive degrees of abstraction. The system for our subject is shown in Figure 21.
There are three dimensions, SHAPE, COLOR and DIRECTION (DIR). For SHAPE
there are only the two features, SPC and BTL. For COLOR, since the subject
appears to see BL and GR as the same for some situations, an intermediate color,
blue-green (BG), is stipulated. This is not to say that the subject has a color name
for this, only that on occasion he does not discriminate between these colors. For
DIRECTION the subject appears to make a discrimination between horizontal (HZ)
and vertical (VT) and then within each between LF and RT, and UP and DN.

The control of the features to be detected and of the detail of these features is
shared between the perceptual system and the STM. Thus, giving the perceptual

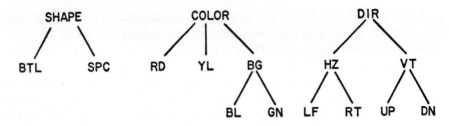

FIG. 21. Hierarchy of features.

object in the instructions determines much of what will be used. The function of LOOK.AT is to obtain additional detail about a perceived object. Thus the initiation of such a quest is under the control of STM. But what detail is seen is under the control of the perceptual system (consonant with the actual display). There is a fixed order to the observation along new dimensions and to the observation down the feature hierarchies of Figure 21. For instance, if the situation were as given in Figure 20 and the instruction (LOOK.AT (OBJ BTL COLOR)) were given, then the result would be (OBS (OBJ BTL RD)). If the instruction were (LOOK.AT (OBJ BTL RD)), the result would be (OBS (OBJ BTL RD HZ)). And if, finally, the instruction were (LOOK.AT (OBJ BTL RD HZ)), the result would be (OBS (OBJ BTL RD RT)).

One aspect of the above example is misleading, and in an important way. Each successive observation with LOOK.AT does not generate a new element, (OBS (OBJ . . .)). Rather, it constitutes an additional observation of an element that already exists (i.e., has been symbolized) in STM. Thus the three observations above constitute modifications of a single observation and the system does not believe that it has seen four distinct things, (OBJ BTL), (OBJ BTL RD), (OBJ BTL RD HZ), and (OBJ BTL RD RT). The instruction (LOOK.AT X1), where X1 = (OBJ BTL), is also successively modified as X1 becomes modified, and it serves to provide all the instructions for additional detail.

LKE has two kinds of perceptual objects, OBJ and SEQ. An OBJ is specified by a set of features; numerous examples have been given above. The features can be given at any level of detail, according to the hierarchies in Figure 21. A SEQ is a sequence of perceptual objects. For example, (SEQ (OBJ BTL) (OBJ BTL)) is a sequence of two bottles. A sequence of two red bottles followed by a green bottle might be given as (SEQ (SEQ (OBJ BTL RD) (OBJ BTL RD)) (OBJ BTL GN)). Thus, recursive structures can be built up. However, the scheme in LKE does not take advantage of the redundancies in patterns. Thus, in terms of symbolization, it is as easy to perceive three different bottles as three identical ones: (SEQ (OBJ BTL RD) (OBJ BTL BL) (OBJ BTL HZ)), or (SEQ (OBJ BTL RD) (OBJ BTL RD) (OBJ BTL RD)). Which of the two will get constructed depends on the constructive processes, and regular sequences may get built whereas heterogeneous ones do not. But the difference is not reflected in the underlying representation.

The search in LOOK.FOR is for an absolute object, that is, for the features as given in the symbolic element labeled ((POBJ.TYPE)), where (POBJ.TYPE):

(CLASS OBJ SEQ). Any relativization to the local situation in the display is to be obtained by constructing the perceptual object that guides the search from the display itself (with LOOK.AT). In particular, the detection of differences in the display is not delegated to the perceptual mechanism.

Similarly, the construction of new perceptual objects, for example, of (SEQ (OBJ BTL) (OBJ BTL)) from two occurrences of (OBJ BTL), is not determined by the perceptual mechanism autonomously, but is done by the formation of the new object in STM. Once such an object is formed, of course, it can be made part of a perceptual instruction and the display perceived in its terms.

Because of the requirements to simulate the environment in a discrete symbolic system (i.e., in L* on a digital computer), there is a finite grain of the display. The display of Figure 20 precludes examining the curvature of the neck of the bottle, though this is possible on the slide, and subjects may even do so on occasion. More detail could be provided if the characterization of the display in terms of a sequence of objects with three attributes did not seem sufficient. However, it would be necessary to extend the types of perceptual objects beyond OBJ and SEQ to cover the types of spatial relations possible: for example, to add WHOLE, whose components are attached parts, each of which is a perceptual object, plus an interfacing connection between parts.

Though the simulation provides a lower bound to the grain, it does not provide an upper bound. Thus, the eyes are located at an object in the display that represents the lowest level of detail. But the perceptual object that is seen from that locus may extend beyond the confines of that single object. SEQ does exactly this.

The structure of LKE, as it stands, permits certain patterns to be formed and not others. Thus, it put some limits in advance on the enterprise of obtaining the pattern descriptions made by the subject (in Table 3). We give in Figure 22 a set of possibilities for the patterns that might be developed in a production system using LKE. Notice, for instance that the characterizations involving numbers, for example, (3 RD), are replaced by extensive lists, like (RD RD RD). One view of this is as a deficiency in LKE, to be rectified by a more adequate perceptual mechanism. A second possible view is that the additional encoding to obtain the codes of Table 3 is done at the conceptual level in developing the linguistic utterance. In this case, the trip from (RD RD RD) to (3 RD) is made conceptually, that is, by productions that count.

We have covered the essential design characteristics of LKE and the kinds of perceptual encodings it admits. The following is a summary of these characteristics, which should be sufficient to understand the behavior of the system:

1. Each perceptual act is initiated by a perceptual operator, either LOOK.FOR or LOOK.AT.

2. Evocation of the perceptual operator is by the production system (interrupts from the environment are possible, but not modeled).

3. Each perceptual act requires an instruction from STM, which is taken to be the initial STM element.

4. Each perceptual act results in the creation of one or more STM elements (which enter STM just as do other elements created by productions) or by

```
              POTENTIAL BEHAVIOR IN PERFORMING ON TASK SCTF

P1: (SEQ (SEQ (OBJ BTL RD)(OBJ BTL RD)(OBJ BTL RD))
         (SEQ (OBJ BTL GN) (OBJ BTL GN)(OBJ BTL GN)))

P2: (SEQ (SEQ (OBJ BTL VT)(OBJ BTL VT)(OBJ BTL VT))
         (SEQ (OBJ BTL HZ)(OBJ BTL HZ)(OBJ BTL HZ)))
;
P3: (SEQ (SEQ (OBJ BTL VT)(OBJ BTL HZ))
         (SEQ (OBJ BTL VT)(OBJ BTL HZ))
         (SEQ (OBJ BTL VT)(OBJ BTL HZ)))

P4: (SEQ (OBJ BTL BL)(OBJ BTL BL))
    (OBJ BTL YL)
    (OBJ BTL YL HZ))
    UNCLEAR WHETHER SUPERORDINATE STRUCTURE IMPOSED

P5: (SEQ (SEQ (OBJ BTL RD)(OBJ BTL RD))
         (SEQ (OBJ BTL BL)(OBJ BTL BL))
         (SEQ (OBJ BTL RD)(OBJ BTL RD)))

P6: (SEQ (SEQ (OBJ BTL YL)(OBJ BTL YL))
         (SEQ (OBJ BTL GN)(OBJ BTL GN))
         (SEQ (OBJ BTL YL)(OBJ BTL YL)))

P7: NO ORGANIZATION ON FIRST PASS

P8: (SEQ (SEQ (OBJ BTL HZ)(OBJ BTL VT))
         (SEQ (OBJ BTL HZ)(OBJ BTL VT))
         (SEQ (OBJ BTL HZ)(OBJ BTL VT)))

P9: (SEQ (OBJ BTL YL)(OBJ BTL YL))

P18: NO SEQUENTIAL ORGANIZATION
     CANNOT CODE NON-SEQUENTIAL ORGANIZATION

P11: (SEQ (SEQ (OBJ BTL RT)(OBJ BTL RT)(OBJ BTL RT))
          (SEQ (OBJ BTL LF)(OBJ BTL LF)(OBJ BTL LF')))
     CANNOT CODE DIRECTION AS IN-OUT

P12: (SEQ (SEQ (OBJ BTL VT)(OBJ BTL HZ))
          (SEQ (OBJ BTL VT)(OBJ BTL HZ))
          (SEQ (OBJ BTL VT)(OBJ BTL HZ)))

P12B: (SEQ (SEQ (OBJ BTL VT)(OBJ BTL HZ))
           (SEQ (OBJ BTL VT)(OBJ BTL HZ))
           (SEQ (OBJ BTL VT)(OBJ BTL HZ)))

P13: NO ORGANIZATION ON FIRST PASS
     (SEQ (SEQ (OBJ BTL LF)(OBJ BTL LF))
          (SEQ (OBJ BTL UP)(OBJ BTL UP))
          (SEQ (OBJ BTL LF)(OBJ BTL LF)))

P14: (SEQ (OBJ BTL VT)(OBJ BTL VT)(OBJ BTL VT)
          (OBJ BTL VT)(OBJ BTL VT)(OBJ BTL VT))
     NOTE: DEPENDS ON WHETHER GROUPS OF 6 CAN BE BUILT UP
           IF NOT, THEN CAN'T CODE NON-SEQUENTIAL ORGANIZATION

P15: (SEQ (SEQ (OBJ BTL HZ)(OBJ BTL VT))
          (SEQ (OBJ BTL HZ)(OBJ BTL VT))
          (SEQ (OBJ BTL HZ)(OBJ BTL VT)))

P16: (SEQ (SEQ (OBJ BTL HZ)(OBJ BTL HZ)(OBJ BTL HZ))
          (SEQ (OBJ BTL VT)(OBJ BTL VT)(OBJ BTL VT)))
```

(Continued)

```
P16B: CANNOT CODE

P17: NO ORGANIZATION ON FIRST PASS
     CANNOT CODE NON-SEQUENTIAL ORGANIZATION OF SECOND PASS

P19: CANNOT CODE NON-SEQUENTIAL ORGANIZATION

P20: (SEQ (SEQ (OBJ BTL YL)(OBJ BTL BL)(OBJ BTL RD))
          (SEQ (OBJ BTL YL)(OBJ BTL BL)(OBJ BTL RD))
          (SEQ (OBJ BTL YL)(OBJ BTL BL)(OBJ BTL RD)))

P20B: (SEQ (SEQ (OBJ BTL HZ)(OBJ BTL VT)(OBJ BTL VT))
           (SEQ (OBJ BTL HZ)(OBJ BTL VT)(OBJ BTL VT))
           (SEQ (OBJ BTL HZ)(OBJ BTL VT)(OBJ BTL VT)))

P21: (SEQ (SEQ (OBJ BTL VT)(OBJ BTL VT)(OBJ BTL HZ))
          (SEQ (OBJ BTL VT)(OBJ BTL VT)(OBJ BTL HZ)))
```

FIG. 22. Possible encodings of displays by system.

modification of elements accessible from the instruction element, for example, the instruction element itself or the perceptual object it contains.

5. The perceptual mechanism retains the memory of the locus of perceptual attention ($\rangle\rangle$) in the display.

6. The perceptual mechanism retains the knowledge of the structure of perceptual features $\langle FTR \rangle$ and no operators currently exist for modifying this from STM or the production system.

7. A perceptual object $\langle POBJ \rangle$ is a symbolic structure of form (OBJ $\langle FTR \rangle \langle FTR \rangle \ldots$) or (SEQ $\langle POBJ \rangle \langle POBJ \rangle \ldots$).

8. The perceptual system can ascertain if a given perceptual object is located in the environment at the point of attention (at $\rangle\rangle$). For (OBJ . . .) it tests the features available at the point of attention. For (SEQ . . .) it takes the point of attention as the leftmost point for the sequence of objects.

9. The perceptual system can add additional knowledge to a given perceptual object, either by increasing the detail of its given features $\langle FT \rangle$ or by adding new dimensions to the perceptual object (for which added detail can then be obtained).

10. LOOK.AT requires a perceptual object. It adds an amount of additional knowledge as specified by the nature of the perceptual mechanism. (Currently it takes N steps of additional detail, N an externally settable parameter.) It does not create a new element in STM, except to indicate termination.

11. LOOK.FOR requires a perceptual object and a direction $\langle EMD \rangle$. It looks for an object in the display along the given direction, taking the perceptual object as fixed and not adding more detail. It creates a new element in STM with the tag (OBS . . .) if it finds the object and (NOBS . . .) if it does not. It also creates a termination element (END LOOK.FOR) if there is no further instruction to look in the given direction.

BEHAVIOR OF THE SYSTEM

The system we have just created, consisting of PSG and LKE, is not in fact immensely complex compared (say) to many existing artificial intelligence systems.

Still, we will only be able to afford the briefest look at its behavior, given the already extended character of this paper. We will not even be able to examine many aspects that are basic to its perceptual and cognitive behavior. In fact, we will set up a single simple system to illustrate how the two parts, the production system and the perceptual system, work together and to suggest some of the problems that exist.

Figure 23 presents the basic specification for behavior in the series completion task (SC3). It includes the various classes, the features, and a display for a particular

```
00100    ; SC3F: SERIES COMPLETION TASK (KLAHR)
00200    ;        REQUIRES LKEF, PSGF, U1F, DICTF, UTILF
00300    ;
00400    DEFINE.SYMBOLS!
00500    ;
00600    SC.CONTEXT SET.CONTEXT!
00700    ;
00800    ; MAKE NAMES AVAILABLE FOR USE IN SC.CONTEXT
00900    RD* RD CHANGE.NAMES!
01000    RT* RT CHANGE.NAMES!
01100    ;
01200    ; DEFINE CLASSES FOR USE IN PRODUCTION CONDITIONS
01300    ;
01400    ; DISPLAY ; CURRENT DISPLAY -- LIST OF OBJECTS
01500    ; BASIC CLASSES DEFINED IN LKEF, FOR REFERENCE
01600    ; <LKOPR>: (CLASS LOOK.AT LOOK.FOR) ; LOOK OPERATORS
01700    ; <EMD>: (CLASS LEFT RIGHT STAY) ; EYE MOVEMENT DIRECTIONS
01800    ; <OBS.TYPE>: (CLASS OBS OBS.AT NOBS) ; OBSERVATION ELM TYPES
01900    ; <NEW.OBS>: (VAR) ; NAME FOR NEW OBSERVATION ELEMENT
02000    ; <END.OBS>: (VAR) ; NAME FOR END ELEMENT
02100    ; <POBJ.TYPE>: (CLASS OBJ SEQ) ; TYPES OF PERCEPTUAL OBJECTS
02200    ; <POBJ>: (<POBJ.TYPE>) ; PERCEPTUAL OBJECTS
02300    ; <NTC.TYPE>: (CLASS END MORE)
02400    ; LKT.ELM: (<NTC.TYPE> <LKOPR>)
02500    ; OBS.ELM: (<OBS.TYPE> <EMD> <POBJ>)
02600    ;
02700    <COLOR>: (CLASS RD GN YL BL BK WH)
02800    <SHAPE>: (CLASS SPC BTL)
02900    <DIR>: (CLASS RT LF UP DN)
03000    <G>:    (CLASS GOAL OLDG)
03100    <SIG>: (CLASS * % + -)
03200    <END>: (CLASS + -)
03300    <COND>: (CLASS -COND +COND)
03400    <OPR>: (CLASS)
03500    <NTC>: (CLASS <LKOPR>)
03600    <OBS>: (CLASS OBS OBS.AT)
03700    ;
03800    DIM.LIST: (SHAPE COLOR DIR)
03900    ;
04000    X1: (VAR)
04100    X2: (VAR)
04200    X3: (VAR)
04300    X4: (VAR)
04400    X5: (VAR)
04500    ;
04600    RD: (FTR COLOR)
04700    YL: (FTR COLOR)
04800    BK: (FTR COLOR)
04900    WH: (FTR COLOR)
05000    BL: (FTR BG)
05100    GN: (FTR BG)
```

(Continued)

```
05200    BG: (FTR COLOR)
05300    COLOR: (FTR)
05400    ;
05500    UP: (FTR VT)
05600    DN: (FTR VT)
05700    VT: (FTR DIR)
05800    LF: (FTR HZ)
05900    RT: (FTR HZ)
06000    HZ: (FTR DIR)
06100    DIR: (FTR)
06200    ;
06300    BTL: (FTR SHAPE)
06400    SPC: (FTR SHAPE)
06500    SHAPE: (FTR)
06600    EDGE: (SPC WH)
06700    ;
06800    ; DISPLAYS USED IN RUN WITH SUBJECT: LM, 28 OCT 70
06900    ;
07000    DSP1: (EDGE (BTL RD RT)(BTL RD RT)(BTL RD RT)
07100          (BTL GN DN)(BTL GN DN)(BTL GN DN) EDGE)
07200    ;
07300    ; SEE FILE SCTF.A00 FOR COMPLETE SET OF TASKS
07400    ;
07500    ;
07600    G1: ((GOAL <END>) --> (GOAL ==> OLDG))
07700    G2: ((GOAL *) ABS AND (GOAL %) --> (% ==> *))
07800    G3: ((GOAL *) AND (GOAL *) --> (* ===> %))
07900    G4: ((GOAL * <OPR>) --> <OPR>)
08000    G5: ((GOAL * <COND>) AND (OLDG <END>) --> (<COND> ==>)
08100         (COND <COND> <END>))
08200    G6: ((COND +COND +) AND (GOAL *) --> (COND ==> OLD COND)
08300         (* ===> +))
08400    G7: ((COND -COND -) AND (GOAL *) --> (COND ==> OLD COND)
08500         (* ===> -))
08600    G8: ((COND) AND (GOAL *) --> (COND ==> OLD COND))
08700    G9: ((MORE) AND (GOAL *) --> (* ===> %))
08800    G10: ((MORE <NTC>) AND (END <NTC>) --> (MORE ==> OLD MORE))
08900    G11: ((GOAL *) ABS AND (GOAL <END> SOLVE) ABS -->
09000         (GOAL * SOLVE))
09100    G12: ((<LKOPR>) --> <LKOPR>)
09200    G13: ((<LKOPR>) AND (END <LKOPR>) --> (<LKOPR> ==> OLD <LKOPR>)
09300         (END ===> OLD END))
09400    ;
09500    ; PS1: TOTAL PRODUCTION SYSTEM
09600    ; PS2: PRODUCTION SYSTEM FOR TASK
09700    ; GS1: HIGH PRIORITY GOAL MANIPULATIONS
09800    ; GS2: BACK UP PRODUCTIONS
09900    ;
10000    GS1: (G13 G1 G3 G10 G9 G5 G6 G7 G8 G4 G2)
10100    GS2: (G11)
10200    PS1: (GS1 PS2 GS2)
10300    ;
10400    STM: (NIL NIL NIL NIL NIL NIL NIL NIL NIL)
10500    ;
10600    "SC3F LOADED (NOTE: DIGITS ARE CHARS)" RETURN.TO.TTY!
10700
10800
10900
```

FIG. 23. SC3F: Basic specification of series completion task.

task. It also includes the basic goal manipulation system used for cryptarithmetic augmented by G12 and G13 to detect and execute perceptual instructions. For completeness, we have added definitions of the basic classes that are defined within LKE itself and are not specific to a task.

Figure 24 gives a short production system (SCP1) for the initial scan of the display. We assume that when the display is flashed on the screen an environment-initiated observation is produced, (OBS NEW DISPLAY). This is the trigger to scan the display and create the initial perceptual organization. This task is not goal directed in an explicit way, but is simply encoded in the set of productions as a direct reaction.

Production PD1 responds to the triggering stimulus and prepares for a left-to-right scan of the display by finding the left-hand edge. It is assumed that the subject has already oriented to the display and thus knows: (a) the display consists of sequences of bottles; (b) the field is bounded by the edge of the slide; (c) the relevant features are global aspects of the bottles; and (d) there is likely to be some sequential organization. This knowledge is embedded in the production system. How this was acquired as a function of instructions and preliminary examples is not touched here.

Production PD2 responds to the positioning of the eyes of the left-hand side by setting up an instruction to look for bottles by scanning to the right. This instruction defines the grain of the perceptual act.

```
00100   ; SCP1: BASIC PRODUCTIONS FOR SERIES COMPLETION TASK (KLAHR)
00200   ;        REQUIRES SC3F, ETC.
00300   ;
00400   ;        (IDENTICAL TO SCPF.E03)
00500   ;
00600   DEFINE.SYMBOLS!
00700   ;
00800   PD1: ((OBS NEW DISPLAY) --> (LEFT (OBJ SPC)) LOOK.FOR)
00900   ;
01000   PD2: ((OBS LEFT (OBJ SPC)) --> (OBS ==> OLD OBS)
01100        (LOOK.FOR RIGHT (OBJ BTL)))
01200   ;
01300   PD3: ((OBS (OBJ BTL)) --> (OBS ==> OBS.AT) LOOK.AT)
01400   ;
01500   PD4: ((<OBS> X1 == (<POBJ.TYPE>)) AND (<OBS> X1) -->
01600        (<OBS> ===> = <OBS>))
01700   ;
01800   PD5: ((<OBS.TYPE>) AND (<OBS> X1 == (<POBJ.TYPE>)) AND
01900        (= <OBS> X1) AND (= <OBS> X1) ABS -->
02000        (<OBS> ===> OLD <OBS>)(= ====> OLD)(OBS (SEQ X1 X1)))
02100   ;
02200   PD6: ((<OBS.TYPE>) AND (<OBS> X1 == (<POBJ.TYPE>)) AND
02300        (= <OBS> X1) AND (= <OBS> X1) AND (= <OBS> X1) ABS -->
02400        (<OBS> ===> OLD <OBS>)(= ====> OLD)(OBS (SEQ X1 X1 X1)))
02500   ;
02600   PS2: (PD4 PD3 PD6 PD5 G12 PD2 PD1)
02700   ;
02800   "SCPF.E03 LOADED" RETURN.TO.TTY!
02900
03000
03100
03200
```

FIG. 24. SCP1: Basic production system for series completion task.

Production PD3 responds to the detection of a bottle by looking at it somewhat closer. This will generate new detail about the bottle in the STM element that represents it. What detail is added is determined by the perceptual system itself and not by the instruction.

Production PD4 recognizes when two adjacent observed objects are the same and notes this fact by marking the second (the one that occurred earlier in time) with an equals (=). There must be a delay in actually organizing the perceived sequence, since subsequent objects have not yet been observed and they may affect the organization.

Productions PD5 and PD6 create perceptual organization by recognizing a sequence of perceived identical objects and encoding it as a SEQ. PD5 creates (SEQ X1 X1) from a pair of identical objects; PD6 creates (SEQ X1 X1 X1) from a triple. The trigger for these actions is not only the requisite sequence of identical objects, but also that a distinct object has been perceived to bound the sequence. There is also a condition that no additional identical objects occur in STM, ((OBS) X1) ABS, which effectively provides a second boundary for the sequence.

In many of the productions (PD3, PD4, PD5, PD6) there is a modification of existing elements in STM by the replacement of one tag by another, for example, (OBS = ⇒ OLD OBS) or (OBS = ⇒ OBS.AT). These modifications serve an essential control function to inhibit the repeated evocation of a production once a set of STM elements has sufficed to evoke it once. If a set of elements does evoke a production, then these same elements are capable of evoking it again (and again). What stops such repeated evocation in general is either some change in these elements, or the new items created evoke a production prior in the ordering. Thus, many productions must take care to modify their evoking inputs.

Figure 25 gives a run of this system on P1, the first display. Tracing through the steps one can see each of the productions playing their role. For instance, G12 locates the first bottle (at 5), which is then examined (at 7) and seen to be red (RD). By 11, two red bottles have been seen whose identity can be noted by PD4. At 18 the observation of a bottle of a different color (BG) permits PD6 to create the sequence of three red bottles (at 21). A similar sequence now occurs with respect to the green bottles until the end of the sequence (NOBS) evokes PD6 at 32 to construct the second sequence. At 36 STM holds both sequences and there is nothing more to do.

Let us try this same system on some additional tasks. Figures 26 and 27 show the behavior of SCP1 on Problems P2 and P3. We give only the display and the final state of STM, from which can be inferred what must have happened. In P2 (Figure 26) we see that no organization at all developed. All elements were seen as the same, since only the color was perceived and that only at the level of BG. Contrariwise, the subject perceived this sequence as three vertical bottles followed by three bottles followed by three vertical ones (see Table 3). In P3 a quite different departure occurred: The system put some yellows together and some blues together, thus constructing an organization that violated the sequential order of the objects. The subject, on the other hand, perceived P3 as a sequence of three pairs, [VT + HZ] (see Table 3).

```
DISPLAY: (EDGE (BTL RD RT) (BTL RD RT) (BTL RD RT) (BTL GN DN) (BTL GN DN) (BTL GN DN) EDGE)
8.  STM: ((OBS NEW DISPLAY) (GOAL * SOLVE) NIL NIL NIL NIL NIL NIL NIL)
PD1  TRUE

DISPLAY: (>> EDGE (BTL RD RT) (BTL RD RT) (BTL RD RT) (BTL GN DN) (BTL GN DN) (BTL GN DN) EDGE)
<NEW.OBS>: (OBS LEFT (OBJ SPC))
<END.OBS>: NIL
2.  STM: ((OBS LEFT (OBJ SPC)) (LEFT (OBJ SPC)) (OBS NEW DISPLAY) (GOAL * SOLVE) NIL NIL NIL
NIL NIL)
PD2  TRUE

4.  STM: ((LOOK.FOR RIGHT (OBJ BTL)) (OLD OBS LEFT (OBJ SPC)) (LEFT (OBJ SPC)) (OBS NEW
DISPLAY) (GOAL * SOLVE) NIL NIL NIL NIL)
G12  TRUE

DISPLAY: (EDGE >> (BTL RD RT) (BTL RD RT) (BTL RD RT) (BTL GN DN) (BTL GN DN) (BTL GN DN) EDGE)
<NEW.OBS>: (OBS RIGHT (OBJ BTL))
<END.OBS>: NIL
5.  STM: ((OBS RIGHT (OBJ BTL)) (LOOK.FOR RIGHT (OBJ BTL)) (OLD OBS LEFT (OBJ SPC)) (LEFT (OBJ
SPC)) (OBS NEW DISPLAY) (GOAL * SOLVE) NIL NIL NIL)
PD3  TRUE

DISPLAY: (EDGE >> (BTL RD RT) (BTL RD RT) (BTL RD RT) (BTL GN DN) (BTL GN DN) (BTL GN DN) EDGE)
<NEW.OBS>: NIL
<END.OBS>: NIL
7.  STM: ((OBS.AT RIGHT (OBJ BTL RD)) (LOOK.FOR RIGHT (OBJ BTL)) (OLD OBS LEFT (OBJ SPC))
(LEFT (OBJ SPC)) (OBS NEW DISPLAY) (GOAL * SOLVE) NIL NIL NIL)
G12  TRUE

DISPLAY: (EDGE (BTL RD RT) >> (BTL RD RT) (BTL RD RT) (BTL GN DN) (BTL GN DN) (BTL GN DN) EDGE)
<NEW.OBS>: (OBS RIGHT (OBJ BTL))
<END.OBS>: NIL
8.  STM: ((OBS RIGHT (OBJ BTL)) (LOOK.FOR RIGHT (OBJ BTL)) (OBS.AT RIGHT (OBJ BTL RD)) (OLD
OBS LEFT (OBJ SPC)) (LEFT (OBJ SPC)) (OBS NEW DISPLAY) (GOAL * SOLVE) NIL NIL)
PD3  TRUE

DISPLAY: (EDGE (BTL RD RT) >> (BTL RD RT) (BTL RD RT) (BTL GN DN) (BTL GN DN) (BTL GN DN) EDGE)
<NEW.OBS>: NIL
<END.OBS>: NIL
10.  STM: ((OBS.AT RIGHT (OBJ BTL RD)) (LOOK.FOR RIGHT (OBJ BTL)) (OBS.AT RIGHT (OBJ BTL RD))
(OLD OBS LEFT (OBJ SPC)) (LEFT (OBJ SPC)) (OBS NEW DISPLAY) (GOAL * SOLVE) NIL NIL)
PD4  TRUE

11.  STM: ((OBS.AT RIGHT (OBJ BTL RD)) (= OBS.AT RIGHT (OBJ BTL RD)) (LOOK.FOR RIGHT (OBJ
BTL)) (OLD OBS LEFT (OBJ SPC)) (LEFT (OBJ SPC)) (OBS NEW DISPLAY) (GOAL * SOLVE) NIL NIL)
G12  TRUE

DISPLAY: (EDGE (BTL RD RT) (BTL RD RT) >> (BTL RD RT) (BTL GN DN) (BTL GN DN) (BTL GN DN) EDGE)
<NEW.OBS>: (OBS RIGHT (OBJ BTL))
<END.OBS>: NIL
12.  STM: ((OBS RIGHT (OBJ BTL)) (LOOK.FOR RIGHT (OBJ BTL)) (OBS.AT RIGHT (OBJ BTL RD)) (=
OBS.AT RIGHT (OBJ BTL RD)) (OLD OBS LEFT (OBJ SPC)) (LEFT (OBJ SPC)) (OBS NEW DISPLAY) (GOAL *
SOLVE) NIL)
PD3  TRUE

DISPLAY: (EDGE (BTL RD RT) (BTL RD RT) >> (BTL RD RT) (BTL GN DN) (BTL GN DN) (BTL GN DN) EDGE)
<NEW.OBS>: NIL
<END.OBS>: NIL
14.  STM: ((OBS.AT RIGHT (OBJ BTL RD)) (LOOK.FOR RIGHT (OBJ BTL)) (OBS.AT RIGHT (OBJ BTL RD))
(= OBS.AT RIGHT (OBJ BTL RD)) (OLD OBS LEFT (OBJ SPC)) (LEFT (OBJ SPC)) (OBS NEW DISPLAY)
(GOAL * SOLVE) NIL)
PD4  TRUE

15.  STM: ((OBS.AT RIGHT (OBJ BTL RD)) (= OBS.AT RIGHT (OBJ BTL RD)) (LOOK.FOR RIGHT (OBJ
BTL)) (= OBS.AT RIGHT (OBJ BTL RD)) (OLD OBS LEFT (OBJ SPC)) (LEFT (OBJ SPC)) (OBS NEW
DISPLAY) (GOAL * SOLVE) NIL)
G12  TRUE

DISPLAY: (EDGE (BTL RD RT) (BTL RD RT) (BTL RD RT) >> (BTL GN DN) (BTL GN DN) (BTL GN DN) EDGE)
<NEW.OBS>: (OBS RIGHT (OBJ BTL))
<END.OBS>: NIL
16.  STM: ((OBS RIGHT (OBJ BTL)) (LOOK.FOR RIGHT (OBJ BTL)) (OBS.AT RIGHT (OBJ BTL RD)) (=
OBS.AT RIGHT (OBJ BTL RD)) (= OBS.AT RIGHT (OBJ BTL RD)) (OLD OBS LEFT (OBJ SPC)) (LEFT (OBJ
SPC)) (OBS NEW DISPLAY) (GOAL * SOLVE))
PD3  TRUE

DISPLAY: (EDGE (BTL RD RT) (BTL RD RT) (BTL RD RT) >> (BTL GN DN) (BTL GN DN) (BTL GN DN) EDGE)
<NEW.OBS>: NIL
<END.OBS>: NIL
18.  STM: ((OBS.AT RIGHT (OBJ BTL RD)) (LOOK.FOR RIGHT (OBJ BTL)) (OBS.AT RIGHT (OBJ BTL RD))
(= OBS.AT RIGHT (OBJ BTL RD)) (= OBS.AT RIGHT (OBJ BTL RD)) (OLD OBS LEFT (OBJ SPC)) (LEFT
(OBJ SPC)) (OBS NEW DISPLAY) (GOAL * SOLVE))
PD6  TRUE
```

(Continued)

```
21.   STM: ((OBS (SEQ (OBJ BTL RD) (OBJ BTL RD) (OBJ BTL RD))) (OBS.AT RIGHT (OBJ BTL BG)) (OLD
OBS.AT RIGHT (OBJ BTL RD)) (OLD OBS.AT RIGHT (OBJ BTL RD)) (= OBS.AT RIGHT (OBJ BTL RD))
(LOOK.FOR RIGHT (OBJ BTL)) (OLD OBS LEFT (OBJ SPC)) (LEFT (OBJ SPC)) (OBS NEW DISPLAY))
G12   TRUE

DISPLAY: (EDGE (BTL RD RT) (BTL RD RT) (BTL RD RT) (BTL GN DN) >> (BTL GN DN) (BTL GN DN) EDGE)
<NEW.OBS>: (OBS RIGHT (OBJ BTL))
<END.OBS>: NIL
22.   STM: ((OBS RIGHT (OBJ BTL)) (LOOK.FOR RIGHT (OBJ BTL)) (OBS (SEQ (OBJ BTL RD) (OBJ BTL
RD) (OBJ BTL RD))) (OBS.AT RIGHT (OBJ BTL BG)) (OLD OBS.AT RIGHT (OBJ BTL RD)) (OLD OBS.AT
RIGHT (OBJ BTL RD)) (= OBS.AT RIGHT (OBJ BTL RD)) (OLD OBS LEFT (OBJ SPC)) (LEFT (OBJ SPC)))
PD3   TRUE

DISPLAY: (EDGE (BTL RD RT) (BTL RD RT) (BTL RD RT) (BTL GN DN) >> (BTL GN DN) (BTL GN DN) EDGE)
<NEW.OBS>: NIL
<END.OBS>: NIL
24.   STM: ((OBS.AT RIGHT (OBJ BTL BG)) (LOOK.FOR RIGHT (OBJ BTL)) (OBS (SEQ (OBJ BTL RD) (OBJ
BTL RD) (OBJ BTL RD))) (OBS.AT RIGHT (OBJ BTL BG)) (OLD OBS.AT RIGHT (OBJ BTL RD)) (OLD OBS.AT
RIGHT (OBJ BTL RD)) (= OBS.AT RIGHT (OBJ BTL RD)) (OLD OBS LEFT (OBJ SPC)) (LEFT (OBJ SPC)))
PD4   TRUE

25.   STM: ((OBS.AT RIGHT (OBJ BTL BG)) (= OBS.AT RIGHT (OBJ BTL BG)) (LOOK.FOR RIGHT (OBJ
BTL)) (OBS (SEQ (OBJ BTL RD) (OBJ BTL RD) (OBJ BTL RD))) (OLD OBS.AT RIGHT (OBJ BTL RD)) (OLD
OBS.AT RIGHT (OBJ BTL RD)) (= OBS.AT RIGHT (OBJ BTL RD)) (OLD OBS LEFT (OBJ SPC)) (LEFT (OBJ
SPC)))
G12   TRUE

DISPLAY: (EDGE (BTL RD RT) (BTL RD RT) (BTL RD RT) (BTL GN DN) (BTL GN DN) >> (BTL GN DN) EDGE)
<NEW.OBS>: (OBS RIGHT (OBJ BTL))
<END.OBS>: NIL
26.   STM: ((OBS RIGHT (OBJ BTL)) (LOOK.FOR RIGHT (OBJ BTL)) (OBS.AT RIGHT (OBJ BTL BG)) (=
OBS.AT RIGHT (OBJ BTL BG)) (OBS (SEQ (OBJ BTL RD) (OBJ BTL RD) (OBJ BTL RD))) (OLD OBS.AT
RIGHT (OBJ BTL RD)) (OLD OBS.AT RIGHT (OBJ BTL RD)) (= OBS.AT RIGHT (OBJ BTL RD)) (OLD OBS
LEFT (OBJ SPC)))
PD3   TRUE

DISPLAY: (EDGE (BTL RD RT) (BTL RD RT) (BTL RD RT) (BTL GN DN) (BTL GN DN) >> (BTL GN DN) EDGE)
<NEW.OBS>: NIL
<END.OBS>: NIL
28.   STM: ((OBS.AT RIGHT (OBJ BTL BG)) (LOOK.FOR RIGHT (OBJ BTL)) (OBS.AT RIGHT (OBJ BTL BG))
(= OBS.AT RIGHT (OBJ BTL BG)) (OBS (SEQ (OBJ BTL RD) (OBJ BTL RD) (OBJ BTL RD))) (OLD OBS.AT
RIGHT (OBJ BTL RD)) (OLD OBS.AT RIGHT (OBJ BTL RD)) (= OBS.AT RIGHT (OBJ BTL RD)) (OLD OBS
LEFT (OBJ SPC)))
PD4   TRUE

29.   STM: ((OBS.AT RIGHT (OBJ BTL BG)) (= OBS.AT RIGHT (OBJ BTL BG)) (LOOK.FOR RIGHT (OBJ
BTL)) (= OBS.AT RIGHT (OBJ BTL BG)) (OBS (SEQ (OBJ BTL RD) (OBJ BTL RD) (OBJ BTL RD))) (OLD
OBS.AT RIGHT (OBJ BTL RD)) (OLD OBS.AT RIGHT (OBJ BTL RD)) (= OBS.AT RIGHT (OBJ BTL RD)) (OLD
OBS LEFT (OBJ SPC)))
G12   TRUE

DISPLAY: (EDGE (BTL RD RT) (BTL RD RT) (BTL RD RT) (BTL GN DN) (BTL GN DN) (BTL GN DN) >> EDGE)
<NEW.OBS>: (NOBS RIGHT (OBJ BTL))
<END.OBS>: (END LOOK.FOR)
30.   STM: ((END LOOK.FOR) (NOBS RIGHT (OBJ BTL)) (LOOK.FOR RIGHT (OBJ BTL)) (OBS.AT RIGHT (OBJ
BTL BG)) (= OBS.AT RIGHT (OBJ BTL BG)) (= OBS.AT RIGHT (OBJ BTL BG)) (OBS (SEQ (OBJ BTL RD)
(OBJ BTL RD) (OBJ BTL RD))) (OLD OBS.AT RIGHT (OBJ BTL RD)) (OLD OBS.AT RIGHT (OBJ BTL RD)))
G13   TRUE

32.   STM: ((OLD LOOK.FOR RIGHT (OBJ BTL)) (OLD END LOOK.FOR) (NOBS RIGHT (OBJ BTL)) (OBS.AT
RIGHT (OBJ BTL BG)) (= OBS.AT RIGHT (OBJ BTL BG)) (= OBS.AT RIGHT (OBJ BTL BG)) (OBS (SEQ (OBJ
BTL RD) (OBJ BTL RD) (OBJ BTL RD))) (OLD OBS.AT RIGHT (OBJ BTL RD)) (OLD OBS.AT RIGHT (OBJ BTL
RD)))
PD6   TRUE

35.   STM: ((OBS (SEQ (OBJ BTL BG) (OBJ BTL BG) (OBJ BTL BG))) (NOBS RIGHT (OBJ BTL)) (OLD
OBS.AT RIGHT (OBJ BTL BG)) (OLD OBS.AT RIGHT (OBJ BTL BG)) (= OBS.AT RIGHT (OBJ BTL BG)) (OLD
LOOK.FOR RIGHT (OBJ BTL)) (OLD END LOOK.FOR) (OBS (SEQ (OBJ BTL RD) (OBJ BTL RD) (OBJ BTL
RD))) (OLD OBS.AT RIGHT (OBJ BTL RD)))
G11   TRUE

36.   STM: ((GOAL * SOLVE) (OBS (SEQ (OBJ BTL BG) (OBJ BTL BG) (OBJ BTL BG))) (NOBS RIGHT (OBJ
BTL)) (OLD OBS.AT RIGHT (OBJ BTL BG)) (OLD OBS.AT RIGHT (OBJ BTL BG)) (= OBS.AT RIGHT (OBJ BTL
BG)) (OLD LOOK.FOR RIGHT (OBJ BTL)) (OLD END LOOK.FOR) (OBS (SEQ (OBJ BTL RD) (OBJ BTL RD)
(OBJ BTL RD))))
END: NO PD TRUE
```

FIG. 25. Run of SCP1 on task P1.

```
DISPLAY: (EDGE (BTL GN UP) (BTL BL UP) (BTL GN UP) (BTL BL LF) (BTL GN LF) (BTL BL LF) EDGE)



31.  STM: ((GOAL * SOLVE) (OLD LOOK.FOR RIGHT (OBJ BTL)) (OLD END LOOK.FOR) (NOBS RIGHT (OBJ
BTL)) (OBS.AT RIGHT (OBJ BTL BG)) (= OBS.AT RIGHT (OBJ BTL BG)) (= OBS.AT RIGHT (OBJ BTL BG))
(= OBS.AT RIGHT (OBJ BTL BG)) (= OBS.AT RIGHT (OBJ BTL BG)))
```

FIG. 26. Run of SCP1 on task P2.

```
DISPLAY: (EDGE (BTL YL DN) (BTL BL RT) (BTL YL DN) (BTL BL RT) (BTL YL DN) (BTL BL RT) EDGE)



34.  STM: ((GOAL * SOLVE) (OLD LOOK.FOR RIGHT (OBJ BTL)) (OLD END LOOK.FOR) (NOBS RIGHT (OBJ
BTL)) (OBS.AT RIGHT (OBJ BTL BG)) (OBS.AT RIGHT (OBJ BTL YL)) (OBS (SEQ (OBJ BTL BG) (OBJ BTL
BG))) (OBS (SEQ (OBJ BTL YL) (OBJ BTL YL))) (OLD OBS.AT RIGHT (OBJ BTL BG)))
```

FIG. 27. Run of SCP1 on task P3.

The sources of these difficulties are not hard to spot. The perceptual system only observes a single additional dimension, whereas the subject obviously is aware of both dimensions of variation. Selection on dimensions of perception is always necessary, and ultimately the relevant dimensions for a task series must become encoded into the STM element that gets formed to look at the display (as provided in SCP1 by PD3). The inappropriate grouping in problem P3 arises simply because SCP1 has no productions that are sensitive to forms other than runs of identical elements.

In addition to these two discrepancies, some other aspects of the system's behavior should be noted. First, we are not having the system actually produce an output (as we did, for example, in the Johnson task), and the encoding of the perceptual objects for output is not given. Thus, in Figure 25, the conversion from (SEQ (OBJ BTL BG) (OBJ BTL BG) (OBJ BTL BG)) to a statement of a sequence of three green bottles is still to be made. The productions to do this are not difficult to envision, but it should be noted that they require an additional look at the stimulus (with LOOK.AT) in order to disambiguate BG to GN. A second feature to notice is that the subsequences are simply left in STM at the end (in both P1 and P3). The subject organizes these into a single perception of the stimulus. Again, this is due to the lack of productions that are sensitive to this final need for organization.

Figure 28 shows a modified production system (SCP2) that attempts to respond to a number of these considerations. We have changed the number of dimensions looked at when adding detail (by LOOK.AT) from one to two. This does not show up in the production system, since it is a feature of the perceptual system. We have added productions PD7 and PD8 to be sensitive to alternations. PD7 recognizes the repetition of an element. Thus, it notes X Y X as indicating an organization into X (Y X). PD8 uses an existing organization to build up additional ones, so that it sees Y X (Y X) as (Y X) (Y X). Normally, the occurrence of Y X would appear to be simply two distinct elements.

It might be thought that PD8 was not needed, since X Y X (Y X) would get transformed to X (Y X) (Y X) in any event by PD7. Indeed this is true, until the last pair occurs, when there is no following X to force the organization. Basically, there must be some reason why Y X looks like a group. Initially it is the fact that following elements repeat (PD7); but eventually it must be that previous elements repeat (PD8). Thus some form of expectation must occur.

```
00100    ; SCP2: MODIFICATION OF SCP1
00200    ;        REQUIRES SC3F, ETC. (I.E., REPLACES SCP1)
00300    ;
00400    ;        (IDENTICAL TO SCPF.E84)
00500    ;        ADDS P7, P8 FOR ALTERNATIONS
00600    ;        ADDS P9, P10 FOR FINAL GROUPING
00700    ;        GOES TO 2 DIMENSIONS OF ADDED DETAIL PER TRY
00800    ;
00900    DEFINE.SYMBOLS!
01000    ;
01100    PD1: ((OBS NEW DISPLAY) --> (LEFT (OBJ SPC)) LOOK.FOR)
01200    ;
01300    PD2: ((OBS LEFT (OBJ SPC)) --> (OBS ==> OLD OBS)
01400         (LOOK.FOR RIGHT (OBJ BTL)))
01500    ;
01600    PD3: ((OBS (OBJ BTL)) --> (OBS ==> OBS.AT) LOOK.AT)
01700    ;
01800    PD4: ((<OBS> X1 == (<POBJ.TYPE>)) AND (<OBS> X1) -->
01900         (<OBS> ===> = <OBS>))
02000    ;
02100    PD5: ((<OBS.TYPE>) AND (<OBS> X1 == (<POBJ.TYPE>)) AND
02200         (= <OBS> X1) AND (= <OBS> X1) ABS -->
02300         (<OBS> ===> OLD <OBS>)(= ====> OLD)(OBS (SEQ X1 X1)))
02400    ;
02500    PD6: ((<OBS.TYPE>) AND (<OBS> X1 == (<POBJ.TYPE>)) AND
02600         (= <OBS> X1) AND (= <OBS> X1) AND (= <OBS> X1) ABS -->
02700         (<OBS> ===> OLD <OBS>)(= ====> OLD)(OBS (SEQ X1 X1 X1)))
02800    ;
02900    PD7: ((<OBS> X1 == (<POBJ.TYPE>)) AND
03000         (<OBS> X2 == (<POBJ.TYPE>)) AND (<OBS> X1) -->
03100         (<OBS> ===> OLD <OBS>)(<OBS> ====> OLD <OBS>)
03200         (OBS (SEQ X1 X2)))
03300    ;
03400    PD8: ((<OBS> X1 == (<POBJ.TYPE>)) AND
03500         (<OBS> X2 == (<POBJ.TYPE>)) AND (OBS (SEQ X2 X1)) -->
03600         (<OBS> ==> OLD <OBS>)(<OBS> ===> OLD <OBS>)
03700         (OBS (SEQ X2·X1)))
03800    ;
03900    PD9: ((NOBS) AND (<OBS> X1 == (<POBJ.TYPE>)) AND
04000         (<OBS> X2 == (<POBJ.TYPE>)) --> (<OBS> ===> OLD <OBS>)
04100         (<OBS> ====> OLD <OBS>)(OBS (SEQ X2 X1)))
04200    ;
04300    PD10: ((NOBS) AND (<OBS> X1 == (<POBJ.TYPE>)) AND
04400          (<OBS> X2 == (<POBJ.TYPE>)) AND
04500          (<OBS> X3 == (<POBJ.TYPE>))) --> (<OBS> ===> OLD <OBS>)
04600          (<OBS> ====> OLD <OBS>)(OBS (SEQ X3 X2 X1)))
04700    ;
04800    PS2: (PD7 PD4 PD3 PD8 PD6 PD5 G12 PD10 PD9 PD2 PD1)
04900    ;
05000    "SCPF.E84 LOADED" RETURN.TO.TTY!
05100
05200
05300
05400
```

FIG. 28. SCP2: Modified system for series completion task.

We have also added productions PD9 and PD10 in SCP2 to group together whatever organization has occurred by the end of the stimulus. However, we have not introduced the second layer of responding, given the perceived organization, for example, to say "3 green." Thus, the output of interest of the system is simply the final state of STM.

Figures 29, 30, and 31 show the results of these modifications on P1, P2, and P3 respectively. P1 and P2 now look fine. However, we failed to obtain the intended result in P3. It did obtain the subsequences, as desired, but it then put two of them together into a higher sequence, rather than all three; and then followed this by the use of PD9 to create an organization of the form (((YX)(YX)(YX))). The reason for this is interesting. The strategy of the SCP1-SCP2 system is to detect organization by delaying until a boundary occurs. The productions PD5 and PD6 respond to a general boundary (⟨OBS.TYPE⟩), since what is important is that the boundary element is different from the existing sequence of elements (the ones marked by =). For instance, PD5 and PD6 need to respond to the occurrence of a NOBS as a boundary. The difficulty this produces can be seen in Figure 32, which shows the critical moment (26) in the run of Figure 31. The occurrence of a new observed object in STM (OBS (OBJ YL VT)) triggers the grouping of the two sequences, since it acts as a perfectly good boundary for PD5. What we want is for the system to delay to see if another subsequence will build up, so that a group of three can be put together. For that to happen the system must either distinguish different kinds

```
DISPLAY: (EDGE (BTL RD RT) (BTL RD RT) (BTL RD RT) (BTL GN DN) (BTL GN DN) (BTL GN DN) EDGE)


39.  STM: ((GOAL * SOLVE) (OBS (SEQ (SEQ (OBJ BTL RD HZ) (OBJ BTL RD HZ) (OBJ BTL RD HZ)) (SEQ
(OBJ BTL BG VT) (OBJ BTL BG VT) (OBJ BTL BG VT)))) (NOBS RIGHT (OBJ BTL)) (OLD OBS (SEQ (OBJ
BTL BG VT) (OBJ BTL BG VT) (OBJ BTL BG VT))) (OLD OBS (SEQ (OBJ BTL RD HZ) (OBJ BTL RD HZ)
(OBJ BTL RD HZ))) (OLD OBS.AT RIGHT (OBJ BTL BG VT)) (OLD OBS.AT RIGHT (OBJ BTL BG VT)) (=
OBS.AT RIGHT (OBJ BTL BG VT)) (OLD LOOK.FOR RIGHT (OBJ BTL)))
```

FIG. 29. Run of SCP2 on task P1.

```
DISPLAY: (EDGE (BTL GN UP) (BTL BL UP) (BTL GN UP) (BTL BL LF) (BTL GN LF) (BTL BL LF) EDGE)


39.  STM: ((GOAL * SOLVE) (OBS (SEQ (SEQ (OBJ BTL BG VT) (OBJ BTL BG VT) (OBJ BTL BG VT)) (SEQ
(OBJ BTL BG HZ) (OBJ BTL BG HZ) (OBJ BTL BG HZ)))) (NOBS RIGHT (OBJ BTL)) (OLD OBS (SEQ (OBJ
BTL BG HZ) (OBJ BTL BG HZ) (OBJ BTL BG HZ))) (OLD OBS (SEQ (OBJ BTL BG VT) (OBJ BTL BG VT)
(OBJ BTL BG VT))) (OLD OBS.AT RIGHT (OBJ BTL BG HZ)) (OLD OBS.AT RIGHT (OBJ BTL BG HZ)) (=
OBS.AT RIGHT (OBJ BTL BG HZ)) (OLD LOOK.FOR RIGHT (OBJ BTL)))
```

FIG. 30. Run of SCP2 on task P2.

```
DISPLAY: (EDGE (BTL YL DN) (BTL BL RT) (BTL YL DN) (BTL BL RT) (BTL YL DN) (BTL BL RT) EDGE)


42.  STM: ((GOAL * SOLVE) (OBS (SEQ (SEQ (SEQ (OBJ BTL YL VT) (OBJ BTL BG HZ)) (SEQ (OBJ BTL
YL VT) (OBJ BTL BG HZ))) (SEQ (OBJ BTL YL VT) (OBJ BTL BG HZ)))) (NOBS RIGHT (OBJ BTL)) (OLD
OBS (SEQ (OBJ BTL YL VT) (OBJ BTL BG HZ)) (OLD OBS (SEQ (SEQ (OBJ BTL YL VT) (OBJ BTL BG HZ))
(SEQ (OBJ BTL YL VT) (OBJ BTL BG HZ)))) (OLD OBS.AT RIGHT (OBJ BTL BG HZ)) (OLD OBS.AT RIGHT
(OBJ BTL YL VT)) (OLD LOOK.FOR RIGHT (OBJ BTL)) (OLD END LOOK.FOR))
```

FIG. 31. Run of SCP2 on task P3.

```
DISPLAY: (EDGE (BTL YL DN) (BTL BL RT) (BTL YL DN) (BTL BL RT) >> (BTL YL DN) (BTL BL RT) EDGE)
<NEW.OBS>: NIL
<END.OBS>: NIL
26. STM: ((OBS.AT RIGHT (OBJ BTL YL VT)) (LOOK.FOR RIGHT (OBJ BTL)) (OBS (SEQ (OBJ BTL YL VT)
(OBJ BTL BG HZ))) (= OBS (SEQ (OBJ BTL YL VT) (OBJ BTL BG HZ))) (OLD OBS.AT RIGHT (OBJ BTL BG
HZ)) (OLD OBS.AT RIGHT (OBJ BTL YL VT)) (OLD OBS.AT RIGHT (OBJ BTL BG HZ)) (OLD OBS.AT RIGHT
(OBJ BTL YL VT)) (OLD OBS LEFT (OBJ SPC)))
PD5   TRUE

29. STM: ((OBS (SEQ (SEQ (OBJ BTL YL VT) (OBJ BTL BG HZ)) (SEQ (OBJ BTL YL VT) (OBJ BTL BG
HZ))) (OBS.AT RIGHT (OBJ BTL YL VT)) (OLD OBS (SEQ (OBJ BTL YL VT) (OBJ BTL BG HZ))) (OLD OBS
(SEQ (OBJ BTL YL VT) (OBJ BTL BG HZ))) (LOOK.FOR RIGHT (OBJ BTL)) (OLD OBS.AT RIGHT (OBJ BTL
BG HZ)) (OLD OBS.AT RIGHT (OBJ BTL YL VT)) (OLD OBS.AT RIGHT (OBJ BTL BG HZ)) (OLD OBS.AT
RIGHT (OBJ BTL YL VT)))
```

FIG. 32. Critical part of run of Figure 35 where evoked PD5.

```
00100   ; SCP3: MODIFICATION OF SCP2
00200   ;        AUGMENTATION TO SCP2
00300   ;
00400   ;        (THUS THE PART OF SCPF.E05 THAT IS DIFFERENT)
00500   ;        ADDS P11 TO PROVIDE BOUNDARY FROM NOBS
00600   ;        MODIFIES P5, P6 TO RESTRICT BOUNDARY TO <OBS>
00700   ;
00800   DEFINE.SYMBOLS!
00900   ;
01000   PD5: ((<OBS>) AND (<OBS> X1 == (<POBJ.TYPE>)) AND
01100        (= <OBS> X1) AND (= <OBS> X1) ABS -->
01200        (<OBS> ===> OLD <OBS>)(= ====> OLD)(OBS (SEQ X1 X1)))
01300   ;
01400   PD6: ((<OBS>) AND (<OBS> X1 == (<POBJ.TYPE>)) AND
01500        (= <OBS> X1) AND (= <OBS> X1) AND (= <OBS> X1) ABS -->
01600        (<OBS> ===> OLD <OBS>)(= ====> OLD)(OBS (SEQ X1 X1 X1)))
01700   ;
01800   PD11: ((NOBS) AND (<OBS> X1 == (<POBJ.TYPE>)) AND
01810         (<OBS> NOBS) ABS --> (<OBS> NOBS))
01900   ;
02000   PS2: (PD7 PD4 PD3 PD6 PD5 G12 PD11 PD10 PD9 PD2 PD1)
02100   ;
02200   "SCPF.E05 ADDITION LOADED" RETURN.TO.TTY!
02300
02400       FIGURE 37. SCP3: MODIFIED SYSTEM FOR SERIES
02500                  COMPLETION TASK TO AVOID WRONG GROUPING
02600
```

FIG. 33. SCP3: Modified system for series completion task to avoid wrong grouping.

of boundaries or (not exclusively) have a more definite expectation of the organization that is coming (i.e., better than PD8).

An unsatisfactory solution, but one that gets the right result in the short run is shown in Figure 33, where alternative versions of PD5 and PD6 are given that restrict the boundaries acceptable to agree with the grouping that is to be done (e.g., all OBJs or all SEQs). Then something must be added to permit the final act of organization at the end. This is provided by PD11, which constructs a boundary element of whatever type is necessary. Figure 34 shows the result.

Although we do not show it, SCP3 continues to operate satisfactorily on P1 and P2. Figures 35, 36, 37, and 38 show the terminal behavior on displays P4, P5, P6, and P7 respectively. The result P7 is satisfactory. In fact, P7 represents a case where the subject does not initially create any organization on the sequence, similar to the

```
DISPLAY: (EDGE (BTL YL DN) (BTL BL RT) (BTL YL DN) (BTL BL RT) (BTL YL DN) (BTL BL RT) EDGE)


41.  STM: ((GOAL * SOLVE) (OBS (SEQ (SEQ (OBJ BTL YL VT) (OBJ BTL BG HZ)) (SEQ (OBJ BTL YL VT)
(OBJ BTL BG HZ)) (SEQ (OBJ BTL YL VT) (OBJ BTL BG HZ)))) (OBS NOBS) (OLD OBS (SEQ (OBJ BTL YL
VT) (OBJ BTL BG HZ))) (OLD OBS (SEQ (OBJ BTL YL VT) (OBJ BTL BG HZ))) (= OBS (SEQ (OBJ BTL YL
VT) (OBJ BTL BG HZ))) (NOBS RIGHT (OBJ BTL)) (OLD LOOK.FOR RIGHT (OBJ BTL)) (OLD END LOOK.FOR))
```

FIG. 34. Run of SCP3 on task P3.

```
DISPLAY: (EDGE (BTL BL UP) (BTL BL UP) (BTL YL UP) (BTL YL RT) (BTL BL RT) (BTL BL RT) EDGE)


39.  STM: ((GOAL * SOLVE) (OBS (SEQ (SEQ (OBJ BTL BG VT) (OBJ BTL BG VT)) (SEQ (OBJ BTL BG HZ)
(OBJ BTL BG HZ)))) (NOBS RIGHT (OBJ BTL)) (OLD OBS (SEQ (OBJ BTL BG HZ) (OBJ BTL BG HZ))) (OLD
OBS (SEQ (OBJ BTL BG VT) (OBJ BTL BG VT))) (OBS NOBS) (OBS.AT NOBS) (OLD OBS.AT RIGHT (OBJ BTL
BG HZ)) (OLD OBS.AT RIGHT (OBJ BTL BG HZ)) (OLD LOOK.FOR RIGHT (OBJ BTL)) (OLD END LOOK.FOR))
```

FIG. 35. Run of SCP3 on task P4.

```
DISPLAY: (EDGE (BTL RD LF) (BTL RD RT) (BTL BL RT) (BTL BL LF) (BTL RD RT) (BTL RT LF) EDGE)


42.  STM: ((GOAL * SOLVE) (OBS (SEQ (SEQ (OBJ BTL BG HZ) (OBJ BTL BG HZ)) (SEQ (OBJ BTL RD HZ)
(OBJ BTL COLOR)))) (NOBS RIGHT (OBJ BTL)) (OLD OBS (SEQ (OBJ BTL RD HZ) (OBJ BTL COLOR))) (OLD
OBS (SEQ (OBJ BTL BG HZ) (OBJ BTL BG HZ))) (OBS NOBS) (OLD OBS.AT RIGHT (OBJ BTL COLOR)) (OLD
OBS.AT RIGHT (OBJ BTL RD HZ)) (OBS.AT NOBS))
```

FIG. 36. Run of SCP3 on task P5.

```
DISPLAY: (EDGE (BTL YL RT) (BTL YL RT) (BTL GN DN) (BTL GN DN) (BTL YL RT) (BTL YL RT) EDGE)


46.  STM: ((GOAL * SOLVE) (OBS (SEQ (SEQ (OBJ BTL YL HZ) (OBJ BTL YL HZ)) (SEQ (SEQ (OBJ BTL
YL HZ) (OBJ BTL YL HZ)) (SEQ (OBJ BTL BG VT) (OBJ BTL BG VT))))) (NOBS RIGHT (OBJ BTL)) (OLD
OBS (SEQ (SEQ (OBJ BTL YL HZ) (OBJ BTL YL HZ)) (SEQ (OBJ BTL BG VT) (OBJ BTL BG VT)))) (OLD
OBS (SEQ (OBJ BTL YL HZ) (OBJ BTL YL HZ))) (OBS NOBS) (OLD OBS (SEQ (OBJ BTL BG VT) (OBJ BTL
BG VT))) (OLD OBS (SEQ (OBJ BTL YL HZ) (OBJ BTL YL HZ))) (OBS.AT NOBS) (OLD OBS.AT RIGHT (OBJ
BTL YL HZ)) (OLD OBS.AT RIGHT (OBJ
BTL YL HZ)))
```

FIG. 37. Run of SCP3 on task P6.

```
DISPLAY: (EDGE (BTL BL UP) (BTL GN UP) (BTL BL UP) (BTL BL DN) (BTL GN DN) (BTL BL DN) EDGE)


32.  STM: ((GOAL * SOLVE) (OBS.AT NOBS) (NOBS RIGHT (OBJ BTL)) (OBS.AT RIGHT (OBJ BTL BG VT))
(OLD LOOK.FOR RIGHT (OBJ BTL)) (OLD END LOOK.FOR) (= OBS.AT RIGHT (OBJ BTL BG VT)) (= OBS.AT
RIGHT (OBJ BTL BG VT)) (= OBS.AT RIGHT (OBJ BTL BG VT)))
```

FIG. 38. Run of SCP 3 on task P7.

performance of SCP1 on P2. Thus, in modifying the program to work more appropriately on P2, it was important not to go so far as to prohibit similar behavior on other displays. Behavior on P6 is partially satisfactory. The system does not have the concept of surrounding, so it cannot obtain the same concept as the subject. It does however, pick up some of the underlying regularity. Behavior on P4 is also partially satisfactory. The production system has no mechanism for breaking off the scan and the behavior of the subject indicates a much stronger expectation for organization than our system provides. However, SCP3 does pick up the first pair and then fails to pick up the pair (say on just color) in the middle. Since it continues (whereas the subject breaks off) it also picks up the second blue pair; and then it puts the two sequences together at the end.[20] The subject's response on task P5 is not within the range of our program, since it does not have the additional direction concepts to permit it to see the first two as a unit in terms of direction as well as color.

CONCLUSION

Let us summarize very briefly where this exploration has taken us. We started with the desire to obtain an explicit control structure for a system that was able to perform tasks involving stimulus encoding. Rather than start fresh we chose to adapt a system that had been developed for describing behavior in problem solving situations, which already came equipped with an explicit control structure.

At the level that has been called sufficiency analysis, the enterprise has been moderately successful. The system developed, PSG + LKE + SC3 + SCP3, does not violate seriously the general characteristics of human cognitive and perceptual organization as we currently understand them. It does encode stimuli and in not unreasonable ways. It does have an explicit control structure and control interface between the perceptual structure and the more central cognitive structure. Furthermore, the control structure plays a significant role in producing behavior. For example, in the Johnson task, it forced us to recode while responding; and in the series completion task it forced us to give up generality on the grouping productions (PD5 and PD6) and to make the system explicitly recognize the end of the sequence.

All the above lends support to the enterprise. On the other hand it is apparent that we hardly understand at all the nature of the system created. Within the confines of this paper we have not even exhibited the behavior of the system along many important dimensions. For example, we have not shown its capability to perceive sequences directly. We might have exhibited it by trying a different processing strategy in place of PD8. It could take the formed sequence as a new instruction for how to look at the display. For instance, we might have labeled sequences as NEW when first created and then used a production such as

---

[20] The careful reader will note that additional cells have been added to STM for the P6 and P4 runs. The exact size of this STM cannot yet be determined, since it holds much control information not accounted for in the usual models. Hence we have set it at whatever size seemed appropriate.

$$(NEW \ OBS \ X1 \ = = \ (SEQ)) \ AND \ (LOOK.FOR \ X2 \ = = \ ((POBJ.TYPE))) \ - \rightarrow$$

$$(NEW \ = \Rightarrow) \ (X2 \ = \Rightarrow \ X1))$$

We did not follow this path, mostly because, like the path we did follow, it simply raises a large number of issues and adjustments in the system before it produces appropriate behavior.

The example above is only one form of unexamined behavior. Others include the ability to adjust the level of detail upward again, after it has been once seen; the ability to match perceived objects so as to create knowledge of their differences; the ability to use a complex perceived object to guide re-perception of the display (as occurs during the remainder of each of the protocols from which our initial utterances were taken); and even the final form of a production system that would do the full gamut of perceptual organization showed by the subject (Table 3).

In all of the above it is not obvious to me (and, I presume, to the reader as well) just what are the capabilities and characteristics of the system. The system does have the power to produce some sorts of performance in all these areas, without further basic modification or augmentation. But experience with even the existing small fragment of its behavior shows it is not easy to arrange to produce a given performance. Although the system has many aspects of a general programming system, it also has definite characteristics of its own that do not permit one simply to state to it in clear terms, so to speak, what is desired. Indeed, it is the very control structure that frustrates this, compared to the sorts of control structures in user-oriented programming languages, which permit absolute local control and protection from unwanted side effects.

To offset the pessimism of the above remarks, one can conclude something about the psychological character of these production systems, even from the small amount of experience that is available. For instance, the natural way to write productions that encode sequences is recursively, from X (SEQ XX) to construct (SEQ X X X). In fact, an earlier production system was constructed this way. This appears to violate the sort of rule that Neal Johnson was attempting to establish, in which one could not peek inside the coded expression. More important, such a production is indeed recursive and there is no way to keep it from constructing coded groups that are as large as you please, for example, X (SEQ X X X X X X) - → (SEQ X X X X X X X). This clearly violates the extensive experience on the use of small encodings that is apparent throughout the data on human encoding. Thus, the present production system admits only finite encodings of two or three. While slightly less elegant, it appears to match more closely what we know of human behavior.

However, despite the above, it would appear that statements about the inadequacies of the system in the light of current psychological knowledge are somewhat premature. My own feelings, upon creating the LKE version, was that the model was psychologically false in a number of obvious ways and that its main excuse for living was that it would at least turn over. I still believe that judgment, but I am no longer prepared to modify the basic structure until more evidence becomes available about the inadequacies of its behavior and whether they are due to not understanding processing strategies, or whether they represent inherent structural features of the system.

Consequently, this paper must end on a note of incompleteness, though one that is hopefully appropriate to a theoretical exploration.

APPENDIX: INTERPRETATION RULES FOR PRODUCTION SYSTEM PSG

Executing a Production System (1—7)

1. A list of productions and production systems is considered a single linear list of productions.
2. Each production is considered in order.
3. Each production constitutes an independent context with respect to assignment of values for variables and class names, all communication between successive evocations of productions occurring via STM.
4. The condition of a production is matched to STM, and the action elements of the production are executed if the match succeeds.
5. If a production is successfully matched then productions are considered again, starting with the first production.
6. Starting-over occurs independently of the actions of the successful production, including termination of the action sequence by a FAIL. The exception is a STOP.PS action, which terminates the production system.
7. If no production is satisfied, the production system terminates.

Matching a Production Condition (8—12)

8. Each condition element is considered in order.
9. Each condition element is matched against each STM element in order.
10. A condition element matches a memory element if:
    10.1 Each symbol in the condition element matches some symbol in the memory element.
    10.2 The symbols in the condition element are considered in order.
    10.3 Memory elements are also considered in order.
    10.4 However, memory elements may be skipped, except the first.
    10.5 If a symbol has a proper name, then the match is on the name of the symbol.
    10.6 Otherwise the symbol is taken as designating another element and the match is executed recursively.
    10.7 A variable can be matched by being assigned, as value, the symbol to which it is being matched, provided that the symbol is in the domain of the variable (if it has one).
    10.8 A class name can be matched by being assigned, as value, the symbol to which it is being matched, provided that the symbol is a member of the class.
    10.9 A variable or class name that has already been assigned a value takes on that value during the remainder of the match.

11. A memory element that has been matched by a condition element is not considered in matching the remainder of the elements.

12. Whether the entire condition matches is determined by considering each condition element in accordance with connectives:

12.1 C1 AND C2   matches if C1 matches and C2 matches.

12.2 C1 OR C2   matches if C1 matches or C2 matches or both.

12.3 C1 ABS   matches if C1 is absent, that is, does not match.

12.4 Any single-level sequence of the above connectives is legal, but embedded expressions are not. For example, C1 AND C2 AND C3 OR C4 AND C5 ABS is legal, but (C1 AND C2) OR (C3 AND C4) is not legal.

Executing Actions after Successful Matching (13–16)

13. All STM elements participating in the match are moved to the front of STM in the order of the condition elements to which they correspond. This happens prior to any of the actions. For example, if (C AND B− → A1) matches STM: (A B C D), then STM is reorganized as STM: (C B A D) before action A1 is executed.

14. Each action element is considered in order.

15. Values of variables and class names assigned prior (in the production) to an action element hold during the execution of an action element.

16. The processing that occurs with an action element depends on what action connective it contains:

16.1 ACTION: FAIL terminates the execution of action elements, thus ending the production.

16.2 ACTION: STOP.PS terminates the production system.

16.3 ACTION: (OPR ...) is an operator and will be executed as a program (which might be a production system).

16.4 ACTION: (X1 = = X2). X1 is either a variable or a class name; it is assigned (or reassigned) the value X2.

16.5 ACTION: (X1 # #). X1 is either a variable or a class name; its value (if it exists) is unassigned.

16.6 ACTION: (X1 X2 ... = ⇒ Y1 Y2 ...). The first element in STM is modified by replacing the sequence X1 X2 ... by the sequence Y1 Y2 .... The identification is only on the first symbol (i.e., on X1), the other symbols (i.e., X2 ...) being in effect simply a way to define an interval of N symbols. If X1 does not exist in the STM element, nothing happens.

16.7 ACTION: (X1 X2 ... = = ⇒ Y1 Y2 ...). The second element in STM is modified analogously to = ⇒.

16.8 ACTION: (X1 X2 ... = = = ⇒ Y1 Y2 ...). The third element in STM is modified analogously to = ⇒.

16.9 ACTION: (NTC X1). X1 is noticed in STM and moved to the front. The match used to identify X1 is the same as that used in the match of condition elements. If X1 is not found in STM, then nothing happens.

16.10 ACTION: (...). In all cases when a specific action connective (as enumerated above) does not exist the action element is taken to be a form for the creation of a new element to go into STM (at the front). A copy of the element is made and all values of variables are replaced by their assigned values. If there are subelements (indicated by symbols that do not have proper names), they too are copied.

REFERENCES

Atkinson, R. C., & Shiffrin, R. M. Human memory: A proposed system and its control processes. In K. W. Spence & J. T. Spence (Eds.), *The psychology of learning and motivation,* Vol. 2. New York: Academic Press, 1968.

Bower, G. H. Mental imagery and associative learning. In L. W. Gregg (Ed.), *Cognition in learning and memory.* New York:Wiley, in press.

Broadbent, D. E. Psychological aspects of short-term and long-term memory. *Proceedings of the Royal Society,* London, 1970, **175,** 333-350.

Chase, W. G., & Simon, H. A. Perception in chess. *Cognitive Psychology,* in press.

Feigenbaum, E. A. The simulation of verbal learning behavior. *Proceedings of the Western Joint Computer Conference,* 1961, 19, 121-132.

Feldman, J. Simulation of behavior in the binary choice experiment. *Proceedings of the Western Joint Computer Conference,* 1961, 19, 133-144.

Feldman, J., Tonge, F. M., & Kanter, H. Empirical explorations of a hypothesis-testing model of binary choice behavior. In A. C. Hoggatt & F. E. Balderston (Eds.), *Symposium on simulation models.* Cincinnati, Ohio: South-Western Publishing Company, 1963.

Hopcroft, J. E., & Ullman, J. D. *Formal languages and their relation to automata.* Reading, Mass.: Addison-Wesley, 1969.

Hunt, E. B. *Concept learning.* New York: Wiley, 1962.

Johnson, E. S. An information-processing model of one kind of problem solving. *Psychological Monographs,* 1964, Whole No. 581.

Johnson, N. F. The role of chunking and organization in the process of recall. In G. H. Bower (Ed.), *The psychology of learning and motivation,* Vol. 4. New York: Academic Press, 1970.

Klahr, D., & Wallace, J. G. The development of serial completion strategies: The information processing approach. *British Journal of Psychology,* 1970, **61,** 243-257.

Leewenberg, E. L. L. Quantitative specification of informat'on in sequential patterns. *Psychological Review,* 1969, 76, 216-220.

McLean, R. S., & Gregg, L. W. Effects of induced chunking on temporal aspects of serial recitation. *Journal of Experimental Psychology,* 1967, 74, 455-459.

Miller, G. A. The magical number seven, plus or minus two: Some limits on our capacity for processing information. *Psychological Review,* 1956, **63,** 81-97.

Minsky, M. *Computation: Finite and infinite machines.* Englewood Cliffs, N. J.: Prentice-Hall, 1967.

Myers, J. L. Sequential choice behavior. In G. H. Bower (Ed.), *The psychology of learning and motivation,* Vol. 4. New York: Academic Press, 1970.

Newell, A. Studies in problem solving: Subject S3 on the cryptarithmetic task DONALD + GERALD = ROBERT. Pittsburgh: Carnegie-Mellon University, 1967.

Newell, A. On the analysis of human problem solving protocols. In J. C. Gardin & B. Jaulin (Eds.), *Calcul et formalisation dans les sciences de l'homme.* Paris: Centre National de la Recherche Scientifique, 1968.

Newell, A., McCracken, D., Robertson, G., & Freeman, P. The kernel approach to building software systems. *Computer Science Research Review,* Carnegie-Mellon University, 1971.

Newell, A., & Simon, H. A. *Human problem solving.* Englewood Cliffs, N.J.: Prentice-Hall, 1972.

Paivio, A. Mental imagery in associative learning and memory. *Psychological Review,* 1969, **76,** 241-263.

Restle, F. Theory of serial pattern learning: Structural trees. *Psychological Review,* 1970, **77,** 481-495

Simon, H. A. Complexity and the representation of patterned sequences of symbols. CIP Working Paper 203, Carnegie-Mellon University, 1972.

Simon, H. A., & Feigenbaum, E. A. An information-processing theory of some effects of similarity, familiarization, and meaningfulness in verbal learning. *Journal of Verbal Learning and Verbal Behavior,* 1964, 3, 385-396.

Simon, H A., & Kotovsky, K. Human acquisition of concepts for sequential patterns. *Psychological Review,* 1963, 70, 534-546.

Simon, H. A., & Newell, A. Human problem solving: The state of the theory in 1970. *American Psychologist,* 1971, 26, 145-159.

Vitz, P. C., & Todd, T. C. A coded element model of the perceptual processing of sequential stimuli. *Psychological Review,* 1969, 76, 433-449.

Waugh, N. C., & Norman, D. A. Primary memory. *Psychological Review,* 1965, 72, 89-104.

Wickelgren, W. A. Multitrace strength theory. In D. A. Norman (Ed.), *Models of human memory.* New York: Academic Press, 1970.

CODING
PROCESSES IN
HUMAN MEMORY

AUTHOR INDEX

Numbers in italics refer to the pages on which the complete references are listed.

SUBJECT INDEX

A

Acoustic level, 308
Adjusted learning technique, 20
Analog representation, 301
AS, *see* Associability scale
Associability scale, 16
Association, 175
    backward, 187
    interitem, 171-172, 187
    remote, 172
Association theory, 171-172, 174-176, 187, 188
Associative model, 174-187
Associative structures, 174-177, 180, 183, 187, 188
Attention
    limited capacity mechanism component of, 36
Attributes, 2
    associative, 6
    discriminative, 6, 7
    frequency, 6
    independence of, 3
    marked-syntactic, 197-198
    orthographic, 3
    retrieval, 6, 7

Attributes *(Cont'd.)*
    semantic, 3, 5, 197
    spatial, 6, 7
    temporal, 6, 172-173
Automatic encoding, 36, 38
Automatic operations, 35
Automatic processing, 33-36
Automatic structure, 33-36

B

Bilingual, 198, 238
Brown-Peterson paradigm, 251-253

C

Categorized lists, 11
Chessboard, recall of, 246-247
Chunking, 184, 369
Chunking task, 396
    production system, 397, 399, 401
    production system trace in, 398, 400, 402
Chunks, 38, 87, 135-140, 162, 170, 171, 186
Clustering, 128-135, 187
    semantic, 253-254
    visual, 253-254

442